Manager's Guide to Corporate Tax

WILLIAM RULAND

A RONALD PRESS PUBLICATION
JOHN WILEY & SONS
New York • Chichester • Brisbane • Toronto • Singapore

Copyright © 1984 by John Wiley & Sons, Inc.
All rights reserved. Published simultaneously in Canada.

Reproduction or translation of any part of this work beyond that permitted by Section 107 or 108 of the 1976 United States Copyright Act without the permission of the copyright owner is unlawful. Requests for permission or further information should be addressed to the Permissions Department, John Wiley & Sons, Inc.

This publication is designed to provide accurate and authoritative information in regard to the subject matter covered. It is sold with the understanding that the publisher is not engaged in rendering legal, accounting, or other professional service. If legal advice or other expert assistance is required, the services of a competent professional person should be sought. *From a Declaration of Principles jointly adopted by a Committee of the American Bar Association and a Committee of Publishers.*

Library of Congress Cataloging in Publication Data:
Ruland, William.
   Manager's guide to corporate tax.

"A Ronald Press publication."
Includes index.
   1. Corporations—Taxation—Law and legislation—United States. 2. Tax planning—United States. I. Title.

KF6464.R85 1984   343.7306'7   84-7344
ISBN 0-471-88179-1   347.30367

Printed in the United States of America
10 9 8 7 6 5 4 3 2 1

Preface

PURPOSE

This book is written for executives interested in the corporation's cash flows, and tax structure. Concerned parties include managers, lenders, and shareholders.

One major objective of this book is to assist in developing a basic understanding of the corporate tax and how tax issues affect the corporation. A second major objective is to help develop an appreciation for tax planning—the conduct of activity directed to minimizing the present value of tax payments. The book should help the manager to recognize tax implications of business decisions, to ask appropriate tax-related questions, and to communicate more effectively with the tax specialist.

Managers involved in line operations, investment decisions, and business planning tend to be aware of the importance of the tax. Few managers, however, understand how the tax is determined and the tax consequences of business decisions. In many cases, tax matters are left to tax experts. The problem with leaving the tax to experts is that tax specialists may not be available when needed—particularly if the manager is not aware of possible tax implications.

The book should be of interest both to managers in large publicly held corporations and to owner/managers in more closely held corporations. In both cases, the tax heavily affects corporate cash flows. The choice of Last-In First-Out (LIFO) and other accounting alternatives, the advantageous timing of sales and other transactions, and the choice of compensation plan alternatives are important in both types of corporations. The manager of the closely held corporation is probably more concerned with ways to remove earnings and minimize double taxation than the large corporation manager. Alternative forms of corporate acquisitions and dispositions, however, should be of interest to managers in both types of corporations.

Outside parties including investors and lenders with an interest in a corporation's financial situation also benefit through an understanding of the corporate tax. Investors and lenders are frequently concerned with estimating the corporation's cash flows. The prediction of cash flows using net income as a point of departure requires a feeling for how tax expense reported in the financial statements relates to the taxes actually payable. This book is also concerned with differences in reported tax expenses and the actual tax liabilities.

THE NATURE OF THIS BOOK

This book on the corporate tax is unique in that it is written for the manager with no tax or legal training and with only a minimal appreciation for accounting. Available work on the corporate tax generally consists of advanced material intended for attorneys or accountants. The more technical material assumes previous background in taxation and contains far too much detail for the practicing manager. Consequently it has not been easy for business managers to obtain a basic appreciation of the corporate tax and how the tax affects business decisions. This book examines the more important general concepts in the taxation of corporations. At the same time, the book is relatively short, and is designed for easy reading. One or more brief examples illustrate important or complex points. The intention is to provide the manager with material that can be mastered in a few evenings. The book will also serve as a reference source for use in management training sessions.

The approach is general in nature. The book does not reference specific court cases or sections of tax legislation. It avoids legal terminology and omits details whenever the simplification or omission is not misleading. The concern is with the tax as it affects business decisions—not in the preparation of tax returns or in the conduct of tax research.

ORGANIZATION

General Concepts in Business Taxation. The first six chapters provide background and summarize basic tax concepts applicable to most businesses. Chapter 1 examines the importance of the tax and provides background. Chapter 2 develops the concept of taxable income, and discusses the actual payment of taxes by the profitable corporation and the possible inflow of cash resulting from the refund of previous tax payments to the loss corporation. Additionally, Chapter 2 introduces a major set of opportunities for deferral or reduction of the tax.

Chapter 3 deals with the acquisition and use of property. Among the topics included in Chapter 3 are the investment tax credit, the unique concept of depreciation used in tax determination, and the tax implications of leasing as an alternative to purchase.

Chapters 4 and 5 are concerned with property sales and other dispositions. These chapters include consideration of capital gains and losses, the nontaxable exchange, and recaptures. These chapters show that the tax rate applicable to the gain on sale is a function of a variety of factors, and that tax planning is particularly important when considering the sale or exchange of property.

Chapter 6 examines the tax deferral opportunities associated with key accounting alternatives including the treatment of inventories, long-term contracts, and installment sales. Chapter 6 also considers the tax implications of employee stock options and pension plans.

Most of the topics covered in Chapters 2 through 6 apply to the tax on noncorporate businesses as well as to corporations. These concepts are included in this book both because they provide necessary background for the study of issues unique to corporate taxation and because they suggest key areas of tax-planning opportunities. The reader who is already familiar with the taxation of noncorporate businesses, however, may wish to concentrate primarily on the tax-planning implications and move quickly to Chapter 7.

Tax Issues Unique to the Corporation. Chapters 7 through 12 are concerned with tax issues unique to the corporation. Chapters 7 and 8 deal with the distribution of funds from the corporation to its owners. Chapter 7 examines dividend payments by corporations. Much of the examination focuses upon the problems created by the taxation of both corporate earnings and the distribution of these earnings to shareholders as dividends; emphasis is directed to reducing the burden of this double taxation. Chapter 8 is concerned with redemptions and liquidations—distributions to shareholders that receive preferential tax treatment. These distributions are of potential importance to both the closely held corporation and the widely held corporation. The discussion of liquidations also provides background for understanding the tax on corporate acquisitions and dispositions. Chapter 9 looks more closely at the corporate form, including the advantages of the corporate form and the tax implications of property contributions to the corporation by shareholders.

Chapters 10 and 11 examine mergers and other acquisitions of corporations. These transactions are of particular interest because of the large potential tax liabilities and because of the sensitivity of tax treatment to the form of the business transaction. These chapters show that minor differences in the terms of the agreement can lead to major differences in tax treatment. Chapters 10 and 11 also examine the conditions under which a tax-free acquisition of another business may or may not result in a desirable form of acquisition. Chapter 12, the final chapter, considers the division of the corporation into two or more smaller corporations through a spin-off or similar mechanism. A division can be tax-free if certain conditions are met.

SCOPE

This short book does not attempt to consider all matters pertaining to the corporate income tax. Many taxation matters are highly specialized and involved. The examination is restricted to topics of more general interest and particularly topics that lead to opportunities for tax planning. In many cases, attention is directed to new developments, including recent changes in the legislation or interpretations. The new developments sometimes provide new problems or opportunities for tax planning that require departures from established practice, and understanding of these is particularly important.

The strength of the book is derived in large part from its simplified treatment of sometimes complex legal phenomena. One consequence of this simplification, however, is that the book does not serve as a comprehensive reference source. The book should facilitate communication with the tax specialist; it is not intended as a substitute for the tax advisor.

WILLIAM RULAND

New York, New York
August 1984

Contents

1   INTRODUCTION   **1**

Importance of the Tax in Business   1
    Tax Planning   3
    The Manager and the Tax Specialist   6
Taxation and the National Interest   7
    Objectives   7
    Tax Theory   8
    Tax Legislation and Administration   9
Summary   10

2   TAX RATES AND TAXABLE INCOME   **12**

The Tax Rates   13
    The Marginal Rate   14
    The Small Corporation   15
Tax Determination   17
    Taxable Income   17
    Taxable Income and Pretax Accounting Income   21
    Tax Credits   23
    Accrual-Basis Accounting   25
    Cash-Basis Accounting   28
    Timing Transactions and Tax Planning   29

Operating Losses	32
The Operating Loss Carryback	32
The Operating Loss Carryforward	34
Operating Losses and the Financial Statements	36
Tax Payments	37
The Estimated Tax	37
Exceptions	38
The Multidivision Corporation	40
Related Taxpayers	42
The Controlled Group	42
Expenditures for the Benefit of a Related Taxpayer	44
The Arms-Length Transaction	45
Summary	46

3 THE ACQUISITION AND USE OF PRODUCTIVE PROPERTY — 50

Property Acquisitions	51
Tax Credits	53
The Investment Tax Credit	53
The Flow-Through and Deferral Methods for Financial Reporting	59
The Investment Tax Credit for Rehabilitated Buildings	61
The Business Energy Credit	64
The Adjusted Basis	65
Construction-Period Interest and Taxes	65
The Allocation of Purchase Price	67
Depreciation	68
The Accelerated Cost Recovery System (ACRS)	69
The Election to Expense	75
Other Capital Expenditures	77

Intangible Assets	77
Mineral Resources	78
Leasing	81
Tax Treatment	81
Purchase versus Lease Treatment	85
The Sale and Leaseback	87
The Finance Lease	88
Related Party Considerations	89
The Investment Tax Credit	90
Depreciation and the Election to Expense	91
Summary	91
Appendix: Nonrecovery Property	95
Estimated Life	95
Residual Value	95
Accelerated Depreciation	97

4 PROPERTY SALES AND EXCHANGES   100

Gains and Losses	101
The Gain	101
The Loss	103
Alternatives to Gain Recognition	108
The Nontaxable Exchange	110
Operation of the Nontaxable Exchange	111
Criteria for the Nontaxable Exchange	112
Problems with the Nontaxable Exchange	113
The Nontaxable Exchange and Boot	118
Loss Transactions	119
Capital Gains and Losses	120
Short-Term and Long-Term Gains and Losses	120
Determining Net Gains and Losses	122
Tax Minimization	125

Fixed Assets	126
Timing Fixed Asset Dispositions	126
Related Party Transactions	127
The Disallowance of Losses on Sales	128
Gains on the Sale of Depreciable Property	129
Summary	129
Appendix: Net Capital Gains and Losses	131
The Procedure	132
Illustrations	132

5 RECAPTURES 139

Depreciation Recapture	139
The Operation of Recapture	139
The Reason for Recapture	140
Property Subject to Recapture	143
Depreciation Recapture and Property Subject to the Investment Tax Credit	143
Recapture and Nonresidential Real Estate	144
Recapture and Residential Real Estate	145
Investment Tax Credit Recapture	146
The Holding Period	146
Applicable Transactions	147
Summary	148

6 ACCOUNTING ALTERNATIVES AND OTHER OPPORTUNITIES FOR TAX REDUCTION AND DEFERRAL 150

Key Accounting Alternatives	151
Inventories	151
Long-Term Construction Contracts	161

Contents xv

      The Installment Method for Sales   164
      The Deferred Tax and the Financial Statements   165
      Bad Debts   169
    Employee Compensation and Benefits   171
      Employee Stock Options   171
      Pension Costs   174
    Additional Tax Credits   175
      The Research and Development Tax Credit   175
      The Targeted-Jobs Credit   177
      The Employee Stock Ownership Tax Credit   177
    Summary   178

7   DIVIDENDS   182

    The Nature of Dividends   183
      The Tax Treatment of Dividends   183
      Earnings and Profits   185
    Double Taxation   189
      Background   189
      Deferred Distributions to Shareholders   192
      Distributions of Earnings at Capital Gains Rates   195
      Distributions Structured as Deductions   198
    Property Dividends   205
    The Corporate Shareholder   207
      Background   207
      The Corporate Dividends Received Deduction   207
    The Stock Dividend   210
      Background   210
      The Tax   210
    Closely Held Corporations—Additional Considerations   212
      The Accumulated Earnings Tax   212

The Personal Holding Company Tax	214
Summary	216

8 RETURNS OF INVESTED CAPITAL — 220

The Return of Investment versus the Distribution of Earnings	221
The Sale	221
Sale Treatment for the Distribution of Accumulated Earnings	223
The Stock Redemption	225
The Tax	225
Criteria for Redemption Treatment	228
The Distribution of Property in Redemption	230
The Partial Liquidation	234
General Characteristics	234
The Tax	236
The Adjusted Basis	238
Criteria for Partial Liquidation Treatment	239
A Comparison of Dividends, Redemptions, and Partial Liquidations	240
The Complete Liquidation	242
The Tax	243
The Sale of Property and Distribution of Proceeds to Shareholders	245
The Basis of Property Received in Liquidation	248
Liquidation of a Controlled Subsidiary	248
Losses in Liquidation	250
The Straddle	251
Additional Considerations	253
The Liquidation and Reincorporation	253
The Collapsible Corporation	255

The Sale of Stock to a Related Corporation	257
Summary	260

9 THE CORPORATE FORM OF ORGANIZATION — 263

Alternative Business Forms	264
Advantages of the Corporate Form	265
The Rights of Stockholders	267
Property Transfers by Shareholders	268
The Shareholders	269
The Corporation	271
Ordinary Loss Treatment for Small Business Stock	272
The S Corporation	273
Taxation of the S Corporation and Shareholders	274
Qualifications for S Corporation Treatment	280
The Minimum Tax	282
The Consolidated Tax Return	283
Advantages	283
Disadvantages	285
Eligibility	286
Summary	286

10 CORPORATE ACQUISITIONS — 289

Forms of Acquisition	290
The Purchase of Assets	291
The Buyer	292
The Seller	292
The Allocation of Purchase Price	299
The Purchase of Stock	302

The Acquired Corporation and Its Shareholders	302
The Buyer	305
The Purchase of Assets versus Stock	310
Interest on Corporate Acquisition Indebtedness	312
Summary	313

11 THE TAX-FREE REORGANIZATION — 315

General Characteristics	316
The Nontaxable Exchange	316
How the Reorganization Operates	318
Forms of Tax-Free Reorganization	319
Common Features	325
Forms of Reorganization	329
The Exchange of Stock for Stock	329
The Exchange of Stock for Assets	330
The Merger and Consolidation	333
The Purchase versus the Tax-Free Reorganization	337
The Recapitalization	340
The Change in Identity or Form	341
Summary	341

12 SPIN-OFFS AND OTHER CORPORATE DIVISIONS — 344

Reasons for Corporate Divisions	345
Criteria for the Tax-Free Division	347
Background	347
Specific Criteria	348
The Form of the Division	350

The Spin-Off	350
The Split-Off	352
The Split-Up	353
The Adjusted Basis of the Distributed Corporation	354
Evaluation of the Tax-Free Division	355
Summary	356

INDEX 359

Chapter 1

Introduction

This book is a nontechnical guide to the U.S. federal corporate income tax. It is designed for the manager with little or no background in taxation. It should also prove useful to the investor or lender interested in evaluating the corporation's financial situation. The objectives are to provide a basic understanding of how tax issues affect the corporation and to develop an appreciation for tax planning.

The book is intended to help people in business recognize situations and decision opportunities with tax implications, to ask appropriate tax-related questions, and to communicate more effectively with the tax specialist. It will also serve as an easy-to-use reference source on the corporate tax.

This chapter provides background concerning the corporate tax. It begins by summarizing the importance of the tax and of tax planning, and then presents a brief overview of tax administration.

IMPORTANCE OF THE TAX IN BUSINESS

The federal income tax is important because of its effect on cash flows. The tax consumes cash that would otherwise be available for investments, loan repayments, dividends, and other purposes. An otherwise positive cash flow from operations may become negative when the tax is considered.

Most business transactions have tax implications. In some cases, as in the sale of merchandise for cash in a retail business, the tax implications are not readily controllable. In other cases, as in the sale of merchandise on credit, the business transaction and sometimes the accounting system can be structured to minimize tax payments. For example, the tax on an installment sale is deferred until the cash is collected. This applies even though the accounting system used to prepare financial statements usually recognizes sales revenue at the time the merchandise is shipped.

Tax considerations also determine the advisability of many key business decisions. The choice of an opening date for a new facility, for example, may result in significant tax deferrals (this will be covered in Chapter 3). As another example, a business may decide to increase the scope of its activity or start up a new business to make use of tax carryovers that would otherwise be lost (discussed in Chapter 10).

Tax considerations also influence the structure of key business transactions. In some cases a business may benefit by selling an unwanted property item outright; in other cases a nontaxable trade-in may be more appropriate (property sales and exchanges are discussed in Chapter 4). As another example, a business may find that seemingly minor differences in the terms of a business acquisition will have major tax implications (explored in Chapters 10 and 11).

This book focuses on the types of transactions that give rise to these tax alternatives, showing that small differences in the form of the transaction can lead to significant differences in the tax. This is particularly true with respect to acquisitions and dispositions. For this reason, emphasis is placed here on acquisitions and dispositions both of individual property items and of entire corporations.

Tax Planning

A major purpose of this book is to facilitate the tax-planning process. Tax planning differs from the process of tax determination. Tax determination entails calculating the tax payable at the end of the year. Tax accountants usually accomplish this task independently by reference to the accounting records. Tax planning involves both engaging in certain transactions and structuring these transactions with the objective of minimizing the present value of tax payments. Tax-planning considerations may also suggest avoidance of particular types of transactions.

Effective tax planning requires the joint participation of the operating manager and the tax specialist. Tax planning is most effective when the operating manager can identify potential planning opportunities and problems and bring these to the attention of the tax specialist. The tax specialist can then consider the overall advisability of the transaction, the form of the transaction, and its timing. Sometimes the specific form of the transaction can be critical. In other cases the timing—such as January 1 versus December 31—can be of major importance. Matters of form and timing, however, cannot be modified at tax-determination time. The signing of the contract, the shipment of the product, the placing of a facility in service represent real events that cannot be altered after the fact. Consequently, effective tax planning takes place continuously rather than just at the time the tax return is prepared.

Tax Minimization. Tax minimization increases cash available for other business purposes, including the replacement of property, growth, repayment of debt, and payment of dividends to shareholders.

The minimization of tax payments is generally regarded as an accepted and prudent business objective. A noted judge ruling on an appeal of a tax case stated, "Anyone may so arrange his affairs that his taxes shall be as low as possible; he is not bound to choose that pattern that will best pay the Treasury; there is not even a patriotic duty to increase one's taxes." Corporations are as concerned with minimizing the tax as they are with minimizing any other expense. As a consequence, corporations frequently devote a great deal of effort to tax-minimization activity. Many corporations engage specialists with responsibility solely for identifying opportunities for tax minimization.

Reduced Tax Rates. One way to minimize the tax is to structure transactions to avoid tax payments entirely. However, this is generally very difficult to achieve.

Tax planning more commonly reduces the amount of tax ultimately payable. This is sometimes accomplished by arranging transactions to provide for taxation at lower tax rates than might ordinarily apply. Small differences in the form of a transaction or its timing, for example, may result in capital gains treatment rather than taxation at higher ordinary income rates. Sales of plant and equipment items can be accelerated or deferred to take place in one tax year or another. Chapter 4 considers the tax impacts of property sales and other dispositions.

Another way to reduce taxes is to structure the transaction to take advantage of various tax credits. Tax credits are examined in Chapters 3 and 6.

Tax Deferral. The reduction of the tax ultimately payable is often not possible. As an alternative, much of tax planning is concerned with deferring tax payments. The amount of tax in this case is not reduced; instead the timing of the tax payments is deferred. The choice of accounting alternatives such as the Last-In First-Out (LIFO) method or the completed contract method of long-term contracts can lead to significant tax deferrals, as shown in Chapter 6. Tax deferrals can also provide a continuing source of business financing, as shown in Chapter 2. Tax deferrals can have the same effect as loans payable without interest.

Importance of the Tax in Business

Tax deferrals reduce the present value of tax payments. The notion of present value relates amounts of funds to the timing of receipt of payment and the interest rate applicable to the time value of money. A $1000 payment, for example, has a present value of $1000 if paid immediately. If payment is deferred for one year at a cost of capital of 12 percent, the present value drops to $893. In other words, $1000 paid now is equivalent to only $893 if payment can be deferred for one year. With a one-year deferral, the $893 could presumably be put to work earning 12 percent interest, or $107. This would provide a total of $1000 at the end of one year.

The present value of a tax deferral for one time period at any interest rate is determined by dividing the amount of the tax deferral by a factor of one plus the interest rate. For two interest periods, the amount deferred is divided again by a factor of one plus the interest rate. For three payments, the amount deferred is divided a third time by the one-plus-the-interest-rate factor. The present value of $893 on the one-year deferral of $1000 was determined by dividing $1000 by a factor of 1.12. A four-period example follows.

EXAMPLE: THE PRESENT VALUE OF A TAX PAYMENT. The Payup Corporation utilizes various tax-planning devices to defer $100,000 in tax for a four-year period. The opportunity cost of funds to Payup is 15 percent.

The present value of the tax payment is $57,175. This is determined by dividing the amount deferred by one plus the interest rate four times as follows:

$$\frac{\$100,000}{(1.15)(1.15)(1.15)(1.15)} = \$57,175$$

An alternative interpretation is that $57,175 for four years at 15 percent will accumulate to $100,000:

Period	Beginning amount	Interest at 15%	Ending amount
Start	—	—	$ 57,175
After 1 year	$57,175	$ 8,576	65,751
After 2 years	65,751	9,863	75,614
After 3 years	75,614	11,342	86,956
After 4 years	86,956	13,044	100,000

Present value concepts are often used to compare the effects of deferrals produced by alternative tax treatments.

The Manager and the Tax Specialist

The manager rarely has either the time or interest to attempt to become a tax expert. Tax legislation is detailed and various provisions are not well-integrated. Some provisions, for example, override other provisions. In addition, tax legislation and interpretations are continuously changing.

The applicability of the various legislative provisions to specific transactions is also subject to continuing question. The courts have ruled in many cases that transactions must be both consistent with the spirit of the law and in literal compliance. Unfortunately these determinations become involved. Tax specialists seek resolution of tax questions by referring to previous court cases involving similar questions. Even then, the eventual disposition of a particular action is not always predictable.

The manager with a grasp of tax fundamentals, however, should be better able to identify potential opportunities and trouble areas and effectively incorporate tax matters in decision-making. An understanding of tax fundamentals should also help the manager to more effectively communicate with the tax specialist.

It should be emphasized that the purpose of this book is not to make prescriptions to the manager. This book is concerned with relatively broad concepts in the interest of brevity and simplicity. Specific courses of action should be decided upon only after consultation with a competent tax specialist.

TAXATION AND THE NATIONAL INTEREST

Objectives

Revenue Objectives. Tax legislation reflects national revenue objectives, economic objectives, and social objectives. With respect to revenue objectives, the income tax is an important source of government financing. The corporate income tax provides a substantial amount of revenue to the federal government.

In recent years Congress has considered a variety of plans to modify the corporate tax. Changes in the corporate tax are popular because the corporate tax provides a mechanism for increasing governmental revenues with no direct effect upon voters (individual taxpayers). On the other hand, business interests lobby against tax increases and have often been successful in winning reductions in the income tax.

Economic Objectives. National economic objectives are also promoted through the income tax. These objectives include measures to increase productive efficiency, primarily through providing increased incentive to invest in productive assets. For example, the investment tax credit reduces taxes for businesses investing in new facilities. The Accelerated Cost Recovery System (ACRS) also increases the cash flows associated with new investments. Both of these topics will be examined in Chapter 3.

The research and development tax credit was also developed to promote economic objectives. This credit reduces taxes for businesses that increase research and development activity. This opportunity for tax reduction will be examined in Chapter 6.

Social Objectives. The tax may also promote a number of national social objectives. For example, the business energy tax credit reduces taxes for businesses that install certain energy-saving devices in the interest of conserving natural resources. Social objectives are also directed toward the welfare of employees and other groups. For example, tax legislation provides incentives for contributions to employee pension plans. Yet another incentive is the existence of tax credits for businesses that hire disadvantaged employees. Chapter 6 will examine many of the tax-reduction opportunities associated with the promotion of social objectives.

Later chapters include examination of tax-reduction and tax-deferral opportunities associated with tax provisions developed to achieve national economic and social objectives.

Tax Theory

Tax legislation evolved over a period of time and in response to diverse and changing economic and political pressures. Consequently there does not seem to be any comprehensive theory explaining current practice. A number of key principles, however, underlie the tax legislation and related interpretations. These include:

Administrative simplicity. The tax should be easy to administer. The concept of the tax return prepared by the taxpayer rather than by the tax authorities probably reduces the cost of administration. Some taxpayers maintain that more should be done to simplify the tax.

Predictability. Taxpayers should be able to predict the amount of the tax. Copies of tax legislation are easily obtained. The Internal Revenue Service (IRS) provides summaries of its position without cost to taxpayers. The IRS sometimes issues advance rulings that outline its position on certain topics in response to taxpayer requests.

Fairness. The administration of the tax should apply equally to all taxpayers in identical circumstances.

Ability to pay. The collection of the tax should coincide with the taxpayer's ability to pay the tax. Corporate taxes are paid in quarterly installments based on the estimate of annual taxes. This seems to be consistent with the ability-to-pay principle. The deferral of taxes on certain transactions until the taxpayer actually receives payment, as in an installment sale, is also consistent with the ability-to-pay principle.

An appreciation of the theory underlying tax administration sometimes helps in understanding the reasons for various provisions of tax legislation. Many of the more complex provisions of tax legislation are designed to facilitate meeting the objectives just described.

Tax Legislation and Administration

Tax Legislation. Tax legislation is the responsibility of the Congress. Today's federal corporate income tax began in the early 1900s. Congress amended the initial legislation on numerous occasions. The U.S. federal tax laws are often referred to as the Internal Revenue Code or just as the Tax Code.

The Treasury. The U.S. Treasury Department administers the Tax Code. Treasury Regulations interpret tax legislation. These Regulations carry considerable weight and sometimes have the force of law.

The IRS. The Internal Revenue Service (IRS) is an agency of the Treasury Department. The IRS is responsible for enforcing tax legislation, interpreting Treasury Regulations, and collecting the tax. The IRS issues rulings in response to taxpayer requests for guidance regarding the tax on proposed transactions. The IRS also audits selected tax returns in the interest of increasing compliance with tax legislation and associated interpretations.

The Courts. Differences of opinion sometimes arise between the taxpayer and the tax-collection authorities. Sometimes these differences concern the meaning of tax legislation. On other occasions, these differences concern the applicability of a particular provision to a given taxpayer situation.

Disputes are usually negotiated by the taxpayer and the IRS. If the negotiations are not successful, the Tax Court, federal district courts, or Claims Court may hear tax cases. Appeals are directed to U.S. Circuit Courts and to the U.S. Supreme Court.

The concepts set forth in court rulings sometimes become important guides for tax planning, as the courts have often undertaken responsibility for protecting the spirit as well as the letter of the tax legislation. In some cases judicial concepts have been formally integrated into the tax legislation by action of Congress.

SUMMARY

Purpose. The purpose of this chapter is to provide background regarding the importance of the federal corporate income tax and its administration.

The Importance of the Tax in Business. Most business transactions have tax implications. In many cases, the tax implications influence the desirability of the transaction. If the transaction is determined to be desirable, tax considerations frequently determine the form of the transaction.

Tax Planning. Corporations assign a high priority to tax planning. Tax-planning activity includes the minimization of

Summary

tax payments by attempting to eliminate the tax entirely, and more commonly, providing for taxation at lower tax rates than might ordinarily apply. Tax planning is also concerned with the deferral of tax payments. Deferrals reduce the present value of tax payments and can be as valuable as loans payable without interest.

Effective tax planning requires a joint effort on the part of the operating management and the tax specialist. Operating managers often contact a tax specialist whenever a potential planning matter arises. A major purpose of this book is to help the operating manager identify major tax-planning opportunities and problems.

The National Interest. The tax is important to the economy because it is responsible for a substantial portion of federal government revenues. The tax also attempts to promote a variety of economic and social objectives. These include measures to increase productivity, to conserve scarce natural resources, and to promote the welfare of employees and disadvantaged jobseekers.

Tax Theory. Tax legislation is complex and not well-integrated. Certain key principles, however, seem to underlie the taxation process. These include administrative simplicity, predictability, fairness, and the taxpayer's ability to pay. Reference to these concepts sometimes facilitates understanding of specific tax-legislation provisions.

Tax Legislation and Administration. Tax legislation is the responsibility of Congress. The Treasury Department through the IRS administers the tax. In cases of differences in interpretation, the courts, including the U.S. Supreme Court, rule on tax matters.

Chapter 2

Tax Rates and Taxable Income

This chapter examines how the tax is determined, and also provides necessary background and introduces some key concepts in tax planning. The examination begins with the structure of tax rates. It is shown that tax rates differ depending upon the amount of taxable income. High-income corporations pay more tax and a higher percentage of taxable income as tax than do low-income corporations. The applicability of different tax rates for different income levels leads to unique tax-planning opportunities for the smaller corporation.

The chapter then examines the calculation of taxable income. Profitable corporations are considered first, including an examination of mechanisms available for tax deferral. Then the loss situation is examined. Loss corporations sometimes receive refunds of taxes paid in earlier years or use current losses to reduce future-year taxes. The benefits of loss carryforwards are sometimes reflected in cash flows, and as will be seen in Chapters 10 and 11, can help to determine the choice among alternative forms of corporate acquisitions.

Consideration of the schedule of tax payments shows that the tax is payable on a periodic basis rather than all at the time the tax return is filed. The pay-as-you-go system has implications for the corporation's financial operations and sometimes leads to substantial borrowing requirements.

The chapter concludes with additional considerations concerning tax rates for the multidivision corporation and an examination of related party considerations.

THE TAX RATES

The amount of the tax is determined by multiplying the corporation's taxable income by a prescribed tax rate. This tax rate depends upon the amount of taxable income. Taxable income is the income computed for purposes of tax determination, and will be examined later in this chapter and in following chapters. The tax rate increases with the corporation's income. This tends to direct the tax burden toward the more successful, higher-income corporations.

The tax rate for corporations is 46 percent of taxable income in excess of $100,000. The rates for lower bracket amounts are:

15% on the first $25,000 of taxable income.

18% on the second $25,000 of taxable income.

30% on the third $25,000 of taxable income.

40% on the fourth $25,000 of taxable income.

The following illustration shows how the amount of the tax is determined.

EXAMPLE: THE TAX COMPUTATION. The Payup Corporation has taxable income of $1,000,000.

Payup's tax is:

	Income	Tax
15% on the first	$ 25,000	$ 3,750
18% on the second	25,000	4,500
30% on the third	25,000	7,500
40% on the fourth	25,000	10,000
46% on the remainder	900,000	414,000
Total	$1,000,000	$439,750

The above calculation shows that the tax rate on amounts below $100,000 is less than the rate on higher income amounts. The tax on the first $100,000 is $25,750—the total of the taxes on the first four tax brackets. Additional income is taxed at the rate of 46 percent. Beginning in 1985, corporations with income exceeding about $1,400,000 are taxed at a 46 percent flat rate. Consequently, only smaller corporations will benefit from the graduated tax.

The Marginal Rate

Taxable income generally changes as the result of business decisions. As income changes, the taxes also change. The marginal rate is the tax rate applicable to income increases or decreases. The marginal rate in the Payup Corporation illustration is 46 percent of the change in taxable income. This is shown in the following illustration.

EXAMPLE: THE MARGINAL RATE. The Payup Corporation determines taxable income as $1,000,000. A $10,000 increase or decrease in taxable income increases or decreases Payup's tax by 46 percent of the amount.

The amount of the change in tax is 46 percent of $10,000, or $4600. The 46 percent marginal rate applies to all increases and decreases unless the decrease reduces taxable income to the lower 40 percent bracket. Then 40 percent becomes the marginal rate.

EFFECT OF A $10,000 REDUCTION IN TAXABLE INCOME

	Tax before reduction		Tax after reduction	
Rate	Income	Tax	Income	Tax
15%	$ 25,000	$ 3,750	$ 25,000	$ 3,750
18%	25,000	4,500	25,000	4,500
30%	25,000	7,500	25,000	7,500
40%	25,000	10,000	25,000	10,000
46%	900,000	414,000	890,000	409,400
Total	$1,000,000	$439,750	$990,000	$435,150

The notion of an average tax rate has limited usefulness for business decisions and is not calculated in the above example. The marginal rate is the relevant rate for business decisions.

The Small Corporation

The reduced tax rates for low-income amounts can be important for small corporations. In fact, one strategy for tax minimization is to adjust the timing of transactions—using devices described later in this chapter—to qualify for taxation at lower rates. The tax on a given amount in income can sometimes be reduced if the distribution of the income between years is changed. An example follows.

EXAMPLE: INCOME DISTRIBUTIONS FOR THE SMALL CORPORATION. The Payup Corporation is just getting started in business and is expected to earn $190,000 in 1985, but only $10,000 in 1986.

Reference to the tax tables indicates that the 1985 income will be taxed at $25,750 for the first $100,000 and 46 percent on the remaining $90,000, for a total tax of $67,150. The 1986 income will be taxed at the 15 percent rate and will amount to $1500. The total tax over both years is $68,650.

As an alternative, Payup should prefer to restructure business transactions to reduce 1985 income by $90,000 to $100,000 and increase 1986 income by the same amount. This type of strategy should both defer tax payments and reduce the total amount of tax ultimately payable. The tax payable in each year under this second alternative will be $25,750 and the total two-year tax will be $51,500 rather than $68,650. The $17,150 saving comes about through taxation of $90,000 at low-bracket amounts rather than at the higher 46 percent rate. A comparison of the two alternatives follows:

TAX WITH AND WITHOUT INCOME DEFERRAL

	Original	With deferral
1985 Tax		
First $100,000	$25,750	$25,750
Next 90,000	41,400	0
1986 Tax		
First $ 10,000	1,500	1,500
Next 90,000	0	24,250
Two-year total	$68,650	$51,500

Tax-saving opportunities through shifting income to lower brackets are available only for lower-income corporations. Large-income corporations cannot benefit through this approach because their marginal tax rate is usually 46 percent every year.

The 46 percent marginal rate applicable to large corporations is assumed to apply in most examples and illustrations used throughout this book even though small-income amounts are sometimes used to simplify the presentation. Managers of lower marginal rate corporations may wish to substitute the rate relevant to their corporations and rework the examples shown here.

TAX DETERMINATION

The tax is determined by multiplying the appropriate tax rate by taxable income and then reducing the tax otherwise payable for the effect of tax credits. The first step is to determine taxable income. Taxable income is the corporation's income remaining after subtracting deductions. The calculation of income and deductions will now be examined.

Taxable Income

Taxable income is the income recognized for tax purposes. Taxable income arises primarily as a result of the recognition of revenues and is reduced primarily through the effect of tax deductions.

Revenue. Revenue is realized when the corporation sells goods or provides services to customers. Examples include revenues from sales, interest, investments, and rents.

Not all receipts of cash qualify as revenues. For example, borrowing funds is a source of cash, but does not result in revenue because the cash is not received from providing goods or services to customers. The net worth of the corporation is not increased as a result of borrowing because the corporation incurs an offsetting liability to pay back the funds at the time the cash is received. The corporation also does not realize revenue on the sale of its own stock to shareholders.

Tax legislation also excludes certain items from income as a matter of national policy. The major exclusion applicable to corporations applies to interest earned on bonds issued by state and local governments. The exclusion of interest income makes the bond more attractive to the investor and may facilitate fund raising by state and local governments. The impact of this exclusion can be seen in the following example.

EXAMPLE: INCOME. The Payup Corporation manufactures office furniture and sells it to a distributor for $3,300,000. The cost of producing the furniture was $2,000,000. Payup also earned $300,000 interest on tax-free State of Nevada bonds and $200,000 on other investments.

Payup's income before deductions is $1,500,000 for tax purposes. This compares to $1,800,000 for purposes of financial reporting. This is determined as:

	Tax determination	Financial reporting
Sales	$3,300,000	$3,300,000
Less: Cost of sales	2,000,000	2,000,000
Gross profit	1,300,000	1,300,000
Add: Interest	200,000	500,000
Gross income	$1,500,000	$1,800,000

Investors are very much aware of the tax-saving potential of municipal bonds and expect to receive less interest on municipals than on equivalent taxable securities. For example, a 7 percent municipal should result in a higher after-tax return to the 46 percent bracket corporation than a 12 percent taxable bond with equivalent risk and maturity. The after-tax return on the 12 percent bond is only 6.48 percent (12 percent less 5.52

Tax Determination

percent—the tax at the 46 percent marginal rate). A convenient rule of thumb in evaluating after-tax returns is to multiply the return before tax by a factor of one minus the tax rate, such as:

$$12\% \times (1 - .46) = 12\% \times .54 = 6.48\%$$

Not all increases in wealth result in revenue. For tax purposes, revenue is generally realized only when goods are transferred as a result of a sale or when services are performed. For example, a corporation's investments may appreciate in value and increase the corporation's wealth. Revenue is not realized, however, until the corporation sells the investments. An illustration of revenue not realized follows.

EXAMPLE: UNREALIZED REVENUE. The Helpum Employment Agency owns an apartment building. The building was acquired in 1931 for $90,000 and now has a market value of about $600,000.

The value of the building has increased by $510,000. Helpum does not realize any of this increase in value as revenue until the building is sold.

The revenue-realization criterion is consistent with the ability-to-pay concept cited in Chapter 1. The revenue is not recognized for tax purposes until received, because the owner does not receive anything in exchange for the increase in value until that time. A second reason for the realization criterion is that a tax on increases in value before the time of sale could be difficult to administer.

Devices to defer revenue realization are common in tax planning. For example, an investor may be interested in selling property in order to purchase similar investment property and cash in on the appreciation in value. The sale of property, however, is a taxable transaction because it results in revenue realization. A better strategy in some cases may be to hold on to the old property for additional appreciation. No matter how large the unrealized or paper gains are on the old property, these gains will not be taxed as income until the property is sold.

Adjustments are then made to revenue to arrive at taxable income. One major category of adjustments consists of deductions.

Deductions. Deductions represent the costs of earning revenue. Common deductions include employee salaries, interest payments, rent payments, and state and local taxes. The repayment of loans is not deductible, since loan repayment does not reduce net worth (both cash and liabilities are reduced in the same amount with a loan repayment). Fines, bribes, and illegal payments are also not deductible. This limitation is imposed in the interest of encouraging certain social objectives.

Some expenditures are expected to provide benefit beyond the end of the year and are not immediately deductible. These costs are referred to as capital expenditures. Examples of capital expenditures include the costs of machinery, equipment, buildings, and vehicles. The cost of additions to buildings and improvements to property such as major overhauls of equipment also qualify as capital expenditures. Taxpayers naturally prefer immediate deductibility of costs and attempt to avoid capital expenditure treatment. For example, taxpayers tend to deduct the costs of certain repairs while the IRS maintains that these expenditures should be capitalized. The problem associated with alternative possibilities for the treatment of repairs is illustrated in the following example.

EXAMPLE: THE TREATMENT OF REPAIRS COMPARED TO THE TREATMENT OF CAPITAL EXPENDITURES. The Highway Trucking Corporation spends $40,000 in March 1985 performing maintenance on its trucks.

If the $40,000 is incurred to perform routine inspections and replacements, the costs are deducted as incurred. If the $40,000

Tax Determination 21

is used to install more fuel-efficient or longer-lasting components, the expenditure would be classified as capital because it increases the value of the property and provides benefit beyond the current year. Certain costs such as the cost of new engines fall in between. In these cases evaluation of the specific facts along with a certain amount of judgement are needed.

Fortunately for the taxpayer, the costs of most capital expenditures are eventually deducted through the depreciation process. The problem, however, is that depreciation does not provide an immediate deduction. Depreciation will be examined in detail in the next chapter.

Taxpayers and the IRS sometimes disagree concerning the proper treatment of certain expenditures. The corporation generally maintains that the expenditure should be deducted currently; the IRS argues for capital expenditure treatment. The amount deducted will be the same in either case. The difference relates to the timing of the deduction. The tax benefit of the capital expenditure may not be fully realized until a considerable amount of time elapses.

Taxable Income and Pretax Accounting Income

The Different Purpose of Different Income Measures. Taxable income differs from pretax accounting income as reported on the corporation's income statement. Taxable income provides the basis for tax determination. Pretax accounting income is the income measured for financial reporting purposes. Taxable income and pretax accounting income differ because different rules are used in determining the two income measures.

The purpose of calculating taxable income is to determine the federal income tax. The purpose of determining pretax accounting income is different. Accounting income is believed to be useful to lenders and investors in making credit and investment decisions. Since the purpose of the two income measures differs, it is not surprising to find that the specific measurement rules also differ.

Differences in Accounting Conventions. Differences between the tax rules and generally accepted accounting principles sometimes require that a given event receive different treatment in each accounting system. For example:

> Fines and illegal payments are not deductible for computing taxable income (to discourage anti-social activity). These payments do reduce pretax accounting income.
>
> Interest revenue from state and municipal bonds is not taxable (to facilitate borrowing by state and local governments). All interest revenue increases pretax accounting income.
>
> Estimated expenses such as expenses for product gurantees are not deductible until paid. Guarantee expenses are deductible only when actually paid (to make the tax easier to administer). Pretax accounting income is reduced by the amount of these estimates. This reduces taxable income relative to pretax accounting income.
>
> Pension expenses for pretax accounting purposes sometimes exceed the amount actually paid to the pension fund. For tax-determination purposes, the deduction is usually the same as the cash paid to the fund.

Differences Due to Taxpayer Choice. The taxpayer choice of different accounting alternatives may also lead to differences between taxable income and pretax accounting income. The use of different estimates such as the estimated life of intangible assets (Chapter 4) also leads to differences in the two income measures.

Taxpayers usually select accounting alternatives and develop estimates that minimize the tax currently payable. The use of accounting alternatives that minimize taxable income is a key element of tax planning. The main choices for the taxpayer are inventory valuation and the choice of the Last-In First-Out

Tax Determination

method (LIFO) to minimize taxable income (described in Chapter 6), the timing of revenue recognition through the use of installment sales or the completed contract method for construction contracts (also described in Chapter 6), and the choice of advantageous depreciation alternatives (covered in Chapter 3). In many cases, the accounting method used in maintaining the corporation's books should also be used for tax-reporting purposes. As a consequence, the corporation chooses an accounting method for tax-reporting purposes and adopts that method in maintaining the books. Key exceptions to the correspondence of accounting methods for tax and financial-reporting purposes are examined later in this book.

The tax otherwise payable is frequently modified by the effect of tax credits. The general impact of tax credits upon the tax payable is examined in the next section. Chapters 3 and 6 consider eligibility for various tax credits in more detail.

Tax Credits

How a Tax Credit Operates. Tax credits such as the investment tax credit reduce the amount of tax otherwise payable. The effect of tax credits upon the tax payable is shown in the following example.

EXAMPLE: TAX CREDITS. The Payup Corporation's tax otherwise payable before considering tax credits is $439,750. Payup qualifies for a $40,000 investment tax credit and $60,000 in other tax credits.

Payup's tax payable is reduced by the amount of the credit as follows:

Tax otherwise payable	$439,750
Less: Tax credits	100,000
Tax payable	$339,750

The Tax Credit Compared to a Tax Deduction. A tax credit differs from a tax deduction and is considerably more valuable. A credit reduces the tax payable. A deduction only reduces taxable income. If taxable income in the above example had been reduced by $100,000, the amount of the tax would be reduced by only $46,000. The following example illustrates the difference between a tax deduction and a tax credit.

EXAMPLE: A TAX CREDIT COMPARED TO A DEDUCTION. The Highpay Corporation reports taxable income before special items of $400,000. Highpay now discovers that it is eligible for a $100,000 tax credit.

The taxable income is $400,000. The tax is determined as:

	Income	Tax
15% on the first	$ 25,000	$ 3,750
18% on the second	25,000	4,500
30% on the third	25,000	7,500
40% on the fourth	25,000	10,000
46% on the remainder	300,000	138,000
Total	$400,000	$163,750
Less: Tax credit		100,000
Tax payable		$ 63,750

If the credit were treated as a deduction, taxable income would be reduced to $300,000. The tax would be determined as:

	Income	Tax
15% on the first	$ 25,000	$ 3,750
18% on the second	25,000	4,500
30% on the third	25,000	7,500

	Income	Tax
40% on the fourth	25,000	10,000
46% on the remainder	200,000	92,000
Total	$300,000	$117,750

The difference between the tax credit and tax deduction, in this case, is $54,000.

Up to this point the chapter has been concerned with the general procedure for determining the tax. The effect of the method of accounting and the tax-deferral opportunities available through the choice of methods will now be examined.

Accrual-Basis Accounting

The accrual basis of accounting gives recognition to the economic impact of a business transaction rather than to the receipt or payment of cash. Most corporations determine the tax using accrual basis accounting systems.

Sales. The accrual basis recognizes revenue when products are sold or services are provided. Revenue is assumed to be earned at the time of sale even though the receipt of cash may come later. The receipt of a customer's promise to pay for merchandise purchased on account, for example, is recognized as revenue under the accrual basis. The accrual basis is illustrated in the following example.

EXAMPLE: SALES REVENUE. The Goodwork Employment Agency maintains its books on the accrual basis. Goodwork provides services and bills customers for $100,000 in 1984. Goodwork receives only $80,000 of this amount in 1984.

Goodwork provides services worth $100,000 and expects to receive this amount in the future. Goodwork's 1984 income is $100,000 under the accrual basis of accounting.

The costs of operating a business break down into a number of components for tax purposes. Nearly all business expenditures will be deductible—the issue is a matter of timing. One category of cost, the cost of buying or producing goods for resale, is not immediately deductible. The costs of selling the merchandise and administering the business, however, are deductible when incurred. The cost of goods sold and selling and administrative costs are examined in the following two sections.

The Cost of Goods Sold. The costs of purchasing materials and subsequent labor costs do not reduce income at the time the cost is incurred in an accrual basis accounting system. These costs are accumulated and classified as inventories. The stock of inventory is then reduced by the amount of these costs at the time of sale. At this point, the cost of purchasing and manufacturing goods is recognized as the cost of goods sold. The income reduction for the cost of goods sold occurs when the items are removed from inventory at the time of sale. The effect is to recognize revenue and much of the cost of producing this revenue at the same point in time.

An illustration of the relationship of purchases, inventories, and the cost of goods sold follows.

EXAMPLE: THE COST OF GOODS SOLD. The Threadbare Corporation begins manufacturing rugs in 1984. During 1984 Threadbare purchases wool and other materials for $30,000. Threadbare's workers produce 500 rugs at an additional labor cost of $70,000. 400 rugs are sold in 1984.

The cost of producing all the rugs available for sale is:

	Materials	$ 30,000
	Labor	70,000
	Total cost	$100,000

The cost of each rug is:
    Cost per unit = $100,000/500 rugs = $200/rug.
This cost is designated as inventory as the rugs are produced.

The total cost of $100,000 breaks down into two components at year-end:

Cost of items remaining:	100 @ $200	=	$ 20,000
Cost of items sold:	400 @ $200	=	80,000
Total cost			$100,000

Gross income from sales is reduced by the $80,000 cost of goods sold. The $20,000 cost of the remaining 100 rugs remains in inventory. This portion of the cost does not reduce gross income for the current period.

Extension of the above situation to the next year shows how the cost of ending inventory eventually becomes the cost of goods sold.

EXAMPLE: INVENTORIES AND THE COST OF GOODS SOLD. The Threadbare Corporation begins manufacturing rugs in 1984. During 1984 Threadbare produces 500 rugs at a cost of $100,000. 400 rugs are sold in 1984; 100 rugs remain in inventory at a cost of $200 per rug. All of the 100 remaining rugs are sold in 1985.

The 1985 cost of goods sold is $20,000—the cost of the beginning inventory.

The example illustrates that all of the inventory cost eventually reduces income. Some of this reduction, however, takes place in a period subsequent to that in which the cost was incurred.

Selling and Administrative Costs. Selling and administrative costs also reduce income. Selling and administrative costs include the cost of advertising, executive salaries, and other items not directly associated with merchandise purchases and the production of goods. Selling and administrative costs are not part of the cost of goods sold.

The distinction between the cost of goods sold and selling and administrative costs is important because the cost of goods sold reduces taxable income only on the sale of merchandise. Selling and administrative costs are deducted as incurred. The difference between the cost of goods sold and selling and administrative costs is illustrated in the following example.

EXAMPLE: SELLING AND ADMINISTRATIVE COSTS. The Threadbare Corporation paid $100,000 to produce rugs during 1984. Only 80 percent of the rugs were sold. Threadbare also incurred $200,000 in 1984 as selling and administrative costs.

Only $80,000 of the cost of production is deducted as 1984 cost of goods sold. The $200,000 selling and administrative costs are all deducted in 1984.

Under the accrual basis of accounting, costs reduce income when the corporation benefits from services and agrees to make payment. The examples developed earlier show that taxable income may be reduced as a consequence even though payment is not made until a future date.

Cash-Basis Accounting.

A cash-basis accounting system recognizes income and subtractions from income when cash is received or paid. Some service corporations find the cash system to be advantageous because it can help in deferring revenue and accelerating expenses. For example, the cash-basis business can defer current-year revenues by deferring customer billings until the beginning of the next year.

A cash-basis business could also reduce taxes by taking deductions for merchandise when paid for rather than when removed from inventory at the time of sale. This would result in taking the deduction before the time of revenue recognition, and could reduce government tax revenues inordinately. As a result, use of the cash basis is restricted.

The cash basis is available for tax purposes only if it is also used in keeping the taxpayer's books. Generally accepted accounting principles prescribe accrual-basis accounting for financial accounting and this generally precludes use of the cash basis for large firms. A second restriction has to do with inventories. If the business uses inventories, as in the case with most manufacturing or merchandising businesses, then the cash basis is not permitted. Most corporations, and particularly larger corporations, do not meet both of these requirements, and as a consequence determine the tax on an accrual basis.

Timing Transactions and Tax Planning

A considerable amount of tax-planning activity is concerned with tax deferral. Significant deferrals, and particularly indefinite deferrals, can contribute a great deal to the efficient use of resources available to the business.

One common mechanism for tax deferral involves postponement of year-end merchandise shipments to the beginning of the new year. The postponement of shipments defers revenues until the next tax year. Here is an illustration.

EXAMPLE: DELAYED SHIPMENTS. The Handwork Corporation receives customer orders that would result in taxable income of

$100,000 in 1984. Handwork delays shipments on 20 percent of the merchandise until early 1985.

Handwork's 1984 taxable income is reduced by $20,000. At the 40 percent tax rate applicable to income amounts between $75,000 and $100,000, the tax deferred is $8000. The calculations follow:

Taxable income		Without deferral	With deferral
Tax:	15% on $25,000	$ 3,750	$ 3,750
	18% on $25,000	4,500	4,500
	30% on $25,000	7,500	7,500
	40% on $25,000	10,000	—
	40% on $5,000	—	2,000
Total		$25,750	$17,750
Tax deferred			$ 8,000

This tax is only deferred because the remaining merchandise will be shipped in 1985 and will increase 1985's taxable income. The value of the deferral can be estimated by assuming that the tax saved represents funds that will not need to be borrowed. For example, if a 12 percent interest rate is assumed, the present value of the tax deferral for one year is 12 percent of $8000 or $960.

The value of tax deferrals is often much greater than the annual interest saving. In many cases it is possible to continue the deferral indefinitely. The deferral then has the same effect as a tax forgiven. This is illustrated in the following example.

EXAMPLE: THE INDEFINITE DEFERRAL. The Handwork Corporation receives customer orders that would result in taxable income of $100,000 in 1984. Handwork delays shipments on 20

Tax Determination   31

percent of the merchandise until early 1985. In 1985 Handwork ships the remaining merchandise and again receives orders that will result in taxable income of $100,000. Handwork ships only 80% of the amount of these new orders in 1985.

1985 taxable income is $100,000, determined as the $20,000 for 1984 orders shipped in 1985 and $80,000 from 1985 orders also shipped in 1985. Taxable income of $20,000 is again deferred for another year.

Handwork's deferral is indefinite. The equivalent of the 1984 income on orders not shipped until the following year will never be taxed until the amount of orders not shipped in the current year drops below $20,000. The $8000 temporary tax saving is deferred indefinitely, providing $8000 in additional capital for the business.

The above illustration shows that the value of year-end tax deferral is often greater than one year's tax savings alone, since some deferrals tend to be indefinite.

Tax deferral can also be achieved through accelerating deductions. For example, corporations commonly accelerate ordering of new office supplies to obtain a current-year deduction. The acceleration of deductions is illustrated as follows.

EXAMPLE: ACCELERATED DEDUCTIONS. The Ajax Corporation normally purchases paper and other office supplies on a weekly basis as supplies are needed. Ajax does not treat the cost of its office supplies as inventories. At year-end, Ajax obtains the usual quantity of supplies and in addition purchases supplies for January and February at an additional cost of $10,000.

The additional $10,000 cost is deductible in the current year. Ajax has accelerated $10,000 in deductions and at the 46 percent marginal rate, defers $4600 in tax for the year. The present value of the tax saving depends on the interest rate. At a 10 percent cost of capital, for example, the interest the taxpayer could earn on $4600 is $460 per year.

If Ajax repeats the above practice every year, the $4600 tax deferral becomes a permanent tax saving. It should be noted, however, that the tax deferral does involve some cost, in that Ajax is acquiring supplies earlier than would normally be the case. The tax deferral will be advantageous only if the cost of carrying the additional supplies is minimal. That would appear to be the case in this example.

The selection of favorable accounting methods also contributes to tax deferral. Alternative accounting methods will be examined in Chapter 6.

OPERATING LOSSES

The discussion thus far has concerned corporations reporting taxable income. In any given year a large proportion of United States corporations report operating losses for tax purposes. Operating losses occur when deductions exceed taxable revenues. These operating losses lead to loss carrybacks and carryforwards. Loss carrybacks result in immediate tax benefit. Carryforwards are potentially valuable assets. Corporations sometimes pay substantial amounts for the use of acquired corporations' carryforwards in acquisition situations.

The Operating Loss Carryback

The operating loss carryback applies to certain corporations in loss years. If the loss corporation previously paid taxes, the corporation may be able to carry the losses of the present period back against previous-year income. This carryback of operating losses results in a refund of taxes previously paid.

The loss-carryback provisions are intended to smooth out the tax effects for corporations reporting profits in some years and losses in other years. The carryback period is limited to three years. The carryback operates as follows.

Operating Losses

EXAMPLE: THE OPERATING LOSS CARRYBACK. The Donin Corporation began business in January 1983. Donin reported taxable income and paid the following taxes:

Year	Taxable income	Tax payments
1983	$20,000	$3,000
1984	30,000	4,650

In 1985 Donin reports a $20,000 loss.

Using the carryback procedure, Donin carries the loss back to 1983. The 1985 loss offsets all of the 1983 taxable income. Donin applies for a refund of the taxes paid in 1983—$3000.

The 1984 income of $30,000 continues to provide carryback eligibility. If Donin's 1985 loss amounted to $50,000, Donin would carry the full $50,000 back against both the 1983 and 1984 income. This would provide a full refund of all taxes paid in both 1983 and 1984.

With a 1985 loss of $20,000, Donin can only carryback this amount. If Donin again reports losses in 1986, Donin will carryback up to $30,000 of these losses against the 1984 income.

The carryback may offset only a portion of earlier-year income. In this case, only a portion of the previous-year taxable income is reduced. This is illustrated in the following example.

EXAMPLE: THE OPERATING LOSS CARRYBACK CONTINUED. The Donin Corporation began business in January 1983. Donin reported taxable income and paid the following taxes:

Year	Taxable income	Tax payments
1983	$20,000	$3,000
1984	30,000	4,650
1985	(20,000)	0

Donin loses $5000 in 1986.

In 1985 Donin carried back the loss and filed for a refund of taxes paid on $20,000 of previous taxable income. In 1986 Donin carries back the $5000 loss against $5000 in of previous taxable income. Since the 1983 carryback entitlement is used up, the 1986 loss is carried back to 1984. The carryback reduces 1984 income by $5000. Donin files for a refund of $900 of 1984 taxes paid. This is determined as:

1984 Original Tax and Tax after Carryback

	Original	After carryback
1984 taxable income	$30,000	$30,000
Less: carryback	0	5,000
Income after carryback	$30,000	$25,000
Tax: 15% on $25,000	$ 3,750	$ 3,750
18% on $ 5,000	900	—
Total	$ 4,650	$ 3,750
Tax refund		$ 900

The operating loss carryback procedure helps to smooth income and losses. The procedure is particularly beneficial for the business that experiences alternative periods of prosperity and disappointment.

The Operating Loss Carryforward

The operating loss carryforward permits offsetting taxable income and losses when carryback entitlement is not available. Carryback entitlement may not be available if it has already been used. This can occur if losses exceed income of the three previous years. Carryback eligibility is also not available for new corporations without any previous tax history.

Operating Losses

The loss carryforward results from current-period operating losses in excess of carryback entitlement. The carryforward offsets taxable income earned in future periods. Losses can be carried forward for a maximum period of 15 years. The operation of loss carryforwards is illustrated in the following example.

EXAMPLE: THE OPERATING LOSS CARRYFORWARD. The Rebound Corporation lost $350,000 in 1984. Rebound had no operating loss carryback entitlement. In 1985, Rebound reports taxable income of $500,000.

The 1984 loss provides carryforward entitlement. In 1985 Rebound applies the $350,000 carryforward entitlement against the 1985 taxable income of $500,000. As a result, the taxes payable are based on only the remaining $150,000 of 1985 income.

1985 taxable income	$500,000
Less: Operating loss carryforward	350,000
Basis for tax determination	$150,000

The carryforward does not necessarily provide tax benefit. The carryforward becomes valuable to the taxpayer only in the event of future profitability. If the loss corporation remains unprofitable, it cannot benefit from the carryforward. In this case, the loss may help to make the loss corporation an attractive acquisition candidate. Chapters 10 and 11 examine conditions under which the loss carryforward entitlement may be used to benefit an acquiring corporation (and increase the value of a loss corporation offered for sale).

Operating loss carrybacks and carryforwards only apply to corporations with a history of operating losses. Successful corporations, however, sometimes report losses for tax purposes as a consequence of liberal tax legislation provisions relating to deductions. As a result, many corporations benefit from utilizing the loss carryback and carryforward procedures.

Operating Losses and the Financial Statements.

The Loss Carryback. Loss carrybacks reduce the amount of loss reported on the financial statements. The effects of the carryback should be considered carefully because the carrybacks will not be recurring items. In other words, the loss from operations will often be greater than the reported net loss due to the favorable influence of carrybacks on the net loss calculation.

The loss carryback disclosure indicates that the corporation has filed for a refund of taxes paid in previous years and has reduced losses by the amount of the refund. The refund receivable appears on the balance sheet as a current asset.

The Loss Carryforward. The loss carryforward represents a potentially valuable contingent asset for the loss corporation. The loss carryforward, however, does not usually appear on the balance sheet. The asset is not recognized on the balance sheet because the carryforward will provide benefit only in the event of future profitability. The existence of an operating loss carryforward is frequently cited in the narrative portion of the annual report or in the notes to the financial statements. A representative loss carryforward situation is shown in the following example.

EXAMPLE: OPERATING LOSS CARRYFORWARD DISCLOSURE. The New Deal Corporation has reported profits for the past several years. In discussing the financial statements with one of the corporation's banks, New Deal's president indicates that the corporation also has a valuable contingent asset that does not appear on the balance sheet. She references a loss carryforward worth approximately $20,000,000.

The loss carryforward probably results from an excess of tax losses over the previous three years' taxable income. New Deal may have losses for tax purposes even though it reports profits to shareholders due to the use of different accounting methods for tax purposes.

New Deal expects that the loss carryforward will reduce taxes payable when New Deal finally becomes profitable for tax purposes. The carryforward will offset taxes on the next $20,000,000 of taxable income. The banker may consider the loss carryforward as equivalent to an asset if the banker feels that the tax benefits will be realized in the future.

The New Deal Corporation example illustrates the disclosure of the tax loss carryforward. The loss carryforward only provides value if the loss corporation eventually reports profits. If the loss carryforward corporation does not become profitable at some time in the future, the loss carryforward will not provide any future benefits.

TAX PAYMENTS

The timing of tax payments is an important determinant of cash flow. Earlier the advantage of deferring the tax from one year to the next was examined. Deferring tax payments within a particular year can also add to temporary increases in cash availability. Lenders are well acquainted with the corporation's need for cash to make quarterly tax payments and sometimes extend short-term loans for tax-payment purposes.

The Estimated Tax

Tax payments during the year are based on estimates of the taxes expected to be payable on that year's taxable income.

__The Quarterly Payments.__ Corporations pay the tax on a quarterly basis. Any deficiency is payable when the return is filed. This quarterly payment system is considered to be consistent with the taxpayer's ability to pay. It also speeds up the availability of funds to the government.

Tax returns are due within two and one-half months after the end of the tax year.

The Amount of Payment. At least 90 percent of the tax liability must be paid during the year. The estimated payments are due in equal installments—that is, one-fourth of the tax is due at the end of the first quarter, a second one-fourth is due at the end of the second quarter, and so on. An illustration follows.

EXAMPLE: THE ESTIMATED TAX. The Payup Corporation expected to report taxable income in 1985 of $1,000,000, with taxes payable of $439,750.
One-fourth of Payup's tax liability is:

$$\$439{,}750/4 = \$109{,}937$$

Of this amount, 90 percent, or $98,944, is payable each quarter. The 90 percent limitation is important, because it provides some opportunity for deferring payment. Since only $98,944 is payable each quarter, the difference between this amount and one-fourth of the tax liability can be put to use for other purposes until the final tax payment is due.

Corporations prefer to delay tax payments as much as possible. As a result, a system of penalties for underpayments has been developed to encourage prompt payment. The underpayment penalty is substantial and provides an incentive for on-time payment.

Exceptions

The underpayment penalties are subject to a number of exceptions. These exceptions recognize the difficulty involved with

Tax Payments 39

estimating annual taxable income early in the year, particularly for small businesses and seasonal businesses.

Annualized Income-to-Date. One exception permits payment of 90 percent of the current year taxes based on the annualized income to date rather than the actual annual income determined at the end of the year. The income-to-date exception is illustrated in the following example.

EXAMPLE: THE INCOME-TO-DATE EXCEPTION. The Payup Corporation reported taxable income of $300,000 in the first half of 1985.

The annualized income at midyear is $600,000. This is determined as twice the half-year amount. Payup must remit a total of 90 percent of the tax due on one-half of $600,000 by the time of the second payment. (A portion of this amount was due previously at the end of the first quarter).

This exception applies even if Payup eventually reports $1,000,000 taxable income for the year. In that case, an extremely large final payment will result.

The seasonal business may also elect to modify the calculation by annualizing income on the basis of the past history of each quarter's income as a percentage of the total annual income. This modification can sometimes be advantageous for the seasonal business.

The Small Corporation. Small corporations are subject to additional exceptions. A corporation is considered small for estimated tax purposes if taxable income did not exceed $1 million in any of the three preceding years. A special exception is available for the small corporation because it often encounters more difficulty in forecasting income.

The small corporation can avoid the penalty if each quarterly installment payment equals at least one-fourth of the tax paid last year. The operation of the exception is shown as follows.

EXAMPLE: THE TAX PAID LAST YEAR. The Payup Corporation is a small corporation. Payup's tax last year was $60,000.

Payup's estimated payments are based on the $60,000 tax paid last year. Only $15,000 is required each quarter.

If Payup actually reports $1,000,000 in taxable income for the year, the tax payable will still be determined in the usual manner. Payup's final payment due with the tax return will be extremely large. Meanwhile, Payup benefits as a result of deferring the tax payment.

The small corporation can also avoid penalty in the case of a tax rate change by making payments based on last year's income and this year's tax rates. An illustration follows.

EXAMPLE: LAST YEAR'S INCOME AT THIS YEAR'S RATES. The Payup Corporation is a small corporation. Payup's tax last year was $60,000. This year, the tax rates have been reduced. If Payup was taxed on last year's income at this year's lower tax rates, the tax payable would be only $50,000.

Payup needs to make quarterly payments equal to only one-fourth of $50,000—the tax that would have been due last year at this year's tax rates. Each quarterly tax payment must equal only $12,500.

The use of last year's rates is generally advantageous only in the event of tax rate reductions, as illustrated in the above example.

THE MULTIDIVISION CORPORATION

This section considers the decision-making implications with respect to the multidivision corporation. The examination shows that the tax rate applicable to the multidivision corporation is the corporation's overall marginal tax rate.

Many of the largest corporations are comprised of semi-autonomous divisions. Some of these divisions may generate high profits while other divisions may be less profitable or even operate at a loss. This leads to the question of which tax rate is the relevant marginal rate for decision-making by an individual department or division.

The relevant tax rate is the rate to the corporation as a whole. If, for example, the marginal tax rate paid by the company is 46 percent, the same rate applies to each division even though some divisions may contribute little if anything to corporate profits. The following example illustrates the tax-planning considerations in the multidivision corporation.

EXAMPLE: THE MARGINAL TAX FOR THE MULTIDIVISION CORPORATION. The Payup Corporation has two divisions—the Chemical Products Division and the Recreation Products Division. The Chemical Products Division generates taxable income of $45,000. The Recreation Products Division generates taxable income of $955,000.

Payup earns $1,000,000 and is taxed $439,750 on this amount. The marginal tax rate relevant to decision making should be the 46 percent effective tax rate to the corporation. A $10,000 reduction in taxable income, for example, reduces corporate taxes by $4600, or 46 percent. This holds whether the reduction in income results from activity associated with the Chemical Products Division or the Recreation Products Division.

The marginal rate applicable to the corporation as a whole applies to all domestic divisions of the corporation including divisions with low profits. If a division operates at a loss, the loss reduces income and taxes for the corporation as a whole. This tax reduction is also determined at the corporation's effective marginal rate.

The tax on overseas operations of the multidivision corporation is complicated by a number of factors. These include the organization of the overseas operations—as a branch of the domestic operation, as a United States subsidiary operating overseas, or as a foreign subsidiary. The particular country in which foreign operations are conducted also determines the tax. These considerations are regarded as beyond the scope of the book. This book is concerned only with the tax on domestic operations.

RELATED TAXPAYERS

One group of related taxpayers is the individual taxpayer and the controlled corporation. Another group of related taxpayers consists of corporations related to each other through common ownership. Related taxpayers receive special tax treatment to reduce the attractiveness of setting up transactions or separate corporations primarily for tax benefit. Thus the related taxpayer provisions impose restrictions upon the concerned parties.

This section considers related taxpayer provisions associated with the concepts developed earlier in the chapter. The provisions examined here pertain to the controlled group, expenditures for the benefit of a related taxpayer, and the arms-length transaction. Additional related party provisions will be examined in later chapters.

The Controlled Group

The tax rate is modified for a group of corporations that qualify as a controlled group.

Background. Prior to the development of a special treatment for the controlled group, businesses sometimes divided into multiple corporations solely to obtain tax benefits. For example, a corporation with $250,000 income would divide into 10 smaller corporations each with income of only $25,000. Total taxable income is not changed. The amount of tax, however, would be drastically reduced. The marginal rate applicable to $25,000 income is only 15 percent as opposed to 46 percent on income in excess of $100,000. Special legislation was enacted to eliminate the tax benefits that would otherwise result from dividing a single corporation into several smaller corporations.

The Tax. The tax for a controlled group is based on the rate applicable to the entire group rather than that of each individual group member. As a consequence, dividing a corporation into multiple corporations will not normally reduce the tax rate. The treatment of the controlled group is shown in the following example.

EXAMPLE: THE CONTROLLED GROUP. Corporation A owns Corporation B. A reports taxable income of $100,000. B reports taxable income of $25,000.

If A and B are members of a controlled group, the tax is determined on the combined income of $125,000. Reference to the tables at the beginning of the chapter indicates that the tax is:

15% on the first	$25,000	$ 3,750
18% on the second	$25,000	4,500
30% on the third	$25,000	7,500
40% on the fourth	$25,000	10,000
46% on the remainder	$25,000	11,500
Total		$37,250

If A and B are not members of a controlled group, the tax is determined on the separate incomes of $100,000 and $25,000 as follows:

Tax on A's $100,000 (determined from the above schedule)	$25,750
Tax on B's $25,000	3,750
Total	$29,500

The controlled group provisions reduce the possibility that related corporations may obtain tax benefit merely by splitting into separate corporations.

Qualifications. A parent–subsidiary is a controlled group if the parent owns 80 percent or more of the voting stock of the subsidiary. If two or more separate corporations are owned primarily by the same shareholders, these corporations may also comprise a controlled group. For example, if two shareholders each own 50 percent of corporations A and B, then A and B are members of a controlled group. As a consequence, many family-run corporation combinations are treated as a single corporation for purposes of determining the applicable tax rates.

The controlled group provisions do not affect the responsibility for the tax. Each corporation in the group files a separate tax return and is responsible for its own tax payments.

Expenditures for the Benefit of a Related Taxpayer

The Actual Payment Requirement. Certain rules for the recognition of income and deduction of costs associated with continuing operations are modified for related taxpayers. A corporation and a shareholder owning more than 50 percent of the stock are related taxpayers. A parent corporation and its subsidiary are also related for purposes of this rule.

Under the accrual basis of accounting, promises to pay interest and other obligations are deductible when the property or services giving rise to the promise is received.

Related Taxpayers

When a taxpayer deals with a related party, the legislation specifies that the costs must actually be paid to qualify as a deduction.

The related taxpayer provisions attempt to discourage the following type of transaction.

EXAMPLE: THE NEED FOR RELATED TAXPAYER PROVISIONS. Mary Smith owns all of the stock in the Federal Motors Corporation. Mary is a cash-basis taxpayer. She starts the corporation by investing a small amount of money for machinery. She rents a factory building to the corporation for $7000 per month. Every month the corporation recognizes an obligation for the rent payment and deducts this amount from taxable income. Over time, the amount of the obligation increases and no cash is paid.

As a cash-basis taxpayer, Mary does not recognize rent income since no cash is received. The corporation, however, deducts the amount from taxable income. Consequently, the combined entity consisting of Mary and the corporation would be receiving tax benefit without giving up anything of value.

If the above situation were permitted, related taxpayers could get together and arrange for large deductions on the part of one party with no offsetting income on the part of the other. The related party provisions discourage the above type of situation. Related parties must actually make the cash payments as a requisite for the deduction.

The Arms-Length Transaction

Another related party rule provides that transactions with related parties must be conducted at arms-length. In other words, the selling price must be the same price that would be determined through bargaining by unrelated taxpayers. If this were not the case, related taxpayers could benefit unfairly by establishing unrealistic selling prices. For example, a taxpayer who owns a corporation taxed at low rates could cause the corporation to sell equipment to the owner at an artificially high price. The corporation's gain would be taxed at a low rate. The owner would then benefit from increased depreciation deductions in later years. The related party rules reduce the potential for this type of transaction.

A major stockholder may sell or rent property to the corporation. The deductions, however, must be based on terms and conditions similar to those that would apply to a rental to unrelated parties. The objective of these related party rules is to minimize the ability to avoid taxes by engaging in transactions that do not change the taxpayer's economic situation except for tax purposes.

SUMMARY

The Tax Rate. The federal income tax is a progressive tax with tax rates beginning at 15 percent of taxable income. The tax rate increases with taxable income. The marginal tax rate for more profitable corporations is 46 percent of taxable income. Small corporations sometimes obtain opportunities for tax planning by timing transactions to benefit from differences in tax rates. For large corporations, the tax on each additional dollar earned tends to remain at the 46 percent marginal rate.

Taxable Income. The tax is based on taxable income. The determination begins with revenues from sales, interest and investment revenue, and rent receipts. Funds obtained through borrowing or issuing the corporation's own stock are not included as income.

Deductions represent the cost of earning income. Typical deductions include employee salaries, interest, rent, and taxes.

Deductions from gross income include most ordinary business expenditures. The cost of property expected to provide benefit beyond the current tax year is classified as a capital expenditure. Capital expenditures are not immediately deductible.

The acceleration of deductions and deferral of income items can lead to significant tax deferrals.

Differences Between Taxable Income and Pretax Accounting Income. Taxable income and pretax accounting income differ because the purposes of the two accounting systems differ. Some income differences result from different accounting rules, and other income differences result from taxpayer choice. The selection of preferred accounting alternatives can also contribute substantially to tax deferrals.

Tax Credits. Credits such as the investment tax credit are subtracted from the tax otherwise payable to determine the required tax payment.

The Accrual Basis. The accrual-basis corporation recognizes revenue when products are sold or services are provided. The deduction of costs is matched with the timing of revenue recognition.

Costs in the accrual-basis accounting system fall into two general categories—(1) the cost of goods sold and (2) selling and administrative costs. The cost of merchandise purchased for resale or the cost of manufactured goods reduces taxable income only when the items are sold. Selling and administrative costs are deducted when the business receives goods or services and agrees to make a future payment.

The cash basis of accounting offers increased flexibility in providing for tax deferrals. Although some smaller service businesses are entitled to use the cash basis of accounting, larger corporations and corporations with inventories are on the accrual basis.

Operating Losses. Operating loss carryovers provide for leveling the tax effects of good and bad years. The operating losses may be carried back against taxable income for the three previous tax years. Operating losses can also be carried forward to offset future income for up to 15 years. Operating loss carryforwards represent potentially valuable contingent benefits if the business subsequently reports taxable income.

The actual value of the carryforward, however, is recognized only if the corporation reports taxable income at some time in the future. Corporations with unused carryforward eligibility may make good acquisition targets if the carryforward can be used by the acquiring corporation.

When the Tax Is Due. The full amount of the tax is due with the tax return on March 15. The tax is due in quarterly installments with penalties for missed or late payments.

Since the actual tax cannot be determined until the end of the year, the legislation provides for waiver of penalties if exceptions are met. One set of exceptions relates to the income to date in relation to the income expected for the year.

Another set of exceptions applies only to the small corporation. The small corporation may avoid penalty by paying in equal quarterly installments an amount equivalent to last year's tax.

The Multidivision Corporation. The tax rate applicable to the multidivision corporation is often important in evaluating investment alternatives and performance. The overall corporate marginal tax rate applies to all domestic divisions of the multidivision corporation.

Related Taxpayers. The tax for a controlled group of two or more corporations is based on the rate applicable for the entire group rather than that of each individual group member.

Parent–subsidiary relationships constitute controlled groups. Two or more separate corporations may also constitute a controlled group if a small number of shareholders own a substantial common ownership in each of the individual corporations.

Expenditures for the benefit of a related taxpayer must actually be paid to qualify as deductions from taxable income. Without this rule, related taxpayers could effectively conduct paper transactions solely for purposes of reducing the tax.

Related taxpayers are free to engage in any business transactions without restriction. Transactions with related parties, however, must be conducted at arms-length to ensure deductions as ordinary business items.

Chapter 3

The Acquisition and Use of Productive Property

Both the acquisition and use of property have significant tax implications. The acquisition of certain types of property leads to direct tax reductions in the form of the investment tax credit and business energy credit. The cost of productive property is then deducted over a period of time.

This chapter begins with the examination of tax credits. The investment tax credit reduces taxes by a percentage of the cost of qualifying property. An investment tax credit also applies to the cost of renovating certain old buildings. The business energy credit is available to businesses that acquire certain energy-saving property. A limited subset of property qualifies for both credits.

Next this chapter considers the deductions associated with the property cost. The cost of productive business property is capitalized rather than deducted immediately. This cost, in most cases, is later deducted gradually as depreciation.

The Accelerated Cost Recovery System (ACRS) determines the depreciation deduction for most property. ACRS provides for accelerated depreciation using relatively short asset lives. Residual value is not considered under ACRS. ACRS generally results in substantial tax deferrals. Corporations may also elect to expense property eligible for ACRS. The expense election results in an immediate deduction, but the amount of qualifying property is limited, and significant disadvantages are also associated with use of this election.

The acquisition of other property such as intangible assets and mineral resources also leads to tax deductions. The treatment of mineral rights is particularly interesting—in some cases the property cost can be deducted several times over the life of the property.

Corporations can also lease productive property as an alternative to purchase. Only certain leases, however, qualify as leases for tax purposes. If the conditions for lease treatment are met, the lease may provide a mechanism for transferring the tax benefit of the investment tax credit and depreciation deduction from one party to another.

A number of important tax-planning implications are associated with property acquisitions and use. For example, the present value of both depreciation and the investment tax credit can be increased by placing property in service at advantageous points in time. Also, the design of a facility, particularly a building, influences eligibility for the investment tax credit. And as mentioned earlier, leasing provides a mechanism for transferring tax benefits from parties that would not otherwise benefit to parties that can effectively use the tax reductions.

PROPERTY ACQUISITIONS

As goods and services are used by the business, the costs of these goods and services are deducted to determine taxable income. The costs of utilities, office rents, employee salaries, and equipment repairs, for example, are deducted as the services are used. The timing of the deduction usually corresponds closely to the timing of the payment for the item. The following example reviews the treatment of currently deductible costs.

EXAMPLE: COSTS DEDUCTED AS INCURRED. The Payup Corporation purchases and uses office supplies costing $9000.

The cost of supplies used reduces taxable income in the period of use. The $9000 cost is deducted to determine the current-year taxable income.

Productive property such as land, buildings, patents, and equipment is treated differently. The cost of productive property does not reduce taxable income immediately.

Productive property is property intended to be used over a period of time for manufacturing, selling merchandise, or providing services. Most businesses need productive property to conduct operations. This type of property is also referred to as a fixed asset—an item that will continue to have value to the business for a period of time. The cost of productive property is capitalized rather than deducted immediately.

The cost of land, goodwill, and other productive property that does not wear out or become obsolete is never deductible. The cost of machinery and buildings and other property that does wear out or become obsolete is deducted over time through a procedure referred to as depreciation. The treatment of depreciable property is illustrated as follows.

EXAMPLE: THE ACQUISITION OF PRODUCTIVE PROPERTY. The Payup Corporation acquires a building for use as a factory in 1985.

The cost of the building is capitalized and is not deductible in 1985. Part of the total cost is assigned to the land, and this portion is never deductible. The portion of the cost attributable to the building is deducted over a period of time.

The acquisition of certain items of productive property gives rise to tax credits. The next section introduces some of the more important tax credits associated with the acquisition of productive property.

TAX CREDITS

Tax credits are available to corporations that acquire certain qualifying property. The stated objective of these tax credits is to provide additional investment incentives to taxpayers.

Credits reduce the tax otherwise payable by the corporation. In so doing, they effectively reduce the cost of acquiring qualified property items. Corporations can often reduce the tax by acquiring property subject to tax credits. Not all property, however, qualifies. Sometimes minor differences in the nature of the property affect its eligibility for tax benefit.

The Investment Tax Credit

The investment tax credit was developed to increase incentives to invest in machinery and equipment in the interest of increased productivity.

The credit is determined as a percentage of the investment in qualifying property. The following example illustrates the computation of the investment tax credit.

EXAMPLE: THE INVESTMENT TAX CREDIT. The Payup Corporation acquires property at a cost of $200,000. A 6 percent investment tax credit applies.

The credit reduces tax payments by 6 percent of $200,000. The net cost of the investment to the buyer is:

Purchase price	$200,000
Less: Investment tax credit	12,000
Net cost	$188,000

Since the credit effectively reduces the cost of the investment, the credit is considered to act as an investment incentive.

Qualifying Property. Qualifying property includes equipment, machinery, and vehicles. The credit is restricted primarily to depreciable, tangible property and does not apply to most real estate. Consequently, fixtures such as gas pumps, grocery store counters, and neon signs qualify for the credit. The gas station building and the grocery store building do not qualify.

Qualifying property generally must be used within the United States. There are no restrictions, however, regarding the place of manufacture.

The benefits of the investment tax credit can be maximized by effective tax planning at the facility design stage. For example, the credit does not apply to buildings or structural components such as walls. Movable partitions in buildings, however, do qualify for the credit while fixed walls do not qualify. Built-in equipment such as a TV in a hotel is considered to be part of the building. Portable TVs used in a hotel, however, do qualify for the credit.

The Amount of the Credit. The amount of the credit depends upon the class of property. Most property qualifying for the credit is either three-year class property or five-year class property. Property in the three-year class consists primarily of automobiles, light-duty trucks, and machinery and equipment used in research and development activities. Other items qualifying for the credit are usually classed as five-year property.

The credit reduces taxes payable by 6 percent of the cost of three-year class property. The credit is 10 percent of the cost of

Tax Credits

other property. The determination of the credit for property in different year classes is shown in the following example.

EXAMPLE: THE INVESTMENT TAX CREDIT. The Payup Corporation invests $1,000,000 in new vehicles classified as three-year property and $2,300,000 in new equipment not in the three-year class.

The maximum elegibility for each class of property is:

3-year class: 6% of $1,000,000	$ 60,000
5-year class: 10% of $2,300,000	$230,000
Total	$290,000

Limitations. The maximum eligibility is subject to limitations and can not always be applied against the tax liability. The total amount of the credit is limited by taxes otherwise payable.

The credit can offset all of the first $25,000 of tax payable, but only 85 percent of the remaining tax. The following example illustrates the restrictions imposed by the taxes payable limitation.

EXAMPLE: THE INVESTMENT TAX CREDIT RESTRICTED BY TAXES PAYABLE. Continuing the Payup Corporation example, assume that Payup's investment in new productive property entitles the corporation to an investment tax credit of $290,000. The tax otherwise payable is only $300,000.

The taxes payable of $300,000 impose a ceiling on the amount of the credit as follows:

100% of first $25,000 of tax	$ 25,000
85% of remaining tax ($300,000 − $25,000)	233,750
Total current-year eligibility	$258,750

Only $258,750 can be deducted from current-year taxes. The difference between this amount and the $290,000 eligibility determined without regard to the tax otherwise payable constraint is $31,250.

The $31,250 credit not used can be applied against previous or future tax payments using a carryback and carryforward procedure. The procedure is similar to that outlined in Chapter 2 for the carryback and carryforward of operating losses.

The purpose of the investment tax credit limitation is to reduce the possibility that profitable corporations may escape tax completely through use of the investment tax credit provision. Corporations that cannot use the investment tax credit directly often arrange to benefit indirectly. One such mechanism is through property leasing. Leasing will be examined later in this chapter.

Used Property. Used property costing up to $125,000 in a given year is eligible for the investment tax credit. The used property entitlement is primarily of interest to smaller corporations. Larger corporations with substantial property acquisitions benefit from the used property eligibility very early in the tax year. Consequently, when computing the marginal tax impact of investment alternatives for large corporations, the used property credit is generally ignored.

The Reduction in Adjusted Basis. The basis of property is important because it affects the depreciation deduction and the gain on sale. These topics will be considered later in this chapter and in Chapter 4. The basis of property eligible for the investment tax credit is reduced as a result of the credit.

The reduction in basis associated with the investment tax credit is equal to one-half the amount of the credit. The following example illustrates the operation of the basis reduction.

EXAMPLE: THE REDUCTION IN BASIS ASSOCIATED WITH THE INVESTMENT TAX CREDIT. The Payup Corporation invests $1,000,000 in new vehicles classified as three-year property and $2,300,000 in new equipment not in the three-year class.

The investment tax credit is determined as:

3-year class: 6% of $1,000,000	$ 60,000
5-year class: 10% of $2,300,000	$230,000
Total	$290,000

The basis of the properties is reduced by one-half the amount of the credit or $145,000. The adjusted basis immediately upon acquisition is:

Cost of property	$3,300,000
Less: ½ investment tax credit	145,000
Beginning adjusted basis	$3,155,000

The basis reduction reduces the benefits associated with the investment tax credit. Prior to 1983, a 10 percent investment tax credit effectively reduced the cost of acquiring property by this amount. This is no longer the case. A 10 percent investment tax credit initially returns 10 percent of the investment cost, but in later years the depreciation deductions are reduced by part of the amount of the credit. The taxable gain on the sale may also be influenced by the reduction of basis.

Corporations may elect to reduce the amount of the credit directly in lieu of the basis adjustment. In the event of this election, the credit is reduced by two percentage points (as from 10 percent to 8 percent). The basis reduction alternative is illustrated in the following example.

Example: Reduction of Investment Tax Credit in Lieu of Basis Adjustment. The Payup Corporation invests $1,000,000 in new vehicles classified as three-year property and $2,300,000 in new equipment not in the three-year class.

The maximum eligibility for each class of property is:

3-year class: 6% of $1,000,000	$ 60,000
5-year class: 10% of $2,300,000	$230,000
Total	$290,000

If Payup elects the reduction in investment tax credit, the credit is reduced by two percent in each case, as follows:

3-year class: 4% of $1,000,000	$ 40,000
5-year class: 8% of $2,300,000	$184,000
Total	$224,000

Payup now maintains the basis of the property at the cost of $3,300,000.

Taxpayers usually maximize the present value of tax savings by claiming the full amount of the credit and taking the basis reduction. The election, however, should simplify record-keeping, and some taxpayers may find it beneficial for this reason.

Accelerated Acquisitions. Sometimes corporations accelerate acquisitions to take advantage of the credit as early as possible. If the business plans to invest in qualified property early in a tax year, it may be beneficial to arrange for delivery and operation before the end of the previous year.

The entire investment tax credit is taken when the property is placed in service. This applies even if the property is placed in service on the last day of the year. The total amount of the credit does not change as a result of this procedure. The accelerated timing, however, acts to defer the tax and provide a source of temporary financing. The Walt Disney Corporation, for example, reportedly accelerated the opening of the only partially completed Epcot Center complex to occur late in its tax year. As a result, Disney received the benefit of the investment tax credit and current year depreciation deductions on the completed portions one year earlier.

The Flow-Through and Deferral Methods for Financial Reporting

For financial accounting purposes two alternatives are used for determining the effect of the credit upon income. These alternatives are the flow-through and the deferral method of accounting. The choice of methods does not affect tax determination. An understanding of the operation of the two methods is important, however, in interpreting financial statements.

The Flow-Through Method. The flow-through method treats the investment tax credit as a reduction in tax expense in the year of acquisition. Tax expense in subsequent years is not affected. In periods of heavy investment, the flow-through method usually provides the largest reduction in tax expense and increases reported income.

The Deferral Method. The deferral method spreads the reduction in tax expense over the expected useful asset life. Compared to the flow-through method, the deferral method reduces current-period tax expense by a lesser amount. In later periods, however, the deferral method results in additional reductions of tax expense.

Although the flow-through method generally reduces tax expense in years of property acquisition, the two methods reduce tax expense by exactly the same amount over the life of the corporation.

Difference in Cash Flows. The choice between the flow-through and deferral methods has no effect whatever upon taxes payable and cash flows. The alternative methods apply only to financial accounting practices. Cash flows are affected only by the actual credit as determined above. The following example illustrates this concept.

EXAMPLE: THE FLOW-THROUGH VERSUS THE DEFERRAL METHOD. The Payup Corporation acquires five-year class property costing $100,000 and qualifying for the investment tax credit. The property has an expected useful life of five-years. Taxes payable before considering the investment tax credit are $25,000 per year.

The five-year class property qualifies for the 10% investment tax credit. The credit is 10% of the $100,000 cost, or $10,000. This reduces taxes in the first year by $10,000, to $15,000.

For financial reporting purposes the business may elect either the flow-through or deferral method of accounting for the investment tax credit. With the flow-through method, first-year tax expense is reported as $15,000. With the deferral method, the reduction in tax expense is spread over the five-year expected property life. This reduces tax expense by only $2000 each year. The year-to-year comparison is shown in the following example:

METHOD USED FOR FINANCIAL REPORTING

Year	Flow-through method tax expense	Deferral method tax expense
1	$ 15,000	$ 23,000
2	25,000	23,000
3	25,000	23,000

Tax Credits

Year	Flow-through method tax expense	Deferral method tax expense
4	25,000	23,000
5	25,000	23,000
Total	$115,000	$115,000

The above example illustrates two important concepts. First, the choice between the flow-through and deferral methods is solely a financial accounting choice and has no impact whatever upon taxes payable or cash flows. Second, the total tax expense (and consequently the total income) over the life of the business should be the same regardless of whether the flow-through or deferral method is used for financial reporting. The choice of methods provides only a temporary effect on income reported for financial accounting purposes.

The Investment Tax Credit for Rehabilitated Buildings

The credit for rehabilitated buildings applies to the cost of renovating certain old buildings. The credit was designed to provide incentive for restoring buildings in downtown areas.

The Three Types of Credits. The amount of the credit depends upon the age and type of the buildings. A three-tier investment tax credit applies to materials, labor, and other costs of rehabilitating old buildings. The minimum age criteria and applicable investment tax credit percentages are:

Property type	Percentage credit
30-year-old building	15%
40-year-old building	20%
Certified historic structure	25%

Only nonresidential buildings are eligible for the 15 percent and 20 percent credits. The 25 percent credit for certified historic structures applies to both residential and nonresidential buildings. Classification of property as a certified historic structure requires either listing in the National Register or location within a designated district that meets National Register standards.

The Impact Upon Adjusted Basis. The impact of the 15 percent and 20 percent rehabilitation tax credit upon the adjusted basis is more severe than that of the regular credit. The entire amount of the rehabilitation credit reduces the depreciable basis of the rehabilitated buildings. For rehabilitations of certified historic structures, the basis is reduced by only one-half the credit, as in the case of the regular investment tax credit.

Qualifications. A rehabilitation expenditure does not qualify for the credit if it includes the cost of acquiring a building, is for the enlargement of a building, or if more than 25 percent of the exterior walls of the building are replaced.

Only major modifications qualify for the credit. In order for a rehabilitation to qualify, the rehabilitation expenditures must exceed the adjusted basis of the property prior to the commencement of the rehabilitation. Then the entire amount of the rehabilitation is subject to the credit. The applicability of the credit is illustrated in the following example.

EXAMPLE: THE REHABILITATION TAX CREDIT. The Payup Corporation invests $2,900,000 to rehabilitate a 50-year-old office building. The interior is stripped of all nonsupporting walls and fixtures and everything is replaced. The adjusted basis of the old building is $300,000.

The rehabilitation should qualify for the rehabilitation tax credit. The rehabilitation does not include the cost of the building, the exterior walls are preserved, and the cost of rehabilitation exceeds the adjusted basis of the building. Since the age of the building exceeds 40 years, the credit is 20 percent of the cost of the rehabilitation, or $580,000.

The adjusted basis of the building after the rehabilitation is:

Old basis	$ 300,000
Add: Rehabilitation	2,900,000
Less: the tax credit	(580,000)
Adjusted basis	$2,620,000

The rehabilitation tax credit provides incentives to building owners to renovate old buildings rather than to abandon old property and move to new locations.

If old buildings are acquired with the objective of renovation, the buyer should be careful to ensure that the purchase price (beginning basis) is less than the expected cost of renovation.

Other Considerations. The provision requiring that rehabilitation expenditures exceed the adjusted basis has been the object of considerable interest. Imaginative taxpayers have devised a variety of mechanisms to better ensure that the rehabilitation qualifies. Several of these mechanisms are noted here as examples of the types of considerations that arise in tax planning. Tax planning suggestions developed to better ensure that the rehabilitation costs exceed the adjusted basis of the property include:

Delay construction until the adjusted basis is reduced through the depreciation process.

If the corporation has recently purchased the property, buy only a partial interest in the property. The remainder of the property retains its old basis, which is probably lower.

If the corporation plans to purchase the property, arrange for purchase of the building and the interior furnishings separately. This also reduces the basis of the building.

Depreciation and considerations relating to property purchases will be examined later in this chapter.

The Business Energy Credit

How the Credit is Determined. Designated energy property is eligible for a 10, 11, or 15 percent business energy tax credit. The investment in energy property can provide very substantial tax reductions because the business energy credit is in addition to the regular investment tax credit. Both credits may be available if the property meets the qualifications for both credits.

Qualifications. Only new property can qualify as energy property. Property that does not qualify for the regular investment tax credit (perhaps because it is a structural component of a building) may still qualify as energy property. Energy property includes solar or wind energy property, ocean thermal equipment, geothermal equipment, certain hydroelectric generating equipment, and certain recycling equipment.

The basis of property qualifying for the business energy credit is reduced by 50 percent of the credit, as with the investment tax credit. The following example illustrates how taxes can be reduced through use of both tax credits.

EXAMPLE: COMBINED TAX CREDITS: The Damit Corporation invests $500,000 in new hydroelectric generating equipment. The equipment qualifies both for the 10 percent investment tax credit and the 11 percent business energy credit.

The combined credits total 21 percent of $500,000, or $105,000. The basis of the property is reduced by one-half the amount of the credits, or $52,500. The beginning adjusted basis is $447,500.

Businesses often find it worthwhile to plan property acquisitions specifically to qualify for the investment tax credit, the business energy credit, or both credits. A discussion of preliminary plans for new facilities with a tax specialist may result in suggestions for changes leading to tax benefits that would not otherwise be available.

THE ADJUSTED BASIS

The adjusted basis of property is a major determinant of future taxes and future tax benefits. The adjusted basis is determined by the property cost and a number of additional factors. The effect of various tax credits upon adjusted basis was examined in the first part of this chapter. The effect of construction-period interest and taxes and the allocation of purchase price upon the adjusted basis will now be considered. Then the reduction in basis associated with the use of the property will be examined.

Construction-Period Interest and Taxes

When new plant and equipment is required for replacement or growth, the new property is often constructed by the corporation. The payments for materials and labor are added to the basis of the property. In some cases, substantial amounts of interest cost and property taxes are also incurred during the construction period.

The costs of interest and property taxes are normally deductible to determine taxable income. An exception relates to interest and tax payments associated with buildings and other property constructed by the corporation. These costs are considered to be part of the cost of the property, and are capitalized along with the cost of materials, labor, and other construction costs. This provision for capitalizing interest and taxes applies only to costs incurred during the construction period. Once the property is ready for use, subsequent interest costs and property tax payments are deducted to determine current-period taxable income. An illustration of the treatment of construction-period interest and taxes follows.

EXAMPLE: THE CAPITALIZATION OF CONSTRUCTION-PERIOD INTEREST AND TAXES. The Smith Brothers Merchandising Corporation decided to expand by adding another department store in a suburban location. Smith Brothers bought a parcel of land, hired an architect and a contractor, and built the new store. Costs associated with the new building are as follows:

Land	$ 500,000
Materials and labor	2,500,000
Architects and contractor	400,000
Interest on construction loan	500,000
Property taxes on land during construction period	100,000
Total costs	$4,000,000

The new store is capitalized at a cost of $4,000,000. None of the above cost elements are immediately deductible. The logic of this approach can be seen by assuming that Smith contracted with a developer to build the store on the developer's own property. The developer would incur costs similar to the above for the land, construction, property taxes, and interest on borrowed money. The selling price to Smith Brothers would likely be $4,000,000 plus the developer's profit. In this case, the total purchase price including interest and taxes during construction would be capitalized.

Corporations usually prefer to deduct rather than capitalize the cost of construction-period interest and taxes. The legislation, however, is specific with respect to the capitalization requirement.

The Allocation of Purchase Price

Sometimes several individual property items are purchased as a package. Examples include land with buildings already constructed and so-called basket purchases of several items of property for one price. In these cases, the buyer calculates the cost of individual items by allocating the purchase price. This procedure is always necessary in the case of land with buildings, since land is not depreciated while the cost of the buildings is depreciated and deducted over time.

The cost of the individual items is determined by allocating the estimated individual market values over the total purchase price. An illustration of the procedure for determining the purchase price of individual items follows.

EXAMPLE: THE ALLOCATION OF PURCHASE PRICE. The Weaver Brothers Knitting Mill acquires a nearby building to be used for factory and office expansion. The new property cost $500,000. Weaver Brothers needs to allocate the cost of the property to the land and to the building. An appraiser estimates that similar land, if acquired separately, would probably cost about $200,000. The appraiser estimates the market value of the building as $600,000. Weaver Brothers apparently obtained the property at a bargain price.

The allocation of purchase price proceeds as follows:

Fair value of land	$200,000
Fair value of building	600,000
Total	$800,000
Fair value of land as a percentage of the total	

(Continued)

($200,000/$800,000)	25%
Fair value of building as a percentage of the total	
($600,000/$800,000)	75%
Cost allocated to land:	
25% of $500,000 purchase price	$125,000
75% of $500,000 purchase price	375,000
Total purchase price	$500,000

The allocation procedure is necessary only when individual property prices are not specified in the contract of sale. Often these prices are specified and if the amount is reasonable, allocation is not necessary.

In the case of land and buildings, the buyer usually prefers to allocate cost to the building. The building is depreciable while the cost of the land is not subject to depreciation.

The first part of this chapter examined tax factors associated with the acquisition of productive property. These include the capitalization procedure, tax credits, treatment of interest and taxes during construction, and the allocation of purchase price. The tax effects of using productive property will now be considered.

DEPRECIATION

The cost of plant and equipment is not deductible upon its acquisition. Instead, the cost of most plant and equipment is deducted gradually over a period of time. This is accomplished through a process referred to as depreciation.

Depreciation is a procedure for deducting the cost of plant and equipment such as machinery and buildings over several tax periods. The objective of depreciation is to provide the taxpayer with an opportunity to recover the cost of the investment as the property wears out or becomes obsolete. Land is not normally subject to depreciation since it does not wear out or become obsolete. The general treatment of property subject to depreciation is illustrated in the following example.

EXAMPLE: DEPRECIABLE PROPERTY. The Payup Corporation purchases office furniture costing $8000.

Only a part of the $8000 cost is deducted in the current year. A portion of the cost will be deducted as current year depreciation. Additional depreciation will be taken in future years, for an eventual total deduction of $8000.

The preceding example assumes that the buyer elects a reduction in the investment tax credit in lieu of the basis reduction. If the election is not made, the basis for depreciation will be reduced by one-half of the investment tax credit, and only the remaining basis can be depreciated.

The Accelerated Cost Recovery System (ACRS)

For most depreciable property, the depreciation deduction is determined using the Accelerated Cost Recovery System (ACRS).

The Depreciation Period. The ACRS depreciation period depends upon the property class. The tax legislation establishes property classes as follows:

> Three-year class—automobiles, light-duty trucks, and machinery and equipment used in research and development activities.
>
> Five-year class—most machinery and equipment.
>
> Ten-year class—certain special-purpose property such as railroad tank cars.
>
> Eighteen-year class—most depreciable real estate.

The relatively short ACRS depreciation period contrasts significantly with the property lives used for depreciation in the corporation's financial statements. The financial statements use expected lives such as 40 years for a building. ACRS uses shorter lives for a number of reasons. One is that the shorter depreciation periods provide faster depreciation and may provide an additional incentive to invest in plant and equipment. A second reason for the shorter ACRS lives is that the ACRS depreciation periods replaced the use of expected lives. Taxpayers and the IRS frequently disagree regarding expected lives. When Congress implemented ACRS, it took away the option of using estimated asset lives. The ACRS provides for lives that are nearly always shorter than the expected useful lives and as a result, was more acceptable to taxpayers.

The Depreciation Rate. The deduction is taken for each class of property each year using prescribed percentages of property cost. The actual expected life of the property is not considered in determining the depreciation deduction. The depreciation period is determined only by the year class and this, in turn, depends only upon the property type. The year class is nearly always less than the actual expected property life.

The amounts of these deductions are different each year for a given property item. The ACRS depreciation schedules prescribe large percentage deductions in early years compared to later years. The same depreciation period and annual percentages apply to both new and used property.

The schedule for five-year class property follows:

COST RECOVERY SCHEDULE
FOR FIVE-YEAR CLASS PROPERTY

Year	Percentage of cost deducted as depreciation
Year placed in service	15%
Second year	22%

Year	Percentage of cost deducted as depreciation
Third year	21%
Fourth year	21%
Fifth year	21%
Total	100%

After the first year, the percentage of cost deducted as depreciation increases, and then declines. The first-year depreciation is less than the second-year amount because the schedule provides only partial depreciation the first year. (The schedule assumes that all acquisitions for the year are purchased at the midpoint of the year). An example showing the application of the five-year class schedule follows.

EXAMPLE: FIVE-YEAR RECOVERY. The Payup Corporation acquires equipment costing $200,000. The expected useful life is 18 years, with expected salvage value of $45,000 after 18 years. The property qualifies for the 10 percent investment tax credit ($20,000).

The equipment falls in the five-year class. The five-year schedule is used to determine the depreciation. The basis for depreciation is $190,000 after subtracting one-half of the 10 percent investment tax credit. Estimated life and salvage value are never considered in the calculations. The annual depreciation is calculated as follows:

COST RECOVERY SCHEDULE
FOR $190,000 FIVE-YEAR PROPERTY

Year	Percentage of basis deducted as depreciation	Depreciation deduction
First year	15%	$ 28,500
Second year	22%	41,800

(Continued)

Year	Percentage of basis deducted as depreciation	Depreciation deduction
Third year	21%	39,900
Fourth year	21%	39,900
Fifth year	21%	39,900
Total	100%	$190,000

The percentages for 18-year property depend on the month of acquisition and require reference to a more detailed schedule.

The Adjusted Basis. The adjusted basis is the carrying value of the property for tax-determination purposes. As depreciation is taken, the adjusted basis is reduced. The effect of depreciation upon the adjusted basis is shown in the following example.

EXAMPLE: THE ADJUSTED BASIS. The Payup Corporation acquires equipment costing $200,000. The expected useful life is 18 years, with expected salvage value of $45,000 after 18 years. The property qualifies for the 10 percent investment tax credit ($20,000).

The depreciation was calculated in the previous example. The adjusted basis is determined as:

Year	Depreciation deduction	Adjusted basis
Year placed in service: beginning of year	0	$190,000

(Continued)

Depreciation

Year	Depreciation deduction	Adjusted basis
end of year	$ 28,500	161,500
Second year	41,800	119,700
Third year	39,900	79,800
Fourth year	39,900	39,900
Fifth year	39,900	0
Total	$190,000	

Figure 3.1 shows the reduction in basis in chart form.

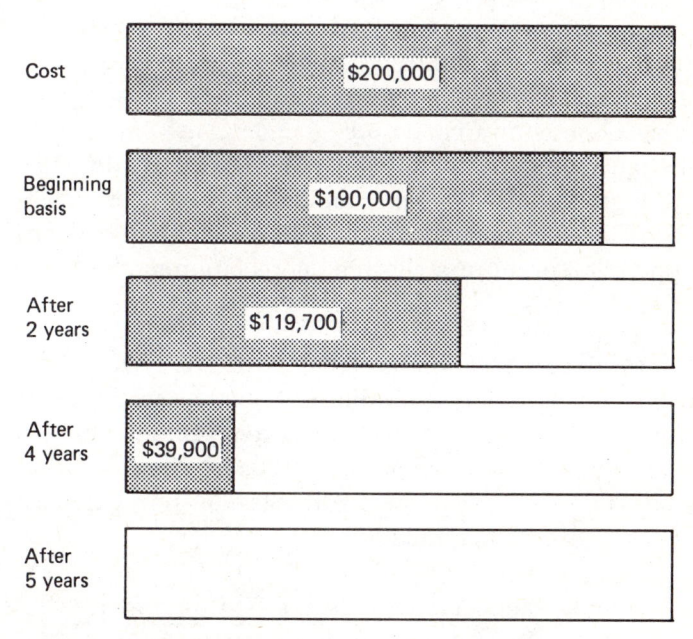

Figure 3.1. The reduction in basis resulting from depreciation and the investment tax credit. Shaded area is remaining basis of $200,000 investment after depreciation and investment tax credit.

The above example shows that when the asset is 100 percent depreciated, the adjusted basis is reduced to zero. The example also illustrates the undesirable effect of the reduction in basis associated with the investment tax credit. The total depreciation deduction over the five-year period is $190,000. If the basis were not reduced by one-half the investment tax credit, the total depreciation deduction would be the $200,000 cost.

Straight-Line Depreciation. The ACRS tables provide for higher depreciation in early years than in later years. (This is not readily apparent in the five-year case because only one-half year depreciation is allowed in the first year. It is more apparent in the case of 10 and 18-year property.)

Taxpayers sometimes find it advantageous to deduct uniform amounts of depreciation each year. (One reason relates to the recapture of depreciation on nonresidential real estate. Recapture is examined in Chapter 5.)

Straight-line depreciation is determined by dividing the beginning property basis by the number of years over which the property is to be depreciated. The following example illustrates the operation of the straight-line depreciation method.

EXAMPLE: STRAIGHT-LINE DEPRECIATION. The Payup Corporation acquires equipment costing $200,000 as in the previous example. The equipment qualifies as five-year class property.

The beginning adjusted basis is $190,000 after reduction for one-half the investment tax credit. Straight-line depreciation over five years is computed as:

$$\text{Annual Depreciation} = \frac{\text{Beginning Adjusted Basis}}{\text{Depreciation Period}}$$
$$= \$190,000/5 \text{ years}$$
$$= \$38,000 \text{ per year}$$

Depreciation

After five years, the adjusted basis of the property will be reduced to zero.

Property Not Subject to Depreciation. Land, art objects, and antiques frequently retain or increase value over time. These types of assets are not subject to depreciation.

Early Acquisitions. Depreciation eligibility for three-year and five-year class property is determined according to the scheduled percentage regardless of when the item is acquired during the year. If property is scheduled for purchase early next year, corporations often purchase the property and place it in service in the current year to minimize current-year tax. The rationale is the same as for the investment tax credit discussed earlier in this chapter.

Nonrecovery Property. Certain property subject to depreciation does not qualify for ACRS and is referred to as nonrecovery property. This includes property acquired before the ACRS system was initiated in 1981. Nonrecovery property is of limited interest for tax planning purposes, since most new depreciable property will qualify as recovery property. The depreciation on nonrecovery property, however, can be important in evaluating financial statements, since all pre-1981 property falls into this category. For this reason, a discussion of nonrecovery property is included in the appendix at the end of this chapter.

The Election to Expense

The cost of a limited amount of qualifying property can be deducted in the year of acquisition as an alternative to capitalization and depreciation. Each corporation can deduct a maximum of $5000.

Qualifying property corresponds to property eligible for the investment tax credit. The election provides for an immediate deduction. If the cost of the property is capitalized, the deductions are spread over a period of time. The advantage, as with any early deduction, is that taxes currently payable are reduced.

The problem with the election to expense is that the amounts treated in this manner are not eligible for the investment tax credit. The election to expense should be desirable if the value of the immediate tax reduction exceeds that of the depreciation/investment tax credit alternative. The calculation should take into account the combined effect of the delayed deduction and the loss of the investment tax credit. The alternatives are illustrated in the following example.

EXAMPLE: THE ELECTION TO EXPENSE. The Payup Corporation acquires new office equipment costing $5,000 in 1986. The cost of the equipment can be deducted immediately if the election is made.

The five-year property is eligible for the 10 percent investment tax credit. This reduces the basis by one-half the credit, or $250. The annual depreciation deduction is then determined as follows:

Year	Percentage of basis deducted as depreciation	Depreciation deduction
First year	15%	$ 713
Second year	22%	1045
Third year	21%	998
Fourth year	21%	997
Fifth year	21%	997
Total	100%	$4750

If the property is depreciated, taxes are reduced immediately by the $500 investment tax credit. Taxes will also be reduced over time by the tax benefit of $4750 in depreciation deductions.

If the cost of the property is deducted immediately, current-period taxes will be reduced by the tax benefit of the $5000 deduction. The investment tax credit, however, will not be available.

The total tax savings will be reduced as a result of the election to expense. The advantage is that the deduction is obtained immediately.

The election to expense provision is of interest primarily to the small corporation. The $5000 limitation renders it relatively insignificant for the larger corporation. In addition, the present value of tax savings will often be increased as a result of retaining the depreciation and investment tax credit alternative and passing up the opportunity to expense the property costs immediately.

OTHER CAPITAL EXPENDITURES

Intangible Assets

Initial Capitalization. Patents, copyrights, and improvements to property leased from others are classified as intangible assets. The costs of intangible assets are capitalized rather than deducted immediately, These costs are later amortized over a period of time.

How Amortization Operates. The cost of intangible assets is amortized over the period of expected useful life. Intangible assets do not fall under the ACRS system and the ACRS schedules do not apply.

The amortization deduction is determined by dividing the asset cost by the expected useful life, as in the case of straight-line depreciation. The following example illustrates the tax treatment of intangible assets.

EXAMPLE: INTANGIBLE ASSETS AND AMORTIZATION. The Catchit Corporation buys a patent for a better mousetrap from an inventor for $40,000. The patent is expected to have a useful life of 10 years.

Catchit's amortization deduction each year is:

$40,000 over 10 years, or $4000 per year

Amortization of $4000 will be deducted each year to determine taxable income for 10 years.

If residual value is applicable, it is taken into account by depreciating only the cost less the residual value. For example, if the residual value in the Catchit example were $10,000, only $30,000 in cost would be depreciated over the 10-year period.

Mineral Resources

Most costs of obtaining mineral rights such as for oil and iron-ore deposits are not immediately deductible. The costs are first capitalized. These costs are then deducted over time as the minerals are recovered. The deduction is determined using a procedure referred to as depletion.

Two methods of calculating depreciation are in use. One is referred to as cost-basis depletion. The other is the percentage depletion method.

Other Capital Expenditures

Cost-Basis Depletion. Cost-basis depletion is similar in operation to depreciation. The cost of obtaining the mineral rights is capitalized as an asset. As the minerals are removed, the cost is recovered as depletion. Using this procedure, when one-half the estimated quantity of minerals is removed for example, one-half of the cost is amortized. The following example shows the operation of cost-basis depletion.

EXAMPLE: COST-BASIS DEPLETION. The Darkdown Mining Corporation paid $1,000,000 for land and mineral rights. Darkdown estimates that 500,000 tons of minerals are available for recovery. In the first year, Darkdown mines 10 percent of this amount.

Darkdown's first-year depletion deduction using the cost basis of depletion is 10 percent of the $1,000,000 cost, or $100,000. If 300,000 tons are recovered in the second year, that year's depletion deduction is 300,000 tons/500,000 tons, or 60 percent of the cost. The second-year depletion will be $600,000. The total amount of depletion is limited to the $1,000,000 cost.

Percentage Depletion. The percentage depletion method is an alternative method for determining depletion. The percentage method applies a specified percentage to the gross income from the property to determine the depletion. This percentage varies for different mineral types, but ranges up to 22 percent for some minerals.

Percentage depletion commonly results in recovering more than the original cost of acquiring the property and preparing it for removal of minerals. For example, it is entirely possible to deduct 22 percent of the cost as depletion each year for 10 years. The generous deduction available under the percentage depletion method was developed to provide additional incentives to mineral exploration and recovery. Percentage depletion is illustrated in the following example.

EXAMPLE: PERCENTAGE DEPLETION. The Darkdown Mining Corporation paid $1,000,000 for land and mineral rights. Darkdown mines 10 percent of the amount of the estimated deposit in the first year and sells the minerals for $2,500,000. The first-year costs of operating the mine total $1,000,000. Darkdown qualifies for the 22 percent depletion allowance.

The gross profit on the mining operation is:

Sales revenue	$2,500,000
Less: Production costs	1,000,000
Gross profit	$1,500,000

Darkdown deducts 22 percent of the $1,500,000 gross profit, or $330,000, as first-year depletion.

The percentage depletion method differs from the cost method in that the amount of minerals mined does not enter into the depletion calculation directly. To operate the cost method, it is necessary to know the amount of minerals recovered relative to the total estimated available reserves. This information does not enter into the percentage of depletion method calculation.

Quite possibly, Darkdown will continue to recover 10 percent of the minerals each year for 10 years with approximately constant costs and sales revenues each year. In this case, the depletion deduction over the 10-year period will be 10 times the first-year amount, or $3,300,000. The cumulative deduction in this case exceeds the original cost by a factor greater than three.

Percentage depletion is subject to a number of specific limitations depending upon the mineral type, the cost of the property, and the type of property holder.

LEASING

Corporations often find it advantageous to lease productive property rather than to purchase the property outright. In some cases, leasing is attractive for business reasons other than tax considerations. In other cases, parties enter into a lease primarily for tax reasons. Machinery, airplanes, buildings, and other property are often leased rather than purchased.

Advantages of leasing include:

Property can sometimes be obtained faster and with less paperwork through leasing compared to the alternative of borrowing and buying the property.

Leasing does not usually require a down payment.

Businesses that are unable to borrow are sometimes able to acquire property through leasing.

If funds are borrowed to buy property, the buyer records a liability in the financial statements. Leasing may permit the lessee (user) to avoid showing the liability.

The use of leases may also reduce the risk to the lessee.

Leasing may also be advantageous for tax purposes. This feature of leasing will be examined later in this section.

Tax Treatment

The Lessee and Lessor. The lessee normally deducts payments for the use of the property as lease or rent expense. The lessor recognizes lease revenue equal to the amount of the lease payments received, and takes the investment tax credit and depreciation deductions. An illustration of the tax treatment by lessee and lessor follows.

EXAMPLE: A LEASE. The Payup Corporation leases all its company cars from the Hurts Corporation. Payments are $5000 per month.

Payup, the lessee, deducts $5000 per month to determine taxable income. Hurts, the lessor, increases taxable income by the same amount.

The lease treatment illustrated in the above example is common for leased office equipment, space in buildings, and many other types of property use situations.

The Depreciation Deduction and Investment Tax Credit. The depreciation deduction is taken by the owner of the property (usually the lessor). The lessor is also entitled to the investment tax credit. If new property is leased, however, the lessor may elect to waive the credit and pass the credit through to the lessee. The investment tax credit pass-through provision can be beneficial if the lessor cannot benefit through use of the credit, as shown in the following example.

EXAMPLE: THE INVESTMENT TAX CREDIT PASS-THROUGH. The Payup Corporation leases new office equipment with a fair market value of $50,000 from the Typit Corporation. Typit is eligible for a 10 percent investment tax credit of $5000. Typit is in a strong financial position, but as a result of large depreciation deductions, has no taxable income.

Since the investment tax credit is limited by taxable income, the credit cannot provide any immediate benefit to Typit. Typit may elect to pass-through the $5000 credit to Payup. In return, Typit should be able to charge more than the usual rental, since the credit is valuable to Payup.

The investment tax credit pass-through applies only to the lease of new property. If the credit could be passed-through for used property, Typit could charge a higher selling price each time the equipment was rented and conceivably benefit indirectly several times through a credit on the same equipment. This would not be consistent with the objective of the credit—to encourage investment in productive property.

The Tax Advantage of Leasing. Leasing can be advantageous for tax purposes because it provides a mechanism for shifting the investment tax credit and depreciation entitlement. Usually this shifts the entitlement from a user unable to take advantage of the credit and depreciation deduction to a lessor who can benefit fully from these items. An example follows.

EXAMPLE: THE UNUSED ACRS DEDUCTION AND INVESTMENT TAX CREDIT. Everest Airlines begins its first year of operations. Income before considering the property acquisition is expected to be $1,000,000. New airplanes with a total cost of $40,000,000 are needed.

The adjusted basis is reduced to $38,000,000 as a consequence of the investment tax credit basis adjustment. Reference to the five-year class recovery schedule shows that first-year depreciation will be 15 percent of the adjusted basis. This results in first-year depreciation of 15 percent of $38,000,000, or $5,700,000.

Since only $1,000,000 of depreciation will reduce income to zero, Everest will be unable to use the remaining $4,700,000 depreciation. Additionally, since the investment tax credit is limited to taxes payable, the investment tax credit potential cannot be used to Everest's advantage.

Everest's solution may be to lease the airplanes from someone that is able to take advantage of the depreciation deduction and investment tax credit.

Leasing can provide tax benefits by effectively tranferring the investment tax credit and depreciation entitlement from the user to the owner (the lessor). The following example illustrates the potential tax benefits of leasing.

EXAMPLE: TAX LEASE. Everest Airlines begins its first year of operations. Income before considering the property acquisition is expected to be $1,000,000. New airplanes with a total cost of $40,000,000 are needed. In continuation of the previous example, Everest Airlines cannot use the additional depreciation and investment tax credit resulting from the purchase of airplanes. Everest arranges with a leasing company for the leasing company to buy the airplanes.

The leasing company will deduct the full amount of depreciation to determine taxable income. At a marginal rate of 46 percent, the leasing company will benefit as a result of the tax deduction of 46 percent on $5,700,000, or $2,622,000 in the first year.

The leasing company, of course, will also claim 10 percent of the property cost as the investment tax credit. The credit will reduce leasing company taxes in the year of acquisition by an additional 10 percent of $40,000,000, or $4,000,000. The total first-year reduction in leasing company tax will thus amount to $6,622,000—the combined savings through additional depreciation deductions and the investment tax credit.

The leasing company will establish lease payments at an amount necessary to obtain a profit on the investment. The profit should incorporate the $6,622,000 first-year savings resulting from the additional depreciation deductions and the investment tax credit as well as the remaining-year tax savings resulting from the depreciation deduction.

A possible problem with the situation just described is that the transaction may fail to qualify for lease treatment for tax purposes and may receive purchase treatment. The treatment of a lease as a purchase rather than a lease is examined in the following section.

Purchase versus Lease Treatment

The Purchase. The tax treatment of a lease depends upon the terms and conditions of the lease agreement. Some kinds of leases effectively serve as property purchases on an installment basis. These leases are treated as purchases for tax purposes. The Everest Airlines example above seems to fall into this category of lease. A second example follows.

EXAMPLE: THE LEASE EQUIVALENT TO A PURCHASE. The Payup Corporation is considering the lease of a machine. The machine has an estimated life of 10 years. If Payup buys the machine it will borrow from its bank and pay $1000 monthly on the note for 10 years. If Payup leases the machine, the lease requires monthly payments of $1000 for 10 years and is not subject to cancellation. The lease also specifies that after 10 years, Payup will receive title to the equipment.

This lease is equivalent to a loan and purchase. The risks of ownership to Payup are similar to those associated with an outright purchase.

When property is purchased, the buyer is eligible for the investment tax credit and takes the periodic depreciation deduction. If a lease transaction is deemed equivalent to a purchase for tax purposes, the lessee treats the transaction as a purchase and takes the investment tax credit and depreciation even though not the legal owner of the property. The lessor is *not* eligible to take the credit or depreciation in this case even though the lessor may be the legal owner.

Criteria for Lease Treatment. Tax legislation provides for lease treatment only when the transaction has the characteristics of a lease rather than a sale. In general this requires that the lessor retain the risks of ownership. The IRS tends to approve lease treatment when the following conditions are met:

> The lessor continues to retain meaningful risks and benefits of ownership. This means that if the property declines in value, the lessor suffers a loss. This condition is not maintained if the property reverts to the lessee at the end of the lease term. The lease will not be considered as a lease for tax purposes if it permits the lessee to purchase the property at a fixed price at the end of the lease term.
>
> The lessee may not contribute to the cost of the property. This would establish the lessee as a co-owner for tax purposes.
>
> The lease must have economic substance independent of tax benefits. One measure of economic substance is the lessor's expectation of receiving a positive cash flow from the lease agreement independent of tax benefits.
>
> The property may not be useful only to the lessee. This would deny the lessor the benefits of the rewards of ownership.

The objective of the above guidelines is to help separate genuine leasing transactions from transactions called leases that for all practical purposes amount to sales. The specific circumstances pertaining to each case are important for purposes of this determination. The Everest Airlines situation has many aspects of a purchase, because the risks of ownership are assumed by the

Leasing

lessee assuming a long-term lease. If lease treatment is desired for tax purposes, a short-term lease (in which the lessor retains risks and benefits of ownership) may be preferred.

The Sale and Leaseback

Background. One variation of the standard lease is the sale and leaseback arrangement. This can also be complicated by the use of funds obtained from a third party—the leveraged lease. Under a sale and leaseback arrangement, a property owner can obtain funds by selling productive property and immediately leasing it back from the buyer. An example of a sale and leaseback arrangement follows.

EXAMPLE: THE SALE AND LEASEBACK. The Payup Corporation sells its factory building in anticipation of closing. Payup then agrees to lease part of the building from the new owner for two years while finishing up operations.

Payup has entered into a sale and leaseback. Although ownership has changed, Payup continues to use the property.

Depreciation and the Investment Tax Credit. With a qualifying sale and leaseback, the new owner is entitled to depreciation. The new owner is entitled to the investment tax credit only if the property is new. The investment tax credit is not available to either party if used property is acquired through a sale and leaseback agreement. This provision helps to discourage setting up sale and leaseback agreements primarily for the purpose of tax benefits.

Some sale and leaseback arrangements will not qualify as leases. An example follows.

EXAMPLE: A SALE AND LEASEBACK DISREGARDED FOR TAX PURPOSES.
Everest Airlines begins its first year of operations as an airline. Taxable income before considering the investment tax credit is expected to be $1,000,000. New airplanes with a total cost of $40,000,000 are needed.

Everest buys the airplanes and shortly afterward sells them to a third party. Everest then leases the airplanes back. The lease cannot be cancelled and is for a period of 20 years. In addition, the terms of the lease call for payments that are similar to those that would be required to pay off a loan if the airplanes were purchased with borrowed funds.

Everest has engaged in a sale and leaseback. This lease, however, seems equivalent to a purchase of property on an installment payment basis. The lessee (Everest) seems to obtain effective ownership. This type of arrangement may well be treated as a purchase for tax purposes.

The Finance Lease

Finance lease treatment is proposed for implementation in 1988. The finance lease is a lease that meets some, but not all usual requirements for lease treatment. The finance lease replaced an arrangement known as safe harbor leasing. Safe harbor leasing assigned lease classification to arrangements with no economic purpose other than tax benefit. Essentially, these provided for transfers of the depreciation deduction and investment tax credit.

The safe harbor lease was developed in 1981 to provide increased investment incentives to loss corporations. Loss corporations cannot benefit directly from ACRS and the investment tax credit. Loss corporations, however, can obtain these benefits indirectly through leasing, as in the earlier example of Everest Airlines. The safe harbor lease was phased out shortly after its inception because it resulted in substantial reductions in tax revenues.

Qualifications. A finance lease is a lease that exists primarily for nontax reasons, but would normally qualify as a purchase because it includes an option to purchase the property at the end of the lease term. A finance lease may also pertain to property that can only be used by the lessee (limited use property).

Restrictions. The finance lease is subject to a number of significant restrictions. The property must be new and it must be subject to the investment tax credit. Consequently, buildings and most other real estate do not qualify for finance lease treatment.

If the criteria for a finance lease are met, the lessor must spread the investment tax credit over five years rather than take the entire credit in the year of the acquisition. Limitations also apply to the total deductions and tax credits associated with leasing and the amount of newly acquired property financed by lease arrangements.

The finance lease was originally planned for 1984. Implementation was delayed to reduce government revenue losses. Additional lease-related legislation is expected in the near future.

RELATED PARTY CONSIDERATIONS

Special tax provisions apply to transactions between related parties. Related parties include shareholders and the closely held corporations that they control. Related parties also include parent—subsidiary combinations and groups of corporations with related ownership. Special provisions were developed to minimize opportunities for related taxpayers to benefit through setting up multiple corporations or entering into certain transactions primarily for tax-minimization purposes.

The Investment Tax Credit

Leases Between Members of a Controlled Group. Normally a lessor can elect to pass the investment tax credit on new property through to a lessee. Since the lessee has not actually paid for the property, assumptions are required to determine the amount of the credit. The usual practice is to base the credit on the fair market value of the property.

If the lessee and lessor are members of a controlled group, one group member could manufacture a property item and lease it to another group member. If the investment tax credit were based on fair market value, the amount of the credit might be far larger than the credit available if based on the lessor's cost.

With lease arrangements between members of controlled groups, the investment tax credit is based upon the adjusted basis rather than the fair market value of the property.

Used Property Acquired From a Related Taxpayer. The investment tax credit is not available on used property acquired from an individual that has control of the corporation. The used property restrictions prevent owners of the corporation from obtaining the benefit of the credit more than once. If this provision did not exist, owners could acquire property and claim the credit. Then after using the property, they could sell the property to a wholly owned corporation which would also be eligible for the credit.

The Controlled Group and Used Property. Corporations are entitled to take the investment tax credit on up to $125,000 of the cost of used property. If members of a controlled group acquire used property subject to the investment tax credit, a single $125,000 limitation on the cost of qualifying used property applies to the entire group.

The purpose of these restrictions is to discourage breaking a single corporation up into smaller corporations to obtain tax benefit.

Depreciation and the Election to Expense

Property Acquired From a Related Party. Members of a controlled group are eligible for ACRS depreciation on property acquired from another member of the group. The election to expense, however, does not apply to property acquired from a related party or another member of a controlled group.

One Election to Expense for the Controlled Group. Taxpayers may elect to deduct up to $5000 of the cost of qualified plant and equipment immediately rather than waiting to take depreciation gradually. However, if members of a controlled group elect to expense property, the group divides a single $5000 deduction.

SUMMARY

Property Acquisitions. The cost of purchasing productive property such as land, buildings, and machinery is not immediately deductible by the buyer.

The cost of productive property is capitalized rather than deducted immediately. The cost of some capitalized property is deducted gradually as depreciation, amortization, or depletion. The costs of certain other items including land and goodwill are never deducted. The costs of these items, however, are considered when the property is sold since the increased basis reduces the taxable gain on sale.

The Investment Tax Credit. The cost of some productive property is effectively reduced by the investment tax credit. The credit reduces the net cost of investing in qualifying property. The credit reduces taxes payable by 6 percent of the cost of qualifying three-year class property and by 10 percent of the cost of other qualifying property.

The credit is available primarily for machinery, equipment, and transportation devices. Most real estate does not qualify. Only a limited amount of used property qualifies for the credit.

The credit is a reduction of taxes payable. If no taxes are payable, no credit can be taken. Additionally, the credit is limited to the first $25,000 in taxes payable and only 85 percent of taxes payable in excess of this amount.

The investment tax credit reduces the adjusted basis of qualifying property. The reduction in basis is equal to one-half the amount of the credit. This provision can be waived if the percent credit is reduced by two percentage points.

The Investment Tax Credit for Rehabilitated Buildings. A credit is also available for qualifying rehabilitation costs of certain older buildings. This credit varies from 15 to 25 percent of the cost of the rehabilitation depending upon the type of building and its age.

The Business Energy Credit. Qualifying energy property is eligible for an additional tax credit of up to 15 percent of property cost. In the case of certain types of property, the energy credit is in addition to the investment tax credit.

Other Factors Influencing the Adjusted Basis. Construction-period interest and taxes are capitalized rather than deducted immediately. This reduces current-period deductions, but increases the adjusted basis of the newly constructed property.

If more than one property item is acquired for a single price, the cost is allocated to determine the adjusted basis of the individual items. The allocation of cost to depreciable property is generally beneficial to the acquiring business.

Depreciation and ACRS. ACRS differs from depreciation for financial reporting purposes. The expected life and salvage value of plant, property, and equipment items is not considered in the depreciation calculation. The depreciation period is relatively short, and the percentage of cost to be depreciated in each year is determined from tables developed for this purpose.

Automobiles, light duty trucks, and machinery and equipment used in research and development activities are depreciated over three years regardless of their useful life. Most other machinery and equipment is depreciated over five years. Real estate is depreciated over 18 years. The calculations apply specified depreciation percentages to the property cost.

The full amount of the investment tax credit and the full amount of the first year's depreciation on three-year and five-year class property apply regardless of when the property is placed in service. Corporations are often able to increase the present value of these tax benefits by accelerating the use of property to an earlier tax year.

The Election to Expense. For limited amounts of property, the taxpayer can elect to deduct the cost currently. The investment tax credit does not apply when this option is elected.

Intangible Assets. Intangible assets include property such as patents and copyrights. The costs of intangible assets are capitalized at the time of acquisition. The cost of the property is later deducted through the amortization process.

Mineral Resources. The cost of acquiring mineral resources is deducted through the depletion process. Two types of depletion are available. Cost-basis depletion determines the deduction on the basis of property cost as the minerals are removed. The calculation is similar to amortization of intangible assets.

Percentage depletion applies a statutory percentage to the gross profits from the drilling or mining operations. The percentage depletion calculation does not depend upon the cost of the property or the amount of minerals recovered. Percentage depletion can result in depletion deductions exceeding the amount of the property cost.

Leasing. Leasing as an alternative to property purchase sometimes offers significant business and tax advantages. The agreement to use property is treated as a lease if the lessor retains the risks and rewards of ownership. Although the determination depends upon the particular circumstances of each case, general guidelines have been established. These guidelines prescribe lease treatment only if the lessee does not hold an interest in the property, and if the lease has economic substance independent of tax benefits. If these conditions are not met, the transaction is treated as a sale by the lessor and a purchase by the lessee.

Sale versus lease treatment has important implications to the lessee and lessor because in many cases, only one party is in a position to benefit from depreciation deductions and the investment tax credit.

The economic owner of the property takes the depreciation on the property. The lessor takes the investment tax credit. In the case of new property, the lessor may elect to pass-through the investment tax credit entitlement to the lessee.

A sale and leaseback is a lease of property with the original owner acting as lessee. The sale and leaseback can qualify for tax lease treatment if it is motivated by economic considerations other than tax avoidance.

A special category of lease referred to as a finance lease will waive some of the above conditions. Finance leases, however, will be subject to a number of restrictions including limitations on the benefits available to the lessor.

Related Party Considerations. When property is leased to a member of a controlled group, the investment tax credit is based on the adjusted basis to the lessor rather than on the fair market value of the property. The investment tax credit is not available on used property acquired from a related taxpayer. The controlled group is also entitled to only one $125,000 allowance for investment tax credit eligibility on used property.

Related parties may take ACRS depreciation on property acquired from another related party. The election to expense, however, is not available on property acquired from a related party. The controlled group is entitled to only one $5000 deduction for the election to expense in lieu of ACRS.

APPENDIX
NONRECOVERY PROPERTY

Certain property subject to depreciation does not qualify for ACRS and is referred to as nonrecovery property. This includes property acquired before the ACRS system was initiated in 1981.

Estimated Life

For nonrecovery property, depreciation is taken over the estimated expected life of the property to the taxpayer. This is usually not advantageous to the taxpayer because the expected life is usually greater than the year-class established for ACRS. Taxpayers usually benefit through taking deductions, including depreciation, as early as possible.

Residual Value

Residual value is the expected value of the property at the time the corporation discontinues its use. In some cases, residual value may represent expected scrap value. In other cases, such as with business cars used for only one or two years before disposition, the residual value may be substantial.

Residual value limits the amount of depreciation that can be taken on nonrecovery property, since nonrecovery property cannot be depreciated below its residual value. The expected residual value is considered in determining depreciation for nonrecovery property as shown in the following example.

EXAMPLE: STRAIGHT-LINE DEPRECIATION FOR NONRECOVERY PROPERTY. The Payup Corporation acquires equipment at a cost of $50,000 and elects to reduce the investment tax credit in-lieu-of the basis reduction. The residual value is $8000 and the expected life is five years. The annual depreciation is determined as:

$$\text{annual depreciation} = \frac{\text{beginning basis - residual value}}{\text{expected life}}$$

$$= \frac{\$50,000 - \$8000}{5 \text{ years}} = \frac{\$42,000}{5 \text{ years}}$$

$$= \$8400 \text{ per year}$$

After five years, the adjusted basis of the property will be reduced to the $8000 residual value. No further depreciation is taken after this time.

Year	Depreciation deduction	Adjusted basis
Year placed in service:		
beginning of year	0	$50,000
end of year	$ 8,400	41,600
Second year	8,400	33,200
Third year	8,400	24,800
Fourth year	8,400	16,400
Fifth year	8,400	8,000
Total	$42,000	

Appendix Nonrecovery Property

Under the ACRS system, the annual depreciation would be $10,000 per year if the straight-line election were made:

$$\text{annual depreciation} = \frac{\text{beginning basis}}{\text{expected life}} = \frac{\$50,000}{5 \text{ years}} = \$10,000 \text{ per year}$$

Use of the prescribed percentages would result in even higher early-year depreciation.

Accelerated Depreciation

Accelerated depreciation is available for most nonrecovery property. Accelerated depreciation is usually computed using the declining balance method. The declining balance method operates by deducting a fixed percentage of the remaining adjusted basis each year. The amount of depreciation declines each year because the adjusted basis declines. Residual value does not enter into the declining balance calculation except that it provides a stopping rule: the basis of the property can never be reduced below the residual value. The operation of the double declining balance method is shown as follows.

EXAMPLE: DOUBLE DECLINING BALANCE DEPRECIATION. The Payup Corporation acquires property not subject to the investment tax credit at a cost of $50,000. The residual value is estimated as $8000. The property is depreciated using the double declining balance method.

The declining balance method provides the following accelerated depreciation schedule:

Year	Beginning basis	Depreciation at 40% of basis	Ending basis
1	$50,000	$20,000	$30,000
2	30,000	12,000	18,000
3	18,000	7,200	10,800
4	10,800	2,800	8,000
5	8,000	0	8,000
Total		$42,000	

The double declining balance method provides for considerably higher depreciation in early years. In this case, the property is depreciated to residual value by the end of the fourth year, and no depreciation is permitted in the fifth. The reasoning is that a greater portion of the benefits to be obtained from the property are obtained in early years, and that new property loses value more quickly in early years. The computations are:

The rate—the depreciation rate for five years is one-fifth, or 20 percent. The double declining balance method computes depreciation at double this rate, or 40 percent.

First-year depreciation—40 percent of beginning adjusted basis of $50,000, or $20,000. This reduces the basis at the end of the year to $30,000.

Second-year depreciation—40 percent of beginning adjusted basis of $30,000, or $12,000. This reduces the basis at the end of the year to $18,000.

Third-year depreciation—40 percent of beginning adjusted basis of $18,000, or $7200. This reduces the basis at the end of the year to $10,800.

Fourth-year depreciation—as a starting point, 40 percent of the beginning adjusted basis of $10,800, or $4320. This would reduce the basis at the end of the year to $6480. The basis, however, cannot be reduced below the $8000 residual value.

Appendix Nonrecovery Property

The fourth-year depreciation in this case is limited to $2800—the amount that reduces the adjusted basis from $10,800 to $8000.

The total depreciation under the declining balance method is the same as for the straight-line method. The declining balance method, however, results in more depreciation in early years and minimizes early-year tax payments. Corporations usually opt for the declining balance method when ACRS is not applicable.

Chapter **4**

Property Sales and Exchanges

This chapter considers the sale and exchange of investments and fixed assets. Investments include stock and bonds issued by other corporations. Fixed assets include machinery, buildings, and other productive property not originally acquired for resale to customers. Investments and fixed assets are sold when no longer needed by the business or when ready for replacement.

The sale of property usually gives rise to gains or losses. Gains on the sale are taxable at the time of sale. The tax rate applicable to a pretax gain or the tax benefit associated with a loss, however, often cannot be determined by looking only at specific property items in isolation. The treatment of gains and losses depends upon the property type, the holding period, and the overall effect of the corporation's other property dispositions for the year.

The estimation of gain or loss in advance of the disposition is an important element of tax planning. The chapter shows that the corporation can often benefit by delaying or accelerating certain dispositions to qualify for more favorable tax treatment.

Property dispositions can also be accomplished through an

Gains and Losses

exchange. Exchanges are sometimes not taxable. The advantages of the nontaxable exchange, however, are at least partially offset by certain undesirable characteristics, including a reduced basis and reduced eligibility for the investment tax credit.

The chapter begins with the calculation of capital gains and losses on a sale. Tax-free exchanges are then considered, and the gain on the sale of fixed assets is examined.

GAINS AND LOSSES

The Gain

The gain or loss on a sale measures the appreciation or decline in value of a property item relative to its carrying value for tax purposes. The gain or loss is an adjustment to taxable income. The amount of the gain or loss is:

Amount realized	xxx
Less: Adjusted basis	xxx
Gain (or loss)	xxx

The amount realized is the cash received plus the fair market value of other property received by the seller. In other words, the amount realized is the total amount received on the sale.

The adjusted basis determination begins with the initial basis. Usually this is the cost. The basis is then reduced for the effect of the investment tax credit and the depreciation previously taken. The general principles applicable to the basis reduction were discussed in the previous chapter.

The Cash Sale. The sale for cash is the most usual and also the most simple form of disposition. An example illustrating the determination of the gain on a sale for cash follows.

EXAMPLE: THE GAIN ON SALE. The Payup Corporation sells land with a basis of $2500 for $6000 cash.

A gain of $3500 results. The adjusted basis of $2500 is subtracted from the $6000 realized on the sale.

Amount realized	$6000
Less: Adjusted basis	2500
Gain on sale	$3500

An illustration is included as Figure 4.1.

The example shows that taxable income is *not* increased by the full amount realized. The amount originally invested after adjustments for depreciation and other factors is first recovered free of tax. Only the gain or the excess of the amount realized over the adjusted basis is taxed.

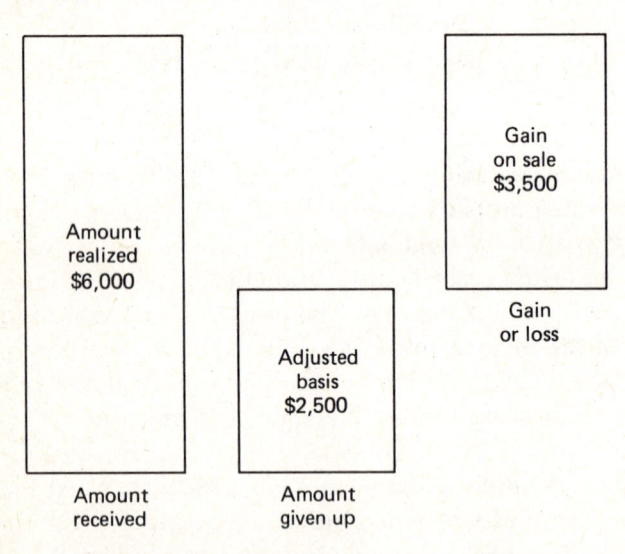

Figure 4.1. The recognition of gain on the property disposition. Land with adjusted basis $2500 sold for $6000 cash.

Gains and Losses

The Sale in Exchange for Property Other than Cash. When the sale is not entirely for cash, the fair market value of the property received is included in the amount realized. The calculation of the amount realized on the receipt of other noncash property is shown in the following xample.

EXAMPLE: THE GAIN ON SALE OF PROPERTY SOLD IN EXCHANGE FOR CASH AND OTHER PROPERTY. The Payup Corporation sells land with a basis of $2500 and receives $6000 cash and other property with a value of $2000.

The amount realized is:

Cash	$6000
Other property	2000
Total	$8000

The adjusted basis of $2500 is subtracted from the $8000 realized on the sale. A gain of $5500 results.

Amount realized	$8000
Less: Adjusted basis	2500
Gain on sale	$5500

An illustration is included as Figure 4.2.

The above example shows that the fair market value of noncash property received increases the amount of the gain.

The Loss

A gain occurs when the amount realized exceeds the adjusted basis. When the amount realized is less than the adjusted basis, the result is a loss. An example of a loss situation follows.

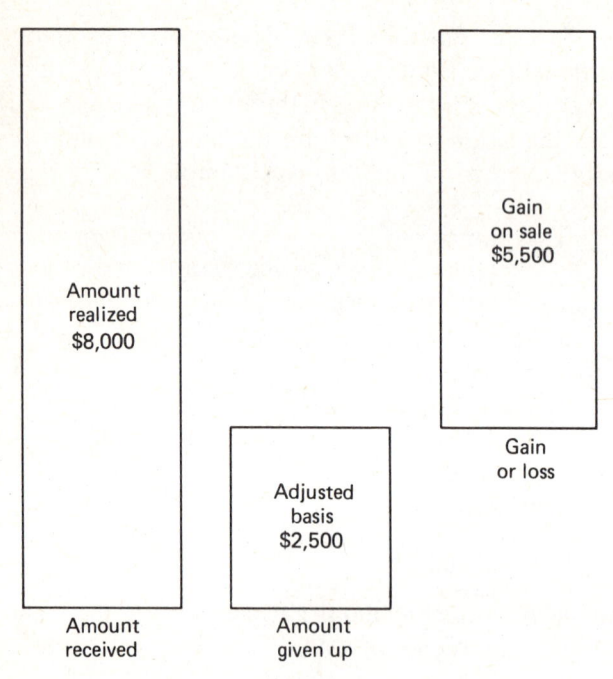

Figure 4.2. The recognition of gain on the property disposition for cash and other property. Land with adjusted basis $2500 sold for $6000 cash plus $2000 other property.

EXAMPLE: LOSS ON A PROPERTY DISPOSITION. The Payup Corporation sells land originally costing $2500 for $1000 in cash and $500 in marketable securities.

The $1500 amount realized represents the total of the cash plus the fair market value of other property received. The gain is determined by subtracting the adjusted basis from the amount realized.

Amount realized	$1500
Less: Adjusted basis	2500
Loss on sale	$1000

Gains and Losses

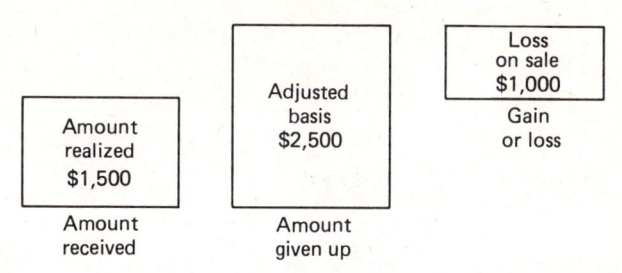

Figure 4.3. The recognition of loss on the property disposition for cash and other property. Land with adjusted basis $2500 sold for $1000 cash plus $500 other property.

Since the amount realized is not as great as the adjusted basis of $2500, the result is a loss. An illustration is included as Figure 4.3.

Property Subject to Depreciation. If property subject to depreciation is sold, the adjusted basis is determined after the reduction for depreciation taken to date. The gain or loss on sale is then determined in the usual manner. The sale of property subject to depreciation is illustrated in the following example.

EXAMPLE: LOSS ON THE DISPOSITION OF DEPRECIABLE PROPERTY. The Payup Corporation sells equipment originally costing $25,000 with $10,000 depreciation to date. Cash and other property with combined fair market value of $7000 is received in exchange.

The adjusted basis is determined as:

Cost	$25,000
Less: Depreciation to date	10,000
Adjusted basis	$15,000

The gain or loss is determined by comparison of the amount realized to the adjusted basis in the normal manner as follows:

Amount realized	$ 7,000
Less: Adjusted basis	15,000
Loss on sale	$ 8,000

Since the amount realized does not exceed the adjusted basis, the result is a loss. Figure 4.4 illustrates this situation.

Property Subject to the Investment Tax Credit. The basis of property subject to the investment tax credit is reduced by depreciation taken and also by part of the investment tax credit. The investment tax credit results in a basis reduction of one-half the amount of the credit. The gain or loss is then determined in the normal manner taking the adjusted basis into account. The effect of the investment tax credit on the gain or loss is shown in the following example.

EXAMPLE: DISPOSITION OF EQUIPMENT SUBJECT TO THE INVESTMENT TAX CREDIT. The Payup Corporation sells equipment originally costing $25,000 with $10,000 depreciation to date. Cash and other property with a combined fair market value of $7000 is received in exchange. A 10 percent investment tax credit was originally taken on the equipment.

The basis is reduced by the total of the depreciation plus one-half the investment tax credit (one-half of $2500) as follows:

Original cost		$25,000
Less: Depreciation	$10,000	
Tax credit basis reduction	1,250	11,250
Adjusted basis		$13,750

```
                                          Loss
                                        on sale
                                         $8,000




                           Adjusted
                            basis
                           $15,000
                                         Gain
                                        or loss



        Amount
        realized
        $7,000






        Amount      Amount
        received    given up
```

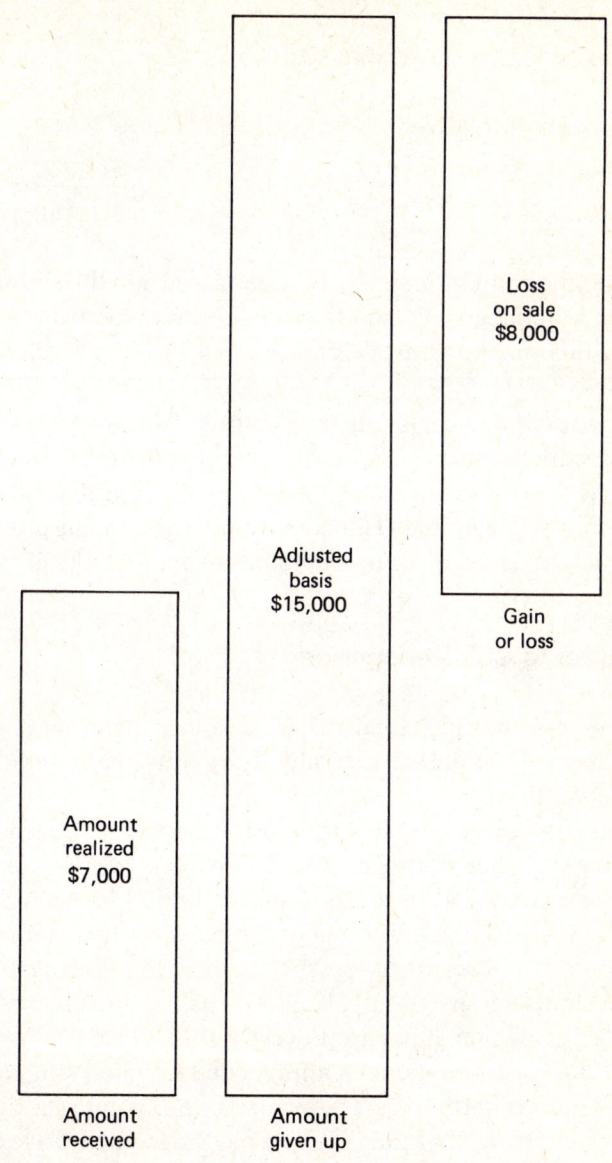

Figure 4.4. The recognition of loss on the disposition of depreciable property. Equipment with adjusted basis $15,000 sold for cash plus other property with combined value $7000.

The gain or loss is determined as:

Amount realized	$ 7,000
Less: Adjusted basis	$13,750
Loss on sale	$ 6,750

The example shows that the gain is increased and the amount of the loss is reduced by the effect of the investment tax credit basis reduction. An illustration is shown in Figure 4.5.

The reduction of basis rule is a compromise. Some legislators felt that reduction in basis for the full amount of the credit would help to increase tax revenues; others maintained that no basis reduction was desirable. The compromise agreement provided for reduction of the basis by one-half the amount of the credit.

Alternatives to Gain Recognition

Since the recognition of gain is taxable, tax planning is often concerned with avoiding the sale of property that would produce a gain on sale.

Businesses often invest temporary excesses of cash in the securities of other corporations. These investments are sold when cash is needed. If a group of diversified investments is made, typically some individual investments will result in gains while others will result in losses. One way to reduce gains on security transactions is to sell either loss securities or those securities on which gains are lowest.

If all the investments have appreciated in value and cash is needed, other alternatives are available. For example, the investor can borrow the funds and pledge the securities as collateral to the lender. This completely avoids the sale and associated gain recognition.

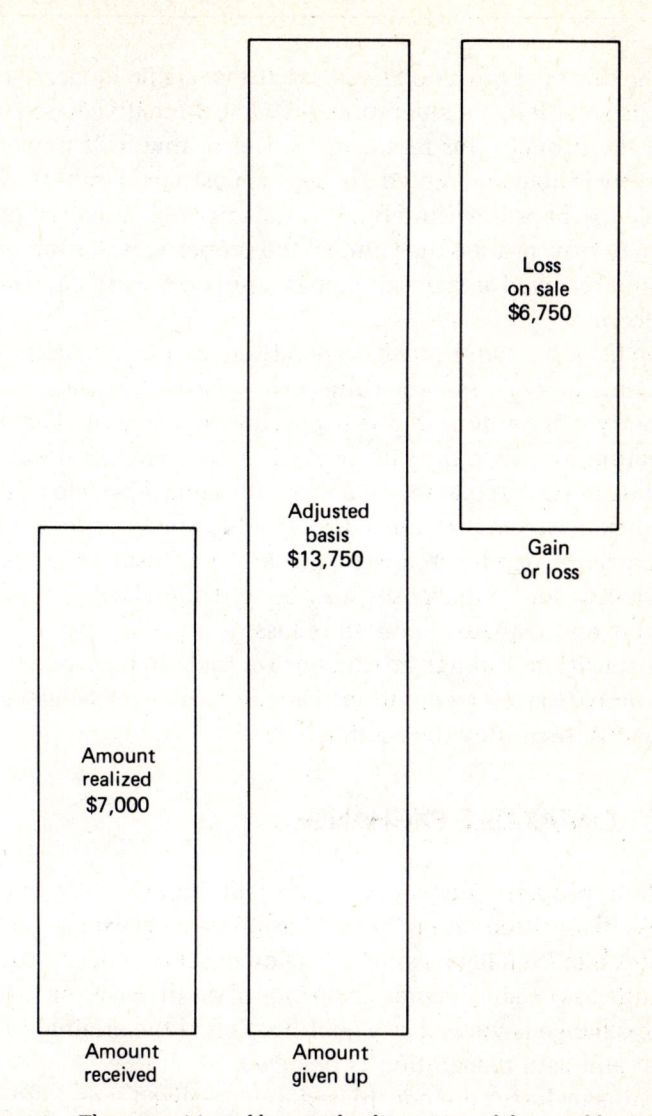

Figure 4.5. The recognition of loss on the disposition of depreciable property subject to the investment tax credit. Equipment with adjusted basis $13,750 sold for cash plus other property with combined value $7000.

109

The sale of appreciated fixed assets that are no longer needed can also result in considerable gain. One alternative to sale is to hold the property for rental instead of selling it. If unwanted property is held and rented, the gain is postponed until the time of sale (perhaps indefinitely). If cash is needed, it may be possible to borrow against the value of the property. A portion of the amount received as rent can then be applied toward payment of the loan.

On the other hand, some corporations are quick to dispose of investments with market value below basis. The sale of loss property can be desirable if it provides tax benefit. The same principle applies to the sale of fixed assets no longer needed by the business. Fixed assets sometimes become obsolete or don't perform up to expectations. The usual tendency is to keep the property on hand perhaps for backup purposes. A preferred alternative for tax purposes may be to dispose of the property quickly and realize a deductible loss.

Dispositions through an exchange or trade-in provide another alternative to gain recognition. The nontaxable exchange is discussed in the following section.

THE NONTAXABLE EXCHANGE

Certain property dispositions are not immediately taxable. These dispositions are referred to as nontaxable exchanges. In a nontaxable exchange, gains on the disposal of property are not included as taxable income at the time of the disposition. Instead, the exchange is viewed as a continuation of the original investment and gain recognition is deferred.

Gains or losses are considered to be realized when property transfers ownership. The realized gain or loss is generally the difference between the fair market value and the adjusted basis. The realized gains, however, are taxable only when recognized for tax purposes. The nontaxable exchange is an example of a gain that is realized, but not recognized.

The Nontaxable Exchange

Operation of the Nontaxable Exchange

Nontaxable exchange treatment is often obtained when new property is obtained at the time of disposal of old property. The following example illustrates the nontaxable exchange in the case of an old car trade-in.

EXAMPLE: A NONTAXABLE EXCHANGE. The Payup Corporation trades in a used car with an adjusted basis of $2000 and a fair market value of $5000. Payup gives $7000 cash and the old car in exchange for a new model. The new car has a fair market value of $12,000.

The gain is determined as the amount realized less the adjusted basis of the property given up and the cash given:

Amount realized		$12,000
Less: Old adjusted basis	$2,000	
Additional cash paid	7,000	9,000
Gain on sale		$ 3,000

The gain is not recognized in the nontaxable exchange. The realized gain is deferred until the replacement car is ultimately sold.

If the old car were first sold with the proceeds used to acquire a replacement, a taxable gain would result. Figure 4.6 illustrates the determination of gain.

Nontaxable exchanges permit indefinite deferrals of tax payments on gains resulting from the disposition of property. This tax deferral helps to finance the cost of the replacement property.

Nontaxable exchange treatment is available only on an exchange. An outright sale will not qualify for nontaxable exchange treatment.

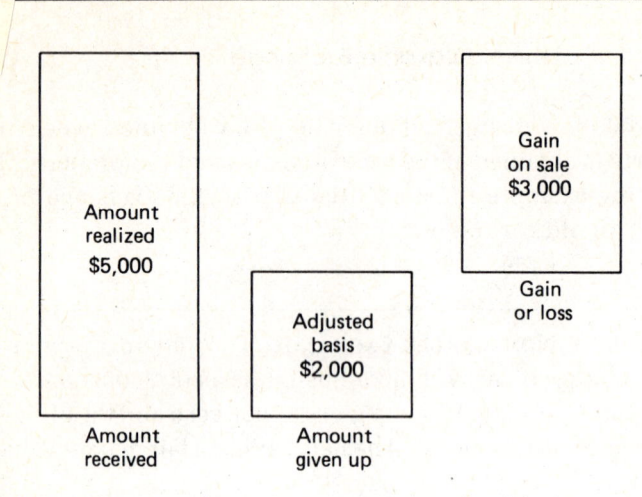

Figure 4.6. The nontaxable transaction. Gain is realized, but not recognized. Property with adjusted basis $2000 and fair market value $5000 exchanged for new property.

Criteria for the Nontaxable Exchange

Property Classes. The property exchanged does not need to be identical to the property received to qualify as a nontaxable exchange. It is only necessary for all property items to fall within the same broadly defined asset class. Two major property classes exist for purposes of the nontaxable exchange. Machinery, equipment, and vehicles all fall within one class. Real estate comprises a second class of property.

Machinery can be exchanged tax-free for other machinery, for equipment, or for vehicles. Real estate held for business purposes can be exchanged tax-free for other real estate.

Nonqualifying Property. Certain types of property items do not qualify for tax-free exchange treatment. These property types include merchandise inventories and securities. The gain on the exchange of these items is always taxable.

The Nontaxable Exchange

Problems with the Nontaxable Exchange

The Reduction in Basis. The nontaxable exchange is not necessarily desirable. The major problem with the nontaxable exchange concerns the basis of the newly acquired property. In cases of increasing new property costs, the basis of the new property is lower in a nontaxable exchange than in a purchase. The new basis is established as the old basis plus any cash or other property given in the exchange. This is shown in the following example.

EXAMPLE: THE REDUCTION IN BASIS. The Payup Corporation trades in a used car with an adjusted basis of $2000 and a fair market value of $5000. Payup gives $7000 cash and the old car in exchange for a new model. The new car has a fair market value of $12,000.

The new adjusted basis is the old basis plus the additional consideration given. The new basis can also be determined as the fair market value of the new property reduced by the amount of gain not recognized. The basis determination using both alternative methods follows:

Method 1:

Old basis	$2000
Additional consideration	7000
Basis of new property	$9000

Method 2:

The gain is determined as the amount realized less the adjusted basis of the property given up:

Amount realized		$12,000
Less: Old adjusted basis	$2000	
Additional cash paid	7000	9,000
Gain on sale		$ 3,000

The entire gain of $3000 is not recognized. The new basis is:

Fair market value of new property	$12,000
Less: Gain not recognized	3,000
Adjusted basis	$ 9,000

Methods 1 and 2 result in the same basis. Both alternative approaches to determining the adjusted basis of the new property are shown in Figure 4.7.

The procedure for determining the basis ensures that the nontaxable exchange does not eliminate the tax. The effect is only to defer recognition of the gain and payment of the tax until the new property is eventually sold. Future depreciation deductions will also be reduced, since these are determined by the adjusted basis. An illustration of the equity of the basis determination procedure follows.

EXAMPLE: THE SALE OF NEW PROPERTY SHORTLY AFTER ACQUISITION BY NONTAXABLE EXCHANGE. The Payup Corporation trades in a used car with an adjusted basis of $2000 and a fair market value of $5000. Payup gives $7000 cash and the old car in exchange for a new model. The new car has a fair market value of $12,000.

The basis of the new car was established as $9000 in the previous examples. If the new car is sold for its fair market value of $12,000 shortly after the exchange, the gain is recognized at that time as:

Amount realized	$12,000
Less: Adjusted basis	9,000
Recognized gain	$ 3,000

This is the same gain that would be taxed in an outright sale of the old property. In that event, the old car with an adjusted basis

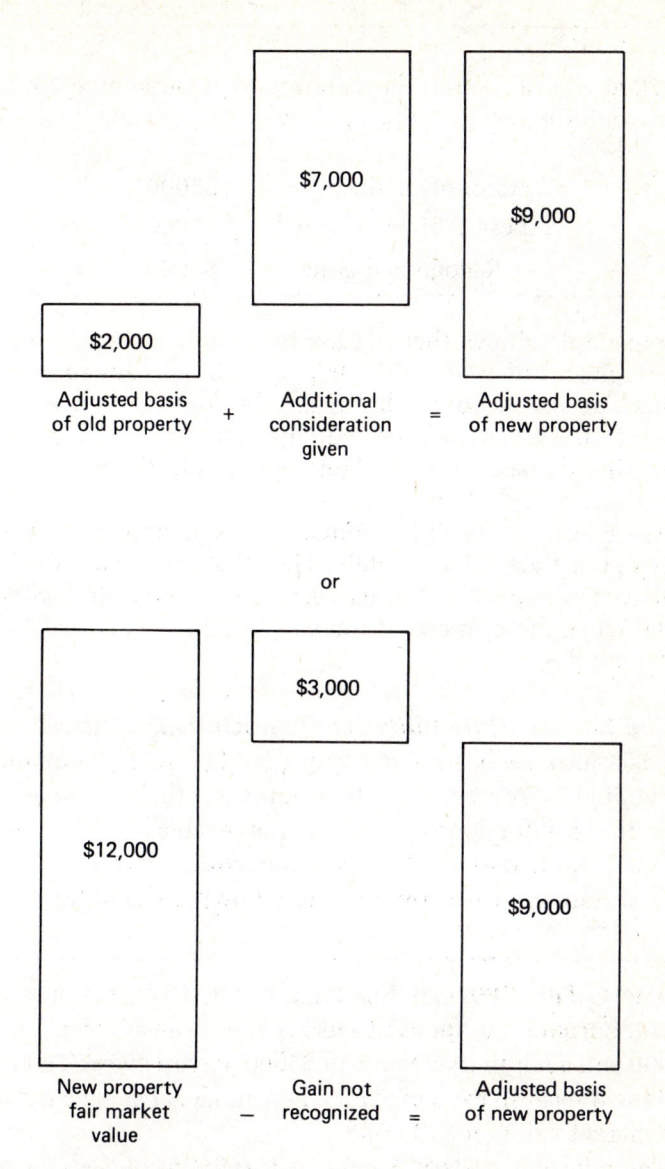

Figure 4.7. The nontaxable exchange and the adjusted basis. Property with adjusted basis $2000 and fair market value $5000 exchanged along with $7000 cash for new property with fair market value $12,000.

115

of $2000 would be sold for its fair market value of $5000. The gain would be recognized as follows:

Amount realized	$5000
Less: Adjusted basis	2000
Recognized gain	$3000

The example shows that the tax in a nontaxable exchange is not forgiven but is merely postponed. If subsequent replacements are also acquired by means of nontaxable exchanges, however, the process is repeated. The basis remains as the beginning adjusted basis increased only by the additional consideration given.

As a result of successive nontaxable exchanges, it is possible to postpone the tax indefinitely. The result, however, will be an adjusted basis far below the market value of appreciated property. If and when the property is finally sold, the gain is likely to be extremely large.

The Reduced Eligibility for Depreciation. The reduction of basis also leads to a reduction in the amount potentially deductible as depreciation. In a purchase, the entire cost provides the basis for depreciation. In a nontaxable exchange, depreciation is limited to the amount of the reduced basis. The depreciation limitation is shown in the following example.

EXAMPLE: THE REDUCED ELIGIBILITY FOR DEPRECIATION. The Payup Corporation trades in a used car with an adjusted basis of $2000 and a fair market value of $5000. Payup gives $7000 cash and the old car in exchange for a new model. The new car has a fair market value of $12,000.

The adjusted basis is $9000. A maximum of $9000 can be deducted as future depreciation. If the new car were purchased outright, depreciation would be based on the $12,000 cost.

The Nontaxable Exchange

The Reduced Investment Tax Credit. An additional disadvantage of the nontaxable exchange is the reduction of the investment tax credit. The credit is based on the sum of the old basis and the additional cash paid rather than on the fair market value of the new property. The following example illustrates the reduced investment tax credit associated with the nontaxable exchange.

EXAMPLE: THE NONTAXABLE EXCHANGE AND THE INVESTMENT TAX CREDIT. The Payup Corporation trades in a used car with an adjusted basis of $2000 and a fair market value of $5000. Payup gives $7000 cash and the old car in exchange for a new model. The new car has a fair market value of $12,000.

If the $12,000 car is purchased outright, a 6 percent investment tax credit of $720 applies. If the car is acquired through a nontaxable exchange, the adjusted basis is $9000. The investment tax credit on 6 percent of this amount is $540.

The preceding discussion assumes the acquisition of new property. If used property is acquired in a nontaxable exchange, the credit is based on only the amount of additional cash paid. The adjusted basis of the old property is disregarded for purposes of determining the credit. The used property situation is illustrated in the following example.

EXAMPLE: THE NONTAXABLE EXCHANGE AND THE INVESTMENT TAX CREDIT ON THE ACQUISITION OF USED PROPERTY. The Payup Corporation trades in a used car with an adjusted basis of $2000 and a fair market value of $5000. Payup gives $7000 cash and the old car in exchange for another car. The acquired car is a used car and has a fair market value of $12,000.

The credit on used property is based only on the $7000 additional cash paid. The credit is only 6 percent of $7000, or $420.

The Nontaxable Exchange and Boot

Cash and other property not qualifying for nontaxable exchange treatment is sometimes received along with property that does qualify. The nonqualifying property is referred to as "boot." Boot is often received if valuable property is given in exchange for property that is less valuable. For example, a business might trade in a high-powered computer for a less valuable model that is easier to operate. In this case, the business would expect to receive boot along with the small computer.

With the receipt of boot, part or all of the gain on an exchange may be taxable. Gains are taxable to the extent of boot received. If the boot received exceeds the gain, however, only the amount of the gain is taxable. The tax treatment of boot is illustrated as follows.

EXAMPLE: A NONTAXABLE EXCHANGE WITH BOOT. The Payup Corporation exchanges a large old building with an adjusted basis of $500,000 for a smaller new building with a fair market value of $200,000. Cash of $400,000 is also received.

The amount realized consists of both the new building and the boot. The total fair market value of the property received is $600,000. The gain is:

Amount realized	$600,000
Less: Adjusted basis	$500,000
Realized gain	$100,000
Recognized as taxable income	$100,000

The entire amount of the gain is taxable because it arises from the receipt of cash and other property not in the same broad property class as the old real estate.

The Nontaxable Exchange

The boot provisions take account of the fact that only a part of the original investment is continued if boot is received. The reasoning is that the taxpayer maintains only a portion of the original investment. Another portion of the investment is converted to cash.

The receipt of boot is not necessarily taxable. Gains are taxable only to the extent of boot received. If there is no gain, the receipt of boot is not taxable. The following example illustrates the receipt of boot without gain.

EXAMPLE: THE RECEIPT OF BOOT WITHOUT THE RECOGNITION OF GAIN. The Payup Corporation exchanges a large old building with an adjusted basis of $500,000 for a smaller new building with a fair market value of $200,000. Cash of $300,000 is also received.

The amount realized consists of both the new building and the boot. The total fair market value of the property received is $500,000. There is no gain, since the amount realized is the same as the adjusted basis. The receipt of boot is not taxed.

Dealers in machinery and certain other property often take exchanges. In the case of real estate or special-purpose property, it is often more difficult to find sellers willing to take used property in exchange. Businesses sometimes find it advantageous to work through brokers who either buy property and take exchanges or find third parties to participate in nontaxable exchanges.

Loss Transactions

Losses on the sale of property can reduce taxable income. For this reason, the deferral of losses using a nontaxable exchange is not generally desirable. If the value of the property is not greater than the adjusted basis, corporations often sell the property outright to recognize the loss.

CAPITAL GAINS AND LOSSES

The chapter to this point has explored the issue of how gains or losses are determined. Now the issue of how gains are taxed will be examined.

Gains and losses are classified as capital gains or as ordinary income. Capital gains, in turn, may be either short-term or long-term. The classification of a gain or loss on sale is important, because capital gains and losses are taxed differently than ordinary gains and losses. Long-term capital gains are subject to a reduced tax rate. Capital gains and losses also receive different treatment with respect to deductibility. Ordinary losses are deductible to determine income. Capital losses are not deductible, but may be used only to offset capital gains.

Short-Term and Long-Term Gains and Losses

The Tax Rates. The maximum tax rate on corporate long-term gains is 28 percent. This compares with the 46 percent tax rate applicable to ordinary income. Since the difference in tax rates is considerable, high marginal rate taxpayers often go to a great deal of trouble to structure transactions to qualify for capital gain rather than ordinary income treatment.

It should be noted that the tax applicable to capital gains can be less than 28 percent. Tax legislation establishes the tax rate on capital gains as the lesser of the ordinary income tax rate or 28 percent. As a result, the ordinary income tax rate sometimes applies to capital gains for the low income tax bracket corporation. (For example, the corporation with total taxable income of $25,000 or less is effectively taxed at the 15 percent rate for both ordinary income and capital gains.) In the interest of sim-

Capital Gains and Losses   121

plicity, however, the discussion of capital gains in this book assumes a 46 percent marginal bracket taxpayer with a 28 percent capital gains tax rate.

Applicable Property. Capital gains are applicable to gains on the sale or exchange of capital assets. Investments in stocks and bonds of other businesses are the most common forms of capital assets. Patents, copyrights, and trademarks are also capital assets.

Fixed assets such as machinery, equipment, and real estate held long-term for the purpose of producing income are not classified as capital assets for tax purposes. Gains on the sale of fixed assets, however, may qualify for capital gains treatment. The disposition of fixed assets will be examined later in this chapter.

The Holding Period. The holding period must be more than six months for gains on sales to qualify as long-term. Since only long-term capital gains are eligible for the reduced tax, businesses sometimes find it advisable to hold capital gain property until six months have elapsed in order to qualify for the reduced tax rate. The gain on appreciated securities held for less than six months, for example, is taxable at the 46 percent rate. If the securities are held for six months and one day, the applicable rate is only 28 percent.

Until 1984 the qualifying holding period was one year. Security brokers and other interested parties lobbied extensively for reducing the long-term holding period to six months. The six-month holding period qualifies more dispositions for capital gains treatment and sometimes encourages more frequent trading.

Capital Losses. Capital gains are subject to tax, but capital losses are not deducted to determine taxable income. Capital losses may only reduce or offset capital gains. This means that in some circumstances a capital loss may not provide tax benefit.

Since capital losses may exceed capital gains in particular years, the tax legislation provides for the carryback of capital losses against previous year capital gains. The procedure is similar to that applicable to net operating losses (discussed in Chapter 2). When capital losses are carried back, the loss corporation files for a refund of taxes previously paid on capital gains. When capital losses are carried forward, the losses offset future capital gains. The carryback period is three years as with the net operating loss. The carryforward period is limited to five years.

The following section on determining net gains and losses addresses the issue of why capital losses may not provide tax benefit in a particular tax year.

Determining Net Gains and Losses

The corporation's net capital gains and losses are calculated using a somewhat involved set of rules. As a consequence, calculations are necessary to determine what tax rate applies to a particular gain or loss when considered in isolation.

Net Long-Term and Net Short-Term Items. The long-term (LT) and short-term (ST) gain or loss is determined by a netting process. First the short-term and long-term gains and losses are grouped as follows:

	Loss	Gain
Holding period: ST	ST loss	ST gain
LT	LT loss	LT gain

Then the net short-term and net long-term items are calculated. Short-term gains are compared to short-term losses, and either a net short-term gain or a net short-term loss results. Then long-term gains are compared to long-term losses, and either a net long-term gain or a net long-term loss results.

Capital Gains and Losses

The net short-term and long-term items are then netted diagonally. Net short-term losses offset net long-term gains. Net long-term losses offset net short-term gains. The following combinations are possible after netting:

Net short-term gains and net long-term gains.

Net short-term losses and net long-term losses.

No other combinations are possible as a result of the netting process outlined above, since short-term items and long-term items are always netted before the diagonal netting takes place. For example, an end result of both net short-term losses and net short-term gains is not possible, since the two items will be netted and only one will survive.

The Tax. The tax is now computed on the above items. Net short-term gains are taxable as ordinary income. Net long-term gains are taxable as capital gains. If the result of netting is a net short-term gain, for example, the gain is taxable as ordinary income. If the result of netting is a net long-term loss, the loss may not provide tax benefit for this tax year. An example follows.

EXAMPLE: NET CAPITAL GAINS and LOSSES. The Payup Corporation sells stock held as investments in other corporations, realizing gains and losses as follows:

Investment A,	short-term gain	$2000
Investment B,	short-term loss	6000
Investment C,	long-term gain	5000
Investment D,	long-term loss	4000

The net short-term items result in a $4000 loss. The net long-term items result in a $1000 gain. The net short-term loss is compared to the net long-term gain and a $3000 net short-term loss results. The loss will not provide current-year tax benefit unless it can be carried back against previous-year capital gains.

The netting procedure is responsible for the inability to determine the tax rate on a particular transaction without considering the other capital transactions. For example, a business may sell shares of stock at a $50,000 gain. Possibly the transaction may increase long-term gains and result in tax at the 28 percent capital gains rate. Another possibility, however, is that the transaction will partially offset short-term losses and have no current-year tax impact (capital losses reduce taxable income only through ability to offset capital gains).

Figure 4.8 summarizes the four possible net gain and loss situations and associated tax implications. Additional illustrations of the netting process are included in the Appendix at the end of this chapter.

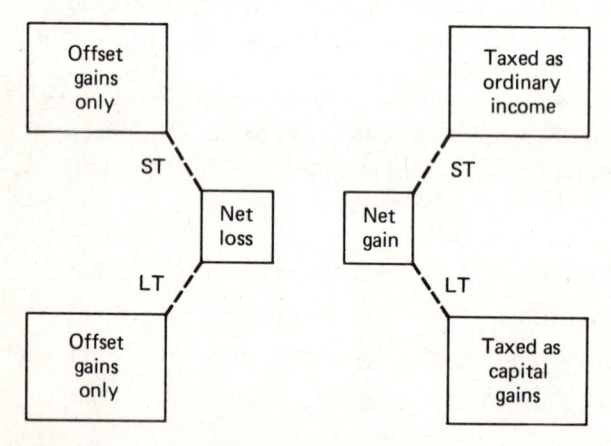

Figure 4.8. Tax implications of net capital gains and losses.

Tax Minimization

The sale of property qualifying for capital gains treatment should be planned carefully to avoid nondeductible losses and to avoid tax on gains at ordinary income rates. One common approach is to minimize taxes on gains by recognizing offsetting losses. This can be done by selling loss investments. The loss on sale offsets the previous gain and reduces the net gain to zero.

Corporations are sometimes faced with the problem of expiring capital loss carryovers. Capital losses provide tax benefit only to the extent that they are offset by gains. If it appears as though a capital loss carryover entitlement will be lost if not applied against a current-year gain, it may be beneficial to sell stocks or other investments and recognize the gains. The gains will not be taxed since they are offset by losses. If the investments are later replaced with similar investments, the result is a step-up in basis with no effective tax cost. An illustration of an effective tax-minimization strategy follows.

EXAMPLE: THE SALE AND REPURCHASE OF INVESTMENTS. The Payup Corporation sells investments, recognizing a short-term gain of $5000, early in 1985. Payup continues to carry a diversified portfolio of investments. The portfolio includes both stocks with unrecognized losses and stocks with unrecognized gains.

At year-end Payup can sell loss investments to offset the $5000 short-term gain. This will eliminate Payup's 1985 taxable gain on securities.

Payup can immediately use the proceeds to buy similar securities. For example, Payup can sell shares in Mobil and immediately repurchase shares in Exxon. Alternatively, Payup can repurchase the same shares if it waits for a period of time before doing so.

Fixed Assets

Gains and losses on the disposition of fixed assets do not qualify directly for capital gains treatment. Gains and losses on the disposition of fixed assets held long-term, however, may contribute to the net capital gain or loss. In computing the corporation's overall gains and losses, gains and losses on net fixed assets are first considered as a group.

The procedure is to total the long-term gains and losses on fixed assets and determine the net long-term gain or loss. If the result is a loss, all long-term losses on fixed assets are deductible from ordinary income, and all gains are taxable as ordinary income. If the result is a gain, the gain is added to other capital gains, with the strong possibility that it will be taxed at preferred capital gains rates. Gains and losses on fixed assets held short-term do not enter into these determinations. These gains and losses are taxed as ordinary income. The rationale for this approach dates back to World War II and may be more political than economic. An illustration of the sale of long-term fixed assets follows.

EXAMPLE: THE SALE OF LONG-TERM FIXED ASSETS. The Payup Corporation sells machinery held long-term at a $5000 gain and a vehicle also held long-term for a $3000 loss.

Both items are long-term fixed assets. The gain and loss is netted, and a $2000 gain results. The gain is included with other long-term capital gains. If the result were a loss, both the gain and loss would be taxable (or deductible) as ordinary income.

Timing Fixed Asset Dispositions

Net capital losses on the disposition of long-term fixed assets are effectively deducted from ordinary income; net gains are taxed at the capital gains rate. Arranging gain and loss recognition carefully can provide the taxpayer with the best possible situation. This is shown in the following example.

EXAMPLE: TIMING LONG-TERM FIXED ASSET DISPOSITIONS. The Payup Corporation sells two parcels of land. A loss of $500,000 is recognized from the sale of parcel A; a gain of $500,000 is recognized on the sale of parcel B.

If the sales take place in the same year, the two dispositions are netted and no tax results. If parcel A is sold the first year and parcel B is sold the second year a net tax saving is obtained as follows:

First year, benefit of deduction on sale of A (46% of $500,000)	$230,000
Second year, tax on gain on sale of B (28% of $500,000)	(140,000)
Net tax benefit	$ 90,000

This tax-saving opportunity is generally available for land and residential real estate. Recapture provisions may preclude substantial savings opportunities for other types of property. (Recapture will be examined in Chapter 5).

RELATED PARTY TRANSACTIONS

Related party transactions apply primarily to the closely held corporation and its owners. Special related party provisions are included in the legislation to prevent related taxpayers from avoiding the tax by undertaking property transactions primarily for tax reasons. Chapters 2 and 3 considered related party provisions associated with the determination of tax rates and the acquisition of productive property. This section briefly considers related party provisions applicable to the sale of property.

The Disallowance of Losses on Sales

Losses on transactions between related parties are not allowable deductions. Gains on sales between related parties, however, are included in income.

The major groups of related parties for purposes of this provision are:

Family members (spouses, brothers, sisters, parents, children, grandchildren, but not in-laws).

Corporations and owners if one owner or group of related owners owns more than 50 percent of the corporation.

An example of a disallowed related party loss transaction follows.

EXAMPLE: THE DISALLOWANCE OF RELATED PARTY LOSSES. Judy Jones owns land with a basis of $400,000 and a fair market value of $100,000. Judy sells the land at its fair market value to the Great Southwestern Corporation, a corporation that she owns.

Judy realizes a loss on the sale determined as:

Amount realized	$100,000
Less: Adjusted basis	400,000
Loss on Sale	($300,000)

If loss recognition were permitted, Judy could benefit by selling property to her corporation whenever the market value drops below cost. The effective ownership of the property would not really change, but Judy would recognize tax benefit as a result of the transaction.

The loss is not recognized by Judy because it is a sale of property to a related party. Judy still has control of the property.

The related party rule was developed because taxpayers were recognizing deductible losses on sales of property that were not effectively changing ownership. One common abuse was the sale of property back and forth between spouses—a practice that will also not provide tax benefit as a result of the related party rules.

Gains on the Sale of Depreciable Property

The related party rules provide that gains on the sale of depreciable property to related taxpayers are taxed as ordinary income. When property that has appreciated in value is sold, the seller may recognize capital gain on the sale. The basis to the buyer becomes the purchase price. If it were not for the special related party provisions, the related taxpayer selling appreciated property could potentially benefit by recognizing the appreciation as capital gain, but then later deducting future depreciation as ordinary income. Taxation on sales to related parties as ordinary income eliminates these potential tax benefits from related party transactions.

SUMMARY

The tax on the disposition of property depends upon a number of factors. These include the type of property, its cost, the selling price, the holding period, the manner of disposition, the investment tax credit, the amount of depreciation taken, and other transactions undertaken by the corporation.

The gain or loss is determined as the difference between the amount realized and the adjusted basis at the time of disposition. If noncash property is received in an exchange, the amount realized is increased by this amount.

The Nontaxable Exchange. The nontaxable exchange defers the recognition of gains indefinitely until the property or its replacement is ultimately sold. Gain is not recognized in a nontaxable exchange unless cash or other nonqualifying property is received in the exchange. Nontaxable exchange treatment applies to exchanges within the same broadly defined class of property.

If boot is received in a nontaxable exchange, the realized gain is recognized to the extent of the boot received.

The basis of property acquired in a nontaxable exchange is determined by reference to the basis of the old property given up. The basis of the new property is equal to the basis of the old property plus the value of any additional consideration given.

The nontaxable exchange does not reduce taxes permanently. It merely defers the recognition of tax. The indefinite deferral of tax, however, can be nearly as valuable as a tax saving.

The investment tax credit in a nontaxable exchange is based upon the adjusted basis of the old property and the value of the additional consideration given in the exchange.

Capital Gains. High marginal tax rate corporations prefer capital gains to ordinary income because a reduced tax rate applies. Sales of capital assets result in capital gains if the holding period of the assets is in excess of six months. Investments in stocks and bonds of other businesses represent the most common form of capital asset.

Machinery, equipment, real estate, and other business property held long-term may also qualify for capital gains treatment. The treatment of gains and losses on long-term fixed assets is determined after grouping all dispositions of these items. If the net effect is a gain, it is added to other capital gains. If the net effect is a loss, the net loss is effectively deducted from ordinary income.

The procedure for calculating capital gains involves grouping to obtain the short-term and long-term gains and losses. The resultant group totals are first netted with the short-term and long-term calculation. The short-term gains are then netted against the long-term losses and the long-term gains are netted against the short-term losses.

Capital Losses. Capital losses are not deductible, but are netted against capital gains. Capital losses can be carried back and carried forward using a procedure similar to that applicable to operating losses.

Related Party Transactions. Special tax treatment applies to certain transactions between related parties. Losses on sales to related parties are not recognized for tax purposes. Gains on the sale of depreciable property to related taxpayers are treated as ordinary income and are not eligible for capital gains treatment.

APPENDIX
NET CAPITAL GAINS AND LOSSES

The tax on the corporation's capital gains and losses is complicated by the netting of long-term gains against short-term losses and short-term gains against long-term losses. The unique treatment given to long-term fixed assets further complicates the calculation. As a result, it is not always clear how a particular item of gain or loss will be taxed. This appendix to Chapter 4 provides two illustrations of the determination of corporate capital gains or losses.

The Procedure

The calculation of capital gains involves specific steps in a specific sequence as follows:

1. Arrange short-term (ST) and long-term (LT) items in separate groups.
2. Identify long-term fixed assets.
3. Determine the treatment of long-term fixed assets.
4. Group the remaining capital items.
5. Net horizontally to obtain net short-term (ST) and long-term (LT) items.
6. Net diagonally to determine net gains and losses.

Illustrations

Two illustrations of the calculation of capital gains on the disposition of a number of property items follow:

EXAMPLE: THE CALCULATION OF NET CAPITAL GAINS. Sales of the following items during the year resulted in short-term (ST) items:

Property A	$(20,000) loss
Property B	(30,000) loss
Property C	10,000 gain
Net ST	$(40,000) loss

Sales of the following items during the year resulted in long-term (LT) items:

Property D	$ 20,000 gain
Property E	70,000 gain

Appendix Net Capital Gains and Losses

Property F	(20,000) loss
Property G (LT fixed)	50,000 gain
Property H (LT fixed)	(60,000) loss
Net LT	$ 60,000 gain

Identify Long-Term Fixed Assets. After the initial grouping, long-term fixed assets are identified. Properties G and H are assumed to fall into this category.

Property H	Property G
$60,000 LT loss	$50,000 LT gain

Gains and losses from the disposition of short-term plant, property, or equipment held for the purpose of producing income are taxed as ordinary income. These do not enter into the determination of capital gain or loss.

Determine the Treatment of Long-Term Fixed Assets.
Now net the long-term items horizontally to determine the net long-term fixed asset gain or loss.

Property H	Property G
$60,000 LT loss	$50,000 LT gain

The result is a net long-term loss of $10,000.

LT Fixed Assets
$10,000 LT loss —

If the net amount is a loss, all long-term fixed asset losses are deductible to determine taxable income and all gains are taxable as ordinary income. In this case, the $60,000 loss is currently deductible. The $50,000 gain is taxed as ordinary income.

If the net long-term fixed assets result in a gain, the long-term gain is included with other long-term capital gains below.

Since the long-term fixed assets do not result in a net gain, they are not considered further in the determination of capital gains.

Group the Remaining Capital Items. Now consider the remaining capital items.

Property A	Property C
$20,000 ST loss	$10,000 ST gain
Property B	Property D
$30,000 ST loss	$20,000 LT gain
Property F	Property E
$20,000 LT loss	$70,000 LT gain

Total the gain and losses in each of the four categories.

Property A	Property C
$20,000 ST loss	$10,000 ST gain
Property B	Property D
$30,000 ST loss	$20,000 LT gain
Property F	Property E
$20,000 LT loss	$70,000 LT gain

The result is:

$50,000 ST loss $10,000 ST gain
$20,000 LT loss $90,000 LT gain

Net Horizontally to Determine Net Short-Term and Long-Term Items. These subtotals are now netted horizontally to determine the net short-term and net long-term items:

$50,000 ST loss	$10,000 ST gain
$20,000 LT loss	$90,000 LT gain

Appendix Net Capital Gains and Losses

The result is:

$40,000 ST loss   —

    — $70,000 LT gain

Net Diagonally to Determine Net Gains or Losses. Finally, short-term and long-term items are netted diagonally. (Short-term and long-term items are never added vertically.)

$40,000 ST loss   —

    — $70,000 LT gain

The result is:

—   —

— $30,000 LT gain

The $30,000 long-term capital gain is taxed at the reduced long-term capital gains rates.

A different set of circumstances might have resulted only in a short-term gain or a short-term gain in addition to the long-term gain. The short-term portion of the gain is taxed as ordinary income.

EXAMPLE: THE CALCULATION OF NET CAPITAL GAINS. Sales of the following property during the year resulted in short-term items:

Property 1	$(40,000) loss
Property 2	20,000 gain
Property 3	50,000 gain
Property 4	(5,000) loss
Property 5	(20,000) loss
Net ST	$ 5,000 gain

Sales of the following items during the year resulted in long-term capital items:

Property 6	$(15,000) loss
Property 7	75,000 gain
Property 8 (LT fixed)	20,000 gain
Property 9 (LT fixed)	$(15,000) loss
Net LT	$ 65,000 gain

First identify long-term fixed assets. Properties 8 and 9 are assumed to fall into this category.

Property 9	Property 8
$15,000 LT loss	$20,000 LT gain

Net the items horizontally to determine the net long-term gain or loss.

Property 9	Property 8
$15,000 LT loss	$20,000 LT gain

The result is a net long-term gain of $5000.

— $5000 LT gain

The long-term gain is included with other long-term capital gains.

Now consider the remaining capital items:

Property 1	Property 2
$40,000 ST loss	$20,000 ST gain
Property 4	Property 3
$ 5,000 ST loss	$50,000 ST gain

Appendix Net Capital Gains and Losses

Property 5 $20,000 ST loss	Property 7 $75,000 LT gain
Property 6 $15,000 LT loss	LT Fixed Assets $ 5,000 LT gain

Total the gains and losses in each of the four categories.

Property 1 $40,000 ST loss	Property 2 $20,000 ST gain
Property 4 $ 5,000 ST loss	Property 3 $50,000 ST gain
Property 5 $20,000 ST loss	Property 7 $75,000 LT gain
Property 6 $15,000 LT loss	LT Fixed Assets $ 5,000 LT gain

The result is:

$65,000 ST loss $70,000 ST gain

$15,000 LT loss $80,000 LT gain

These are netted horizontally to determine the net short-term and net long-term items:

$65,000 ST loss	$70,000 ST gain
$15,000 LT loss	$80,000 LT gain

The net short-term and long-term items are:

    — $ 5,000 ST gain
    — $65,000 LT gain

Normally the net short-term and long-term items are netted diagonally. Netting diagonally in this case does not affect the outcome. The end result is still both a short-term and a long-term gain. (Short-term and long-term gains are never added.) The short-term portion of this gain is taxed as ordinary income. The long-term portion is taxed at the more favorable capital gains rates.

Chapter 5

Recaptures

Long-term gains on the sale of investments are taxed at the preferred capital gains rates. The gain on sale of fixed assets, however, is frequently taxed as ordinary income. The ordinary income rates on the sale of fixed assets arise from the operation of recaptures. Recaptures are often responsible for ordinary income treatment even though the property might otherwise qualify for capital gains treatment.

A different type of recapture applies to the investment tax credit. The investment tax credit is offered as an incentive for business to invest in new plant and equipment. If the new plant and equipment is held for only a short period of time, the investment tax credit is recaptured or paid back.

This chapter overviews the recapture of depreciation and the investment tax credit.

DEPRECIATION RECAPTURE

The Operation of Recapture

With recapture, some or all of the gain on the disposition of property may be taxed at ordinary income rates. The amount of recapture is the lesser of the gain or the depreciation previously taken.

In practice, the depreciation previously taken is often large compared to the gain. Consequently, the entire gain is taxed as ordinary income. The following example illustrates the operation of depreciation recapture.

EXAMPLE: DEPRECIATION RECAPTURE. A building with an original cost of $100,000 and depreciation to date of $100,000 is sold for $100,000.

The adjusted basis of the building is zero since all of the $100,000 cost has been depreciated.

The gain on the sale is:

Amount realized	$100,000
Less: Adjusted basis	0
Gain on sale	$100,000

Since the gain equals the depreciation previously taken, all of the gain is subject to recapture. The entire $100,000 gain is taxed as ordinary income.

It should be noted that recapture only applies to the tax rate on the gain. It does not increase the amount of the gain. In other words, the recapture cannot exceed the amount of the gain.

The Reason for Recapture

Without depreciation recapture, taxpayers could deduct depreciation at ordinary income rates and later sell the property with tax on the gain payable at reduced capital gains rates. In the absence of this provision, tax benefits could result merely from

Depreciation Recapture

owning equipment. The reason for the concept of recapture is shown in the following example.

EXAMPLE: THE REASON FOR DEPRECIATION RECAPTURE. A building with an original cost of $100,000 and depreciation to date of $100,000 is sold for $100,000 as in the earlier example.

The gain on the sale was determined as $100,000. The net tax advantage before recapture of the property ownership is:

	Tax effect
Previous tax reductions from depreciation ($100,000 at 46%)	$46,000
Less: Tax on gain ($100,000 at 28%)	28,000
Net tax advantage	$18,000

Recapture effectively precludes this treatment. With recapture, the $100,000 deducted at ordinary income rates is responsible for the $100,000 gain in the above example. The gain is also taxed at ordinary income rates for a total tax of $46,000. Consequently, there is no net tax advantage other than that associated with the time value of money.

In some cases, recapture applies to the entire gain. In other cases, recapture applies to only a portion of the gain because depreciation previously taken is less than the amount of the gain. An illustration follows.

EXAMPLE: A PORTION OF THE GAIN SUBJECT TO DEPRECIATION RECAPTURE. A building with an original cost of $100,000 has depreciation to date of only $60,000. The selling price is $150,000.

Only a portion of the gain in this case is subject to recapture, since the gain on sale exceeds the total depreciation to date. The gain is calculated as follows:

Cost of building	$100,000
Less: Depreciation taken to date	60,000
Adjusted basis	$ 40,000
Amount realized	$150,000
Less: Adjusted basis	40,000
Gain on sale	$110,000
Recaptured and taxed as ordinary income	$ 60,000
Taxed as capital gains	$ 50,000

Figure 5.1 illustrates the components of the gain in chart form.

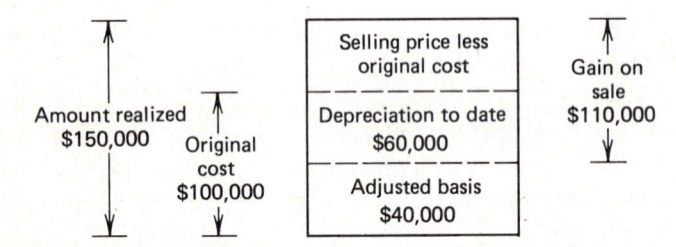

Figure 5.1. Depreciation recapture. Depreciation is recaptured to the extent of depreciation previously taken. Property sold for $150.000. Cost, $100,000; depreciation to date, $60,000. The gain is taxed as:

1. Capital gain. The appreciation of property above original cost—$50,000.
2. Ordinary income. The recapture of depreciation previously taken—$60,000.

Depreciation Recapture

In practice, the gain is often less than the depreciation previously taken and the full amount of gain is subject to recapture. The result is that gains on the sale of depreciable business property are often taxed as ordinary income.

Property Subject to Recapture

Property subject to recapture consists of assets subject to depreciation or amortization. Recapture property includes machinery, equipment, vehicles, buildings, patents, and copyrights.

Depreciation Recapture and Property Subject to the Investment Tax Credit

Effective with acquisitions in 1983, the gain attributable to the reduction in basis associated with the investment tax credit is also subject to recapture. The operation of recapture with property subject to the investment tax credit is shown as follows.

EXAMPLE: RECAPTURE AND THE BASIS REDUCTION ATTRIBUTABLE TO THE INVESTMENT TAX CREDIT. The Small Corporation sells a vehicle for $15,000. The vehicle originally cost $10,000 in 1984 and was subject to a 6 percent investment tax credit. The basis was reduced by one half of 6 percent or $300 at the time of purchase.
Depreciation to date is $4000.

The adjusted basis at the time of sale is:

Cost		$10,000
Less: Depreciation	$4000	
One-half the tax credit	300	4,300
Adjusted basis		$ 5,700

The gain on sale is:

Amount realized		$15,000
Less: Adjusted basis		5,700
Gain on sale		$ 9,300

The gain is taxed as:

Ordinary income at 46%		
Depreciation	$4000	
One-half the tax credit	300	$4300
Capital gain at 28%		$5000

The recapture of the gain attributable to the investment tax credit basis reduction is important in the above example only because the gain exceeds the amount of depreciation to date. If the gain does not exceed the depreciation to date, the basis reduction will affect the amount of the gain, but will not be subject to recapture.

Recapture and Nonresidential Real Estate

The recapture rules for real estate differ from those applicable to other property. Most gains on the sale of real estate depreciated using straight-line depreciation are not subject to recapture. The recapture on real estate depreciated using the straight-line method is limited to 15 percent of the gain that would be recaptured if the item were personal property. Under ACRS the taxpayer can elect straight-line depreciation. As a consequence, the recapture provisions serve as a major motivation for selecting straight-line depreciation for real estate rather than using the ACRS percentages. The 15 percent recapture increases to 20 percent beginning in 1985.

Evaluation. Accelerated depreciation using the ACRS tables results in greater early-year depreciation and increases early-year cash flows. On the other hand, straight-line depreciation results in an increased basis and a reduced tax on sale assuming the property is sold at a gain. Additionally, in the case of nonresidential real estate, much or all of the gain on sale is taxed as a capital gain rather than as ordinary income.

The likelihood of a gain, the expected holding period, and the time value of money should all be considered when determining whether or not to elect straight-line depreciation for nonresidential real property.

The following steps are suggested when evaluating the choice of depreciation method for nonresidential real estate:

1. Determine the annual depreciation and final adjusted basis under each alternative.
2. Estimate the gain or loss on the eventual sale.
3. Apportion the expected gain to ordinary income and capital gain.
4. Estimate the associated tax.
5. Determine the present value of the tax savings resulting from accelerated depreciation compared to the increased tax associated with recapture for each alternative.

Recapture and Residential Real Estate

A second exception to the usual recapture rules applies to the case of residential property such as an apartment building held for rental. Recapture primarily applies to the excess of accelerated depreciation over that allowable using the straight-line method for residential rental property. On the disposition of residential real estate, 15 percent of the straight-line depreciation is also subject to recapture as in the case of nonresidential real estate. The following example compares the tax situation for residential and nonresidential real estate.

EXAMPLE: PREFERENTIAL TREATMENT FOR INVESTMENTS IN RESIDENTIAL REAL ESTATE. The Ajax Management Corporation owns two rental properties. One is an office building, and the other an apartment house. Both are sold at gains of $2,000,000 and both have accelerated depreciation to date exceeding the amount of the gain.

All the gain on the sale of the office building is subject to recapture and is taxable at the 46 percent ordinary income rate. Only a portion of the gain on the sale of the residential rental property is subject to recapture.

The tax on the sale of residential real estate is generally less than the tax on the sale of nonresidential real estate as a result of more favorable recapture provisions.

INVESTMENT TAX CREDIT RECAPTURE

Recapture of the investment tax credit can result in substantial tax assessments when property is sold or otherwise disposed of. When property subject to the investment tax credit is disposed of prematurely, a portion of the investment tax credit is subject to recapture. If the property has not met the necessary holding requirements, a portion of the credit, in effect, must be paid back.

The Holding Period

The holding period corresponds to the ACRS depreciation class. For most property, the required holding period for full investment tax credit entitlement is five years. The required holding period is three years for property in the three-year depreciation class.

Depreciation Recapture

The amount of recapture is 2 percent of the qualifying property cost for each year less than the required holding period. The operation of investment tax credit recapture is shown in the following example.

EXAMPLE: INVESTMENT TAX CREDIT RECAPTURE. Five-year property qualifying for the investment tax credit is acquired for $100,000. The property is subsequently sold at the end of two years.

The purchaser was originally entitled to a credit of 10 percent of $100,000, or $10,000. The property was held for only two years of the required five-year holding period. Two percent of the investment tax credit is retained for each year during which the property was held. Two percent is returned as recapture for each year of the required holding period that the property was not held.

Four percent of the purchase price is considered to be earned. Six percent or $6000 of the investment tax credit is subject to recapture.

If the property were held for four years, only 2 percent of the cost, or $2000, would be subject to recapture.

Businesses sometimes find it advantageous to hold property subject to investment tax credit recapture rather than to dispose of it prematurely. One approach is to lease unwanted property to another party and continue to maintain ownership until the investment tax credit holding period has elapsed. This avoids investment tax credit recapture.

Applicable Transactions

Investment tax credit recapture generally applies to sales and all other property dispositions. These include property liquidations, foreclosures, stolen property, and even property given away as gifts.

Exceptions. In event of a change in the form of doing business, recapture may not be required. An example is the incorporation of a partnership and transfer of old property to the new corporation.

Recapture is not required for changes in business form if all of the following conditions are met:

The property is retained as qualifying property in the same trade or business.

The previous owners retain a substantial interest in the business.

Substantially all assets are transferred to the new business.

The property retains the same basis in the new business as in the old.

Most asset dispositions do not meet the above criteria and are subject to investment tax credit recapture.

The Adjustment of Basis. The basis of property eligible for the investment tax credit is reduced by one-half the amount of the credit on acquisition. If the credit is later recaptured, one-half the amount of the recapture is added back to the property basis to determine the gain or loss on the sale.

SUMMARY

Depreciation Recapture. Depreciation recapture results in the taxation of gains on the sale of depreciable property at ordinary income rates. Recapture applies to the extent of depreciation previously taken. The portion of the gain attributable to the reduction in basis associated with the investment tax credit is also subject to recapture.

Recapture applies only in part to nonresidential real estate if depreciation is taken using the straight-line method. Recapture also applies only in part to residential real estate held for rental even if accelerated depreciation is taken using ACRS tables.

Investment Tax Credit Recapture. Investment tax credit recapture effectively results in the return of a portion of the investment tax credit. Recapture applies to the investment tax credit if the property is not held for the required three or five-year holding period.

The nature of investment tax credit recapture differs from that applicable to depreciation. With the recapture of depreciation, the portion of the gain equal to depreciation previously taken is taxable as ordinary income. Recapture only applies in the case of a gain.

With the investment tax credit, recapture recovers a portion of the credit previously taken without reference to gains or losses. Investment tax credit recapture may be applicable even in the case of a loss on the sale.

Chapter **6**

Accounting Alternatives and Other Opportunities for Tax Reduction and Deferral

This chapter examines additional mechanisms available for tax reduction and deferral. These include the choice of accounting alternatives, modifying the form of employee compensation, and additional tax credits. The choice of favorable alternative accounting treatments can contribute to tax deferral. The cases examined here concern inventories, long-term contracts, installment sales, and bad debts. With respect to inventories, the chapter illustrates the advantages of the lower of cost or market method, the Last-In First-Out (LIFO) inventory valuation method, and of maintaining LIFO layers. The potential advantages of installment sales treatment and the allowance method of accounting for bad debts are also illustrated.

With respect to employee compensation, the form of the transaction can determine whether or not a payment is deductible. The tax implications of employee stock options and employee pension plans are discussed in this context.

The chapter concludes with examination of the key tax credits other than those relating to property acquisitions. These are the research and development tax credit, the targeted jobs credit, and the employee stock ownership tax credit.

KEY ACCOUNTING ALTERNATIVES

One characteristic of accrual-basis accounting is the availability of alternative accounting methods for a given transaction. Alternative accounting treatments are sometimes available because the accrual-basis measurement of income necessitates reliance upon sometimes arbitrary or controversial assumptions regarding the timing of income recognition. The first topic considered here is inventories.

Inventories

Inventories include items purchased for processing and resale. A merchandising business generally maintains inventories of goods purchased for resale. The department store, for example, maintains inventories of clothing and household items. A manufacturing business maintains a number of different inventory categories. As another example, an automobile manufacturer maintains inventories of raw materials such as steel, tires, and paint. The manufacturer also maintains an inventory of work in process. Work in process includes partially completed products such as engines and partially assembled autos. The inventory of finished goods awaiting shipment to dealers represents a third general category of inventory.

The accounting problem for inventories arises because businesses typically incur different inventory purchase or manufacture costs over time for a given inventory category and are not able to specifically identify which items are sold and which remain on hand. In this case, assumptions are necessary to determine the cost of items sold during the period and the cost of the items remaining in ending inventory.

The Cost of Goods Sold. The cost of inventory is initially capitalized at the time of purchase or manufacture. The cost is deducted only when the product is sold. At this time, the cost of inventory sold is subtracted from sales revenues to obtain gross income. An illustration contrasting the cost of goods sold with the amount actually expended on purchases follows.

EXAMPLE: THE COST OF GOODS SOLD. The Kool Off Corporation opens a store and stocks a line of room air conditioners. Kool Off obtains air conditioners costing $70,000 in the spring of 1984. Kool Off sells half of the air conditioners for $60,000 during the spring and summer.

Kool Off initially classifies the air conditioners as inventory with a cost of $70,000. None of the $70,000 purchase cost is deductible immediately.

When the goods are sold, Kool Off determines the cost applicable to the goods sold. Since one-half of the goods are sold in 1984, Kool Off's cost of goods sold is one-half of the $70,000 cost, or $35,000.

Goods available for sale	$70,000
Explained by:	
Sold (½ amount available)	35,000
Remaining in inventory	35,000

The 1984 gross income from air conditioner sales is:

Sales	$60,000
Less: Cost of goods sold	35,000
Gross income	$25,000

Key Accounting Alternatives

The ending inventory is the $35,000 cost of units not sold. This becomes the beginning inventory for 1985.

The Lower of Cost or Market Method for Carrying Inventory. Inventories are initially recorded on the books at the historical cost of purchase or manufacture. Frequently the market value of at least some items drops below cost due to improvements in technology or increased competition. The selling price of pocket calculators, home computers, and old textbooks, for example, sometimes drops below original dealer cost.

In cases where the market value of inventory drops below cost, the lower of cost or market method can be used to determine inventory carrying value. With the lower of cost or market method, the cost of inventory is reduced to market value and income is reduced by the same amount. The operation of lower of cost or market valuation is illustrated in the following example.

EXAMPLE: THE LOWER OF COST OR MARKET METHOD. The selling price of one of the Kool Off Corporation's air conditioner models dropped below Kool Off's cost for competitive reasons. These particular items cost $5000. The selling price was reduced to $4500.

With the lower of cost or market valuation, the books are adjusted to reflect the lower market price. The market price is reduced by $500. The inventory carrying value is reduced to only $4500.

Reductions in inventory carrying value also reduce taxable income. Income is reduced by the $500 reduction in inventory value to the lower of cost or market. Businesses usually prefer to carry inventory at the lower of cost or market rather than always at original cost, because this reduces the carrying value of some inventory items.

The lower of cost or market procedure only applies to reductions in market value. Increases in inventory value do not lead to writeups.

The Importance of Alternative Inventory Flow Assumptions. When inventory items are acquired at different costs, the determination of inventory cost and the cost of goods sold requires assumptions regarding the flow of inventory. The need for inventory flow assumptions is shown in the following example.

EXAMPLE: THE NEED FOR COST FLOW ASSUMPTIONS. Excell Industries started a new department this year. The new department acquired 40 merchandise items in four purchases, as follows:

	Quantity	Unit price	Total cost
Purchase 1	10	$3	$ 30
Purchase 2	10	4	40
Purchase 3	10	4	40
Purchase 4	10	5	50
Total	40		$160

The new items are physically identical to the old items and were mixed in with the old items at the time of delivery. Thirty units are sold during the year. Ten units remain in ending inventory. The challenge is to determine the cost of goods sold and the cost of goods remaining in ending inventory.

If the first units purchased are sold, gross income is reduced by the cost of the first purchases. On the other hand, the last units purchased may be sold first. In this event, possibly the cost of the last purchases should determine the reduction in gross income.

Key Accounting Alternatives

In most cases, sales include some combination of early and recent purchases and available records do not indicate which goods were sold at a particular point in time. This determination requires assumptions to identify the cost of the ending inventory and to separate the cost of goods sold from the cost of the ending inventory. Even if records are available to identify specific units sold, taxpayers usually find it advantageous to choose a cost-flow assumption.

The First-In First-Out Method. Usually the physical flow of goods corresponds to a First-In First-Out (FIFO) system. Supermarkets, for example, hope to sell the initial purchases while the merchandise is fresh before selling the items purchased as replacements. The FIFO inventory method assigns the cost of the first purchases to the cost of goods sold.

The Operation of LIFO. Sometimes the physical flow of goods corresponds to a Last-In First-Out (LIFO) system. LIFO assigns the cost of the most recently acquired inventory to the cost of goods sold. The following example compares the FIFO and LIFO inventory conventions.

EXAMPLE: THE FIFO AND LIFO SYSTEMS. The Excell Industries example is continued. Excell started a new department this year. The new department acquired 40 merchandise items in four purchases, as follows:

	Quantity	Unit price	Total cost
Purchase 1	10	$3	$ 30
Purchase 2	10	4	40
Purchase 3	10	4	40
Purchase 4	10	5	50
Total	40		$160

Thirty units are sold during the year, for a total selling price of $140. Ten units remain in ending inventory.

The FIFO costing system assigns the cost of the first 30 units purchased as the cost of goods sold (the first units in are the first units sold). The cost of the first 30 units is the total of purchases one, two, and three—$110. Taxable income with a FIFO costing system is:

Sales	$140
Less: Cost of goods sold (FIFO)	110
Taxable income	$ 30

LIFO costing assigns the cost of the most recent units purchased to the cost of goods sold. The cost of the last 30 units is the total of purchases two, three, and four, or $130. Income under LIFO is determined as:

Sales	$140
Less: Cost of goods sold (LIFO)	130
Taxable income	$ 10

LIFO should be advantageous for tax determination in the above example because it reduces taxable income from $30 to only $10. LIFO is advantageous here because prices are increasing. In times of rising prices, the recent acquisitions have higher costs. When prices are rising and the units purchased during the period at least equal the units sold, LIFO provides a higher cost of goods sold. The higher LIFO cost of goods sold results in lower taxable income and lower taxes.

LIFO and Decreasing Prices. Prices sometimes decrease in industries such as the computer equipment business. In that case, the FIFO/LIFO situation is reversed. LIFO results in a lower cost of goods sold and higher taxable income than FIFO in times

Key Accounting Alternatives

of falling prices. The following example illustrates the operation of LIFO in times of falling prices.

EXAMPLE: LIFO AND FALLING PRICES. The Elec Tech Corporation began selling high fidelity sound systems in 1984. Purchases during the first and second half of the year are:

	Quantity	Unit price	Total cost
First half	1000	$60	$60,000
Second half	1000	20	$20,000
Total	2000		$80,000

During the year, Elec Tech sells 1000 units.

Under FIFO, Elec Tech's cost of goods sold is the $60,000 cost of the first 1000 units purchased. The cost of the ending inventory is $20,000.

Elec Tech's LIFO cost of goods sold will only be $20,000, with $60,000 remaining in inventory. The cost of goods to be deducted is $80,000 with either inventory method. FIFO, in this case, takes most of the deduction in the current tax year. LIFO results in deferral of the deduction to later tax periods. The FIFO/LIFO difference is shown in the following summary:

FIFO cost of goods available	$80,000
Explained by:	
FIFO cost of goods sold	$60,000
FIFO ending inventory	20,000
LIFO cost of goods available	$80,000
Explained by:	
LIFO cost of goods sold	$20,000
LIFO ending inventory	60,000

Elec Tech's cost of goods sold is decreased by $40,000, and taxable income is increased by the same amount, as a result of using LIFO.

The LIFO Election. LIFO is often used for tax determination purposes when the physical flow of goods corresponds more closely to FIFO. LIFO is still applicable in this case. The taxpayer can elect to switch to LIFO at any time without specific permission.

LIFO and Dipping Into Inventory Layers. LIFO always results in lower taxable income than FIFO when (1) prices are rising and (2) the inventory level is not decreased. If the level of inventory declines during a period of rising prices, a portion of the potential LIFO benefits will be lost. Decreases in inventory quantity are referred to as dipping into a LIFO layer. Dipping into layers assigns the costs of old inventory to the cost of goods sold. This results in a low cost of goods sold and increases taxable income. The consequences of dipping into a layer are illustrated in the following example.

EXAMPLE: DIPPING INTO A LAYER. The new Excell Industries department ended its first year in business with an ending LIFO inventory of 10 units at $3. In the second year, 58 units of inventory are purchased at $5, but 60 units are sold.

The new department dips into two units of the previous year layer in the second year. The cost of the 60 units sold is:

Purchased year 1:	58 units	@$5 per unit	$290
Purchased year 2:	2 units	@$3 per unit	6
Total	60 units		$296

The sale of two units from the beginning inventory reduces the cost of goods sold compared to the cost if all 60 units sold were

Key Accounting Alternatives   159

acquired in the second year. In that case the cost of the units sold would be:

   Purchased year 2:   60 units   @ $5 per unit $300

Dipping into the layer reduces the cost of goods sold by $4, which is the difference between the second-year cost of the items taken from previous inventory and the inventory carrying value (2 units at a cost difference of $2 per unit).

In the absence of layer dipping, the cost of goods sold would be greater by $4. The two alternatives can be summarized as follows:

Cost of goods sold	With dipping into layer	Without dipping into layer
58 @ $5	$290	—
2 @ $3	6	—
60 @ $5	—	$300
Total	$296	$300

Dipping into LIFO layers in times of rising prices reduces the cost of goods sold and increases taxable income. LIFO corporations sometimes find it advantageous to obtain funds for inventory replacement or delay end-of-year shipments of finished goods to avoid dipping into inventory layers.

LIFO Conformity for Financial Reporting. Tax legislation specifies that LIFO must be used for financial accounting purposes if used for purposes of tax determination. As a consequence of this conformity requirement, the use of LIFO to defer taxes also reduces financial reporting income. Businesses are sometimes reluctant to use LIFO for this reason even though it improves cash flows. LIFO increases cash flows, but reported net income, the common indicator of financial performance, is reduced with LIFO.

The use of LIFO for financial reporting purposes when used for tax determination has also led to the intentional liquidation of layers. An earlier example showed that layer liquidation increases taxable income and increases the tax. Layer liquidation also increases financial reporting income. Corporations that "need" income for the financial statements have been known to intentionally liquidate LIFO layers to increase reported income even at the cost of additional tax payments. Generally accepted accounting principles call for the disclosure of layer liquidations in footnotes to the financial statements.

The use of LIFO also leads to another consequence for financial reporting purposes. In times of rising prices the LIFO corporation will appear to have a lower inventory valuation on the balance sheet.

The difference in FIFO and LIFO-reported inventories can be seen by reference to the previous Excell Industries example with the situation repeated as follows:

	Quantity	Unit price	Total cost
Purchase 1	10	$3	$ 30
Purchase 2	10	4	40
Purchase 3	10	4	40
Purchase 4	10	5	50
Total	40		$160

Thirty units are sold during the year for a total selling price of $140. Ten units remain in ending inventory.

Inspection of the purchases reveals that the FIFO ending inventory is the cost of the last units purchased, or $50. The

LIFO ending inventory is determined as the cost of the first purchase, or $30.

In practice, balance sheets of LIFO corporations appear to be weaker than those of FIFO corporations. The difference, however, is often attributable to the choice of accounting methods. The above data reveal that the LIFO $30 ending inventory and the FIFO $50 ending inventory both represent the same physical inventory units with the same fair market value.

Long-Term Construction Contracts

The sale of goods produced under a long-term contract differs from other sales because the sale is made in advance of construction and the selling price is known at that time. When contracts are signed for road construction, shipbuilding, and other long-term projects, the contract costs are estimated before bids are even submitted. The contractor sets a target level of contract income and then submits a bid consistent with this income estimate. An example of a long-term construction contract follows.

EXAMPLE: THE LONG-TERM CONSTRUCTION CONTRACT. The Big Pump Corporation contracts to build a pipeline. Big Pump negotiates a contract price of $575,000,000. This is a fixed price agreed upon before construction begins. The estimated cost to Big Pump is $500,000,000. Big Pump estimates profit as:

Contract price	$575,000,000
Less: Construction costs	500,000,000
Estimated gross profit	$ 75,000,000

Although the profit is not completely earned until the project is complete, some accountants feel that revenue is earned gradually as a project is completed rather than all at once on completion. Other accountants feel that profit is not assured until the project is complete and that revenue recognition should be deferred until that time. As a consequence, two major accounting alternatives have been developed to conform to alternative views regarding the earnings process. These are the completed contract method and the percentage of completion method.

The Completed Contract Method. The completed contract method recognizes revenue at the time the project is completed and accepted by the customer. The completed contract method recognizes gross profit on the contract only upon completion of the contract even if progress payments are received on the contract. If the contract takes five years to complete, revenue is not recognized until the end of five years. As a result, tax payments on the profits are deferred until this time. An example of the completed contract method follows.

EXAMPLE: THE COMPLETED CONTRACT METHOD. The Big Pump Corporation contracts to build a pipeline. The expected profit is $75,000,000 and the project duration is expected to be three years. One-third of the work is completed in the first year.

The revenue from the contract is recognized when the project is completed. As a result, $75,000,000 gross income is recognized in the third year. No revenue is recognized prior to that time.

The Percentage of Completion Method. The percentage of completion method is an alternative method of accounting for long-term construction contracts. Construction companies often use the percentage of completion method of accounting in preparing financial statements. Under the percentage of completion method, revenue is recognized gradually over the life of the contract.

Key Accounting Alternatives 163

The percentage of completion method incorporates estimates of total gross profit on the contract. This total gross profit is apportioned to each year of the contract period based on the work done on the contract each year.

In the case of a profitable contract, revenue is recognized gradually over the period of the contract. This approach tends to reflect the economic realities of the situation. It recognizes the favorable effect of the contract upon the contractor's financial situation on a period-by-period basis. The percentage of completion method is illustrated in the following example.

EXAMPLE: THE PERCENTAGE OF COMPLETION METHOD. In continuation of the Big Pump Corporation example, Big Pump contracts to build a pipeline. The expected profit is $75,000,000 and the project duration is expected to be three years. One-third of the work is completed in the first year.

The percentage of completion method recognizes one-third of the revenue when one-third of the work is completed. First-year taxable income increases by one-third of the expected profit, or $25,000,000.

The completed contract method is generally advantageous for tax determination purposes. It defers the recognition of revenue until the project is completed. Some small corporations, however, prefer the percentage of completion method because it spreads revenue over time and minimizes the bunching of income all in the year of completion. If income is bunched, all income over $100,000 is taxed at the 46 percent marginal rate (Chapter 2). If the income is spread over a period of years, a small corporation may benefit through lower-bracket taxable income resulting from the reporting of nominal amounts of taxable income each year.

Corporations are free to use one method of accounting for long-term contracts for financial reporting purposes and another method for tax determination. Often corporations choose the completed contract method for tax determination and the percentage of completion method for financial reporting.

The Installment Method for Sales

Retail sales of appliances and other items are often made on an installment basis. An installment sale usually consists of a down payment followed by periodic monthly payments. Sales of real estate or other property may also provide for payment in two or more installments.

The installment method of accounting recognizes sales revenue gradually as payments are received. With the installment method, for example, when one-half of the cash is collected, one-half of the revenue is recognized. This is in contrast to the usual method of revenue recognition where revenue is recognized at the time of sale whether or not cash is actually received at that time. An example of the installment method follows.

EXAMPLE: THE INSTALLMENT METHOD. The Coolit Corporation sells appliances to consumers on the installment basis. The terms of sale are 10 percent down and the balance in low monthly installments. In late 1984, Coolit sells a $900 washing machine to Mr. Smith. The cost of the appliance to Coolit was $400.

In the case of a sale for cash or on a short-term receivable, Coolit recognizes revenue at the time the merchandise is shipped. Gross profit resulting from the sale is:

Sales revenue	$900
Less: Cost of goods sold	400
Gross profit	$500

Under the installment method, Coolit recognizes gross profit gradually as cash is received. The 10 percent down payment results in recognition of 10 percent of the gross profit, or $50.

Key Accounting Alternatives   165

Taxable income in 1984 is increased by only $50 as a result of this sale.

The installment method results in taxable income of $50 compared to taxable income of $500 resulting from a sale for cash. The remaining $450 in gross profit will be recognized gradually over time as the remaining payments are received. For example, when the second $90 is collected, gross profit will be increased by an additional $50.

Advantages. The installment method provides relief to the taxpayer in the sense that the tax is deferred until the taxpayer collects the cash. If the installment method were not available, accrual-basis corporations would be taxed prior to receipt of the cash needed to make the tax payment. The installment method is consistent with the ability-to-pay principle.

Taxpayers doing business on the installment basis are not required to use the installment method. They are free to recognize all sales as income in the current year. The installment method, however, defers revenue recognition and is generally more advantageous for tax purposes than immediate recognition of income. The installment method is permitted only for tax purposes and is not usually acceptable for financial reporting.

Occasional Sales. The installment basis also applies to sales of productive property no longer needed in the business. The installment basis of accounting is usually advantageous in this case as it acts to defer recognition of a portion of the gain on sale.

The Deferred Tax and the Financial Statements

The "deferred tax" on the financial statements arises from the use of accounting methods that differ for financial accounting and tax-determination purposes. The deferred tax is the difference between the tax actually payable and the tax payable if the same accounting methods were used for both financial reporting and tax determination. The difference in tax resulting from use of a more favorable accounting alternative for tax purposes is referred to as a deferred tax credit. If the tax difference results from use of a less favorable accounting alternative for tax-determination purposes, it is referred to as a deferred tax charge.

The deferred tax credit appears on the liability and shareholder equity section of the balance sheet. The deferred tax charge resembles a prepayment of taxes in some respects, and appears with assets on the balance sheet. The deferred credit is more common than the deferred charge. The following example illustrates an installment sale situation—a situation that frequently gives rise to a deferred tax credit.

EXAMPLE: INSTALLMENT SALES AND THE DEFERRED TAX. The Watchit Corporation sells color televisions on the installment basis. First-year sales are $800,000. The cost of the merchandise to Watchit is $500,000. Watchit collects only $200,000 cash in the first year on these sales. The remainder is receivable in the second year.

Watchit recognizes revenue at the time of sale for financial reporting purposes and uses the installment method for purposes of tax determination.

Gross income reported on the financial statements for the first year is determined as the sales less the cost of the merchandise sold, or $300,000. With a 46 percent tax rate, the tax normally payable would be $138,000.

The installment method results in less taxable income since only 25 percent of receivables are collected the first year. The taxable income is determined as 25 percent of $300,000, or $75,000. At the 46 percent rate, the tax payable is only $34,500. Although the tax currently payable is $34,500, $138,000 should eventually be payable when all installment receivables are col-

Key Accounting Alternatives 167

lected. The difference between these two amounts appears on the balance sheet as the deferred tax credit.

The deferred tax credit is the tax that has been deferred as a result of using a more advantageous system for tax-determination purposes.

The Deferred Tax as a Liability. Under some circumstances it may be appropriate to regard the deferred tax as a liability because payment may eventually be required. This is common in the case of occasional installment sales of unwanted plant, property, and equipment items as seen in the following example.

EXAMPLE: THE DEFERRED TAX AS A LIABILITY. In continuation of the Watchit example, assume no new sales in the second year and that all first-year receivables are collected.

The gross income from first-year sales was $300,000. Second-year taxable income is 75 percent of the $300,000 gross income, or $225,000. The tax at 46 percent is $103,500. In this case, the $103,500 deferred tax is paid the next year.

An Amount Not Likely to be Paid. In other circumstances it is not appropriate to regard the deferred tax as a liability because the tax is never paid. The following example assumes continued sales year after year.

EXAMPLE: THE CONTINUOUS DEFERRAL OF DEFERRED TAX. In continuation of the above examples, Watchit's installment sales in the second year are also $800,000, with the cost of merchandise also $500,000. As in the first year, 25 percent of installment receivables are collected in the year of sale and the remaining 75 percent are collected the following year.

The first-year sales resulted in tax payable of $34,500 with deferred tax of $103,500.

The effect of the second-year sales is identical to that of the first year. The tax payable resulting from second-year sales is $34,500 and the new deferred tax is $103,500. In addition, the collection on first-year installment receivables requires payment of the first-year deferred tax of $103,500. The first-year deferred tax was paid, but was immediately replaced with a new deferred tax representing sales for the second year. The result is continuation of the $103,500 deferred tax.

The preceding example shows that the first-year deferred tax is immediately replaced with a second-year deferred tax as it becomes payable. Extension of the example to third-year and future periods provides the same result. As long as installment sales continue at the same level, the deferred tax will continue to be replaced and will never be repaid. Consequently, many analysts feel that the deferred tax should not be considered a liability since it may never come due.

Depreciation and the Deferred Tax. In practice, the largest determinant of the deferred tax is the use of different depreciation calculations for tax and financial accounting purposes. This is particularly true for corporations that do not do business on the installment basis.

It should be emphasized that the deferred tax is of interest only when interpreting the financial statements. The actual tax liability depends upon the corporation's taxable income for that period and is not affected by the deferred tax. The deferred tax, however, may provide an indication of the trend of expected future tax payments. The extent to which the deferred tax is indicative of future tax payments depends upon the probability of continuation of circumstances that gave rise to the deferred tax.

Key Accounting Alternatives

Bad Debts

Most business transactions involve the use of credit. Businesses find it difficult to insist on payments in cash if the competition extends credit.

Businesses that extend credit are aware that some proportion of credit sales will never be collected. The amount of these bad debts can be controlled through use of a tight credit policy. Tight credit policies, however, generally lead to reduced sales. The result is that businesses extend credit with the expectation that some portion of the credit sales will not be collectible. These bad debt losses represent a significant loss of revenue for these types of businesses.

Corporations can determine the bad debt deduction using either of two methods. One is the direct write-off method. The second is the allowance method.

The Direct Write-Off Method. With the direct write-off method, bad debts are not deducted until specific accounts are deemed to be uncollectible. This may take several years. When the bad debt is written off, the amount of the receivable is reduced and taxable income is reduced by the same amount.

The Allowance Method. Corporations usually find it advantageous to use the allowance method of accounting for bad debts. With the allowance method, a percentage of the current period's outstanding accounts receivable is classified as probably uncollectible. This estimate is deducted as the cost of bad debts. The bad debt deduction is based upon the corporation's previous loss experience. (This is one of the few instances in which a deduction is permitted for an estimated cost. Generally a deduction requires that the cost must actually be incurred.)

The procedure for determining the bad debt deduction is illustrated as follows.

EXAMPLE: THE BAD DEBT DEDUCTION. The Lucky Sales Corporation begins business near the end of 1984. Outstanding accounts receivable at the end of 1984 are $4000. The management estimates that about 2 percent of the outstanding accounts receivable will not be collected.

Lucky Sales will deduct 2 percent of the outstanding receivables of $80 as bad debts in 1984. Lucky Sales will also establish an allowance equal to this amount. The allowance will be reduced in 1985 and later years as specific accounts receivable are deemed to be uncollectible.

The above example shows the procedure for estimating the expected bad debts at the end of the year. After the first year of operations, each year will begin with a bad debt deduction. The actual write-offs of bad debts also need to be considered. At the end of each year, the remaining allowance is compared with the allowance estimated to be needed to cover outstanding receivables. The difference is the amount of the current year bad debt deduction. The procedure is shown in the following example.

EXAMPLE: THE BAD DEBT DEDUCTION CONTINUED. The Lucky Sales Corporation estimates that about 2 percent of year-end accounts receivable will not be collected. Lucky Sales began 1985 with an allowance for uncollectible accounts of $80. The writeoff of uncollectibles during the year used up all except $20 of this allowance. Outstanding receivables at the end of 1985 are $7000.

Lucky Sales will require an allowance at year end equal to 2 percent of outstanding receivables, or $140. The bad debt deduction is determined as:

Required allowance	$140
Less: Remaining allowance	20
Increase in allowance	$120

The $120 increase in the allowance is deductible as bad debts for 1985.

The illustration of the allowance method shows that bad debts are deducted as the allowance is increased. No deduction is taken at the time specific uncollectibles are actually written off. The expected amounts of uncollectibles were already deducted in a previous tax year when the allowance was established.

EMPLOYEE COMPENSATION AND BENEFITS

The manner in which a transaction is structured sometimes influences tax effects, including the extent to which a payment may be deductible. This section examines key alternatives in structuring employee stock option and pension plans.

Employee Stock Options

Stock options are often made available to key employees as incentives for performance and as alternatives to compensation in cash. Employees sometimes prefer stock options to cash because the potential gains to the employee may be greater and because receipt of the option is not taxable. The advantages to the corporation include the possibility of increased employee incentive to performance and the ability to compensate employees with no direct cash outflow.

General Operation. A stock option gives the employee the right to buy a specified number of shares of the corporation's stock. The price and time period are also specified at the time the option is granted. An illustration follows.

EXAMPLE: THE STOCK OPTION. The Wild West Corporation granted executive stock options to Jane Johnson. The options provided for the purchase of 1000 shares of Wild West Corporation stock for $10 per share anytime within the next five years. The Wild West Corporation stock presently sells for $8 per share.

It will not be beneficial for Jane to exercise the options as long as the market price of the stock remains below the $10 per share exercise price.

If the market price of the stock increases to more than the $10 option price, it may be desirable to exercise the options. For example, if the market price increases to $40, Jane can obtain 1000 shares of stock for $10 per share or $10,000. She can receive stock valued at $40,000 in exchange for the options and her $10,000 payment.

The Incentive Stock Option. One particular type of stock option is the incentive stock option. An incentive stock option must meet certain requirements, including that of an option price not less than the fair market value of the stock at the time the option is granted. For example, if the market price is $10, the option price may not be less than $10 at the time the option is issued.

The incentive stock option is not taxable to the employee at the time of receipt or exercise. This assumes that the employee continues employment until at least shortly before the date of exercise and does not dispose of the stock for at least two years after the option is granted.

If the preceding conditions are met, the employee is taxed only on the capital gain at the time the stock is finally sold. This gain is the difference between the fair market value of the stock at the time of sale and the original exercise price. If the employee does not exercise the option, there is no gain and no tax. The advantages to the employee are that compensation is not recognized on receiving the option, if the option is exercised gain is not recognized until the stock is later sold, and the gain is taxable as a capital gain rather than as ordinary income assuming a sufficient holding period.

The incentive stock option, however, is not necessarily an advantageous way to compensate the employee from the corporation's view. The corporation does not receive a deduction with respect to incentive stock options. If the corporation were to issue stock to outside parties for cash and then pay the cash to employees as compensation, the compensation expense would be deductible.

As an alternative to the incentive stock option, the corporation can grant a nonqualified stock option. The exercise of the nonqualified option results in a compensation deduction to the corporation. The nonqualified stock option is examined in the following section.

The Nonqualified Stock Option. Options not meeting the conditions prescribed for incentive stock options are referred to as nonqualified stock options. In a nonqualified plan, the employee recognizes gain at the time of exercise. The gain is based on the difference between the fair market value of the stock when exercised and the option price. This gain is taxed at ordinary income rates. When the stock is finally sold, capital gain is recognized as the difference between the fair market value of the stock and the adjusted basis (the amount paid for the stock).

The advantage of the nonqualified stock option from the corporation's view is that the corporation deducts the amount of compensation from taxable income at the time the option is exercised. The deduction is equal to the employee's gain on exercising the option. An illustration of the nonqualified stock option follows.

EXAMPLE: THE NONQUALIFIED STOCK OPTION. The Bluebird Corporation is considering granting George Jones a nonqualified stock option. The option will permit George to obtain shares of stock for $10,000 at any time within the next three years. The stock price is currently $30,000. The stock price increases to $60,000 at the time of exercise.

The option cannot qualify as an incentive stock option because the market price when the option is issued exceeds the option price. The employee recognizes compensation at the time the option is exercised. The employer, in this case, is entitled to deduct the employee gain on exercise as compensation.

The tax to George at the time of exercise is:

Market value of stock at time options exercised	$60,000
Less: Exercise price	10,000
Recognized gain	$50,000
Tax on ordinary income at the 50% individual tax rate	$25,000

George recognizes $50,000 as taxable income on exercise of the option. The corporation also deducts the same $50,000 as employee compensation expense at the time of exercise.

Some corporations offer nonqualified options rather than incentive stock options in order to benefit from the compensation deduction. The exercise of the option provides a deduction to the corporation with no associated outlay of cash.

Pension Costs

Pension plans provide for future employee pension benefits. In an employer-sponsored plan, the employer makes payments to a pension fund that provides benefits to employees on retirement. The employee does not recognize income until benefits are actually received on retirement.

Employer payments to qualified pension plans are deductible in the year of payment. The interest earned by the pension fund is not taxed to the corporation.

A qualified plan may not discriminate in favor of officers, directors, or highly paid employees. A qualified plan must also be vested. In a vested plan employees are entitled to coverage after a prescribed period of service whether or not they continue as employees until retirement. This provision was developed for the benefit of employees. As a result, corporations cannot terminate employees just before retirement and avoid pension payments.

ADDITIONAL TAX CREDITS

Tax credits reduce the tax otherwise payable. The investment tax credit and business energy credit are associated with investments in new productive property and were covered in the Chapter 2 examination of property acquisitions. Other tax credits include the research and development tax credit, the targeted-jobs credit, and the tax credit for employee stock ownership plans.

The Research and Development Tax Credit

The research and development tax credit is a relatively new credit designed to provide incentives to conduct additional research and development. The credit applies to additional research and development activity over and above that of previous periods.

The Amount of the Credit. The credit is 25 percent of the increase in research and development costs over the costs of a three-year base period. The qualifying costs pertain mainly to personal services, materials, and rentals. The costs of acquiring land and depreciable property are not included.

The credit is limited to the tax liability. Excess research and development credits can be carried back three years and carried forward fifteen years. An example of the research and development tax credit determination follows.

EXAMPLE: THE RESEARCH AND DEVELOPMENT TAX CREDIT. The Jersey Chemicals Corporation is determining the 1985 research and development tax credit. The 1985 research and development expenditures are $500,000. Research and development expenditures for the most recent three years are:

1984	$ 475,000
1983	450,000
1982	425,000
Total	$1,350,000

The average of the research and development expenditures over the three-year period is $450,000 per year. Entitlement to the credit is determined as the excess of 1985 research and development expenditures over those of the previous three-year base period.

1985 research and development	$500,000
Less: Base period amount	450,000
Eligibility for credit	$ 50,000
Credit at 25%	$ 12,500

The credit is a direct reduction of taxes otherwise payable by Jersey Chemicals.

Implications for Tax Planning. Corporations sometimes find it advantageous to rent facilities and equipment needed for research and development for purposes of maximizing the tax

Additional Tax Credits

credit. The amount paid as rent is classified as a research and development cost. If the property is purchased, the purchase price does not qualify for the research and development tax credit. Depreciation on purchased property also does not qualify for the credit. A switch to a policy of renting rather than owning research and development property increases qualifying research and development expenditures. This switch can provide a research and development tax credit even if the actual amount of research and development activity does not change from one year to the next.

The Targeted-Jobs Credit

The targeted-jobs credit reduces taxes of corporations that hire new employees from certain population groups. Qualified employees must come from one of several specified economically disadvantaged groups. The objective of the credit is to increase incentives to hire disadvantaged employees.

The credit is based on employee wages. The credit is 50 percent of the first $6000 of first-year wages, and 25 percent of the first $6000 of second-year wages. As a result, a corporation can reduce taxes by up to $3000 in the year that it hires the disadvantaged worker and up to $1500 in the following year.

The Employee Stock Ownership Tax Credit

An Employee Stock Ownership Plan (ESOP) is an employer-funded plan that invests in the corporation's securities for the benefit of employees. The employer contributes stock to the plan. This provides benefits to employees and entails no cash outlay on the part of the employer.

The Amount of the Credit. The credit is based on the value of the stock contributed to the plan. A contribution of stock valued at $100,000 can result in a $100,000 tax credit. The maximum credit is limited by the amount of the corporation's payroll. The amount of the credit is limited to 0.5 percent of the payroll. The payroll-based tax credit replaces a previous provision that increased the investment tax credit that could be claimed by businesses contributing to ESOPs. That provision is no longer available.

The Employee Tax. The employee is not taxed until stock is actually distributed by the plan. Increases in the market price of the stock are taxable at capital gains rates when the employee eventually sells the stock.

The ESOP as a Source of Financing. ESOPs are sometimes used to obtain financing for the corporation as well as for purposes of employee benefit. When the ESOP is used to obtain financing, the ESOP plan borrows funds and uses the funds to buy shares of stock from the corporation. The corporation ends up with the borrowed funds.

SUMMARY

Accounting Alternatives. Taxpayers are sometimes able to choose between selected accounting alternatives. The selection of favorable accounting alternatives can result in significant differences in taxable income.

Accounting for Inventories. Corporations that use inventories in their business may elect the lower of cost or market convention. Under this convention, if inventory replacement costs fall below the original purchase price, the inventory is written down to the lower replacement cost and the amount of the writedown reduces taxable income. The lower of cost or market alternative reduces taxable income and defers the tax.

Corporations may also choose between the First-in First-Out (FIFO) and Last-in Last-out (LIFO) cost flow alternatives. FIFO inventory valuation assigns the cost of the first units acquired to the cost of goods sold. LIFO inventory valuation assigns the cost of the most recently acquired inventory to the cost of goods sold. In times of rising prices, LIFO usually increases the cost of goods sold and reduces taxable income.

LIFO corporations are careful to avoid dipping into inventory layers. Dipping into layers effectively recaptures some of the previous advantage obtained through the use of LIFO and increases taxable income.

LIFO can be advantageous for corporations subject to rising prices. If industry prices tend to decrease, LIFO may result in higher tax.

Long-Term Construction Contracts. Businesses with long-term construction contracts can use either the completed contract or percentage of completion method of accounting. The completed contract method defers recognition of contract revenue until all work is completed. This can result in a major deferral of tax for the corporation involved in long-term construction contracts. Businesses in the construction industry frequently use the completed contract method for tax purposes and the percentage of completion method for financial reporting.

Installment Sales. The installment method of accounting recognizes income as cash is received from installment sales rather than when the exchange of property takes place. This results in the deferral of income recognition and is usually beneficial to the taxpayer. The installment method is available when merchandise is sold on the installment basis. It is also applicable to occasional sales of productive property.

The Deferred Tax. The deferred tax on the financial statements arises from the use of different accounting methods for financial-accounting and tax-determination purposes. The deferred tax is the difference between the tax actually payable and the tax payable if the same accounting methods were used for both financial reporting and tax determination. The deferred tax credit is the tax that has been deferred as a result of taking more deductions or recognizing revenue more slowly for tax-determination purposes. The specific circumstances giving rise to the deferred tax should be considered in determining whether to regard the deferred tax as a liability or as an amount that will not be paid in the foreseeable future.

Bad Debts. The allowance method of accounting for bad debts provides for a deduction at the time of sale based on estimated bad debts. This results in recognition of the bad debt deduction prior to the time when specific accounts receivable are deemed to be uncollectible. Use of the allowance method reduces taxable income earlier than with the direct write-off method alternative.

The Employee Stock Option. Stock options are often made available as incentives for performance and as alternatives to compensation in cash. The incentive stock option is not taxable to the employee at the time of receipt or exercise if various holding-period requirements are met. The employee is taxed only at the time the stock is finally sold and then at capital gains rates. An incentive stock option must have an exercise price that is not less than the fair market value of the stock at the time the option is granted. The corporation does not normally receive a deduction with respect to incentive stock options.

Options not meeting the conditions prescribed for incentive stock options are referred to as nonqualified stock options. In a nonqualified plan, the employee recognizes gain at the time of exercise. The corporation deducts the amount of compensation from taxable income at the time the option is exercised.

Pension Plan Contributions. Most pension plans are organized as qualified pension plans. Employer payments to qualified pension plans are deductible in the year of payment. The interest earned by the fund is not taxed to the corporation.

A qualified plan may not discriminate in favor of officers, directors, or highly paid employees. The qualified plan must also be vested.

The Research and Development Tax Credit. The research and development tax credit provides a tax reduction of 25 percent of the current year's additional research and development expenditures over the expenditures of a previous base period.

The Targeted-Jobs Credit. The targeted-jobs credit reduces the tax for businesses that hire workers from certain disadvantaged groups.

The Employee Stock Ownership Tax Credit. Employers contributing stock to an employee stock ownership plan are eligible for a tax credit. The amount of the credit is based on the amount of stock issued and the size of the employer payroll. Corporations have sometimes used the credit to provide a source of financing as well as to reduce taxes payable.

Chapter 7

Dividends

Shareholders invest funds in the corporation with the expectation of later receiving distributions in return. These distributions are usually in the form of cash or property that shareholders can convert to cash.

One form of distribution to shareholders is a dividend. A dividend is a distribution of the corporation's earnings. Shareholders are taxed on the receipt of dividends as ordinary income. Another type of distribution is the return of amounts originally invested. The return of amounts originally invested is often not taxed.

Shareholders generally try to avoid dividend treatment because dividend payments often result in the double taxation of corporate earnings. Effective tax planning includes a number of mechanisms to reduce the impact of double taxation. Available mechanisms include deferred distributions, the distribution of earnings at capital gains rates, distributions structured as deductions, and the S corporation.

This chapter examines the nature of dividends and the tax on these dividend distributions. Emphasis is directed to mechanisms used to reduce the impact of double taxation. The development also includes the special situation of the corporate shareholder. The corporate shareholder deducts from taxable income most or all of the dividends received from domestic corporations.

The first part of the chapter examines dividends in general, double taxation, and the taxation of individual shareholders. The chapter then looks at the tax on corporate shareholders receiving dividends. The final part of the chapter considers special taxes designed to encourage the payment of dividends by corporations with accumulated earnings.

Nondividend distributions to shareholders will be examined in Chapter 8.

THE NATURE OF DIVIDENDS

The Tax Treatment of Dividends

A dividend is a distribution of corporate earnings to the shareholder. Most returns to shareholders take the form of dividends. Figure 7.1 illustrates the distribution of dividends.

The Shareholder Tax. The receipt of dividends is taxable to shareholders. These distributions are taxed as ordinary income.

The Distributing Corporation. The payment of cash dividends is *not* deductible by the distributing corporation. An illustration of dividend treatment follows.

EXAMPLE: THE DISTRIBUTION OF CASH DIVIDENDS. The Payup Corporation pays cash dividends of $100 to shareholders. The shareholders receiving the dividends are taxed at ordinary income rates. Payup does not claim the dividend payment as a deduction from taxable income.

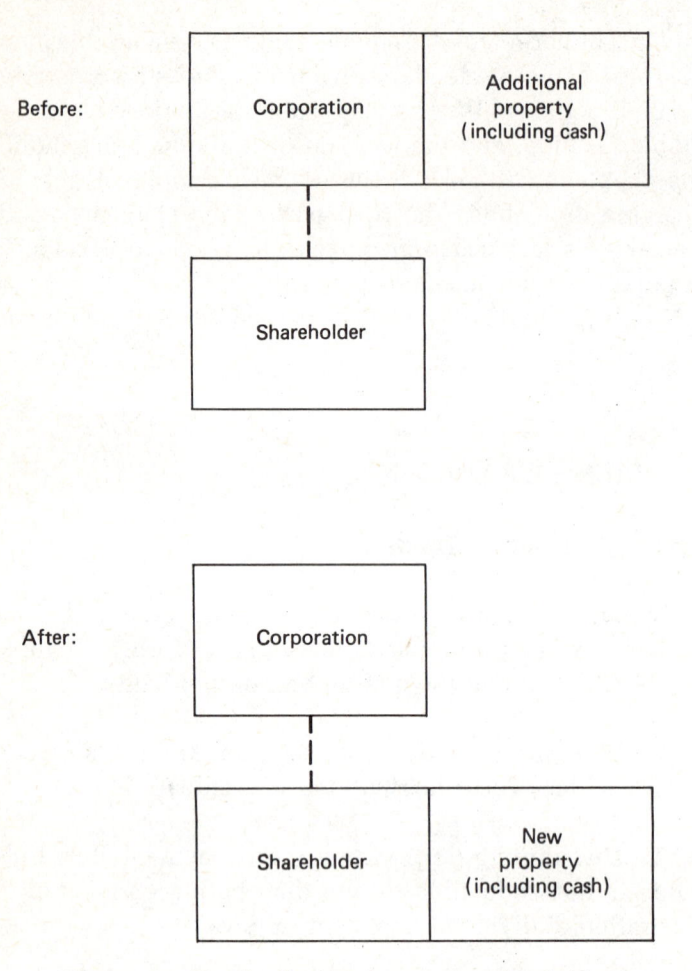

Figure 7.1. The distribution of property to shareholders.

Not all distributions to shareholders qualify as dividends. Only distributions of earnings and profits qualify as dividends. Earnings and profits are examined in the next section.

Earnings and Profits

Earnings and profits represent the after-tax earnings of the corporation reduced by the amounts paid out as dividends. Earnings and profits are the earnings accumulated by the corporation.

The rationale underlying the concept of earnings and profits is that increases in earnings and profits reflect increases in corporate wealth. The intent is to tax distributions as dividends if the economic situation of shareholders improves as a result of the distribution. If shareholders merely receive a return of amounts originally invested, their economic situation may not be changed.

How Earnings and Profits Are Measured. The measurement of earnings and profits begins with total taxable income summed over the life of the corporation. The taxable income is then reduced by taxes paid. Other adjustments are also made to consider the corporation's ability to pay dividends.

For example, interest earned on tax-exempt municipal bonds does not increase taxable income. However, the amount of the interest revenue is added to taxable income to determine earnings and profits. The interest revenue is added to obtain earnings and profits because the cash received as interest does increase the corporation's ability to pay dividends. This adjustment increases earnings and profits relative to the amount of accumulated after-tax income.

Another adjustment is made for depreciation method. ACRS depreciation (Chapter 3) provides for faster depreciation in early years compared to late years. This increases current-period deductions and reduces taxable income for corporations maintaining investments in productive property. Straight-line depreciation, however, is assumed for purposes of computing earnings and profits. This adjustment increases earnings and profits relative to the cumulative income after tax.

After total earnings available for dividends are determined, dividends paid since the formation of the corporation are subtracted to arrive at the accumulated earnings and profits. The following example illustrates the distribution of earnings and profits.

EXAMPLE: THE DISTRIBUTION OF EARNINGS AND PROFITS. The New Frontier Corporation was formed in 1984 with a shareholder investment of $2000. Combined 1984 and 1985 income after tax payments is $300. Dividend distributions are $100.

The after-tax earnings increase earnings and profits. The dividends represent distributions of earnings and profits. Shareholders are taxed on the $100 in dividend distributions at ordinary income rates. The earnings and profits are reduced from $300 to $200, as illustrated in Figure 7.2.

Earnings and Profits Compared to Retained Earnings. Retained earnings on a corporate financial statement represent the aggregate income earned over the life of the business less the dividends paid to shareholders. Retained earnings, however, usually differ from earnings and profits. One cause of the difference is the adjustment to earnings and profits for depreciation and other factors. Another factor responsible for the difference between earnings and profits and retained earnings is the use of different principles for measuring taxable income and financial reporting income. (Key accounting differences are summarized in Chapter 9.)

Other Distributions. Distributions in excess of earnings and profits are not taxed as ordinary income. The return of original investment, for example, is not taxable to the shareholder. The return of investment is illustrated in the following example.

The Nature of Dividends

```
                    ┌─ ─ ─ ─ ┐      ┌─────────┐
┌──────────┐        │        │      │ Dividends│
│          │        ├────────┤      │  $100   │
│  Income  │        │Earnings│      └─────────┘
│ after tax│        │and profits│
│   $300   │        │  $200   │
│          │        ├────────┤
└──────────┘        │        │
                    │        │
                    │Original│
                    │investment│
                    │ $2,000 │
                    │        │
                    └────────┘
    →                            →
    In                           Out
```

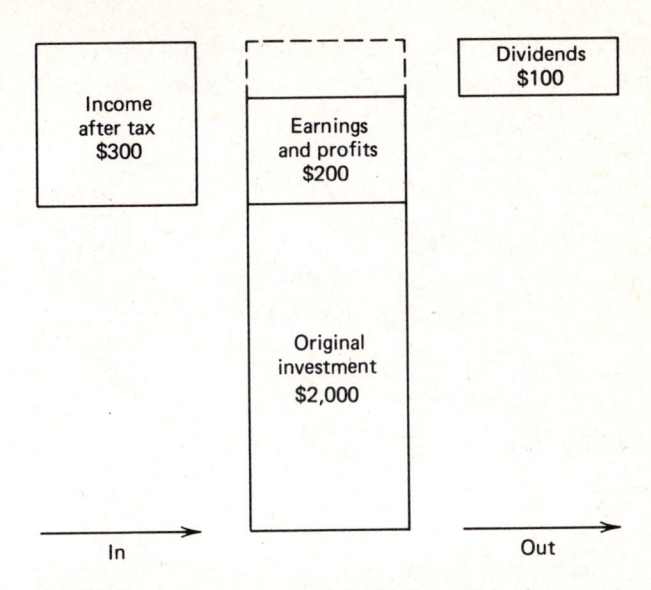

Figure 7.2. The distribution of earnings and profits.

Original investment	$2000
Earnings after tax	300
Available for distribution	$2300
Less distributions	100
Ending amount	$2200
Original investment	$2000
Ending earnings and profits	$ 200

EXAMPLE: THE DISTRIBUTION OF EARNINGS AND PROFITS AND THE RETURN OF SHAREHOLDER INVESTMENT. The New Frontier Corporation was formed in 1984 with a shareholder investment of $2000. Combined 1984 and 1985 income remaining after tax payments is $300. The earlier example is modified to provide for 1984 and 1985 distributions totaling $500 to shareholders.

The distribution includes $300 of earnings and profits taxable at ordinary income rates. The remaining $200 represents a non-taxable return of the shareholder's original investment, as illustrated in Figure 7.3.

Total income after tax	$300
Less: Total dividends	300
Ending earnings and profits	$ 0
Distribution of original investment	$200

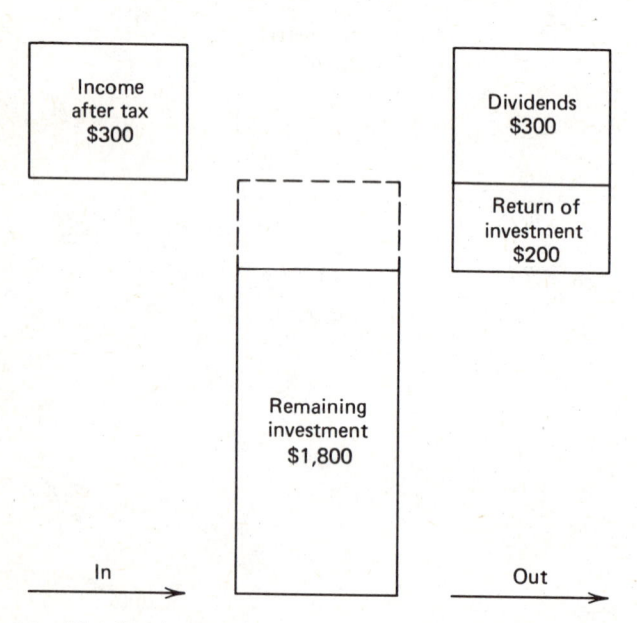

Figure 7.3. The distribution of earnings and profits and return of the shareholder's original investment.

Original investment	$2000
Earnings after tax	300
Available for distribution	$2300
Less distributions	500
Ending amount	$1800
Remaining investment	$1800
Ending earnings and profits	$ 0

> The return on investment reduces the shareholder's basis from $2000 to $1800.

The preceding example reveals that distributions to shareholders are not always taxable. Distributions are only taxable as dividends to the extent of earnings and profits. If the corporation does not have earnings and profits, the distributions are not dividends. The distributions, in this case, are regarded as returns of amounts originally invested rather than returns on investment. These types of distributions will be considered in more detail in the next chapter.

It should be emphasized that the concept of earnings and profits relates to the distributing corporation rather than to a particular investor. For example, an investor might buy all the shares in a corporation that immediately declares a dividend. If the corporation previously had earnings and profits, the distribution is taxable to the shareholder as a dividend.

DOUBLE TAXATION

Background

The double taxation of corporate earnings can result in the receipt and retention of only a small portion of pretax corporate earnings by the shareholder. This section examines double taxation and alternative planning mechanisms used to alleviate the double taxation problem. The examination of double taxation begins with an overview of tax rates applicable to both the corporation and the individual investor.

The Marginal Rates for Individual and Corporate Shareholders. The problem of double taxation arises through the joint effect of the corporate tax on earnings and the individual investor's tax on dividends. The tax rates applicable to individuals differ from those applicable to corporations. The marginal tax rates for high-bracket individual and corporate shareholders are summarized as follows:

MARGINAL TAX RATES FOR HIGH-BRACKET INDIVIDUAL AND CORPORATE SHAREHOLDERS

	Individual shareholders	Corporate shareholders
Ordinary income	50%	46%
Long-term capital gains	20%	28%

The summary shows that the maximum tax rate is approximately 50 percent for both individual shareholders and corporations. The tax rate on long-term capital gains is considerably lower than that applicable to ordinary income for both groups of shareholders.

The examples in this chapter and those that follow continue to use small dollar amounts in the interest of simplicity. The examples, however, assume the above marginal tax rates which generally apply to high-income individuals and corporations.

How the Double Tax Arises. The tax on dividend distributions is responsible for the double taxation on corporate earnings. The corporate earnings are taxed twice in the sense that the distributing corporation is initially taxed on earnings. The shareholders are then taxed again on the receipt of dividends. The following example illustrates the problem of double taxation.

EXAMPLE: DOUBLE TAXATION. The New Frontier Corporation has 1984 taxable income of $100 and is taxed at the 46 percent marginal tax rate. New Frontier distributes all the after-tax income to its shareholders, as shown in Figure 7.4.

The first tax is that paid by New Frontier at the 46 percent marginal rate—46 percent of $100, or $46. The shareholders receive $54 ($100 less the $46 tax). The shareholders are then

Double Taxation

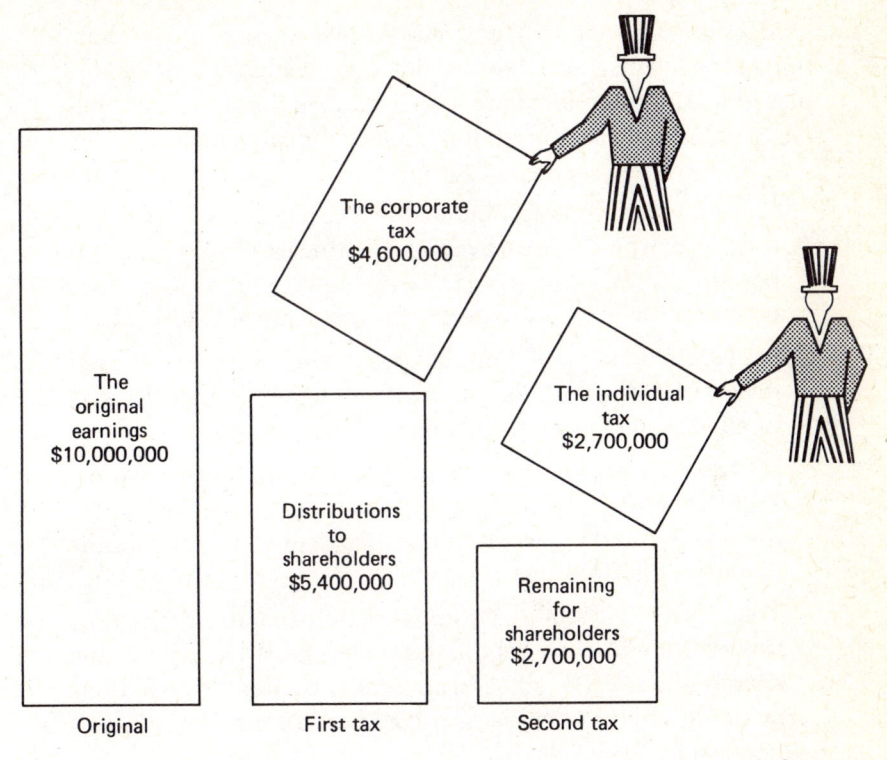

Figure 7.4. Double taxation. First the corporation's earnings are taxed; then shareholders are taxed on the distribution to them.

taxed on this dividend income at their 50 percent marginal rate. The second tax, then, is 50 percent of $54, or $27.

The original earnings have now been taxed twice. The combined tax is $73. Only $27 of the original $100 in earnings is available to shareholders after payment of the corporate and individual shareholder taxes.

As a consequence of this double taxation, individuals in the 50 percent marginal tax bracket can retain only 27 percent of corporate profits ($27 after tax on corporate pretax earnings of $100). The corporate and individual taxes are responsible for the remaining 73 percent of earnings.

Minimization of the Effects of Double Taxation. Minimization of the effects of double taxation takes a high priority in tax planning. Common techniques to minimize the impact of double taxation fall into the following general categories:

> Defer Distributions to Shareholders. Distributions to shareholders can be deferred by accumulating earnings in the corporation. This alternative is available only to shareholders who don't need the dividends for other purposes.
>
> Distribute Earnings at Capital Gains Rates. Actions by either the distributing corporation or by the shareholders can result in effective taxation of earnings at capital gains rates.
>
> Structure Distributions as Deductions. Corporations can sometimes structure distributions to shareholders as payments deductible by the corporation rather than as nondeductible dividend distributions.
>
> The S Corporation Election. The S corporation's income flows through to shareholders and in most cases only the shareholders are taxed. As a consequence, double taxation is avoided. This election is restricted to more closely held corporations.

The first three alternatives are examined in this chapter. The S corporation will be considered in Chapter 9.

Deferred Distributions to Shareholders

One method of minimizing the effect of double taxation is to defer the distribution of dividends to shareholders. Shareholders are not taxed until earnings are paid in the form of dividends.

Shareholders not in need of immediate dividend income can defer the tax by investing in profitable corporations that do not pay dividends. This defers the effect of double taxation of dividends. The dividend payment and nondividend payment alternatives are now examined.

Future Growth. If dividends are not paid, the funds saved should provide a source of growth. Generally the value of the corporation increases as a result. The retention of earnings alternative is illustrated in the following example.

EXAMPLE: THE RETENTION OF EARNINGS COMPARED TO THE DIVIDEND PAYMENT. John Smith invests $4000 as the sole shareholder of the Smith Products Corporation. The corporation earns $1000 after taxes. John does not need the income currently. John can take the $1000 as a dividend and invest the funds in a new business venture. Alternatively, John can let the earnings accumulate in the Smith Products Corporation. Smith Products may then expand the business.

If John earns the same returns on the investment in the new corporation as Smith Products earns on the additional capital, the choice of alternatives may not be important to John except for tax purposes.

For example, John may believe he can earn a 25 percent return on investment if he invests in a new corporation. If John can also earn 25 percent by leaving the investment in the Smith Products Corporation, however, he may benefit by not declaring a dividend.

If John takes the $1000 dividend, he is taxed at the 50 percent noncorporate taxpayer rate, and only $500 remains for investment in new business ventures. If John leaves the funds in the corporation, no tax is currently payable.

Eventually John will demand cash in return for his investment and both the $1000 initial earnings and all additional interest earned will be taxable at that time.

John may be retired by that time and his marginal tax rate may be reduced. Alternatively, John may employ other tax-planning alternatives to reduce the tax impact. These will be examined later in this chapter.

The principles relating to earnings accumulations also apply to the investor who owns only a portion of the corporation's stock. The small investor case is illustrated in the following example.

EXAMPLE: EARNINGS REINVESTMENT. Suzan Murphy pays $50 per share for 100 shares of Growth Corporation common stock. Growth has a policy of not paying dividends. Growth retains all earnings and expands the size of the business. Growth's annual return on shareholder investment is 20 percent.

In the first year, Growth earns 20 percent, or $10 on each share of Suzan's $50 stock. If the earnings are distributed as a dividend Suzan is taxed at the 50 percent ordinary income rate, for a tax of $5.

If the earnings are not paid as a dividend, the investment should increase in value by the amount of the undistributed earnings as in the previous case of the Smith Corporation. The investment value should increase from $50 to $60 per share.

Potential Problems. Corporations often prefer to accumulate earnings as an alternative to dividend distribution to reduce the double taxation problem. Care is required in the case of closely held corporations, however, to remain clear of special taxes established to encourage the corporation to distribute earnings. The tax on accumulated earnings and the personal holding company tax have been developed for this reason. These taxes are discussed under "Closely Held Corporations—Additional Considerations" later in the chapter.

Shareholders can defer dividends in conjunction with a second alternative—the distribution of earnings at capital gains rates. This provides for a reduced tax rate on the distribution and is examined in the following section.

Distributions of Earnings at Capital Gains Rates

The Receipt of Earnings at Capital Gains Rates. Investors can sometimes receive cash returns on investments and recognize the distribution at capital gains rates. This can be accomplished through following a strategy of investing in growth corporations that do not pay dividends. The stock is then sold when cash is desired. This approach is sometimes referred to as a "bailout" or removal of earnings at capital gains rates.

Sale Treatment. When investors sell stock, they receive a return on investment determined as the difference between the selling price and amount originally paid. The important difference between a dividend and a sale is that in a sale, the return of the investment is not taxed. The appreciation in stock price in a sale is a capital gain and is taxed at capital gains rates.

The reinvestment of dividends by the corporation and subsequent sale of stock by the shareholders provides a means for converting ordinary income into capital gains. This reduces the problem associated with the double taxation of income.

The shareholder does not need to sell the entire interest in the corporation's shares to benefit from the appreciation in value. The occasional sale of a small percentage of the shares held may provide a satisfactory return on investment. An illustration follows.

EXAMPLE: THE SALE OF STOCK AS AN ALTERNATIVE TO DIVIDENDS. Suzan Murphy, in an earlier example, paid $50 each for 100 shares of the Growth Corporation's common stock. Growth earned $10 and reinvested the earnings. The stock value increased to $60. Suzan now requires cash.

If Growth distributes $10 per share in dividends, Suzan's tax on the $1000 distribution is $500 at the marginal rate of 50 percent. Only $500 will be available to Suzan after tax.

As an alternative Suzan can sell shares for the new market

value of $60. For example, Suzan can sell 16 shares of stock at $60 and realize $960 before tax. Suzan will then recognize gain as:

Amount realized on sale of 16 shares	$960
Less: Cost of 16 shares @ $50	800
Recognized gain	$160
Tax on capital gain at 20%	$ 32

The return of investment is not taxed. The gain is taxed at capital gains rates. Suzan will realize $928 from the $960 sale after payment of $32 in tax. This compares with only $500 realized after tax on the receipt of $1000 in dividends.

Since only 16 shares are sold, Suzan's original investment is maintained and even increases slightly, to $5040 (this is determined as 84 remaining shares valued at $60 per share). If the stock price continues to appreciate as a result of earnings reinvestment, Suzan can continue the process by selling shares whenever she needs cash.

Growing corporations often reinvest most or all of their earnings in expansion activity as an alternative to dividend payment. Many investors prefer to hold stock in high-growth corporations and to realize returns as capital gains on the sale of the stock rather than at ordinary income rates on the receipt of dividends.

The Loss of Control. The sale of stock alternative is available primarily to shareholders who are not averse to giving up part of their interest in the corporation. This generally applies to shareholders in large, publicly owned corporations.

The owners of more closely held corporations also desire sale treatment, but are frequently not willing to give up control of the business. Many of the tax problems dealing with corporations arise from attempts by shareholders to bail out earnings at capital gains rates without reducing their interest in the corporation. One such device that has been the subject of specific legislation is the preferred stock bailout. This is examined in the next section.

The Preferred Stock Bailout. The preferred stock bailout is designed to remove dividends at capital gains rates and at the same time maintain the shareholder's interest in the corporation. Tax-legislation provisions now make it difficult to use this device effectively. The preferred stock bailout is discussed here for two reasons. First, it provides an example of the emphasis shareholders have placed on removing earnings at capital gains rates. Second, the discussion shows that this particular approach to avoid double taxation now seems to be blocked.

Some corporations have more than one class of outstanding stock. One class is common stock with unlimited rights to receive dividends. Other classes of stock have certain preferences and restrictions. These classes of stock are referred to as preferred stock. Corporations sometimes issue preferred stock which is nonvoting. The use of nonvoting preferred stock permits the existing owners of the corporation to raise additional capital without giving up control.

In one form of preferred stock bailout, the corporation issues nonvoting preferred stock to shareholders as a dividend. The shareholders are not taxed on receipt of the preferred stock dividend. The shareholders then sell this stock to third parties and receive sale treatment with gains taxable at capital gains rates. This effectively results in the distribution of cash to shareholders. The shareholders retain control of the corporation, since the ownership of voting stock does not change. The buyers of the stock later sell the preferred back to the corporation at prearranged prices. At the completion of the cycle, the shareholders have the cash and the corporation retires the preferred stock.

The bailout was previously used to avoid the tax on dividends. Tax legislation now provides that when preferred stock issued as a dividend is later sold by the shareholder, the fair market value of the preferred stock when issued is recognized as ordinary income. This removes the advantage of the preferred stock bailout. An illustration follows.

EXAMPLE: THE PREFERRED STOCK BAILOUT. The Johnson Corporation issues preferred stock as a nontaxable stock dividend to its sole owner, Harold Johnson. Harold then sells the preferred stock to a third party for $5000. Harold's objective is to receive sale treatment with tax only on the gain and at capital gains rates.

This transaction falls within the definition of a preferred stock bailout. Harold will likely be taxed on the receipt of the $5000 at ordinary income rates when he sells the preferred stock.

The prohibition of the preferred stock bailout does not prevent shareholders from bailing out earnings at capital gains rates. Corporations and investors continue to develop ways to avoid dividend treatment. The preferred stock bailout provisions, however, do make it more difficult to obtain sale treatment while at the same time maintaining the same proportionate interest in the corporation. The removal of earnings at capital gains rates is important in tax planning, and much of the next chapter is concerned with additional mechanisms that can be used to accomplish this objective.

Distributions Structured as Deductions

Another way to minimize double taxation is to structure corporate distributions as deductible payments by the corporation. If payments to shareholders are deductible to the distributing corporation, these payments effectively cancel the same amount of pretax income. Thus, the effect is a distribution on which the earnings were not originally taxed to the distributing corpora-

Double Taxation

tion. One approach is to distribute funds to shareholders in the form of interest rather than dividends. This option is available to all corporations. Closely held corporations have additional opportunities to minimize double taxation through arranging offsetting deductions by the distributing corporation. Available alternatives include structuring distributions as rent payments or owner salaries.

The Deduction for Interest Expense. If funds are borrowed, the borrowers will require a return on capital. The return on borrowed funds takes the form of interest, a deductible expense to the corporation. In contrast, when investment funds are obtained from shareholders, the return to shareholders is not deductible. The inability to deduct dividend payments on invested funds results in double taxation. The corporation is taxed on the entire amount of earnings; the shareholders are then taxed again on the reduced amount received by them.

The following example compares the tax effects of a payment to shareholders as interest and as a dividend.

EXAMPLE: THE DEDUCTION FOR INTEREST. The New Frontier Corporation needs $20,000. Alternatives are to issue additional shares of stock or to borrow by issuing long-term notes. In either case, the investors or lenders will require a 20 percent annual return on investment ($4000 per year).

If New Frontier issues stock, the dividends distributed to shareholders in return for the use of the funds are not deductible. If New Frontier issues debt in exchange for the $20,000, the $4000 in interest payments on the notes is deductible by the distributing corporation.

The distinction between a payment of interest and as a dividend is primarily of interest to the distributing corporation. Assuming that the shareholder is not another corporation, the form of the contribution is not particularly important for tax purposes. Both dividend income and interest income are taxed at ordinary income rates. (If the shareholder is another corporation, the form of the distribution is important, because receipts of dividends are subject to the 85 percent or 100 percent dividends received deduction discussed later in this chapter.)

The tax advantages of debt to the corporation are illustrated further in the following example.

EXAMPLE: THE TAX ADVANTAGES OF DEBT. The New Frontier Corporation needs $20,000 to construct new facilities. The funds can be raised either by borrowing or through the sale of stock. Both the investors and lenders will receive a 20 percent return on their investment. New Frontier is expected to earn $10,000 annually before considering financing costs. The two corporations are interested in the effect of the alternative forms of financing upon their existing shareholders.

The new investors and lenders will each receive 20 percent of the $20,000 investment ($4000) as returns on investment. The investors and lenders are both taxed on the receipt of interest and dividends at ordinary income rates. New Frontier will deduct the interest payments to determine taxable income. The dividend payments, however, are not deductible. The effects upon New Frontier's original shareholders are as follows:

	Issue stock	Borrow
Income before interest	$10,000	$10,000
Deduct: Interest	0	4,000
Taxable income	$10,000	$ 6,000
Deduct: tax @ 46%	4,600	2,760
Remaining	$ 5,400	$ 3,240
Dividends to new shareholders	4,000	0
Remaining for original shareholders	$ 1,400	$ 3,240

The return to New Frontier's original shareholders resulting from borrowing is more than double that resulting from the issuance of stock. The debt is a tax-deductible expense. As a result, New Frontier's taxable income is reduced and the after-tax cash available for dividend payments is increased.

If the same funds are obtained through selling stock the dividends paid on the stock are not deductible.

The interest payment is preferred to the dividend payment for tax purposes because the payment of interest is deductible by the distributing corporation. The interest is deductible and the payment does not result in a double tax since taxable income is reduced by the amount of the interest expense.

The Substitution of Debt for Equity. The substitution of debt for equity can help to minimize the impact of double taxation. Taxpayers have sometimes tried to take advantage of the distinction between dividend payments and interest by setting up corporations with only token amounts of stock and enormous amounts of debt. This is unrealistic from a business point of view, as debt is not usually available to a corporation unless shareholders also have a substantial interest. The courts have maintained that if the debt effectively acts as equity, it will be treated as equity for tax purposes. In this case, the interest payment will be reclassified as a nondeductible dividend and the corporation will lose the interest deduction.

Debt may be considered to act as equity if the corporation has a high amount of debt in relation to owners' equity or if debt is held by shareholders in the same proportion as their relative equity holdings. Lack of a definite maturity date for a loan is also more characteristic of equity than of debt. An example follows.

EXAMPLE: THE SUBSTITUTION OF DEBT FOR EQUITY. Shareholders M and N each invest $15,000 and each hold one-half of the No Deal Corporation's common stock. No Deal also owes $100,000 to outside lenders. The corporation borrowed $50,000 from M and $50,000 from N. The debt does not have a definite maturity date.

No Deal's debt has many of the same characteristics of equity. The ratio of debt to equity is $200,000 debt to only $30,000 equity:

	Debt	Equity
Shareholder's investment	—	$30,000
Shareholder's loans	$100,000	—
Outside loans	100,000	—
Total	$200,000	$30,000

The debt held by shareholders is also in the same proportion as their stock ownership. If the investors had each invested $65,000 in stock, both their ownership interest and the availability of capital to No Deal would be the same. The IRS may maintain that the two $50,000 loans by shareholders should be considered as investments in additional shares of stock rather than as debt. In this case, the interest deduction would not be allowed.

If the debt has a definite maturity date and if it is not held by shareholders in proportion to their equity interest, the corporation's case for deducting the interest is improved.

Distributions in the form of Rent. A second mechanism for making deductible distributions to shareholders is to structure distributions as rent. This option is open primarily to the closely held corporation. Rent payments are deductible by the corporation. The advantage of structuring distributions as rent is shown in the following example.

EXAMPLE: DISTRIBUTIONS IN THE FORM OF RENT. The Roundabout Delivery Corporation needs new delivery vans costing

$100,000. Roundabout is already deeply in debt and the only available source of funds is from M, the sole owner. Roundabout earns 20 percent on invested funds. Profits are expected to increase by about 20 percent, or $20,000 annually, as a result of the expansion.

One option is for M to contribute $100,000 to the corporation in exchange for additional shares of stock. Roundabout's earnings are expected to increase by $20,000 annually, and Roundabout can distribute these earnings to M. The problem is that Roundabout will not be able to deduct the distribution to M and the earnings will be effectively taxed twice.

Alternatively, M can loan the funds to Roundabout. This amounts to an investment in stock as it is likely that loan treatment will be denied. Roundabout is already heavily in debt and the proposed loan would be held in the same proportion as equity.

Another option is for M to acquire the new vans as a personal investment. M will then rent the vans to Roundabout for $20,000 per year. M will recognize taxable income of $20,000 in any of the three cases. The very significant advantage of the rental arrangement is that the corporation deducts the $20,000 payments to M as rental payments. This effectively avoids double taxation. If the $20,000 is paid as dividends, no deduction is permitted. The end result is similar to that occurring if M had made a $100,000 loan to the corporation. The advantage of a rental is that the corporation is less likely to risk denial of the deduction.

The rental of property directly to the corporation by shareholders is common in closely held corporations. The widely held corporation is less likely to rent property from shareholders. The rental of property from outsiders, as an alternative to selling shares and buying property, however, provides the widely held corporation with advantages similar to those resulting from debt. The interest or rent payments are deductible to the corporation—dividends to shareholders are not deductible.

The Deduction for Owner Salaries. The closely held corporation often uses another approach to minimize double taxation. This is the payment of salaries to owners in lieu of dividends. Salary payments to employees including owner-employees are deductible expenses to the corporation. An example follows.

EXAMPLE: SALARY PAYMENTS TO OWNER-EMPLOYEES. Sally Smart is the sole owner of the Smart Publishing Company. Smart Publishing's earnings average about $200,000 annually. Sally's needs for cash are modest and she draws a $25,000 annual salary. Smart Publishing is taxed at the 46 percent rate on earnings, and $108,000 remains after tax. Sally declares annual dividends of $108,000 and invests the distribution in stocks and real estate. Sally's taxable income is:

Salary	$ 25,000
Dividend income	108,000
Total income	$133,000

Sally's income from the business is all taxable as ordinary income. Sally has other investment income sufficient to bring her marginal tax rate to 50 percent. The amount available from the publishing business after tax is:

Total income	$133,000
Less: Tax @ 50%	66,500
Remaining after tax	$ 66,500

Sally can utilize a number of alternative devices to reduce tax. One is to increase her salary. Assume that she grants herself a $200,000 raise to $225,000. This reduces the corporation's earnings to zero and as a result, the corporation is not taxed. Sally will be taxed on the salary at ordinary income rates. The advantage is that her after-tax earnings are increased because the corporation escapes tax. In other words, there is no double taxation.

Salary	$225,000
Tax @ 50%	112,500
Remaining after tax	$112,500

The amount remaining after tax compares to the $66,500 remaining under the modest salary alternative.

The IRS sometimes challenges high owner salaries on the grounds that they are unreasonable. In the case of a challenge, the IRS suggests dividend treatment for the amount of the salary regarded as excessive. Owners sometimes need to document the value of their services to the corporation. This may require demonstrating that the salary is reasonable compared to salaries of executives with comparable responsibilities and accomplishments.

PROPERTY DIVIDENDS

Dividends are sometimes distributed in the form of property rather than in the form of cash. Any type of property can be distributed in a property dividend. As a practical matter, however, the property should be easily divisible. Shares of stock held as investments by the corporation often serve as appropriate property dividends. An example follows.

EXAMPLE: THE PROPERTY DIVIDEND. The New Frontier Corporation distributes securities of other corporations to its shareholders. The fair market value of the securities is $800.

The New Frontier shareholders receive $800 as a property dividend.

The Shareholder Tax. Shareholders recognize taxable income from property dividends as the fair market value of the distributed property. Shareholders are taxed on property dividends at ordinary income rates. In other words, the shareholder tax is the same as the tax on an equivalent amount of cash.

The Distributing Corporation's Tax. In most cases, the distributing corporation is taxed on any gain realized on appreciated property distributed as a dividend. This represents a recent change to the tax legislation. Prior to 1984, property dividends did not lead to gain recognition.

Summary of Corporate Distributions to Shareholders. The following table summarizes the tax implications of corporate distributions to the shareholder and the distributing corporation. The summary will be updated as additional types of distributions are examined.

SUMMARY OF CORPORATE DISTRIBUTIONS TO SHAREHOLDERS

Distribution	Type SH	SH tax	DC tax	Basis of property received
Cash dividend	All	Inc	None	Amount received
Property dividend	All	Inc	Gain	Fair value

NOTE: SH refers to the shareholder
DC refers to the distributing corporation
Inc refers to ordinary income treatment

The first portion of this chapter was concerned with the taxation of dividends paid to the individual shareholder. The second portion of the chapter examines the tax implications of dividends paid to corporate shareholders.

THE CORPORATE SHAREHOLDER

Background

Both individuals and other corporations can hold shares of stock in corporations. Corporations invest in the shares of other corporations for a variety of reasons. These include the investment of temporary excess cash balances, growth, diversification, control of material supplies, and assured markets for products. In some cases only small amounts of stock in other corporations are purchased. In other cases, a corporation may acquire a 100 percent interest in a second corporation.

When the shareholder is a corporation, dividends received are taxable at the corporate ordinary income rate of 46 percent. The amount of taxable dividends, however, is reduced by the corporate dividends received deduction.

The Corporate Dividends Received Deduction

The Need for Relief. The double taxation of corporate earnings presents a special problem when the shareholder is another corporation. This occurs because the passage of dividends between corporations before transfer to shareholders could result in triple or higher-order taxation without special provisions. The following example demonstrates the need for special provisions to avoid triple taxation.

EXAMPLE: THE NEED FOR SPECIAL PROVISIONS TO AVOID TRIPLE TAXATION. The New Frontier Corporation has 1984 taxable income of $100 and is taxed at the 46 percent marginal tax rate. New Frontier distributes the remaining $54 to its sole shareholder, Consolidated Industries.

Without relief from the triple taxation problem, Consolidated would be taxed at its 46 percent marginal rate on the dividend income, and would keep only $29 after its tax of $25.

Finally, the third tax would fall upon Consolidated's individual shareholders. They would lose 50 percent of the $29 dividend as tax and keep only 50 percent, or $14.50 after tax.

In summary:

First tax:	$100 @ 46%	$46.00
Second tax:	54 @ 46%	25.00
Third tax:	29 @ 50%	14.50
Total tax		$85.50

The situation outlined above does not occur in practice because of the deduction for dividends received from another corporation.

The 85-Percent Dividends Received Deduction. Corporations receiving dividends from other domestic corporations deduct 85 percent of the dividends received to determine taxable income. As a consequence, only 15 percent of the dividends received are effectively taxed.

The 100-Percent Dividends Received Deduction. Corporations receiving dividends from certain affiliated corporations may benefit from an even more generous deduction. Members of affiliated groups may deduct 100 percent of the dividends received from another group member. Affiliated group status requires 80 percent ownership of the subsidiary. Criteria for the affiliated group are similar to those for the controlled group. Affiliated corporations are usually controlled groups, but meet additional criteria including status as taxable corporations and as domestic corporations.

As a result of the 100 percent dividends received deduction, the parent corporation is not taxed at all on the receipt of dividends from the affiliated corporation. The rationale for the dividends received deduction is that the individual shareholders of the parent corporation will eventually be subject to tax when dividends are passed through to them.

The Deferral of Double Taxation.   The dividends paid by the controlled subsidiary to the parent should eventually flow through to the parent's investors. When this occurs, the dividends will be taxable. Thus the corporate dividends received deduction does not really eliminate double taxation to the individual shareholder. The dividends received deduction merely prevents triple or higher-order taxation which could make the problem even worse. An example illustrating the benefit of the dividends received deduction follows.

EXAMPLE: THE CORPORATE DIVIDENDS RECEIVED DEDUCTION. The New Frontier Corporation receives $100 in cash as dividends from the Small Corporation. New Frontier does not hold a controlling interest in Small.

The receipt of dividends is taxable to New Frontier. The tax is determined as:

Dividends received	$100
Less: 85% deduction	85
Taxable income	$ 15
Tax @ 46%	$ 6.90

This tax represents only a small portion of the $46 tax that would be payable without the dividends received deduction. In the absence of the deduction, all $100 would be taxable at the 46 percent tax rate.

The tax to shareholders is deferred rather than avoided in the above case. The shareholders will be taxed when the dividends from the subsidiary eventually flow through to them.

THE STOCK DIVIDEND

Background

Corporations that are unable to pay cash dividends sometimes declare stock dividends. Stock dividends are paid by issuing one additional share of stock for each specified number of shares held by the investor. The stock dividend is illustrated in the following example.

EXAMPLE: THE STOCK DIVIDEND. One hundred shares of New Frontier Corporation stock are outstanding. The shares were originally issued for $2000 and the fair market value is now $3000. New Frontier issues a 20 percent stock dividend.

The 20 percent stock dividend results in an increase in the number of shares outstanding by 20 percent. The number of shares outstanding increases from 100 to 120 shares.

Shareholders do not receive anything except shares in a stock dividend. The market value of the 120 shares generally remains at about the market value of the original 100 shares (the market price of each share is reduced).

The 100 shares each had a market value before the dividend of $3000/100 shares, or $30 per share. After the stock dividend, the market value of each share will probably be reduced to $3000/120 shares, or $25.

This example shows that shareholders do not receive anything of real value from the corporation in a stock dividend. Shareholders end up with more shares, but each share has a reduced market value.

The Tax

Usual Treatment. The corporation is not taxed on the issuance of its own shares. The shareholders are also not taxed on

The Stock Dividend

receipt of a simple stock dividend since their wealth is not increased. The original basis is prorated over the old and new shares so that the adjusted basis of each share is reduced. The overall adjusted basis does not change. The rationale for this approach can be seen in the following example.

EXAMPLE: THE STOCK DIVIDEND AND THE ADJUSTED BASIS. One hundred shares of New Frontier Corporation stock are outstanding. The shares were originally issued for $2000 and the fair market value is now $3000. New Frontier issues a 20 percent stock dividend. Shareholder N later sells 12 of the new shares for $40 per share.

The 100 shares of New Frontier Corporation are increased to 120 shares as a result of the 20 percent stock dividend.

The old shares had a basis of $2000/100 shares, or $20 per share. After the stock dividend, the 120 shares have a basis of $2000/120 shares, or $16.67 per share.

The 12 shares sold at $40 apiece result in a gain of:

Amount realized	$480
Adjusted basis (12 @ $16.67)	200
Gain on sale	$280

If there had not been a stock dividend, N would sell only 10 shares. The value of each share would be 120 percent of $40, or $48. The same gain would result:

Amount realized (10 @ $48)	$480
Adjusted basis (10 @ $20)	200
Gain on sale	$280

Consequently, N has not received anything of real value as a stock dividend. N does not recognize income and the combined basis of his shares does not change.

The Dividend Payable in Either Cash or Stock. Exceptions to the tax-free treatment of shareholders may apply in cases where the stock dividend does not result in a pro rata increase in the number of common shares. For example, dividends are sometimes payable in either cash or in stock at the option of the shareholder.

The dividend payable in cash or stock may change the proportionate interest of shareholders in the corporation. After the dividend, shareholders who take cash will have a smaller percentage ownership in the corporation than shareholders who take additional shares of stock. Dividends payable in either cash or stock are taxable to all shareholders including those that elect to receive stock. Shareholders electing to receive stock are considered to receive something of value, since their proportionate interest in the corporation's ownership is increased.

CLOSELY HELD CORPORATIONS—ADDITIONAL CONSIDERATIONS

The discussion earlier in this chapter indicated that the accumulation of earnings can be employed as a device to avoid the double tax on corporate income. The use of the corporation to minimize the effects of taxation is discouraged by two provisions in the tax legislation: the tax on accumulated earnings and the personal holding company tax.

The Accumulated Earnings Tax

Background. The closely held corporation could avoid the tax on dividends entirely through a policy of accumulating earnings indefinitely and not paying dividends. This could be particularly effective for the smaller corporation taxed at a low marginal rate. The accumulated earnings tax discourages this alternative.

The Tax. The accumulated earnings tax rate is 27.5 percent on the first $100,000 of additional accumulated income, and 38.5 percent on additional increases in accumulated income. The tax is applied to the amount of current-year earnings retained in the business. The tax is based on the excess of the current-year earnings retained over that required for reasonable business needs.

The legislation provides that up to $250,000 may be accumulated over the life of the business without penalty. Additions to accumulated earnings in excess of reasonable business needs are subject to the tax after taking the $250,000 allowance into account. An illustration of the application of the tax follows.

EXAMPLE: THE ACCUMULATED EARNINGS TAX. The Savit Corporation has accumulated earnings and profits of $340,000 at the beginning of 1984. During 1984, taxable income is $60,000 with no dividend declarations. The 1984 regular tax is $25,000. Savit needs to retain $150,000 for reasonable business needs.

Ending accumulated earnings are $375,000 determined as:

Beginning		$340,000
Taxable income	$60,000	
Less: Regular tax	25,000	35,000
Ending accumulated earnings		$375,000

The ending accumulated earnings exceed both the reasonable business needs and the allowable amount of $250,000. The portion of 1984 income retained in excess of the amount required for reasonable business needs is subject to the accumulated earnings tax. In this case, the $35,000 of after-tax excess accumulated earnings is taxable to Savit in 1984 at the rate of 27.5 percent. This tax is in addition to the regular corporate tax and any other taxes.

The tax is based only upon the current-year increase in accumulated earnings and profits. The beginning-of-year accumulated earnings and profits in excess of reasonable business needs were presumably taxed in previous years.

Reasonable Business Needs. Earnings accumulated for reasonable business needs are not subject to the tax. Reasonable business needs include:

Working capital for operations.

Future business expansion.

Retirement of indebtedness.

Self-insurance and contingencies.

Corporations tend to distribute accumulated earnings as dividends rather than pay the tax. This is consistent with the intention of the accumulated earnings tax provisions.

The accumulated earnings tax is normally a problem only for the closely held business. However, the tax is also applicable to the widely held business.

The Personal Holding Company Tax

The personal holding company tax is designed to discourage investors from setting up corporations to avoid individual taxes on investment income.

Background. Prior to the development of the personal holding company tax, investors could reduce the regular income tax on investments by setting up corporations to hold the investments. The interest received by the corporation was taxed at the lower rates applicable to corporations. The dividend revenue was subject to the deduction for dividends received from another corporation. The individual was not taxed until the cash was removed from the corporation.

Closely Held Corporations—Additional Considerations

The personal holding company tax discourages use of the corporation to avoid taxes on investment income. The tax is levied on the personal holding company—a corporation primarily in the business of holding passive investments.

Criteria. A corporation may qualify as a personal holding company if five or fewer individuals own more than half the stock and 60 percent or more of the income consists of interest, rents, dividends, and other types of passive income.

The personal holding company criteria were established in order to provide dividend payment incentives to corporations that might escape the tax on accumulated earnings. For example, the accumulated earnings tax exempts accumulations of less than $250,000. The personal holding company tax does not provide for exemptions.

The Tax. The personal holding company penalty tax rate is 50 percent. This is in addition to the regular corporate income tax. The tax is assessed on additions to accumulated taxable income after tax and after dividend payments. The tax provides a strong incentive to declare dividends. An illustration of the operation of the personal holding company tax follows.

EXAMPLE. The Big Buck Corporation, a personal holding company, reports taxable income of $100,000 in 1984. Big Buck does not pay dividends. Federal income taxes amount to $73,000. The tax is determined as the total of the regular corporate tax and the personal holding company tax as follows:

The corporation's regular tax is 46 percent of $100,000, or $46,000. Of the original $100,000, $54,000 remains after tax.

The personal holding company penalty tax is:

$$50\% \text{ of } \$54{,}000 = \$27{,}000$$

The total tax payable by Big Buck is:

	Regular tax	$46,000
	Penalty tax	27,000
	Total tax	$73,000

The personal holding company tax is avoided by declaring dividends. If dividends of $54,000 are declared, Big Buck is not taxed. The shareholders are taxed on the dividend income at ordinary income rates as in the case of a dividend.

Corporations have sometimes qualified unexpectedly for personal holding company status. For example, Chapter 10 discusses the sale of all assets of the corporation. Corporations selling assets often invest the proceeds temporarily in securities, possibly with the objective of liquidating and distributing the securities to shareholders. The income from these securities will then consist entirely of passive investment income and may be subject to the personal holding company tax. Corporations that sell assets should plan to quickly dispose of the proceeds either by distribution to shareholders or by reinvestment in new productive business property.

If the personal holding company tax is imposed, the accumulated earnings penalty tax does not apply.

SUMMARY

Dividends are distributions of earnings and profits to shareholders. These distributions are taxable to shareholders.

Earnings and profits are the cumulative after-tax earnings of the corporation after certain adjustments and less the dividends paid. Distributions that do not represent earnings and profits may not be taxable to shareholders.

Double Taxation. Double taxation occurs when the corporation is taxed on earnings and the shareholders are taxed again when the earnings are distributed as dividends. Shareholders can minimize the impact of double taxation by investing in corporations that accumulate earnings and do not pay dividends if the accumulated earnings tax and personal holding company tax can be avoided. Corporations can minimize the problem of double taxation through policies of deferring dividend distributions, and structuring distributions as deductible items.

Accumulated Earnings. Double taxation is deferred when earnings are accumulated by the corporation rather than paid out as dividends. Growth corporations often accumulate earnings and reinvest them in other projects in lieu of dividend payments.

Distribution of Earnings at Capital Gains Rates. The distribution of earnings at capital gains rates often occurs in the case of growth stocks. As the earnings are accumulated, the stock price increases. If investors then sell the stock, the increase in stock value (attributable to the earnings) is recognized as a capital gain.

Deductions as Alternatives to Dividends. Double taxation of earnings can also be avoided by setting up the capital structure to provide for payments for the use of capital in the form of deductions rather than as dividends. The use of debt rather than stock as a means of raising capital is consistent with this objective. The rental of property to the corporation by owners also minimizes the effect of double taxation. Interest and rent payments are deductible by the corporation. Dividend distributions to shareholders are not deductible.

Owners of closely held corporations can also provide for corporate deductions on distributions by structuring distributions as salary rather than as dividends.

Property Dividends. The fair market value of property received as a dividend distribution is taxable to shareholders. The distributing corporation is usually taxed on the gain resulting from the appreciation of property distributed as a property dividend.

Dividend Distributions to Corporate Shareholders. The problem of double taxation is minimized for corporations receiving dividends from other corporations. Corporations are entitled to deduct 85 percent of dividends received from domestic corporations to determine taxable income. If the receiving corporation is a member of an affiliated group of corporations, 100 percent of the dividends received from another member of the group may be deducted to determine taxable income. Corporate shareholders may prefer dividend treatment over capital gains treatment due to the dividends received deduction.

Additional Considerations for Closely Held Corporations. The accumulated earnings tax provides an incentive for the closely held corporation to distribute any cash not needed for business purposes to investors as dividends. The tax is an add-on tax, and is based on the amount of after-tax earnings accumulated in excess of those needed for future business purposes.

The personal holding company tax applies to closely held corporations with income received primarily from holding passive investments. The tax was intended as a penalty tax to discourage setting up corporations to hold investments in order to recognize income at reduced tax rates and to discourage accumulating earnings in the corporation. The tax reduces investor incentives to set up personal holding companies. Corporations, however, still need to be alert to situations that could give rise to the tax.

Chapter 8

Returns of Invested Capital

Corporate distributions to shareholders fall into two general classifications. The first is the distribution of earnings and profits. This is a dividend taxable to the shareholder as ordinary income. All other distributions fall into a second general classification. This includes the return of the shareholder's investment. The return of investment is treated as a sale of stock back to the distributing corporation. Sale treatment gives rise to capital gains or losses. Additionally, only the excess of the distribution over the adjusted basis is taxable to the shareholder. The return of the original investment is tax-free.

The tax legislation provides for sale treatment if the investor reduces his or her proportionate interest in the corporation or if the corporation engages in certain transactions to reduce its capital requirements. Over the years, however, shareholders have employed a variety of mechanisms to obtain sale treatment for distributions that effectively act as distributions of earnings. Shareholders of closely held corporations in particular have been concerned with bailing out earnings at capital gains rates without giving up any interest in the corporation. The sale of stock is often not acceptable to the shareholder because it may require giving up control in the corporation.

The law attempts to distinguish between distributions of

earnings and other types of distributions. Specific types of distributions are eligible for sale treatment. These include certain redemptions, partial liquidations, and complete liquidations. Distributions not meeting specific criteria are classified as dividends to the extent of earnings and profits.

This chapter begins with background material and an overview of the return on investment. This is followed by discussion of the stock redemption, the partial liquidation, and the complete liquidation.

THE RETURN OF INVESTMENT VERSUS THE DISTRIBUTION OF EARNINGS

The Sale

The return of investment is treated like a sale. The portion of the distribution corresponding to the amount originally invested is not taxed. The excess of the distribution over the amount of the original investment is recognized as taxable income. The tax is then determined at preferred capital gains rates. This section compares the outright sale of stock and the return of investment by the distributing corporation in redemption of stock.

The Sale of Stock to Other Investors. The sale of property including stock was examined in Chapter 4. The tax on the sale of securities is determined by the gain recognized on the sale. The following example reviews the tax treatment applicable to the sale of securities.

EXAMPLE: THE SALE OF INVESTMENT. Harry Jones originally bought shares in the New Frontier Corporation for $11,000. Harry now sells the stock for $20,000.

Harry recognizes gain as follows:

Amount realized	$20,000
Less: Adjusted basis	11,000
Recognized gain	$ 9,000

The gain is a capital gain if Harry holds the stock for the required period.

The Sale of Stock Back to the Corporation. Certain distributions to shareholders that do not represent earnings and profits qualify as returns of investment. The return of investment is treated in the same manner as a sale of stock as shown in the following example.

EXAMPLE: THE RETURN OF INVESTMENT. The New Frontier Corporation distributes $20,000 to shareholders as a return of investment. The shareholders turn in shares of stock originally issued by New Frontier. The shareholders originally paid $11,000 for the stock.

The shareholders receive the return of the original investment free of tax. The shareholders receive $9000 in excess of the original investment. This is taxed as a capital gain as in the previous example. New Frontier is not taxed on the return of investment.

Sale treatment is preferable to a dividend (assuming a distribution to an individual shareholder). If the transaction receives dividend treatment, the entire amount of the distribution is taxable. A second disadvantage of dividend treatment is that the tax is determined at ordinary income rather than at capital gains rates.

Sale Treatment for the Distribution of Accumulated Earnings

Most profitable corporations reinvest at least a portion of their earnings as an alternative to the payment of dividends. The reinvestment of earnings provides the corporation with additional financing and tends to increase the value of the corporation's stock. Investors can share in corporate profits at capital gains rates by following a policy of investing in corporations that reinvest earnings.

A Review of Sale Treatment for Appreciated Stock. An illustration in Chapter 7 showed how the accumulation of earnings can lead to an increase in stock price. A summary of the previous illustration follows.

EXAMPLE: DIVIDEND REINVESTMENT. Suzan Murphy, a shareholder in the Growth Corporation, paid $50 for each share of Growth Corporation common stock. Growth doesn't pay dividends, but reinvests all earnings. Growth earned $10 on Suzan's investment of $50. If the earnings were distributed as a dividend, Suzan would be taxed $5 on the $10 dividend at the ordinary income rate.

The investment increased in value from $50 to $60. Suzan later sells the investment and recognizes gain as:

Amount realized	$60
Less: Adjusted basis	50
Recognized gain	$10

Suzan is taxed on the $10 capital gain at the preferred 20 percent rate. The tax is only $2 compared to a $5 tax on a dividend distribution.

The earnings have been removed from the corporation in a transaction qualifying for sale treatment.

The above situation illustrates one way that shareholders can reduce the burden of double taxation. The amount realized on the sale of the stock in a growth corporation includes earnings that would be taxed as ordinary income if paid as dividends. In other words, the sale of appreciated stock can result in the removal of earnings at capital gains rates.

The Sale of Widely Held Stock. The sale of stock provides a simple and effective means of removing earnings of widely held corporations at capital gains rates. Stock sales, in most cases, can be easily arranged. Shareholders may sell only a few shares at a time—it is not necessary to sell all the stock. If the shareholder desires to continue ownership in the corporation, the shares can be repurchased later.

The Sale of Stock in Closely Held Corporations. The sale of shares in a closely held corporation may not always be desirable. One problem is that the sale of stock reduces the shareholder's interest in the corporation. Shareholders of closely held corporations are often reluctant to sell stock and give up control. A second problem is that shares may not have an established market value and may be more difficult to sell.

The sale of shares back to the corporation may provide a solution to both of the above difficulties. The sale to the corporation, however, leads to problems in determining whether the transaction acts as a sale or merely as a device to remove profits at capital gains rates.

The Legal Distinction between a Dividend and a Return of Investment. Taxpayers have exercised considerable ingenuity in structuring distributions as returns of investment rather than as dividends. Closely held corporations, in particular, attempt to arrange sale treatment while at the same time permitting existing shareholders to retain control of the corporation.

Tax legislation specifies that all returns to shareholders receive dividend treatment unless the shareholder can establish that the distribution should be treated in some other manner. Tax legislation is very much concerned with distinguishing between dividends and the return of capital. Redemptions, partial liquidations, and liquidations represent returns of capital and receive sale treatment. The relevant provisions of these types of distributions are examined in this chapter.

THE STOCK REDEMPTION

The stock redemption is one form of return of investment. A redemption takes place when a shareholder sells stock back to the issuing corporation. Corporations sometimes redeem stock for the convenience of the shareholder. A minority shareholder, for example, may want to sell shares that don't have an established market value, Figure 8.1 illustrates the stock redemption.

Corporations may also redeem shares for their own convenience or for the benefit of existing shareholders. For example, the corporation may repurchase shares for later distribution to employees exercising stock options. This is an example of a redemption for business purposes. Alternatively, the corporation may buy back shares to prevent the loss of control that other shareholders might experience if shares are sold to an outside party. This redemption would be for the benefit of the shareholders.

The Tax

The Shareholder Tax. A qualifying redemption receives sale treatment. The return of the shareholder's investment is not taxed. Any excess received by the shareholder over the amount invested is taxable to the shareholder as a capital gain.

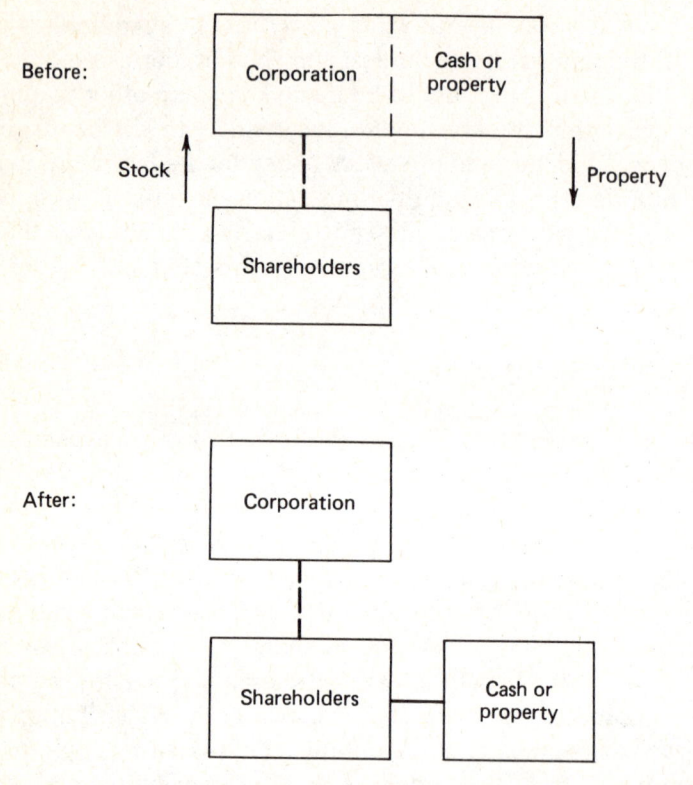

Figure 8.1. The redemption. The corporation distributes property to selected shareholders in exchange for stock.

The Redemption for Cash and the Distributing Corporation Tax. Shareholders may receive either cash or other property in exchange for shares in redemption. The distributing corporation does not recognize gain or loss on the distribution of cash. An illustration of a redemption follows.

EXAMPLE: A QUALIFYING STOCK REDEMPTION. Sharon Smith invested $200 in the New Frontier Corporation. Several years later, Sharon turned in all stock in New Frontier and received $300 in return.

If this qualifies as a redemption, the tax to Sharon is determined as:

Amount realized on redemption	$300
Less: Adjusted basis of stock	200
Recognized gain (capital gain)	$100
Tax @ 20 percent	$ 20

If Sharon sells the stock to a third party for $300, the same treatment results. Sharon will also recognize a capital gain of $100. Shareholders receive the same tax treatment in a redemption that would apply to a sale of stock to a third party for the same price.

The distributing corporation does not recognize gain or loss on cash redemptions because income was recognized earlier when the corporation earned the cash.

Nonqualifying Redemptions. If the transaction fails to qualify as a redemption, the amount of the distribution is an ordinary dividend (to the extent of accumulated earnings and profits). An example follows.

EXAMPLE: A DIVIDEND. Sharon Smith invested $200 in the New Frontier Corporation. Several years later, Sharon and all other shareholders turned in 10 percent of their stock in New Frontier. Sharon received $300 in return. Assume that Sharon's $300 does not qualify as a redemption.

The entire $300 distribution to Sharon must then be treated as a dividend (assuming that the corporation has sufficient earnings and profits). The dividend is taxable as ordinary income. Sharon's tax is 50 percent of $300, or $150. This compares to a tax of only $20 on the same distribution in redemption.

Since sale treatment is usually preferred to treatment as a dividend, the criteria for redemption treatment are important to shareholders. The next section examines the criteria for stock redemption.

Criteria for Redemption Treatment

The Reduction in Proportionate Interest. The concept of a redemption is based on the notion that the shareholder effectively sells the stock and gives up the corresponding interest in the corporation. Consistent with this notion, the distribution to shareholders must *not* be made in proportion to the stock held. To qualify as a redemption, there must be a meaningful reduction in the shareholder's proportionate interest in the corporation. An example follows.

EXAMPLE: A QUALIFYING STOCK REDEMPTION. The New Frontier Corporation has 3000 shares of stock outstanding. New Frontier now distributes $200 to Nancy Jones in redemption of 1000 shares of Nancy's 1500 shares of stock. Nancy's holdings are reduced to only 500 shares. None of the other shareholders receive distributions in redemption. Figure 8.2 gives an illustration.

Prior to the redemption, Nancy held 1500 shares, or 50 percent of the outstanding shares. After the redemption, Nancy only holds 500 shares, or 25 percent of the 2000 shares now outstanding.

This should qualify as a redemption because the distribution is not proportionate to each stockholder's interest. Nancy's interest was reduced from 50 percent to 25 percent. The interest of the other shareholders increased to 75 percent of the outstanding shares.

The redemption legislation also contains provisions that make it difficult for shareholders to go through the motions of a redemp-

The Stock Redemption

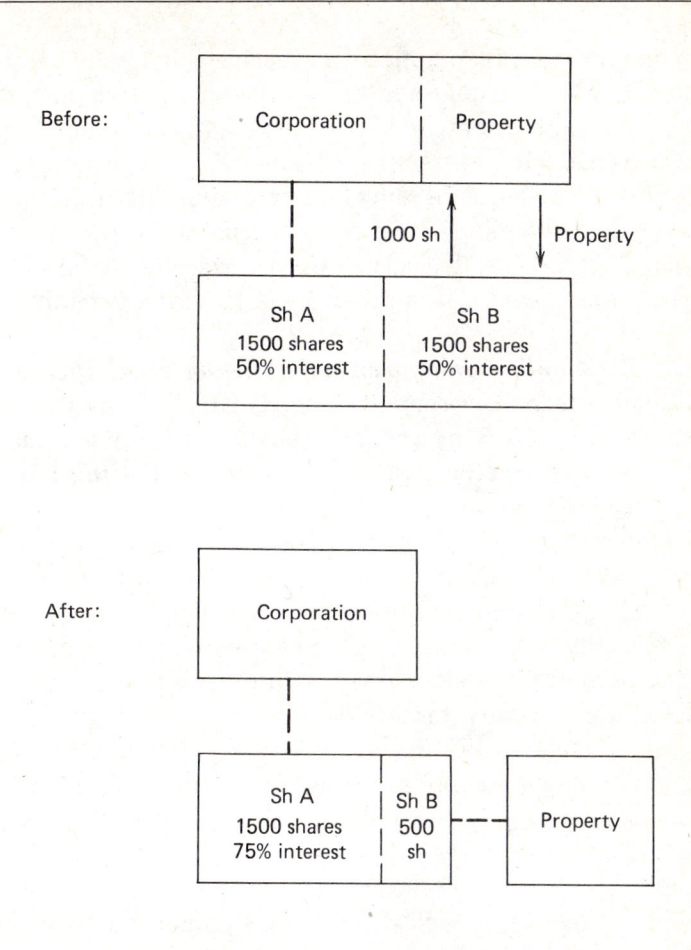

Before:

```
         ┌─────────────┬─────────────┐
         │ Corporation │  Property   │
         └─────────────┴─────────────┘
               │      ↑        │
               │  1000 sh   Property
               │      │        ↓
         ┌─────────────┬─────────────┐
         │    Sh A     │    Sh B     │
         │ 1500 shares │ 1500 shares │
         │ 50% interest│ 50% interest│
         └─────────────┴─────────────┘
```

After:

```
         ┌─────────────┐
         │ Corporation │
         └─────────────┘
               │
         ┌─────────────┬──────┐      ┌──────────┐
         │    Sh A     │ Sh B │ ──── │ Property │
         │ 1500 shares │ 500  │      │          │
         │ 75% interest│  sh  │      └──────────┘
         └─────────────┴──────┘
```

Figure 8.2. The reduction of proportionate interest. Shareholder B turns in 1000 shares and the ownership percentage is reduced.

tion without effectively giving up an interest in the corporation. Conceivably this could be done by turning in stock at the same time another family member buys the same amount of stock. For example, if a husband and wife each own a 50 percent interest in the corporation, the wife could "sell" her interest back to the corporation via a redemption and receive sale treatment. The family would then continue to own the corporation since the husband would then own 100 percent of the outstanding shares. The constructive ownership provisions of the legislation provide that the meaningful reduction in interest criterion applies to the shareholder and to related parties including the immediate family and controlled corporations. Consequently, the situation outlined above will not usually qualify as a redemption.

The Redemption Compared to the Dividend. Corporations and shareholders have sometimes tried to disguise dividends as stock redemptions. This was accomplished by turning in shares of stock in return for the dividend and merely calling the transaction a redemption.

Dividend distributions are ordinarily granted on a per-share basis, with each share receiving the same amount of the dividend. The proportionate interest of each shareholder remains the same after the dividend as before the dividend payment.

The proportion of stock ownership test associated with the redemption separates the dividend and the redemption. The corporation may call in shares of stock and seem to go through the motion of a redemption, but unless a shareholder's proportionate interest is reduced, the distribution will not qualify as a redemption. For example, a corporation could call in one-half of its stock and distribute $300 per share for each share received. If after the redemption, each shareholder's proportionate interest in the corporation remained unchanged, the distribution would receive dividend treatment rather than sale treatment. The fact that stock is turned in to the corporation does not by itself determine the treatment of the distribution.

The Distribution of Property in Redemption

Distributions in redemption may take the form of either cash or other property. The redemption for cash was examined earlier in this chapter. The redemption for property introduces additional considerations.

The Shareholder Tax. If appreciated property is distributed in redemption, the amount realized by the shareholder is the fair market value of the property received. The shareholder recognizes gain on the excess of the amount realized over the adjusted basis of the stock. As far as the shareholder is concerned, the tax on a property distribution in redemption is the same as the tax on a cash distribution.

The New Adjusted Basis. The adjusted basis of property received in redemption is the fair market value—the amount realized by the shareholder on receipt of the distribution.

The Distributing Corporation's Tax. The distributing corporation is not taxed in a redemption for cash. The distributing corporation, however, does recognize gain on the redemption of stock for property. Gain is recognized by the distributing corporation as though the property were sold for cash prior to the redemption.

The fair market value of the distributed property nearly always differs from the adjusted basis. As a consequence, the corporation distributing property in redemption recognizes gain or loss on the appreciation of the transferred property. This effectively treats the transaction as a sale from the corporation's view.

The gain recognized by the distributing corporation is a capital gain assuming a sufficient holding period. Recaptures apply as in a sale. The calculation of gain on the distribution of property in redemption is shown in the following example.

EXAMPLE: THE PROPERTY REDEMPTION. The New Frontier Corporation distributes property with a fair market value of $400 to

John Smith in redemption of John's shares. The property has an adjusted basis of $200 with $50 depreciation taken to date. The basis of John's stock to him is $100. Figure 8.3 illustrates the situation.

John recognizes $300 capital gain as follows:

Amount realized	$400
Less: Adjusted basis of stock	100
Capital gain	$300

New Frontier realizes gain as $200

Amount realized	$400
Less: Adjusted basis	200
Realized gain	$200
Subject to recapture	$ 50
Capital gain	$150

The amount recaptured is the lesser of the gain or the depreciation taken to date. The recapture is taxed at ordinary income rates. The remaining $150 of gain is taxable to New Frontier as a capital gain.

An exception to the gain recognition requirement pertains to the distribution of stock in a subsidiary corporation. Gain is not recognized by the distributing corporation if the corporation distributes stock in a subsidiary corporation to certain individual shareholders.

Losses on Redemption. The recognition of gain provision by the distributing corporation on the property redemption does not apply to losses. Ordinarily a loss is recognized if the fair market value of property transferred is less than the adjusted

The Stock Redemption

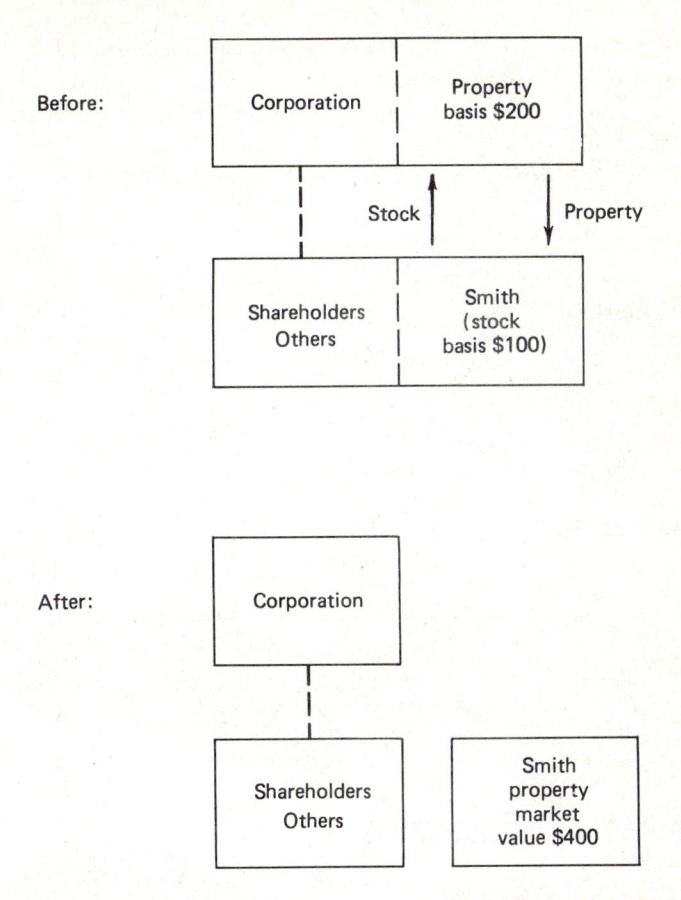

Figure 8.3. The property distribution in redemption. Shareholder Smith turns in stock and receives property with fair market value $400.

basis. The distributing corporation, however, does not recognize loss on the transfer of property distributed as a property redemption. Consequently it is not usual for corporations to distribute loss property to shareholders. Property with a fair market value below basis is usually sold directly to recognize the loss.

The summary of corporate distributions to shareholders continued from the previous chapter on dividends follows:

SUMMARY OF CORPORATE DISTRIBUTIONS TO SHAREHOLDERS

Distribution	Type SH	SH tax	DC tax	Basis of property received
Cash dividend	All	Inc	None	Amount received
Property dividend	All	Inc	Gain	Fair value
Redemption	**All**	**Capital gain**	**Gain**	**Fair value**

NOTE: SH refers to the shareholder
DC refers to the distributing corporation
Inc refers to ordinary income treatment
Ind refers to individual shareholders only

THE PARTIAL LIQUIDATION

General Characteristics

A liquidation is similar in some respects to a redemption. In both cases, owners receive at least a portion of their original investment from the corporation.

In a partial liquidation, shareholders turn in some shares in exchange for a distribution of property. In a complete liquidation, all property is distributed to shareholders, and the corporation ceases to exist. Liquidations sometimes arise from insolvency, but profitable businesses also undergo liquidations.

The Importance of Distributing Corporation Circumstances. The criteria for partial liquidation treatment relate to the circumstances of the distributing corporation. This differs from the case of redemptions, where shareholder considerations (the reduction of proportionate interest) determine the tax to the shareholder.

Partial liquidations are major contractions in the size of the business. Partial liquidations often result from the disposition of a business by a corporation originally in two or more lines of business. The following example illustrates one set of circumstances that may lead to a partial liquidation.

EXAMPLE: PARTIAL LIQUIDATION RESULTING FROM A CASUALTY. The Fit Rite Corporation manufactures men's clothing. It sells some of its products in a nearby factory outlet retail store. The factory outlet has been more profitable than the factory.

The Fit Rite factory is damaged by fire and management decides to focus more attention on the retail operation and not to rebuild the factory. The insurance proceeds are distributed directly to the shareholders.

This distribution may qualify as a partial liquidation of the business. Part of the original investment is returned to shareholders in a genuine contraction of the business.

Sometimes corporations decide to discontinue an ongoing business while continuing to carry on another business. A car dealer, for example, may discontinue the used car sales operation. The dealer might then sell the used car operation for cash and distribute the cash to shareholders in partial liquidation. The distribution of business assets by a corporation that continues another business may also qualify as a partial liquidation. The car dealer, for example, might distribute the used car sales operation to a shareholder in partial liquidation of the corporation.

The Individual Versus the Corporate Shareholder. Partial liquidation treatment applies only to noncorporate shareholders. Corporations that receive distributions in partial liquidation treat the distribution as a dividend. This dividend is then subject to the dividends received deduction.

The Tax

The Distributing Corporation. Corporations may distribute either cash or other property in partial liquidation. The distributing corporation does not recognize gain or loss on the distribution of cash in partial liquidation. If property is distributed, the distributing corporation recognizes gain on the distribution as in a redemption. An example follows.

EXAMPLE: THE DISTRIBUTING CORPORATION GAIN IN A PARTIAL LIQUIDATION. The Cargo Corporation operates a car dealership that consists of several businesses—domestic new cars, imports, and used cars. Cargo distributes the used car business to shareholders in partial liquidation. The used car business is carried on Cargo's books at $2000. The fair market value of the business is $2500.

Cargo recognizes gain on the Sale as:

Fair market value	$2500
Adjusted basis	2000
Realized gain	$ 500

The shareholders take the $2500 fair market value of the property as their basis. They recognize gain as the excess of this amount over the basis of the stock given up. Recaptures of the investment tax credit and depreciation apply as in a sale for cash.

Exceptions for Distributions to Certain Shareholders. The distributing corporation does not always recognize gain on distributions in partial liquidation. Gain is not recognized by the distributing corporation if the distribution is made with respect to qualified stock. Qualified stock is stock held by a noncorporate shareholder who held at least ten percent of the value of the distributing corporation's stock during the previous five year period. If the corporation was in existence for less than five years, the shareholder must have held the stock since the time of incorporation.

The Shareholder Tax. The shareholder tax depends upon the type of shareholder. As indicated previously, the corporate shareholder treats the distribution in partial liquidation as a dividend.

The noncorporate shareholder treats the receipt of a distribution in partial liquidation as a sale. The return of investment is not taxable. Any excess received over the amount invested is taxable to the shareholder as a capital gain. The effect upon the shareholder is the same as in either a redemption or sale of stock to a third party. The tax in a partial liquidation is illustrated in the following example.

EXAMPLE: SHAREHOLDER TAXATION IN A PARTIAL LIQUIDATION. The Fit Rite Corporation is damaged by fire, and insurance proceeds received and distributed to shareholders are $16,000. Shareholders turn in one-third of their stock with an adjusted basis of $12,000 in a partial liquidation.

If the shareholder is an individual, sale treatment applies as follows:

Amount realized by shareholders	$16,000
Less: Adjusted basis	12,000
Recognized gain	$ 4,000
Tax @ 20 percent	$ 800

If the distribution to the individual shareholder does not qualify as a partial liquidation, it is taxed as an ordinary dividend. At the 50 percent individual tax rate, the tax on the $16,000 dividend is $8000.

The Adjusted Basis

The amount realized and the adjusted basis of property received by the noncorporate shareholder in a partial liquidation is the fair market value of the property. The shareholder treatment is illustrated in the following example.

EXAMPLE: THE PARTIAL LIQUIDATION OF PROPERTY TO SHAREHOLDERS. The Shine-Up Corporation discontinues its chain of shoe outlets and distributes property to shareholders in partial liquidation. The property consists primarily of shelving and displays with a fair market value of $1000. Their basis to Shine-Up is $700, and depreciation to date is $100. The property is distributed to Shine-Up's primary shareholder, Mr. Robert Socks. Mr. Socks plans to go into the shoe business. He turns in stock with a basis of $400 in partial liquidation.

Mr. Socks recognizes capital gain as:

Amount realized	$1000
Less: Adjusted basis of stock	400
Recognized gain	$ 600

The Partial Liquidation

The basis of the property to Mr. Socks is the fair market value of $1000.

The gain realized by Shine-Up is:

Fair market value of property	$1000
Less: Adjusted basis	700
Realized gain	$ 300

Of the $300 gain $100 is subject to recapture as ordinary income. The remaining $200 is recognized as a capital gain by Shine-Up.

The corporate shareholder treats the distribution received in partial liquidation as a dividend. The fair market value of the property dividend is taxed as ordinary income. The adjusted basis to the new owner is the property fair market value.

Criteria for Partial Liquidation Treatment

To qualify as a partial liquidation, at least one of the following criteria must be met:

> The distribution represents a genuine contraction in the size of the business. The fire-damaged factory example meets this criterion.
>
> An entire trade or business is distributed. The trade or business must have been actively conducted and the distributing corporation must also continue to operate another active business. The Cargo Corporation situation seems to meet these criteria.

In practice, it is often difficult to distinguish between genuine contractions of the business and dividend distributions. All dividend distributions reduce the property available to the business and in a general sense result in corporate contractions.

The entire trade or business criterion is more definite. To qualify, a separate business must be transferred to shareholders in liquidation. The transfer of parts of a business such as selected stores or manufacturing facilities will not necessarily qualify.

Most distributions to shareholders do not qualify as partial distributions. For example, corporations routinely receive insurance proceeds from casualty losses and routinely discontinue certain operations. Normally these events do not qualify for partial liquidation treatment.

A Comparison of Dividends, Redemptions, and Partial Liquidations

The Dividend. Dividends are distributions of earnings and profits. If the corporation does not have earnings and profits, the distribution is not taxable as a dividend. With positive levels of earnings and profits, individual shareholders will not usually prefer dividend treatment since the entire amount received is taxable as ordinary income.

Other Types of Distributions. Redemptions and partial liquidations represent returns of investment. These are taxable only to the extent that the distribution exceeds the shareholder's adjusted basis. The gain is taxed as a capital gain, except for the partial liquidation to the corporate shareholder, which receives dividend treatment.

The Redemption. Redemption treatment is available if the distribution is substantially disproportionate across shareholders. The circumstances of the shareholder rather than of the distributing corporation determine eligibility for redemption treatment.

The Partial Liquidation

The Partial Liquidation. Partial liquidation treatment is available to individual shareholders only. Partial liquidations usually represent the disposition of an entire business by a corporation previously operating two or more separate businesses. The situation of the distributing corporation rather than of the shareholder determines whether partial liquidation treatment applies. The distribution can either be to selected shareholders or proportionate to the number of shares held.

The tax on the corporation distributing property is generally the same for a redemption and partial liquidation. The distributing corporation recognizes gain on the appreciation of distributed property. The gain is usually treated as a capital gain subject to recapture provisions.

Individual and corporate shareholders obtain a basis step-up on property received as a property dividend or received in a redemption or partial liquidation. This represents a recent change in the tax legislation with respect to the property dividend. Prior to 1984, the gains on appreciated property were not recognized by the distributing corporation and corporations receiving property dividends obtained a carryover basis for the property.

SUMMARY OF CORPORATE DISTRIBUTIONS TO SHAREHOLDERS

Distribution	Type SH	SH tax	DC tax	Basis of property received
Cash dividend	All	Inc	None	Amount received
Property dividend	All	Inc	Gain	Fair value

(Continued)

Distribution	Type SH	SH tax	DC tax	Basis of property received
Redemption	All	Capital gain	Gain	Fair value
Partial liquidation	Ind	Capital gain	Gain	**Fair value**

NOTE: SH refers to the shareholder
DC refers to the distributing corporation
Inc refers to ordinary income treatment
Ind refers to individual shareholders only

THE COMPLETE LIQUIDATION

In a complete liquidation, the liquidating corporation distributes all property to shareholders and ceases to exist, as shown in Figure 8.4.

Corporations liquidate for a variety of reasons. These include the following:

Creditors sometimes force corporations to dispose of assets and liquidate to satisfy their claims (an involuntary liquidation).

In acquisitions, acquiring corporations sometimes find it advantageous to liquidate the acquired corporation.

Closely held corporations are sometimes liquidated when the owners reach retirement age.

Corporations sometimes find it advantageous to liquidate and continue operating as sole proprietorships or partnerships.

The Complete Liquidation

Before: Corporation
          |
         Shareholders

After: No corporation,
         No shareholders.

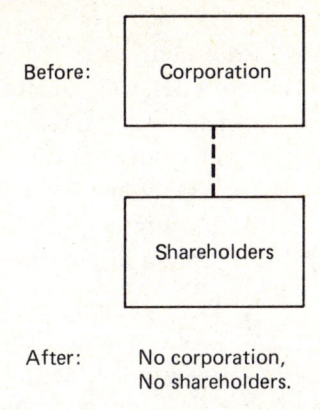

Figure 8.4. The complete liquidation. The corporation distributes all property to shareholders and dissolves.

An involuntary liquidation in bankruptcy is only one of many factors that may motivate the decision to liquidate.

The Tax

The Shareholders. Shareholders receive sale treatment on a complete liquidation. The shareholders turn in their stock and receive the proceeds on liquidation from the corporation. The shareholders then recognize gain on the excess of the amount realized over the adjusted basis of their stock.

If the shareholders receive property, the amount realized is the fair market value of the property. The tax to shareholders is the same as in a sale of stock, a redemption, or a partial liquidation.

The Liquidating Corporation. The liquidating corporation recognizes gain only on depreciation and investment tax credit recaptures and other special items when it distributes property. One special gain item is the difference between the carrying value of LIFO inventory and its carrying value assuming FIFO. Since, as discussed in Chapter 6, LIFO defers taxes relative to FIFO, the tax deferral is eliminated and gain is recognized on distribution of the inventory. Another special gain item applies to the distribution of installment notes receivable. The installment method results in profit deferral. The income is recognized upon distribution of the installment note. Gains are also recognized on the distribution of mortgaged properties, and on distribution of previously expensed items such as supplies (which have no basis to the distributing corporation). The following example illustrates the complete liquidation.

EXAMPLE: THE COMPLETE LIQUIDATION. The Donin Corporation's property consists entirely of land with an adjusted basis of $1000. The fair market value is $5000. Donin liquidates by distributing all property to shareholders. The basis of the stock to shareholders is $3000.

The gain realized by the distributing corporation on liquidation is $4000. This is determined as:

Fair value of property	$5000
Less: Adjusted property basis	1000
Gain on liquidation	$4000

Donin does not recognize any of the realized gain on the liquidation.

The shareholders obtain sale treatment. The gain recognized by shareholders is:

Amount realized	$5000
Less: Adjusted basis of stock	3000
Recognized gain	$2000

The following example illustrates the operation of recaptures in a liquidation.

EXAMPLE: DEPRECIATION RECAPTURE IN A COMPLETE LIQUIDATION. The Donin Corporation's property consists entirely of buildings

The Complete Liquidation

with an original cost of $4000 and accelerated depreciation to date of $3000 (adjusted basis, $1000). The fair market value of the property is $5000. The basis of the stock to shareholders is $3000.

The gain to Donin on liquidation is $4000. This is determined as:

Fair value of property	$5000
Less: Adjusted basis	1000
Gain on liquidation	$4000
Subject to recapture	$3000
Gain not recognized	$1000

Only the recapture is taxable to the distributing corporation. The tax is at ordinary income rates. The recapture results in tax to the corporation at the 46 percent ordinary income rate on $3000, or $1380.

The Donin Corporation example illustrates the importance of recapture in a liquidation. Liquidating corporations have sometimes found themselves with large tax liabilities resulting from recapture or other special-gain items and no resources available to pay the tax. The need for cash to pay taxes is one factor responsible for the sale of property by the corporation to a third party prior to liquidation. This is examined in the next section.

The Sale of Property and Distribution of Proceeds to Shareholders

Liquidating corporations sometimes sell property to a third party and then distribute all property to shareholders in complete liquidation. This procedure may be necessary to provide cash for the tax on recaptures. The sale of property by the distributing corporation may also occur if the corporation receives an offer to buy property while attempting to determine its value. For example, an expert brought in to appraise the property may make an attractive offer to buy it. Also, corporations are often better equipped than individual shareholders to find buyers and negotiate sales.

It may also be more convenient for the corporation to sell property outright rather than attempt to portion it out to shareholders. Additionally, shareholders may not be able to use or store certain property such as locomotives and specialized industrial equipment. As a consequence, it is common for the liquidating corporation to sell some or all property directly.

The Tax Implications. When a corporation sells property and distributes all property to shareholders in complete liquidation within a 12-month period, the distributing corporation does not recognize gain or loss. Only the gains on recaptures and a small number of other special-gain items are subject to tax.

The shareholders recognize gain on the distribution of proceeds received in liquidation in the same manner as with the transfer of property. Both the corporation and shareholders are taxed as though the liquidating corporation distributed the property directly to shareholders.

To qualify for nonrecognition of gain on property sold pursuant to liquidation, the liquidating corporation must sell all property and distribute proceeds to shareholders within a 12-month period. When these conditions are not met, the distributing corporation recognizes gain on the sale of the property in the usual manner. An illustration of the sale of property and distribution of proceeds in complete liquidation follows.

EXAMPLE: THE SALE OF PROPERTY AND DISTRIBUTION OF PROCEEDS IN COMPLETE LIQUIDATION . The Allover Corporation sells all its property consisting exclusively of appreciated land for $5000. The adjusted basis is $1000. The proceeds of the sale are then distributed to shareholders in liquidation.

The Complete Liquidation

If the transaction is treated as an ordinary sale, the tax to the Allover Corporation is determined as:

Amount realized from the sale	$5000
Less: Adjusted basis	1000
Recognized gain	$4000
Tax @ 28 percent	$1120

If the transaction qualifies as a sale of property followed by liquidation of the distributing corporation, the corporation does not recognize gain. The shareholders receive the entire proceeds of the liquidation. The shareholders then apply sale treatment to the amount received in liquidation. The shareholders determine gain as the difference between the amount received in liquidation and the adjusted basis of their shares.

The Sale of Some Property and Distribution of Other Property Directly to Shareholders. The sale of property and distribution to investors within 12 months qualifies for liquidation treatment even if the corporation distributes some property directly to shareholders.

The after-tax proceeds to shareholders are the same for the direct property distribution and for the sale of property with the distribution of proceeds to shareholders. A comparison of the two alternatives follows.

EXAMPLE: PROPERTY VERSUS CASH DISTRIBUTIONS IN COMPLETE LIQUIDATION. The Allover Corporation's property consists entirely of appreciated land with a fair market value of $5000 and an adjusted basis of $1000, as in the earlier example. The shareholders originally paid $2000 for the Allover stock.

If Allover distributes the land to shareholders in liquidation, the shareholders recognize gain as:

Fair market value of property	$5000
Less: Adjusted basis of stock	2000
Recognized gain	$3000
Tax @ 20 percent	$ 600

If Allover sells the land and distributes the $5000 proceeds to shareholders, the shareholders still recognize a gain of $3000, as determined above. The shareholders in this case receive cash instead of land. Allover is not taxed if the transaction qualifies as a sale and liquidation. The tax to the shareholders is $600 in either case.

The sale of property by the corporation in a qualifying sale and liquidation is an alternative to the transfer of property directly to shareholders. The liquidating corporation does not normally recognize gain except for recapture and other special gain items in either case.

The Basis of Property Received in Liquidation

The basis of property received by shareholders in a complete liquidation is the fair market value of the property received. This applies to corporate as well as to noncorporate shareholders. An exception applies to the liquidation of a controlled subsidiary by the parent corporation. The liquidation of a controlled subsidiary is examined in the next section.

Liquidation of a Controlled Subsidiary

The Nonrecognition of Gain. When a parent corporation liquidates a controlled subsidiary, the parent corporation turns in its stock and receives the assets of the subsidiary. The tax treatment in this case differs from the more general treatment applicable to other liquidations. Gain is not recognized by a parent corporation when it liquidates a controlled subsidiary. The reasoning is that the corporation continues to hold the same property—now directly rather than indirectly through the subsidiary.

The Basis. The parent takes the basis of the subsidiary property as its basis in the property when it liquidates the subsidiary (the subsidiary basis carries over to the parent). The parent's basis in the subsidiary stock disappears. This is also consistent with the continuation of property ownership rationale.

EXAMPLE: LIQUIDATION OF A CONTROLLED SUBSIDIARY. The Roughwater Corporation liquidates its subsidiary, the Nomore Corporation, by transferring Nomore's property to itself. The property has a basis of $500 to Nomore. The fair market value of the property is $2000.

Roughwater does not recognize gain on the liquidation. The new basis to Roughwater is Nomore's former basis of $500.

The equity of this approach can be seen by assuming that Roughwater subsequently sells the property for its fair market value. Roughwater will then recognize gain as:

Amount realized	$2000
Less: Adjusted basis	500
Recognized gain	$1500

Nomore would realize the same gain if it sold the property to a third party initially. The liquidation of a controlled subsidiary does not usually provide an opportunity for permanent tax benefit. It merely defers gains on transfers until the property is eventually disposed of to external parties.

Recapture and other special gain items do not apply when a corporation liquidates its controlled subsidiary. The provisions relating to liquidation of a controlled subsidiary prevent the parent corporation from obtaining a basis step-up by liquidating subsidiaries and transferring property to itself.

Losses in Liquidation

When the fair market value of property sold is less than the adjusted basis, a loss results. The liquidating corporation does not recognize either gain or loss in a distribution pursuant to a liquidation. Corporations with loss property usually sell the property outright to recognize the loss. The same consideration applies to the distribution of loss property as a property dividend or in a redemption. Loss property is generally sold rather than distributed to shareholders.

SUMMARY OF CORPORATE DISTRIBUTIONS TO SHAREHOLDERS

Distribution	Type SH	SH tax	DC tax	Basis of property received
Cash dividend	All	Inc	None	Amount received
Property dividend	All	Inc	Gain	Fair value
Redemptions	All	Capital gain	Gain	Fair value
Partial liquidation	Ind	Capital gain	Gain	Fair value

The Complete Liquidation

Distribution	Type SH	SH tax	DC tax	Basis of property received
Liquidation	All	Capital gain	Recap	Fair value
Liquidation controlled subsidiary	Corp	None	None	Old basis

NOTE: SH refers to the shareholder
DC refers to the distributing corporation
Inc refers to ordinary income treatment
Ind refers to individual shareholders only
Recap refers to recapture and other gain items
Corp refers to corporate shareholders only
Old basis includes gain recognized by the DC

The Straddle

Frequently a liquidating corporation will have some property that can be sold for a gain and other property that can be sold at a loss. This provides the opportunity for a straddle.

In a straddle, loss property is sold before the plan of liquidation becomes effective. As a result the distributing corporation recognizes loss on the disposition. Then the gain property can be disposed of free of tax as part of the complete liquidation.

EXAMPLE: THE STRADDLE. The Fedup Corporation liquidates property with a fair market value of $5000 and an adjusted basis of $3000. Part of the property with an adjusted basis of $1500 has a market value of only $800. The remainder of the property can be sold for $4200.

If Fedup transfers all property to shareholders, gain is realized as:

Fair market value of property	$5000
Less: Adjusted basis	3000
Realized gain	$2000

None of the gain is taxable to the corporation in liquidation.

As an alternative, Fedup can employ the straddle. Prior to filing the plan of liquidation, Fedup sells the loss property and realizes a loss as follows:

Amount realized on sale	$ 800
Less: Adjusted basis	1500
Realized loss	$ 700

The loss is then treated the same as any other loss on disposition of fixed assets, as examined in Chapter 4. The loss offsets capital gains, thereby reducing taxable income. If aggregate losses on the disposition of fixed assets exceed aggregate gain on fixed assets, the losses are fully deductible from ordinary income. The $2700 gain on the distribution of the remaining property will be greater in a straddle, but the gain will not be recognized if the property is distributed in complete liquidation (except for recaptures and other special-gain items).

The straddle provides the best of possible situations. Losses are recognized on a property sale. Following this, the corporation commences liquidation and either sells gain property or distributes gain property to shareholders without itself recognizing gain. The IRS examines the straddle closely, but straddles have been successful when the timing of the sale occurs before the commencement of the liquidation.

ADDITIONAL CONSIDERATIONS

Corporations have sometimes liquidated solely to obtain tax benefit. Two devices used for this purpose are the liquidation and reincorporation and the collapsible corporation. Corporations have also bailed out earnings by selling stock to related corporations. Liquidation and reincorporation will now be examined, followed by a look at the collapsible corporation and sale of stock to related corporations.

The Liquidation and Reincorporation

Corporations have sometimes successfully removed earnings from the corporation through a process of liquidation and reincorporation.

How the Liquidation and Reincorporation Works. In a liquidation and reincorporation, the corporation distributes all property to shareholders in complete liquidation. The shareholders recognize gain applying sale treatment. The basis of the property received is its fair market value.

The shareholders keep the cash and contribute the noncash property to a new corporation in exchange for new shares of the corporation's stock.

Shareholder Benefits. One result of the above procedure is the bailout of cash at capital gains rates. A second feature of the liquidation and reincorporation is the step-up in basis of corporate property to its fair market value. This occurs because the basis of the property received by shareholders in liquidation is the fair market value. When the property is contributed to the new corporation, it receives its basis from the basis in the hands of the shareholders—the fair market value. An illustration of a liquidation and reincorporation attempt follows.

EXAMPLE: LIQUIDATION AND REINCORPORATION. The Greatguns Corporation has a long history of successful operations. The shareholder's adjusted basis in the stock is $2000. Greatguns has $2000 in cash and land with a fair market value of $3000. (The combined fair market value of property is $5000.) The adjusted basis of the land is $2000. Greatguns desires to distribute a dividend to its shareholders.

If Greatguns declares a $2000 dividend, shareholders are taxed on the amount received at ordinary income rates. The shareholders net only $1000 after tax at their 50 percent tax rate.

As an alternative, the closely held corporation can liquidate and reincorporate. The stockholders then receive all property in liquidation. The distributing corporation is not taxed. The tax consequences to the shareholders are:

Cash and fair market value of Other property received	$5000
Less: Adjusted basis of stock	2000
Recognized gain	$3000
Tax at 20 percent	$ 600

The shareholders then keep the cash and contribute the property to a new corporation in exchange for new shares of stock.

The liquidation and reincorporation provides two types of benefits to shareholders. First, the tax is reduced on the same amount of the cash distribution (from $1000 to $600). Second, future corporate taxes will be reduced due to the step-up in basis of the property contributed to the corporation (from $2000 to a new basis of $3000). For land or other property not subject to depreciation, the basis step-up reduces the gain on the eventual sale. For depreciable property, the additional depreciation deduction resulting from the basis step-up provides additional tax benefit.

Additional Considerations

The IRS frequently challenges the liquidation and reincorporation. Sometimes the IRS classifies the property distribution as a dividend. In other cases, the IRS prevents the step-up in basis. The liquidation and reincorporation, however, is not always easy to detect. The liquidation and reincorporation is sometimes used successfully if accomplished through a series of involved transactions and if it takes place over a period of time.

The Collapsible Corporation

The collapsible corporation is a corporation that liquidates or is sold before it has realized a substantial portion of the taxable income to be derived from the property.

Background. The collapsible corporation was often used in the motion picture industry. On completion of a motion picture, a film corporation distributed the film rights to shareholders in liquidation. The fair market value of the film rights was established as the amount expected to be received through future rentals. The amount received on liquidation also became the adjusted basis of the film rights to shareholders.

Shareholders were taxed on the distribution at capital gains rates. As the royalties were received from showing the film, the shareholders then amortized the film rights and reduced their adjusted basis. The shareholders did not recognize income because the deduction obtained from the amortization of the film rights was the same as the amount received as royalties. If the total royalties corresponded exactly with the estimates, the adjusted basis was reduced to zero by the time the royalties stopped.

As a result, all of the profits on the film were recognized at the time the film was completed and the original corporation was liquidated. None of the income was recognized at ordinary income rates—it was recognized as a capital gain. Furthermore, the corporation itself recognized no income. Only the shareholders recognized income. Consequently, double taxation was avoided.

The collapsible corporation treatment proved to be highly successful in the motion picture industry and was extended to a variety of other types of businesses.

The Tax. Tax legislation now provides for taxation of gains resulting from the collapsible corporation as ordinary income rather than as capital gains. The gain is taxed as ordinary income either if the shareholder sells the stock or if the corporation distributes its assets in liquidation.

An example of the collapsible corporation applied to the case of land development follows.

EXAMPLE: A COLLAPSIBLE CORPORATION. George Brown forms a corporation and purchases farmland for $100. The corporation improves the land and develops it into building lots with a fair market value of $2100.

If the corporation sells the lots to a single buyer and distributes the proceeds to George in liquidation, the distributing corporation does not recognize income. George receives sale treatment with gain determined as:

Amount received	$2100
Less: Cost of sales	100
Gain	$2000

The shareholder's gain in an ordinary liquidation is taxed at capital gains rates. If the corporation is deemed to be collapsible, however, George's gain is taxed as ordinary income.

If George sells stock in a collapsible corporation for $2100, a $2000 gain would also result. The gain in this case would also be taxed as ordinary income.

When Collapsible Corporation Treatment Applies. Collapsible corporation treatment applies, in general, to property manufactured, constructed, or produced by the taxpayer.

Collapsible corporation treatment does not apply if any of the following conditions are met:

More than two-thirds of the corporation's income potential has been realized.

The property is held for at least three years after the completion of manufacture, production, or purchase.

The property is depreciable business property such as machinery or equipment.

Taxpayers can still receive capital gains treatment by holding property long enough to disqualify the corporation as collapsible.

The Sale of Stock to a Related Corporation

Background. The sale of stock to a related corporation previously provided for the bailout of earnings at little or no immediate tax consequence and with no loss of control. This is now classified as a special type of redemption—a redemption through the use of a related corporation. Specific tax-legislation provisions are designed to eliminate the tax advantage associated with this practice. An illustration of the bailout attempt follows.

EXAMPLE: AN ATTEMPT TO BAIL OUT EARNINGS AT CAPITAL GAINS RATES. Smith owns all the stock in both Corporation X and Corporation Y. The basis of the stock to Smith in each corporation is $300.

Smith now sells the stock in Y to X for $400. Smith receives $400. After the exchange, Smith owns X and X owns Y. (Smith continues to control X and Y.) The important difference is that

Smith receives a distribution of $400 at very little tax cost. The tax is determined as:

Amount realized from X on sale	$400
Less: Adjusted basis in Y	300
Gain recognized on sale	$100
Tax @ 20%	$ 20

The above treatment would apply to sales to unrelated corporations. If the two corporations are related as in this case through common ownership by Smith, Smith would have bailout potential. This would occur because cash would be received at capital gains rates without Smith effectively giving up ownership of Y.

The Related Corporations Rules. The sale of stock to a related corporation now receives special attention in the tax legislation. The amount received by the shareholder is treated as a dividend. The dividend treatment is modified to provide for taxation of the entire amount distributed as ordinary income even if the distribution exceeds accumulated earnings and profits.

This provision also is designed to eliminate the potential tax benefits associated with setting up new corporations without earnings and profits and then selling stock in established corporations to these new corporations. The distribution by the new corporation would not otherwise be taxable as a dividend, since dividends are limited to accumulated earnings and profits. An illustration of the related corporation treatment follows.

EXAMPLE: REDEMPTIONS THROUGH THE USE OF RELATED CORPORATIONS. Smith owns all the stock in both Corporation X and Corporation Y. The basis of the stock to Smith in each corporation is $300. Smith now sells the stock in Y to X for $400, as illustrated in Figure 8.5.

Additional Considerations 259

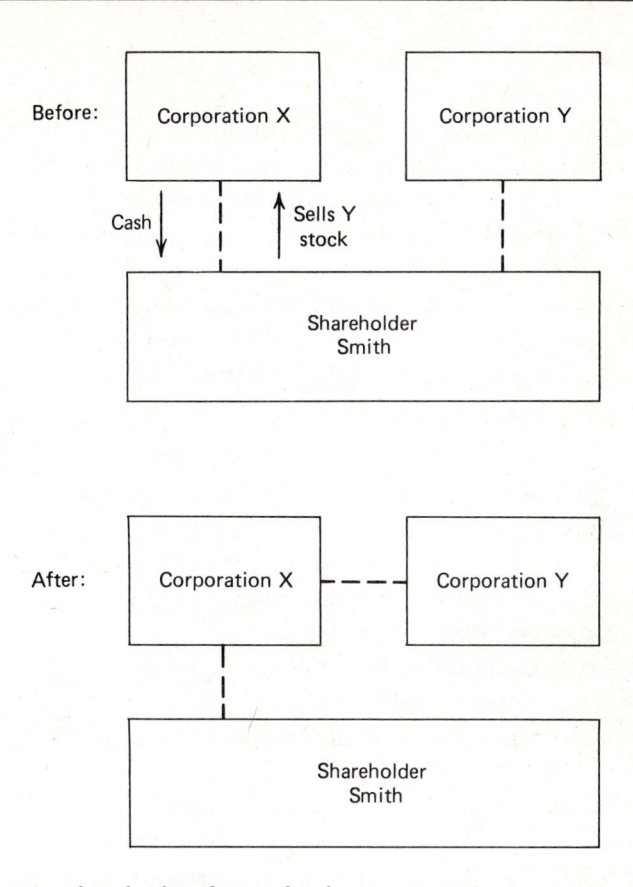

Figure 8.5. The sale of stock to a related corporation. The shareholder sells all Corporation Y stock to Corporation X for cash.

Smith treats the $400 as a dividend in accord with the provisions applicable to sales of stock to related corporations. Corporations X and Y are related by the fact of Smith's effective common ownership of both corporations.

A sale of stock to a related corporation should no longer provide tax benefit, unless the transaction meets the necessary criteria for a redemption—a reduction in interest in both corporations.

SUMMARY

The distinction between the distribution of earnings and other distributions is important because the distribution of earnings is fully taxable. Other distributions usually receive sale treatment.

Shareholders sometimes find it advantageous to attempt to obtain sale treatment while keeping their interest in the corporation. For this reason, specific criteria have been developed to identify transactions eligible for sale treatment. Key nondividend distributions include the stock redemption, the partial liquidation, and the complete liquidation.

The Stock Redemption. A redemption is a sale of stock back to the issuing corporation. The shareholder receives sale treatment. The return of investment is not taxable to the shareholder. The excess of the return over the amount originally invested is taxed at reduced capital gain rates.

A distribution qualifies for redemption treatment if it is not in proportion to the stock held. In other words, a redemption represents a meaningful reduction of the shareholder's proportionate interest in the corporation.

The appreciation of property distributed in redemption is taxable to the distributing corporation. This is the same as for the property dividend on which gains are also now taxable to the distributing corporation.

The Partial Liquidation. A partial liquidation represents a significant reduction in the size of the corporation and the scope of its activity. Noncorporate shareholders receive sale treatment on the receipt of distributions in partial liquidation. The distributions are not taxed except to the extent that they exceed the amounts originally contributed. The additional amount of the distribution is taxed as a capital gain.

Distributions in partial liquidation to corporate shareholders receive dividend treatment. The dividend is subject to the dividends received deduction.

The distributing corporation recognizes gain on the appreciation of property distributed to shareholders in partial liquidation.

The Complete Liquidation. In a complete liquidation, the liquidating corporation distributes all property and ceases to exist. The distributing corporation does not usually recognize gain on liquidation except with respect to recapture and other special-gain items. The shareholders receive sale treatment on a distribution received in complete liquidation.

As an alternative to distributing property directly to shareholders, the liquidating corporation can elect to sell the property and distribute the proceeds in liquidation. The distributing corporation is not taxed on the sale of property except for recaptures and other special-gain items, if the sale and distribution of proceeds to shareholders in complete liquidation takes place within a 12-month period. The shareholders, however, recognize gain on the amount received by them as in the receipt of cash.

Liquidation of a Subsidiary. If a parent liquidates a controlled subsidiary, gain or loss is not recognized. The parent takes the former basis of assets to the subsidiary as its new basis in the acquired assets.

Liquidation and Reincorporation. In a liquidation and reincorporation, the corporation distributes all property to shareholders in complete liquidation. The shareholders recognize gain on the sale. The basis of the property received is its fair market value. The shareholders then keep the cash and contribute the noncash property to a new corporation in exchange for shares of the new corporation's stock.

One result of the above procedure is the bailout of cash at capital gains rates. A second feature of the liquidation and reincorporation is the step-up in basis of corporate property to its fair market value. This occurs because the property contributed to the corporation receives its basis from the basis in the hands of the shareholders—the fair market value.

Liquidation and reincorporation is usually regarded as a device to avoid tax. The legislation and courts discourage liquidation and reincorporation.

The Collapsible Corporation. The collapsible corporation is a corporation that is sold or liquidates before it has realized a substantial portion of the taxable income to be derived from the property. Gains resulting from the collapsible corporation are taxed as ordinary income rather than as capital gains.

Collapsible corporation treatment can be avoided if minimum holding period and income recognition requirements are met.

The Sale of Stock to a Related Corporation. The sale of stock to a related corporation previously provided for the bailout of earnings at little or no immediate tax consequence and with no loss of control. This procedure no longer provides tax benefit. The distribution to the shareholder is taxed as ordinary income.

Chapter 9

The Corporate Form of Organization

Unique opportunities and problems are associated with the corporate form of business. Chapters 7 and 8 focused on dividends and other distributions by the corporation. The shareholder tax on distributions from the corporation leads to the use of mechanisms to reduce or eliminate the double tax on corporate earnings.

This chapter considers additional opportunities and problems. The chapter begins with an examination of the corporation in general—the advantages and disadvantages of the corporate form and why a business might decide to incorporate. The chapter then considers the transfer of property to the corporation. Businesses begin with the investment of capital by owners. The investment of cash does not create tax problems. The contribution of other property, however, may result in taxable gain to the shareholder as in a sale. The chapter examines the general concepts underlying the tax-free contribution of property to the corporation by shareholders.

Following this, the treatment of losses on the disposition of stock in certain small corporations is covered. If both the corporation and the investors in a small corporation meet prescribed criteria, shareholders can sometimes deduct losses on small business stock from ordinary income.

Another topic of interest to many corporations and shareholders is the S corporation. The S corporation election is available to certain closely held corporations. The S corporation's earnings are allocated to shareholders and each shareholder reports his or her proportionate share of corporate earnings as personal income. Consequently, shareholders in an S corporation are not subject to double taxation of corporate earnings. A second important advantage of the S corporation is that corporate losses are passed through to shareholders and reduce shareholder taxable income. Shareholders in regular corporations do not obtain direct tax benefit from corporate losses.

The chapter concludes with the minimum tax and the consolidated tax return. The minimum tax applies to corporations that benefit substantially from investment incentives provided in tax legislation. Corporations that would report considerably higher taxable income if it were not for the effect of deductions resulting from investment incentives may be subject to a minimum tax.

The consolidated tax return election is available to groups of affiliated corporations. The consolidated return includes the income of all controlled subsidiaries and can result in reduced tax. Use of the consolidated return, however, limits the corporation's ability to benefit through loss carrybacks and increases the complexity of tax determination and tax planning.

ALTERNATIVE BUSINESS FORMS

Common forms of business organization include the single owner proprietorship, the multiple owner partnership, and the corporation. The corporate form is elective. The business desiring to incorporate files an application for a charter with the state in which incorporation is desired. Approval of the charter permits the corporation to issue shares of stock.

Advantages of the Corporate Form

Businesses organize as corporations primarily to obtain the advantages of limited liability and to facilitate raising capital. Nearly every business requires capital prior to beginning operations. Additional capital is often needed to finance business growth.

The corporation obtains capital from investors. In exchange, the corporation issues shares of stock in the corporation. The shareholders are the owners of the corporation.

The corporate form facilitates raising capital for a number of reasons including the limited liability of shareholders, the possibility of ownership by small investors, the ease of acquiring and disposing of shares, and possible tax advantages.

Shareholders in the Corporation Have Limited Liability. The corporation is liable for all debts incurred by it. The shareholders themselves, however, are not liable for corporate debts. The result is that shareholders in a corporation can lose only the amount of their investment.

The limited liability feature of the corporation contrasts with the liability associated with the single owner proprietorship or partnership. Individual owners or partners can be assessed for the liabilities of the business. Investors are reluctant to subject themselves to liability for potential business problems when they are not personally involved in the business operation. As a result, investors usually prefer a limited liability situation.

Small Investors Can Purchase Shares. Investors can buy shares in a corporation by contributing only small amounts of capital. Investors desiring to make only a minimal investment may acquire only a few shares of stock. This feature of the corporate form facilitates raising capital because it increases the pool of investors that have the funds to invest.

The ability to acquire only a small amount of ownership also permits investors to remain diversified and not tie up too much capital in a single investment.

Ownership Interests Can be Acquired and Disposed of Easily. If the investor desires to sell shares in the corporation, the disposition can often be accomplished easily and without permission from other shareholders. In many cases, shares trade on the New York Stock Exchange or another organized exchange and may be bought or sold merely by contacting a stockbroker.

In cases of closely held corporations, it may be more difficult to locate buyers and sellers. A sale of shares, however, will often be easier to accomplish than the sale of a partnership interest. The sale of a partnership interest often requires a change in the partnership agreement. This can require the approval of all other partners and may involve extensive legal work.

Tax Advantages. The corporate form may also provide tax advantages to the shareholder. One advantage is that the shareholder is not taxed on corporate income until the corporation distributes something to the shareholder. Partners are taxed on the partnership profits even if none of the profits are distributed to the partners.

The tax implications of the corporate form, however, are complex. Substantial tax penalties including "double taxation" are associated with the corporate form. An additional disadvantage is that shareholders may be taxed on the removal of property that they previously contributed to the coporation. Thus while the corporate form is sometimes beneficial for tax purposes, this is not necessarily the case.

Most large United States businesses are organized as corporations. The advantages of limited liability and greater ease in raising capital are probably responsible for the selection of this business form in the vast majority of cases.

The Rights of Shareholders

The shareholder obtains potentially valuable benefits as a result of investing in the corporation. These include:

> The Right to Share in Corporate Profits. Profit distributions take the form of dividends from the corporation to the shareholder. Profitable corporations may pay dividends if cash is available for this purpose. If the corporation turns out to be extremely profitable, a small investment can provide extremely high returns.
>
> The Right to Vote for the Board of Directors. The board of directors appoints management and oversees the affairs of the corporation. The right to vote for directors permits the shareholder to influence the affairs of the corporation.
>
> The Right to Share in the Proceeds on Liquidation of the Corporation. Shareholders are entitled to the return of part or all of the investment if the corporation decides to liquidate. (This payment assumes, of course, that funds are available after payment to creditors.)

Stock ownership is risky in the sense that dividends depend on earnings and in many cases will never be available to shareholders. Many investors are willing to accept this risk and hope for a high future dividend payout. In some cases, small investments have turned out to be extremely profitable.

The decision to incorporate a business is usually followed by the contribution of capital to the business by shareholders. This capital contribution is examined in the next section.

PROPERTY TRANSFERS BY SHAREHOLDERS

Ordinarily property owners recognize gain or loss on the disposition of property. Gain is not necessarily recognized, however, on the transfer of property to a controlled corporation.

New corporations are often started by incorporating a business previously operated as a proprietorship or partnership. The previous owners transfer title of the machinery, buildings, and other property to the corporation in exchange for stock. The original owners of the property continue to own the property, but now through the corporation. The recognition of gain on the transfer of property to a corporation owned by the taxpayer could discourage the incorporation of businesses seeking limited liability and other advantages of the corporate form. A partnership, for example, may manufacture products in a factory building that has doubled in value since its acquisition. Recognition of gain on the transfer of the building to the new corporation could discourage formation of the corporation. For this reason, relief provisions have been developed that permit the tax-free transfer to a controlled corporation.

Tax legislation protects the shareholder from gain recognition on the appreciation of property contributed to the controlled corporation. Figure 9.1 illustrates the transfer of property to the controlled corporation. The gain is not taxed, because the shareholder has not liquidated the original investment. The reasoning is similar to that underlying the nontaxable exchange (covered in Chapter 4).

The protection from gain recognition, however, does not apply to all exchanges for stock. For example, an attorney may agree to provide legal services in exchange for stock in the corporation. The attorney would recognize taxable compensation based on the fair market value of the stock received. The value of the stock received on the contribution of services to the corporation is taxable to the shareholder as income. The cost of services is not a continuation of an original investment in modified form.

Property Transfers by Shareholders

```
                    ┌──────────────┐
                    │  Corporation │
                    └──────────────┘
           Issues  │                 ▲  Contributes
           stock   ▼                 │  property
                    ┌──────────────┐
                    │ Shareholders │
                    └──────────────┘
```

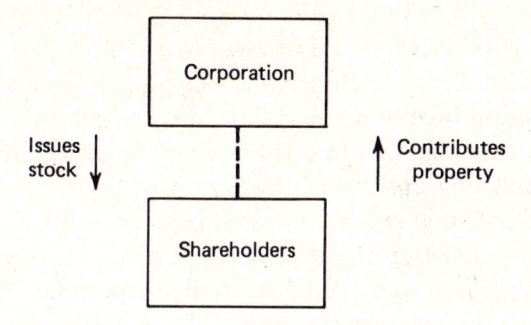

Figure 9.1. Property transfers to the controlled corporation. The gain is not recognized if certain conditions are met.

The Shareholders

Taxable Income. Normally taxable sale treatment applies to contributions of property to a corporation. The shareholder recognizes gain based on the difference between the fair market value of the property and its adjusted basis.

When shareholders transfer property to a controlled corporation, no gain or loss is recognized if the transfer is solely in exchange for stock or securities and the persons transferring property have at least 80 percent control of the corporation immediately after the transfer. If the transfer meets these criteria it is treated as a continuation of the shareholder's original investment in a new form. The increase in property value is not taxable to the shareholder.

The Basis of the Stock. When property is transferred tax-free to a corporation, the shareholder receives stock. The shareholder takes the basis of the property transferred as the basis in the newly received stock. An example of the tax-free transfer follows.

EXAMPLE: THE TAX-FREE TRANSFER OF PROPERTY TO THE CORPORATION. Dorothy Smith, the sole proprietor of a newspaper publishing business, decides to incorporate to obtain the advantage of limited liability. The business assets consist primarily of a building and printing equipment with a fair market value of $2,000,000 and an adjusted basis of $500,000.

Assuming that Dorothy receives only stock in exchange for contributing the newspaper assets to the corporation, the transfer is tax-free to her. Dorothy owns 100 percent of the corporation's stock immediately after the transfer. Her basis in the stock is the $500,000 former basis in the business assets.

If the transaction does not qualify as a tax-free transfer, Dorothy would recognize gain as follows:

Fair market value	$2,000,000
Less: Adjusted basis	500,000
Recognized gain	$1,500,000

Much of the gain in a taxable transaction will be subject to recapture and subject to tax at ordinary income rates since Dorothy is transferring depreciable property.

The rationale for nontaxable treatment stems from the fact that since the transferor owns the corporation's stock immediately after the transfer, the investment is not liquidated. Only the form of the investment changes. The ownership changes from individual ownership to ownership of shares in a corporation.

The transfer to a controlled corporation provisions also apply to transfers by two or more persons. These provisions often come into play when two or more businesses combine interests and form a corporation. The transfer of property by two shareholders is illustrated in the following example.

EXAMPLE: CONTROL BY TWO OR MORE SHAREHOLDERS. Dorothy Smith, the owner of a newspaper, agrees to merge business interests with Tom Jones, the proprietor of a small magazine publishing house. Neither original business is a corporation. Both parties contribute their business property to the new Smith-Jones Corporation in exchange for stock.

This contribution will probably be tax-free to both parties. Both receive only stock for an interest in a company that they jointly control immediately after the exchange.

If property other than cash, stock, or securities is received by the shareholder, this property is treated as boot. If gain is realized, it is recognized to the extent of the boot received (Chapter 4).

Loss Property. The nonrecognition of gain provisions also apply to losses. If loss property is to be transferred, the transferor should consider selling the property at a loss. The transferor can recognize the loss with the associated tax benefits. The corporation should then be able to buy the same property or similar property at its fair market value.

The Corporation

The corporation is not taxed on the receipt of property contributed by shareholders. The basis of the property to the shareholders carries over and becomes the basis to the corporation in the tax-free exchange.

The carryover basis treatment is not advantageous to the corporation in the case of appreciated property. Other factors being equal, it may be beneficial for the corporation to issue stock for cash and use the cash to buy the property, possibly from another supplier. The disadvantage is that the shareholder is then taxed on the gain. The benefits of gain recognition, however, may offset the disadvantages for a low-tax-bracket shareholder.

Evaluation. The provisions for gain recognition apply only to the contribution of property other than cash. The shareholder will never recognize gain on the transfer of cash in exchange for stock.

It is relatively easy for a controlling shareholder to defer gain on the contribution of appreciated property to the corporation. Problems sometimes arise with the contribution of property by a shareholder who does not individually control the corporation. This problem can usually be avoided by ensuring that all major shareholders contribute some property to the corporation at the same time.

ORDINARY LOSS TREATMENT FOR SMALL BUSINESS STOCK

Small business stock refers to the shares of stock held in a qualifying small business corporation. The small business stock provision was designed as an incentive for investors to purchase shares in small (frequently risky) businesses and acts to the benefit of owners of certain small businesses. It should be noted that small business stock is not the same as stock in an S corporation (sometimes called a small business corporation).

As a rule, shareholders realize capital gains on the sale of stock. With qualifying small business stock, shareholder gains are capital gains, but losses are wholly deductible from ordinary income. If the business fails to perform up to expectations, shareholders may deduct losses of up to $50,000 per shareholder as ordinary income. As a result, in the event of gains, shareholders are taxed at a marginal tax rate of only 20 percent. In the event of losses, however, the shareholder deducts the loss from ordinary income and effectively reduces taxes at the 50 percent rate.

This increases the probability of a favorable after-tax return, since the after-tax impact of the loss is reduced. An illustration of small business stock treatment follows.

EXAMPLE: THE INVESTMENT IN SMALL BUSINESS STOCK. James Henry invests $100,000 and receives one-half of the stock of the Everest Building Corporation. The price of the stock later drops and James sells all shares for $60,000. James recognizes a loss of $40,000.

Normally the loss would be a capital loss and helpful for tax purposes only in offsetting capital gains. The offsetting of capital gains usually provides tax benefit only at reduced capital gains rates. Additionally, if current period capital gains are not sufficient, most of the loss will be subject to capital loss carryover rules and may not result in any immediate tax benefit.

The Everest stock seems to qualify as small business stock. In this case, the entire loss is currently deductible from ordinary income.

The small business stock provision applies to the first $1,000,000 of stock issued in the business. If the business later grows, additional amounts of stock do not qualify for small business stock treatment. The advantages of small business stock are restricted to individual shareholders only. Corporations holding stock in a small business cannot benefit from the small business stock designation.

THE S CORPORATION

The S corporation is a regular corporation that receives special tax treatment. The S corporation benefits from limited liability and other advantages of the corporate form, but is not normally subject to tax. Consequently, the S corporation operates as a corporation, but avoids the problem of double taxation.

The S corporation provisions were designed to permit the closely held business to incorporate without incurring tax penalty.

Taxation of the S Corporation and Shareholders

The Tax to the Corporation. The S corporation itself does not normally recognize income. The S corporation income or loss flows through to the shareholder tax returns and contributes to shareholder income.

The Shareholder Tax. S corporation shareholders recognize income or loss on a basis proportionate with their stock ownership. If a shareholder owns half the stock, the shareholder recognizes half of the corporation's income as personal taxable income. The corporation itself, in most cases, does not recognize income or pay tax. Consequently double taxation is not applicable. An example of the profitable S corporation follows.

EXAMPLE: THE S CORPORATION. Mary Jones has taxable income from wages of $50,000. She also owns a one-half interest in an insurance firm which is taxed as an S corporation. The insurance firm earns $60,000.

Mary includes one-half the S corporation income, or $30,000, with her other income. She reports total taxable income of $80,000. The S corporation itself is not taxed.

The Tax Rates. The regular earnings of an S corporation are taxable to shareholders at ordinary income rates.

Income and losses qualifying as capital gains also flow through to shareholders as capital gains or losses. Shareholders are taxed at the preferred capital gains rates on these items. The separate flow-through of ordinary income and of capital gains is illustrated in the following example.

EXAMPLE: THE S CORPORATION WITH TWO SOURCES OF INCOME. The Longline Corporation is an S corporation. Each of two shareholders owns one-half of the corporation's stock. Longline earns $400,000 in 1985. Of this amount, $300,000 is ordinary income and $100,000 represents a long-term capital gain.

Longline does not recognize income. Each shareholder recognizes $150,000 as additional ordinary income and $50,000 as additional capital gains income.

Operating Losses. The flow-through of operating losses to the shareholder is a major advantage of the S corporation. Losses flow through in proportion to shares held in the same manner as income. This is in contrast to the conventional corporation, where losses do not provide immediate benefit to the shareholder.

The amount of the shareholder's investment including loans made to the S corporation limit the amount of the loss flow-through. This provision operates by placing a lower limit on the basis of the S corporation stock to the shareholder. The basis of the stock is increased for earnings and decreased for dividends and loss flow-throughs. The loss limitation provides that loss flow-throughs cannot reduce the combined basis in the stock and loans to the corporation to less than zero. The result is that shareholders sometimes need to make additional contributions to the corporation as stock or loans in order to receive the tax benefit of loss flow-throughs. An illustration of an S corporation with operating losses follows.

EXAMPLE: THE LOSS CORPORATION. Frank Harris invested $10,000 in the Dim Sum Corporation, an S corporation in early

1984. Dim Sum reported operating losses in both 1984 and 1985. Franks's share of the operating losses was $6000 in 1984 and $7000 in 1985.

Frank's personal taxable income is reduced by the $6000 loss flow-through in 1984. Since Frank's investment totaled only $10,000, the 1985 operating loss flow-through is limited to only $4000 ($10,000 less $6000 in 1984). A summary of the losses and amount of loss flow-through follows:

Transaction	Loss flow-through	Basis of stock
Initial investment		$10,000
1984 loss—$6000	$6000	4,000
1985 loss—$7000	4000	0
1985 loss in excess of basis		$ 3,000

Frank can receive tax benefit from the remaining amount of the 1985 loss if he either invests or lends an additional $3000 to Dim Sum in 1985.

Cumulative operating losses in excess of basis can be carried forward by S corporation shareholders until additional investments increase the basis of the investment above zero. The tax benefit of these operating loss carryforwards can be lost on termination of the S corporation election, however, if the basis is not restored to a positive amount before that time.

Distributions of Earnings to Shareholders. The distribution of cash is generally not taxable to shareholders. This is subject to an exception for the S corporation previously taxed as a regular corporation. For example, regular corporations with accumulated earnings and profits may elect S corporation status. The earnings previously accumulated by the new S corporation were previously recognized by the corporation, but not by the shareholders. The S corporation shareholders will recognize income on receipt of any dividends representing pre-S-corporation earnings. An illustration follows.

EXAMPLE: ACCOUNTING FOR EARNINGS DISTRIBUTIONS. The General Manufacturing Corporation has operated as a regular corporation for several years and has accumulated earnings and profits. In 1984 General Manufacturing elected S corporation status. General Manufacturing reported operating losses for 1984 and 1985. In 1985 General Manufacturing distributes cash dividends to shareholders.

The S corporation shareholders deduct their proportionate share of 1984 and 1985 losses. The shareholders also recognize taxable dividend income on the receipt of the dividends in 1985.

Ordinarily the distribution of earnings is not taxable to shareholders because they previously recognized income on the flow-through of earnings. The receipt of dividends is taxable in this case because the earnings were not previously recognized by the shareholders. The income did not flow through to the shareholders because the corporation elected S corporation status subsequent to the time the earnings were reported.

Long-Term Capital Gains. The treatment of long-term capital gains represents an exception to the general rule of no tax to the S corporation itself. Long-term capital gains may be taxable directly to the S corporation if the corporation reports taxable income, the gains are large in comparison to the taxable income, and the corporation has been an S corporation for only a short length of time and is not a new corporation.

The capital gains provision was included to discourage corporations from electing S corporation treatment on a one-time basis to avoid the corporate tax on capital gains.

The reason for special treatment of long-term capital gains and the operation of this provision is shown in the following two examples.

EXAMPLE: DOUBLE TAXATION AND CAPITAL GAINS. The East Bend Corporation has operated for 50 years as a conventional corporation. In 1985 East Bend sells property not subject to depreciation for $5,000,000. The property was originally donated to East Bend by the city as an incentive to locate in the area and has no adjusted basis.

East Bend realizes a gain of $5,000,000. If East Bend is taxed as a conventional corporation, the $5,000,000 gain is taxable at the corporate capital gains rate. The shareholders are then taxed again on any dividends they receive as a result of the distribution.

The capital gains tax to East Bend is 28 percent of $5,000,000, or $1,400,000. The amount available for distribution to shareholders is reduced by the $1,400,000 tax on the gain.

Amount realized from sale	$5,000,000
Less: Tax on gain	1,400,000
Available for dividends	$3,600,000

The amount retained by shareholders is then further reduced by the shareholder tax:

Amount received by shareholders	$3,600,000
Less: Tax on dividends at 50% ordinary income rates	1,800,000
Remaining for shareholders	$1,800,000

Special provisions for the treatment of S corporation capital gains limit the ability of regular corporations to improve their

The S Corporation

tax situation by converting to S corporations for short periods of time. Basically these provide for taxation of certain S corporation long-term capital gains to both the corporation and the shareholder as in a regular corporation. The operation of these provisions is shown in the following example.

EXAMPLE: CAPITAL GAINS AND THE NEW S CORPORATION. The East Bend Corporation has operated for 50 years as a conventional corporation. In 1985 East Bend sells property not subject to depreciation for $5,000,000. The property does not have any adjusted basis. East Bend elects S corporation status just for one year, 1985.

East Bend realizes a gain of $5,000,000. If East Bend elects S corporation status, the $5,000,000 gain to the corporation normally flows through to the shareholders.

The shareholders recognize capital gain taxed at the 20 percent individual taxpayer rate, with 80 percent of the $5,000,000 distribution, or $4,000,000, remaining available for shareholders after tax.

Since East Bend recently elected S corporation status, the tax determination is more complicated. The provision relating to capital gains removes much of the advantage from the "one-shot" S corporation election. If East Bend becomes a S corporation for the year, the gain is taxable to East Bend at corporate capital gains rates. The shareholders are then taxed again on the amount of the gain reduced by the tax paid by the corporation.

The tax is determined as:

Corporate tax on $5,000,000	$1,400,000
Shareholder tax	
Corporation's gain	$5,000,000
Less: Corporate tax paid	1,400,000
Gain to shareholder	$3,600,000
Tax at 50%	$1,800,000

The total tax is $3,200,000. This leaves only $1,800,000 available to shareholders. This is the same amount that would have been available after sale by a regular corporation with double taxation on the amount distributed to shareholders.

It should be noted that the above example is somewhat oversimplified because the S corporation tax on capital gains applies only to gains over a prescribed minimum amount. As a result, there may be a small advantage to the one-shot election.

The provisions relating to capital gains do permit the S corporation shareholders to obtain capital gains treatment on property sales. The special capital gains provisions are intended only to prevent regular corporations from avoiding double taxation on gains by electing S corporation status for years of major asset dispositions. This reasoning is responsible for taxing gains to the corporation only if the corporation has recently elected S corporation status.

Qualifications for S Corporation Treatment

The Criteria. Although S corporations tend to be small, size alone does not determine S corporation eligibility. The number of shareholders and nature of operations are the determining factors. Key qualifications include the following:

The corporation must be a domestic business incorporated in the United States. Foreign corporations do not qualify.

The corporation may have a maximum of 35 shareholders.

The stock must be owned by individuals, estates, or specific types of trusts. The stock may not be owned by corporations, partnerships, or regular trusts.

All shareholders must originally agree to elect S corporation status.

Loss of Election. The election is lost if any of the qualifications for S corporation status are no longer met, or if shareholders holding more than 50 percent of the shares revoke the election.

EXAMPLE: QUALIFICATIONS FOR S CORPORATION STATUS. The Longline Corporation is an S corporation. In 1985, one of Longline's shareholders sells part of her shares to the General Engines Corporation.

Longline is no longer owned entirely by noncorporate shareholders. Longline loses its S corporation status.

Changes in the History of S Corporation Treatment. Prior to 1981, S corporation treatment was not as advantageous. One problem was that the maximum individual tax rates on income were considerably higher than corporate tax rates. (The highest bracket marginal tax rate was 70 percent of taxable income.) Many eligible corporations opted for regular corporation treatment taxable at the lower corporate rate. In 1981, the maximum tax on individual income was reduced to 50 percent.

Also, in 1982, a number of restrictions and tax traps were removed. Previous restrictions sometimes led to taxation of shareholders twice on the same income.

The S corporation can be advantageous in that it minimizes the double taxation problem. The flow-through of operating losses to shareholders can also be important, particularly for the new corporation. New corporations anticipating early-year losses often initially elect S corporation status. The losses are then deductible by shareholders. When the business becomes profitable, the shareholders revoke the election, particularly if the corporation's marginal tax rate is low compared to that of the shareholders.

THE MINIMUM TAX

Corporations with large deductions relative to taxable income can be subject to the minimum tax.

The minimum tax applies to the corporation that has reduced taxable income through the use of tax deductions resulting primarily from investment incentives. The minimum tax increases the likelihood that profitable corporations taking advantage of available investment incentives will pay at least some tax.

The minimum tax is 15 percent of the amount of tax-preference items. The tax only applies to the amount of tax-preference items in excess of the greater of (1) $10,000 or (2) the regular tax for the year less certain credits. Tax-preference items arise through:

> Accelerated depreciation, depletion, and amortization in excess of that applicable using the straight-line method for real estate, mineral rights, and pollution control facilities.
>
> Bad debt deductions of financial institutions in excess of actual loss experience. Banks may sometimes take bad debt deductions in excess of their actual loss experience. The additional tax benefit is a tax preference item.
>
> A portion of the excess of net long-term capital gains over net short-term losses. Net long-term capital gains receive favorable tax treatment. A portion of this amount is classified as a tax-preference item.

The minimum tax is an add-on tax. This tax is in addition to the regular tax liability. An example follows.

EXAMPLE: THE MINIMUM TAX. The Turtle Corporation reports taxable income of $700,000 and a regular tax of $300,000. Turtle does not qualify for any tax credits. Included among the deductions is $5,000,000 for ACRS depreciation on real estate. The straight-line depreciation would have been only $3,000,000.

Turtle has $2,000,000 in tax-preference items. This amount is determined as the excess of accelerated depreciation over straight-line depreciation on the real estate.

The $2,000,000 in preference items exceeds the $300,000 regular tax by $1,700,000. The add-on minimum tax is 15 percent of this excess, or $255,000. The total tax is:

Regular tax	$300,000
Minimum tax	255,000
Total tax	$555,000

The minimum tax only applies to those corporations with large amounts of tax preferences. The tax, however, can be significant for these businesses, and particularly for expanding businesses that make heavy use of investment incentives such as ACRS depreciation.

THE CONSOLIDATED TAX RETURN

The consolidated tax return is a relief provision available to certain related corporations. A parent–subsidiary group may elect to file one consolidated tax return in lieu of separate tax returns for each individual corporation. The consolidated entity is then taxed as a single corporation.

Advantages

One advantage of the consolidated return is that operating losses of some affiliated corporations are offset against gains of other affiliated corporations. An illustration of the advantageous use of a consolidated return follows.

EXAMPLE: THE ADVANTAGE OF THE CONSOLIDATED RETURN. Corporation A recognizes taxable income of $25,000,000. Corporation B, a subsidiary, has a long history of losses. The current year loss is $20,000,000.

If Corporations A and B file separate returns, A is taxed on the $25,000,000 earnings. B receives no immediate tax benefit, assuming that loss carryback eligibility is exhausted.

If A and B file a consolidated return, consolidated taxable income is:

Corporation A	$25,000,000
Corporation B	(20,000,000)
Consolidated taxable income	$ 5,000,000

With the consolidated return, taxable income is reduced to only $5,000,000.

A second advantage of the consolidated return relates to the elimination of gains on sales to other members of the group. Income is determined only on sales outside the group. Sales by a parent corporation to a consolidated subsidiary corporation are not subject to tax. This is shown in the following illustration.

EXAMPLE: THE CONSOLIDATED RETURN AND INTERCOMPANY SALES. The Hi Test Corporation operates a number of petroleum refineries. Hi Test also operates the Chemplex Corporation as a subsidiary corporation. Chemplex packages and markets chemicals obtained as a by-product of the refining process.

Chemplex bought raw materials from Hi Test during Chemplex's first year of operation. Hi Test's profit on these purchases was $500,000. Chemplex repackaged the products and sold half of the chemicals to outside buyers.

If Hi Test and Chemplex are taxed as two separate corporations, all $500,000 of Hi Test's profit on the sales to Chemplex represent taxable income to Hi Test. This includes the profit on goods not yet sold by Chemplex.

If Hi Test and Chemplex file a consolidated return, the intercompany sales revenue is not recognized until Chemplex sells the remaining product to outside parties.

The ability to defer profits on intercompany sales serves as a very significant advantage of the consolidated return.

The consolidated return may also provide increased opportunities to take advantage of the investment tax credit and other deductions and credits. Additional investment tax credits, for example, are not beneficial to loss corporations. If profit and loss corporations consolidate, all credits may be taken as long as the consolidated entity as a whole is sufficiently profitable.

Disadvantages

The consolidated return is not always advantageous. One problem occurs when some member corporations have operating loss carryback eligibility. If the consolidated corporation is profitable, the carryback eligibility of individual group members cannot be utilized. The problem in a carryback situation is illustrated in the following example.

EXAMPLE: THE LOSS CARRYBACK AND THE CONSOLIDATED RETURN. Corporation A reports a 1985 loss of $100,000. Corporation A is eligible to carryback the entire amount of the loss and file for a refund of taxes previously paid on $100,000 of taxable income. Corporation B reports a 1985 gain of $400,000. A and B file a consolidated tax return.

The consolidated taxable income is $300,000. Since the result is a positive income amount, corporation A cannot claim the refund on the loss carryback.

A second disadvantage of the consolidated return relates to the complexity of the consolidated tax situation. Extra cost and time are needed to determine the tax. Tax planning also becomes more involved as the tax situation applicable to the entity as a whole must be considered whenever planning alternatives are evaluated.

Eligibility

A parent–subsidiary affiliated group may elect to file on a consolidated basis if the parent controls the subsidiary. Foreign corporations and certain other types of corporations with special tax circumstances cannot be included in consolidated returns.

SUMMARY

The Corporate Form of Organization. Businesses organize as corporations because of the limited liability feature and because the corporate form facilitates raising capital. The corporation usually finds it easier than the partnership to raise capital because the liability of shareholders is limited, small investors can more easily acquire ownership interests, and in many cases, investors can easily sell and purchase shares.

Tax considerations can also motivate a business to incorporate, but incorporation may not be advantageous for tax purposes because of the double taxation problem.

The Rights of Shareholders. Shareholders invest in corporations for a variety of reasons. These include the right to share in corporate profits, the right to vote, and the right to share in the proceeds upon liquidation of the corporation.

Property Transfers to the Controlled Corporation. Gain is not recognized on property transfers that are solely in exchange for stock or securities by persons who control the corporation. This type of transfer is treated as a continuation of the shareholder's original investment in a new form.

When property is transferred tax-free to a corporation, the shareholder receives stock. The shareholder takes the basis of the property transferred as the basis in the newly received stock.

If the transferrers do not control the corporation, they recognize gain on the transfer as on a sale. The transferrers also recognize gain if they contribute services to the corporation for stock or if they receive cash or other property from the corporation in addition to stock.

Ordinary Loss Treatment for Small Business Stock. Small business stock pertains to investments in certain small corporations by certain types of shareholders. When qualifying small business stock is sold, shareholder gains are capital, but losses are wholly deductible from ordinary income. Losses up to $50,000 are deductible by each shareholder in a small business corporation as ordinary income.

The S Corporation. The S corporation is a regular corporation that receives different tax treatment. The S corporation provisions were designed to permit the closely held business to incorporate without incurring tax penalty. The S corporation election permits the business to operate as a corporation and at the same time avoid the problem of double taxation. A second important advantage is that losses in an S corporation flow through directly to shareholders.

The S corporation itself does not normally recognize income. The income or loss of the S corporation flows through directly to the shareholder tax returns and contributes to shareholder income. Shareholders of the S corporation recognize income or loss on a basis proportionate with their stock ownership.

Income and losses qualifying as capital gains also flow through to shareholders as capital gains. Shareholders are taxed at the preferred capital gains rates on these items.

The distribution of cash is generally not taxable to shareholders. One exception concerns regular corporations with accumulated earnings and profits that elect S corporation status.

Although most S corporations tend to be small, size alone does not determine S corporation eligibility. The number of shareholders and nature of operations are the determining factors. The corporation must be a domestic business with a maximum of 35 shareholders. None of the shareholders may be a corporation.

The Minimum Tax. The minimum tax applies to corporations with large amounts of tax preferences relative to taxable income. Tax preferences arise primarily through the benefit of capital gains, accelerated depreciation, and other investment incentives. The minimum tax is an add-on tax—it is in addition to the regular tax. The minimum tax may be particularly significant in the case of expanding corporations with low taxable income and large tax preferences.

The Consolidated Return. The consolidated entity is taxed as a single corporation rather than taxed separately as individual corporations. With a consolidated return, operating losses of some member corporations are offset against gains of other member corporations.

The consolidated return also eliminates gains on sales to other members of the group. Income is determined only on sales outside the group. This can reduce taxable income substantially for affiliated corporations that regularly transact business with each other.

Disadvantages of the consolidated return include the inability to benefit from loss carrybacks in cases where the consolidated entity as a whole is profitable, and the increased complexity of accounting and tax planning.

Chapter 10

Corporate Acquisitions

Corporations acquire other businesses for a variety of reasons. These include the desire to grow, to diversify, to obtain operating efficiencies, and to obtain improved distribution for products.

These corporate acquisitions are of particular tax interest because the amount of the tax can be substantial and because small differences either in the form of the transaction or in the intent of the parties can determine the tax consequences. Additionally, the interests of the acquiring corporation are usually totally opposed to the interests of the acquired corporation or its shareholders. When the form of the transaction produces favorable tax consequences for the acquiring corporation, the impact upon the acquired corporation or its shareholders tends to be adverse.

Common forms of acquisition include the purchase of either assets or stock. Assets are purchased directly from the acquired corporation. The transaction is sometimes taxable to the seller at capital gains rates and sometimes as ordinary income. Buyers often prefer the purchase of assets because it results in a basis step-up. Buyers also favor assignment of a high proportion of the selling price to inventories and depreciable assets. Sellers, on the other hand, favor the allocation of purchase price to land, goodwill, and other items taxable at capital gains rates.

With a purchase of stock, the selling shareholder recognizes gain. The buyer obtains a carryover basis for the acquisition. The buyer may elect to step up the basis of assets immediately after acquisition, but this may entail the recognition of gains on the part of the buyer.

This chapter examines acquisitions of assets and stock of other corporations and illustrates the concepts cited above. Corporations can also acquire other corporations in a tax-free transaction. The tax-free reorganization will be considered in Chapter 11.

FORMS OF ACQUISITION

Corporate acquisitions take a variety of forms. One general method of acquisition is the purchase. In a purchase the acquiring corporation can purchase either the assets of the acquired corporation or its stock. In either case, the acquiring corporation will obtain additional assets, additional income, and other benefits of ownership.

In an asset acquisition, the assets are obtained from the acquired corporation. If stock is purchased, the stock is obtained from the acquired corporation's shareholders.

The acquiring corporation gives cash, other property, its own stock, or some combination of these in exchange. Unique tax consequences are associated with the following general forms of acquisition:

The purchase of assets (for cash).

The purchase of stock (for cash).

The acquisition of assets or stock in exchange for stock.

An illustration of the purchase of assets follows.

EXAMPLE: AN ACQUISITION BY PURCHASE. The New Frontier corporation acquires the Lowsale Corporation's assets including factories, offices, and inventories by paying cash to Lowsale.

This is a purchase of assets for cash. New Frontier, the acquiring corporation, obtains Lowsale's assets. Lowsale continues to exist as a separate corporation with only one asset—the cash received from New Frontier. Lowsale is free to distribute the cash to shareholders and liquidate or to use the cash to acquire new assets and continue in business.

The exchange of stock operates differently. Following is an example of the exchange of stock for stock.

EXAMPLE: AN ACQUISITION OF STOCK FOR STOCK. The New Frontier Corporation acquires the Lowsale Corporation's common stock from Lowsale's shareholders. New Frontier gives 10,000 shares of its own common stock to Lowsale's shareholders in exchange.

This is an exchange of stock for stock. New Frontier now controls Lowsale. The expanded New Frontier Corporation is now owned jointly by its original shareholders and the former shareholders of Lowsale.

The remainder of this chapter concentrates on the first case, the acquisition by purchase. Particular emphasis is directed to the basis of assets to the buyer, the allocation of purchase price, and the role of recaptures.

THE PURCHASE OF ASSETS

If payment is primarily in the form of cash or property other than the acquiring corporation's stock, the acquisition is referred to as a purchase. The purchase is not normally taxable to the acquiring corporation.

A purchase by one party involves a sale by the other. The corresponding sale is taxable to the seller assuming that it results in the recognition of gain. The taxable gain is based on the difference between the proceeds on the sale and the adjusted basis of the property sold.

In a purchase, the buyer acquires either the assets of the acquired corporation or its stock. Assets include cash, receivables, inventory, equipment, real estate, and other property. In a purchase of assets, the acquired corporation is the seller. The acquired corporation, in this case, receives cash or other consideration and ceases to be a party to any future transactions. Only those assets and liabilities specifically provided for in the purchase agreement are transferred. The buyer is protected against assuming hidden liabilities.

In a stock purchase, the buyer deals with the acquired corporation's shareholders. The buyer may negotiate with the shareholders or may merely buy available shares on the market. The acquired corporation itself is not involved directly. The acquired corporation retains its identity unless the buyer chooses to liquidate the acquired corporation and take title to its assets.

The Buyer

The buyer is never taxed on a purchase of assets. The buyer carries assets acquired by purchase at their purchase price (fair market value).This serves as the basis for depreciation and for future gain or loss on the sale. The purchase of assets is illustrated in Figure 10.1.

The Seller

The seller receives sale treatment and recognizes gain or loss in the normal manner on the sale of assets (Chapters 4 and 5). The purchase of assets is illustrated in the following example.

The Purchase of Assets

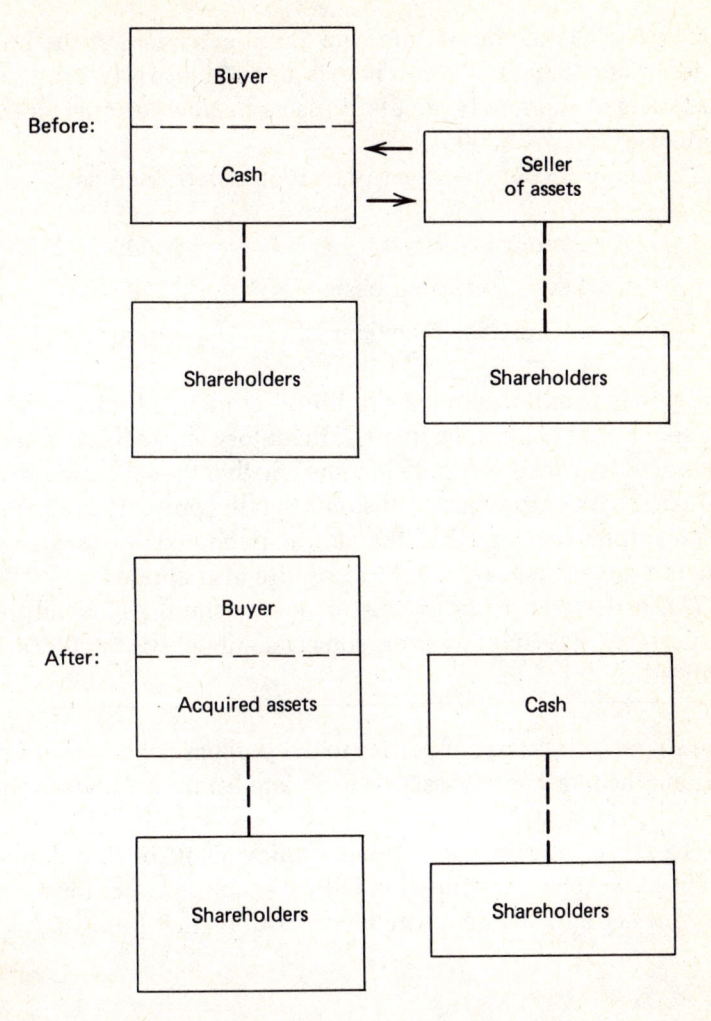

Figure 10.1. The purchase of assets. The acquiring corporation gives cash to the selling corporation.

EXAMPLE: THE PURCHASE. The New Frontier Corporation acquires the assets of the Lowsale Corporation for $3000. Lowsale's assets consist entirely of land, with an adjusted basis $2000.

Lowsale's land comes onto New Frontier's books at the purchase price of $3000. The purchase is not taxable to New Frontier. The basis of the newly acquired assets to New Frontier is the purchase price of $3000.

The seller recognizes a gain of $1000 determined as:

Amount realized	$3000
Less: Adjusted basis	2000
Gain recognized on sale	$1000

The gain is a capital gain if the holding period is sufficient and if the seller did not hold the items as inventory for resale. The gain on inventory sale is ordinary income whether the sale is made to a single buyer or to separate customers. If the property is subject to recapture, part or all of the gain may be taxed as ordinary income. Investment tax credit recapture also applies.

The seller continues to exist as a corporation. The selling corporation's assets, however, consist solely of the $3000 cash realized on the sale.

The shareholders are not parties to the purchase of assets transaction. The purchase of assets is negotiated entirely between the two corporations.

The sale of all assets is frequently followed by the liquidation of the seller. This complication will be examined after the summary of tax effects in corporate acquisitions that follows.

SUMMARY OF CORPORATE ACQUISITIONS

Transaction	A tax	B tax	B SH tax	Basis to A
Purchase assets	**None**	**Gain**	**None**	**Fair value**

NOTE: A is the acquiring corporation
B is the acquired corporation

The Sale of Assets Followed by Liquidation of the Seller.
The sale of property can result in double taxation. Generally gains on the sale of property are taxable. Double taxation results when the acquired corporation sells assets (and pays tax) and distributes the proceeds to shareholders. The shareholders are again taxed on the distribution by the corporation. This amounts to a 73 percent tax on the gain (46 percent to the corporation plus one-half of the remaining 54 percent), as discussed in Chapter 7. A major challenge to the seller's shareholders is to ensure that the gains are not taxed twice.

Double taxation can be avoided if the acquired corporation prepares a plan of liquidation and disposes of all assets (as described in Chapter 8). The usual procedure is to sell the assets and distribute the proceeds to the shareholders in a qualifying sale and liquidation, as illustrated in Figure 10.2. If the distribution is completed within 12 months of the date of the plan of liquidation, only the shareholders are subject to tax on any gain realized by them. The liquidating corporation does not usually recognize gain with the exception of recapture (see Chapter 8). The sale of assets followed by liquidation is illustrated in the following example.

EXAMPLE: THE SALE OF ASSETS FOLLOWED BY LIQUIDATION. The Lowsale Corporation sells land with a basis of $2000 to the New Frontier Corporation for $3000. The basis of Lowsale's stock to its shareholders is $2000. Lowsale then liquidates by distributing all proceeds to shareholders.

Lowsale does not recognize gain and is not taxed on the sale. Lowsale's shareholders are taxed when they receive cash in exchange for their shares (liquidation of the corporation). Lowsale's shareholders recognize gain as:

Amount received on liquidation	$3000
Adjusted basis of stock	2000
Gain on sale	$1000

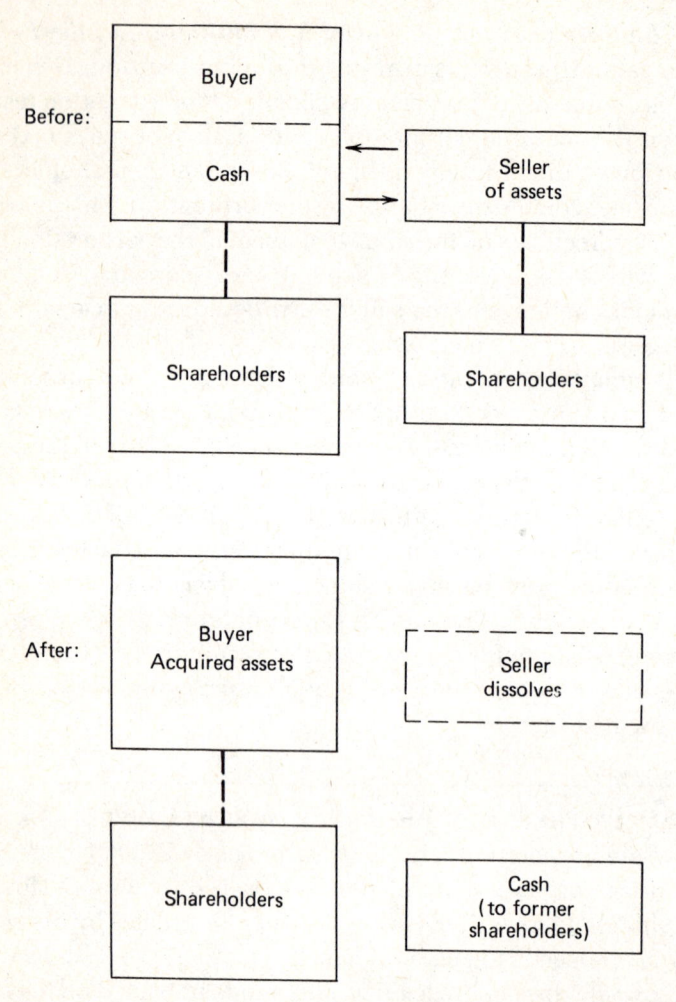

Figure 10.2. The purchase of assets followed by liquidation of the selling corporation.

If the sale of property and transfer of proceeds to shareholders does not qualify for liquidation treatment, both the corporation and the shareholders recognize taxable gains.

The Sale of Assets by Shareholders. As an alternative to sale by the corporation in liquidation, the corporation can distribute the assets to shareholders in liquidation. The shareholders may then sell the assets to the acquiring corporation.

In both cases, the acquired corporation itself does not recognize gain other than that associated with recapture and other special-gain items. (The recognition of gain by the distributing corporation on liquidation is examined in Chapter 8.) The shareholders recognize capital gain on the excess of the fair market value of the property received over the adjusted basis of their stock. The fair market value of the property then becomes the new basis to the shareholders. The shareholders will not recognize additional gain if they later sell the property for the original amount realized, since the selling price will be the same as the basis.

The shareholder tax is the same in the liquidation and sale of assets by shareholders and in the sale of assets by the corporation followed by the distribution of proceeds to shareholders.

Recapture. Recapture applies whenever property subject to depreciation or amortization is sold (Chapter 5). If the corporation sells the assets, recapture applies to the corporation. If the corporation distributes the property to shareholders and liquidates, recapture still applies. In other words, recapture cannot be avoided by transferring property to shareholders. The operation of recapture in a sale of assets situation is shown in the following example.

EXAMPLE: THE SALE OF ASSETS FOLLOWED BY LIQUIDATION WITH RECAPTURES. The New Frontier Corporation buys the assets of Lowsale for $3000, as in the previous example. Lowsale's assets consist of depreciable machinery with a basis of $2000 ($2300 cost less $300 accumulated depreciation). The basis of the stock to Lowsale's shareholders is $2000.

New Frontier carries the newly received assets at the fair market value of $3000. New Frontier is not taxed on the purchase. The basis for future depreciation is $3000. Lowsale realizes a $1000 gain. The gain is recognized, however, only on the $300 recapture. The tax at ordinary income rates is $138.

Lowsale's shareholders will receive only $2862 of the proceeds on sale since Lowsale pays $138 corporate tax on the $300 gain. Lowsale's shareholders recognize gain as:

Amount realized	$2862
Less: Adjusted basis of stock	2000
Gain on sale	$ 862

Assuming individual shareholders holding stock for more than one year, this gain is taxable at the 20 percent capital gains rate. The tax is 20 percent of $862, or $172.

The total tax to the selling corporation and its shareholders is:

Tax to Lowsale	$138
Tax to Lowsale shareholders	172
Total	$310

If the acquired corporation does not liquidate, the corporation's tax is usually increased because the full amount of the gain is taxable. An updated summary of the tax impacts of corporate acquisitions follows:

SUMMARY OF CORPORATE ACQUISITIONS

Transaction	A tax	B tax	B SH tax	Basis to A
Purchase assets	None	Gain	None	Fair value

Transaction	A tax	B tax	B SH tax	Basis to A
Purchase assets, B liquidates	None	Recap	Gain	Fair value

NOTE: A is the acquiring corporation
B is the acquired corporation

The above summary indicates that with the purchase of assets, the acquiring corporation is never taxed. The acquired corporation can avoid tax except with respect to recaptures on the gain if it distributes the proceeds to shareholders in liquidation. In this case, the shareholders are subject to tax on their gains.

The Allocation of Purchase Price

In a sale of assets, it is common practice to negotiate the total selling price of the business. For tax purposes it is then necessary to allocate the overall selling price to individual property items. These allocations are important to the buyer because the basis of acquired property determines future depreciation and the eventual gain or loss on the sale. The seller is concerned with the allocation of purchase price because it directly impacts upon the tax on the sale.

Depreciation and Recaptures. The buyer generally prefers to allocate the purchase price to depreciable property such as equipment. This provides increased depreciation deductions during the holding period or if the holding period is short, reduces the gain on sale. The seller's interests are directly opposed. The seller prefers allocation to land, goodwill, and other items that result in capital gains with no recapture when sold. These items are not depreciable by the buyer for tax purposes. An illustration of the importance of purchase price allocation follows.

EXAMPLE: THE ALLOCATION OF PURCHASE PRICE. The New Frontier Corporation buys the assets of the Lowsale Corporation for $3000, as in the previous example. Lowsale's assets consist of depreciable machinery with a basis of $2000 ($2300 cost less $300 accumulated depreciation). The basis of the stock to Lowsale's shareholders is $2000.

New Frontier asserts that the acquired equipment has a fair market value of $3000. Lowsale maintains that the equipment is worth only $2000 and that the remainder of the purchase price represents goodwill.

The New Frontier proposal:

	Equipment	Goodwill
Amount realized	$3000	$ 0
Adjusted basis	2000	0
Gain on sale	$1000	$ 0

New Frontier will carry the equipment at $3000. Lowsale recognizes $300 gain on recapture equal to the amount of depreciation previously taken. This proposal is more advantageous to New Frontier because it results in a higher basis for depreciation. The problem is that Lowsale is taxed on recapture.

Lowsale's proposal:

	Equipment	Goodwill
Amount realized	$2000	$1000
Adjusted basis	2000	0
Gain on sale	$ 0	$1000

In this case, New Frontier will record the equipment at only $2000. New Frontier assigns $1000 of the purchase price to goodwill. None of Lowsale's gain on sale is subject to recapture, since goodwill is not depreciated for tax purposes.

Goodwill represents part of the excess of the purchase price over the fair market value of the acquired assets. The problem with goodwill from the buyer's view is that it is not subject to depreciation.

In cases where the seller agrees not to set up a competing business for a period of time, part of the excess of selling price can be assigned to a covenant not to compete. The covenant not to compete is subject to amortization and is deductible by the buyer. The problem from the seller's view is that the sale of the covenant is taxed at ordinary income rates.

Allocations to Inventories. The allocation between items taxable at capital gains rates and inventories is also important. The sale of inventory is taxed as ordinary income. When inventory is included in a sale of assets, the sellers prefer to assign a low basis to inventory because the sale of merchandise is taxable as ordinary income. The seller prefers proportionately more cost allocation to items taxable to the seller at capital gains rates.

The buyer prefers to maximize the allocation to inventory. A high basis for inventory reduces the buyer's taxable profit when the inventory is later resold.

The timing of the deductions is also important to the buyer. The tax savings resulting from a reduced profit on the merchandise resales provides current-year benefit to the buyer. The tax savings resulting from additional depreciation will be recognized gradually since depreciation takes place over a relatively long period of time. As a consequence, the buyer may prefer to allocate more of the purchase price to inventory than to depreciable property. The same reduction in taxable income occurs. The deduction, however, takes place earlier in the case of merchandise sales.

Ideally, the allocation of purchase price should be established such that the present value of the combined buyer and seller tax payments is minimized. If this is done, the selling price may need to be adjusted to compensate one of the parties for additional tax payments.

The IRS tends to accept reasonable purchase price allocations included in the contract of sale and used by both parties. In the absence of such an agreement, the IRS may suggest its own allocations.

THE PURCHASE OF STOCK

Corporate acquisitions accomplished through the purchase of stock are also common. In a purchase of stock, the buyer usually deals with the acquired corporation's shareholders. The management of the acquired corporation need not be a party to the transaction. The purchase of stock is illustrated in Figure 10.3.

Stock is often acquired when:

The acquired corporation's management does not approve of the takeover.

The acquired corporation must retain its corporate identity to retain a franchise or other benefit.

The acquired corporation is carrying forward previous operating losses. These would be lost with the purchase of assets (the carryover of operating losses will be examined later in this chapter).

The sellers prefer a sale of stock for their own tax reasons.

The Acquired Corporation and Its Shareholders

The Acquired Corporation. The acquired corporation continues to operate as a separate corporation (controlled by the acquiring corporation). The acquired corporation does not sell property, and consequently never recognizes gain. The acquired corporation operates as a subsidiary and keeps its own set of books. The acquired corporation may continue to file its own tax return, or the acquiring corporation may file a consolidated tax return for the combined entity.

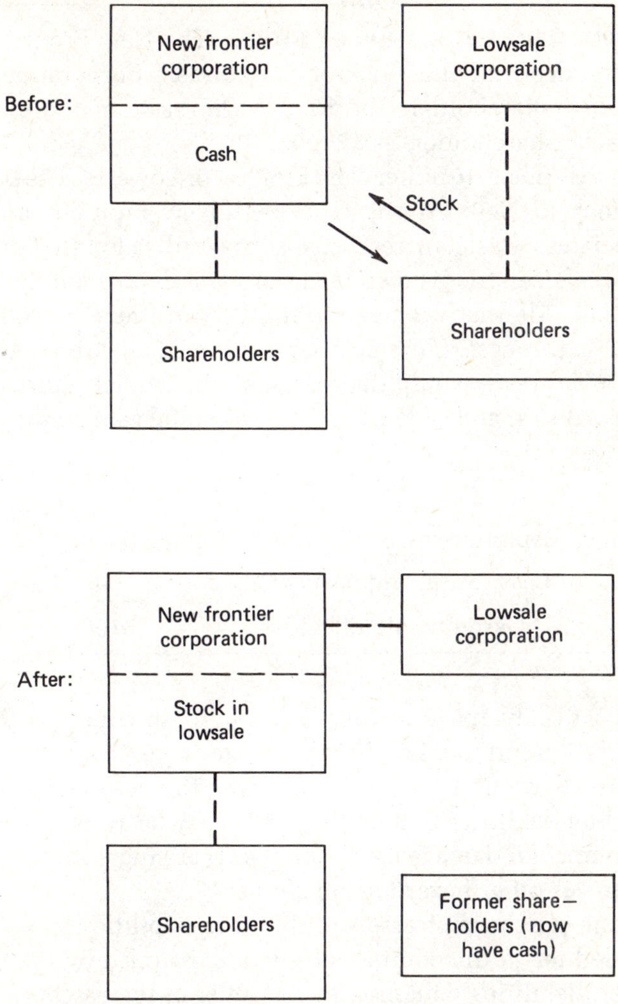
Before:
New frontier corporation
Cash
Lowsale corporation
Stock
Shareholders
Shareholders
After:
New frontier corporation
Stock in lowsale
Lowsale corporation
Shareholders
Former share—holders (now have cash)

Figure 10.3. The purchase of stock. The acquiring corporation purchases stock from the acquired corporation's shareholders.

The Shareholders. The acquired corporation's shareholders sell their stock. They recognize capital gain on the sale. The acquisition of stock is shown in the following example.

EXAMPLE: THE ACQUISITION OF STOCK. The New Frontier Corporation acquires the stock of the Lowsale Corporation from Lowsale's shareholders for $3000. The basis of the stock to Lowsale's shareholders is $2000.

There is no tax to either New Frontier or Lowsale. The basis of the stock to New Frontier is $3000. New Frontier does not depreciate Lowsale's assets because they still belong to Lowsale.

Lowsale can file its own tax return and depreciate the assets as before. Alternatively, New Frontier can file a consolidated return. In this case, Lowsale's depreciation deduction is still the same as Lowsale would deduct on an individual return.

Lowsale's shareholders recognize a capital gain on the sale of stock.

Amount realized	$3000
Less: Adjusted basis of stock	2000
Gain on sale of stock	$1000

A chief disadvantage of the stock purchase concerns the acquired corporation's liabilities. In a stock purchase, the buyer obtains all property and also receives the seller's liabilities, including liabilities that neither party may be aware of such as environmental damage claims or claims arising from the use of asbestos or other hazardous materials.

In the purchase of assets, only those liabilities specifically provided for in the contract of sale are assumed by the buyer. Hidden liabilities remain with the seller of the assets.

SUMMARY OF CORPORATE ACQUISITIONS

Transaction	A tax	B tax	B SH tax	Basis to A
Purchase assets	None	Gain	None	Fair value

Transaction	A tax	B tax	B SH tax	Basis to A
Purchase assets, B liquidates	None	Recap	Gain	Fair value
Purchase stock	**None**	**None**	**Gain**	**Carryover**

NOTE: A is the acquiring corporation
B is the acquired corporation

The Buyer

When stock is acquired, the acquiring corporation carries the cost of the stock as an investment. The buyer is not taxed on the acquisition.

Operating Loss Carryforwards. Operating loss carryforwards result from operating losses not carried back against previous-period taxable income. This occurs when losses exceed carryback eligibility. (Loss carrybacks and carryforwards were explained in Chapter 2.)

Operating loss carryforwards of the acquired corporation sometimes serve as an important motivation for an acquisition. The possibility of reducing future taxes as a result of the carryforward can help to make a loss corporation an attractive acquisition target.

The provisions relating to retention of operating loss carryforwards in acquisitions are involved because they are determined largely by case law. In very simple form:

Carryforwards do not come with the purchase of assets. They remain with the acquired corporation. If the acquired corporation liquidates, the carryforwards are lost. The reasoning is that only the assets are acquired, not the corporation itself.

Carryforwards are lost if a stock purchase is followed by the election to step-up basis (the basis step-up is discussed later in this chapter).

Carryforwards are still available to the acquired corporation if its stock was acquired and the acquired corporation continues to operate as a separate corporation. In this case, the original corporation remains intact.

Carryforwards may be available if the acquisition is by tax-free reorganization (tax-free reorganization will be discussed in Chapter 11).

There are many ways for the buyer to use the seller's carryforwards. One of the simplest mechanisms is for the buyer to buy stock in a loss corporation. The buyer might then transfer a business to the loss corporation that is sufficiently profitable to ensure that the newly expanded acquired corporation reports a profit. The loss carryforwards will offset the taxable income of this profitable corporation.

The summary of key tax implications includes an indication of the ability of the acquired corporation to retain operating loss carryforwards as indicated above. The acquired corporation's operating losses are never carried forward in a purchase of assets. It is sometimes possible to carry forward operating losses, however, with a purchase of stock.

SUMMARY OF CORPORATE ACQUISITIONS

Transaction	A tax	B tax	B SH tax	Basis to A	**Loss carryover**
Purchase assets	None	Gain	None	Fair value	**None**
Purchase assets, B liquidates	None	Recap	Gain	Fair value	**None**
Purchase stock	None	None	Gain	Carryover	**Possible**

NOTE: A is the acquiring corporation
B is the acquired corporation

With a purchase transaction, the acquiring corporation's loss carryforward can be obtained only if stock is purchased. There are other ways, however, to benefit from loss carryforwards. One is for the loss corporation to buy the assets of a profitable corporation. The combined taxable income then will be completely or partially offset by the loss corporation's previous carryovers.

Review of the Importance of the Acquired Corporation's Basis. Earlier the importance of purchase price allocation upon the buyer's basis was examined. The buyer generally prefers a transaction that results in a high basis, particularly for inventory and depreciable assets. The following example considers the importance of basis in a purchase of stock.

EXAMPLE: THE IMPORTANCE OF THE ACQUIRED CORPORATION'S BASIS. The New Frontier Corporation is interested in acquiring the Lowsale Corporation for $3000. Lowsale's assets have an adjusted basis of only $2000. The fair market value of Lowsale's assets is $3000. All of the assets are eligible for depreciation.

If New Frontier acquires net assets for $3000 the purchase price becomes the future basis for depreciation. New Frontier will later benefit through $3000 in depreciation deductions.

If New Frontier acquires Lowsale's stock for $3000, Lowsale's future depreciation deductions are generally limited to Lowsale's existing basis of $2000, unless an election is made to step up the basis.

The basis step-up can be obtained only if the purchase price exceeds the book value of the acquired corporation's net assets. If the purchase price is less than the book value, a step-down results. The step-down is not desirable.

The Election to Step Up Basis. The purchase of stock results in carryover of the seller's old basis to the buyer. In the usual case where the purchase price is higher than the carrying value of the assets to the seller, the procedure results in a relatively low basis.

Tax legislation contains a provision whereby the acquiring corporation can elect to step up the basis of a newly acquired subsidiary to fair market value. The election must be made shortly after acquisition. This permits the acquiring corporation to carry the subsidiary as though it had made the acquisition through a purchase of assets.

The following example illustrates the election to step up the basis.

EXAMPLE: THE ELECTION TO STEP UP THE BASIS. The New Frontier Corporation is interested in acquiring the Lowsale Corporation for $3000. Lowsale's assets have an adjusted basis of only $2000. The fair market value of Lowsale's assets is $3000. The New Frontier Corporation acquires all Lowsale's stock for $3000, as in the previous example. New Frontier then elects to step up the basis of the acquired assets.

The basis is increased from the old basis of $2000 to the $3000 purchase price as a result of the election.

Advantages of the basis step-up include:

> For depreciable assets, a higher basis for depreciation.
>
> For depreciable assets, depreciation under ACRS with shorter depreciable lives compared to the previously used depreciation method.
>
> For assets to be disposed of in the near future, a higher basis and reduced gain on sale.

The basis step-up, however, is not always desirable. Consequences include the following:

> The acquired corporation is subject to recapture as though it sold the property outright in a sale of assets. The importance of recapture depends upon the amount of the gain and depre-

ciation previously taken. If the property is land, recapture will not apply. However, if the property is appreciated plant and equipment, the impact of recapture may be considerable.

Operating loss carryforwards of the acquired corporation are lost in a basis step-up. The acquisition is treated as a purchase of assets for purposes of determining carryforward eligibility.

The prospect of recapture associated with the step-up in basis election presents a potentially serious difficulty to the buyer of stock. In a basis step-up the acquired corporation recognizes taxable gain due to recapture. Since the acquiring corporation owns the acquired corporation, this amounts to a tax on the buyer. The basis step-up with recapture is illustrated in the following example.

EXAMPLE: RECAPTURE AND THE ELECTION TO STEP UP THE BASIS. The New Frontier Corporation acquires all Lowsale stock for $3000, as in the previous example. Lowsale's assets originally cost $2600 with $600 depreciation to date. New Frontier elects to step up the basis of the acquired assets.

The basis is increased from the old basis of $2000 to the $3000 purchase price. Lowsale realizes gain as the difference between the fair market value of the assets and the previous basis. The $600 gain attributable to depreciation taken to date is recognized and recaptured as ordinary income.

The burden of recapture falls on the buyer, since the buyer is the new owner of the acquired corporation. In many cases the buyer will need additional financing over and above the acquisition cost to raise the cash needed to pay the tax on the recapture.

The buyer generally seeks to avoid recapture by arranging for a purchase of assets. In the purchase of assets, the seller is subject to recapture at the time of the sale.

Buyers, however, are often willing to assume the burden of recapture if the additional tax is taken into account when the selling price is negotiated. The cost of recapture depends upon the nature of the assets, their age, the amount of depreciation previously taken, and the buyer's marginal tax rate. The effective tax cost will be quite low if most of the assets are not subject to recapture or if the buyer has a low marginal tax rate.

Another consideration is the investment tax credit. The credit is available on the purchase of up to $125,000 in used property (Chapter 3). The investment tax credit is not available to the buyer of stock or on property acquired by the purchase of stock followed shortly thereafter by the election to step up the basis. The investment tax credit may be important to smaller corporations that have not yet met the $125,000 entitlement for used equipment. The investment tax credit consideration will probably not be of interest to larger businesses that will quickly use the entitlement on other purchases.

Summary of Corporate Acquisitions

Transaction	A tax	B tax	B SH tax	Basis to A	Loss carryover
Purchase assets	None	Gain	None	Fair value	None
Purchase assets, B liquidates	None	Recap	Gain	Fair value	None
Purchase stock	None	None	Gain	Carryover	Possible
Purchase stock, basis step-up	None	Recap	Gain	Fair value	None

NOTE: A is the acquiring corporation
B is the acquired corporation

The Purchase of Assets versus Stock

The previous discussion considered the purchase of assets and the purchase of stock with and without a basis step-up. This section summarizes the advantages and disadvantages associated with the purchase of stock.

The New Basis. In a purchase of assets, the buyer and the selling corporation are the parties to the transaction. The purchase price becomes the basis of the newly acquired assets. The selling corporation recognizes gain.

In a purchase of stock, the buyer deals with the acquired corporation's shareholders. The basis of the acquired assets does not change in a stock acquisition unless the buyer elects a basis step-up. The basis step-up causes the buyer to recognize gain on recapture.

If both corporations are aware of the tax implications, they may arrange the transaction so that the corporation with the lower marginal tax rate recognizes the gain. In this case the selling price will be adjusted to reflect the additional tax (or tax saving).

In some cases, including the sale of land and residential real estate, recapture is not applicable or not significant. In this event, the buyer can step up the basis on a stock acquisition without recognizing gain. This may affect future depreciation and will also reduce the gain when the property is subsequently sold.

The Seller. With respect to the seller, the sale of stock versus assets determination depends upon whether the acquired corporation's shareholders wish to continue the affairs of the acquired corporation. This determination will likely be influenced by comparing the basis of the stock and the basis of the assets disposed of. If the basis of the stock is low in comparison to the basis of the assets, the shareholders may stand to recognize a large gain on the sale of the stock. In this case the shareholders may be reluctant to sell stock and recognize gain on the sale.

As an alternative to the sale of stock, the acquired corporation can sell assets, recognize gain on the sale, and continue to operate as a corporation. This might be attractive in the case of a low shareholder basis for the stock and a high basis for assets to the corporation. The corporation's gain in this case could be small compared to that of the shareholders. The shareholders might then be better off by continuing their stock ownership and having the corporation invest in new business undertakings.

The above discussion assumes the usual case of assets with fair market value in excess of their adjusted basis. If the fair market value is below the adjusted basis, the situation reverses. In this case, the buyer may prefer stock and the seller may prefer to sell assets and recognize a loss on sale.

The final topic included in the chapter relates to deductions for interest on amounts borrowed to acquire another corporation.

INTEREST ON CORPORATE ACQUISITION INDEBTEDNESS

Interest payed on amounts borrowed is normally fully deductible to determine taxable income. An exception applies to interest when large amounts of funds are borrowed to finance certain corporate acquisitions.

Congress became concerned at one time with the number of acquisitions of stock of large corporations financed primarily through issuing notes or bonds to the shareholders of the acquired corporation rather than by issuing shares of its own stock. The interest on the notes was financed through the earnings of the acquired corporation. Often the original sellers insisted on debt convertible to stock in the acquiring corporation. This practice resulted in increased financial risk for acquiring corporations, reduced taxes because of the deductibility of interest payments, and no clear benefit to the economy.

If borrowed funds are used to acquire stock or assets of another corporation, the interest deduction available to the corporation may be limited. The purpose of the limitation is to discourage corporate acquisitions with borrowed funds.

The limitation applies only if interest deductions are in excess of $5,000,000, if the debt is convertible to stock, and if the result is a very heavily leveraged acquiring corporation.

SUMMARY

Forms of Acquisition. Acquisitions take a variety of forms. The acquisition can be either by purchase or by tax-free reorganization. The acquiring corporation can acquire either stock or assets. The acquiring corporation can give cash, its own stock, or other property. The acquiring corporation is not taxed on an acquisition unless it elects to step up the basis in a purchase of stock.

The Purchase of Assets. The buyer usually prefers a purchase of assets. With a purchase of assets, the buyer obtains only desired assets, assumes only specified liabilities, and obtains a basis step-up with no tax cost to the buyer.

The Purchase of Stock. With a purchase of stock, the buyer operates the acquired corporation as a subsidiary. The previous depreciable basis of the assets continues as the new basis. The buyer may also elect to step up the basis of the assets to the purchase price. The step-up provides a higher basis for depreciation and subsequent sale. In this case, the buyer recognizes gain on recapture and possibly on other special-gain items.

Operating loss carryforwards are lost both in a purchase of assets and in a stock purchase with basis step-up.

The Sale. The seller can sell either stock or assets. If shareholders sell stock, the transaction is simple. Gain is recognized as the difference between the amount realized and the adjusted basis of the shareholder's stock.

If the corporation sells assets, double taxation becomes a very real possibility. Double taxation can be avoided if the sale is followed by a disposition of all proceeds to shareholders in liquidation. The shareholders are then free to sell the assets. The seller is also subject to recapture on eligible property as in the case of any sale of individual property items.

The Allocation of Purchase Price. The allocation of purchase price is important in a purchase and sale because it affects the tax on the gain to the seller and also the basis of individual assets to the buyer. Generally buyers attempt to allocate as much cost as possible to depreciable assets and inventories. Sellers generally prefer to allocate the cost to land and other assets on which the gains will qualify for capital gain treatment.

Since the interests of buyers and sellers usually conflict, the allocation of purchase price is often negotiated.

Interest Deductions for Corporate Acquisition Indebtedness.
The interest deduction available to the corporation may be limited if the borrowed funds are used to acquire stock or assets of another corporation. The purpose of the limitation is to discourage corporate acquisitions with borrowed funds.

Chapter 11

The Tax-Free Reorganization

The preceding chapter examined the taxable sale of a corporation. This chapter is concerned with the tax-free reorganization—a form of acquisition not usually taxable to the acquired corporation or its shareholders.

Tax-free reorganization differs from purchase in that the acquiring corporation issues shares of its own stock to obtain assets or stock of the acquired corporation. The acquired corporation usually prefers tax-free treatment because it does not cause either the acquired corporation or its shareholders to recognize gain on the exchange of stock. The shareholders of the acquired corporation continue to hold their investment, although the form of the holding is modified. The basis of the stock or assets given up carries over to the stock received in exchange. Consequently, the transaction is tax-deferred rather than truly tax-free. The concept resembles the nontaxable exchange applicable to the trade-in of individual property items (discussed in Chapter 4).

Acquiring corporations usually try to avoid the tax-free reorganization. The basis of property acquired in a tax-free reorganization carries over. If the acquiring party structures the transaction as a purchase, a more desirable basis step-up results in the case of appreciated property.

Transactions qualifying for tax-free reorganization treatment must meet two separate sets of conditions. First, tax legislation prescribes specific forms of acquisition. Second, the spirit of the transaction must be consistent with a number of judicial concepts, including the existence of a business purpose for the transaction and maintenance of a continuity of interest by the acquired corporation's shareholders.

This chapter develops and illustrates the above concepts. The chapter begins with review of the nontaxable exchange. The criteria for tax-free reorganizations are then examined, followed by comparison of purchase versus tax-free reorganization. As will be seen, "tax-free" acquisitions are not necessarily preferable to taxable transactions.

GENERAL CHARACTERISTICS

The tax-free reorganization is a type of nontaxable exchange. This section first reviews the nontaxable exchange. Then the tax-free reorganization is introduced.

The Nontaxable Exchange

The nontaxable exchange considers the exchange of property as a continuation of the original investment rather than as a sale. In this case, the transaction is not taxable. The basis of the newly acquired property is established as the basis of the old property plus the amount of any additional consideration given. Examples of the sale and nontaxable exchange follow.

EXAMPLE: A TAXABLE SALE. The Prestige Corporation sells the president's limousine and buys a new model. The old limo has an adjusted basis of $2000 and a fair market value of $8000. The

General Characteristics

new limo costs $48,000. Prestige sells the old limo and pays $48,000 cash for the new one.

The gain on sale is:

Amount realized	$8000
Less: Adjusted basis	2000
Gain recognized on sale	$6000

The $48,000 cost becomes the basis of the replacement property.

As an alternative to sale, the transaction could be set up as a nontaxable exchange:

EXAMPLE: THE NONTAXABLE EXCHANGE. The Prestige Corporation exchanges the president's limousine for a new model. The old limo has an adjusted basis of $2000 and a fair market value of $8000. The new limo costs $48,000. Prestige trades in the old limo and gives $40,000 cash in exchange for the new one.

The nontaxable exchange does not result in gain recognition. The realized gain is $6000 as on the sale in the previous example. All of the $6000 gain is deferred.

The deferral operates through establishing the basis of the new property as the basis of the old property plus the additional cash paid:

Old basis	$ 2,000
Add: Cash paid	40,000
New basis	$42,000

This could also be determined as:

New fair market value	$48,000
Less: Gain not recognized	6,000
New basis	$42,000

If the new limo is sold for $48,000 shortly after the exchange, the $6000 deferred gain is recognized at that time:

Amount realized	$48,000
Less: Adjusted basis	42,000
Recognized gain	$ 6,000

The above example shows that the tax is not forgiven in a nontaxable exchange. The tax is merely deferred until the time of future property disposition. The same reasoning applies to the tax-free reorganization.

How the Reorganization Operates

The tax-free reorganization is an exchange of investments in two or more corporations. Gain is not recognized at the time of the exchange. The new investment is considered to be a continuation of the old investment in modified form. The basis of the old investment carries over and becomes the basis of the new investment. The basis carryover is shown in the following exchange of stock for stock illustration.

EXAMPLE: THE NONTAXABLE EXCHANGE OF INVESTMENTS. The New Frontier Corporation acquires the Lowsale Corporation. The Lowsale shareholders receive stock in New Frontier in exchange for their Lowsale stock. The Lowsale shareholders originally paid $2000 for their stock. The fair market value of the stock received in New Frontier is $3000.

The amount realized is the fair market value of the New Frontier stock.

The gain realized on the transaction is:

Amount realized	$3000
Less: Adjusted basis	2000
Realized gain	$1000

The gain is not recognized currently in a tax-free reorganization.

The $2000 previous basis of the Lowsale stock to its shareholders carries over and becomes New Frontier's basis in the newly received stock. If the New Frontier stock is later sold, gain is recognized at that time.

The subsequent sale of the newly received stock is shown as follows.

EXAMPLE: THE CARRYOVER BASIS IN THE NONTAXABLE EXCHANGE. In continuation of the above example, Lowsale's former shareholders later sell the New Frontier stock with a basis of $2000 for $3000 cash.

The gain realized on the transaction is:

Amount realized (sale of stock)	$3000
Less: Adjusted basis	2000
Realized gain	$1000

The entire $1000 gain is recognized at the time of sale. The gain from the "tax-free" exchange is not forgiven. It is merely deferred.

The concepts underlying the tax-free reorganization are similar to those associated with the nontaxable exchange. The transaction is not taxed as long as it represents a continuation of the original investment.

Forms of Tax-Free Reorganization

Only certain prescribed forms of reorganization qualify for tax-free status. The first three types of tax-free reorganization apply to acquisitions, and are summarized briefly here. Specific qualifications for these reorganization forms will be examined later in this chapter. Two additional types of tax-free reorganization apply to modifications of corporate form or ownership and are not usually associated with acquisitions. These are considered near the end of this chapter. A sixth type of tax-free reorganization applies to corporate divisions and is the subject of the next chapter.

The Exchange of Stock for Stock. In an exchange of stock for stock, A, the acquiring corporation, issues shares of its stock to shareholders of B, the acquired corporation. B's shareholders then transfer their shares in B to the acquiring corporation. The exchange of stock for stock is illustrated in Figure 11.1.

As a consequence, B's former shareholders become shareholders in A. A holds all of B's stock. Exchanges of stock are common because the transaction is simple, cash is not required for payment, and the acquired corporation is maintained intact. Additionally, the acquiring corporation may not need to deal with B's management. The transaction takes place between the management of the acquiring corporation and the shareholders of the acquired corporation. B's management is not involved.

The Exchange of Stock for Assets. The exchange of stock for assets is another common form of tax-free acquisition. A, the acquiring corporation issues shares of its stock to B and receives all of B's assets. B's only assets after the exchange consist of its stock in A. This stock is sometimes distributed to B's shareholders in liquidation of B, as shown in Figure 11.2. B's former shareholders now become shareholders in A. The negotiations are conducted by the managements of the two corporations. B, however, may need to obtain the permission of its shareholders.

Merger or Consolidation. The merger or consolidation is the third major form of tax-free acquisition. In a merger, the acquired corporation, B, becomes part of the acquiring corporation, as shown in Figure 11.3. In a consolidation, both A and B combine into a new corporation, C. The former shareholders of

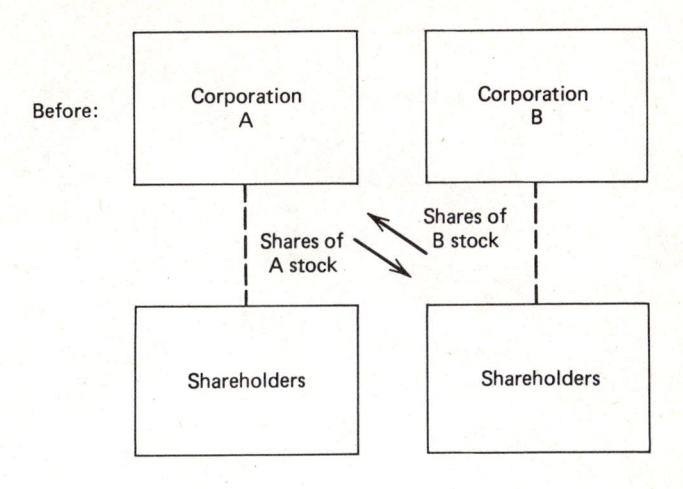

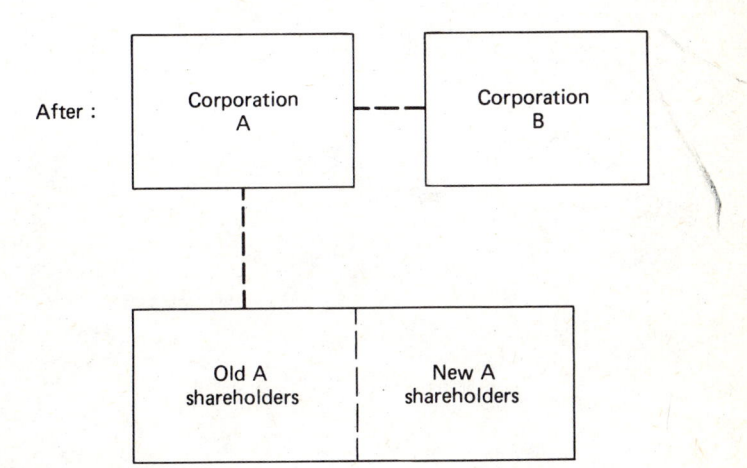

Figure 11.1. The exchange of stock for stock. The acquiring corporation gives shares of stock in exchange for shares of the acquired corporation.

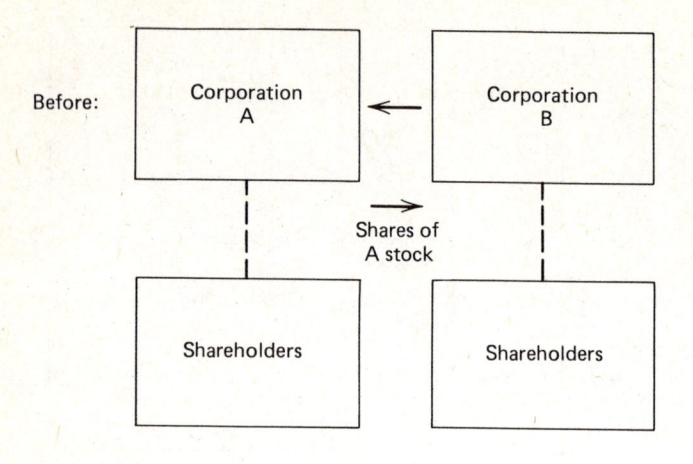

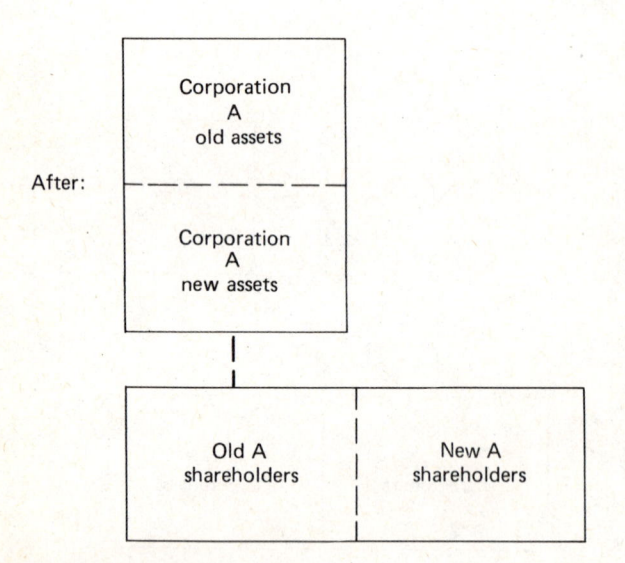

Figure 11.2. The exchange of stock for assets followed by liquidation of the acquired corporation.

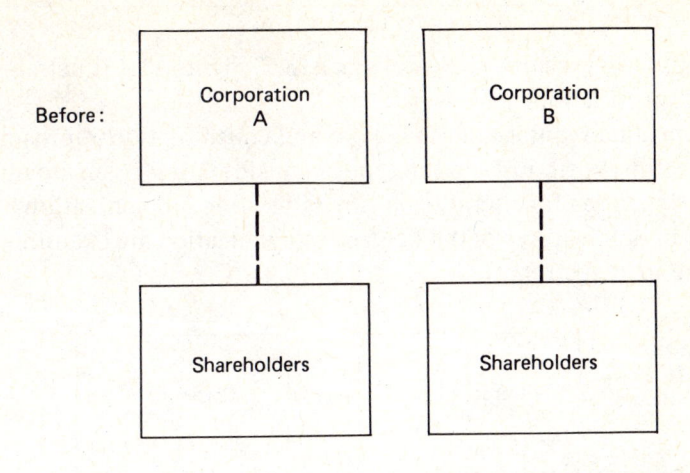

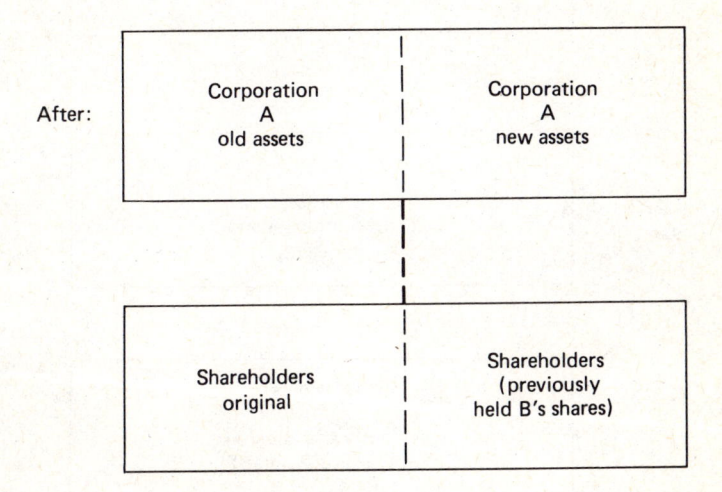

Figure 11.3. The merger. The interests of two or more corporations combine and one corporation dissolves.

323

A and B each receive shares of stock in C. Figure 11.4 illustrates the consolidation.

A major advantage of the merger and consolidation approach is that the restrictions on the type of consideration given are not as stringent as for the other forms of tax-free reorganization.

Common features of the tax-free reorganization are examined in the next section.

Before:

Corporation A	Corporation B
Shareholders	Shareholders

After:

Corporation C
(old corporations A and B)

Shareholders
(previously shareholders corporations A and B)

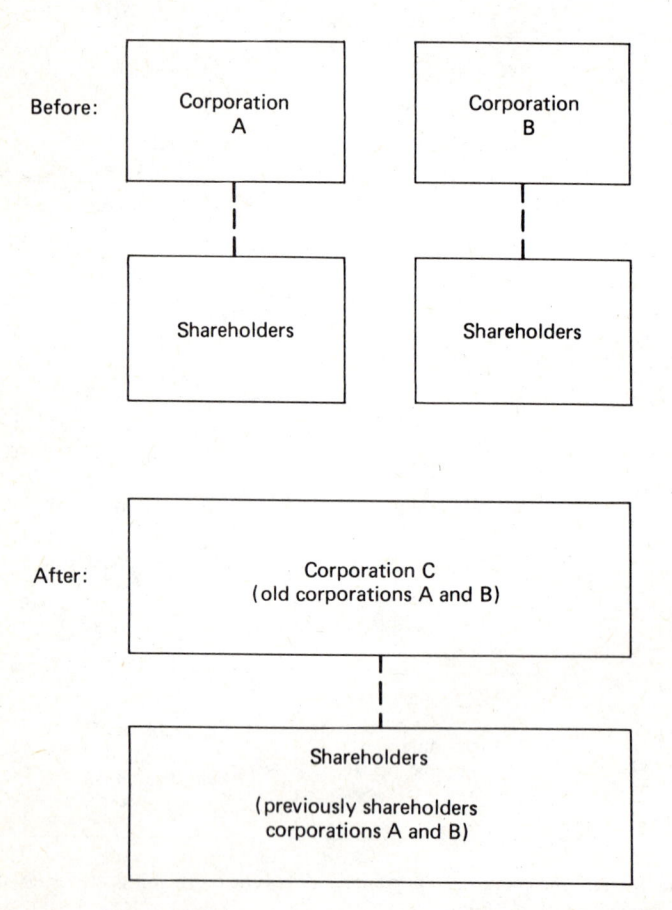

Figure 11.4. The consolidation. The interests of two or more corporations combine and both corporations dissolve.

Common Features

In a tax-free reorganization, the acquired corporation's former shareholders continue their investment in the newly expanded corporation. Tax-free reorganizations possess the following additional common features:

> Business Purpose. A qualifying reorganization should be motivated by a business purpose other than tax avoidance. Business reasons for acquisitions include expansion, diversification, increased ability to raise capital, and integration of a small business into a larger business that can operate more efficiently. Tax-avoidance motives would include changes in form designed to produce tax benefits with little evidence of true business purpose. The acquisition of a nonoperating corporation without assets in order to obtain operating loss carryforward benefits, for example, would qualify as a tax-avoidance motive.
>
> Controlling Interest. The acquiring corporation obtains control of either the acquired corporation's stock or its assets. Acquisitions of small percentage ownerships do not qualify. Tax-free treatment is available only for significant changes in corporate ownership and only as the result of an acquisition or an action taken by the corporation. Exchanges of stock between shareholders do not receive tax-free treatment. Exchanges between shareholders are treated as sales.
>
> Continuing Interest. The acquired corporation's shareholders must maintain a continuing equity interest in the acquiring corporation. In other words, shareholders do not sell their interest, but exchange their interest for stock in the acquiring corporation. The receipt of bonds or other promises to pay does not constitute a continuing equity interest.

The following is an example of a reorganization that is not tax-free because it does not meet all of the necessary conditions.

EXAMPLE: A TAXABLE ACQUISITION. The New Frontier Corporation acquires 30 percent of the Downturn Corporation's assets for cash.

This is not a tax-free reorganization. The 30 percent ownership does not provide control. Additionally, if New Frontier merely buys out Downturn's shareholders for cash, Downturn's former owners do not maintain a continuing interest in the acquiring corporation.

If New Frontier acquires 95 percent rather than 30 percent of Downturn's assets and gives stock rather than cash, the transaction may not be taxable to Downturn.

The Step-Transaction Doctrine. The operation of tax-free reorganizations is complicated by judicial considerations. The business purpose and continuing interest doctrines outlined earlier in this chapter have developed as a result of sensitivity to the spirit as well as the letter of the law. The legislation, in many cases, does not specify the need for a business purpose or continuing interest. The courts, however, tend to rule against transactions that seem to meet the necessary criteria but do not meet the spirit of the law.

The courts also apply a step-transaction doctrine. An exchange of stock for stock, for example, may be followed by a liquidation with the acquiring corporation receiving the assets. The combined effect of the two transactions will be equivalent to an acquisition of assets and may be treated that way for tax purposes. The courts have ruled that when two separate transactions appear to act as related steps in the same transaction, they will be treated as a single transaction. The courts have sometimes treated transactions differently than the treatment claimed by taxpayers due to the step-transaction doctrine.

The general criteria outlined above apply to all tax-free reorganizations. More detailed criteria apply to specific types of tax-free reorganizations. Each type of tax-free reorganization is examined separately following the outline of tax consequences.

Consequences of the Tax-Free Reorganization. The impact of the tax-free reorganization differs considerably from that associated with the taxable transaction. The tax-free reorganization entails consequences to both the acquired party and the acquiring party.

The acquired corporation is not taxed on the receipt of stock resulting from a tax-free reorganization. If the acquired corporation receives stock in exchange for assets, it does not recognize gain. If the acquired corporation's shareholders receive new stock in exchange for their old stock, their gain is not recognized until they eventually sell the stock received in the reorganization. Recaptures are also not recognized in a tax-free reorganization.

Qualification as a tax-free reorganization is important to the acquiring corporation for the following reasons:

The basis of stock or assets received carries over from the basis of stock to the acquired corporation's shareholders or the basis of assets from the acquired corporation. In the case of appreciated property, the carryover basis results in reduced depreciation deductions to the acquiring corporation.

Tax attributes such as operating loss carryforwards may carry over to the acquiring corporation. Loss carryforwards are not obtained in a purchase of assets.

The shareholders of a corporation acquired through an exchange of stock do not recognize gain on the exchange of stock. Consequently they usually prefer a tax-free reorganization to the taxable sale of shares.

The following example illustrates the consequences of tax-free versus taxable status.

EXAMPLE: THE CONSEQUENCES OF THE TAX-FREE REORGANIZATION. The New Frontier Corporation acquires all the assets of the Lowsale Corporation for stock in New Frontier. Lowsale's basis in the assets was $2000. Lowsale receives stock with a value of $3000.

If the acquisition qualifies as a tax-free reorganization, neither corporation recognizes gain at the time of the acquisition.

The basis of the New Frontier stock to Lowsale is the $2000 adjusted basis of the assets given up. The basis of the assets to New Frontier is their $2000 previous basis to Lowsale.

Lowsale's operating loss carryforward entitlement may carry over to New Frontier.

If the transaction is not tax-free, Lowsale recognizes gain on the sale of assets and the basis of the property to New Frontier is $3000 rather than $2000.

The Chapter 10 summary of different forms of acquisitions updated for the general consequences of the tax-free reorganization follows:

SUMMARY OF CORPORATE ACQUISITIONS

Transaction	A tax	B tax	B SH tax	Basis to A	Loss carryover
Purchase assets	None	Gain	None	Fair value	None
Purchase assets, B liquidates	None	Recap	Gain	Fair value	None
Purchase stock	None	None	Gain	Carryover	Possible
Purchase stock, basis step-up	None	Recap	Gain	Fair value	None
Tax-free reorganization	None	None	None	Carryover	Possible

NOTE: A is the acquiring corporation
B is the acquired corporation

More specific criteria for the five specific types of tax-free exchange considered in this chapter follow.

FORMS OF REORGANIZATION

The Exchange of Stock for Stock

The exchange of stock for stock comprises one common form of corporate acquisition. The exchange of stock takes place between the acquiring corporation and the shareholders of the acquired corporation. The acquired corporation itself is not involved in the exchange. The acquired corporation's former shareholders maintain a continuing interest in the acquired corporation indirectly through ownership of the acquiring corporation's shares.

Criteria. To qualify as a tax-free stock for stock reorganization:

> The acquiring corporation may only give voting stock. Any other consideration disqualifies the transaction.
>
> The acquiring corporation must control the acquired corporation immediately after the exchange. Control is defined as an 80 percent interest in the acquired corporation.

The tax-free exchange of stock for stock was illustrated earlier. An example of an exchange that would *not* qualify for tax-free status follows.

EXAMPLE: A TAXABLE STOCK FOR STOCK EXCHANGE. The New Frontier Corporation grants common stock to the Lowsale Corporation's shareholders in exchange for all of Lowsale's voting stock. M, a former Lowsale shareholder, insists upon payment of $200 in cash because he is opposed to certain New Frontier Corporation policies.

The transaction does not qualify as a tax-free reorganization because the solely-for-voting-stock condition is not met. The payment of even small amounts of cash disqualify the exchange of stock for stock for tax-free reorganization treatment.

Tax Treatment. The acquired corporation's shareholders do not recognize taxable income in a qualifying tax-free reorganization.

In a stock for stock transaction, both corporations continue to maintain their identities. The acquired corporation operates as a subsidiary of the acquiring corporation. The basis of the acquired corporation's assets does not change. The previous basis of the acquired corporation's stock to its shareholders carries over as the new basis of the stock to the acquiring corporation. The basis of the acquiring corporation's stock received by the acquired corporation's shareholders is the same as the basis of their stock given to the acquiring corporation.

The Exchange of Stock for Assets

The exchange of stock for assets may also qualify as a tax-free reorganization. The acquiring corporation receives the assets of the acquired corporation. It gives its own stock in exchange. The acquired corporation then distributes all assets including the stock in the acquiring corporation to its shareholders and liquidates. Neither the acquired corporation nor its shareholders are taxed on the distribution of stock to the shareholders.

Criteria. In a tax-free exchange of stock for assets, substantially all of the assets must be transferred to the acquiring corporation (thereby insuring control). Small amounts of cash or other property may be transferred by the acquiring corporation under certain conditions, but the consideration must be restricted primarily to voting stock. (This ensures continuity of an equity interest on the part of the acquired corporation's shareholders.)

Forms of Reorganization

Tax Treatment. In an exchange of stock for assets, the acquired corporation recognizes gain only to the extent of cash and other property received (boot). Gain is recognized on the receipt of boot because the shareholders are effectively cashing in on a portion of their investment.

After the exchange, the acquired corporation's assets will consist primarily of the acquiring corporation's stock. This stock is usually distributed to shareholders in liquidation of the acquired corporation. In this case, the acquired corporation's former shareholders maintain a continuing interest in the acquired corporation.

EXAMPLE: A TAX-FREE STOCK FOR ASSETS EXCHANGE. The New Frontier Corporation acquires all the assets of the Lowsale Corporation. The assets have a fair market value of $3000 and an adjusted basis of $1000. The adjusted basis of the Lowsale stock to its shareholders is $2000. New Frontier gives Lowsale voting stock with fair market value $3000.

The realized gain to Lowsale is:

Amount realized	$3000
Less: Adjusted basis	1000
Realized gain	$2000

This transaction should qualify as a tax-free exchange of stock for assets since substantially all assets are acquired and the consideration given is voting stock. In this case, Lowsale will not be taxed.

The adjusted basis of the stock received by Lowsale is $1000. The basis of the assets received by New Frontier is $1000—the previous basis of the assets to Lowsale.

If Lowsale distributes the New Frontier stock to its shareholders as part of the reorganization, Lowsale's shareholders will also not recognize gain.

Evaluation. The tax-free stock for assets exchange requires the acquisition of substantially all assets. The stock for stock exchange requires that control of the acquired corporation be attained. The high percentage ownership of the acquired corporation is a dominant feature of the tax-free reorganization. As indicated previously, acquisitions to obtain only a relatively small partial interest do not qualify for favorable tax treatment.

The stock for assets exchange is less restrictive than the stock for stock exchange because the acquiring corporation can give some cash and other property. Another advantage is that the acquiring corporation does not need to assume all the acquired corporation's liabilities. Corporations are often concerned with acquiring hidden liabilities such as subsequent lawsuits arising from asbestos manufacture or toxic waste dumping. Liabilities arising from subsequent tax audits of preacquisition years have also occurred. The acquiring corporation does not assume liabilities if only the assets are acquired.

A chief business reason for the stock for stock exchange is that the management of the acquiring corporation need not approve of or even be a party to the transaction. A stock for stock exchange may also be useful when the acquiring party wants to maintain the corporate identity of the acquired corporation. Certain leases and franchises, for example, may remain in effect only for the corporation to which originally granted. Thus it may be necessary to preserve the acquired corporation to retain nonassignable leases, franchises, or other privileges.

The basis of the acquired corporation's assets compared to the shareholder's basis in its stock should also be considered in evaluating the desirability of the exchange of stock for assets or for stock. In an exchange of stock for assets, the acquired corporation's basis in the newly acquired stock is the basis of the acquired assets. In the acquisition of stock for stock, the acquired corporation's basis in the newly acquired stock is the previous basis to shareholders. If the basis of the assets is higher than the basis of the stock to shareholders, the acquiring corporation will prefer to acquire assets. If the basis of the stock is higher than that of the assets, the acquiring corporation will prefer to acquire stock. The role of basis is illustrated in the following example.

EXAMPLE: THE ROLE OF BASIS IN THE ASSETS VERSUS STOCK ALTERNATIVE. The New Frontier Corporation acquires the Lowsale Corporation by giving stock. Lowsale's assets have a basis of $2000. Lowsale's shareholders bought their stock in 1945 at a cost of only $500.

If New Frontier acquires assets, the basis of the assets will be $2000. If New Frontier acquires stock, the basis of the stock carries over from that of the previous shareholders as only $500.

This basis aspect is not important to Lowsale's shareholders, since their basis in the New Frontier stock is determined by their basis in the Lowsale stock and remains at $500 in any event.

The above example represents a situation in which an alternative that benefits the acquiring corporation does not act to the disadvantage of the acquired corporation's shareholders. This type of situation is relatively rare in corporate acquisitions. In most cases, the interests of the parties are directly opposed.

The Merger and Consolidation

General. The statutory merger or consolidation is a third common type of tax-free acquisition. A merger or consolidation is statutory when it meets all legal requirements for a merger in the state of incorporation.

A merger takes place when the acquiring corporation gives stock or other property in exchange for the acquired corporation's stock. The acquired corporation then transfers all assets and liabilities to the acquiring corporation and liquidates.

A consolidation takes place when a newly created corporation gives stock to acquire the stock of two or more corporations.

The former corporations then transfer all assets and liabilities to the new corporation and liquidate.

Criteria. The consideration given by the acquiring corporation in a merger or consolidation can consist of both stock and other property. A substantial portion of the consideration should be stock to ensure that the acquired corporation's shareholders maintain a continuing interest in the acquiring corporation. The acquired corporation's shareholders cannot merely sell their stock tax-free to the acquiring corporation for cash even if state law designates the transaction as a merger.

Tax Treatment. As with the other forms of acquisition by tax-free reorganization, the transaction is tax-free except with respect to the treatment of boot. The statutory merger is illustrated in the following example.

EXAMPLE: A STATUTORY MERGER. The New Frontier Corporation gives stock with fair market value of $3000 to shareholders of the Lowsale Corporation. Lowsale then merges into New Frontier and liquidates. Lowsale's shareholders originally paid $2000 for their stock.

If the acquisition qualifies as a statutory merger, gains or losses are not recognized on the transaction unless property other than stock or securities is received.

The gain to Lowsale's shareholders is determined as:

Amount realized	$3000
Less: Adjusted basis	2000
Gain not recognized	$1000

If the merger does not qualify as a tax-free reorganization, the acquired corporation's shareholders recognize the $1000 gain.

The basis of the New Frontier stock to Lowsale's shareholders is $2000. This is also the basis of the newly acquired assets to New Frontier.

The merger treatment resembles the stock for stock exchange. An important difference is that in a merger, cash and other property can also be given in addition to voting stock.

The Receipt of Boot. Cash and other property is sometimes distributed in addition to stock in merger situations. Some shareholders, for example, may receive cash for their shares while others receive the acquiring corporation's stock. This type of merger can be more attractive to the acquired corporation's shareholders.

Consideration other than stock or long-term debt is classified as boot. When boot is received, realized gain is taxable to shareholders to the extent of the boot received as in the nontaxable exchange. The rationale is that the receipt of boot does not represent continuation of the original investment, but acts as a form of payment to shareholders. In other words, shareholders exchange part of their investment and sell part of the investment for boot. The part of the transaction resembling a sale is taxable.

A limited amount of boot may also be given in an exchange of stock for assets. In this case, the realized gain is recognized to the extent of boot received in the same manner as in the merger. The treatment of boot received in a merger is shown as follows.

EXAMPLE: A STATUTORY MERGER WITH BOOT. The New Frontier Corporation gives $500 cash and stock with a fair market value of $2500 to shareholders of the Lowsale Corporation. Lowsale then merges into New Frontier and liquidates. Lowsale's shareholders originally paid $2000 for their stock.

If this qualifies as a statutory merger, gains or losses are recognized only to the extent of the value of property received that is not stock or securities.

Amount realized	$3000
Less: Adjusted basis	2000
Gain realized	$1000
Gain recognized (realized gain to the extent of boot received)	$ 500

Evaluation. A primary advantage of the merger and consolidation over other forms of tax-free reorganization is that fewer restrictions apply to the form of consideration given. Some shareholders, for example, can receive cash while others receive stock. This would disqualify an exchange of stock for assets transaction and cause the disposition to be taxable. A disadvantage of the merger or consolidation is that it may be necessary to obtain shareholder approval and to comply with various provisions of applicable state law to qualify.

Summary of Alternative Forms of Acquisition by Tax-Free Reorganization. The stock for stock exchange permits only voting stock to be given in exchange for control of the acquired corporation.

The stock for assets exchange specifies that the consideration given be primarily voting stock in the acquiring corporation. Substantially all the acquired corporation's assets must be transferred in a stock for assets exchange. The exchange of stock for assets acquisition can be attractive because the acquiring corporation does not assume responsibility for liabilities of the acquired corporation.

The merger or consolidation is less restrictive in some respects than the other forms of tax-free reorganization. The merger permits payment of a greater portion of the consideration in cash or other nonstock property. A major disadvantage of the merger or consolidation is that stockholders of both the acquiring and acquired corporations must vote in favor of the merger. This can be difficult and time-consuming. The need to comply with all applicable state laws may also add time and cost to the merger transaction.

The Purchase versus the Tax-Free Reorganization

An acquisition may be structured either as a purchase or as a tax-free reorganization by establishing the terms of payment as either voting stock or as cash or its equivalent. The choice between purchase and tax-free reorganization is important to both the acquiring and acquired corporations.

The Acquiring Corporation. The acquiring corporation generally prefers a purchase. The purchase is not taxable to the buyer since if gain is recognized, it is recognized by the seller.

Property acquired by purchase takes the purchase price as the basis. Usually the purchase price exceeds the seller's basis and a step-up in basis results. The step-up consideration was examined in detail in Chapter 10. It provides a higher basis for depreciation and results in increased depreciation deductions. The step-up will also reduce recognized gain when the property is eventually sold (assuming the property is not fully depreciated by that time).

In a tax-free reorganization, the basis of acquired property carries over from the acquired corporation. There is no basis step-up. Other factors equal, buyers are often willing to pay more for appreciated property acquired by purchase. This assumes of course, that the property has appreciated in value. If the fair market value is less than the basis, a step-down would result.

The Acquired Corporation and Its Shareholders. The sale of the acquired corporation's property is taxable to the corporation or its shareholders.

Capital gains are recognized on a sale. The gains are computed as the difference between the amount realized and the adjusted basis of the acquired corporation. Neither party is taxed on the tax-free reorganization assuming that boot is not exchanged. Other factors equal, the buyer should be less willing to acquire by tax-free reorganization and the seller should be willing to trade for shares with less value to benefit through a tax-free reorganization.

If the basis of the property exceeds its fair market value, the reverse situation should apply. In this case, the seller may prefer to recognize a loss on the sale. This can be accomplished through a sale transaction rather than through a tax-free reorganization.

Fortunately, however, the concerned parties often agree on terms. The acquiring corporation, for example, may not have a positive amount of taxable income and may not be subject to tax anyway. In this case, the basis step-up has no immediate value since the additional depreciation deductions will not be available anyway. Thus the form of the transaction may not be too important to the buyer.

Alternatively, the seller may have a history of capital losses that will merely offset any gains recognized on the sale. If the gains aren't taxable, they may be of no concern to the seller.

In some cases, the sellers will not want to maintain a continuing interest in the acquiring corporation as called for in a tax-free reorganization. The sellers may prefer to receive cash, pay the tax, and terminate their interest completely. In this case, the sellers will prefer an outright sale.

Differences in Shareholder Basis. The purchase versus tax-free reorganization decision is sometimes complicated when the interests of shareholders conflict. One cause of conflict results from the previous acquisition of stock by shareholders at different prices. An illustration of a situation giving rise to shareholder conflict follows.

Forms of Reorganization

EXAMPLE: THE PROBLEM PRESENTED BY DIFFERENT BASES FOR DIFFERENT SHAREHOLDERS. The New Frontier Corporation expressed interest in acquiring the Lowsale Corporation's stock from Lowsale's shareholders. The fair market value of Lowsale is established as $3000. New Frontier offers to purchase the stock or to exchange its stock tax-free. It is not willing to consider a merger, because that would require time-consuming approval from its stockholders.

Two shareholders each own 50 percent of Lowsale's stock. Shareholder M purchased her shares in 1920 for $300. Shareholder N purchased the other 50 percent of the shares in 1983 for $1,700.

If New Frontier purchases the stock for cash, the consequences to M and N are as follows:

Shareholder M:

Amount realized	$1500
Adjusted basis of stock	300
Recognized gain	$1200

Shareholder N:

Amount realized	$1500
Adjusted basis of stock	1700
Recognized gain/ (loss)	$(200)

Shareholder M will attempt to avoid gain recognition and will favor a tax-free reorganization. Shareholder N, on the other hand, will prefer to recognize the loss and reduce taxable income accordingly. Shareholder N prefers a sale.

New Frontier will find it difficult to please both parties as the tax-free exchange of stock does not permit a cash payment to N.

One alternative is for N to accept the New Frontier stock in a tax-free reorganization. N is then free to later sell the stock and realize the loss at that time.

The purchase versus tax-free reorganization decision is important to both the acquired corporation and the acquiring corporation. The interests of the two parties often conflict. If one party is not aware of the tax implications associated with the acquisition, the consequences can be serious. On the other hand, parties familiar with the tax consequences can generally work out compromises satisfactory to everyone concerned.

The Straddle. The straddle permits the seller to realize gains tax-free and at the same time provides for the immediate recognition of losses. In a straddle, the acquired corporation first sells those assets with a basis above fair market value. This results in the recognition of deductible losses. Then, as a second step, the acquired corporation transfers its stock in a tax-free reorganization. As a result, the acquired corporation recognizes losses, but the shareholders do not recognize gains.

The operation is similar to the straddle by the liquidating corporation examined previously in Chapter 8.

The Recapitalization

Two additional forms of tax-free reorganization not involving acquisitions are the recapitalization and the change in identity or form. The recapitalization is considered first.

General. A recapitalization represents a change in the corporation's capital structure. Debt and preferred stock issues are sometimes convertible into shares of common stock. The conversion of these types of securities by the lender or shareholder is one form of recapitalization. Corporations sometimes have difficulty making interest payments on debt. A restructuring to effect the conversion of debt into an equity interest represents a second type of recapitalization.

The doctrines of business purpose, continuity of interest, and the step transaction generally continue to be applicable to this type of tax-free reorganization.

The issuance of debt by the corporation in exchange for stock does not qualify as a tax-free recapitalization because the former shareholder does not maintain a continuing equity interest.

Tax Treatment. Parties to the recapitalization do not normally recognize gain on the transaction.

The Change in Identity or Form

Corporations undergo changes in identity or form for a variety of reasons. One common example is the legal liquidation of a corporation in one state followed immediately by incorporation of the same business in another state. This change in identity or form is tax-free to the involved corporation.

SUMMARY

The Tax-Free Reorganization. Acquisitions by tax-free reorganization can be accomplished through the exchange of stock for stock, stock for assets, or through merger. For a reorganization to be tax-free, the acquired parties maintain a continuing interest in the acquired corporation. This means that a major part of the payment must be in the form of stock.

Qualifications. Qualification as a tax-free reorganization also requires that the acquiring corporation obtain control of the acquired corporation and that one or both corporations must be involved. Transactions taking place solely between shareholders do not qualify as tax-free reorganizations. The acquiring corporation must also have a business purpose other than tax avoidance in order for the transaction to qualify for tax-free treatment. The judicial considerations of continuity of interest, business purpose, and the step transaction also apply.

Tax Treatment. Gain is not recognized at the time of the acquisition. The basis of assets received by the acquiring corporation is the old basis to the acquired corporation. The basis of stock received by the acquiring corporation carries over from the basis of its former shareholders. The basis of stock received by the acquired corporation or its shareholders is the basis of the property or stock given to the acquiring corporation in exchange.

Types of Tax-Free Reorganization. Acquisitions by tax-free reorganization commonly take the form of acquisitions of assets, acquisitions of stock, or acquisitions by merger or consolidation.

The Acquisition of Stock. The acquisition of stock usually takes place between the acquiring corporation and the shareholders of the acquired corporation. The acquired corporation is not involved and no accounting entries are made on its books. The basis of the assets does not change. Only voting stock can be given by the acquiring corporation when stock is acquired in a tax-free reorganization.

The Acquisition of Assets. The acquisition of assets takes place between the acquiring corporation and the acquired corporation. Title to the assets is transferred to the acquiring corporation. The basis of the assets continues as the previous basis to the acquired corporation. In an acquisition of assets, the consideration given by the acquiring corporation must be primarily voting stock.

The Merger or Consolidation. In a merger or consolidation, two corporations come together and one or both of the involved corporations loses its identity. Consideration other than stock or securities can be given in a qualifying merger or consolidation, as long as the acquired corporation's shareholders maintain a substantial continuing interest. The acquired corporation or its shareholders recognize gain to the extent of the boot received.

The Purchase Versus the Tax-Free Reorganization. The seller's tax is deferred in a tax-free reorganization. The seller, however, often prefers an outright sale in order to cash in on the investment. In this case the seller will not have a continuing interest and the transaction will be taxable. Sellers also prefer a purchase and sale transaction in cases where the fair market value of their investment is less than the adjusted basis. In this case, the seller can recognize the loss on sale.

The buyer generally prefers a purchase since it results in a step-up of basis. If the property has a high basis relative to fair market value, however, the buyer may prefer a tax-free reorganization to retain the high basis. The possibility of using loss carryforwards also affects the buyer's preference. The probability of using the acquired corporation's loss carryforwards is increased in a tax-free reorganization.

The Recapitalization. The recapitalization represents a change in the corporation's capital structure. Examples include the conversion of preferred stock or debt into common stock.

The Change in Identity or Form. The change in identity or form may occur when a corporation liquidates and immediately reincorporates in another state or under another name. The change in identity or form is generally tax-free as long as the judicial conditions for a tax-free reorganization are met.

Chapter 12

Spin-Offs and Other Corporate Divisions

Corporations sometimes divide into two or more active businesses. Some of the mechanisms that can be employed to accomplish the division include:

A taxable dividend distribution of property to shareholders (covered in Chapter 7).

A taxable redemption or liquidation of corporate property resulting in sale treatment to shareholders. The distributing corporation usually recognizes gain in a redemption or liquidation (described in Chapter 8).

This chapter focuses upon another mechanism for the corporate division: the tax-free division. The tax-free division is accomplished through the distribution of the stock of a subsidiary corporation to the distributing corporation's shareholders. The subsidiary corporation may be an established subsidiary. Alternatively, the distributing corporation can transfer property to a new subsidiary and then distribute stock in the new subsidiary to shareholders.

The tax-free distribution of a subsidiary corporation's stock to shareholders permits a corporation to divide for good business reasons without tax penalty. The tax-free division, however, may not necessarily provide the most advantageous mechanism for division. Tax-free treatment results in a carryover basis for assets. Tax-free treatment also does not permit recognition of possible losses by shareholders.

This chapter examines the division of the corporation into two or more smaller corporations. The chapter begins with consideration of reasons for corporate divisions. The criteria for tax-free treatment are then introduced. Following this, specific forms of tax-free divisions are examined.

REASONS FOR CORPORATE DIVISIONS

Corporations sometimes find it either necessary or desirable to divide into two or more corporations and to sever all ties between the separate corporations. Common reasons include:

> A diversified corporation decides to separate a regulated business, such as a bank or utility, from its nonregulated businesses.
>
> New legislation prevents the corporation from continuing all of its existing business activities.
>
> Shareholders disagree on how to run the business.
>
> Antitrust action forces a division of the corporation.
>
> A business is divided and each part is operated independently to increase administrative efficiency.

For example, a public utility may decide to divest itself of certain parts of the business, as illustrated in the following example.

EXAMPLE: CORPORATE DIVISION FOR ANTITRUST PURPOSES. The American Telephone and Telegraph (AT&T) Corporation manufactured telephones and switching equipment, operated long-distance facilities, and owned local operating telephone companies. AT&T was cited for reducing competition in the communications industry as a result of its size and scope of activity.

AT&T divested certain operations by transferring stock in subsidiary corporations to its shareholders. The basic businesses continue, but no longer under any of the original parent company influence. The shareholders now own these subsidiaries directly. The parent corporation continues to operate with reduced size.

Alternatively, a corporation may divide a business in the interests of increased operating efficiency:

EXAMPLE: CORPORATE DIVISION TO REDUCE COSTS AND INCREASE OPERATING EFFICIENCY. The Move-On Motors Corporation owns six regional General Motors dealerships. The corporation began as a single dealership and grew as the founder's children started up dealerships in nearby towns. The corporation is now owned by six grandchildren each of whom operates one of the dealerships. The grandchildren feel that each can operate more efficiently as a separate corporation.

The grandchildren divide Move-On into six separate corporations. Each of the six new corporations issues stock to one of the grandchildren in exchange for the grandchild's stock in Move-On. Move-On is dissolved.

Both of the above divisions share characteristics of the ordinary dividend distribution in that the corporation's property is distributed to shareholders. Ordinarily the value of stock distributed to shareholders is taxable to the shareholders at ordinary income rates.

Under certain conditions the distribution of part of the business can also qualify as a partial liquidation. In a partial liquidation only the portion of the distribution representing the gain is taxable. The gain in a partial liquidation is taxed at capital gains rates. If assets were distributed rather than stock in the above examples, the transactions might qualify as partial liquidations.

The above transactions may also qualify as tax-free reorganizations. In this case, shareholders are not taxed on receipt of the distribution. The situations developed in the preceding examples are not taxable if specific conditions are met. The next section considers the criteria for the tax-free division.

CRITERIA FOR THE TAX-FREE DIVISION

Background

The principles underlying the tax-free corporate division were designed to provide tax-free treatment to corporate divisions that merely continue the original investment in changed form. The rationale is similar to that applicable to the tax-free reorganization in an acquisition situation.

In both examples cited earlier, the original investment continues in changed form. A corporation divides into two or more smaller corporations. The original shareholders continue as shareholders in two or more corporations rather than in just a single corporation. All original shareholders can continue to hold stock in all separate corporations, as in the AT&T illustration, or the distribution may be non-pro-rata, as in the case of Move-On Motors.

Specific criteria relating to corporate divisions help to ensure that tax-free status is awarded only when the original ownership continues. Otherwise division could be used to circumvent the dividend provisions and act as a device to distribute earnings at capital gains rates. A nonqualifying distribution is illustrated in the following example.

EXAMPLE: A TAXABLE CORPORATE DISTRIBUTION. The Sharp Corporation desires to distribute $1,000,000 in dividends to its shareholders. The dividends will be taxable to the investors at the individual taxpayer rate of 46 percent.

As an alternative to the dividend, Sharp considers transferring investments with a basis and market value of $1,000,000 to a new corporation. Sharp will then distribute stock in the new corporation to its shareholders. Sharp anticipates that the shareholders can then sell the investments at market value and, in effect, realize the distribution at reduced capital gains rates. Shareholders who do not need cash can continue to hold the investments with no gain recognition until the time of sale.

This attempted bailout of earnings does not meet the spirit of the tax-free provisions. The substance of the distribution resembles a two-step distribution of cash to shareholders. This distribution will probably be taxable to shareholders as a dividend at ordinary income rates.

Specific Criteria

The distributing corporation separated its assets into two groups in the preceding example. One group consisted of the assets needed for continuing operations. The second group consisted of the assets it desired to distribute to shareholders—the investments. The example illustrated an obvious attempt to distribute earnings and profits to shareholders at capital gains rates.

Specific criteria have been developed in an attempt to differentiate between the continuation of investment in changed form and the device for distributing earnings and profits. A summary of key specific criteria follows.

Business Purpose. The division must have a business purpose other than tax minimization. The business purpose must be for the benefit of the corporation rather than primarily for the benefit of the individual shareholders. The separation of assets as in the Sharp Corporation example would probably not meet the business purpose test. Divestiture of a particularly risky business or a court-ordered divestiture would be examples of business purpose.

Two or More Active Businesses. Both the parent corporation and any new corporations resulting from the division must be active businesses with a five-year minimum history of business operation. Additional restrictions apply if one business has been recently acquired. Passive investments in securities or real estate are not regarded as active businesses. As a consequence, the Sharp Corporation situation would also fail this criterion.

The active business requirement also makes it more difficult for the primary business to invest cash in a second business with the intent of later distributing the second business to shareholders. If a separate business is initiated, considerable time must pass to develop a history of business operation.

Continuity of Interest. The original shareholders must continue to maintain an interest in the newly received corporation. Some shareholders may sell stock, but if too much stock is sold, the distribution may be deemed taxable. A sale of stock to third parties prearranged to occur shortly after the division is not consistent with the continuity of interest provision.

Control and Transfer to Shareholders. The distributing corporation must have control of the distributed corporation prior to the distribution. The tax-free division applies to the distribution of shares of investments only if the distributing corporation held a majority of the outstanding shares. All stock in the distributed corporation must then be transferred to the shareholders.

The distributing corporation may distribute stock of an established subsidiary corporation. Alternatively, the distributing corporation may transfer part of its own assets (representing a separate active business) to a newly created corporation, and distribute the stock of this newly created corporation to shareholders.

THE FORM OF THE DIVISION

A tax-free division may take the form of a spin-off, a split-off, or a split-up. Neither the distributing corporation nor the shareholders recognize gain or loss on the transaction if any of the three forms of distribution meet the previously cited criteria.

The Spin-Off

In a spin-off, the parent corporation distributes stock of a subsidiary corporation to shareholders, as illustrated in Figure 12.1. The distribution can consist of stock in an established subsidiary or in a newly created subsidiary. The shareholders now hold stock in both the original corporation (now reduced in size) and in the second corporation. An illustration of the nontaxable spin-off follows.

EXAMPLE: A NONTAXABLE SPINOFF. The Forward Corporation, an auto manufacturer, determines that its steel-producing operation requires too much management attention. Forward sets up a new corporation, the United Steel Corporation, and transfers the steel-producing property to United. All of the United Steel Corporation stock is distributed to Forward's shareholders.

This may qualify as a nontaxable spinoff. Forward's shareholders do not recognize gain on the receipt of the stock. For-

The Form of the Division 351

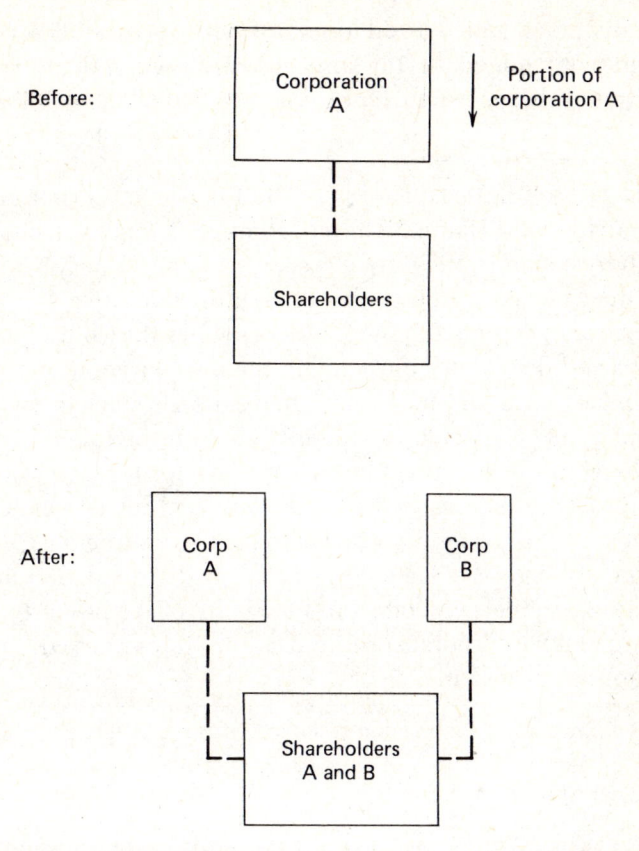

```
                    ┌──────────────┐    Portion of
  Before:           │ Corporation  │ ↓  corporation A
                    │      A       │
                    └──────┬───────┘
                           │
                    ┌──────┴───────┐
                    │ Shareholders │
                    └──────────────┘


                 ┌───────┐         ┌───────┐
  After:         │ Corp  │         │ Corp  │
                 │   A   │         │   B   │
                 └───┬───┘         └───┬───┘
                     │                 │
                   ┌─┴─────────────────┴─┐
                   │    Shareholders     │
                   │       A and B       │
                   └─────────────────────┘
```

Figure 12.1. The spin-off. The corporation divides and transfers stock to its shareholders.

ward's original shareholders continue to own the original Forward Corporation, now divided into the Forward Corporation and the United Steel Corporation. United Steel, however, is completely separate from Forward, the auto manufacturer.

If a spin-off does not qualify as tax-free, the consequences to the shareholder can be severe. In a spin-off, the shareholder does not turn in any shares. As a result, the entire distribution is treated as a dividend and is taxable as ordinary income. The consequences of a nonqualifying spin-off are shown in the following illustration.

EXAMPLE: A TAXABLE SPIN-OFF. The Big Burger Corporation is owned by Mrs. Hamm. The corporation operates a chain of hamburger stands. Big Burger receives an offer from Mr. King to buy the Chicago region stands at an attractive price.

Instead of selling, Big Burger incorporates the Chicago region stands and distributes the stock in the new corporation to Mrs. Hamm as a spinoff. Mrs. Hamm then sells the stock to Mr. King and attempts to recognize a capital gain on the sale.

The spin-off will probably not qualify for tax-free status. It will probably be regarded as a device used for tax-avoidance purposes. The corporation seems to be distributing the Chicago region stands to Mrs. Hamm as a property dividend. She should recognize dividend income on the receipt of the property. This plan to remove corporate profits at capital gains rates will probably not be successful.

The Split-Off

In a split-off, the shareholders turn in some of their shares of the parent in exchange for shares in a second corporation. Otherwise, the split-off is the same as the spin-off. The nontaxable split-off is illustrated as follows.

EXAMPLE: A NONTAXABLE SPLIT-OFF. In an earlier example, the Forward Corporation set up a new corporation, the United Steel Corporation. Forward transfers the steel producing property to United. All of the United Steel Corporation stock is distributed to Forward's shareholders. The example is modified slightly to provide for the exchange of shares by Forward's shareholders.

Forward's shareholders turn in one share of Forward stock for each five shares held. In return they receive one share of stock in the new United Steel Corporation.

This will probably be a nontaxable split-off. The effect is the same as in a spin-off, except that the parent corporation's shareholders turn in shares in exchange for shares of the distributed corporation.

The Split-Up

A split-up is the division of the parent corporation into two or more separate corporations. These corporations then distribute stock to the original corporation's shareholders. Figure 12.2 illustrates the split-up. The parent corporation liquidates and shareholders now hold stock only in the new corporations. An example of a split-up follows.

EXAMPLE: THE NONTAXABLE SPLIT-UP. Some time ago, the Elite Stores Corporation began selling closeout merchandise in a factory warehouse sale. Gradually the warehouse sale activity expanded into a continuous operation totally unrelated to any of Elite's regular merchandising activity. Elite then decided to divide the two activities into two separate corporations.

Elite divided the corporation by setting up two new corporations, the Fashion Stores Corporation and the Toolow Corporation. Elite's shareholders turned in their shares of stock in return for shares in Fashion and Toolow. This may also qualify as a tax-free division.

The treatment of a taxable split-off or split-up is less severe than that applicable to the taxable spin-off. Generally taxable split-offs and split-ups are treated as either liquidations or redemptions. In either event, taxable income is based upon only the gain rather than the entire distribution. With a taxable spin-off, the shareholder receives dividend treatment.

354   Spin-Offs and Other Corporate Divisions

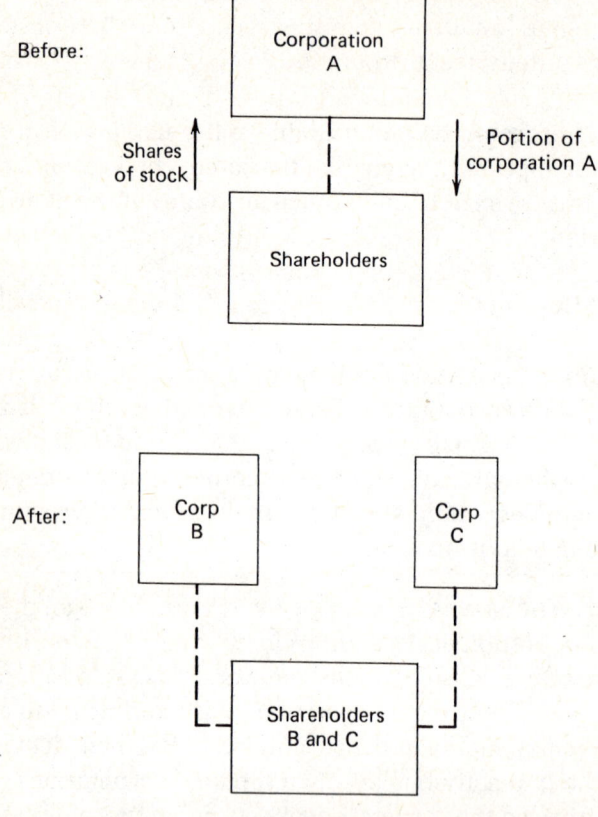

Figure 12.2. The split-up. The corporation divides into two or more separate corporations and distributes all stock to shareholders.

The Adjusted Basis of the Distributed Corporation

Two questions arise with respect to the adjusted basis of the newly distributed corporation. First, what is the adjusted basis of the assets to the distributed corporation? The answer is that the assets retain the same basis they had in the parent corporation at the time of their distribution, as with any distribution of stock. As a consequence, depreciation, for example, will continue with the previous depreciation schedule.

The second question relates to the basis of the stock in both the original corporation and the new corporation or corporations. The original basis is prorated between the original corporation stock and the new corporation stock in proportion to market values. In other words, the original adjusted basis of the stock to shareholders is divided up between the stocks of the original corporation and the new corporation or corporations.

Evaluation of the Tax-Free Division

The qualified spin-off, split-off, or split-up provides a tax-free mechanism for dividing the business. In many cases, tax-free treatment will be preferred and the concern will be with meeting both the specific criteria for the tax-free division and also the general requirements for a tax-free reorganization.

In some cases, however, treatment as a dividend or liquidation may be preferable due to basis considerations or the desire of shareholders to recognize losses. This section examines the pros and cons of the tax-free division.

The Basis of the Distributing Corporation. The basis of the distributing corporation's assets does not change upon tax-free transfer of the corporation's stock. If the assets themselves are distributed as a property dividend, however, the basis to the noncorporate shareholder is the fair market value. In some cases, the distribution of a dividend entails little or no tax cost. For example, the corporation making the distribution may have no earnings and profits. Since dividends are taxable only to the extent of earnings and profits, the distribution will not be taxable. Consequently, the shareholder may be able to step up the basis of assets at no tax cost with a property dividend.

Loss Recognition. The taxable split-up and distribution of assets to shareholders with no portion of the original corporation remaining may qualify as a complete liquidation. The shareholders receive sale treatment in a complete liquidation. They recognize gain or loss as the difference between the fair market value of the stock received and the adjusted basis of their stock.

If the fair market value of the stock received by the shareholders is less than their basis in the stock, the shareholders recognize capital losses on receipt of property in liquidation. The desirability of recognizing losses may also lead shareholders to prefer the taxable distribution of assets rather than the tax-free distribution of stock in the event of declines in the market value of property.

SUMMARY

General. Corporations can be divided tax-free by distributing stock in a subsidiary corporation to shareholders if certain requirements are met.

Types of Distributions. Tax-free divisions can take the form of a spin-off, split-off, or split-up. The distributing corporation does not recognize gain or loss in a qualifying spin-off, split-off, or split-up. If the division qualifies as tax-free, the shareholders receiving the distribution do not recognize gain or loss. The shareholder's basis in the combined holdings does not change. The basis of property held by the corporation also does not change.

The Spin-Off. In a spin-off, the parent corporation distributes stock of a subsidiary corporation to shareholders.

The Split-Off. In a split-off, the shareholders of the parent turn in part of their original shares before receiving shares in the new corporation. Otherwise, the split-off is identical to the spin-off.

The Split-Up. In a split-up, all the parent corporation's assets are transferred to two or more new corporations. These corporations then distribute stock to the original corporation's shareholders.

Criteria. Requirements for tax-free treatment include:

A business purpose other than tax minimization and division for the benefit of the business rather than the shareholders.

Both the parent corporation and any new corporations resulting from the division represent active businesses with a history of business operation.

A continuity of interest on the part of the shareholders.

Control by the parent of the corporation that is distributed, and the distribution of stock to the parent corporation's shareholders.

Nonqualifying Distributions. Nonqualifying distributions are treated as dividends, redemptions or liquidations with gains taxable to the shareholders.

Sometimes it is advantageous to structure distributions in a manner that ensures that the transaction is taxable. Key considerations include the tax to shareholders on receipt of a dividend or other taxable distribution, the adjusted basis, and the possibility that shareholders may recognize losses on a distribution received in liquidation.

Index

Accelerated Cost Recovery System, 69, 70
Accelerated depreciation:
  ACRS, 69, 70
  minimum tax, 282, 283
Accounting alternatives, 22, 23
Accounting method:
  accrual basis, 25, 26
  cash-basis, 28, 29
Accrual basis accounting, 25, 26
Accumulated earnings, 192–196
  preferred stock bailout, 197, 198
  problems with, 194
  sale treatment, 223
  S corporation, 276, 277
  tax, 194, 212–214
Acquisition indebtedness, 313
Acquisitions, 51, 52
  acquired corporation, 302–304
  acquired liabilities, 304
  basis step-up, 307
  borrowed funds, 312
  capital gain, 304
  form of, 300, 301
  loss carryforward, 305–307
  reasons for, 302
ACRS, 69, 70
  basis, 72–74
  depreciation rate, 70–72
  early acquisition, 75
  property class, 70, 71
  straight-line depreciation, 74, 75

Add-on minimum tax, 282, 283
Affiliated corporation, 42, 89, 257–259
  consolidated tax return, 283–285
  liquidation of, 248–250
Allocation:
  acceptability of, 302
  purchase price, 67, 68
  selling price, 299–301
Allowance:
  bad debts, 169–171
Alternative business forms, 264, 265
Alternatives:
  accounting, 22, 23
Amortization, 77, 78
Amount realized, 101
Asset purchase, 291–294
  allocation of selling price, 299–301
  basis, 292
  basis step-up, 307
Asset sale, 291–294
  allocation of selling price, 299–301
  capital gain, 294
  liquidation of seller, 294, 295, 297
  recapture, 294
  shareholders, 297

Bad debts, 169–171
  allowance method, 169
  minimum tax, 282

Bailout, preferred stock, 197, 198
Basis:
  ACRS, 72, 74
  adjusted, 65
  advantages of step-up, 308
  asset purchase, 292, 307
  carryover in liquidation of
      subsidiary, 249, 250
  form of acquisition, 338, 339
  gain or loss, 101–106
  interest and taxes during
      construction, 65–66
  investment tax credit, 106, 108
  liquidation, 243, 248, 297
  liquidation and reincorporation,
      253–255
  nontaxable exchange, 113, 114,
      116, 117, 271
  partial liquidation, 238, 239
  property redemption, 231
  property transfer, 269, 270
  recapture, 308
  reduction for investment tax
      credit, 56, 57
  rehabilitation tax credit, 62, 63
  spin-off, 354, 355
  split-off, 354, 355
  split-up, 354, 355
  stock, 311
  stock for assets decision, 332
  stock dividend, 210, 211
  stock purchase, 307–310
  tax-free reorganization, 318, 319,
      327, 328, 337, 338
Bond, tax-free, 18, 22
Boot:
  nontaxable exchange, 118, 119,
      330–332, 334–336
  tax-free reorganization, 331, 332,
      334–336
  transfer to controlled corporation,
      271
Business energy credit, 64
Business form, 264, 265
Business history, tax-free division,
    349

Business purpose:
  tax-free division, 349
  tax-free reorganization, 325

Capital, ability to raise, 265
Capital contribution, 265, 266
  S corporation, 275, 276
Capital expenditure, 20, 21
Capital gain, 120, 123–125, 223
  allocation of selling price for,
      299–301
  applicable property, 121
  computation of, 122, 123,
      132–138
  flow-through in S corporation,
      274, 275
  holding period, 121
  liquidation, 243, 244
  liquidation and reincorporation,
      253–255
  minimum tax, 282
  nonqualifying division, 353
  partial liquidation, 234–237
  recapture, 139
  redemption, 225–227, 231, 232
  sale of assets, 294
  sale of stock, 195, 196, 220, 222
  sale to related party, 129
  S corporation, 277–279
  small business stock, 272–273
  tax rate, 190
Capitalization, cost, 52
Capital loss, 120, 121
  carryforward and carryback, 122
  tax-free reorganization, 338
Capital structure, recapitalization,
    340, 341
Carryback:
  capital loss, 122
  consolidated return, 285
  financial statements, 36
  operating loss, 32–34
Carryforward:
  basis step-up, 308, 309
  capital loss, 122
  financial statements, 36, 37

Index

operating loss, 34, 35
S corporation loss, 275, 276
Carryover basis:
  liquidation of subsidiary, 249, 250
  nontaxable exchange, 271
  partial liquidation, 239
  spin-off, 354, 355
  split-off, 354, 355
  split-up, 354, 355
  tax-free reorganization, 318, 319, 337, 338
  transfer to corporation, 269, 270
Cash, stock for stock reorganization, 330, 333
Cash-basis accounting, 28, 29
Cash flow, effect of tax on, 1, 2
Certified historic structure, tax credit, 62
Change in identity or form, tax-free organization, 341
Charter, corporate, 264, 265
Closely held corporation, 196
  accumulated earnings tax, 212–214
  double taxation, 212–216
  loan from shareholder, 199–201
  passive investment income, 215
  personal holding company tax, 214–216
  rental from shareholders, 202, 203
  salary to shareholders, 201, 202
  sale to, 127–129
  sale of stock in, 224, 257–259, 266
  S corporation, 273, 274
Code, tax, 9
Collapsible corporation, 255, 256
  criteria, 257
  holding period, 257
  income potential, 257
Compensation, for stock, 268
Completed contract method, 162
Consolidated tax return, 283–285, 304
  advantages and disadvantages, 283–285
  eligibility, 286

operating loss, 285
tax credit, 285
Consolidation, 320, 324
  boot received, 334–336
  shareholder approval, 336, 337
  tax-free reorganization, 333–337
Contingent asset, loss carryforward, 36, 37
Contribution:
  capital, 265, 266
  capital in S corporation, 275, 276
  shareholder, 268–271
Control:
  loss on sale of stock, 196
  tax-free division, 349
  tax-free reorganization, 325, 326, 329
Controlled corporation, 42
  dividends received, 208, 209
  transfer to, 268–271
  transfer for services, 268
Controlled group, 42–44, 89, 90, 257–259
  consolidated tax return, 283–285
  election to expense, 91
Controlled subsidiary, liquidation of, 248–250
Corporate form, advantages, 265
Cost allocation, depreciation, 68, 69
Cost of goods sold, 26–28, 152
Cost recovery, depreciation, 68, 69
Cost-basis, depletion, 79
Covenant not to compete, allocation to, 301
Credit, tax, 23–25, 53
Credit sales, bad debts, 169–171

Debt:
  compared to equity, 201
  corporate acquisition, 312
  deductibility of, 199–201
  when equivalent to equity, 201, 202
  recapitalization, 340, 341
Deduction, 20, 51, 52
  acceleration of, 31, 32

Deduction (*Continued*)
　　capital expenditure, 20, 21
　　dividend from affiliated
　　　　corporation, 208, 209
　　dividends received, 207, 208
　　minimum tax, 282, 283
　　related taxpayer, 44, 45
　　timing of, 26
Deferral:
　　cash-basis accounting, 28, 29
　　dividends received, 209
　　gain, 319
　　investment tax credit, 59–61
　　nontaxable exchange, 111, 112
　　revenue recognition, 19
　　tax, 4, 5, 30
　　tax payment, 37, 38
　　tax planning, 29–32
Deferred tax, 165–168
　　depreciation, 168
　　liability, 167
Depletion:
　　cost-basis, 79
　　mineral resources, 78
　　percentage-basis, 79–80
Depreciable property, 52
　　allocation of selling price, 299–301
　　sale to related party, 129
Depreciation, 52, 68, 69, 91
　　ACRS, 69, 70
　　deferred tax, 168
　　early acquisition, 75
　　election to expense, 75–77
　　leased property, 81–85
　　minimum tax, 282, 283
　　nonrecovery property, 75
　　nontaxable exchange, 116
　　property class, 69, 70
　　recapture, 74, 294, 297, 298
　　recapture in basis step-up, 308–310
　　straight-line method, 74–75
Depreciation rate, ACRS, 70–72
Depreciation recapture, 139–143
　　investment tax credit, 143, 144

　　liquidation, 244, 245
　　partial liquidation, 237
　　property subject to, 143
　　real estate, 144–146
　　redemption, 231, 232
　　tax-free reorganization, 327, 328
Directors, 267
Diversification, investment, 265, 266
Dividend, 183, 184, 202, 267
　　affiliated corporation, 208, 209
　　from another corporation, 207–209
　　compared to partial liquidation, 241
　　compared to redemption, 230
　　corporate shareholder, 207, 239
　　criteria, 224, 225
　　deferral of, 192–197
　　nondeductibility of, 199–201
　　sale of stock in related corporation, 258, 259
　　stock, 210–212
　　taxable spin-off, 351, 352
Dividend received deduction, 207, 208
Division:
　　reasons for, 345–347
　　tax-free reorganization, 345, 346
Double taxation, 189–191, 266
　　closely held corporation, 212–216
　　debt, 199
　　deductions, 198, 199
　　loan to corporation, 199–201
　　minimization of, 192
　　owner salary, 204, 205
　　personal holding company, 214–216
　　problem with, 190
　　property dividend, 205, 206
　　rental, 202, 203
　　S corporation avoids, 274
　　S corporation income, 276–280

Earnings, bailout, 197, 198
Earnings accumulation, 195, 196
　　passive investment income, 215

Index

personal holding company tax, 214–216
Earnings distributions:
  dividends, 183, 184
  property dividend, 205, 206
Earnings and profits, 185–189
Earnings reinvestment, 195, 196
Election:
  basis step-up, 307, 308
  expense, 75–77, 91
  reduce investment tax credit, 57, 58
  S corporation, 280, 281
Employee benefits, 171
Employee compensation, 171
Employee stock option, 171
Employee Stock Ownership Plan, 177, 178
Energy credit, 64
Equity, compared to debt, 201
ESOP tax credit, 177, 178
Estimated expense, 22
Estimated tax, 37, 38
Exchange:
  controlled corporation, 268–271
  nontaxable, 110–111
  services, 268
Exclusions, 18
Expense, estimated, 22

Fair market value, services, 268
FIFO inventory, 155, 156
Finance lease, 88–89
Financial reporting, 21, 22
  installment method, 165
  LIFO balance sheet, 161
  LIFO conformity, 159, 160
  percentage completion method, 163
Financial statements:
  deferred tax, 165–168
  loss carryback, 36
  loss carryforward, 36, 37
Fine, 20, 22
First-in First-out method, 155, 156
Fixed assets, 52
  allocation of purchase price, 67, 68

recapture, 139
sale of, 126–129
Flow-through:
  capital gain in S corporation, 274, 275
  income in S corporation, 274
  investment tax credit, 59–61
  operating loss in S corporation, 275, 276

Gain, 101–106, 292
  capital, 120, 294
  collapsible corporation, 255, 256
  consolidated tax return, 283–285
  liquidation, 245–248, 251, 252
  liquidation of controlled subsidiary, 248–250
  partial liquidation, 236, 237
  recognized, 106, 110, 118, 119
  redemption, 231, 232
  related party, 129
  S corporation, 277–280
  small business stock, 272, 273
Gain deferral:
  nontaxable exchange, 111, 112
  tax-free reorganization, 319
Gain recognition:
  nonqualifying division, 353
  partial liquidation, 237
  property transfer, 268–271
  transfer of services, 268
Goodwill:
  allocation of selling price, 299–301
  not depreciable, 301
Growth stock, 193, 223
Guarantee, deduction for, 22

Hidden liabilities, exchange of stock for assets, 332
Holding period, capital gain, 121

Illegal payment, 20, 22
Improvement, 20
Incentive stock option, 172, 173
Income, 21, 22
  deductions, 20

Income (*Continued*)
  flow-through in S corporation, 274
  pretax, 21, 22
Incorporation, 264, 265
Installment method, 164, 165
Installment receivables, liquidation of corporation, 244
Intangible asset, 77, 78
Interest:
  construction period, 65, 66
  when debt equivalent to equity, 201, 202
Internal Revenue Service, 9, 10
Inventory, 26–28, 151, 152
  allocation of selling price to, 301
  FIFO, 155, 156
  flow assumptions, 154
  LIFO, 155, 156
  liquidation, 244
  lower of cost or market, 153, 154
  sale of, 294
  specific identification, 155
Investment:
  return of, 220
  S corporation, 275, 276
  for services, 268
  shareholders, 268, 269
  small business stock, 272, 273
Investment income, personal holding company tax, 214, 215
Investment tax credit, 53, 54
  amount of, 54, 55
  basis reduction for, 56, 57
  cash flow, 60, 61
  consolidated tax return, 285
  election to expense, 75–77
  election to step-up basis, 310
  financial reporting of, 59
  leased property, 81–85
  limitation of, 55, 56
  nontaxable exchange, 117
  qualifying property, 54
  recapture, 146–148, 294
  recapture in liquidation, 244
  recapture in partial liquidation, 237

  recapture on redemption, 231, 232
  reduction of, 57, 58
  rehabilitated building, 61, 62
  tax planning, 54, 58, 59
  used property, 56, 90
Investor, diversification of, 265, 266
IRS, 9, 10

Land, allocation of selling price, 299, 300
Last-in First-out method (LIFO), 155, 156
Layers, LIFO inventory, 158, 159
Lease, 81, 88, 202, 203
  advantage of, 81
  criteria for, 86
  finance lease, 88–89
  vs. purchase, 85
  from related taxpayer, 89
  safe harbor lease, 88, 89
  sale and leaseback, 87–88
  tax advantage, 83–85
  tax treatment, 81–85
  used property, 90
Liabilities:
  acquired in acquisitions, 304
  exchange of stock for assets, 332
Liability, limited, 265
LIFO inventory, 155, 156
  balance sheet, 161
  conformity, 159, 160
  decreasing prices, 156–158
  layers, 158, 159
  liquidation, 244
  switch to, 158
  tax advantage of, 156
Limited liability, shareholders', 265
Liquidation, 242
  basis of property, 248
  change in identity or form, 341
  collapsible corporation, 255, 256
  controlled subsidiary, 248–250
  loss, 250
  merger or consolidation, 333, 335
  nonrecognition of gain, 243
  property, 297

Index

reincorporation, 253–255
sale of assets, 294, 295
after sale of assets, 295, 297
sale by distributing corporation, 245–248
sale treatment, 237, 243, 244
split-off, 353
split-up, 353
straddle, 251, 252, 340
tax-free reorganization, 331
Loan, shareholder, 199–201
Long-term capital gain:
   minimum tax, 282
   S corporation, 277–280
Long-term construction contracts, 161, 162
Loss, 101, 103–106, 271
   capital, 120, 121
   consolidated tax return, 283–285
   flow-through in S corporation, 275–276
   liquidation, 250
   nontaxable exchange, 119
   operating, 32
   related party sale, 128, 129
   small business stock, 272, 273
   straddle, 251, 252, 340
Loss carryback, 32–34
   consolidated return, 285
   financial statements, 36
Loss carryforward, 34, 35, 305–307
   basis step-up, 308
   financial statements, 36, 37
   S corporation, 275, 276
   tax-free reorganization, 327, 328
Lower of cost or market, 153, 154

Marginal tax rate, 14, 15, 190, 311
   capital gain, 120, 121
   controlled group, 42–44
   form of acquisition, 338
   multidivision corporation, 40–42
   ordinary income, 120, 121
Market value, 67, 68
Merger, 320, 323, 333–338
   boot received, 334–336

   shareholder approval, 336, 337
Mineral resources, 78–79
Minimum tax, 282, 283
Multidivision corporation, marginal tax rate, 40–42

Nondepreciable property, allocation of selling price, 299–301
Nonqualified stock option, 173, 174
Nonrecognition of loss, related party, 128, 129
Nonrecovery property, ACRS, 75
Nontaxable exchange, 110, 111, 316–318
   boot, 118, 119, 271
   controlled corporation, 268–271
   depreciation, 116
   followed by sale, 114, 116
   investment tax credit, 117
   loss, 119
   problems with, 113, 114, 116, 117
   qualifications for, 112

One-shot election, S corporation, 277–280
Operating loss, 32
   carryback of, 32–34
   carryforward of, 34, 35, 305–309
   consolidated tax return, 283–285
   financial statements, 36
   flow-through in S corporation, 275–276
Ordinary income:
   collapsible corporation, 255, 256
   dividends, 183, 184
   nonqualifying redemption, 227
   partial liquidation, 236, 237
   preferred stock bailout, 197, 198
   property dividend, 205, 206
   recapture, 139
   sale of stock to related corporation, 258, 259
   tax rate, 13, 14, 190
Ordinary loss, small business stock, 272, 273

Overhaul, 20, 21
Owner salary, deductible to corporation, 205

Partial liquidation, 234–236
  basis, 238, 239
  compared to dividend or redemption, 241
  corporate shareholder, 239
  criteria, 239, 240
  gain recognition, 236–237
  sale treatment, 237
Partnership, compared to corporation, 266
Passive investment, tax-free division, 349
Passive investment income, 215
Payment, tax, 37, 38
Penalty:
  exceptions to, 38, 39
  underpayment, 38
Pension deduction, 22
Pension plan, 174, 175
Percentage completion method, 162, 163
Percentage depletion, 79–80
Personal holding company tax, 194, 214–216
Planning, tax, 3, 29–32
Preferences, minimum tax, 282, 283
Preferred stock, recapitalization, 340, 341
Preferred stock bailout, 197, 198
Present value, 5, 6
Pretax income, 21, 22
  loss carryback, 36
  loss carryforward, 36, 37
Progressive tax, 13, 14
Property acquisition, 52
Property class, depreciation, 69, 70
Property dividend, 205, 206
  corporate shareholder, 207
Purchase:
  vs. lease, 85–86
  stock, 266

  vs. tax-free reorganization, 337, 338
Purchase of assets, 291–294
  allocation of selling price, 299–301
  basis, 292
  basis step-up, 307
Purchase of stock:
  acquired corporation, 302, 304
  acquired liabilities, 304
  basis step-up, 307–310
  capital gain, 303, 304
  loss carryforward, 305–307
  reasons for, 302
Purchase price, allocation, 67, 68

Qualified pension plan, 174, 175
Qualified stock, 237

Recapitalization, tax-free reorganization, 340, 341
Recapture:
  basis step-up, 308–310
  depreciation, 74, 139–143, 294, 297, 298
  investment tax credit, 146–148, 294
  liquidation, 244, 245
  partial liquidation, 237
  property subject to, 143
  redemption, 231, 232
  sale of assets, 295
  tax-free reorganization, 327, 328
Receipt, compared to revenue, 17
Receivables, liquidation, 244
Recognition:
  alternatives to, 108, 110
  loss in nontaxable exchange, 120
  loss with straddle, 340
Recovery of cost, depreciation, 70, 71
Redemption, 225
  basis, 231
  compared to dividend, 230
  compared to partial liquidation, 241

Index

constructive ownership, 228–230
  criteria, 228–230
  dividend treatment, 227
  loss, 232, 233
  nonqualifying, 227
  property, 230, 231
  split-off, 353
  split-up, 353
  stock in related corporation, 257–259
  tax on, 225–227
Refund, operating loss, 32–34
Regulations, Treasury, 9
Rehabilitation tax credit, 61, 62
  basis, 62, 63
  qualification for, 62–64
Reincorporation, following liquidation, 253–255
Reinvestment of earnings, 195, 196
Related corporation, sale of stock to, 257–259
Related party, 42–45
  sale to, 127–129
  special considerations, 89–91
Rental, related corporation, 45, 46, 202, 203
Repair, 20, 21
Research and development tax credit, 175–177
Retained earnings, compared to earnings and profits, 186
Retention of earnings, 192–196
Return of investment, 224, 225
Revenue, 17
  realization, 17, 19
  recognition, 17, 22
  sales, 25
  unrealized, 19
Ruling, IRS, 9, 10

Salary:
  for stock, 268
  unreasonable, 205
Sale:
  alternative to liquidation, 250
  fixed assets, 126–129

  installment method, 164, 165
  liquidation, 245–248
  related corporation, 45, 46
  stock, 221, 266
  stock *vs.* assets, 310, 312
Sale of assets, 392
  allocation of selling price, 299–301
  capital gain, 294
  liquidation of seller, 295–297
  recapture, 294
  shareholders, 297
Sale and leaseback, 87–88
Sale of stock:
  acquired corporation, 302–304
  acquired liabilities, 304
  capital gain, 304
  loss carryforward, 305–307
  reasons for, 302
Sale treatment, 221, 222
  liquidation and reincorporation, 253–255
  redemption, 225–227, 231
  stock to related corporation, 257–259
Sales revenue, 25
S corporation:
  advantages, 281
  distributions of earnings, 276, 277
  earnings prior to election, 276, 277
  history, 281
  income flow-through, 274
  loss of election, 281
  one-shot election, 277–280
  qualifications, 280
  reason for, 273, 274
Seasonal business, estimated tax, 39
Shareholder:
  benefits, 267
  investments, 268, 269
  loan to corporation, 199–201
  S corporation, 279
Small business, estimated tax, 39, 40
Small business stock, loss on, 270, 271

Small corporation:
  tax rates, 15, 16
  used property tax credit, 56
Small investor, 349
Spin-off:
  active businesses, 354, 355
  basis, 354, 355
  business purpose, 349
  continuity of interest, 349
  control, 349
  loss recognition, 355, 356
  nonqualifying distribution, 351, 352
  passive investment, 349
  transfer to shareholders, 349
Split-off:
  active businesses, 349
  basis, 354, 355
  business purpose, 349
  continuity of interest, 349
  control, 349
  loss recognition, 355, 356
  passive investment, 349
  transfer to shareholders, 349
Split-up:
  active businesses, 349
  basis, 354, 355
  business purpose, 349
  continuity of interest, 349
  control, 349
  loss recognition, 355, 356
  nonqualifying distribution, 353
  passive investment, 349
  transfer to shareholders, 349
Statutory depletion, 79, 80
Step-transaction, 326
Stock, 264, 265
Stock basis, 311
  form of acquisition, 338, 339
Stock dividend, 210–212
Stock option, 171
  incentive stock option, 172, 173
  nonqualified, 173, 174
Stock ownership, 266
  S corporation, 280

Stock purchase:
  acquired corporation, 302, 304
  acquired liabilities, 304
  basis step-up, 307–310
  capital gain, 303, 304
  loss carryforward, 305–307
  reasons for, 302
  recapture in basis step-up, 308–310
Stock redemption, 225
  compared to the dividend, 240, 241
  compared to partial liquidation, 230
  criteria, 228–230
  gain, 231, 232
  loss, 232, 233
  nonqualifying, 227
  recapture, 231, 232
  split-off, 353
  split-up, 353
  tax on, 225–227
Stock sale, 221
  acquired liabilities, 304
  capital gain, 304
  concerned parties, 303
  loss carryforward, 305–307
  partial liquidation, 237
  reasons for, 302
Straddle:
  liquidation, 251, 252
  tax-free reorganization, 340
Subsidiary corporation:
  basis, 307, 308
  consolidated tax return, 283–285
  liabilities, 304
  liquidation of, 248–250
  loss carryforward, 305–309
  purchase of stock, 302, 304
  reasons for, 302
  spin-off, 350, 351
  split-off, 352, 353
  split-up, 353
  tax-free division, 345–347

Index

Targeted-jobs tax credit, 177
Tax, 212–214
   accumulated earnings, 65, 66
   construction period, 214–216
   personal holding company, 214–215
Taxable income, 17, 21, 22
Tax administration, 9, 10
Tax bracket, 13, 14
Tax Code, 9
Tax Court, 10
Tax credit, 23–25, 53
   business energy, 64
   consolidated tax return, 285
   ESOP, 177, 178
   investment, 53–59
   research and development, 175–177
   targeted-jobs, 177
Tax deferral, 4, 5, 29–32, 165–168
   dividends received, 209
   revenue recognition, 19
Tax determination, 17
Tax expense:
   investment tax credit, 59–61
   loss carryback, 36
   loss carryforward, 36, 37
Tax-free division, 345–347
   basis, 354, 355
   business history, 349
   business purpose, 349
   continuity of interest, 349
   control, 349
   criteria for, 347, 348
   spin-off, 350–352
   split-off, 352, 353
   split-up, 353
   transfer to shareholders, 349
Tax-free exchange, 110, 111
Tax-free reorganization:
   basis carryover, 327, 328
   business purpose, 325
   change in identity or form, 341
   consequences of, 327, 328
   consolidation, 320, 324, 333–337
   continuing interest, 325–326

   control, 325, 326, 329, 333
   criteria, 329, 330, 333
   gain, 318, 319
   loss carryforward, 327, 329
   merger, 320, 324, 333–337
   vs. purchase, 337, 338
   recapitalization, 340, 341
   recapture, 327, 328
   step-transaction, 326
   stock for assets, 320, 330–332, 336
   stock for stock, 320, 329, 330, 333
   tax rate, 338
   voting stock, 329, 330, 333
Tax legislation, 9
Tax loss:
   carryback of, 32–34
   carryforward of, 34, 35
   financial statements, 36
Tax minimization, 3, 4
Tax payment, 37, 38
Tax planning, 3, 29–32
Tax preferences:
   minimum tax, 282, 283
Tax rate, 4, 13, 14
   capital gain, 120–125, 190
   controlled group, 42–44
   corporate, 190
   form of acquisition, 338
   individual, 190
   marginal, 14, 15
   ordinary income, 120, 122
   small corporation, 15, 16
Tax refund, 32–34
Tax return, consolidated, 283–285
Tax theory, 8, 9
Trade-in, nontaxable exchange, 110, 111
Treasury Department, 9
Treasury Regulations, 9
Triple taxation, 207, 208
Twelve-month liquidation, 245–248

Underpayment:
   exceptions, 38, 39
   penalty, 38

Undistributed earnings,
    accumulated earnings tax,
      213–215
Used property:
  controlled group, 90
  investment tax credit, 56, 117
  leased from related taxpayer, 90

Vesting, pension plan,
  175
Voting rights, 267
Voting stock:
  in exchange of stock, 329
  tax-free reorganization,
    330, 333

Sistema binario de signos, *véase*
  Sistema sígnico
Sistema sígnico
  binario 24, 83, 175
  ternario 24, 83, 175-6, 212, 224
Sócrates 239-41, 244-6
"Solución final" 268, 278
Steiner, G. 275
Stoessel, M. 59-61, 83
Sueño 16, 40, 53-7, 63, 78, 94-6, 135, 143, 179, 189-95, 198-203, 209-10, 215, 221, 226, 241, 249-50, 275-6
  y despertar 96, 137, 163, 189-92, 198, 215, 226
Szondi, P. 32

Taxonomía 83, 247
Teoría Crítica 18-20, 119, 128, 281-3
Teoría feminista 121, 128, 133
Tiempo 47-8, 52, 112, 145, 190, 232, 257
  homogéneo, vacío 43, 48
Topografía 40, 59, 78, 91-3, 135-7, 168, 180, 189-90, 195, 200, 215, 223-7
Traducción 55, 100, 170-1, 179, 213, 227-32, 247
  sin el original 167, 179, 221, 249, 254
  teoría benjaminiana de la 215-22, 229-33
Transición entre el sueño y el despertar 137, 163
  del sistema binario a ternario 24, 83, 175
Triángulo edípico 61, 133-4
  origen 80, 85, 88-91, 204-6, 254
  el Otro 123-5, 167-71, 176, 180, 250, 273, 281
  el otro sexo 123, 154, 168, 175
  el lenguaje del otro 167-8, 171, 176, 179-80
Tropos 21, 143

Umbral 96, 137, 148, 162-3, 180, 186, 189, 192
  entre el sueño y el despertar 96, 137, 189

Warburg, A. 246-7, 252-4
  Mnemosyne 247, 252
Wittgenstein, L. 281-3
Wohlfarth, I. 30-2

Yates, F. A. 175, 244

del grupo colectivo 40, 198-200,
203, 227, 243
estudio contemporáneo acerca de
la 239, 243
modelo topográfico de la 16, 186-
9, 192, 198-200, 213, 223, 227
pictórica 246-7, 250-4
y escritura 239-43
Mesianismo 16, 20-2, 37, 67, 105,
110, 254-7, 265
Metáfora 13, 34, 37, 45, 48-52, 103,
112, 135, 237, 241, 283
Mímesis 37, 61, 64, 131-3, 150, 223
Mitchell, W. 100
Mito 121, 125, 135-9, 155, 160, 173,
180, 190, 233, 239-41, 266, 276-8
Mnemotécnica 241-4

Nacionalsocialismo 268-70, 273-6,
279, 283
Nieztsche 69, 74, 86-8, 91-3, 250
*Vom Nutzen und Nachteil der
Historie für das Leben* 89

Olvido 22, 64-6, 203, 207, 252

Pasajes/galerías 53-5, 91, 162-3, 180,
189-90, 200
Pensar en imágenes [*Bildenken*]11-
6, 37, 43, 55, 74, 80, 100-13, 126-
8, 139, 145, 148, 157-8, 185, 188,
226, 255, 265-6, 283
Personificación 163, 175, 180
Pintura 57-9, 100, 103, 138, 171,
243-4, 24Pizarra mágica
[*Wunderblock*] 112, 179, 190, 241
Platón 71-2, 239-41
Fedro 239-41, 244
Política y arte 33-6
de las imágenes 39
Postestructuralismo 18-20, 128
Presencia de espíritu 30, 39-40, 64
Prostituta [*Hure*] como figura 16,
145, 148, 152, 162-5, 180 *véase
también* ramera

Proust 66, 74, 98, 196, 207-9
Proveniencia 44, 88-9
Psicoanálisis 16, 22-4, 39-40, 55, 67,
94, 133-4, 137, 141, 167, 179, 189,
195, 201-4, 213, 225, 241, 249, 273

Ramera [*Dirne*] *véase también*
Prostituta [*Hure*] 145, 152-4, 157,
162-3, 180
Recuerdo 45, 61, 85, 101, 185-6, 196,
226, 243, 247-9, 254-5
Redención 22, 24, 67, 138, 219, 230-
2, 235, 254-7
Reik, T. 196
Representación distorsionada 163-7,
179, 193-5, 200, 210-3, 225, 249,
252
Retórica 11, 103, 237-9, 243-4
Retorno/vuelta 23, 67, 112, 146, 213,
230-2, 254, 278
Revelación 144, 186, 223
distancia de la 218-9, 227-32
Revolución 33, 43-5, 47
Revolución Francesa 42-3, 93

Schmitt, C. 18, 262-3
Scholem, G. 107-9, 139, 255-7, 265
Semejanza, *véase también* Similitud
24, 59, 82-3, 97, 98-100, 105, 207-
10, 222-5, 227, 249
Semiótica 129-33, 148
Shock /Chock 63-4, 185, 196
Símbolo del deseo 40, 78, 163, 198-
200, 227, 255
Símbolo mnémico 40, 193-5, 200,
209, 213, 216, 249, 275
Similitud 11, 59, 69, 82-5, 94, 100,
131-3, 175-6, 212, 223-5
distorsionada 24, 85, 209-10,
216, 225
no sensorial 24, 60, 82, 85, 100,
131, 149, 186, 209-12, 216,
222-5
Síntoma 22, 193-5, 207, 249, 252,
273-5

Índice histórico 16, 176, 200, 255
Inervación 39, 52, 55, 96, 165, 198, 204
Inmediatez 36-7, 43, 61, 82-3, 131, 210-2, 216-9, 222, 225, 229, 255
Inspección [*Beaugenscheinigung*] 111, 137-8
Irigaray, L. 150

Jeroglíficos 179
Jetztzeit 39, 43, 48, 137, 255-7
Jung, C. 201

Kafka, F. 20, 64-7, 74, 160-2, 180, 207, 232, 252-4
  La colonia penitenciaria 66, 252
Kant, I. 263
Klee, P. 109-112
  Angelus Novus 100, 106-9, 112, 139, 157-8, 265
Kracauer, S. 203
Kraus, K., 163
Kristeva, J. 18-20, 119, 129-37, 154
  Des Chinoises 134, 150
  Historias de amor 134

Laberinto 146-8, 189-92, 206, 226-7, 241
Lacan, J. 133-4, 157, 221
Lavater, J. 248-9
Lectura
  la teoría de Benjamin de 40, 78, 93, 103, 126, 135-8, 178-9, 186, 198-203, 213-5, 222, 225-7, 232, 254
Legibilidad 13, 16, 42, 74, 76-8, 85, 94, 97, 185, 193, 198-200, 209-13, 244-6, 249-50
Lenguaje 78-85, 100, 105, 126, 129-33, 145, 148-50, 154, 176, 192, 210-2, 233-5, 249-52
  adámico 61, 82, 100, 149, 218, 232
  como discurso 78, 85, 93
  como literatura 78-80, 83-5, 176, 225

crítica de Wittgenstein sobre el 283
de la conciencia 24, 40, 55, 66, 163, 181, 193, 200, 203-4, 210, 213-6, 221, 225, 249, 2⁻3
de las cosas 100, 212, 215, 216, 225
del cuerpo 23, 63, 66, 150, 249, 252
puro 23, 218-9, 222, 233
teoría benjaminiana del 15, 18, 24, 37, 82, 131, 135, 148-50, 209, 215-33
Levi, P. 268
Literatura 74, 78-80, 83-5, 103, 16⁻, 176, 207, 244, 265, 281
Lo femenino 24, 61, 117-28, 143, 158-60, 168
Lo lésbico como figura 72, 152
Lo mesiánico 15, 22, 37, 106, 232-8
  el fin de la historia 230
  intensidad de 106, 146, 235, 25⁻
Lo que ha sido 16, 48, 96, 98, 126, 137-8, 158-60, 163, 185, 189-90, 201, 213-5, 226-7, 254-5
Lo simbólico 129-34
Löwith, K. 263

Madre 61, 128, 133-4, 155, 162
Marx, K. 40, 263
  El 18 de Brumario de Luis Bonaparte 42-5
Marxismo 40, 203-4
Materialismo histórico 22, 33, 36, 39-42, 103, 106
Mémoire involontaire 66
Memoria
  concepto benjaminiano de 18, 24, 45, 185-9, 196-8, 203-9, 213-5, 223, 226, 255
  concepto freudiano de la 112, 192-200, 249
  corpórea 55, 244, 247-50, 254
  cultural 16, 175, 243, 246, 250

Fuerzas contrarias, véase
gegenstrebige Tügung

Geertz, C. 246
Gegenstrebige Fügung 107, 148, 235, 264
Genealogía 32, 71, 88-9
Género:
    diferencia genérica 16, 72, 117, 143, 148, 154, 158, 168
    discurso de los géneros 117
    lenguaje y 119
    relaciones genéricas 117-21, 154, 168
Genio 149, 155-7, 233
Gestos 30, 61, 62-3, 132, 212, 247, 252
Ginzburg, C. 193-5
Goethe, W. 74
Gramatología 101
Greenblatt, S. 69
Guattari, F. 250

Habermas, J. 18, 32-7, 238
Habitantes de los umbrales 24, 47-8, 52, 112, 145, 162-3, 190, 232, 257
Hegel, G.W.F. 101, 263
Heidegger, M. 20, 176, 276
Historia 57, 67-9, 77, 80, 85-94, 103, 110-2, 133, 137-8, 141, 189-90, 233-7, 254, 257-61
    como escenario 93-4
    el concepto benjaminiano de la historia 42, 45, 76-7, 86, 232, 261-5
    imágenes de 13, 40-2, 59, 76, 93, 186, 265
    representación dialéctica de la 42
    un *continuum* 42-3, 74, 86, 110, 138
Historikerstreit 273
Historiografía 67, 86, 93, 138, 185-6, 203, 255, 265

Hölderlin, F. 20, 23, 74, 101, 112-3, 227, 230-2
Homosexualidad 72
Horkheimer, M. 123, 135, 180, 263, 266, 276, 283
    Dialéctica del Iluminismo 123, 265-8, 271, 276-8, 283
Huella 93, 163, 186, 189, 193-5, 198, 201, 207-9, 212-3, 223, 241, 247
Huella mnémica 193, 200, 225, 247, 275
Huella permanente/duradera 66, 93, 112, 193, 204, 250
Husserl, E. 20
Hyppolite, J. 86

Iluminación profana 13, 39, 48, 52, 55, 66, 257
Iluminismo, dialéctica del 121-5, 135-7, 266-8, 276, 279-81
Imagen arcaica 52, 126, 201
Imagen de pensamiento [*Denkbild*] 11-16, 37, 43, 55, 74, 80, 100, 113, 146-8, 165, 238
Imagen del espacio (*Bildraum*) 13, 34-9, 42, 45, 50, 57-9, 61, 89, 137, 165, 254
Imagen dialéctica 20-3, 48, 52-5, 59, 93, 96-7, 100, 106, 110, 125-8, 137-48, 152, 157, 165, 178, 201, 254-7, 265
Imagen mnémica 59, 98, 103, 185, 189, 209, 227
Imagen onírica 40, 53-5, 59, 96, 98, 103, 160, 275
Imágenes desconcertantes 23, 131, 201-3, 210-3, 215-6, 221, 223, 227
Imaginación 94-6
Impacto 63-64, 185, 196
Inconsciente 39-40, 55, 66-7, 93, 112, 135-7, 168, 179-80, 190-3, 198, 203-4, 241, 250
    del grupo colectivo 57, 198, 201-3, 223;
    véase también lenguaje

de la conciencia y del inconsciente 16, 22, 24, 193, 209, 250
Disimultaneidad 105, 109-12, 135, 139, 146, 150, 255-7
Distorsión 22-4, 42, 61, 66-7, 93, 96, 162-3, 179-80, 193-5, 198, 207-12, 216, 221, 223-5, 227-9, 232, 252-5
Durero, A. *Melancolía* 100

"El jorobado" 67, 232
El libro del Génesis 82-3, 149, 215, 225
Emergencia 88-93
Ensamblaje de fuerzas contrarias 37, 105-6, 146, 235, 264
Escena de la historia 39, 42, 91, 94
    de la memoria 94, 158, 186-8, 192, 206-7, 223, 275
    de la escritura 93, 158, 179, 241
Escena primaria/primigenia 82, 91, 134-5, 160, 265
Escritura 168, 176, 180-1, 188, 192, 200-1, 206, 209-16, 222, 225-7, 230-2, 239-46, 254, 265
    alegoría como una forma de la escritura 176-8, 180-1
    de las cosas 83-5, 212, 215-6, 225
    en asombro 276, 183
    excitante 24, 176, 204, 212
    imágenes de la 97, 100-3, 178, 212
    memoria como 193, 213 y memoria 239-43
    transformación de la existencia en 146, 213, 226-7, 230-2, 254
Escuela de Frankfurt 18, 128
Espacio del cuerpo 39, 48, 57, 61, 64, 165
Espacio del cuerpo y de la imagen [*Leib- und Bildraum*] 13, 23, 24, 30, 39, 47-57, 60-6, 86, 89, 137, 143, 163-7, 180, 204

Espíritu del lenguaje [*Sprachgeist*] 83, 131
    la expulsión del paraíso del espíritu del lenguaje 82, 83, 216-8, 229
Estado de excepción 261
Excitación 15, 42, 63, 193, 204, 209, 247-9, 283

Falsa conciencia 42, 112, 203
Fascismo 57
Filosofía 11, 103, 263-6, 270-3, 281-3
    historia de la 22, 42, 105-6, 110, 235, 255-7, 262-5
Fisonomía 195, 247-9
Flâneur 48, 168
Fórmulas patéticas 247, 253
Foucault 18-20, 69-96, 129, 145, 175-6, 225
    Arqueología del saber 77
    La historia de la sexualidad 69-72, 77
    "Introducción" al libro de Binswanger *Traum und Existenz* 94-6
    Las palabras y las cosas 16, 74, 77-85
    "Nietzsche, la genealogía, la historia" 86-91
Fragmento 80, 245
Freud 16-20, 39-40, 59, 61, 66, 93, 96, 112, 133, 163, 179-80, 188, 190-212, 215, 249-54, 273
    "El trabajo del sueño" 203
    estudios de Benjamin sobre 61, 195-6
    La interpretación de los sueños 40, 94-6, 193, 221, 250
    Más allá del principio de placer 192, 196
    "Notas sobre la 'pizarra mágica'" 112, 192
    Totem y tabú 203

"La obra de arte en la época de
su reproductibilidad técnica"
63-4
"La obra de los Pasajes" 18, 24,
40-2, 52-7, 66, 74, 78-80, 86,
93-6, 126, 145-8, 152, 160-2,
168, 176-8, 185-6, 189, 192,
193-8, 201-6, 209, 223, 213-5,
226, 254-5, 261
"La tarea del traductor" 215-22,
227-33
"Nach der Vollendung" ["Después
de la terminación definitiva"]
128, 155
"París, capital del siglo XIX"
198, 227
"Sobre algunos temas en
Baudelaire" 185, 193-8
"Sobre el concepto de historia"
22, 40-3, 47-8, 57, 67, 86, 103-9,
148, 185, 236, 254-5, 259-65
"Sobre el lenguaje en general y
el lenguaje de los humanos"
59, 148, 216-8, 225, 230
"Sobre la capacidad mimética"
60, 149, 186, 209, 215-6
"Sócrates" 154
"Una imagen de Proust" 66, 98,
203, 207-9
"Para una crítica de la violencia"
19
Bergson, H. 197
Binswanger, L. 94
Bloch, E. 235-7
Brecha [*Bahnung*] 23, 96, 129, 197,
204-6, 226
Brecht, B. 34-6
Buci-Glucksmann, C. 126
Burckhardt, J. 69

Cábala 83-5
Capacidad mimética 15, 82, 101,
129-31, 148- 209-12, 222-3
Caso límite [*Grenzfall*] 260-5, 268-
70, 275, 283

Cercanía 50-2, 63, 145, 163-5, 201
Cita 15, 42-5, 80-2, 93, 138
Ciudad 55, 71, 78, 135, 158-60, 167-
8, 180, 189-92, 198-200, 213-5
modernidad de la 53, 74, 189,
192, 212, 223
Computer 241-3
Concepto benjaminiano de la
imagen 11, 59, 97-100, 185, 207
como lo tercero 11-3, 97-8
Consideración por las condiciones
de representabilidad 40, 179,
192, 203
Constelación 11, 20, 42-3, 50, 53, 93,
98-100, 106, 109, 112, 120, 126,
133-4, 137, 145-6, 201, 209, 265,
278
Contrapartida 105
Corporeidad 56, 160, 163, 167, 171,
180, 247
Creación
intelectual 128, 152-5
mito de la 57, 131-3, 149
Crítica ideológica 15, 32-3, 71
Crítica salvadora 20, 32, 112, 143,
155, 176
Cuerpo 23, 30, 39, 50-5, 59-67, 71,
86-9, 125, 134, 137, 141, 150, 165,
204, 207, 232, 247-50
como escenario 88, 179, 250
del grupo colectivo 50-2, 53-5,
61, 165
lenguaje del 23, 66, 150, 247-9,
252

Deleuze, G. 250
De Man, Paul 233-8
Derrida, J. 18-20, 93, 103
Descorporeización 63, 171
Deconstrucción 20
Deseo de la imagen 14, 20, 98, 110-2
despertar 16, 55, 95, 112, 126, 137,
139, 145, 163, 189, 200
Dialéctica 13, 96, 101, 107, 123-6,
133, 139, 189

Índice analítico

Abismo 85, 152, 175-8, 227-9, 231
Actualidad 13, 29-46, 48-50, 64
Adorno, G. 18, 32, 123, 135, 196,
    263, 266-83, 276, 283
    Diálectica del Iluminismo 123,
        265-8, 271, 276-8, 283
    Dialéctica negativa 271-3
    "El ensayo como forma" 270
    *La crítica de la cultura y la
        sociedad*, 270
    Mínima Moralia 266-8, 271
Ahora de la cognoscibilidad 39, 52,
    76, 96, 126, 137, 178, 200-1, 254-5
Alegoría 16, 112, 143, 148, 163-181,
    188, 190, 204, 226, 243
Antisemitismo 268-70
Archivo 43, 72, 77, 103, 143, 146,
    160-3, 175, 209, 212, 241
Arendt, H. 268
Ariadna 148, 160, 226
Aristóteles 15, 241-4
Arqueología 71, 186
Arquitectura 53, 57, 78, 103, 135,
    168, 180, 189, 206
Ars memoriae 174, 241-4
Arte de la memoria 243
asombro/estupor 259-65, 276, 281-3
Aura 60-1, 163, 180, 201
Auschwitz 266-75

Bachmann, I. 276-83
    A los treinta años 281-3

Das Lächeln der Sphynx ["La
    sonrisa de la esfinge"] 276-83
Malina 119-21, 275-6, 283
Bachofen, J. 160-2, 196
Baudelaire, Ch. 64, 71-4, 152, 163,
    176, 180, 216
    Tableau parisiens 217
Benjamin, W.
    "Agesilaus Santander" 158
    "Crónica de Berlín" 162, 186-9,
        192, 204-6, 223, 226
    Charles Baudelaire 15, 64-6, 69-
        72, 143, 148, 162
    "Das Tagebuch" 105, 145-6
    Dirección única 55, 148, 157,185,
        204
    *El origen del drama barroco
        alemán* 16, 39, 57, 77, 88-94,
        171-8, 181, 212
    "El surrealismo" 30, 33-4, 37-9,
        47-57, 63-6, 86, 204
    "Fragmento teológico-político"
        105-6, 110, 145, 233-7, 257
    "Franz Kafka" 22, 64-7, 146,160-2,
        180, 207, 213, 229-32, 235,
        252-5
    Infancia en Berlín hacia el 1900
        59, 97-8, 148, 158-62, 188-9,
        209, 226
    "La conversación" 144-5, 154
    "La enseñanza de lo semejante"
        60, 186, 209, 215-6, 223

— (1994a): *Bilder des kulturellen Gedächtnisses: Beiträge zur Gegenwartsliteratur*, Dülmen-Hiddingsel, Tende.
— (1994b): "The wreathed beard of Moses: body language between interpretation and reading", en S. Schade (comp.): *Andere Körper/Different Bodies: Katalog der Ausstellung im Offenen Kulturhaus Linz*, Viena, págs. 36-45.
— (1995a):"Aby Warburg's *Schlangenritual*: reading culture and reading written texts", *New German Critique* 65 (primavera/ invierno de 1995), págs. 135-153.
— (1995b):*Flaschenpost und Postkarte: Korrespondenzen zwischen Kritischer Theorie und Postestrukturalismus*. Colonia, Böhlau.
— (1996): "Reading/writing the feminine city: Calvino, Hessel, Benjamin", en G. Fischer (comp.): *With the Sharpened Axe of Reason: Approaches to Walter Benjamin*, Oxford, Berg, págs. 85-98.
Weigel, Sigrid (comp.) (1992): *Leib- und Bildraum: Lektüren nach Walter Benjamin*, Colonia, Böhlau.
Wiegmann, Jutta (1989): *Psychoanalytische Geschichtstheorie: Eine Studie zur Freud-Rezeption Walter Benjamins*, Bonn, Bouvier.
Wind, Edgar (1980): "Warburgs Begriff der Kulturwissenschaft und seine Bedeutung für die Ästhetik", en A.Warburg: *Ausgewählte Schriften und Würdigungen*, (comp. por D.Wuttke), Baden-Baden, Koerner.
Wohlfahrt, Irving (1993): "The measure of the possible, the weight of the real and the heat of the moment: Benjamin's actuality today", *New Formations* 20, (verano), págs. 1-20.
Yates, Frances A. (1966): *The Art of Memory*, Londres, Routledge/ Kegan Paul.
Yerushalmi, Yosef Hayim (1982): *Zachor. Erinnere Dich! Jüdische Geschichte und jüdisches Gedächtnis*, Berlín, Wagenbach, 1988.

Schlaffer, Heinz (1989): *Faust Zweiter Teil: Die Allegorie des 19. Jahrhunderts*, Stuttgart, Metzler.

Schmitt, Carl (1934): *Politische Theologie. Vier Kapitel zur Lehre von der Souveranität*, Berlín, 1990.

Scholem, Gershom (1963): "Zum Verständnis der messianischen Idee im Judentum" (1953), en *Judaica I*, Francfort, Suhkamp, págs. 7-74.

— (1973): *Zur Kabbala und ihrer Symbolik*, Francfort, Suhrkamp.

— (1980): *Die jüdische Mystik* (1941), Francfort, Suhrkamp.

— (1983): *Walter Benjamin und sein Engel*, Francfort, Suhrkamp.

Starobinski, Jean (1983): "Brève histoire de la conscience du corps", en R. Ellrodt: *Genèse de la conscience moderne*, París, PUF, págs. 215-229.

Steiner, George (1987): "The Long Life of Metaphor: An Approach to the *Shoah*", *Encounter* 68 (2), págs. 55-61.

Stoessel, Marlen (1983): *Das vergessene Menschliche: Zu Sprache und Erfahrung bei Walter Benjamin*, Múnich/Viena, Hanser.

Taubes, Jacob (1987): *Ad Carl Schmitt. Gegenstrebige Fügung*, Berlín.

Unseld, Siegfried (comp.) (1972): *Zur Aktualität Walter Benjamins: Aus Anlass des 80. Geburtstags von Walter Benjamin*, Francfort, Suhrkamp.

Warburg, Aby (1980): *Ausgewählte Schriften und Würdigungen*, (comp. por D.Wuttke), Baden-Baden, Koerner.

Weber, Samuel (1978): *Rückkehr zu Freud. Jacques Lacans Entstellung der Psychoanalyse*, Francfort/Viena/Berlín, Ullstein; nueva edic.: Francfort, Fischer, 1992.

Weigel, Sigrid (1983): "Der schielende Blick: Zur Geschichte weiblicher Sprachpraxis", en Inge Stephan y Sigrid Weigel: *Die verborgene Frau*, Berlín, Argument.

— (1987): *Die Stimme der Medusa: Schreibweisen in der Gegenwartsliteratur von Frauen*, Dülmen/Hiddingsel, Tende; nueva edic.: Reinbeck/Hamburgo, Rowohlt, 1989.

— (1990): *Topographien der Geschlechter: Kulturgeschichtliche Studien zur Literatur*, Reinbeck/Hamburgo, Rowohlt.

Marx, Karl (1960): *Der achtzehnte Brumaire des Louis Bonaparte*, Berlín, MEW 8.
— (1971): *El 18 Brumario de Luis Bonaparte* (trad. O. P. Safont), Barcelona, Ariel.
Menke, Bettina (1991): *Sprachfiguren: Name-Allegorie-Bild nach Walter Benjamin*, Múnich, Fink.
Menninghaus, Winfried (1980): *Walter Benjamins Theorie der Sprachmagie*, Francfort, Suhrkamp.
Mitchell, W. J. T. (1984): "What is an image?", *New Literary History* XV (primavera de 1984), 3, págs. 503-537.
Nägele, Rainer (1991): *Theater, Theory, Speculation: Walter Benjamin and the Scenes of Modernity*, Baltimore/Londres, Johns Hopkins University Press.
Nietzsche, Friedrich (1969): *Werke* (comp. por K. Schlechta), Francfort/Viena/Berlín, Ullstein.
— (1988): *Sämtliche Werke. Kritische Studienausgabe in 15 Einzelbänden* (comp. por G. Colli y M. Montinari), Berlín/Nueva York, DTV/de Gruyter.
Nora, Pierre (1986): *Les lieux de mémoire*, París, Gallimard.
Pfotenhauer, Helmut (1985): "Benjamin und Nietzsche", en B. Lindner (comp): *Walter Benjamin im Kontext*, Königstein, Athenäum, (2ª ed. ampl.), págs. 100-126.
Platón (1949): "Fedro o de la belleza" (trad. de Patricio de Azcárate), en *Apología de Sócrates/Diálogos*, Buenos Aires, El Ateneo.
Plumpe, Gerhard (1979): "Die Entdeckung der Vorwelt: Erläuterungen zu Benjamins Bachofenlektüre", en Walter Benjamin: *Text+Kritik*, 31/32 (comp. por H. L. Arnold), Múnich, *Text+Kritik*, págs. 19-27.
Raulff, Ulrich (comp.) (1986): *Vom Umschreiben der Geschichte: Neue historische Perspektiven*, Berlín, Wagenbach.
Saxl, Fritz (1980): "Die Ausdrucksgebärden der bildenden Kunst" (1932), en Aby Warburg (comp.): *Ausgewählte Schriften und Würdigungen* (comp. por D. Wuttke), Baden-Baden, Koerner, págs. 419-432.
Schade, Sigrid; Wagner, Monika y Weigel, Sigrid (comps.) (1994): *Allegorie und Geschlechterdifferenz*, Colonia, Böhlau.

Kott, Jan (1990): *Das Gedächtnis des Körpers: Essays zu Theater und Literatur*, Berlín, Alexander.

Kristeva, Julia (1974a): *Des Chinoises*, París, Éd. des Femmes.

— (1974b): *La révolution du langage poétique*, París, Seuil.

— (1976): "Die Produktivität der Frau: Interview mit Elaine Boucquey", en *Das Lächeln der Medusa* (alternative 108/09), págs. 166-172.

— (1983): *Histoires d'amour*, París, Denoël. [Ed. cast.: *Historias de amor*, México, Siglo XXI, 1992.]

Kuhn, Hugo (1979): "Allegorie und Erzählstruktur", en W. Haug (comp): *Formen und Funktionen der Allegorie*, Stuttgart, Metzler, págs. 206-128.

Kurnitzky, Horst (1978): *Ödipus. Ein Held der westlichen Welt: über die zerstörerischen Grundlagen der Zivilisation*, Berlín, Wagenbach.

Lachmann, Renate (1990): *Gedächtnis und Literatur: Intertextualität in der russischen Moderne*, Francfort, Suhrkamp.

Laplanche, J. y Pontalis, J.-B. (1967): *Diccionario de psicología*, Barcelona, Labor.

— (1985): *Fantasme originaire: fantasme des origines, origines du fantasme*, París, Hachette.

Lavater, Johann Kaspar (1775): *Physiognomische Fragmente zur Förderung der Menschenkenntnis und Menschenliebe*, Stuttgart, Reclam, 1984.

Levi, Primo (1963): *La tregua*, Turín, Einaudi.

Lindner, Burkhardt (comp.) (1985): *Walter Benjamin im Kontext*, Königstein, Athenäum (2ª ed. ampl.).

Lindner, Burkhardt (1992): "Engel und Zwerg: Benjamins geschichtsphilosophische Rätselfigur und die Herausforderung des Mythos", en L. Jäger y y Th. Regehly (comps.): *'Was nie geschehen wurde, lesen': Frankfurter Benjamin-Vorträge*, Bielefeld, Aisthesis, págs. 236-265.

Löwith, Karl (1949): *Sämtliche Schriften*, vol.2: *Weltgeschichte und Heilgeschehen: Zur Kritik der Geschichtsphilosophie*, Stuttgart, Kohlhammer, 1983.

cast.: *La proposición del fundamento*, Barcelona, Ediciones del Serbal, 1991.]
Heine, Heinrich (1993): *Sämtliche Gedichte in zeitlicher Folge* (comp. por K.Briegleb), Francfort/Leipzig, Insel.
Heinrich, Klaus (1985): "Das Floss der Medusa", en R. Schlesier (comp.), *Faszination des Mythos: Studien zu antiken und modernen Interpretationen*, Basilea/Francfort, Roter Stern, págs. 335-398.
Heller, Agnes (1993): "Die Weltzeituhr stand still: Schreiben nach Auschwitz? Schweigen nach Auschwitz? Philsophische Betrachtungen eines Tabus", *Die Zeit*, 7 de mayo de 1993, pág. 61.
Hofmann, Werner; Syamken, Georg y Warnke, Martin (1980): *Die Menschenrechte des Auges: über Aby Warburg*, Francfort, EVA.
Hölderlin, Friedrich (1992): *Sämtliche Werke und Briefe* (comp. por M. Knaupp), Múnich, Hanser, 3 tomos.
Horkheimer, Max y Adorno, Theodor W. (1947): *Dialektik der Aufklärung. Philosophische Fragmente*, Francfort, Fischer, 1969. [Ed. cast.: *Dialéctica del Iluminismo*, Buenos Aires, Sudamericana, 1987.]
Irigaray, Luce (1977): *Ce sexe qui n'en est pas un*, París, Minuit. [Ed. cast.: *El sexo que no es uno*, Madrid, Saltes, 1982.]
Jameson, Fredric (1984): "Postmodernism, or the cultural logic of late capitalism", *New Left Review* 146, págs. 53-93.
Kafka, Franz (1971): *Sämtliche Erzählungen*, Francfort, Fischer.
Kemp, Wolfgang (1985): "Fernbilder, Benjamin und die Kunstwissenschaft", en B. Lindner (comp.):*Walter Benjamin im Kontext*, Königstein, Athenäum (2ª ed. ampl.), págs. 224-257.
Kemp, Wolfgang (comp.) (1989): *Der Text des Bildes: Möglichkeiten und Mittel eigenständiger Bilderzählung*, Múnich, Text+Kritik.
Kippenbrg, Hans G. y Luchesi, Brigitte (comps.) (1978): *Magie: Die sozialwissenschaftliche Kontroverse über das Verstehen remden Denkens*, Francfort, Suhrkamp.
Klee, Paul (1990): *50 Werke aus 50 Jahren (1890-1940)*, comp. por W.Hofmann (catálogo de la exposición), Hamburgo.

Freud, Sigmund y Breuer, Josef (1970): *Studien zur Hysterie*, Francfort, Fischer.
Fürnkäs, Josef (1988): *Surrealismus als Erkenntnis: Walter Benjamin – Weimarer Einbahnstrasse und Pariser Passagen*, Stuttgart, Metzler.
García Düttmann, Alexander (1991): *Das Gedächtnis des Denkens: Versuch über Heidegger und Adorno*, Francfort, Suhrkamp.
Geertz, Clifford (1973):*The Interpretation of Cultures: Selected Essays*, Nueva York, Basic Books. [Ed. cast.: *La interpretación de las culturas*, Barcelona, Gedisa, 1988.]
Ginzburg, Carlo (1986): *Miti emblemi spie. Morfologia e storia*, Turín, Einaudi. [Ed. cast.: *Mitos, emblemas e indicios*, Barcelona, Gedisa, 1997.]
Habermas, Jürgen (1972): "Bewusstmachende oder rettende Kritik – Die Aktualität Walter Benjamins", en Siegfried Unseld (comp.), *Zur Aktualität Walter Benjamin. Aus Anlass des 80. Geburtstags von W. Benjamin*, Francfort, Suhrkamp, págs. 173-223.
— (1973): *Kultur und Kritik*, Francfort, Suhrkamp.
— (1989): "Verwunderte Nation-oder lernende Gesellschaft?", *Frankfurter Rundschau*, 11 de abril de 1989, pág. 9.
Harth, Dietrich (comp.) (1991a): *Die Erfindung des Gedächtnisses*, Francfort, Keip.
— (1991b): "Der aufrechte Gang – Monument der Kultur? Über die Lesbarkeit des Leibes und einige andere Voraussetzungen der Kulturanalyse", en A. Assmann y D. Harth (comps.): *Kultur als Lebenswelt und Monument*, Francfort, Fischer, págs. 75-111.
Hass, Ulrike (1993): *Militante Pastorale: Zur Literatur der antimodernen Bewegungen im frühen 20. Jahrhundert*, Múnich, Fink.
Haug, Walter (comp.) (1979): *Formen und Funktionen der Allegorie*, Stuttgart, Metzler.
Haverkamp, Anselm y Lachmann, Renate (comps.) (1991): *Gedächtniskunst: Raum-Bild-Schrift. Studien zur Mnemotechnik*, Francfort, Suhrkamp.
— (1993): *Memoria: Vergessen und Erinnern. Poetik und Hermeneutik XV*, Múnich, Fink.
Heidegger, Martin (1957): *Der Satz vom Grund*, Pfullingen, [Ed.

— (1991): *Gesten: Versuch einer Phänomenologie*, Düsseldorf/Bensheim, Bollmann.

Foucault, Michel (1966): *Les mots et les choses: Une archéologie des sciences humaines*, París, Gallimard. [Ed. cast.: *Las palabras y las cosas*, Barcelona, Tusquets, 1987.]

— (1969): *L'archéologie du savoir*, París, Gallimard. [Ed. cast.: *La arquelogía del saber*, México, Siglo XXI, 1984.]

— (1971a): *L'ordre du discours*, París, Gallimard. [Ed. cast.: *El orden del discurso*, Madrid, Siglo XXI, 1997.]

— (1971b): "Nietzsche, die Genealogie, die Historie", en W. Seitter (comp.): *Von der Subversion des Wissens*, Francfort, Fischer, 1974. [Ed. cast.: *Nietzsche, la geneaología, la historia*, Valencia, Pre-Textos, 1997.]

— (1976): *Histoire de la sexualité. 1. La volonté de savoir*, París, Gallimard. [Ed. cast.: *Historia de la sexualidad. La voluntad de saber*, t. I, Madrid, Siglo XXI, 1998.]

— (1984a): *Histoire de la sexualité. 2. L'usage des plaisirs*, París, Gallimard. [Ed. cast.: *Historia de la sexualidad. El uso de los placeres*, t. II, Madrid, Siglo XXI, 1998.]

— (1984b): *Histoire de la sexualité. 3. Le souci de soi*, París, Gallimard. [Ed. cast.: *Historia de la sexualidad. La inquietud de sí*, t. III, Madrid, Siglo XXI, 1998.]

— (1992): "Einleitung", en L. Binswanger, *Traum und Existenz* (1954), Berna/Berlín, Gachnang und Springer, págs. 7-93.

Fox Keller, Evelyn (1986): *Liebe Macht und Erkenntnis: Männliche oder weibliche Wissenschaft*, Múnich, Hauser.

Freud, Sigmund (1952): *Gesammelte Werke, chronologisch geordnet* (comp. por Anna Freud y otros), Londres, Imago Publishing Co., 18 tomos. [Ed. cast.: *Obras Completas*, Buenos Aires, Amorrortu, 1978-1985.]

— (1969): *Studienausgabe* (comp. por Alexander Mitscherlich y otros), Francfort, Fischer, 1969-1975.

— (1986): *Briefe an Wilhelm Fliess, 1887-1904*, Francfort, Fischer.

— (1987) *Gesammelte Werke*, volumen suplementario: *Texte aus den Jahren 1885-1938* (comp. por Anna Freud y otros), Francfort, Fischer.

De Certeau, Michel (1980): *L'invention du quotidien, 1. Arts de faire*, París, Gallimard.

Deleuze, Gilles y Guattari, Félix (1972/3):*Capitalisme et schizophrénie, l'Anti-Oedipe*, París, Minuit. [Ed. cast.: *El antiedipo. Capitalismo y esquizofrenia*, Barcelona, Paidós, 1995.]

De Man, Paul (1986): "Conclusions: Walter Benjamin's 'The task of the translator'", en *The Resistance to Theory*, Minneapolis, MN, University of Minnesota Press, págs. 73-105.

Derrida, Jacques (1967a): *De la grammatologie*, París, Hachette. [Ed. cast.: *De la gramatología*, México, Siglo XXI, 1976.]

— (1967b): *L'écriture et la différence*, París, Seuil. [Ed. cast.: *La escritura y la diferencia*, Barcelona, Anthropos, 1989.]

— (1990): "Force de loi: Le 'fondement mystique de l'autorité'"/ "Force of law: The 'mystical foundation of authority'", *Cardozo Law Review* 11 (1989-1990), págs. 919-1045.

Diner, Dan (comp.) (1988): *Zivilisationsbruch: Denken nach Auschwitz*, Francfort, Fischer.

Diner, Dan (1992): "Historical understanding and counter-rationality: the *Judenrat* as epistemological vantage", en S. Friedlander (comp.): *Probing the Limits of Representation: Nazism and the "Final Solution"*, Cambridge, MA, Harvard University Press.

Douglas, Mary (1973): *Ritual, Tabu und Körpersymbolik: Sozialanthropologische Studien in Industriegesellschaft und Stammeskultur*, Francfort, Suhrkamp, 1986.

Duden, Anne y Weigel, Sigrid (1989): "Schrei und Körper - Zum Verhältnis von Bildern und Schrift: Ein Gespräch über Das Judasschaf", en Thomas Koebner (comp.): *Laokoon und kein Ende: Der Wettstreit der Künste*, Múnich, Text+Kritik, págs. 113-141.

Duden, Barbara (1989): "A repertory of body history", en M.Feher y otros (comps.), *Zone 5. Fragments for a History of the Human Body* 3, Nueva York, Urzone, págs. 470-578.

Flusser, Vilém (1987): *Die Schrift: Hat Schreiben Zukunft?*, Gotinga, Immatrix.

Profane Erleuchtung und rettende Kritik, Würzburg, Königshausen und Neumann.
__ (1986): *Antike und Moderne: Zu Walter Benjamins 'Passagen'*, Würzburg, Königshausen und Neumann.
Bolz, Norbert y Witte, Bernd (comps.) (1984): *Passagen: Walter Benjamins Urgeschichte des XIX. Jahrhunderts*, Múnich, Fink.
Briegleb, Klaus (1988): "'Paris, den...': Heinrich Heine Tagesberichte. Eine Skizze", *Der Deutschunterricht* 40, 1, págs. 39-50.
__ (1993): "Leo Löwenthal - Literatursoziologie unmittelbar zur Epoche", *Mitteilungen des Instituts für Sozialforschung* 3, págs. 12-29.
Buci-Glucksmann, Christine (1984): *Walter Benjamin und die Utopie des Weiblichen*, Hamburgo, VSA. (Contiene la traducción al alemán de dos artículos de la autora: "Féminité et modernité: Walter Benjamin et l'utopie du Féminin" y "Walter Benjamin et l'ange de l'histoire: une archéologie de la modernité").
Buck-Morss, Susan (1989): *The Dialectics of Seeing: Walter Benjamin and the Arcades Project*, Cambridge, MA, MIT Press. [Ed. cast.: *Didáctica de la mirada*, Madrid, Visión, 1996.]
Bulthaup, Peter (comp.) (1975): *Materialen zu Benjamins Thesen "Über den Begriff der Geschichte": Beiträge und Interpretationen*, Francfort, Suhrkamp.
Burgard, Peter J. (1992): "Adorno, Goethe, and the politics of the essay", *Deutsche Vierteljahrschrift für Literaturwissenschaft und Geistesgeschichte*, 66, 1, págs. 160-191.
Châtelet, François (1975): "Die Geschichte", *Geschichte der Philosophie*, VII, Francfort/Viena/Berlín, Ullstein.
Clair, Jean y Szeemann, Harald (comps.) (1975): *Junggesellenmaschinen/Les Machines Célibataires* (Catálogo de la Exposición), Berna.
Claussen, Detlev (1988): "Nach Auschwitz: Ein Essay über die Aktualität Adornos", en D. Diner (comp.), *Zivilisationsbruch: Denken nach Auschwitz*, Francfort, Fischer, págs. 54-88.
Cysarz, Herbert (1924): *Deutsche Barockdichtung: Renaissance, Barock, Rokoko*, Leipzig, Haessel.

___ (1991b) *Mnemosyne: Formen und Funktionen der kulturellen Erinnerung*, Francfort, Fischer.
Assmann, Jan y Hölscher, Tonio (comps.) (1988): *Kultur und Gedächtnis*, Francfort, Fischer.
Axeli-Knapp, Gudrun (1988): "Die vergessene Differenz", *Feministische Studien*, 6.1: 12-31.
Babylon. Beiträge zur jüdischen Gegenwart, Francfort, 1986 y años sigs.
Bachmann, Ingeborg (1978): *Werke* (comp. por Christine Koschel, Inge von Weidenbaum y Clemens Münster), 4 tomos, Múnich/Zúrich, Piper.
___ (1983): *Wir müssen wahre Sätze finden: Gespräche und Interviews* (comp. por Christine Koschel e Inge von Weidenbaum), Múnich/Zúrich, Piper.
___ (1963): *A los treinta años*, Barcelona, Seix Barral, 1963.
Bachofen, Johann Jakob (1948): *Das Mutterrecht* (comp. por Meuli), Basilea, Schwabe.
Benhabib, Seyla (1986): *Critique, Norm and Utopia*, Guildford, Nueva York, Columbia University Press.
Benjamin, Walter (1974/1989): *Gesammelte Schriften* (comp. por Rolf Tiedemann y Hermann Schweppenhäuser), 7 tomos (en 14 libros), Francfort, Suhrkamp.
___ (1978): *Briefe* (comp. por Gershom Scholem y Theodor Adorno), 2 tomos, Francfort, Suhrkamp.
___ (1979): *Text+Kritik* 31/32 (comp. por H. L. Arnold), Múnich, Text+Kritik.
___ (1980): *Illuminationen*, Francfort, Fischer.
Blumenberg, Hans (1981): *Die Lesbarkeit der Welt*, Francfort, Suhrkamp.
Bohleber, Werner (1990): "Das Fortwirken des Nationalsozialismus in der zweiten und dritten Generation nach Auschwitz", *Babylon: Beiträge zur jüdischen Gegenwart 7*, págs. 70-84.
Bohn, Volker (comp.) (1990): *Bildlichkeit: Internationale Beiträge zur Poetik 3*, Francfort, Suhrkamp.
Bolz, Norbert y Faber, Richard (comps.) (1985): *Walter Benjamin:*

Bibliografía

Adorno, Theodor W. (1949): *Prismen. Kulturkritik und Gesellschaft*, Francfort, Suhrkamp, 1963. [Ed. cast.: *Prismas. La crítica de la cultura y la sociedad*, Barcelona, Ariel, 1962.]
— (1951): *Minima moralia. Reflexionen aus dem beschädigten Leben*, Francfort, Suhrkamp, 1969. [Ed. cast.: *Mínima moralia*, Madrid, Taurus, 1988.]
— (1959): *Noten zur Literatur*, Francfort, Suhrkamp, t. I. [Ed. cast.: *Notas de literatura*, Barcelona, Ariel, 1962.]
— (1966): *Negative Dialektik*, Francfort, Suhrkamp, 1975. [Ed. cast.: *Dialéctica negativa*, Madrid, Cuadernos para el diálogo, 1975.]
Agamben, Giorgio (1990): "Das unvordenkliche Bild", en V. Bohn (comp.), *Bildlichkeit: Internationale Beiträge zur Poetik 3*, Francfort, Suhrkamp, págs. 534-553.
— (1992): "Noten zur Geste", en J.Georg-Lauer (comp.): *Postmoderne und Politik*, Tubinga, Edition Diskord, págs. 97-107.
Arendt, Hannah (1986): *Zur Zeit: Politische Essays* (comp. por M. L. Knott), Berlín, Rotbuch.
Aristóteles (1978): *Acerca del alma* (trad. de T. Calvo Martínez), Madrid, Gredos, 1994.
Assmann, Aleida y Hardmeier, Jan-Christof (comps.) (1983): *Schrift und Gedächtnis: Archäologie der literarischen Kommunikation I*, Múnich, Fink.
Assmann, Aleida y Harth, Dietrich (comps.) (1991a): *Kultur als Lebenswelt und Monument*, Francfort, Fischer.

figuras de pensamiento y símbolos mnémicos relacionados con la parte de culpa radiada del presente de nuestra conciencia. Se trata, pues, de una literatura a la sombra de una "dialéctica negativa" que trata de moverse, por lo tanto, en un rincón oscuro de ese ámbito.

En el conjunto de su obra en prosa, sin embargo, el relato *Das Lächeln der Sphinx*, así como la novela *Malina*, se encuentran en una situación de vasos comunicantes, tanto en lo que respecta a la crítica programática de Horkheimer y Adorno como a la negación benjaminiana a reconocerle estatuto filosófico al estupor en vista de lo sucedido en la historia reciente de Alemania.

Así, en el famoso episodio del cartero Kranewitzer en *Malina*, por ejemplo, se retoma nuevamente el mismo motivo conductor. Con la historia de este "cartero por vocación", quien, reflexionando sobre "el secreto de la correspondencia" [*Briefgeheimnis*] y "el problema del Correo" [*das Problem der Post*], cae en el más franco estupor y a partir de allí ya no puede seguir repartiendo las cartas, el texto comenta el mito fundante del discurso filosófico. En las múltiples capas de connotación de la relación Yo-Malina, ese Yo femenino innombrado ocupa en la novela no sólo el lugar del recuerdo, de la excitación y lo Otro de la Razón, sino también el lugar del asombro: "…pues mi estupor está hecho de curiosidad (¿pero Malina tiene en absoluto capacidad de asombro?, yo cada vez lo creo menos) y también de inquietud…"(Bachmann, 1978: III.22). En la relación de las posiciones entre Malina y el personaje Yo, lo que importa es, entre otras cosas, la conexión dialéctica entre el saber de Malina "sin admiración" (1978: III.23) y la postura del Yo ante el asombro. Sólo la representación de esta relación permite a Ingeborg Bachmann desarrollar una "escritura en asombro", y ello sucede en una novela que en su totalidad marca en múltiples sentidos un caso límite.

estudiante de filosofía salga una escritora que desarrolle una poética del "escribir en asombro", Ingeborg Bachmann va a pasar por muchas etapas que implicarán también otros tantos desvíos entre los terrenos de la filosofía y la literatura –pues, como afirmó Benjamin, "el método es el desvío"–. Su muy publicitado paso de la lírica a la prosa presenta una gran complejidad, no bien se lo mire con atención. Su prosa nace, en verdad, de una nueva postura y modo de escribir que proviene de una simultaneidad entre discurso filosófico y poesía. Su compromiso con la crítica al lenguaje emprendida por Wittgenstein, así como su postulado de una estructura lógica de la lengua como límite del mundo, por una parte, sumado al pasaje hacia un campo literario que se halla más allá de esa estructura (es decir, el lenguaje metafórico de la lírica), por otra, se manifiestan de carácter complementario. En este sentido, ello es comparable a la relación entre el *topos* de lo indecible y la simultánea metaforización acerca de Auschwitz en la literatura en lengua alemana después de 1945.

Sólo la prosa abre a Ingeborg Bachmann un campo donde se anula la oposición existente entre el ocuparse de la actualidad del pasado y seguir concretamente las huellas de la memoria y los problemas de representación en la historia póstuma del Nacionalsocialismo. Aunque algunos de sus relatos aparecidos en 1960 aluden a las coordenadas filosóficas en la herencia de Wittgenstein, tratando de ejercer una crítica desde adentro, es decir, de deconstruirlas, su compromiso literario se halla, en rigor, contra lo que generalmente se opina, en una línea muy clara que la comunica con la Teoría Crítica,[25] especialmente con el libro programático de 1947 y con Benjamin, mucho más que dentro de la herencia wittgensteiniana.[26] Sin embargo, no se trata en su caso de una prosa filosófica, sino de un trabajo literario con

---

25. El interés de Bachmann por esta corriente se documenta en la cantidad de títulos de Adorno y Benjamin que se han hallado en su biblioteca personal.
26. Para la relación de Bachmann con Benjamin, véase Weigel (1994a: 81-110).

pero, sin embargo, la creadora de enigmas no deja de permanecer hasta el final enigmática, como parte de algo No conocible, No Explicable. La Esfinge es la imagen de lo Otro de la Razón, que no es accesible a la racionalidad y que aquí aparece como la protección para los muertos, una sombra que no precede a la razón, sino que se manifiesta como el efecto y lo irreductible de la historia del Iluminismo.

Si hay que leer esta sonrisa de la Esfinge, en realidad, como una especie de comentario a la parábola de una crítica a la civilización precedente, podría afirmarse también que en la imagen final se hace evidente una posición que se enlaza de modo oculto y no consciente con una correspondencia que remite a Benjamin. Pues este final del relato temprano se perfila a modo de anuncio de un estilo peculiar de la autora según asoma en su prosa *después* del período lírico, por ejemplo, en el volumen de relatos titulado *A los treinta años*, de 1960. La conquista de un lugar literario por el paulatino pasaje a través de postulados filosóficos, que son desarrollados primeramente con el ejemplo de Wittgenstein, aparecerá aquí verificado en referencia a reflexiones del ámbito de la filosofía de la historia con respecto a la Teoría Crítica. En este sentido, en *Das Lächeln der Sphinx* su autora se coloca en una postura que la acerca a la idea de Benjamin en torno a un estupor no filosófico. Y, aunque Bachmann entra en contacto con la obra de Benjamin más tarde, después de la primera edición completa de sus textos que aparecen en 1955, este relato puede valer como premisa y condición de posibilidad para el interés creciente en este autor durante los años posteriores en la creación de la escritora.

Leído de tal modo, el relato *Das Lächeln der Sphinx* se presenta como una mónada para el proyecto *Todesarten* ["Formas de morir"] de Ingeborg Bachmann donde, por cierto, las relaciones entre la Razón y lo Otro se multiplican a través de vías de posicionamiento del sujeto femenino.[24] Pero antes que de la

---

24. Para un análisis de la contribución de Ingeborg Bachmann a una dialéctica femenina de la Ilustración, véase Weigel (1990).

inicia un camino propio que la aparta de las correspondencias filosóficas inspiradoras, para conquistar *otro* lugar en el pasaje de la Ilustración hacia la mitología. En este sentido, la realización de la tercera tarea en el cuento se caracteriza como revelación, de modo tal que la narración toma la forma de una parábola, dado que no se incita a una enseñanza inmediata: "La revelación de esta vía dio como resultado...". Por un lado, hay que decir que la Esfinge no aparece victoriosa, sino como "sombra" que protege a los muertos de volverse objetos de resolución de enigmas en ocasión de nuevos mensajes. De modo paralelo se afirma en un texto que habría llevado el título ensayístico de *Auf das Opfer darf keiner sich berufen* ["Nadie debe apelar a las víctimas"]:

> Él vio cómo la sombra de ella se desplegaba como una capa sobre los muertos, que ahora no podían declarar nada de lo que había que decir, porque la sombra los había cubierto para protegerlos. (Bachmann, 1978: IV. 335)

Con este gesto, que protege a los cuerpos de los muertos de la "moraleja de la historia" o de la traducción en afirmaciones, se conserva también un resto del mito que es irreductible. De este modo, no se cumple sólo ese pasaje de la Ilustración a la mitología, sino también, al mismo tiempo, se postula en cierta medida el fracaso del propio Iluminismo, pero no como un fracaso en sentido negativo, sino más bien en el sentido de una acotación de los límites entre Iluminismo y la crítica a ese mismo Iluminismo. En rigor, entonces, este costado irreductible nace de ese esclarecimiento de un movimiento esclarecido, en tanto en el relato de Ingeborg Bachmann nacen briznas de sentido que no pueden ser reducidas mediante el patrón de la racionalidad. "La ola que bate en un mar de secretos" y golpea sobre el rostro de la Esfinge, su sonrisa y su desaparición de los límites de ese territorio cierra el relato. Esos elementos parecen volverse los signos de *otra* posición, donde cobra sentido aquello a lo que se dirige el deseo de lograr el desencantamiento. La constelación que se forma entre el Señor y la Esfinge comporta, por un lado, esa voluntad de saber por medio de la que debe expulsarse la angustia ante la sombra,

ser, sin lugar a dudas, considerado un paso en la crítica a la civilización con medios literarios, representa, al mismo tiempo, una ilustración a la Ilustración, una iluminación del Iluminismo. En este sentido, cuatro años después del final de la guerra, este texto se presenta tomando posición frente al Nacionalsocialismo como representación concreta de un modo más claro que la propuesta filosófica. No hay que olvidar, por cierto, que el texto de Bachmann utiliza un lenguaje simbólico, que habría de tornarse sintomático de la temática de la eliminación masiva después de Auschwitz, con la tendencia a la utilización de metáforas universales de muerte junto con imágenes del horror. La obra lírica que produce paralelamente Ingeborg Bachmann no deja de formar parte de esta tendencia hacia la metaforización sobre Auschwitz:

Sieben Jahre später,
in einem Totenhaus,
trinken die Henker von gestern
den goldenen Becher aus
Die Augen täten dir sinken.
"*Früher Mittag*", 1952

[Siete años después,
en una Casa de los Muertos,
beben los verdugos de ayer
en la copa de oro hasta el final
Tus ojos se sumergirían.]
De *Früher Mittag* (Bachmann 1978: I.44)

La coincidencia con una referencia histórica exacta (siete años después de 1945), por una parte, y el plan de una metaforización que escenifica un horror determinado (*Henker, Totenhaus*), por otra, son características en este poema de la problemática de una reelaboración lírica del pasado, algo que habría de ser para Ingeborg Bachmann un momento clave en su decisión de fines de la década del cincuenta: abandonar la poesía para dedicarse a la prosa.

El final del relato *Das Lächeln der Sphinx* indica que su autora

angustia y *su* obsesión por lograr la ruptura del hechizo en que se halla el mundo, y que son la causa de la aparición de la Esfinge, dado que si se siguiera una interpretación psicoanalítica el monstruo mítico saldría de sus propias proyecciones, pues como dice el texto: "…que él mismo ha invocado a la sombra que quizás encerraba una amenaza, debiendo conjurarla para que tomara vida, para poder así combatirla". Cuando el texto sostiene que el Señor del lugar conjura a la Esfinge para conjurarse a sí mismo, resulta claro que las preguntas que ella ha de formularle brotarán de su propia voluntad de saber. En el desarrollo de las tres tareas ha de hacerse reconocible que el Señor quiere con todas sus fuerzas el desencantamiento del mundo que le permita penetrar con la mirada lo escondido para poseerlo, registrarlo y controlarlo, mientras la racionalidad se manifiesta como el instrumento para llevar a cabo este cometido, incluso si hay que pagar para ello el precio de la muerte. La tarea de los científicos y de sus asistentes que trabajan en la elaboración de las respuestas se presenta de modo creciente como una "mímesis con la muerte" –citada en la *Dialéctica del Iluminismo*–, de modo que al llegar a la tercera labor sus prácticas ya se han vuelto una maquinaria mortífera:

> Poco tiempo después el mandato ordenó a los hombres trabajar en grupos según los lugares donde habían sido instaladas guillotinas altamente especializadas, hacia las que cada uno era convocado con una exactitud obsesiva para ser enviado así de la vida a la muerte. (Bachmann, 1978: III.21-22)

Sobre todo con la mención de elementos de una matanza realizada en grupos y cumplida en lugares acondicionados especialmente para ello, así como con la representación de la matanza como trabajo, esta puesta en escena despierta la imagen de un exterminio irracionalmente motivado, pero racionalmente llevado a cabo como sucedió con la "Solución final". Con miras a que el hecho sea perfecto y completo –nos dice el texto–, el Señor del lugar ha de entregar a las máquinas también a quienes colaboraron en su funcionamiento.

Hasta este punto, el relato de Ingeborg Bachmann, que puede

luto. Este relato que se inspira en el esquema de interpretación de una crítica a la racionalidad según había sido planteada por la *Dialéctica del Iluminismo*, sufre claramente la influencia de ese texto programático de la teoría de la cultura de la Escuela de Frankfurt, que había nacido bajo el efecto causado por el Nacionalsocialismo durante el exilio californiano.[23] De modo similar al capítulo sobre Ulises de Horkheimer y Adorno, el texto de Bachmann presenta la lectura de una escena mítica, pero esta vez no como un comentario de filosofía de la historia, sino como narración, cuya estructura misma se refiere a aspectos míticos hasta desembocar finalmente en una reescritura del mito.

El texto de Bachmann se refiere a ese conocido mito fundante donde la Esfinge, una figura monstruosa que asedia las puertas de una ciudad, se presenta, al mismo tiempo como creadora de enigmas y dragón devorador, mientras la victoria le llega al héroe gracias a la obtención del saber. En lugar de Edipo, en el relato de Bachmann aparece el *Herrscher eines Landes* ["Señor de un país"] que no tiene un correlato histórico. Sin embargo, de lo que se trata es de una constelación paradigmática, como aclara el comienzo del texto: "En un tiempo en que todos los gobiernos peligraban" (Bachmann, 1978: II.19). Con la intranquilidad y temor frente a una amenaza desconocida que no venía, con todo, desde abajo, sino desde "exigencias e indicaciones no expresas, que creía tener que obedecer, pero que no conocía", el Señor aparece como la encarnación de la "angustia del hijo auténtico de la civilización moderna", del que se habla al comienzo de la *Dialéctica del Iluminismo* (Horkheimer y Adorno, 1966: 4).

La transformación del mito en *Das Lächeln der Sphinx*, que implica que sucumba el Señor, no se construye simplemente por el cambio de una estructura narrativa, sino que resulta legible como in-versión en tanto es como si el Dominador fuera vencido con sus propias armas. Esas armas son las de la racionalidad que se revelarán para él mortales. El punto de partida lo constituyen, en rigor, *su*

---

23. Este texto fue publicado en 1947 en Amsterdam, bajo el sello editorial Querido.

(Bachmann: 1978: III. 230). El significado de la primera piedra señala "vivir en asombro" [*Staunend leben*]; el de la segunda, "escribir en asombro" [*Schreiben im Staunen*], y de la tercera sólo se sabe que el personaje ha de conocer el mensaje después de su liberación.

Esta escena que alude al asombro benjaminiano puede ser entendida, por cierto, como alegoría de la escritura de la propia Ingeborg Bachmann, que retoma en el giro "*Satz vom Grund*"* –título de una obra de Heidegger (Heidegger, 1957)– un motivo que había aparecido veinte años antes, al comienzo de su carrera literaria, como una crítica de la razón y de la racionalidad. Ahora bien, cuando en la novela *Malina* se opera una sustitución de la "frase sobre la razón" (dado que resulta ilegible) siendo reemplazada por el mensaje de "escribir en asombro", puede entenderse esto como un texto cifrado: Benjamin ha pasado a ocupar definitivamente el lugar de la tácita fascinación por las figuras heideggerianas –como, por ejemplo, la de la "angustia" [*Angst*]–. Ello puede verse, además, no sólo como el rechazo definitivo de Heidegger por parte de Bachmann, sino también como un comentario autorreferencial sobre la crítica de la razón de sus comienzos, que se encuentra reforzado ahora en el momento de una lectura de la *Dialéctica del Iluminismo*.

En 1949, la joven estudiante de filosofía Ingeborg Bachmann contaba con 23 años, cuando, a la par de su investigación doctoral sobre la recepción de Heidegger, publicaba en un diario vienés, *Die Wiener Tageszeitung*, un relato que llevaba por título *Das Lächeln der Sphinx* ["La sonrisa de la Esfinge"], donde se tematizaba el pasaje de la Ilustración a la mitología y el carácter destructor de una racionalidad que se imponga de modo abso-

---

* Este título da lugar a varios juegos lingüísticos debido a la ambigüedad de los términos. *Satz* significa "la frase gramatical", "lo que se pone", "lo que queda"; y *Grund*, "fondo", "base"; ambas palabras forman, además, un compuesto: *Grundsatz* que se traduce como "principio fundamental", de modo tal que el título heideggeriano podría entenderse como un chiste de orden metalingüístico donde se desmenuza el vocablo compuesto. [N. del T.]

"LA ESCRITURA BAJO EL ESTUPOR" DE INGEBORG BACHMANN COMO CASO LÍMITE EN LA LITERATURA

La incapacidad para asimilar conscientemente los hechos así como los rastros de un golpe traumático en la posterior historia del Nacionalsocialismo estructuran el capítulo del sueño en la novela de Ingeborg Bachmann, *Malina*, aparecida en 1971. En ese texto se manifiesta la otra cara de la medalla de una "dialéctica negativa", dado que muestra las huellas y síntomas que se ocasionan a causa de esa incapacidad de la conciencia para asumir la culpa.[22] El capítulo del sueño lleva la impronta especialmente de los síntomas de un retorno de lo totalitario reprimido. En las imágenes oníricas se representan escenarios que apuntan a una total ruptura de la civilización en las relaciones de los sexos y a una caída del deseo femenino en las redes del complejo de culpa. A partir de citas dispersas en cada una de las imágenes oníricas de elementos tomados de un rígido lenguaje simbólico del exterminio –como "cámara de gas", "rieles", "tubos", etcétera–, este decorado se torna legible como escenario de una memoria después de Auschwitz, sin que *Malina* contenga un discurso *sobre* Auschwitz. Son justamente esos momentos que se resisten a entrar en lo histórico, como huecos de la conciencia y síntomas o símbolos mnémicos, los que dotan al texto de Bachmann de su lugar en la historia.

En uno de los episodios oníricos, la que sueña se presenta como escritora –aunque se trata de una mujer que se halla prisionera y a quien se le prohíbe escribir–, mientras intenta registrar la "frase sobre la razón" [*Satz vom Grunde*]. Ese texto, sin embargo, en lugar de encontrar su camino hacia la escritura sobre un papel se inscribe sobre su carne y, de ese modo, se torna ilegible, mientras que junto a ella se hacen visibles ahora tres piedras que han sido arrojadas por "la Suprema Instancia"

---

22. Para un análisis detallado de estos aspectos, véase Weigel (1994a: 232-263).

encontrar su modo de descripción dentro de una crítica de la razón instrumental ni de una dialéctica de la Ilustración en su tentativa de explicar la simultaneidad de una racionalidad en la realización del exterminio junto con una irracionalidad e incomprensibilidad en sus motivaciones y justificación. Si el Holocausto puso en tela de juicio de modo flagrante la "relación entre premisas racionales, la capacidad de comprender y la reconstrucción plena de sentido" (Diner, 1992: 142)[21] a nivel de filosofía de la historia; al mismo tiempo, en definitiva, existe una incapacidad de "pensar Auschwitz", que no puede llamarse a descanso en un "pensamiento después de Auschwitz" y que no encuentra su salida del atajo en ningún discurso, ya se trate del filosófico, del historiográfico o del literario. Por ese motivo, George Steiner ha desplazado el campo donde se discute el problema de la singularidad del Holocausto —desde su historización a su comprensión— al manifestarse en contra de la tentativa de integrar el hecho de la *Shoah* en "la historia normal de la humanidad" con el objeto de normalizar la comprensión (Steiner, 1987: 87).

Esta problematización y las figuras de una reflexión posible han producido un movimiento con muchos desvíos hacia un "pensamiento después de Auschwitz" que se sienten conectados entre sí frente a la imposibilidad de una integración de los acontecimientos en la noción existente de Historia —es decir, la variante historiográfica del trauma—, con una postura que podría describirse con la ayuda de la negación benjaminiana de un estupor filosófico. Esos debates se desplazan entre los lugares de un caso límite, como lo ha representado Benjamin ya en su tesis VIII.

---

21. Dan Diner postula una "historia negativa" para el conocimiento histórico (cf. Diner, 1992: 142).

aparece caracterizada como portadora del trauma. La *Dialéctica negativa* puede entenderse, entonces, como intento de mantener la correspondencia con esta constelación todavía dentro de los límites del discurso filosófico, pero en este movimiento la filosofía *pasa a ser* ella misma el caso límite, en tanto y en cuanto el no poder asumir la culpa a nivel consciente remite a una figura que va a moldear la posterior historia del Nacionalsocialismo en los años después de la guerra.

Los diferentes signos de un *retorno* a una culpa no asumida por la conciencia habrían de marcar la historia subsiguiente del discurso y la repercusión del Nacionalsocialismo de manera extrema, lo que se manifiesta en primera instancia en el paradigma del trauma que se ha ido haciendo cada vez más evidente desde los años setenta.[19] El lugar común de un "hablar después de Auschwitz" –que dejó su impronta largo tiempo en el discurso cultural alemán inmediatamente después de la guerra– había colaborado para que se postergara un enfrentamiento más radical con los aspectos centrales de un "pensar después de Auschwitz", que hubiera obligado a no dejar de lado las categorías universales de lo indecible frente a la especificidad del Holocausto. Esta problemática ha ganado nueva visibilidad sólo a consecuencia de la lucha [*Historikerstreit*] dentro del revisionismo histórico alemán. Por una parte, esta contienda tiene que ver con lo irreconciliable de los lugares de enunciación en la historia posterior del Nacionalsocialismo, es decir, que la memoria de los sobrevivientes y de los descendientes de las víctimas no puede ser asociada con la de los herederos del grupo colectivo de los agentes, con el objeto de crear un cuadro histórico coherente.[20] Por otra parte, esto concierne también a los intentos de lograr una representación histórica de la política de exterminio: un proyecto que siempre arriba a una contradicción insoluble que no puede

---

19. Bohleber brinda un enfoque general del tema (1990).
20. Una de estas disputas fue conocida en Alemania como el "debate Broszat-Friedländer". Para el lugar común de "Escribir después de Auschwitz", véanse los matices en las diferentes formas del silencio en Heller (1993).

de acusar el golpe, y cuanto más profundamente y con más fuerza gane nuevos territorios, tanto mayor será el recelo de que se está alejando de lo que ella en realidad es. (Adorno, 1966: 357) (El destacado es mío.)

Aun cuando esta *Dialéctica negativa* lleva a un extremo radical la reflexión sobre la herencia del Siglo de las Luces que había aparecido en *Dialéctica del Iluminismo* como una "autorreflexión del pensamiento" [*Selbstreflexion des Denkens*] o como un pensamiento dialéctico que obliga a "un pensar también contra sí mismo" (1966: 358), sin embargo, queda todavía un residuo que no llega al nivel de la conceptualización. Que el hecho de no poder tomar *plenamente* conciencia sea la razón de ser de la necesidad de la filosofía conduce a cuestionarse por las manifestaciones, el estatuto, las posibilidades de conocimiento y la práctica real frente a esos aspectos de la culpa que la conciencia no puede asumir. Dado que la figura de "aspectos" que no son asumibles en la conciencia coincide exactamente con el concepto freudiano de trauma, lo que Adorno está describiendo aquí no es otra cosa que *lo Otro* de la conciencia: esos "aspectos" pueden leerse tan sólo como signos mnémicos, como síntomas y otros modos de un lenguaje del inconsciente. De esta manera, justificar la necesidad de la filosofía en base a este sentimiento de culpa, al mismo tiempo, significa señalar los límites de la filosofía. Esto no sucedería, sin embargo, si la filosofía hiciera suya las concepciones del psicoanálisis y los procedimientos de otra lectura de un lenguaje del inconsciente, lo que llevaría, naturalmente, a un nuevo tipo de acto de filosofar, donde se verían implicadas otras maneras de pensar. Con la referencia a un no poder asumir plenamente la culpa a nivel de la conciencia, Adorno toca un problema central. En este movimiento parece profundamente llamativo, además, que en la misma tirada en la que el autor muestra su desconocimiento de la estructura psicoanalítica de la figura de pensamiento que está utilizando, cargue a la filosofía con el impacto sentido por los sobrevivientes ("La filosofía no puede dejar de acusar el golpe..."), con lo que la misma filosofía

Dentro de la historia de la génesis de los textos adornianos, sólo en 1966 llega a ser una constelación filosófica central el último peldaño de la relación dialéctica o el caso límite de una crítica cultural tematizada indirectamente en ella, una situación que se había postulado ya en 1949 en su *Crítica de la cultura y la sociedad*. En el famoso tercer capítulo de la tercera parte, titulado "Meditaciones sobre metafísica", de la *obra magna* de Adorno, *Dialéctica negativa*, la figura de un "después de Auschwitz" llega a ser, finalmente, el modelo de esa dialéctica negativa. A pesar de esto, la estructuración del libro deja abierta la no identificación entre un discurso filosófico y el lugar señalado en el texto como un "después de Auschwitz". En el diseño gráfico de la página aparece la frase "después de Auschwitz" [*Nach Auschwitz*] más bien como nombre en el tope superior que como verdadero título, es decir, como un nombre no integrable al texto filosófico y que, por lo tanto, mantiene con el título del capítulo una relación de particular tensión: una constelación que se coloca, concretamente en el diseño gráfico, en la postura de un pensamiento que piensa contra sí mismo, según se postula en esta *Dialéctica negativa*, como cierre del apartado 1 que lleva en el tope de página la indicación "Después de Auschwitz".

En esta obra se retoma el tema de la culpa que había aparecido quince años antes en el prólogo-dedicatoria de *Minima Moralia* para venir a determinar el inicio de otra filosofía. Es la posición del que ha salido con vida y siente "la culpa de vivir" frente a los que han muerto, lo que ahora adquiere el estatuto de una condición de necesidad para la filosofía, una filosofía que contiene en sí misma la desconfianza ante sí:

> La culpa de vivir, que como hecho puro roba el aliento ya a la otra vida, y siguiendo una simple estadística, sustituye una suma inconmensurable de asesinados por una mínima cantidad de salvados, como si hubiera entrado en los cálculos de probabilidades; sin embargo, esta culpa ya no puede congraciarse con la vida. *Cada culpa se reproduce a sí misma sin descanso, porque en ningún momento puede tomar plenamente conciencia de sí misma. Esto, y no otra cosa, obliga a la tarea filosófica*. La filosofía no puede dejar

después de Auschwitz significa la barbarie"[16] aparece después de dos puntos, para caracterizar una situación frente a la que se encuentra la crítica cultural contemporánea y que el mismo Adorno califica de: "el último peldaño de la relación dialéctica entre la cultura y la barbarie".[17] "Ella carcome" –según afirma Adorno– "el conocimiento que expresa por qué se ha tornado imposible escribir poesía hoy en día."[18] (1949: 26).

Para el caso de la filosofía, en cambio, Adorno no va a formular ninguna afirmación semejante de tal radicalidad. Sus escritos que discuten cuestiones *fundamentales* de la relación entre literatura y filosofía –como, por ejemplo, el trabajo sobre "El ensayo como forma", de 1957–, o ponen sobre el tapete la razón de existir de la filosofía –como, por ejemplo, "¿Para qué es necesaria la filosofía?", de 1962– no acusan el menor rastro de un pensamiento después de Auschwitz. No puede negarse, sin embargo, que la metáfora de una "estrella amarilla"* en el estudio de 1957 hace clara alusión a la persecución de los judíos. Esta alusión permanece, con todo, a nivel abstracto, en tanto aquí el género ensayo es definido como "impuro" [*unrein*] y, en consecuencia, expulsado de la "cofradía <porque no llena los requisitos> como filosofía" [*Zunft als Philosophie*; 1959: 10], dado que no cumple con las premisas de sistematicidad, verdad, unidad de origen, etcétera. Esta caracterización del ensayo como género lo lleva, en definitiva, a una cercanía metafórica con la imagen de los judíos en el discurso antisemita (Burgard, 1992). Debatiendo sobre "la cofradía como filosofía", a Adorno no se le ocurre dirigir sus asociaciones hacia la "filosofía como cofradía" [*die Philosophie als Zunft*].

---

16. En alemán: "*nach Auschwitz ein Gedicht zu schreiben, ist barbarisch*". [N. del T.]
17. En alemán: "*letzte Stufe der Dialektik von Kultur und Barbarei*". [N. del T.]
18. En alemán: "*Diese frisst die Erkenntnis an, die ausspricht, warum es unmöglich wird, heute Gedichte zu schreiben*". [N. del T.]
* Literalmente: "de una mancha amarilla" [N. del T.]

Iluminismo (1947) de los últimos textos benjaminianos (1940) todavía no ha sido motivo de una toma de conciencia epistemológica en su condición de hiato histórico. En este sentido, a la inversa, parecería que el texto de Benjamin –posiblemente a causa de deber su origen a la inmediatez con la experiencia de persecución– acreditara en su haber una mayor cercanía con respecto a la idea de peligro, y, por ello, estuviera mejor preparado para meditar a nivel epistemológico acerca de un caso límite que resultaría apropiado como condición de posibilidad para pensar *a posteriori* la mencionada cesura histórica. Un pensamiento "después de Auschwitz", en todo caso, no podrá evitar considerar ese asombro y horror, que Benjamin ha elevado a caso límite, considerándolo el comienzo para un nuevo modo de conocimiento. Eso produce necesariamente consecuencias para el discurso filosófico después del Holocausto [*Shoah*].[14]

Las reflexiones críticas de Adorno sobre su propio lugar tanto como las consecuencias que representa el nombre de Auschwitz para el pensamiento se encuentran ligadas, por el contrario, desde hace mucho a la cuestión de cómo se puede hablar sobre lo indecible, así como al hecho de discutir acerca de un paradigma que se resumiría en un "hablar después de Auschwitz" en relación con determinados géneros y disciplinas. En esto llama la atención que el fin diagnosticado para algunos géneros literarios como tales –como, por ejemplo, para la sátira[15] o para el poema– no ha valido para la filosofía. Por cierto que la apreciación de Adorno sobre la poesía después de Auschwitz no formula un postulado (en contraste con la trivializada historia de su recepción que ha tendido a sacarla de su contexto), sino que describe una constelación crítico-cultural que se podría ver como un caso límite, dado que se habla del último peldaño de una relación dialéctica. Esa afirmación adorniana "escribir una poesía

---

14. Un detallado análisis con respecto a Adorno después de Auschwitz en relación con la obra *Germanien* de Heidegger, puede encontrarse en García Düttmann (1991).
15. Cf. Adorno, 1951: 280-283, bajo el título de "El error de Juvenal".

La perplejidad acotada *a posteriori* en el texto a causa del conocimiento obtenido se transforma en virulencia cuando se dan referencias concretas al Nacionalsocialismo que quedan circunscriptas a los campos de concentración; allí no se mencionan ni la "Solución final" [*Endlösung*] ni los lugares de exterminio [*Vernichtungslager*]. Y éste es un enfoque típico para la perspectiva de los reintegrados a la sociedad alemana, como es el caso también de Hannah Arendt, que en su ensayo *Wir Flüchtlinge* ["Nosotros, los fugitivos"] de 1943 afirmaba: "Evidentemente nadie está interesado en saber que la historia actual ha creado un nuevo género humano: personas que han sido puestas en campos de concentración –por los enemigos– y en campos de internación –por los amigos–." (Arendt, 1986: 9). En esta declaración se nota todavía la ausencia de la idea de aniquilación de grupos específicos del "género humano", una experiencia incomprensible y que no puede ser apaciguada con ninguna explicación como la que caracteriza a las anotaciones de los sobrevivientes, según puede verse en los textos de Primo Levi, por ejemplo. Tampoco la *Dialéctica del Iluminismo*, cuya tesis central en torno al retroceso de la Ilustración hacia una época mítica fue siendo elaborada en relación con los fenómenos que mostraba el Nacionalsocialismo entre 1942 y 1944, parece acusar los rastros del conocimiento de la "Solución final". Incluso los "elementos de antisemitismo" que surgen en el contexto de un vasto proyecto de investigación entre el grupo de emigrantes alemanes residentes en California con el objeto de constituir una "historia filosófica primigenia del antisemitismo" (Horkheimer y Adorno, 1969: 6), deberían ubicarse dentro de un *antes de* Auschwitz, dado que se basan en material obtenido antes de saber que allí los judíos habían sido exterminados según un plan sistemático organizado con una concienzuda división de tareas.[13]

La "Solución final" (1942) como cesura objetivamente histórica (a la luz de datos fehacientes) que separa la *Dialéctica del*

---

13. Lo mismo vale todavía para el libro de Leo Löwenthal *Individuum und Terror* (1944). Para la posición de una autoseparación frente a la Teoría Crítica, véase Klaus Briegleb (1993: 12-29; esp. 24 y sigs.).

tual en la emigración", desde donde Adorno reflexionaba sobre los movimientos históricos que "consisten en la disolución del sujeto sin permitir todavía que salga de allí uno nuevo",[10] la contemporaneidad de esas notas con lo que sucedía en Auschwitz en 1944 aparece siete años después bajo una luz completamente diferente,[11] y a esto se refiere Adorno en el prólogo de 1951 en su comentario de "la aniquilación que representaron para el sujeto los campos de concentración" (1951: 8).

La experiencia de una vida dañada en las anotaciones surgidas *en el exilio* había sido marcada por el maltrato de la memoria cultural del emigrante:

> La vida pasada del emigrante queda anulada, como es sabido [...] Esa vida así violentada es exhibida, además, en la marcha triunfal llevada a la rastra sobre un automóvil por los operadores de Estadísticas Unidos; e incluso lo pasado ya no está seguro frente al presente, que lo consagra una segunda vez al olvido en el acto de recordarlo. (Adorno, 1951: 52-53)[12]

Este lugar de la experiencia desde la vuelta a Alemania y con la información paulatina y fidedigna sobre la inmensidad de lo sucedido con la aniquilación de los judíos europeos, produce ahora una reflexión no exenta del sentimiento de culpa:

> Escribí el libro en su mayor parte durante la guerra, en condiciones contemplativas. La violencia que me había empujado me vedaba, al mismo tiempo, una visión más completa. Todavía no podía confesarme mi propia parte de culpa, que es la que rodea a quien en conocimiento de lo indecible que le sucedió al conjunto, habla en absoluto de temas individuales.

10. Véase Adorno, 1951: 11 y 8.
11. Véase al respecto Claussen (1988: 54-68). De todos modos, hay que señalar que Claussen desdibuja los perfiles en su representación de la distancia histórica entre las obras de Adorno *Minima moralia* y *Dialéctica negativa* (1966), es decir, la genealogía de la configuración adorniana de sus pensamientos y lenguaje en relación con Auschwitz.
12. En este pasaje se puede escuchar un eco de la tesis VI de Benjamin de "Sobre el concepto de historia": "*tampoco los muertos* han de estar seguros frente al enemigo, si triunfa" (*G.S.,* I.2.695).

LOS LÍMITES DE LA FILOSOFÍA DESPUÉS DE AUSCHWITZ: ADORNO

En alguna medida, la *Dialéctica del Iluminismo* (1947) que fue escrita inmediatamente después e inspirándose en las tesis benjaminianas –especialmente en el capítulo dedicado a Ulises, donde una lectura de escenas primigenias[9] de la mitología se corresponde con un acercamiento textual a la transición entre el mito y la Ilustración– es una obra que tomó su forma gracias a exigencias sobre un nuevo modo de conocimiento. Sin embargo, sus autores retroceden ante la radicalidad del procedimiento benjaminiano que extrae imágenes de pensamiento del *continuum* del discurso filosófico, declarando que su concepción de la historia "es una crítica de la filosofía que, por lo tanto, rehúsa abandonar el terreno de la filosofía", según se lee en el prólogo de la reedición de 1969 (Horkheimer y Adorno, 1969: X). Mientras ambos autores se hallaban ocupados en la redacción de esa obra conjunta, Adorno, por su parte, trabajaba (a partir de 1944) en sus *Reflexionen aus dem beschädigten Leben* ["Reflexiones desde una vida dañada"], que luego pasaría a ser el subtítulo de su libro *Minima moralia*, el texto que más se aleja del procedimiento estructural coherente del discurso filosófico entre todos los escritos adornianos. Sin embargo, Adorno afirma allí que "las partes no podrían aprobar un examen de filosofía de la que, con todo, ellas forman parte" (Adorno, 1951: 12), justificando esta impertinencia filosófica por la íntima relación del texto con los aspectos subjetivos.

La dedicatoria a Marx Horkheimer en forma de prólogo, colocada en ocasión de la publicación del libro (1951), puede ser leída en el contexto de la repatriación de los miembros de la Escuela de Frankfurt, cuando era el momento de reflexionar sobre la escritura en el exilio con cierta distancia temporal. Mientras que, por un lado, se trataba de la posición del "intelec-

---

9. Para el concepto de escena primaria [*Urszene*], véase Laplanche y Pontalis (1985).

percibe la catástrofe. En este caso la catástrofe no es la excepción, sino que es lo inabordable para nuestra mirada acostumbrada a la progresión continua. La mirada del ángel –la otra mirada o lo otro de nuestra percepción– aparece ahora como la condición de posibilidad para percibir la catástrofe en la historia.

El modo de pensar tanto como la manera de escribir benjaminianos en estos pasajes surgidos a partir de un asombro no filosófico (o post-filosófico) van estrechamente unidos: la representación de una idea en una imagen de pensamiento o en una imagen dialéctica,[7] y la constelación específica de que aquí se trata –la tensión y oposición entre filosofía de la historia y mesianismo judío–.[8] El asombro como un caso límite lleva, al mismo tiempo, a las fronteras con el discurso filosófico; es decir, al fin de la filosofía como un meta-discurso y hacia el inicio de un nuevo tipo de escritura. El modo diferente de conocimiento implica un modo diferente de escritura, que no puede ya ser descrito en términos formales. En la obra de Benjamin ese modo toma su configuración no sólo por el uso textual de imágenes de pensamiento, sino también por su transgresión de las fronteras entre los géneros y las disciplinas –es decir, entre las fronteras entre literatura, filosofía e historia–, en un intento teórico todavía amorfo por reproducir los más diversos fenómenos, cosas y escrituras, que son leídos como imágenes de la historia.

7. Para una lectura de la tesis IX sobre el "Ángel de la Historia" como imagen dialéctica, véase el capítulo 4 del presente estudio.
8. Al analizar la historia y la salvación, Karl Löwith se refiere al libro de Hermann Cohen *Religion der Vernunft aus den Quellen des Judentums* ["La religión de la razón a partir de las fuentes del judaísmo"], pero borra las diferencias entre la escatología cristiana y el profetismo judío (Löwith, 1983: 28). Por este motivo, su crítica de la filosofía de la historia permanece dentro de la inmanencia, refiriéndose al concepto de crisis. Por el contrario, Gershom Scholem muestra la tendencia de excluir el apocalipsis en la tentativa de Maimónides por describir la revelación judía como un sistema consistente de una religión de la Razón (Scholem, 1963). Sin embargo, la incompatibilidad y la "radical diferencia entre el mundo irredento de la historia y el de la salvación mesiánica" (1963: 36) estructura el pensamiento benjaminiano y es la base para sus tesis "Sobre el concepto de historia".

analizadas dentro de un discurso de filosofía de la historia. Explícitamente Benjamin formula esto en la Reflexión XIII, afirmando que no le interesa solamente realizar una crítica a la "idea de Progreso", sino que lo que importa es que la crítica a la idea de marcha [*Vorstellung des Fortgangs*] debe ser la base de esta crítica (*G.S.*, I.2.701). Se trata, entonces, aquí de la construcción de la historia, justamente de un "concepto de historia", que en la propuesta de Horkheimer y Adorno para titular este último texto benjaminiano como *Geschichts-philosophische Thesen* ["Tesis histórico-filosóficas"] estaba desconociendo el lugar epistemológico radical que le correspondía. Dado que Benjamin no desarrolla aquí precisamente tesis histórico-filosóficas, sino a lo sumo tesis *sobre* filosofía de la historia, y en la medida en que reflexiona sobre limitaciones, situándolas como caso límite a nivel epistemológico, el problema del título bajo la corrección de la Escuela de Frankfurt no hace más que acentuar el desconocimiento de la argumentación central del texto benjaminiano, lo que ha condicionado a la recepción posterior de modo que tampoco captara este punto clave.

En el apartado que sigue inmediatamente a la tesis sobre el estupor no filosófico, en la famosa Reflexión IX donde aparece el "Ángel de la Historia", Benjamin ha emprendido la tarea de representar este caso límite epistemológico como una imagen de pensamiento. Ni el primer ángel (de la poesía de Scholem) que formula un deseo del regreso basado en una teleología negativa de la historia, ni el boquiabierto *Angelus Novus* de ojos inconmensurables –una imagen mítica que acentúa los aspectos del horror en su asombro– posibilitan otra idea de la historia. Sólo en la figura de un ensamblaje de fuerzas que se dirigen en direcciones opuestas [*die Figur einer gegenstrebigen Fügung*] –en la mirada del ángel asustado, que es arrastrado por la tormenta del progreso hacia el futuro, sin poder mirarlo a los ojos, y que aparece posicionado de modo asincrónico hacia la cadena de hechos que se presentan ante nosotros–, sólo en esa constelación logra representación esa idea. Todo lo que vemos son las cosas que siguen su curso, mientras que es la mirada del ángel y sólo ella la que

regla o de la regla definida como razonable. En este sentido, el estupor como postura engendrada por la actividad filosófica, ha venido a dar a una posición que se halla más allá del discurso filosófico; es decir, se trata de una postura que resulta de un efecto de la historia de la filosofía. Sólo el paso que lleva a tomar con seriedad este asombro y comprenderlo como límite de la filosofía tradicional abre otra posibilidad de concepción: no un retroceso hacia un estupor original, *quasi* pre-filosófico, sino una negación del asombro filosófico para permitir el nacimiento de otra vía de conocimiento.

Al mismo tiempo, Benjamin postula la insostenibilidad de una filosofía de la historia asociada a los aspectos de totalidad, desarrollo e interpretación de sentido [*Sinnesdeutung*].[5] Con la afirmación de insostenibilidad de una "concepción de la historia específica" [*eine spezifische Vorstellung von Geschichte*] Benjamin está marcando no sólo la frontera de un concepto concreto de historia –por ejemplo, el concepto de Progreso– sino, a la vez, de una idea fundamental de "historia", como un decurso que se va cumpliendo en el tiempo de modo significativo. Ésta es una concepción que se halla en la base de toda filosofía de la historia que hace de la reconocibilidad de la razón [*Erkenntbarkeit der Vernunft*] en el devenir histórico la premisa para la dotación de sentido filosófico a esa ciencia, lo que abarca desde la doctrina de la salvación cristiana, pasando por Kant, Hegel y Marx hasta Löwith.[6] La crítica al Progreso y a la razón del devenir histórico mismo, la crítica hacia esos fenómenos que Horkheimer y Adorno han de denominar –en alusión a las tesis de Benjamin– "dialéctica del Iluminismo", lleva a la razón a una red de contradicciones que ya no pueden ser

---

5. "Como unidad y totalidad, tiene un *sentido* el tiempo que comienza y concluye, el ámbito del discurso histórico: y esto en una doble significación, pues tiene, a la vez, una *dirección* y una *inteligibilidad*." (Châtelet, 1975: VII.205)

6. Por ejemplo, la descripción de Karl Löwith en su *opus magnum* de filosofía de la historia analiza los problemas del pensamiento escatológico en la Modernidad, basándose sobre el paradigma de la *crisis* en lugar de reflexionar sobre los límites de la filosofía de la historia.

De este modo, si en el uso de Carl Schmitt se entiende el término como un concepto general de las ciencias políticas [*Staatslehre*], Benjamin, por su parte, toma de ello lo relacionado con un caso límite (conceptual), pero, al mismo tiempo, se aleja de esta posición al transponerlo al territorio de la filosofía de la historia. Y con el estupor, que marca la frontera en el ámbito de filosofía de la historia, el pensamiento benjaminiano entra en un dominio que ya no puede relacionarse con la teología política de Carl Schmitt. El asombro aparece en el contexto benjaminiano justamente en el lugar donde en la obra de Schmitt se le da espacio a la fase decisionista: "La decisión sobre la excepción es decisión en todo el sentido de la palabra" (Schmitt, 1934: 11, n.3). Para Benjamin, por el contrario, la introducción del verdadero estado de excepción no se da asociada a una decisión, sino a una cesura epistemológica, es decir, a otra concepción de la historia que aparece posibilitada por un estupor no filosófico y que, al mismo tiempo, diferencia un asombro por lo vivenciado en el siglo XX de la figura de lo que es "todavía" posible.

En relación con el concepto de la historia esto produce las siguientes consecuencias: 1) un corte frente a la síntesis entre estupor y discurso filosófico; y 2) una cesura con la filosofía de la historia tradicional.

Si, como ha transmitido el mito fundante de la filosofía, el asombro se hallaba en el origen de la actividad filosófica, entonces, ha sido a través de la filosofía *como disciplina* que él se introduce en el *logos*, siguiendo las reglas de un discurso racional y lógico. La necesidad de esclarecimiento de fenómenos enigmáticos les ha quitado mucho también del horror que ellos causaban. *To thambos* —es decir: "estupor", "asombro" y "horror"— pasó a un discurso que se consideró dirigido hacia el interés por el conocimiento, el esclarecimiento y la verdad, integrándose los valores del estupor en un orden accesible a la razón, hasta llegar así a superar lo enigmático. Cuando después de esta tarea de iluminación sobreviene nuevamente el asombro, entonces éste es completamente diferente del asombro original, dado que ha devenido tal a través de la desviación de la razón tomada como

VIII sostiene que se trataría de arribar a un concepto de la historia que fuera coherente con la doctrina que afirma "que la 'situación de excepción' en la que vivimos es la regla", entrecomillando ese concepto, Benjamin pone de relieve a modo de cita una idea difundida que más adelante va a contrastar con el concepto de un "verdadero estado de excepción".

Si los acontecimientos (del fascismo) –que, siguiendo el sentido común, se consideran como situación de excepción– son la regla, entonces lo que le importa a Benjamin con la "introducción de un verdadero estado de excepción" es romper con esa norma. Esta ruptura no significa, sin embargo, una simple transformación de una teleología del Progreso en una negativa. Del mismo modo que la conocida frase de los Pasajes, "que la cosa 'siga así', ésa es la catástrofe" (*G.S.*, V.1.592),[4] no implica una afirmación sobre la normalidad de la catástrofe; sino que, a la inversa, lo importante aquí es lo catastrófico de esa norma. Esto es, entonces, la otra cara de la regularidad de los fenómenos que se prefiere adscribir a un estado de excepción. "La introducción de un verdadero estado de excepción" que postula Benjamin exige por ello una ruptura con ese concepto de la historia que se basa en la idea de Progreso como regla y que califica así a todo lo que se escapa a esa regla como excepción, retroceso, barbarie, irracionalidad o cosas por el estilo.

También para Carl Schmitt se relaciona este estado de excepción con un concepto límite y un caso límite:

> Soberano es aquel que decide sobre el estado de excepción. Esta definición sólo puede hacerle justicia al concepto de soberanía como concepto límite. Pues concepto límite no significa un concepto confuso, como es usado en la terminología poco clara de la bibliografía corriente, sino un concepto de una esfera de las más elevadas. Esto se corresponde con que su definición no pueda dar cuenta del caso normal, sino del caso límite. (Schmitt, 1934: 11)

---

4. En alemán: "*Dass es 'so weiter' geht, ist die Katastrophe*" (Anotaciones y materiales para "La obra de los pasajes", Block N9a,1; *G.S.*, V.1.592). [N. del T.]

se elevan a rango de norma tanto un giro negativo de la historia como el hecho catastrófico, de modo tal que la crítica benjaminiana al concepto de Progreso, en definitiva, aparece transformada en una teleología negativa de la historia.

Una lectura más atenta de la cita de Benjamin, sin embargo, permite ver que su autor no se promueve en contra del estupor en sí, sino que más bien está negándole estatuto filosófico. En esa frase aparecen dos palabras realzadas por Benjamin: el "todavía" [*noch*] entrecomillado obtiene así el carácter de un lugar común, un "se dice que" que se torna el signo de una "idea de Progreso" que está en la base, es decir, que implica a este estupor específico (sobre lo todavía posible); la cursiva utilizada para la negación subraya la negatividad del *status* filosófico de ese asombro. Pero no se trata de que el estupor mismo fuera rechazado. En lugar de rechazo, lo que se expresa en el asombro es la única condición para la posibilidad de conocimiento, como lo aclara la continuación del pasaje: El asombro "no se halla al comienzo de un acto de conocimiento, salvo que se trate de ese conocimiento por el cual la idea de la historia de la que proviene no pueda sostenerse".[3]

Si el estupor, entonces, se halla en un comienzo posible de conocimiento sobre una idea insostenible de la historia que lo gestó, eso significa que ese estupor marca, al mismo tiempo, justamente el fin de esa idea de la historia. De este modo, el asombro obtiene la caracterización de un caso límite [*Grenzfall*]. Valorado como *no* filosófico, define el corte frente a una historiografía que mida los acontecimientos contemporáneos en el decurso progresivo de la historia y los considere inadecuados o retrógrados en su forma. Considerado *no* filosófico, el estupor se torna así la condición de posibilidad de otro tipo de conocimiento.

La importancia del asombro como caso límite se corresponde con el modo en que Benjamin utiliza en este apartado el concepto de situación de excepción. Cuando al comienzo de esta reflexión

---

3. En alemán: "[*Das Staunen*] steht nicht am Anfang einer Erkenntnis, es sei denn der, dass die Vorstellung von Geschichte, aus der es stammt, nicht zu halten ist". [N. del T.]

11. El estupor no filosófico o la escritura en perpetuo asombro
La posición de Benjamin después del Holocausto

EL ESTUPOR BENJAMINIANO COMO CASO LÍMITE DE LA FILOSOFÍA DE LA HISTORIA

La observación de Benjamin acerca del estupor en su "Sobre el concepto de historia", que escribió en 1940 poco antes de su fuga frustrada y su muerte, se halla entre las más citadas frases de todos sus escritos:

> El estupor sobre el hecho de que las cosas que experimentamos en el siglo XX "todavía" son posibles, *no* es filosófico. (Reflexión VIII, "Sobre el concepto de historia", I.2.697)[1]

A menudo se cita esta afirmación con la intención de hacer hincapié sobre la forma en que nos acostumbramos a la violencia, la aniquilación y la destrucción en el contexto de nuestra percepción cotidiana, con la intención de dirigirse en contra de la postura del asombro y del horror. Al hacerlo, se trata de dar un lugar en la lógica del desarrollo histórico a los numerosos fenómenos de los desastres causados por el hombre. Según la posición tomada habrá diferencias en el modo de hacer la referencia, pero siempre ella conllevará una valoración negativa.[2] En este tipo de enfoques

---

1. En alemán: "*Das Staunen darüber, dass die Dinge, die wir erleben, im zwanzigsten Jahrhundert 'noch' möglich sind, ist* kein *philosophisches*". [N. del T.]

2. Esto sucede en posturas que defienden el capitalismo, el patriarcado, la destrucción de la naturaleza, el colonialismo o la revolución científica.

contribución de Scholem. Analizando esto en relación con las consecuencias que le traen al individuo, Scholem se centra en la problematicidad de la idea del vivir en esperanza como una vida de constante diferir (1963: 73).

Desde la perspectiva de las teorías modernas del sujeto, en particular desde el posicionamiento psicoanalítico del individuo, sin embargo, la vida aparece determinada ya como diferida, en los aspectos de la figura del deseo, la añoranza, la pasión y la expectativa. La versión benjaminiana de lo mesiánico puede ser entendida justamente en este marco, por ejemplo, cuando Benjamin habla de una "intensidad mesiánica" para describir la posición y las actitudes del sujeto de la historia. A pesar de ello, la espera puede tornarse para Benjamin la experiencia de una iluminación profana, así como la lectura solitaria, el acto de pensar, el deambular [*Flanieren*] y la soledad. En este sentido, Benjamin radicaliza la concepción por la que la llegada del Mesías habría de coincidir con el fin de la historia, para obtener a partir de la asincronicidad entre la historia y la redención un tercer elemento: su concepto de *Jetztzeit*, una estructura del tiempo que explota del *continuum* y que coloca al sujeto en la actitud de la intensidad mesiánica, en el centro de un mundo irredento, en el medio del orden de lo profano. Con todo, el desfasaje entre el período mesiánico de Benjamin y su preocupación por la filosofía de la historia –cuyos primeros atisbos se ubican hacia 1920 con el "Fragmento teológico-político"– parece plasmarse como enfoque reflexivo veinte años después, cuando toma forma la idea de una figura psicoanalítica de la memoria: no ya bajo el aspecto de la superación [*Aufhebung*] de los extremos, sino de una imagen para la representación de la disimultaneidad, según se muestra en la lectura que hace del "Ángel de la Historia" como imagen dialéctica.

imágenes de pensamiento que consideraba todavía inmaduras para publicar, esta idea aparece, sin embargo, ahora en la siguiente variación: "Sólo a la humanidad redimida [...] su pasado puede serle citado en cada uno de sus momentos" (Reflexión III, "Sobre el concepto de historia"; *G.S.*, I.2.694), donde se da la escandalosa unión del mesianismo y el psicoanálisis de un modo ya difícil de disimular.

En su trabajo *Zum Verständnis des messianischen Idee im Judentum* ["Para la comprensión de la idea mesiánica en el judaísmo"], Scholem hace hincapié en lo profano del mesianismo judío en oposición a la honda interioridad del concepto cristiano de redención (Scholem, 1963). En este texto, su autor investiga el modo en el que el mesianismo relaciona la catástrofe con la redención, la restauración y la utopía, el tiempo primigenio y el fin de los tiempos, el horror y la consolación, todo como variaciones expresivas en la historia de las ideas y los movimientos mesiánicos. La pretensión de laicismo, por una parte, y la "ausencia de toda transición entre historia y redención", por otra, no conducen más que a una constelación aporética, dado que esto significaría que no puede existir "progreso hacia la redención y la historia", sino más bien, una "diferencia radical entre el mundo irredento de la historia y el de la redención mesiánica" (Scholem, 1963: 36). Scholem mismo subraya esta situación al subtitular una de las partes de su texto "El precio del mesianismo", donde se dice: "La grandeza de la idea mesiánica corre paralela a la infinita debilidad de la historia del judaísmo que no estaba preparado para entrar a la palestra histórica en el exilio" (1963: 73). El difícil *status* histórico-filosófico del mesianismo en la Modernidad, sintetizado como "la crisis de la pretensión mesiánica" (1963: 74), no aparece de ninguna manera mejorado en la

---

el texto famoso que conocemos como "Sobre el concepto de historia" ha partido de una idea genérica de tesis —en la tradición de las tesis de Marx sobre Feuerbach— para ir transformándose durante las reelaboraciones en algo más afín con la personalidad de Benjamin y asumir la forma de "reflexiones", que es la designación que aparece preferentemente en esta traducción. [N. del T.]

Photos]–. Es decir, pasa a primer plano lo que provoca la cognoscibilidad y visibilidad de las imágenes, pues:

> El indicio histórico de las imágenes dice solamente que pertenecen a una determinada época; dice, sobre todo, que han arribado a la legibilidad en una determinada época. (Anotaciones y materiales para "La obra de los pasajes", Block N3,1; *G.S.*, V.1.577)

Lo que en este proceso es descifrable son no tanto el saber y las intenciones de épocas pasadas, sino "los residuos de un mundo onírico" [*Rückstände einer Traumwelt*], los símbolos del deseo de una época que se encuentra en ruinas "antes de que se hallan desintegrado los monumentos que ellos representan" ("París, la capital del siglo XIX"; *G.S.*, V.1.59).

Ya en la terminología se produce una sobreimpresión de enfoques mesiánicos y psicoanalíticos, y esto se observa no sólo en el ensayo sobre Kafka, donde se ponen claramente en juego dialéctico categorías como distorsión y redención. El concepto del "ahora de la cognoscibilidad" viene a confluir con la relación entre la imagen dialéctica y la redención, según se hace visible en los Pasajes y en las reflexiones "Sobre el concepto de historia". Cuando Benjamin caracteriza el "tiempo del ahora" [*Jetztzeit*], cuya estructura perceptiva se corresponde con el modelo psicoanalítico de la legibilidad de las huellas mnémicas, como "modelo de una época mesiánica" (Reflexión XVIII, "Sobre el concepto de historia"; *G.S.*, I.2.703), ello significa que la perspectiva de una redención siempre participa de la legibilidad, es decir, del indicio histórico de las imágenes de "lo que ha sido". Pero no sucede como meta, sino en la inmediatez de cada instante, así como Scholem definió el tiempo mesiánico como "la inmediatez divina de cada día" [*Gottesunmittelbarkeit eines jeden Tages*] (Scholem, 1963: 26). Por otra parte, en los esbozos para "Sobre el concepto de historia" se encuentra la siguiente afirmación: "La imagen dialéctica debe definirse como el recuerdo involuntario de una humanidad redimida" (*G.S.*, I.3.1233).* Incorporada a las

---

* La presencia de la palabra "tesis" para estos esbozos permitiría suponer que

memoria corporal, sobre todo en el proyecto de los Pasajes y en las tesis "Sobre el concepto de historia". La teoría de *la imagen dialéctica* benjaminiana pone el acento sobre la práctica de la lectura, dado que en primera instancia es el único modo de darle estatuto a "lo que ha sido", presentándolo como imagen. Aquí nos hallamos no ya frente a una memoria *de las* imágenes o de un recuerdo dentro y con las imágenes, sino que la estructura misma del recuerdo aparece trasladada a un espacio de la imagen [*Bildraum*], por lo que obtiene así un carácter figurativo. De este modo, la relación entre "lo que ha sido" y "el ahora" se define como figurativa y dialéctica. Y así la imagen dialéctica no es, en realidad, una variación de la imagen, sino la imagen en sí:

> La imagen es aquella en la que lo que ha sido entra en contacto con el ahora para formar una constelación de modo rápido como un destello.[...] La imagen leída significa la imagen en el "ahora de la cognoscibilidad", cuando es portadora en sumo grado del sello del instante crítico y peligroso que se halla en toda lectura.(Anotaciones y materiales para "La obra de los pasajes", Block N3,1; *G.S.*, V.1.578)

En este modelo de legibilidad se produce una superación de la diferencia cuantitativa entre memoria e historiografía, con la apoyatura de una tradición judía (cf. Yerushalmi, 1982), y, al mismo tiempo, se establece una analogía entre la construcción de la historia y la estructura del recuerdo, que refuerza la incompatibilidad de la oposición entre filosofía de la historia y mesianismo. La imagen de "lo que ha sido" es el efecto de un recuerdo, como se formula en la difundida frase de Benjamin: "Articular históricamente el pasado significa [...] apoderarse de un recuerdo" (Reflexión VI, "Sobre el concepto de historia"; *G.S.*, I.2.695).

Al mismo tiempo, en este modelo se hace patente un último corte radical con la categoría de *intentio*. En ese movimiento gana una importancia central lo que determina las condiciones para el "ahora de la cognoscibilidad" –Benjamin utiliza aquí las metáforas de la "iluminación" [*Illumination*], de la "carga explosiva" [*Ladung*], o de la "revelación de una foto" [*Entwicklung eines*

Warburg de memoria en imágenes como síntomas, comparándolos con los corporales de Freud, o sea como símbolos mnémicos que se manifiestan en una representación distorsionada, entonces la cercanía entre las concepciones de Warburg y Benjamin sería mayor. Pero justamente es en este punto, en la comprensión del carácter simbólico específico de las "fórmulas patéticas", donde se bifurcan los caminos en la recepción de la obra de Warburg. Sea como fuere, siguen existiendo marcadas diferencias entre la explícita mención de Warburg a tradiciones humanísticas (especialmente en su comprensibilidad) y la ruptura benjaminiana con una historia basada en la idea de progreso, pero también entre la búsqueda de Warburg de una configuración donde encuentra su forma la tensión entre un grado medio del símbolo, pronunciado "con recaudos" [*vorbehaltend*], por una parte, y la imagen dialéctica o el método alegórico benjaminianos, por otra, donde la base está dada por una extracción de la imagen de un *continuum*.

La idea de mesianismo en el pensamiento benjaminiano tiene su más clara manifestación justamente en el ensayo sobre Kafka, donde se produce un juicio de valor frente a la *distorsión*, siendo ésta apreciada tanto como *diferencia* hacia la redención como hacia el origen olvidado. Para Benjamin, los personajes kafkianos sufren una pérdida para acceder a la escritura, esa escritura cuyo estudio promete la redención. Así, si en Freud la distorsión es una traducción sin original, lo cual produce la consecuencia de querer parafrasear este original por medio de asociaciones, en el caso de Benjamin este concepto significa la lejanía de un lugar perdido e inalcanzable, al que se dirige en la figura de la "Vuelta" [*Umkehr*], pues "la vuelta es la dirección del estudio que transforma la existencia en escritura" (*G.S.*, II.2.437). La existencia *como* escritura, que se forma gracias a la vuelta, a la postura del que recuerda, se evidencia justamente en las distorsiones (en la esperanza de la salvación).

En el caso de la memoria de imágenes, Benjamin ha procedido dando mayores matices a su trabajo acerca de la teoría de la legibilidad por lo menos más que lo que había hecho para la

espalda de los culpables, superponiendo incisiones y amontonando ornamentos, hasta que la espalda de los culpables se torna vidente y puede descifrar ella misma la escritura, en cuyas letras el culpable puede deducir el nombre de la culpa desconocida. Es entonces la espalda la que carga con la culpa. (*G.S.*, II.2.432)

DISTORSIONES, IMÁGENES DIALÉCTICAS Y REDENCIÓN

En el ensayo sobre Kafka, donde Benjamin analiza los gestos y las reacciones de los personajes de la obra de ese autor como distorsiones, al mismo tiempo que define este concepto como "la forma que toman las cosas en el olvido" (*G.S.*, II.2.431) –partiendo de la idea de que lo olvidado se mezcla con aquello ya olvidado antes en un mundo anterior [*Vorwelt*]–, es justamente el cuerpo el que aparece como el medio de las distorsiones. En este sentido, Benjamin puede sostener igualmente que el cuerpo les es ajeno [*fremd*] a los hombres, pues se ha tornado lo extraño [*die Fremde*] por antonomasia. Siguiendo con esta idea, el término de "distorsión" [*Entstellung*] –tanto como expresión y como lenguaje– se carga también en este texto de una connotación psicoanalítica, desplazando así la lectura cercana a la de crítica ideológica que podía tener la idea afín de "alienación" [*Entfremdung*].[16]

Se podría comparar esta lectura del lenguaje del cuerpo con el proyecto del atlas ilustrado de Warburg, donde se daba una concentración de la memoria figurativa en relación con los gestos expresivos. Hay que decir, sin embargo, que en el caso de Benjamin el material proviene, en cambio, de textos *literarios* y que, por lo tanto, su método de lectura ha aprovechado las enseñanzas de Freud. Benjamin reflexiona justamente sobre los gestos de los personajes kafkianos, pero no solamente desde el punto de vista del olvido (es decir, de la memoria), sino también como fases de una representación distorsionada. Por supuesto que si se quisiera "leer" las túnicas en movimiento del método de

---

16. Para un panorama de la terminología psicoanalítica alrededor de 1930, véanse los capítulos 8 y 9 del presente estudio.

manera excluyente pero no esquemática. En el contexto de la concepción psicoanalítica aquí expuesta no se trataría tanto de la distinción entre la participación consciente e inconsciente, como más bien de un esfuerzo hacia la legibilidad de la memoria figurativa y del cuerpo, para dotarla con aquello con que se han enriquecido las concepciones que se sirven de una analogía entre el lenguaje y la estructura del inconsciente.

Estas reflexiones no son sólo importantes en el caso de la memoria individual. Como campo de lucha y territorio de simbolizaciones, el cuerpo juega un papel central también en la memoria colectiva. Especialmente bajo el aspecto de la situación de víctima [*Opferstruktur*] en la historia de la civilización, Nietzsche calificó el dolor como "el más poderoso instrumento de lo mnemónico" [*mächtigstes Hilfsmittel der Mnemonik*], al mismo tiempo, que afirmaba en 1887 que "nunca nada se daría sin sangre, martirio y sacrificios cuando al hombre le pareciera necesario crearse una memoria" (Nietzsche, 1969, II:3.248). Su idea de dejar la marca de la quemadura inserta [*Einbrennen*] o de producir una incisión [*Einprägen*] expresa cabalmente el proceso que hoy en día se caracteriza como "inscripción" [*Einschreibung*] y es precisamente en este contexto en el que Deleuze y Guattari se refieren a la crueldad diciendo: "La crueldad no tiene nada que ver con una violencia cualquiera o natural que se encargaría de explicar la historia del hombre; ella es el movimiento de la cultura que se opera en los cuerpos y se inscribe sobre ellos, trabajándolos" (Deleuze y Guattari, 1972/1973: 170).

El ejemplo más llamativo de esto aparece en la imagen de ese engranaje, según lo imagina Kafka en *La colonia penitenciaria*, que escribe en las espaldas de los prisioneros las leyes de los dominadores de la colonia. La tarea de esa maquinaria está organizada de tal modo que el sentenciado llegará a descifrar la escritura formada por las propias heridas cuando lo alcance la agonía, es decir, la decodificación total coincide con su propia muerte:

> En *La colonia penitenciaria*, sin embargo, los que mandan se sirven de una antiquísima maquinaria que graba letras alambicadas en la

Darstellung), una traducción sin el original, como Freud la definió paradigmáticamente en el caso del lenguaje onírico. Este lenguaje coloca, tanto al que lo revela como al que se pone a considerarlo, frente a la tarea de un desciframiento, es decir, ante el caso de su legibilidad, de modo que aparece como un lenguaje donde la autoría se torna problemática. En *La interpretación de los sueños* la significación del cuerpo como fuente del sueño u otros procesos anímicos sufre un retroceso, para tornarse, en cambio, importante como escenario en el que se manifiestan estos mismos procesos:[15] el cuerpo es así el lugar de enfrentamiento y el campo de las simbolizaciones.

En esta concepción no se trata ni de que el cuerpo *tenga* una memoria –así como tampoco nosotros *tenemos* un cuerpo– ni que el cuerpo represente a la memoria. Más bien se trata de que la memoria aparece inscripta en el cuerpo en forma de huellas duraderas [*Dauerspuren*], que en virtud de determinadas percepciones estructuran la repetición de afectos y las imágenes mentales asociadas con esos rastros. En este contexto, es necesario agregar que esta repetición nunca comporta la reiteración de lo mismo, sino que siempre se produce otro retorno que, en definitiva, es el retorno de lo Otro. Esto se refiere, sin embargo, sólo a las huellas duraderas que se fijan en el inconsciente que, a su vez, deben diferenciarse de ideas conscientes, siguiendo un *dictum* del mismo Freud en carta a Fliess (del 6 de diciembre de 1896), quien indicaba que conciencia y memoria se excluían (Freud, 1986: 217). Esta relación aparecerá concretizada en el sistema freudiano, más adelante, y finalmente será reformulada como una incompatibilidad en los modos de funcionar de los dos sistemas: la conciencia surgirá en lugar de la huella del recuerdo (Freud, 1969: III.235).

De este modo, la memoria figurativa y del cuerpo [*Bild- und Körpergedächtnis*] aparecen aquí estrechamente ligadas. Ambas participan de la relación dialéctica entre la conciencia y el inconsciente, donde los territorios aparecen distribuidos de

---

15. Este proceso aparece en la mira de Jean Starobinski (1983).

LA MEMORIA CORPORAL Y FIGURATIVA EN EL PSICOANÁLISIS

Por otro lado también hay que acotar aquí que en algunos ámbitos del actual discurso sobre el cuerpo, el mito de un verdadero lenguaje corporal es un tema que suscita una virulenta disputa, incluso cuando ya no se trate de características fisonómicas, sino mayormente de síntomas patológicos. En la historia de las reflexiones acerca del cuerpo como medio de expresión se dio, por lo menos desde el psicoanálisis freudiano, una ruptura frente a la idea de una clara interpretabilidad y una homologización de lo corporal y lo anímico.[13] Y esto sucede sobre todo por el hecho de que en la obra de Freud la relación entre cuerpo y lenguaje, soma y sema (*soma-sema*), aparecen en el marco de una conceptualización dentro de una compleja estructura de la memoria. Tanto como la concepción de una representación del interior en el exterior, Freud refuta también la localización de "nociones del intelecto" [*Sinnesvorstellungen*] en lo físico, y, en su lugar, parte de que lo psíquico es un proceso paralelo a lo físico, en cuya base no se encuentra ninguna relación de similitud.[14] En este contexto, Freud considera que la modificación fisiológica producida por un estímulo es la posibilidad para un recuerdo, es decir, del resurgimiento de la idea asociada con el estímulo. De ese modo, el síntoma histérico, por ejemplo, era para Freud un símbolo del recuerdo.

Los síntomas, como articulaciones corporales por excelencia, son así parte de un lenguaje del inconsciente y, por ello, siguen la estructura de *una representación distorsionada* [*einer entstellten*

---

13. Naturalmente que Freud no fue el primero en rebatir las viejas concepciones; véanse al respecto las críticas contra Lavater en su misma época en la pluma de Lichtenberg y Lessing. Otras concepciones fueron, por ejemplo, la de Bergson –acerca de las imágenes de experiencias pasadas que estarían almacenadas de modo sensomotriz, y que se podrían interpretar como recuerdo "háptico" o del tacto [*haptische Erinnerung*]– o la de Nietzsche.

14. Véase al respecto la monografía de Freud sobre la afasia que data de 1891 (Freud, 1969: III.165-167).

Aun cuando los gestos se lean como la encarnación de pasiones y sufrimiento, sin embargo, esta lectura de la memoria corporal no se rige por el fantasma de las interpretaciones fisonómicas que pretendían poder deducir del exterior del cuerpo lo que sucedía adentro. Un cometido semejante, como era trascender las perturbaciones sobre los aspectos no visibles o no aprehendibles del sujeto con la ayuda de interpretaciones de rasgos de la configuración corporal –ya sean denominados "el alma", "el interior" o "el espíritu"–, tiene, en efecto, una larga tradición. En uno de los clásicos de la Fisonomía, Johann Kaspar Lavater (1741-1801), es muy evidente que su concepción tiene como base una consideración de la memoria corporal, donde ella aparece como "engrama", como si se tratara de una copia del interior reflejada especularmente. Así en el cuerpo, especialmente en los rasgos del rostro de un individuo, se habrían grabado sus cualidades caracterológicas y, por lo tanto, serían legibles como signos unívocos. El procedimiento de Lavater ha obtenido un lugar dentro de la historia de los métodos de identificación criminal, en tanto se remitía a una imagen del cuerpo en estado de quietud, así como a la medición y la catalogación de la estructura corporal y del rostro.

La relación entre lenguaje y cuerpo es en este punto especialmente problemática, porque la imagen corporal es entendida, en cierto sentido, como lenguaje, y en ese carácter ocupa un lugar exclusivo, dado que aparece situado más allá de los lenguajes simbólicos como si fuera comprendido en tanto representación idéntica de lo inmaterial. Ese operativo de la Fisonomía pone en escena el mito del (otro) lenguaje que sugeriría una vía de escape de la inseguridad sobre la comprensibilidad y verdad del lenguaje escrito y hablado, a partir del hecho de que la relación entre palabra y significado se ha tornado cuestionable.

simbólico tradicional, que hoy se subsumiría bajo la idea de "intertextualidad", se presenta en este método como un volver a acordarse de formas preconfiguradas y de las vivencias que ellas conllevan.

Especialmente con su atlas ilustrado que apareció bajo el título de *Mnemosyne*, donde se habían seleccionado láminas con expresiones afines o similares que reproducían imágenes de diferentes épocas y géneros de las artes plásticas, Aby Warburg logró que su empresa llevara la impronta de una colección de la memoria en imágenes como memoria de los gestos y del lenguaje del cuerpo.[10] La gesticulación –más exactamente: los gestos representados en las imágenes– es catapultada así al rango de una forma simbólica, cuya importancia no se mide por la posibilidad de traducción a una lengua, sino sólo por el recuerdo de la forma y experiencia así actualizadas. El nacimiento de una marca figurativa en forma de los gestos expresivos del cuerpo, la así llamada "fórmula patética" [*Pathosformel*], se pone en relación con un estímulo a la vez que se la compara con la huella que algo deja en su recorrido, y, en este sentido, es completamente análoga a la descripción psicoanalítica de una huella mnémica (cf. Wind, 1980: 174). La empresa de insertar las fórmulas patéticas en un atlas ilustrado según grupos y determinadas configuraciones de gestos expresivos del cuerpo da como resultado no precisamente una clasificación enciclopédica del conocimiento que siga el modelo de tablas taxonómicas,[11] sino la (re-)construcción de huellas mnémicas en la que cada repetición contiene también una variación.[12]

---

10. Cf. especialmente Saxl, 1980: 419-432.
11. Para la importancia de las tablas taxonómicas en el orden del conocimiento en la Edad de la Representación, véase Foucault, 1966.
12. Sólo recién a partir de la recepción de la corriente fundada por Warburg o desde el establecimiento de una Escuela Warburg se ha originado la tendencia a la codificación de las fórmulas patéticas y a la fijación de una enciclopedia de ellas que, por otro lado, son leídas más bien como símbolos que como huellas mnémicas.

figurativos como gestos corporales y modos de conducta, que resultan por dicha lectura un "conjunto de textos" [*Ensemble von Texten*]. La legibilidad surgiría, entonces, gracias a una postura que Geertz denomina "*thick description*", es decir, un modo de percibir que se apoya en las experiencias nacidas en el trato con lenguajes simbólicos. La capacidad para una lectura entrenada y sistemática se traslada de ese modo a los así llamados textos culturales, que pueden referirse a culturas exóticas o alejadas ya sea temporal o geográficamente, pero también a la memoria cultural de la propia cultura así como a ámbitos extraeuropeos.

EL ATLAS ILUSTRADO DE LOS GESTOS EXPRESIVOS: ABY WARBURG

Como ejemplo de los esfuerzos ya realizados en torno a la idea de legibilidad se podría mencionar también el proyecto llevado a cabo por Aby Warburg, fundador de la Kulturwissenschaftliche Bibliothek [Biblioteca Científico-Cultural] y un instituto, cuya tarea consistía en descifrar *la memoria figurativa* [*Bildgedächtnis*] de la historia del arte europeo.[8] Partiendo de la tentativa de comprender la recepción del lenguaje antiguo en imágenes en el arte del Renacimiento y de interpretarlo, es decir, partiendo del esfuerzo, entonces, de "hacer *hablar* a una imagen que ya no se entiende *de modo directo*"[9] (Wind, 1980: 168) (El destacado es mío.) Durante su actividad, Warburg formulaba preguntas a las imágenes (pictóricas) con respecto a lo que en ellas se presentaba como un trabajo de recuerdo. El procedimiento de la cita, de la apropiación y de la reformulación de un lenguaje figurativo y

---

8. Aby Warburg fundó dicha Biblioteca en Hamburgo en 1909, pero a comienzos de los años veinte se transformó en un instituto público. En 1933 debió ser rescatado de esa sede, por la llegada del nazismo al poder, y llevado a Londres, donde todavía existe bajo el nombre de Warburg Institute; cf. Warburg (1980); Hofmann, Syamken y Warnke (1980).

9. En alemán: "*Ein Bild, das man nicht mehr unmittelbar versteht, zum Sprechen zu bringen*". [N. del T.]

preocupación se vincula más bien con la existencia de las palabras o cuadros concretos que tan pronto como se han alejado del creador es como si se escaparan a su posibilidad en el control de las significaciones: "Lo que una vez está escrito, rueda de mano en mano, pasando de los que entienden la materia a aquellos para quienes no ha sido escrita la obra." (Platón, 1949: 184).

LEGIBILIDAD

Lo que está aquí en juego es la comprensibilidad y *legibilidad* de textos particulares, en el sentido del peligro de una lectura *no autorizada* –un peligro que Sócrates situaba desde la perspectiva del orador–, es decir, de una lectura más allá de la *intentio* del autor (y probablemente muy alejada de ella). Pero cuando uno se aproxima desde otro ángulo a esta conclusión, la escritura aparece como la condición de posibilidad de lecturas diferentes y cambiantes, de la posibilidad de decodificación y legibilidad también de los textos apócrifos o deteriorados, fragmentarios o transmitidos fuera de su contexto.

En este sentido, es decir, en asociación con una lectura que aparezca reglamentada por tales signos y verificada en ellos, el texto y la escritura se han tornado hoy en día, en la antropología y en la semiótica de la cultura, los paradigmas para el modo de leer civilizaciones alejadas y extrañas. La legibilidad de esas culturas es, por ejemplo, para Clifford Geertz como

> [...] si se tratara de leer un manuscrito (en el sentido de "construir una lectura") que es extraño y está desvaído, lleno de elipsis, incoherencias, correcciones sospechosas y comentarios tendenciosos, pero no escrito en signos fonéticos convencionales, sino con ejemplos efímeros de conductas aceptadas. (Geertz, 1973: 10)

Una lectura tal no tiene nada que ver con una interpretación arbitraria individual, sino que exige un procedimiento metodológicamente fundamentado, puesto que se esfuerza en descifrar construcciones de sentido culturales, tanto de signos lingüísticos y

Así Frances Yates, en su análisis subtitulado en alemán *Mnemonik von Aristoteles bis Shakespeare* ["Lo mnemónico desde Aristóteles a Shakespeare"] investiga la historia tardía de la técnica mnemónica en el arte de la Edad Media y del Renacimiento (Yates, 1966), donde aparecía como clave para categorizar los cuadros alegóricos, y así esta investigadora ha venido a subrayar con su trabajo una vez más el significado de ese proceso. Con la vinculación entre *imagines agentes* –que a menudo son definidas como imágenes corpóreas [*körperhafte Bilder*] o comparaciones– y la capacidad figurativa [*Bildlichkeit*] del discurso, las primeras aparecen descubiertas, o redescubiertas, en el origen de la retórica (dentro de la que encontramos la metáfora), puesto que la *memoria* ya había sido proclamada tradicionalmente el instrumento para el análisis en ese ámbito. En las investigaciones sobre la memoria provenientes de Yates, juegan un gran papel ahora los análisis de las formas y las imágenes del discurso figurativo en ejemplos de la literatura europea, así como la búsqueda de procedimientos mnemotécnicos en diferentes artes hasta llegar a la Modernidad.[7]

La memoria del cuerpo, en cambio, tiene una presencia llamativamente marginal en ese debate. El significado central que poseen las imágenes, por el contrario, se explica en este contexto por el hecho de que rara vez se encuentran los argumentos platónicos que se hallan también en el diálogo antes citado, cuando Sócrates, para reforzar sus reservas contra la escritura, la compara con la pintura: "Éste es, mi querido Fedro, el inconveniente así de la escritura como de la pintura; las producciones de este último arte parecen vivas, pero interrogadlas, y veréis que guardan un grave silencio" (Platón, 1949: 183). No está claro aquí qué es lo que produce la inquietud de Sócrates, pero parecería que tuviera que ver con la comprensibilidad y necesidad de aclaración inherentes tanto a la escritura como a la pintura. Al proseguir con su argumentación, sin embargo, se explica que su

---

7. Cf., por ejemplo, el caso de Klaus Reichert para el *Ulysses* de Joyce, en Haverkamp y Lachmann, 1991: 328-355.

IMÁGENES DEL ARTE DE LA MEMORIA

En este arte de la memoria las imágenes juegan ahora un papel descollante, tanto las imágenes mentales [*Vorstellungsbilder*] como la capacidad figurativa [*Bildlichkeit*] del discurso, de la retórica, de la emblemática, de la *alegoresis*, pero también las imágenes materializadas, es decir: pinturas y esculturas. Partiendo de la determinación aristotélica que establece que no hay pensamiento sin imágenes de la imaginación (Aristóteles, 1978: 431a16; 431b3 y 432a9) y que el recuerdo significa mirar algo como a una imagen, en la mnemotécnica se trata de las reglas para la reproducción *voluntaria* de tales imágenes como arte del recuerdo (cf. Aristóteles, 1978: 427b20). La creación de imágenes mnemotécnicas (las así llamadas *imagines agentes*, que pueden depositarse en lugares de un edificio imaginado) sigue, con el objeto de garantizar sus aspectos activos por una parte, el principio de la llamatividad, de lo particularizante, de lo inhabitual, de lo digno de verse; pero, por otra parte, sigue también el principio de la onomatopeya, de la asociación fonética o semántica. En todos los casos, en suma, esta técnica adhiere a los principios de una codificación arbitraria, con el fin de cumplir con la función substitutiva de las imágenes en la cosa o la palabra que se recuerda.

La contracara de la función retentiva [*Merkfunktion*] de las imágenes de la memoria, partiendo de que han sido efectivamente registradas, es, sin embargo, su indescifrabilidad para quien no conozca las claves. También la escritura de esta *ars memoriae* o la de los esquemas gráficos tradicionales de las imágenes mnémicas permanecen así –tanto como su discurso– asociadas con el autor. En este sentido, la *memoria* aparece como participando de la historia de los discursos en torno al poder y al saber, dado que al ser comprendida como la primera virtud en la vía hacia el conocimiento (como *prudentia*) entra en vinculación con una autorización e institucionalización de la actividad mnémica. En tanto arte de puestas en clave, la *ars memoriae* tiende, no por azar, a volverse una parte integrante del saber hermético.

En rigor, la mayoría de los numerosos trabajos y monografías que han aparecido en los últimos años sobre la memoria se concentran en las técnicas de la así llamada "memoria artificial", por ejemplo la mnemotécnica como *ars memoriae* [o *ars-memoria*]: técnicas del arte de la memoria y de las artes como memoria. En los esfuerzos por encontrar formas de materializar e institucionalizar la cultura o por fundar una memoria cultural en forma de ritos, modos de vida, imágenes, textos, instrumentos, monumentos, ciudades, paisajes, etcétera,[5] se trata siempre de una preocupación particular del plano académico y, en parte también, de tradiciones herméticas de ese arte de la memoria o arte-memoria que tiene que ver fundamentalmente con lo *literario*.[6]

Con los cambios de paradigma de "discurso como recuerdo" [*Erinnerungsdiskurs*] a "discurso como memoria" (*Gedächtnisdiskurs*), según se muestra en las investigaciones más recientes, el interés se desplaza desde una memoria individual a una cultural, a una memoria como cultura y a la cultura de la memoria. Con este proceso parece repetirse también la constelación paradójica de una transición (en lugar de desde "el discurso" a "la escritura" se marcha desde "la cultura" a "la técnica"). Considerando la función de almacenamiento insuperable de los *computers*, se hace de nuevo presente la habilidad y la erudición de la tradición mnémica asociada a la escritura. Sin embargo, con la mnemotécnica se acentúa nuevamente la función de la retención [*Merkens*] y de almacenamiento [*Speicherns*], aunque ahora con la mirada no puesta en la cantidad, sino en la habilidad: una especie de desfasaje dentro de la constelación de la rivalidad.

---

5. Cf. por ejemplo: De Certeau (1980), Assmann y Hölscher (1988), y Assmann y Harth (1991b)

6. Especialmente en Yates (1966), Lachmann (1990), Assmann y Harth (1991a), y Haverkamp y Lachmann (1991).

inmaterialidad, la inteligibilidad e invisibilidad de la memoria humana –desde la de "sello sobre la cera" (Aristóteles) o "tablilla encerada del alma"(Platón), pasando por "templo", "biblioteca", "casa del tesoro", "libro", "palimpsesto", "depósito", "archivo", "edificio", "espacio", "teatro", "laberinto", "topografía", hasta llegar a "huella", "pizarra mágica" y "escritura"– la última se ha tornado dominante, desde que con el psicoanálisis el interés por la memoria se concentró en el inconsciente y el lenguaje onírico. Con la llegada victoriosa de la elaboración electrónica de datos –los nuevos "medios"– la cosa cambia. Juntamente con la creciente significación de la escritura como el medio más importante se pone ahora en entredicho su función de metáfora de la memoria, dado que se le sobreimpone súbitamente la idea de almacenamiento [*Speicher*].

Con este proceso, sin embargo, parece que nos encontráramos de nuevo en el punto de partida, dado que había sido la función de la conservación, la que Sócrates había acordado esencialmente a la escritura, no la de la introspección o recuerdo.* Y aquí surge la pregunta de si no podrían las palabras socráticas con los conceptos intercambiados ("escritura" en vez de "discurso"; "*computer*" en lugar de "escritura") volver a expresar el miedo frente a una nueva invención: que esta nueva creación insufle en los que aprenden más bien olvido e indiferencia hacia el medio anterior (ahora la escritura), porque, confiando en sus *computers*, ejercerán sus recuerdos desde el exterior por medio de signos extraños, en lugar de acordarse por sí mismos.[4] Y, por ello, la popularidad de la que goza la memoria en las ciencias actuales también podría valer como recuerdo y autoaseguramiento de una capacidad y habilidad que no se agota en la idea de almacenamiento.

* En alemán la palabra *Er- inner-rung*, lleva consigo etimológicamente la idea de "interiorización". [N. del T.]

4. Realmente el paradigma antiguo no ha perdido, por lo visto, nada de su atractivo a pesar de la nueva constelación de transición que vivimos; cf. la oposición escritura como huella *vs.* "el corazón vivo de la memoria", en Nora (1986).

gaciones recientes que se ocupan de *memoria y escritura*.[1] La disputa parece concentrarse en la cuestión de si en la situación actual, en la que la creciente importancia de los medios electrónicos proclama la muerte de la cultura escrita, como el fin de una cultura en la que la escritura resultó como el medio dominante y confiable para el traspaso de la tradición, una mirada retrospectiva al mito de su origen debería servirnos nuevamente para recordar su historia. La reserva mencionada aparece en la investigación reciente especialmente enarbolada para caracterizar la oposición que Sócrates mostraba entre los caracteres extraños de la escritura y "el discurso vivo y animado, que reside en el alma del que está en posesión de la ciencia" (Platón, 1949: 184), como rudimento de una conciencia en una cultura preescrituraria.[2] La constelación de una mirada retrospectiva hacia un momento de transición (del discurso oral a la escritura) que aparece en Platón, no sin un atisbo de paradoja, lleva la marca de la forma en que nos han llegado esos textos: Platón *narra* en su obra un *diálogo*, en el que Sócrates, por su parte, *informa* acerca de una *conversación* mantenida entre el rey Thamus y el dios Theut en Egipto, que había *oído contar* y que trataba sobre la *escritura*.

Partiendo de ese mito, la investigación más reciente se ocupa especialmente de la historia de la compleja conexión entre escritura y memoria, en la que ambos términos se han tornado, en gran medida, intercambiables. La escritura se considera ahora la memoria de la cultura, mientras que la memoria se define como escritura o también como "escenario de la escritura".[3] En la serie de metáforas a través de las que se intenta reiteradamente asir la

---

1. Entre los primeros que abrieron la serie al respecto, habría que citar a Assmann y Hardmeier (1983), pero también Yates (1990), Lachmann (1990) y Harth (1991a).

2. De modo más acentuado esta corriente aparece en Derrida, quien define su teoría de la *écriture* –la *grammatologie*– en oposición al mito de una verdad del alma que se manifestaría en el *logos*, pero, sin embargo, rechaza justamente la idea de un sistema sígnico que se hubiera hallado antes de la escritura; cf. Derrida, 1967a: 23 y sigs.

3. Cf. "Freud et la scène de l'écriture" (Derrida, 1967b: 293-340).

10. Legibilidad
El lugar de Benjamin en los enfoques contemporáneos sobre la memoria corpórea y pictórica

Puesto que la categoría de "memoria" en la configuración teórica actual de los estudios culturales parece llamada a atraer la atención –por lo menos en el ámbito de habla alemana–, ha de tratarse en las páginas que siguen la ubicación de este concepto en la reelaboración benjaminiana y la importancia de la memoria en el campo de diferentes enfoques del discurso respectivo así como su prehistoria.

LA MEMORIA Y LA ESCRITURA

Ella <la escritura: *grámmata*> no producirá sino el olvido en las almas de los que la conozcan, haciéndoles despreciar la memoria <*mneme*>; fiados en este auxilio extraño abandonarán a caracteres materiales el cuidado de conservar sus recuerdos, cuyo rastro habrá perdido su espíritu. Tú no has encontrado un medio de cultivar la memoria, sino de despertar reminiscencias <*hypómnesis*>; y das a tus discípulos la sombra de la ciencia y no la ciencia misma. (Platón, *Fedro o de la belleza*, 1949: 182-183)*

Esta reserva de Sócrates frente a la escritura, transmitida por Platón, puede seguir encontrándose masivamente en las investi-

---

* Se ha elegido en este caso la traducción al castellano realizada por Patricio de Azcárate. [N. del T.]

La lectura que ocupa el lugar de la traducción 237

Puesto que vimos que lo que aquí es llamado político e histórico se debe puramente a razones lingüísticas, podemos reemplazar en este pasaje "político" por "poético", en el sentido de una poética. Dado que ahora comprendemos que lo no mesiánico, no sagrado, esto es el aspecto político de la historia, es el resultado de una estructura poética de la lengua, entonces lo político y poético ocuparán uno el lugar del otro, estando lo poético en oposición a la noción de lo sagrado. Hasta tal punto que dicha poética, dicha historia es no mesiánica, no es una teocracia; sino una retórica, no hay allí espacio para ciertas nociones históricas tales como la noción de la Modernidad, que siempre es dialéctica, esto es decir que es una noción esencialmente teológica. (De Man, 1986: 93)

Si junto con lo mesiánico lo que se consigue aquí es desembarazarse de lo dialéctico en la teoría benjaminiana, puede verse como una ironía de la historia de la recepción de los textos de Benjamin el hecho de que la interpretación de Paul de Man venga a confluir con aquella que al comienzo del presente estudio se puso en evidencia en el caso de Habermas, sobre todo cuando se piensa que Habermas y Paul de Man se encuentran en posiciones diametralmente opuestas en las filiaciones académicas. En efecto, las dos posiciones coinciden en el rechazo de lo mesiánico en el texto benjaminiano, a la vez que en la equiparación de lo político con lo poético, pero, en tanto en la una se le da una valoración negativa en el contexto de una filosofía social de la teoría de la comunicación, en el caso de Paul de Man se asocia ese proceso positivamente haciéndolo encajar en el proyecto de una retórica deconstructiva. Sea como fuere, lo cierto es que en cada caso el pensamiento en imágenes de Benjamin –que Habermas trataba como "metáforas", y Paul de Man simplemente como "tropos"– pierde su significado genuino para la formación de una teoría original.

Geist der Utopie ["El espíritu de la utopía"] de Bloch"; Paul de Man traduce al inglés del siguiente modo: "To have denied the political significance of theocracy, *to have denied the political significance of the religious, messianic view, to have denied this* with all *desirable* intensity is the great merit of Bloch's book 'The Spirit of Utopia'." (En cursiva se registran los agregados).[10]

En su interpolación, De Man llega a igualar la teocracia (el Reino de Dios) con la mirada mesiánica [*der messianische Blick*], mientras que, en rigor, Benjamin está criticando la confusión y la fusión entre política y religión, justamente con la idea de reelaborar una relación entre lo histórico y lo mesiánico. Y se trata precisamente del significado político de la mirada mesiánica lo que ha de ser, de una enorme importancia en su trabajo, en un ámbito que se ubica en y frente a la historia, como se hace evidente en sus tesis sobre teoría de la historia ("Sobre el concepto de historia"), en las que se continúa tratando la relación entre lo mesiánico y lo histórico.

Dado que en el caso del texto de Paul de Man se trata de la transcripción de una conferencia, podría ser que con la ayuda de otra entonación su autor hubiera hecho claras las acotaciones declarándolas como suyas en el pasaje de Benjamin que estaba citando, y que los responsables de la edición, por su parte, no hubieran verificado los dos planos del proceso entre lo propio y lo ajeno. Pero, puesto que lo que importa resaltar ahora no es la historia de una falsificación, sino que más bien se trata de destacar en la polémica en torno a Benjamin el desconocimiento de su trabajo en la relación de lo mesiánico y lo histórico, entonces estos agregados interpretativos adquieren la categoría de síntomas de una lectura que rechaza en la teoría benjaminiana el nivel de lo mesiánico. En mi opinión, Paul de Man debe anular ese plano para así poder asimilar los escritos de Benjamin a una propia teoría de la retórica, como indica el siguiente pasaje:

---

10. De Man toma la cita de la edición alemana titulada *Illuminationen*, Francfort, 1980: 262.

En esta traducción de Paul de Man se producen varias transformaciones: 1) *"vollenden"* se considera como si fuera *"beenden"* (*to put an end*): "terminar"; 2) *"erlösen"* como *"befreien"* (*to free*): "liberar"; 3) *"Messias"* como *"es"* (*it*): "eso"; y 4) *"schaffen"*- "crear", queda sin traducir.

Semejante interpretación llevaría a la siguiente versión:

> Sólo el mesías mismo pone fin a la historia, en el sentido de que libera y cumple completamente la relación de la historia con lo mesiánico.

Del mismo modo cuando Benjamin, al continuar con su argumentación, afirma que el Reino de Dios no es *telos,* ni meta, sino "la terminación de lo histórico" [*das Ende des Historischen*], o cuando niega que pueda dársele a la teocracia un sentido político, entonces ello sucede porque en lugar de debatir la relación compleja entre los dos elementos, Benjamin representa en una imagen el nexo entre lo profano y lo mesiánico, como una "pieza pedagógica de la historia de la filosofía" [*Lehrstück der Geschichtsphilosophie*] que alcanza su figuración en la constelación de un ensamblaje de fuerzas que marchan en sentido contrario [*gegenstrebige Fügung*].[9] La relación entre el dinamismo de lo profano y la intensidad mesiánica obtiene aquí su representación como movimiento sobre una trayectoria de dos fuerzas, que a pesar de poseer direcciones opuestas imprimen una a la otra un impulso en su respectiva dirección. Se trata de una figura que en el ensayo sobre Kafka se reitera bajo la forma de un galope contra la tormenta.

Ahora bien, para imponer su interpretación de una historia depurada de lo mesiánico, Paul de Man continúa con su aviesa traducción en la forma de un agregado. Así mientras que en el texto de Benjamin se dice: "Haber negado el significado político de la teocracia con la mayor intensidad es el mayor mérito de *Der*

---

9. Para el tratamiento específico de este aspecto, véase el capítulo 4 del presente estudio.

autor, es de notar que en esta interpretación se pierde lo dialéctico inherente a la teoría del lenguaje benjaminiana, puesto que en Benjamin la relación entre "lo puro" y "lo poético" ofrece mayores matices. Y, por lo demás, en Benjamin no se trata de separación, sino de distancia [*Abstand*] y lejanía [*Entfernung*]. Paul de Man, por su parte, continúa su argumentación del siguiente modo:

> Dentro de este conocimiento negativo de su relación con el lenguaje de lo sagrado es donde se inicia la lengua poética. Esto es, si se quiere, una fase necesariamente nihilista que es necesaria en cualquier comprensión de la historia.
> Benjamin expresó esto en forma terminante, no en este ensayo, sino en otro texto denominado "Fragmento teológico-político", del que voy a citar a modo de conclusión un breve pasaje. (De Man, 1986: 92)

En el "Fragmento teológico-político", sin embargo, no se trata –como opina De Man– de una separación entre lo histórico y lo mesiánico, sino de su relación dialéctica, es decir: de la convergencia de todo lo histórico *en* lo mesiánico. La realización [*Vollendung*] del acaecer histórico a través del Mesías aparece introducida como una figuración, que debería definirse, al mismo tiempo, como rescate [*Erlösung*], cumplimiento [*Vollendung*] y creación [*Schaffung*] de la relación entre ambos polos. Así se expresa Benjamin al respecto:

> Sólo el Mesías mismo realiza todo el acaecer histórico, y esto sucede en el sentido de que sólo él mismo rescata, lleva a su cumplimiento y crea su relación con lo mesiánico.

> [*Erst der Messias selbst vollendet alles historische Geschehen, und zwar in dem Sinne, dass er dessen Beziehung auf das Messianische selbst erst erlöst, vollendet, schafft.*] (*G.S.*, I.1.203)

Veamos ahora cómo traduce Paul de Man este pasaje:

> Only the messiah himself puts an end to history, in the sense that it frees, completely fulfills the relationship of history to the messianic. (De Man, 1986: 93)

perturbación que representa lo mesiánico en los textos de Benjamin para Paul de Man tiene quizás que ver con la asociación errónea del término, propia del lenguaje corriente, que implica lo mítico –en el sentido de un mito del genio y de la creación que ve al poeta como una figura sacralizada– según puede verse en el ejemplo que el mismo Paul de Man trae a colación: el caso del poeta alemán Stefan George (De Man, 1986: 77). Así se llega a la operación de querer eliminar lo mesiánico, para ejecutar en la lectura de Benjamin la propia norma de una separación estricta entre el lenguaje poético y sagrado. La molestia ante lo mesiánico que se percibe al comienzo del texto de Paul de Man converge al final en la tentativa de eliminar completamente este aspecto de la teoría benjaminiana de la traducción, tomando como trampolín al propio Benjamin. Para este fin, De Man se desliza hacia otro texto benjaminiano (el "Fragmento teológico-político"; *G.S.*, II.1.203-204), citándolo en una traducción inexacta, completada con su interpretación. Esto es particularmente llamativo, dado que, por lo demás, el aporte de Paul de Man es conocido por la precisión de sus observaciones lingüísticas y su crítica a traducciones erradas del mismo ensayo benjaminiano.

El "Fragmento teológico-político" –surgido probablemente hacia 1920-1921, que se ubica realmente en el mismo período del ensayo sobre la traducción–, le sirve a Paul de Man de apoyatura para realizar una rigurosa separación entre "la lengua poética" y "la lengua pura" [*reine Sprache*]:

> La historia como la concibe Benjamin no es ciertamente mesiánica, dado que consiste en la rigurosa separación y actuación de la separación de lo sagrado y lo poético, la separación de la *reine Sprache* (*lengua pura*) y la lengua poética. La *reine Sprache*, el lenguaje sagrado, *no* tiene *nada en común* con la lengua poética; la lengua poética *no* se le parece; la lengua poética *no* depende de ella; la lengua poética *no* tiene *nada* que ver con ella. (De Man, 1986: 92) (El subrayado es mío.)

Dejando de lado la retórica empleada en las negaciones, llamativamente forzada, que muestra a las claras el interés de su

la disolución del sentido, sino en el reestablecimiento de las distorsiones, para las que en Kafka y en Benjamin "el jorobado" [*der Bucklige*] provee la configuración de un prototipo:

> Este hombrecillo es el habitante de la vida distorsionada; ha de desaparecer cuando llegue el Mesías, del que un gran rabino ha dicho, que Él no había de desear cambiar el mundo por medio de la violencia, sino enderezarlo solamente un poquito. [...] Nadie dice, claro, que las distorsiones que el Mesías ha de venir a enderezar, sean sólo las de nuestro espacio. Ellas son también las del tiempo. (*G.S.*, II.2.432-433)

Si este enderezar se refiere aquí tanto a las distorsiones del cuerpo, del espacio y del tiempo, entonces ello abarca todas las dimensiones de una lectura y de una escritura mnémica, en la que se encuentra también absorbido lo mesiánico –después del retorno de lo mimético olvidado–. En el concepto de distorsión en el ensayo sobre Kafka convergen una teoría lingüística reformulada al modo psicoanalítico como el aspecto mesiánico de la teoría histórica de Benjamin, pues la distorsión marca tanto la distancia del original desaparecido en el trabajo onírico como también la distancia hacia la revelación *y* la salvación. En la génesis de su configuración teórica le cabe al concepto de salvación en la teoría de la traducción la tarea de introducir lo mesiánico –absorbido en la teoría de la lectura y sustituido por ella– dentro de la escritura de los textos tardíos. La lectura que viene a ocupar el lugar de la traducción lleva su impronta.

EL RECHAZO DE PAUL DE MAN DE LO MESIÁNICO

Ha llegado el momento de analizar lo mesiánico en Benjamin, tomando como ejemplo el intento de Paul de Man en una de sus últimas conferencias, en gran medida dudoso, de depurar al ensayo benjaminiano sobre la traducción de todo rastro de mesianismo.[8] La

---

8. Esta conferencia de 1983 apareció, luego publicada bajo el título de "Walter Benjamin's 'The Task of the Translator'" (De Man, 1986: 73-105).

concepción allí dominante acerca de la no comunicabilidad. En ese ensayo se hace de esta idea un *Leitmotiv* para la teoría de la traducción, donde la distancia hacia la revelación se conjuga con la figura de la salvación [*Erlösung*] y, de este modo, al final del texto en un movimiento hacia el prototipo e ideal de toda traducción que la acerca a "la versión interlineal del texto sagrado" (*G.S.*, IV.1.21), resulta integrado [*aufgehoben*] el concepto de la no comunicabilidad. Precisamente en el momento de la disolución de toda comunicación y de todo sentido se produce una inversión de la distancia hacia la revelación en una figura mesiánica: la salvación. Esta salvación, con todo, no se hace reconocible al considerar el "fin mesiánico de la historia", sino en la mirada nostálgica hacia la revelación que supone el conocer la distancia que separa de ella. Esto significa, entonces, una mirada a ese texto que es, al mismo tiempo, prototipo e ideal como representante tanto de la escritura perdida como también de la nunca alcanzada: la versión interlineal del texto sagrado. Quizás habría que representarse el lenguaje adámico perdido –la traducción de la creación divina en palabras– como *una* variación posible, es decir, como la variación perdida de tal versión interlineal.

Las traducciones hölderlinianas de Sófocles no ocultan en el ensayo sobre la traducción sólo la idea de vuelta, ellas marcan, al mismo tiempo, en el movimiento del texto de Benjamin el límite antes de la precipitación en el silencio, el sostén ante el abismo y el pasaje hacia el texto sagrado: "Pero existe un sostén. Ese sostén no está dado por ningún otro texto además de los textos sagrados". La figura de la Vuelta, que en el ensayo sobre Kafka se manifiesta sin reservas, se torna aquí en el contexto de la traducción una figura que debe su razón de ser a *otra* traducción: la metamorfosis de la existencia en escritura. Si se trata ahora de aceptarla en medio de una tormenta, entonces no puede existir la promesa de ningún sostén, pues con esto caducaría también la empresa de marchar en su contra.

En el conocimiento acerca de que lo que separa de la revelación no es sólo una distancia, sino también que ésta está marcada por una distorsión, aparece la salvación ahora ya no en

tormenta. Y en esta situación ya no habrá ningún sostén. Más precisamente sólo habrá un movimiento contrario que será "un marchar en su contra" [*ein Dagegenangehen*]. El estudio que habrá de oponerse a la tormenta que sopla del olvido sólo puede hacer suya la figura de la Vuelta: "La vuelta es la dirección del estudio que transforma la existencia en escritura" (*G.S.*, II.1.437).

También esta figura del ensayo sobre Kafka (1934) puede leerse como un *Schibboleth*, es decir como el signo de reconocimiento de un recuerdo del ensayo sobre la traducción (1914-1922/1923), y como signo de la sustitución de las figuras de pensamiento allí dominantes por otras. La Vuelta aparece, entonces, en el segundo ensayo en lugar del no mencionado nombre del autor, que en el primero era nombrado como el creador de prototipos de traducción, cuando se decía: "Las traducciones de Hölderlin son prototipos de su forma" (*G.S.*, IV.1.21). Pues claro está que la alusión se dirige en múltiples sentidos a Hölderlin, donde en su poética retorna siempre la figura de *la vuelta* como se dice en sus versos: "La vuelta de todos los modos de imaginación y formas" [*Umkehr aller Vorstellungsarten und Formen*] (Hölderlin, 1992: II.375).[7] Para el poeta *die Umkehr* tenía la función –en sus traducciones de las tragedias griegas– de hacer resaltar lo que en ellas había de "oriental" (Hölderlin, 1992: 925). En la formulación benjaminiana, Hölderlin no tenía la intención solamente de helenizar la lengua alemana, sino, además, como si se tratara de un estrato anterior que hubiera que rescatar, de orientalizar la lengua griega.

Sin embargo, el concepto de *Umkehr* no aparece explícitamente mencionado en el ensayo benjaminiano sobre la traducción, sino que queda como una alusión oculta de las traducciones llevadas a cabo por Hölderlin. Como contrapartida, el texto mismo de Benjamin realiza la figura de la Vuelta. Tendiendo un puente –como se ha mencionado ya– con la fórmula concluyente del ensayo sobre el lenguaje de 1916 ("Sobre el lenguaje en general y sobre el lenguaje de los humanos") que contiene la

---

7. Al respecto véase el capítulo 4 de este estudio.

distancia hacia la revelación [*Offenbarung*], parece aquí pensable la figura de un acortamiento de esa lejanía, aunque ella siga presentándose como inalcanzable. Así si la distancia a la revelación significa un criterio para la teoría de la traducción, al mismo tiempo esta última contiene en sí el atisbo de un prototipo [*die Ahnung eines Urbildes*] y, por ello, la idea de un original sin más o de un original al que se refiera lo oculto de cada traducción particular:

> Pero existe un sostén. Ese sostén no está dado por ningún otro texto además del texto sagrado, donde el sentido ha dejado de ser la divisoria de aguas entre el fluir de la lengua y el fluir de la revelación. (IV.1.21)

El sostén significa en este contexto un aferrarse ante la posibilidad de extraviarse en el abismo de "las infinitas profundidades de la lengua", en tanto ese acto permite a la inmediatez, perdida después de la expulsión del paraíso del espíritu del lenguaje, manifestarse de nuevo, una inmediatez cuyo retorno en el texto después del desmoronamiento del sentido se vuelve ahora el criterio de la traducibilidad: "En el caso en que el texto pertenezca, *de modo inmediato* y sin un sentido mediado, en su literalidad de lenguaje verdadero, a la verdad o a la doctrina, ese texto será eminentemente traducible" (*G.S.*, IV.1.21). Si suscribimos a esta interpretación, entonces la figura del aferrarse [*ein Halten*] en el ensayo sobre Kafka, de diez años más tarde, se ha reforzado en un movimiento contrario, pasando a ser un galope contra la tormenta. Así si ahora se dice que se trata de "una tormenta que sopla desde el olvido", y que el estudio es "un galope que marcha en contra de ella" ("Franz Kafka", *G.S.*, II.2.436), mientras que en otro pasaje del mismo texto se define la distorsión como "la forma que las cosas toman en el olvido" (*G.S.*, II.2.431), entonces, se puede decir que en el caso de las distorsiones la distancia hacia la revelación ha cambiado completamente, del mismo modo que ha cambiado la idea con ello asociada de un peligro: no se está expuesto ya al peligro de precipitarse en un abismo, sino al de ser arrastrado por la

ya se había perfilado al final del ensayo benjaminiano sobre la traducción como precipicio, según se insinúa en el abismo de las traducciones del griego hechas por Hölderlin: "En ellas se precipita el sentido de abismo en abismo hasta amenazar con *perderse en las infinitas profundidades de la lengua* " (*G.S.*, IV.1.21). (El destacado es mío.)

La idea del perderse [*sich-verlieren*] provoca evidentemente la asociación con la lectura. Sin embargo, se ha producido aquí un pasaje que va desde la idea de capas profundas del lenguaje y del recuerdo a un patrón topográfico de la memoria, es decir: de un peligro a un ejercicio o a una actividad desempeñada con arte (*kunstvolle Tätigkeit*). Esta actividad se produce en beneficio de esa postura del leer por la que la existencia se metamorfosea en escritura. En la situación de la confusión de lenguas, Benjamin había adjudicado a la traducción primeramente la tarea que consistía en verificar, hablando de los idiomas: "A qué distancia se encuentra su aspecto oculto hasta llegar a la revelación, y en qué medida puede actualizarse [*gegenwärtig werden*] el conocimiento de esa distancia" (*G.S.*, IV.1.14). En correspondencia con esta idea podría considerarse aquel "errar el camino con arte" en el laberinto de la ciudad como prueba acerca de la actualidad [*Gegenwärtigkeit*] "de lo olvidado y de 'lo que ha sido' " [*des Vergessenen und Gewesenen*] dentro del conocimiento de un mundo distorsionado en situación de similitud, es decir: una postura de lectura auténtica.

PARA LA VUELTA DE LA REVELACIÓN HACIA LO MESIÁNICO

En el ensayo sobre la traducción se ponía en escena también, a pesar de todo, una idea de "salvación" ante la caída en el precipicio del sentido en tanto se permitía la asociación del afirmarse [*des Haltens*], y esto sucedía a través del gesto lingüístico al que le es inherente cierta seguridad: "Pero existe un sostén" [*Aber es gibt ein Halten*]. Dado que las condiciones de necesidad y posibilidad de la traducción se hallan fundamentadas en la

cuyas primeras huellas estaban en el laberinto del papel secante en mis cuadernos escolares. Bueno, no las primeras, pues antes hubo una que ha sobrevivido a todas. El camino en este laberinto, donde no ha faltado una Ariadna, me llevaba a atravesar el puente Bendler cuya suave curva era para mí la vivencia del primer flanco de una colina. No lejos de su comienzo estaba la meta: Friedrich Wilhelm y Reina Luise. Sobre sus pedestales redondeados sobresalían de los canteros como bajo el hechizo de curvaturas mágicas que ante ellos dibujaba un hilo de agua sobre la arena. Más que dirigirme a los soberanos yo me dirigía a sus pedestales, puesto que lo que acaecía en ellos, si bien confuso en relación con el conjunto, se hallaba más cerca. (*G.S.*, VII.1.393-394)

En medio de la topografía urbana, entonces, el laberinto se torna a través del arte de perderse, donde no se sigue el trazado del orden del plano de la ciudad, la imagen del recuerdo de una huella mágica de la palabra, que remite a la mudez lingüística de la naturaleza, desde cuyo fondo se destacan los símbolos de una memoria colectiva, como monumentos que han devenido piedra. De ellos se puede decir lo mismo que Benjamin en su *exposé* "París, capital del siglo xix" (de 1935) decía de "las ruinas de la burguesía": que los símbolos del deseo del último siglo yacen en ruinas antes de que los monumentos que los representaban se hubieran desintegrado (*G.S.*, V.1.59).

Las huellas laberínticas de los borroneos sobre el papel secante, por el contrario, simbolizan los rastros de aquellas distorsiones, que han sido posibles gracias a la superposición de numerosas escrituras erradas e invertidas del pasado. Apuntan también a las imágenes desconcertantes que se hacen visibles en la imagen gráfica [*Schriftbild*]. Para descifrarlas, hace falta igualmente un arte de la errancia, un errar no por la ciudad, sino en la escritura: ese arte tiene ya un nombre y éste es la lectura. La lectura, entonces, define esa postura frente a lo escrito y frente al lenguaje que ya no se halla bajo el signo de Babilonia, sino bajo el del laberinto.

Desde Babilonia al laberinto: "confusión" [*Verwirrung-Verirrung*] de lenguas o de caminos, un juego verbal que en alemán puede darse con la desaparición de una letra (w) y que do su punto de partida de una confusión de lenguas bajo el nombre de Babel (ya el nombre señaliza la condición lingüística representada, dado que la etimología hebrea de esa palabra remite a *balal* en el sentido de "confundir"), se inicia aquí un movimiento en la consideración teórica benjaminiana que tiene que ver con "errar [el camino]" [*sich verirren*], una acción que aparece contextualizada en la imagen del laberinto. Esta figura, entonces, puede aparecer haciendo sistema como alegoría de un esfuerzo para representar el concepto de memoria [*Gedächtnis*], dado que es justamente en esta imagen donde más claramente pueden leerse las huellas de las superposiciones que tienen lugar en ese proceso, así como sus desplazamientos: por ejemplo, en el laberinto de los edificios en la ciudad, que es comparado con una topografía de sueño y despertar ("La obra de los Pasajes"- "Esbozos tempranos"; *G.S.*, V.2.1046), mientras se lo interpreta como sueños de la Antigüedad transformados ahora en reales (Primeras anotaciones para "La obra de los Pasajes"; *G.S.*, V.2.1007). O también el laberinto como imagen mental, en cuya reflexión se transforma la representación del recuerdo desde una figura de árbol genealógico en un sistema de apertura de brechas, es decir, en una escritura mnémica ("Crónica de Berlín"; *G.S.*, VI.491). El laberinto es así la imagen dialéctica por excelencia. A través del medio del recuerdo –con la mirada puesta en "lo que ha sido", en la vuelta como dirección del estudio– se produce la metamorfosis de la existencia en escritura.

Así en una imagen de pensamiento que se encuentra en *Infancia en Berlín*, bajo el título de "Jardín Zoológico" aparece el laberinto como lugar de un errar el camino con arte [*eines kunstvollen Verirrens*]:

> No saber cómo encontrar lugares en una ciudad no significa gran cosa. Pero equivocar el camino en una ciudad, como uno yerra en un bosque, requiere entrenamiento. En ese caso los nombres de las calles deben sonarle al errante como el chasquido de una rama seca y las callejuelas en el núcleo antiguo han de reproducirle las horas del día como lo haría una oquedad en la ladera de una montaña. Yo he aprendido este arte tardíamente; ello ha venido a cumplir un sueño

una similitud distorsionada o no sensorial.[6]

Esta segunda cesura tiene validez sobre todo para marcar el esfuerzo teórico en torno al psicoanálisis, al acotar también la diferencia de la teoría lingüística benjaminiana de los años treinta frente a su teoría temprana de la magia del lenguaje. Dado que los dos cortos ensayos de 1933 se siguieron leyendo –lo que es lo más corriente– como simples suplementos o continuaciones del ensayo sobre el lenguaje de 1916, de ese modo desaparece justamente ese aspecto que puede ser resumido como una reformulación psicoanalítica de la teoría lingüística. En el concepto de la similitud distorsionada se entrecruzan, por cierto, dos rastros de un esfuerzo teórico lingüístico: por una parte, el inherente al concepto de similitud en las reflexiones sobre la magia del lenguaje (que se originan en una lectura del libro del Génesis) y, por otra parte, el inherente al concepto de un lenguaje del inconsciente ligado a la noción de distorsión, del que Benjamin se ha ido apropiando durante sus estudios sobre la memoria. La escritura de la existencia [*die Schrift des Daseins*] y la escritura de las cosas [*die Schrift der Dinge*] en la topografía de la Modernidad aparecen, entonces, no sólo separadas por la primera cesura del lenguaje de las cosas en la magia del lenguaje, sino, además, por un segundo hiato que está asociado a la figura de la distorsión. Se trata, entonces, de un retorno de una escritura distorsionada de las cosas, cuya similitud lanza un destello en lo visible.

BABEL Y EL LABERINTO

En el curso de las explicitaciones de teoría lingüística (que ponen el acento sobre el carácter escriturario de todo lo percibido), en la obra benjaminiana la lectura desplaza a la traducción. Del mismo modo, la imagen de pensamiento en cuyo signo se produce esta sustitución y transformación es el laberinto. Toman-

---

6. En la obra de Benjamin la formulación de la similitud distorsionada se encuentra en el ensayo sobre Proust y en *Infancia en Berlín hacia 1900*.

puesto que esta similitud no sensorial obra en todo acto de leer, entonces se abre en esta capa profunda un acceso hacia el llamativo doble sentido de la palabra *leer* como su significado profano pero también mágico. ("La enseñanza de lo semejante"; *G.S.*, II.1.208-209)

Sin embargo, esto no debería leerse sólo como un retorno de los aspectos de la mímesis en las reflexiones benjaminianas sobre teoría del lenguaje a posteriori de la reelaboración del esquema de la memoria, que implicara las figuras topográficas (en los Pasajes y en los esbozos tempranos) para pasar al escenario de la memoria como otro tipo de registro ("Crónica de Berlín", por ejemplo) hasta llegar a las huellas legibles de un inconsciente colectivo en la topografía urbana de la Modernidad. El párrafo citado podría leerse también como representación de un regreso de la mímesis olvidada, que ha sido posible gracias al concepto de distorsión (como un lenguaje del inconsciente). La distorsión, por lo tanto, es *la* forma en la que la similitud perdida se torna oculta y reconocible a la vez.

Las similitudes distorsionadas pueden leerse, entonces, no sólo –en el sentido de un retorno de lo reprimido– como signo de una escritura que se hace visible a partir de las huellas de la memoria, sino que ellas mismas provocan el recuerdo de una condición lingüística perdida. Por otro lado, un punto de referencia histórico para la similitud no sensorial de Benjamin lo representan la escritura de las cosas y el sistema sígnico ternario, cuya desaparición Michel Foucault colocaba en el momento de transición de *l'âge classique*, analizándola como la época de la representación.[5] El recuerdo de esta similitud perdida con el medio de un lenguaje de la literatura (como una especie de contra-discurso) y su resurgimiento en la Modernidad no reestablecen (como si fuera la segunda cesura), entonces, la similitud perdida o la inmediatez mágica. Más bien lo que se inscribe en el retorno de la similitud es la figura de la distorsión:

---

5. Véase el capítulo 3 del presente estudio.

La lectura que ocupa el lugar de la traducción 223

nueva incomunicabilidad que se torna el criterio de la traducibilidad: "Allí donde el texto pertenece a la verdad o a la doctrina, de modo inmediato y sin un sentido mediador, en la literalidad del verdadero lenguaje, en ese momento ese texto es por excelencia traducible" (*G.S.*, IV.1.21). Se trata ahora, por lo tanto, sobre todo del aspecto de lo no comunicable por lo que es reestablecida aquí la relación con la revelación, pero también con la lengua paradisíaca o con la magia del lenguaje.

Ya en el intento de formulación con el que Benjamin al final de su ensayo trata de articular la idea de la dialéctica de un lenguaje *después de* la expulsión del paraíso y esa idea de una función del lenguaje que se ha perdido, que ha sido reprimida, pero que, con todo, permanece presente en ella y en su relación con el lenguaje, aparece concentrando los aspectos perdidos en lo no comunicable, sin hacer mención de la similitud ni de lo mimético ni de la magia:

> El lenguaje no consiste, por cierto, en todo caso sólo en la comunicación de lo comunicable, sino, al mismo tiempo, es símbolo de lo no comunicable. Este costado simbólico de lo no comunicable depende de su relación con el signo... (*G.S.*, II.1.156)

Al retomar esta misma configuración de 1916 en el texto "La enseñanza de lo semejante", de 1933, donde ahora se desarrolla el esquema de la "similitud no sensorial", habrán de volver a reestablecer una relación dialéctica la magia y la mímesis:

> Este aspecto mágico, si se quiere, tanto del lenguaje como de la escritura no corre paralelo, sin embargo, sin ton ni son en pos del otro, el semiótico. Todo lo mimético del lenguaje es más bien una intención asentada sobre un fondo [*eine fundierte Intention*] que en general sólo puede manifestarse en conexión con algo extraño, justamente con lo semiótico, lo comunicativo del lenguaje como su reservorio [*Fundus*]. Así el texto literal de la escritura es el fondo en el que sólo y únicamente puede formarse la imagen desconcertante. Así la relación de sentidos, que se halla inserta en los sonidos de la oración es el fondo del que puede brotar sólo de modo vertiginoso, como en un destello, lo similar en lo instantáneo del sonido. Pero

perfecto archivo de las similitudes no sensoriales" ("La enseñanza de lo semejante"; *G.S.*, II.1.209). En este sentido, la lectura sería la forma, que habría tomado la traducción "en un mundo distorsionado en la situación de similitud" ("Una imagen de Proust"; *G.S.*, II.1.314).

EL RETORNO DE LA MÍMESIS OLVIDADA

En este sentido podría leerse el concepto de "similitud no sensorial" también como figura de un retorno de lo reprimido. Pues Benjamin había partido en su teoría lingüística temprana sobre todo de la oposición irreconciliable entre el paradigma de la arbitrariedad en "la consideración burguesa del lenguaje" y la afirmación de una igualdad esencial entre palabra y cosa en la teoría mística del lenguaje (*G.S.*, II.1.150), para integrar esta oposición, finalmente, en una relación dialéctica historizante. Por otra parte, en su descripción de la situación *después de* la expulsión del paraíso desaparece de su propio texto el aspecto de lo mimético. Más bien, aparecen subrayados –como ya se ha dicho– la sobredenominación [*Überbenennung*] y mudez de la naturaleza, y en relación con el mito de la torre de Babel se destaca la confusión de lenguas, como motivo conductor en su teoría de la traducción. En rigor, lo mimético tampoco tiene importancia en el ensayo sobre la traducción. Lo mismo sucede con el concepto de la similitud que no tiene aquí un claro perfil, pues su significado aparece superado por el de "afinidad" [*Verwandtschaft*] (*G.S.*, IV.1.13). Así es que a través de la afinidad íntima y oculta entre los idiomas, a través de su participación en lo puro del lenguaje –fundada en el aspecto de lo no comunicable– las múltiples lenguas permanecen atadas a un común ideal nunca alcanzable: dar esa "versión interlineal del texto sagrado" que es definida como "el prototipo y el ideal de la traducción" (*G.S.*, IV.1.21). Sólo en un estrato del lenguaje, en el que "cada acto de comunicación [*Mitteilung*], cada sentido y cada intención [...] están destinados a disolverse" (*G.S.*, IV.1.19), aparece una

puede ser percibido, entonces, como huella mnémica de ese gesto convocante; donde, en definitiva, ha desaparecido la relación con el original. Y justamente esto se halla ya instaurado en la imagen del eco, pues éste representa siempre un retorno diferente, así como el lenguaje del inconsciente, que puede entenderse como la traducción sin un original.

De modo análogo a lo que sucede con la idea de transitoriedad de la "traducción" en Benjamin también podría debatirse en torno de lo pasajero del concepto en *La interpretación de los sueños* de Freud, donde su autor compara la relación entre los pensamientos de los sueños y su contenido con la relación que habría entre un original y su traducción (Freud, 1969: 280). En la medida, sin embargo, en que el libro de Freud se concentra en una escritura figurativa del sueño como un modo de representación específico y siempre distorsionado, conceptualizándolo así bajo la dominación en crecimiento del lenguaje del inconsciente, el original en la versión freudiana termina haciéndose cada vez más irreconocible. En este sentido, a la metáfora de la traducción en *La interpretación de los sueños* le son propios rasgos de una distorsión; distorsión que sólo podría adquirir todo su valor en la reformulación lacaniana del lenguaje del inconsciente como "traducción sin original".

Frente a una traducción sin original, sin embargo —y en este sentido habría que entender las imágenes desconcertantes de las cosas en la Modernidad–, existe sólo *una* postura consecuente: la de la lectura. Así puede decirse que la lectura debe entenderse como la postura que resulta de un concepto de la traducción para la que ha desaparecido el original. También desaparece el sentido del original, si la teoría de la lectura ha venido a instalarse *en el lugar* [*an die Stelle*] de la teoría de la traducción, y con ello también se desvanecen todas las ideas que se orienten hacia la pregunta de "cómo ha sido realmente".

En este recorrido la traducción, entretanto, no ha desaparecido, sino que ha quedado absorbida dentro de la lectura, dado que, según afirma Benjamin, la capacidad mimética del hombre ha emigrado "a la lengua y la escritura" para crearse allí "el más

extrañeza de las lenguas" (*G.S.*, IV.1.14), entonces lo hace no sólo porque esta redención nunca podría ser alcanzada totalmente. Su referencia a la transitoriedad apunta quizás también a lo provisorio del concepto de traducción. Pues la extrañeza de la lengua consiste, por cierto, no sólo en una extrañeza de los diferentes idiomas entre sí, dado que tomados individualmente los idiomas se caracterizan también por la extrañeza, y dicha cualidad no puede ser superada con la traducción. Se trata, en rigor, de otra manera de la extrañeza, que en realidad se refiere a la confusión de los signos, de la que se habla al final del ensayo benjaminiano sobre el lenguaje y que es la que fundamenta la mencionada cesura, sin que, con todo, este concepto haya alcanzado en la teoría de la traducción desarrollada más tarde un significado relevante.

Sin embargo, cuando se enfrentan la práctica lingüística, la comunicación, la comprensión y la lectura no sólo a la extrañeza de las lenguas, sino también a la confusión y condición enigmática de sus signos y símbolos, entonces, las posibilidades del concepto de traducción elaborado por Benjamin en 1921 llegan quizás al límite de su fuerza. Y este límite está relacionado con lo que he denominado la segunda cesura. Esta ruptura, en realidad, no tiene nada que ver con el problema de la traducción de un original, sino con las traducciones sin original o cuando el original ha desaparecido.

En "La tarea del traductor" Benjamin describe la tarea de la traducción con una imagen, traducir sería conjurar el eco del original en el idioma al que se traduce, o con sus propias palabras:

> La traducción [...] convoca [...] al original a ese lugar < en el interior del bosque del lenguaje (*im innern Bergwald der Sprache*) > al único lugar donde en cada caso el eco puede dar en el propio idioma la resonancia de una obra en otra lengua. (*G.S.*, IV.1.16)

Para permanecer en ese campo de imágenes, se podría decir que el límite del concepto aquí apuntado se haría justamente visible donde se percibe ese eco y donde la percepción de la conjuración se ha hecho invisible e inaudible; donde el eco de la expulsión del paraíso. La extrañeza de las lenguas (*G.S.*, IV.1.14) que se ha originado por la multiplicidad de los idiomas, aparece evaluada en este ensayo sobre todo también en relación con su distancia de la revelación [*Entfernung von der Offenbarung*] y, por ello, del lenguaje paradisíaco. Por este motivo, Benjamin puede afirmar en el mismo estudio, por una parte, "la extrañeza de las lenguas" y, por otra parte, que "las lenguas no son extrañas entre sí" (*G.S.*, IV.1.12), dado que se hallarían referidas al lenguaje puro en una "afinidad suprahistórica" (*G.S.*, IV.1.13) y en un plano de comunidad virtual. La extrañeza de las lenguas en la historia se corresponde, así, con una afinidad de las lenguas *antes* de la historia. En esta constelación no le compete a la traducción justamente la tarea de allanar esa extrañeza o de anular aquella cesura, sino, más bien, de acentuar el conocimiento de la distancia hacia la revelación o de realizar la verificación de ese saber:

> Si, sin embargo, esos <lenguajes> crecen de tal modo hasta llegar a los confines mesiánicos de la historia, entonces es la traducción la que produce el fuego en la eterna vigencia de las obras y en la infinita renovación de las lenguas. La traducción sigue haciendo constantemente la prueba sobre ese sagrado crecimiento de las lenguas: en qué medida lo que tienen de oculto se encuentra distante de la revelación, cuán presente puede tornarse esto en el conocimiento de esta distancia. (*G.S.*, IV.1.14)

Después de la cesura, en la que se perdió la inmediatez, y cuando el lenguaje se encontró en la situación de la mediatez y de la comunicabilidad, le toca a la traducción la tarea de orientarse hacia la no comunicabilidad; tarea que Benjamin coloca en la cercanía de la redención: "*Redimir* cada lenguaje puro, que se halla bajo el exorcismo de los extraños, en el suyo propio, así como liberar ese lenguaje encarcelado en la obra en el acto de repoetización [*Umdichtung*]: ésa es la tarea del traductor." (*G.S.*, IV.1.19) (El destacado es mío.)

Cuando Benjamin en este ensayo declara que "toda traducción es sólo un modo transitorio de algún tipo para enfrentarse con la inmediatez que acompaña a la "expulsión del paraíso del espíritu del lenguaje" y a la aparición de la multiplicidad y confusión de las lenguas –como si se tratara de un fenómeno secundario de la expulsión–. Esta aparición, por cierto, es la condición para la necesidad de otro tipo de traducción, para la traducción de un idioma a otro, es decir, esa traducción de la que trata la teoría benjaminiana:

> Después de la expulsión del paraíso que, al hacer mediata la lengua, había sentado la base de su multiplicidad, sólo podía distar un paso hacia la confusión de las lenguas. Dado que los hombres habían dañado la pureza del nombre, sólo faltaba un alejamiento de esa contemplación de las cosas, mediante la cual su lenguaje se introduce en el hombre, para robarle a ese mismo hombre la base común del espíritu del lenguaje ya vacilante. Los *signos* se han de confundir siempre que las cosas se enreden. A la esclavitud del lenguaje en la charla vana corresponde la esclavitud de las cosas en la extravagancia casi como su consecuencia inevitable. En este alejamiento de las cosas que se originó en la esclavitud surgió el proyecto de construir una torre y con ese proyecto la confusión de las lenguas. ("Sobre el lenguaje en general y sobre el lenguaje de los humanos"; *G.S.*, II.1.154)

Además de esas tres significaciones que Benjamin le atribuye a la expulsión del paraíso del espíritu del lenguaje: la aparición del carácter semiótico (es decir, la mediatez del lenguaje), el surgimiento de una nueva magia (es decir, la del juicio) y el nacimiento de la abstracción (o sea: de la separación en bueno y malo), hay que mencionar, entonces, también la confusión de los signos y del lenguaje que marcan esa cesura con la que el lenguaje se ve separado de su situación adánica de la inmediatez, una situación que se había dado antes del comienzo de la historia. Esta ruptura es la que hace necesaria una teoría de la traducción. Al mismo tiempo es una mirada retrospectiva la que determina la dirección de su estudio.

En tanto Benjamin coloca su teoría de la traducción en el dominio "de la vigencia de la obra" [*des Fortlebens der Werke*], sitúa la traducción sin más *dentro de la historia*, es decir: después

las cosas al del hombre" (*G.S.*, II.1.150). Sin embargo, en el caso de esta cesura no se trata de la misma de la que se hablaba en el ensayo sobre el lenguaje de la primera época.

En relación con esa primera cesura catalogada como "expulsión del paraíso del espíritu del lenguaje" que había sido interpretada como origen del carácter semiótico, de la abstracción y de la existencia de multitud de idiomas, la segunda ruptura comporta marcas de algo que había quedado pendiente, tanto en el sentido de un estatuto teórico como también dentro de la génesis de las figuras benjaminianas de pensamiento. Como consecuencia para la teoría benjaminiana acerca de la traducción se revela que con este segundo corte la lectura ha venido a ocupar el lugar de la traducción, y esto sucede tanto en lo que respecta a su importancia teórica como también a la relación con los textos de Baudelaire. Si el ensayo de Benjamin acerca del traductor se inscribe en el contexto de las traducciones benjaminianas de *Tableaux parisiens*, entonces son estos mismos textos franceses no ya el punto de partida para la traducción, sino un paradigma para una lectura de la Modernidad donde las cosas devienen escritura.

ACERCA DE LA DOBLE EXTRAÑEZA DEL LENGUAJE

Si, por un lado, es cierto que las ideas sobre "la traducción del lenguaje de las cosas al del hombre" o "del lenguaje mudo al sonoro", o aun "del sin nombre al del nombre" (*G.S.*, II.1.150 y sigs.) están ligadas al momento inmediato, es cierto también que esta traducción del francés recibió en la mente de Benjamin el *status* de un modelo para su teoría de la traducción en el artículo que denominó "La tarea del traductor". Esto se torna explícito en la orientación de la traducción a "lo no comunicable" [*das Nicht-Mitteilbare*], "ese núcleo del mismo lenguaje puro"[4] (*G.S.*, IV.1.19). Al mismo tiempo, sin embargo, se produce la pérdida de la

---

4. En alemán: "*jener Kern der reinen Sprache selbst*". [N. del T.]

contexto de sus estudios de la Modernidad vuelva a sus reflexiones sobre la teoría lingüística y que trabajando en los dos pequeños artículos de 1933 recuerde su ensayo de diecisiete años antes sobre el lenguaje de la magia. En esos dos artículos de 1933 Benjamin desarrolla, en efecto, su concepto de la "similitud no sensorial", y este término marca exactamente también el punto de fuga en el que se entrecruzan los andamiajes de una escritura del inconsciente y de la magia del lenguaje en sus reflexiones teóricas. La "similitud no sensorial" (en otros textos se habla también de una "similitud distorsionada") indica ese lugar en los escritos benjaminianos donde en el plano de una filosofía del lenguaje se produce una reformulación del lenguaje del inconsciente y, viceversa, una relectura psicoanalítica de su teoría de la magia del lenguaje.

La expresión de "similitudes distorsionadas" contiene, al mismo tiempo, el *Schibboleth*,* que la diferencia menciona por su nombre: la diferencia entre un lenguaje de las cosas (definido en el ensayo "Sobre el lenguaje en general y sobre el lenguaje de los humanos" como lenguaje paradisíaco) y el lenguaje de las cosas en la Modernidad. Ambos deben ser leídos como imágenes desconcertantes y como símbolos mnémicos. La *distorsión* marca una cesura inescatimable, que separa, en el segundo caso, la existencia legible como una escritura en la "historia primigenia de la Modernidad" de "la palabra muda en la existencia de las cosas" (II.1.152) y distingue, en el primer caso, lo que proviene de las palabras en el mito de la creación. Es justamente la distorsión —como si fuera la inmediatez en la revelación de lo mudo— la que ha interrumpido la inmediatez de "la traducción del lenguaje de

---

* La palabra hebrea *Schibboleth* (que significa "espiga" o "río", entre otras acepciones) aparece en el Antiguo Testamento ("Jueces", XII, 6) en el centro de la historia de la lucha contra los efrainitas, a quienes se reconocía porque no podían pronunciarla correctamente (diciendo "Sibboleth"). El poeta judío Paul Celan la utiliza en una de sus poesías, "*In Eins*" ("En uno"), insertándola en el texto en alemán; a esta misma poesía Jacques Derrida le dedica una interpretación en una conferencia dada en inglés y luego reelaborada en francés, bajo el título de "Schibboleth pour Paul Celan" (París, Galilée, 1986), donde hace una reflexión sobre el judaísmo a partir de este término. [N. del T.]

durante ese período y donde se perciben rastros claros de una lectura de Freud.[3]

Pero si en este contexto Benjamin trabaja en una teoría de la lectura, con cuya apoyatura se pueden descifrar las imágenes desconcertantes de lo banal así como las imágenes de "lo que ha sido", entonces debe destacarse también que en este período se ocupó igualmente de una *escritura de las cosas* [*Schrift der Dinge*], que se diferencia radicalmente de ese *lenguaje de las cosas o de la naturaleza* [*Sprache der Dinge bzw. der Natur*], según el propio Benjamin lo había definido en su teoría temprana acerca de la magia del lenguaje: como un lenguaje mudo que se revelaba de modo inmediato por la traducción al lenguaje del hombre, pues "La traducción del lenguaje de las cosas al del hombre no es solamente la traducción de lo mudo a lo sonoro, sino de lo innombrado a un nombre" ("Sobre el lenguaje en general y sobre el lenguaje de los humanos"; *G.S.*, II.1.151).

Puesto que el concepto benjaminiano de traducción se funda en la lectura realizada durante 1916 del libro del Génesis en el contexto de una elaboración teórica del lenguaje "en la capa más profunda de la teoría lingüística" (*G.S.*, II.1.151), a la par que su artículo de 1921 titulado "La tarea del traductor" se refiere a esta etapa, hay que reconocer que la idea de un lenguaje mudo de las cosas es esencial para su concepción sobre el tema. Y el pasaje de su interés desde ese lenguaje a *la escritura de las cosas* ha de ser de grandes consecuencias para su concepto de la traducción formulado en 1921. Partiendo de este hecho, se ha de tratar en las páginas que siguen la hipótesis de la naturaleza transitoria del concepto de traducción de 1921 en el marco de una génesis de la formación teórica benjaminiana o, en otras palabras, de una transformación de su concepto de traducción que habría de ser sustituido por un modelo de lectura en los trabajos de los años treinta.

No es, pues, una casualidad que Benjamin justamente en el

---

3. Para esta lectura de Freud, véase el capítulo 8 del presente estudio.

gestos y las palabras, las cosas y los acontecimientos, todo *como forma de escritura*, y, por lo tanto, lee.[2] Se trata justamente de esa postura frente a la lectura aludida en el proyecto de los Pasajes, donde se dirige la atención hacia la topografía de la ciudad y a "las imágenes desconcertantes de lo banal" [*Vexierbilder des Banalen*] en la Modernidad. Allí la legibilidad y la descifrabilidad de esa escritura aparecen conceptualizadas de modo análogo al lenguaje del inconsciente del psicoanálisis.

Este patrón de escritura se corresponde con una concepción topográfica de la memoria, que considera los signos visibles como símbolos mnémicos, como productos de una reelaboración psíquica y como representaciones distorsionadas; como una escritura, por lo tanto, en la que las huellas de la memoria nunca llegan a ser inmediatas ni completamente visibles. Puede decirse, por un lado, que este modelo escriturario de un lenguaje del inconsciente (de la multitud) sirve de base al proyecto de los Pasajes en su segunda y mayor fase (1934-1940); pero, también, que Benjamin partía, en cambio, en las primeras anotaciones y esbozos para el proyecto (entre 1927 y 1929) de una concepción espacialmente topográfica, en la que aparecen reproducidas las esferas del sueño y del despertar como dimensiones de signo opuesto en calidad de algo así como una duplicación de la topografía urbana. El tiempo intermedio –entre los años 1929 y 1934– le sirvió a Benjamin para la reelaboración de su concepto específico de la memoria (es decir: fue la época de un trabajo teórico con la representación, con los modos funcionales y con el lenguaje de la memoria), que puede reconstruirse gracias a los ensayos, reseñas y esbozos que Benjamin siguió escribiendo

---

2. La mayor oposición frente a los escritos tempranos se da justamente en estos textos. Así, por ejemplo, si en *Das Tagebuch* ["El diario íntimo"], de 1913, se está rodeado del acontecimiento *como* por un paisaje (*G.S.*, II.1.99), entonces el acontecimiento se percibe allí dentro de una estructura mítica, en la que la historia aparece como naturaleza. Los esfuerzos de Benjamin para integrar la mitología en un espacio histórico (*G.S.*, V.1.571) están en la base de su concepción de la lectura, donde las imágenes de "lo que ha sido" se vuelven descifrables en el contexto de una escritura de la memoria.

9. La lectura que ocupa el lugar de la traducción
La formulación psicoanalítica de la teoría sobre la magia del lenguaje

LA ESCRITURA DE LA EXISTENCIA

"La vuelta es la dirección del estudio que transforma la existencia en escritura" (*G.S.*, II.2.437). Esta metamorfosis de la existencia en escritura de la que habla Benjamin en su ensayo sobre Kafka puede ser comprendida como una forma de traducción que se conjura bajo la figura de "Vuelta" [*Umkehr*]. Si la existencia es propiamente legible sólo *como escritura*, es decir cuando se ha tornado escritura o es percibida como tal, su transformación en escritura o su estudio bajo esa condición depende, en todo caso, de una figuración determinada. La vuelta, caracterizada como dirección del estudio, marca una postura de la lectura [*Lektüre-Haltung*] frente a "lo que ha sido", que se encuentra en relación con una concepción de la memoria en la base de los trabajos de Benjamin en el territorio de los Pasajes[1] y que al comienzo de la década del treinta ha ganado en sus escritos una configuración teórica muy elaborada. La transformación que se cumple en la "existencia", para que ella pueda devenir escritura, es el producto de una postura que se debe solamente a la actividad de decodificación de quien percibe o estudia. Es este individuo el que contempla las imágenes y huellas de "lo que ha sido", las configuraciones duraderas y efímeras de la vida, los

---

1. Estos trabajos han sido caracterizados por el propio Benjamin como de su segundo ciclo productivo, que seguiría a su ciclo "germanista" (donde todavía se hallaba su ensayo sobre el traductor), al que venían a sustituir.

la Modernidad, representan así *una escritura de las cosas* [*eine Schrift der Dinge*] o, alternativamente, de las configuraciones de la vida, que es radicalmente diferente del *lenguaje de las cosas o de la naturaleza* [*Sprache der Dinge bzw. der Natur*] en la inmediatez de la magia del lenguaje, como Benjamin la definió para el lenguaje paradisíaco. Esto significa que no es sólo diferente a nivel histórico, sino que se halla en otro territorio teórico.[20]

La percepción o la legibilidad de las similitudes y de las imágenes desconcertantes (que se dan con la vertiginosidad de un destello) activan, por otro lado, una vieja capacidad que ya en la época del sistema ternario de signos era corriente, y que Benjamin en su libro sobre el drama barroco había rescatado, en el momento en que estaba desapareciendo, en forma de esa "escritura excitante" (puesta de manifiesto gracias a la mirada alegórica): una lectura de las imágenes como escritura, que intensifica la capacidad mimética del hombre. Tal lectura, que sabe de una decodificación de similitudes no sensoriales y de representaciones distorsionadas y donde entran en contacto la memoria del lenguaje y el lenguaje de la memoria, constituye así la aparición de esa postura con la que se hacen reconocibles y legibles los restos, las imágenes, las cosas, las palabras, los gestos y las imágenes de la escritura en tanto huellas. Esto es, como dice Benjamin, "la postura de un recuerdo auténtico" [*die Haltung echter Erinnerung*].

---

20. En cuanto a este tema, véase el capítulo siguiente del presente estudio.

de la percepción [*Merkwelt*] del hombre moderno contiene muchas menos de esas correspondencias mágicas" ("La enseñanza de lo semejante"; *G.S.*, II.1.206) parece recordarle al propio Benjamin su trabajo de 1916 dedicado a la magia del lenguaje.[19] Allí la inmediatez que primeramente era vista en la traducción del lenguaje mudo de la naturaleza a la lengua sonora del hombre, inherente al lenguaje paradisíaco perdido, puede ser entendida ahora como una cualidad mimética desaparecida, que, sin embargo, habría emigrado hacia la relación entre escritura y lengua:

> Todo lo mimético del lenguaje es más bien una intención asentada sobre un fondo [*eine fundierte Intention*] que en general sólo puede manifestarse en conexión con algo extraño, justamente con lo semiótico, lo comunicativo del lenguaje como su reservorio [*Fundus*]. Así el texto literal de la escritura es el fondo en el que sólo y únicamente puede formarse la imagen desconcertante. ("La enseñanza de lo semejante"; *G.S.*, II.1.208-209)

En esta conceptualización de la relación entre la función semiótica del lenguaje y las similitudes que aparecen en conexión con ella, se entrecruzan reflexiones sobre el lenguaje de la memoria con otras sobre la memoria del lenguaje. Puesto que las imágenes desconcertantes son distorsiones que son leídas no solamente como signos de una escritura que se manifiesta desde las huellas de la memoria, sino que, al mismo tiempo, traen el recuerdo de un estado de lenguaje perdido, entonces, el archivo de las similitudes no sensoriales que es el lenguaje provee una memoria del lenguaje, que en la Modernidad puede tornarse fructífero para el desciframiento de las huellas de la memoria.

Las imágenes desconcertantes, que pueden leerse como los perfiles de lo banal visto por Benjamin en la topografía urbana de

---

19. Véase el pedido de Benjamin en carta a Scholem, donde le comunica su deseo de que le envíe "como comparación de estas anotaciones [...] aquellas anteriores" sobre el lenguaje, dado que en su huída de Alemania debió de haberlas dejado entre sus "papeles de Berlín" (Benjamin, 1978: 575).

dialéctica entre conciencia e inconsciente. Pues la percepción de la similitud

> [...] se halla asociada en cada caso con un destello. Pasa vertiginosamente al lado, puede quizás volverse a ver, pero no puede atraparse como otras percepciones. Se ofrece a la vista justamente de modo efímero, pasajero como una constelación estelar. La percepción de las similitudes aparece, por ello, ligada a un instante. ("La enseñanza de lo semejante"; *G.S.*, II.1.206-207)

La percepción de lo similar caracteriza, así, precisamente el momento de la legibilidad de huellas de la memoria, que Freud había descrito como el destello de la conciencia en el instante de la percepción. En tanto esto hace corresponder una percepción presente con las brechas en la memoria, al mismo tiempo se produce una asociación a través de "una similitud de toma de posesión o de excitación" [*eine Besetzungs- oder Erregungsähnlichkeit*], que no puede ser representable en ninguna conformación duradera (ni en ninguna capacidad figurativa idéntica), sino que –como demuestra Benjamin– puede ser reconocible en su calidad de similitud no sensorial. Este término –comparable al de *similitud distorsionada*– es, por lo tanto, una tentativa de describir los modos de influencia de las similitudes gracias al medio que representa el lenguaje del inconsciente, es decir: por medio de una representación distorsionada. Por otra parte, también Freud había adjudicado a las relaciones de semejanza un papel destacado durante el trabajo onírico.[18]

En la obra de Benjamin, la cualidad de reconocer similitudes aparece situada en una historia de la capacidad mimética, siendo esta cualidad evaluada como un rudimento de la capacidad perdida de tornarse similar. Se trata, entonces, de una cualidad para la que se encuentran ejemplos tomados del dominio de los ritos y del ocultismo. La indicación de que parece que "el mundo

---

18. Compárese aquí el Apartado VI.C sobre los medios de representación del sueño ["Die Darstellungmittel des Traums"] en *La interpretación de los sueños* de Freud.

de buscar una reformulación para el concepto de distorsión, que, entretanto, había estado elaborando.

LA SIMILITUD DISTORSIONADA: EL LENGUAJE DE LA MEMORIA Y LA MEMORIA DEL LENGUAJE

Las imágenes del recuerdo en *Infancia en Berlín* aparecen completamente creadas de manera tal que dejen ver las *huellas* de la memoria, en tanto se suministran los caminos asociativos que permiten la anexión de diferentes imágenes, escenas, palabras y nombres. Aunque a ellas se les otorga algo así como la jerarquía de sustitutos de procesos de excitación o el estatuto de símbolos del recuerdo registrados por medio del lenguaje, sin embargo, su significado no concluye en esa cuestión de sentido, que se resume en *qué* debe entenderse, como, por ejemplo, la formula el maestro Knoche en el párrafo titulado "Dos imágenes enigmáticas" [*Zwei Rätselbilder*], de *Infancia en Berlín* (*G.S.*, VII.1.401). Más bien las huellas pueden comprenderse de modo tal que se siga la cadena asociativa, en cuyo surgimiento entran en juego similitudes variadas, que, por cierto, son más exactamente reconocibles en constelaciones y figuraciones, dado que son sensorialmente muy poco perceptibles o visibles en forma de objeto.

Estas constelaciones son las que conforman ese "archivo de similitudes no sensoriales", que Benjamin encuentra en el lenguaje y la escritura, y que en el correr de la historia habría sido el lugar al que habría ido a dar la capacidad mimética del hombre (*G.S.*, II.1.209). Efectivamente, Benjamin sostiene estas ideas en sus dos pequeños artículos sobre teoría del lenguaje –"La enseñanza de lo semejante" y "Sobre la capacidad mimética"– que surgen en 1933 en el contexto del trabajo con las imágenes del recuerdo para *Infancia en Berlín*. El modo en que Benjamin describe aquí la percepción de similitudes se corresponde exactamente con esa constelación de la legibilidad que se ve estructurada por la relación

miento de los recuerdos individuales en la literatura, por el contrario, Benjamin asocia el concepto de "distorsión" con la figura de similitud. Ya en el ensayo sobre Proust (de 1929) nos encontramos con la formulación de nostalgia "por un mundo distorsionado en situación de similitud" [*nach der im Stand der Ähnlichkeit entstellten Welt*], con lo que Benjamin sugiere que en la obra de Proust a cada similitud (estructurada por las huellas del recuerdo) siempre se la inscribe en una fase de la distorsión, o, en otras palabras, del trabajo onírico:

> La similitud de lo Uno con lo Otro con la que nosotros contamos y que nos ocupa cuando estamos despiertos, es una simple sugestión de las más *profundas similitudes* del mundo onírico, donde lo que sucede no surge de modo idéntico, sino similar: impenetrablemente similar a sí mismo. [...] así era Proust de insaciable; esa puerta disimulada (*die Atrappe*), el Yo (*das Ich*), había que vaciarlos de un solo golpe, para volver a llenarlos con ese tercer elemento: la imagen, que apaciguaba su curiosidad, no, no su curiosidad, sino su nostalgia. Yacía en el lecho, destrozado por la nostalgia, nostalgia por *un mundo distorsionado en la situación de similitud*, en la que irrumpe el rostro verdadero surrealista de la existencia. A ese mundo le corresponde [...]: la imagen.(*G.S.*, II.1.314) (El destacado es mío.)

Así, por un lado, resulta importante la relación de imagen y de similitud (distorsionada), para el concepto benjaminiano de imagen. Por otro lado, también es interesante este ensayo sobre Proust, en tanto dirige su mirada a un modelo de memoria y porque, además, se encuentra en proximidad temporal con los esbozos tempranos para los Pasajes. Con este proyecto lo une la idea que da profundidad espacial a los sueños. Pero si en este ensayo Benjamin no hace más que seguir en la metáfora de la profundidad la propia imaginería proustiana, hay que acotar que al retomar la figuración de similitud distorsionada en las imágenes del recuerdo, ello proviene de la propia cosecha de Benjamin. Así en su obra *Infancia en Berlín hacia 1900*, de pocos años después, donde Benjamin declara: "Yo estaba distorsionado por la similitud"[17] (*G.S.*, VII.1.417), se muestra al autor en la empresa

---

17. En alemán: "*Ich war entstellt von Ähnlichkeit*". [N. del T.]

Así, si, por una parte, en la tentativa arqueológica para representar la memoria se produce el pasaje de una imaginación estratificada [*Schichtenvorstellung*] hacia la escritura, ahora, por otra parte, el laberinto conforma aquí el medio para el desplazamiento de una imagen genealógica –que recuerda a las representaciones referidas al origen y a la proveniencia– hacia un modelo de brechas con ramificaciones como huellas de la memoria. En este sentido, la "Crónica de Berlín" se torna legible como un texto de tal densidad, que permite reconocer las huellas de la metamorfosis desde un escenario de la memoria espacialmente topográfico a uno que lo es de modo escriturario.

Para el significado creciente del concepto de *distorsión* existen en este contexto muchos ejemplos. La distorsión aparece definida en el ensayo sobre Kafka (de 1934) como la forma que toman las cosas cuando llegan al territorio del olvido. Es característico el papel que el término juega en este artículo, en el que Benjamin reflexiona sobre el sentido de la gesticulación en los textos kafkianos, considerando nuestro cuerpo como "el país extranjero más olvidado" [*die vergessenste Fremde*] (*G.S.*, II.2.431), como si fuera el material y la matriz de una representación de lo olvidado, que aquí, al mezclarse con lo olvidado del mundo anterior [*Vorwelt*] apunta hacia una lejanía mítica. Ya sea que lo olvidado aparezca cargado en el cuerpo o en él inscripto, de todos modos sus signos sin palabras pueden leerse como un lenguaje de la memoria. No cabe duda de que el término "distorsión" del ensayo sobre Kafka se refiere realmente a Freud, en tanto puede documentarse que el pequeño texto de 1931 que le precede y que lleva el título de *F.K.: Beim Bau der Chinesischen Mauer* ["Franz Kafka: en la construcción de la muralla china"], donde las distorsiones kafkianas se describen como representación de "signos, indicaciones y síntomas de desplazamientos" [*Zeichen, Anzeichen und Symptome von Verschiebungen*] *G.S.*, II.2.678), se construye sobre la derivación de una relación entre el olvido y la culpa (*G.S.*, II.2.682). Esto sirve aquí de evidencia acerca de que el uso del término "distorsión" en el ensayo más tardío se está refiriendo claramente al uso freudiano. En el contexto de las reflexiones sobre los modos de funciona-

imagen topográfica de la memoria que se basa en el patrón de las "brechas".

En cuanto a la idea de laberinto, su punto de partida es la idea de que las imágenes de los escenarios a menudo se sobreimprimen en el recuerdo con las imágenes de los individuos. A partir del intento de paliar ese olvido personal por medio de un esquema gráfico de la vida, en el que pueda establecerse documentadamente la significación curricular de las personas, su representación (que se había originado en una serie de árboles genealógicos) se transforma, con todo, en un laberinto. Y, si el laberinto no aparece aquí ya como en los esbozos tempranos para el proyecto de los pasajes, como un pasado petrificado –aunque más no fuera como realización de una "ciudad soñada por los antiguos" (*G.S.*, V.2.1007)–, sino como imagen en la que la historia del individuo es representable en una figura de la memoria, al mismo tiempo se trata de un laberinto con entradas que conducen a su interior, que es lo primero que llama la atención, para pasar, luego, a una contemplación de los caminos transversales y las brechas. En este mecanismo, las entradas no cobran significado en relación con su acceso hacia el interior, sino en virtud de las ramificaciones de sentido que posibilitan:

> [...] preferiría hablar de un laberinto. Lo que se alberga en la cámara de su enigmático centro –el Yo o el Destino– no debe preocuparme ahora, pero tanto más me inquietan, sin embargo, las muchas entradas que conducen a su interior. Esas entradas las denomino yo amistades primigenias [*Urbekanntschaften*] [...] Dado que la mayoría de estas amistades primigenias –por lo menos, esas que permanecen en nuestra memoria– traban, por su parte, nuevos contactos, abriéndose a nuevas amistades con otras personas, así entonces, en cierto tiempo, se ramifican esos pasillos hacia sus costados (hacia la derecha pueden dibujarse los masculinos, y hacia la izquierda los femeninos). Si, en definitiva, se abren nuevas brechas por caminos transversales de uno de esos sistemas hacia los otros, todo depende de las ramificaciones de nuestro paso por la vida. ("Crónica de Berlín"; *G.S.*, VI.491)

datan de estos años.[14] Partiendo de este punto, el concepto de "inervación"[15] va dejando su rastro para conectarse con una lectura posterior de Freud, cuando acapara el interés de Benjamin el lenguaje del inconsciente, donde vuelve a obtener un lugar central la relación entre excitación (o "inervación") y producción de imágenes, como sucede en los textos freudianos clásicos. Así, por ejemplo, en un pasaje sobre las imágenes mentales en *Dirección única*: "No hay imaginación sin inervación" [*Keine Vorstellung ohne Innervation*] (*G.S.*, IV.1.116-117).

Y tampoco el carácter de escritura de la alegoría en el libro sobre el drama barroco habría sido posible evidentemente sin el concepto de "excitación" [*Erregung*], dado que allí se sostiene que la mirada alegórica transforma a las cosas y a las obras en una "escritura excitante" [*erregende Schrift*] (I.1.352). En otro contexto, como, por ejemplo, en el caso de los recuerdos del individuo nos encontramos con el término de "brecha" [*Bahnung*]. Así sucede en "Crónica de Berlín", justamente en un texto donde el autor prueba diferentes imágenes para representar la actividad del recuerdo, desarrollando una maqueta topográfica para el individuo[16] que aparezca separada de modelos autobiográficos, normalmente asociados con las ideas de proveniencia, el continuo decurso de la vida, secuencia, etcétera. De modo similar a lo que sucedía con la alegoría arqueológica antes mencionada donde funcionaba como representación de la memoria que desembocaba en la idea de escenario en la idea de otra escritura, también el laberinto se transforma en estas anotaciones en una

14. Véase el capítulo 2 del presente estudio.
15. Compárese aquí la formulación de una "inervación motora" en las "Notizen zu einer Theorie des Spiels" ["Anotaciones para una teoría del juego"], que datan de los años 1929/1930 (*G.S.*, VI.188), y están en la proximidad temporal de las "inervaciones del grupo colectivo" mencionadas en el ensayo sobre el surrealismo, al mismo tiempo que prenuncian las observaciones sobre la memoria reflexiva del jugador en los estudios sobre Baudelaire.
16. La topografía del recuerdo individual aparece aquí diferenciada del recuerdo de la ciudad que se muestra como grabado en el suelo ("Crónica de Berlín"; VI.489), para reaparecer de modo acentuado en las imágenes del recuerdo en *Infancia en Berlín hacia 1900*, mostrando justamente las correspondencias entre el recuerdo del sujeto y la topografía urbana.

que debería ser analizada bajo la ley de la represión: "Los productos de la falsa conciencia se asemejan a imágenes desconcertantes en las que lo central se asoma detrás de nubes, hojas y sombras" (*G.S.*, III.223). Esta tentativa de reformular cuestiones derivadas del marxismo con la apoyatura de una mirada entrenada psicoanalíticamente será uno de los *Leitmotive* del proyecto de los Pasajes, y en el texto mencionado se halla en conexión con las publicaciones aparecidas en 1930, en las que Benjamin, en vísperas de la irrupción del Nacionalsocialismo, ve una posibilidad para trabajar en un programa para la politización de los intelectuales.

En este contexto se encuentra, por ejemplo, junto a la reseña citada el texto sobre el surrealismo del año anterior, donde, de manera afín con el concepto de "espacio del cuerpo y de la imagen", se utiliza el término de "inervaciones". Aquí se trata de un concepto que en Freud es entendido como "documentaciones de los estímulos" [*Erregungsaufzeichnungen*], y cuya matriz se halla en su teoría de los trayectos nerviosos [*Nervenbahnen*] que data de trabajos tempranos dominados por la neurología, como "Proyecto de psicología" (*Entwurf einer Psychologie*; Freud, 1887).* De ese modo, el término que Freud transfirió luego a las "brechas" [*Bahnungen*] abiertas en el inconsciente o a las "huellas duraderas" o permanentes [*Dauerspuren*], vuelve a adquirir en la formulación benjaminiana su significación primera más corpórea cuando en su obra se habla de "las inervaciones corpóreas del grupo colectivo" y sus descargas [*Entladungen*] revolucionarias. La variante neurológica más antigua dentro del psicoanálisis en la que los procesos corpóreos tenían una mayor relevancia estaba ejerciendo una influencia significativa, entonces, en la época en que Benjamin se dedicaba al estudio de Freud en Berna, como lo demuestran las anotaciones sobre antropología que

---

* Según lo aclara Lacan (*Écrits*, Du Seuil, París, 1966: 45, nota 1), ese texto temprano formaba parte de las cartas dirigidas a Fliess hacia 1895. Es importante señalar aquí que ese texto de Freud no debe confundirse con su tardío *Esquema del psicoanálisis* [*Abriss der Psychoanalyse*] aparecido póstumamente. [N. del T.]

de la historia y la matriz para una historiografía dialéctica. Al mismo tiempo, esta anotación para el proyecto de los Pasajes contiene indicios de la lectura por parte de Benjamin de los ensayos freudianos "El trabajo del sueño", de 1900, y *Totem y tabú*, de 1912/1913.

EL ASEGURAMIENTO DE LAS HUELLAS EN UNA LECTURA DE FREUD

Sin embargo, las huellas de figuras de pensamiento psicoanalíticas en los textos de Benjamin se pueden interpretar no tanto como indicios para una recepción de títulos particulares de Freud, sino como indicaciones de un trabajo intensivo con determinados conceptos freudianos.

Si ya en los esbozos tempranos para los Pasajes surgía el motivo del olvido (por ejemplo: O°, 50; *G.S.*, V.2.1031), ello se va transformando cada vez más en una dialéctica del recuerdo y del olvido, como sucede en el ensayo sobre Proust, que data de 1929, donde se define el quehacer proustiano conectando "el tejer de su recuerdo" [*das Weben seiner Erinnerung*] y "los ornamentos des olvido" [*die Ornamente des Vergessens*].

En el contexto de las reflexiones sobre la memoria colectiva, sin embargo, los conceptos del inconsciente y de la *represión* se van tornando cada vez más importantes. Así se refiere Benjamin explícitamente a la "ley de la represión" [*das Gesetz der Verdrängung*] en la discusión de los huecos que el marxismo ha dejado en sus explicitaciones. Esto sucede, por ejemplo, en el comentario sobre el libro de Siegfried Kracauer sobre los empleados (de 1930), en el que Benjamin, aprovechando tangencialmente el género "reseña", desarrolla su visión de una integración de los paradigmas del ser y la conciencia –desde el marxismo– y de la conciencia y el inconsciente –desde el psicoanálisis–. Partiendo así de "la creación de falsa conciencia" [*Erzeugung falschen Bewusstseins*] –una categoría que de ahí en adelante desaparece de sus escritos–, la considera como una producción de imágenes superficiales (*G.S.*, V.1.47), en tanto el trabajo onírico del grupo colectivo ha ido dejando aquí sus rastros. En el concepto de huella, además, se encuentra implícito el proceso de una escritura pasada, que ha dejado sus huellas, con la práctica presente de la decodificación, el ahora de la cognoscibilidad, donde Huella y Aura son vistas como conceptos de fuerzas contrarias:

> Huella y Aura. La Huella es una cercanía, por más lejano que sea lo que ha dejado tras sí. El Aura es manifestación de una lejanía, por más cercano que sea lo que ella provoca. En la Huella nos apropiamos de la cosa, en el Aura ella nos domina. (Anotaciones y materiales para "La obra de los Pasajes", Block M16a,4; *G.S.*, V.1.560).

De todos modos, este proceso de apropiación posibilitado por la huella lleva consigo rasgos de una actividad, en tanto se lo describe como desciframiento. Pero, al mismo tiempo, este "estar persiguiendo huellas" se parece a una postura que proviene del psicoanálisis y que Benjamin traslada al lenguaje de las cosas o de las imágenes desconcertantes [*Vexierbilder*] de lo banal:

> Es más fácil ir metiéndose en el interior de las cosas desechadas para descifrar como imágenes desconcertantes los perfiles de lo banal [...] El psicoanálisis hace rato que descubrió las imágenes enigmáticas como esquematismos del trabajo onírico. Por nuestra parte, sin embargo, no estamos tan seguros sobre las huellas del alma como sobre los de las cosas. El árbol totémico de los objetos lo buscamos en la espesura de la historia primigenia. (Block I1,3; *G.S.*, V.1.281)

¡Estar detrás de las huellas de las cosas más que de las del alma!: aquí se produce justamente el traslado de un proceso psicoanalítico a una decodificación de la escritura en imágenes del sueño; es decir, ello significa una consideración de las condiciones de representabilidad de un lenguaje del inconsciente del *grupo colectivo* (o de la memoria colectiva), re-materializándolo y transponiéndolo como si se lo llevara al plano cultural. En ese recorrido el proceso de una lectura entrenada psicoanalíticamente llega a ser el modelo para una consideración

[*Besetzung*]* que regula la conexión entre los diferentes sistemas del aparato psíquico en Freud, se establece aquí la relación entre lo pasado y lo presente, dado que Benjamin la comprende como un nexo figurativo y no temporal: "La imagen es aquello, donde 'lo que ha sido' entra con la velocidad de un destello en contacto con el ahora para formar una constelación".[13] Y esta convergencia vertiginosa ocurre en el lenguaje, pues como agrega Benjamin: "Sólo las imágenes dialécticas son auténticamente históricas, es decir no arcaicas, y el lugar en el que uno las encuentra es el lenguaje." (Anotaciones y materiales para "La obra de los Pasajes", Block N2a,3; *G.S.*, V.1.576).

El giro en contra de las imágenes arcaicas es indicio de una voluntaria diferenciación con la obra de Jung, con cuyo patrón de un "inconsciente colectivo" [*des kollektiven Unbewussten*] no tiene nada en común la idea benjaminiana de un inconsciente del grupo colectivo [*vom Unbewussten des Kollektivs*]. Aun cuando en el patrón de lectura benjaminiano para una consideración histórica *las imágenes* de "lo que ha sido" jueguen un papel dominante, Benjamin va a partir de un modelo de escritura con huellas de la memoria, como cuando, entre otros momentos, describe las imágenes dialécticas como imágenes leídas (Block N3,1; *G.S.*, V.1.578) o también como imágenes oníricas ("París, capital del siglo XIX"; *G.S.*, V.1.55). Pues su lectura de las imágenes se corresponde con una maqueta de la escritura en imágenes del sueño como si se tratara de un lenguaje. Así también se refiere allí a "configuraciones de la vida" que son duraderas y a la vez

---

* El término freudiano *Besetzung* ha sido traducido al francés como *investissement* y en inglés como *cathexis*. Alude a la energía psíquica que se halla unida a una representación, una parte del cuerpo, un objeto, etc. Una discusión sobre las acuñaciones de Freud puede verse en Anthony Wilden, *Speech and Language in Psychoanalysis*. Jacques Lacan, Baltimore (Londres), The Johns Hopkins University Press, 1968, pág. 199. [N. del T.]

13. En alemán: "*worin das Gewesene mit dem Jetzt blitzhaft zu einer Konstellation zusammentritt*". [N. del T.]

hecho espacial y pétreo. Ella debe ser leída como la de una memoria colectiva donde en su lectura se revelan los símbolos del recuerdo y las huellas. Y el sueño ya no será considerado un ámbito separado del despertar (un espacio, un estrato, o algo similar), sino un modo de representación (o un lenguaje) del inconsciente.

En este decurso encontramos en las reflexiones de Benjamin acerca de la teoría y conceptualidad de su proyecto exactamente esos aspectos que caracterizan el patrón topográfico de la memoria en Freud. La *legibilidad* de las huellas de la memoria, que en Freud vincula el hacerse visible [*Sichtbarwerden*] y el desaparecer de la escritura con el destellar y extinguirse de la conciencia durante el acto perceptivo (Freud, 1969: III. 368), se presenta en Benjamin referida a las imágenes de "lo que ha sido". La legibilidad de las imágenes se señala así como su "*index* histórico",[12] a la vez que aparece bajo la impronta del "ahora de la cognoscibilidad":

> Lo que diferencia a las imágenes de las "esencialidades" de la fenomenología es su *index* histórico. [...] El *index* histórico de las imágenes declara no solamente que ellas pertenecen a una determinada época, sino que revela sobre todo que ellas llegan a la legibilidad en una época determinada. Y este "arribar a la legibilidad" constituye un específico punto crítico en el movimiento contenido en su interior. Cada presente está así determinado por esas imágenes que aparecen en sincronía con él: cada ahora es el ahora de una determinada cognoscibilidad. (Anotaciones y materiales para "La obra de los Pasajes", Block N3,1; *G.S.*, V.1.577-578)

De una manera análoga al proceso de la toma de posesión

---

12. Para esta noción de una relación figurativa entre el ahora y "lo que ha sido", puede servir traer a cuento un pasaje similar en la obra de Freud, donde aparece su concepto de la "marca temporal" [*Zeitmarke*] entre el sueño diurno y la fantasía: "Pues lo pasado, lo presente y lo futuro se apiñan como las cuentas en el hilo del rosario del deseo que corre atravesándolas", en "El creador literario y el fantaseo" (Freud, 1969: II, 483).

Si aquí el sueño aparece asociado con el motivo freudiano del símbolo del deseo, también las huellas de lo visible de la ciudad resultan de una reelaboración en la que entran en contacto lo pasado y lo presente. Lo que queda tallado en piedra –Benjamin habla de "ruinas de la burguesía" (*G.S.*, V.1.59)– se vuelve, en este contexto de la topografía de una memoria colectiva, una escritura, cuya legibilidad y decodificabilidad sigue el patrón freudiano de la memoria:

> El desarrollo de las fuerzas productivas derribó los símbolos del deseo del último siglo antes de que los monumentos que los representaban se hubieran desintegrado. [...] A esta época corresponden los pasajes e interiores, los pabellones de exposición y dioramas. Ellos son restos de un mundo onírico. La evaluación de los elementos del sueño al despertar es un caso ejemplar del pensamiento dialéctico. Por ello es el pensamiento dialéctico el órgano del despertar histórico. ("París, capital del siglo XIX"; *G.S.*, V.1.59)[11]

En la conexión entre ruinas, símbolos del deseo y monumentos, Benjamin establece una consideración de la historia que aparece como una lectura de los signos de una representación previa, con respecto a la cual la decodificación presente no se hallaría de ningún modo en una relación especular, pero tampoco podría entenderse como de aseguramiento de las huellas o método de desciframiento, sino como lectura de huellas de la memoria y representaciones distorsionadas.

La topografía de la ciudad deja de ser un pasado que se ha

---

11. El despertar se torna un punto central en la constelación de la memoria sólo cuando se entrecruzan de modo explícito escenas literarias (especialmente a partir de la lectura de Proust) con la teoría freudiana del sueño. Sin embargo, Benjamin no dejó de prestar atención de modo evidente a lo nuevo de su *desideratum* de un psicoanálisis del despertar, como se documenta de modo expreso en sus preguntas en carta a Adorno de junio de 1935: "¿No tiene usted presente, por otra parte, un psicoanálisis del despertar en su obra <de Freud> o en la de sus discípulos? ¿O estudios sobre el tema?" (*G.S.*. V.2.1121). En rigor, en *La interpretación de los sueños* aparece una vez el despertar como una constelación *in flagranti*, en la que se podría apresar la "traslación de pensamientos en imágenes" [*Umsetzung von Gedanken in Bilder*] (Freud, 1969: II, 483).

Baudelaire) ninguna mención explícita de esa teoría. Y todavía más esencial que el registro de una lectura de Freud parece ser reconstruir el trabajo benjaminiano en la concepción de la memoria, que ha de servir de base a los textos de los Pasajes de la década del treinta, en la génesis de las figuras de pensamiento y de representación. Pero veamos primero este último aspecto antes de pasar al aseguramiento de huellas.

LOS PASAJES: UNA LECTURA DE LAS HUELLAS DE LA MEMORIA EN EL GRUPO COLECTIVO

Mientras que en los esbozos tempranos para los Pasajes, como he indicado antes, el paradigma de sueño y vigilia no estructura *todavía* la concepción del inconsciente y su representación, describiéndose las casas, en parte, como formaciones de sueños, Benjamin habla, por otra parte, en su *exposé* (surgido en 1935) bajo el título de "París, capital del siglo XIX", sobre el inconsciente del grupo colectivo:[10]

> En el sueño, en el que cada época se adelanta a la siguiente en las imágenes, aparece la última en maridaje con elementos de la prehistoria de la humanidad, es decir: una sociedad sin clases. Sus experiencias, que tienen su repositorio en el *inconsciente del grupo colectivo* [*im Unbewussten des Kollektivs*], procrean, en penetración con lo Nuevo, la Utopía: una Utopía que ha dejado sus *huellas* en miles configuraciones de la vida, desde las instalaciones duraderas hasta las modas efímeras. (*G.S.*, V.1.47) (El destacado es mío.)

---

10. La concepción del inconsciente es también significativa en el artículo "Pequeña historia de la fotografía", de 1931, donde se relaciona lo "inconsciente instintivo" [*Triebhaft-Unbewusstes*] del psicoanálisis con lo "inconsciente óptico" [*Optisch-Unbewusstes*] de la fotografía (*G.S.*, II.1.371), así como en el ensayo sobre la obra de arte (de 1938), que retoma esta reflexión conectándola ahora con el cine (*G.S.*, I.2.500).

a la relación entre memoria [*Gedächtnis*] y recuerdo [*Erinnerung*]. Esta anotación, por lo tanto, puede pertenecer a un estadio previo[9] y puede valer como preludio de la ya mencionada cita central de *Más allá del principio de placer* y la teoría freudiana del "Chock" en el ensayo sobre Baudelaire de 1939, donde Benjamin, además de reflexionar sobre la concepción freudiana de la memoria, lo hace, sobre otros aportes, como los de Bergson, Reik y Proust, a la par que cita a Freud, señalando que su punto de partida estaría en "que 'la conciencia surgiría en el lugar de la huella del recuerdo'"(*G.S.*, I.2.612).

Puesto que Benjamin cita de modo distorsionado el pasaje del ensayo de Freud –transformando "en lugar de" por "en el lugar de"– puede suponerse que, aunque se está refiriendo a los datos editoriales de la tercera edición (Viena, 1923, página 31), la frase fue extraída de propias anotaciones que habría tomado en el momento de una lectura anterior o simplemente más lejana. Mi tesis, por consiguiente, consiste en que entre los primeros esbozos (entre 1927 y 1929), cuando la lectura de Freud era menos consciente y sistemática, y la segunda importante fase de trabajo en el proyecto de los Pasajes (entre 1939 y 1940) habría habido una lectura más intensiva de la obra de Freud. Dicha suposición, que trataré de fundamentar aquí siguiendo de cerca los rastros de esta lectura –por supuesto, en el sentido de un método filológico de búsqueda de indicios– se apoya en primera instancia en la terminología de palabras freudianas utilizada por Benjamin (como "brecha" [*Bahnung*], "inconsciente" [*Unbewusstes*], "represión" [*Verdrängung*], "inervación" [*Innervation*] o "distorsión" [*Entstellung*]), cuya aparición es documentable en los textos benjaminianos del período mencionado sin que medie (como, por ejemplo, en el ensayo sobre

---

9. Esto significa que puede ser datada a partir de la época en que Benjamin retoma su trabajo en el proyecto de los Pasajes (1934) y el comienzo del ensayo sobre Baudelaire, que es una ramificación del proyecto principal (1937). Estas dataciones hacen verificable una lectura consciente y sistemática por parte de Benjamin de la teoría psicoanalítica de la memoria a mediados de los años treinta.

un seminario sobre Freud dado por Paul Häberlein en Berna),[7] como también de los textos freudianos sobre "la doctrina del inconsciente" [*Lehre vom Unbewussten*] en su reseña sobre un silabario infantil (*Frankfurter Zeitung*, 13 de diciembre de 1930) bajo el título de "Chichleuchlauchra" (*G.S.*, III.271) y el estudio sobre el narcisismo[8] en su reseña titulada "Kolonialpädagogik" ["Pedagogía colonial"], que apareció en el mismo diario una semana más tarde (*G.S.*, III.273). Además de los casos mencionados, existen informes sobre la lectura del artículo de Freud "Psicoanálisis y telepatía" (de 1934) según una carta dirigida a Gretel Adorno en 1935 (*G.S.*, II.3.953) y, por último, la nota de homenaje acerca de la "Escuela freudiana" en el ensayo sobre Bachofen, del mismo año (Benjamin, 1979: 28). También en 1935 Benjamin escribe a Adorno que se propone abordar el estudio de Freud (*G.S.*, V.2.1121), como si no fuera consciente de cuánto le deben sus ideas a la teoría freudiana. Esta observación dirigida a Adorno podría tomarse, sin embargo, como una indicación del interés en Freud, cuyo estudio por esta época estaba tomando un carácter más sistemático o estaba aportando rasgos conceptuales para su teoría de la memoria, como aparece sugerido por una variedad de anotaciones en los Pasajes. Así, por ejemplo, en el Block K (*Traumstadt und Traumhaus*: "ciudad de los sueños y casa de sueños") encontramos bajo el encabezamiento de "Para una teoría psicoanalítica del recuerdo" la cita de Reik que ha de reaparecer en la sección sobre teorías de la memoria en "Baudelaire" y en la que Reik reflexiona sobre su lectura de Freud en referencia

---

7. Compárese el texto en *G.S.*, VI.674; y Scholem (1975: 75). Véanse también las sátiras universitarias ("Acta Muriensa") intercambiadas con Scholem después de la común permanencia en Berna (*G.S.*, IV.1.2.442) que contienen indicaciones sobre el estudio del libro de Freud acerca del chiste (aparecido en 1905), con el que Benjamin estuvo en contacto seguramente también más adelante, según lo documenta la anotación en un esquema para los trabajos previos al ensayo sobre Kraus de 1931 (cf. *G.S.*, II.3.1097).

8. Evidentemente se trata aquí del texto de Freud titulado exactamente "Introducción del narcisismo" de 1914.

de Freud), que Ginzburg junto con los *indicios* (*indici*; en el caso de Sherlock Holmes) y las marcas pictóricas (*segni pittorici*; en el caso de Morelli) subsume en la categoría de *huellas* (*tracce*; Ginzburg, 1986: 165), deben distinguirse dentro del sistema freudiano frente a este nuevo uso. En efecto, los síntomas para Freud'eran entendidos como signo de un retorno de lo reprimido y, de tal modo, definidos como resultados de una reelaboración psíquica, que estructuralmente era pensada como análoga a la distorsión durante el trabajo onírico. Esto significa que los síntomas en Freud remiten a un pasado, que ha dejado sus huellas en el inconsciente, y estas huellas se vuelven legibles sólo en forma de síntomas –signos de una representación distorsionada en lo visible–, y, por lo tanto, funcionan como símbolos del recuerdo.

En relación con el desciframiento de diferentes huellas del pasado, residuos, ruinas, fragmentos, testimonios, etcétera, lo importante va a ser si ellas podrán ser interpretadas en el sentido de un aseguramiento de las huellas en el contexto del paradigma de evidencias o, por el contrario, como símbolos visibles del recuerdo en el esquema psicoanalíticamente reformulado de las huellas de la memoria, es decir: como sustituto visible de huellas duraderas ilegibles.

Benjamin puede colocarse, por cierto, en un claro plano de afinidad con Freud en su elaboración de una teoría de la memoria. Su atención por correspondencias topográficas y por el significado de los puntos de pasaje se concentra en figuras de pensamiento que pueden ser consideradas condiciones previas para la aceptación de la topografía freudiana de la memoria. Por otro lado, sin embargo, resulta más difícil reconstruir con exactitud el modo en que Benjamin leyó a Freud, dado que raramente hay indicaciones explícitas a su obra ni se informa particularmente sobre su lectura, y mucho menos en los casos donde los rastros de las figuras de pensamiento freudianas están obrando marcadamente en Benjamin.

Así, por ejemplo, existen indicaciones sobre una lectura de Freud en la época estudiantil (en 1918 Benjamin había asistido a

tiempo que supone que esta escritura se corresponde con la forma de una representación distorsionada.

3. Este último sería el tercer momento donde la *distorsión* es la característica para la estructura del inconsciente en Freud, también significativo para otros fenómenos como el sueño y para otros lenguajes del inconsciente. Así, por ejemplo, cuando Freud comprende el síntoma histérico o corpóreo como símbolo del recuerdo, es decir como huella corpórea de la memoria, que no puede ser interpretada como "engrama" [*Engramm*] o copia.

En el plano semiótico estas tres características son las que determinan la concepción freudiana de la memoria: la figuración "en el lugar de" en la relación de conciencia y huellas duraderas, la legibilidad asociada con el destello [*Aufleuchten*] y el fenómeno de la representación distorsionada en el signo visible o legible de las huellas de la memoria. Estas características son también las que diferencian su concepción de las huellas de aquella del paradigma de los indicios, cuya historia ha seguido Carlo Ginzburg bajo el lema de "aseguramiento de las huellas". En la prehistoria y surgimiento del psicoanálisis freudiano se encuentran realmente, por cierto, aquellas formas de desciframiento de claves, huellas y síntomas a nivel criminal y médico, que Ginzburg ha colocado con los ejemplos del método Morelli (para la identificación de la autoría de cuadros)[6] en un amplio marco donde figuran la detección, los estudios fisonómicos, la grafología y las marcas digitales, caracterizando así un paradigma de indicios para el aseguramiento de las huellas: "un modelo que hemos llamado en cada caso, según el contexto, adivinatorio, conjetural y semiótico" (Ginzburg: 1986: 184).

Sin embargo, justamente en el hecho de que en los ejemplos de Ginzburg se trate siempre de métodos de proporcionamiento de la identidad aparece fundamentada la diferencia de la teoría freudiana con este paradigma. Los *síntomas* (*sintomi*; en el caso

---

6. Para la lectura freudiana del método Morelli, véase especialmente "El Moisés de Miguel Ángel" (Freud, 1969: X, 195-220); y también Weigel (1994b).

huellas duraderas [*Dauerspuren*] y de estímulos que han dejado allí su marca [*aufgezeichnete Erregungen*], mientras que el sistema percepción-conciencia estaría siempre dispuesto a absorciones de nuevos estímulos [*Reize*] o percepciones [*Wahrnehmungen*], al mismo tiempo que se encargaría de la protección contra determinadas excitaciones [*Reizschutz*].

2. Esta característica se manifiesta también esencialmente por una *relación* de los dos sistemas, que puede ser llamada dialéctica, en tanto "la conciencia surgiría en el lugar de la huella del recuerdo"[5] (Freud, 1969: III, 235), teniendo en esta frase la palabra "*Stelle*" tanto valor de sustantivo ("el lugar") como de frase prepositiva ("en lugar de"). En este último sentido, la conciencia lanza luz y se extingue en el momento en que, a causa de la puesta en funciones del sistema percepción-conciencia (que se origina de modo discontinuo), surge una conexión entre la huella duradera y la percepción. Sin embargo, si "las huellas duraderas" aparecen caracterizadas "como base de la memoria" y su legibilidad se asocia con ciertas condiciones, Freud, al mismo tiempo, define aquí estas huellas de la memoria como escritura –que, con todo, nunca es escritura propiamente dicha y, aunque lo fuera, ni siquiera sería completamente legible–. En este sentido, su *legibilidad* se ve estructurada por la dialéctica entre la conciencia y las huellas del recuerdo, siendo definida como destello instantáneo (o visibilidad momentánea).

Para considerar el aspecto de la *descifrabilidad* de esta escritura, habría que recurrir a otros textos de Freud, por ejemplo a su *Interpretación de los sueños* (1900),* donde "considerando las condiciones de representabilidad" [*mit Rücksicht auf Darstellbarkeit*] su autor analiza los modos de representación del sueño como escritura en imágenes [*Bilderschrift*], al mismo

---

5. En alemán: "*Bewusstsein entstehe an Stelle der Erinnerungsspur*". [N. del T.]

* La autora, como la mayoría de los estudiosos, da aquí la fecha de 1900, aunque –como es sabido– Freud publicó la obra a fines de 1899; pero no queriendo adscribirla espiritualmente al siglo xix, la hizo figurar premonitoriamente como del inicio del siglo xx. [N. del T.]

hecho con los nombres de las calles, elevándolo a la esfera del lenguaje, tomándolo de la red de calles para pasar a la (x)[4] la designación (x) dentro de la lengua. (Primeras anotaciones para "La obra de los Pasajes", f.13 y f.19; *G.S.*, V.2.1007)

El hecho de prestar semejante atención a la esfera del lenguaje anuncia ya una perspectiva que se va a dar en las siguientes investigaciones benjaminianas. Pues es llamativo, por supuesto, que en esta fase de la labor en el proyecto de los Pasajes, Benjamin todavía no utilice el concepto y la apoyatura del inconsciente, sino que se refiera a la relación de sueño y vigilia (o de sueño y conciencia) transportándola a un dominio espacial. Al hacerlo, con todo, Benjamin se refiere explícitamente también a la teoría psicoanalítica, poniendo el acento sobre la idea de la "condición fluctuante de una conciencia siempre dividida de modo múltiple entre la vigilia y el sueño" (Primeras anotaciones para "La obra de los Pasajes", Gº,27; *G.S.*, V.2.1012), una concepción que intenta trasladar del individuo al grupo colectivo. Cuando uno compara, por lo tanto, el escenario topográfico del acto de recordar –que Benjamin descubre en la metrópolis de la Modernidad– con la concepción freudiana, se pueden notar, ya al final de la década del veinte, tanto puntos de contacto como divergencias.

LECTURA *VS.* ASEGURAMIENTO DE HUELLAS

Varias características relevantes que aparecen en el patrón topográfico de la memoria en Freud, según ha sido definido en *Más allá del principio de placer* (1920) y en "Notas sobre la 'pizarra mágica'" (1925), merecen cierta consideración para nuestro análisis:
1. La *diferenciación* de los dos sistemas del aparato psíquico que son entre sí incompatibles en su funcionamiento, de los cuales el del inconsciente serviría para absorber ilimitadamente

---

4. El signo (x) indica una palabra que se ha dejado sin transcribir porque en el manuscrito era ilegible.

apunta al concepto de "correspondencias" que va a desarrollar luego, y que aquí señala los nexos entre mito y ciudad, por un lado, y la relación entre sueño y vigilia, por otro:

> En la antigua Grecia se indicaban lugares, en los que se podía bajar al territorio infernal. También nuestra existencia en la vigilia es un ámbito en el que, en sitios escondidos, se desciende a los subsuelos del mundo, con zonas completamente imperceptibles donde confluyen los sueños. Durante el día pasamos junto a ellos sin darnos cuenta, pero apenas llega el sueño, enseguida los buscamos tanteando con mano presta para perdernos en sus oscuros corredores. El laberinto de casas de la ciudad se parece a la conciencia durante la claridad diurna; los pasajes (esas son las galerías que conducen a su existencia pasada <de la ciudad>) desembocan durante el día en las calles sin que nadie lo note. Por la noche, bajo la oscura masa de los edificios, sin embargo, su oscuridad más compacta arroja su perfil aterrorizante; y quien se aventura por allí tardíamente [*der späte Passant*] apura su paso, salvo que lo hayamos incitado a seguir su viaje por la callejuela estrecha. ("La obra de los Pasajes"- "Esbozos tempranos", aº, 4; *G.S.*, V.2.1046)

Cuando se trata, entonces, de lugares [*Stellen*] donde los sueños desembocan en la existencia de la vigilia o los pasajes llevan a las calles, allí Benjamin hace ya hincapié sobre la idea de ubicación −como lo hará sobre los sitios de los hallazgos en la ya mencionada imagen arqueológica de la "Crónica de Berlín"−, pero no sobre el lugar exacto del encuentro (o de la búsqueda), sino sobre el punto preciso del pasaje: el umbral que marca el acceso al pasado. En otra anotación caracteriza así casas y laberintos de edificios como una formación onírica [*Traumgebilde*], es decir, como sueños antiguos que se han tornado piedra y han logrado configuración, y que han entrado en el lenguaje por los nombres de las calles:

> La apariencia más oculta de las grandes ciudades: ese objeto histórico de la metrópolis con sus calles uniformes e hileras de casas interminables posee la arquitectura soñada por los antiguos: el laberinto hecho realidad. [...] Lo que la metrópolis de la época moderna ha hecho de la antigua concepción del laberinto. Lo ha

ejemplar del acto de recordar" (*G.S.*, V.2.1057)– abre el acceso a otro tipo de saber sobre el pasado: hacia un "conocimiento todavía no sabido de 'lo que ha sido'" (*G.S.*, V.2.1014) o hacia una configuración onírica del pasado que ha dejado sus marcas en el presente (aunque Benjamin todavía en este estadio no utiliza el concepto de "huella"):

> Existe una experiencia singular de la dialéctica. La experiencia compulsiva y drástica que contradice todo lo que sea "la gradualidad" del devenir [*Allgemach des Werdens*] y que revela todo aparente "desarrollo" como una transformación dialéctica eminentemente artificiosa es el despertar de un sueño [...] Y así presentamos el método nuevo, dialéctico de la historia: ¡atravesar "lo que ha sido" con la intensidad de un sueño, para vivenciar el presente como el mundo de la vigilia al que se refiere el sueño! (Y cada sueño se refiere a ese mundo de la vigilia. *Todo* lo anterior debe ser penetrado históricamente.) (*G.S.*, V.2.1006)

En estas afirmaciones no sólo se da una oposición a concepciones lineales del tiempo y a modelos de desarrollo histórico, sino que se le niega entidad temporal de modo absoluto a la relación entre "lo que ha sido" y el presente, para reflexionar, en su lugar, sobre la conexión entre sueño y "mundo de la vigilia" [*Wachwelt*] –que logra su representación en la topografía de la ciudad–, otorgándoles a ambos, finalmente, un estatuto espacial. En este proceso, sin embargo, la topografía de la ciudad no sirve para la *representabilidad* [*Darstellbarkeit*] del mundo del sueño y de la vigilia, así como, por ejemplo, la utiliza Freud, al presentar su "Notas sobre la pizarra mágica" como alegoría para la representación del intercambio de dos sistemas del aparato psíquico diferentes: Percepción-Conciencia (*Wahrnehmung-Bewusstsein;* en abreviatura: *W-Bw*), por un lado, e Inconsciente (*Unbewusstes;* en abreviatura: *Ubw*), por otro. Benjamin compara más bien determinados fenómenos, figuras y sitios en la topografía real de la ciudad con el sueño y la conciencia, *redescubriendo* también la relación entre estos territorios de manera material en esa topografía. Ello significa un método de observación que

serie de glosas berlinesas en "forma suelta y subjetiva" (*G.S.*, VI.476), había estado precedida por los primeros esbozos y anotaciones para el proyecto de los Pasajes, en los que las galerías parisienses habrían de aparecer como paradigmas de "un pasado hecho espacio" [*raumgewordene Vergangenheit*] ("Esbozos tempranos"; *G.S.*, V.2.1041). En tanto la topografía y la arquitectura de la ciudad se considera como "espacio de la memoria colectiva" [*Gedächtnisraum des Kollektivs*], aparece allí ya una topografía de la memoria materializada, en la que la parte externa –la ciudad moderna– entra en contacto con el modo representativo de la topografía de la memoria en el psicoanálisis: un modo de observación que, sin embargo, sólo consigue una configuración diferenciada gracias al pasaje por el desvío de las imágenes del recuerdo de la infancia berlinesa y otros trabajos que van desde fines de la década del veinte a comienzos de la década siguiente. En las páginas que siguen, entonces, el tema principal será reconstruir esta elaboración del patrón de memoria benjaminiano.

PARA UNA TOPOGRAFÍA DEL SUEÑO Y LA VIGILIA

En los esbozos tempranos para los Pasajes Benjamin trabaja utilizando un modo de observación dialéctica, que él mismo caracteriza como "giro copernicano en la consideración histórica"[2] (*G.S.*, V.2.1057),[3] a la par que descubre su relación entre el sueño y el inconsciente en la constelación del despertar: en el umbral, entonces, entre el sueño y la vigilia. El giro en esta consideración histórica de la que habla Benjamin debe comprenderse de tal modo que el despertar –que aparece como "el caso

2. En alemán: "*kopernikanische Wende in der geschichtlichen Anschauung*". [N. del T.]
3. Compárese la situación freudiana de su "innovación científica" como "tercera perturbación del egoísmo humano", después de la cosmológica debida al descubrimiento de Copérnico y la biológica causada por la teoría de la descendencia, en Freud: "Sobre la historia del movimiento psicoanalítico" (1914), en *Gesammelte Werke*, X, 43-113. Véase al respecto: Weber (1978: 223 y sigs.).

el movimiento de la búsqueda lleva a su descubrimiento, en la continuación del pasaje Benjamin relativiza inmediatamente su valor:

> [...] y se engaña a sí mismo en lo mejor, quien documenta sólo el inventario de los hallazgos y no también la oscura suerte del lugar exacto del encuentro. La búsqueda inútil tiene tanta importancia como la exitosa y, por ello, el recuerdo no debe proceder contando, ni mucho menos informando, sino, en sentido estricto, como en el modo épico y rapsódico: hincando su pala siempre en otros lugares, investigando siempre en capas más profundas en comparación con las viejas. (*G.S.*, VI.486-487)

Bajo la idea de memoria como escenario este intento de representación nos lleva, a partir de una estructura narrativa –la vuelta repetida hacia el comienzo–, pasando por los movimientos de la excavación que persiguen piezas individuales muy significativas, finalmente hacia un catálogo de los lugares de los hallazgos o también de la búsqueda vana, que –en tanto se la diferencia del *inventario* de lo rescatado– aparece como si fuera otra documentación por escrito, desde la que el movimiento de la búsqueda ahora también se describe como otra repetición, pero efectuada siempre en otros lugares y en capas más profundas. Así en esta representación del escenario de la memoria –que es una imagen de pensamiento por excelencia– se produce la doble exposición de una alegoría arqueológica, cuya capacidad para la imagen se asocia con un patrón en estratos, con un modelo escriturario, según lo había caracterizado Freud en su concepción topográfica de la memoria, donde ella aparecía como "otro escenario" [*ein anderer Schauplatz*].

"Crónica de Berlín", como esbozo previo para lo que sería después *Una infancia en Berlín hacia 1900* (desde 1933 en adelante), es ese texto de Benjamin en el que su autor, probando diferentes alegorías para la representación (junto a la excavación, por ejemplo, también la idea del árbol genealógico y el laberinto), ha trabajado de manera más intensa sobre *su* patrón representativo del recuerdo. Esta intención, que se remonta a un pedido para una

anotaciones e imágenes de pensamiento de la "Crónica de Berlín" (1932), que se hallan apoyadas teóricamente en una reformulación psicoanalítica de la teoría del lenguaje benjaminiana en los dos pequeños artículos de 1933 ("Sobre la capacidad mimética" y "La enseñanza de lo semejante"), donde se fundamenta la categoría de la "similitud no sensorial".

Al registro de la arqueología, por otro lado, se refiere la imaginería de esos párrafos sobre la memoria en la "Crónica de Berlín", donde Benjamin pone el acento sobre la relevancia del lugar preciso del encuentro con las cosas y que puede ser significativo para la legibilidad así como para la relación entre las huellas y los residuos. La "postura de los recuerdos auténticos" [*Haltung echter Erinnerungen*] se describe en este contexto en la imagen de la excavación como actividad arqueológica, mientras que lo que interesa no es tanto lo que se encuentra cuanto más bien los caminos que llevan a la búsqueda. En tanto se considera que los recuerdos no deben espantarse "de volver una y otra vez a la misma situación",[1] se le adscribe a la actividad del recordar la figura de una repetición, que, por cierto, con la denominación *de lo mismo* no ha descubierto todavía su objeto, sino sólo el punto de partida de su movimiento:

> Pues las situaciones objetivas son simplemente estratos, capas, que sólo después del rastreo más riguroso proporcionan lo que hace a los verdaderos valores que están ocultos en el interior de la tierra: las imágenes que, desprendidas de sus anteriores relaciones, se levantan como objetos preciosos en los sobrios aposentos de nuestra tardía comprensión: así como despojos o torsos en la galería del coleccionista. ("Crónica de Berlín"; *G.S.*, IV.486)

Si aquí se califica, en una comparación con los objetos preciosos o piezas de coleccionista, esas imágenes desprendidas de anteriores relaciones como si fueran los objetos deseados o de culto del recuerdo —es decir: como residuos significativos—, que

---

1. En alemán: "*immer wieder auf ein und denselben Sachverhalt zurückzukommen*". [N. del T.]

acerca de los Pasajes (1927-1929) para volver a aparecer en el momento en que Benjamin retoma su proyecto a partir de 1934. Se podría decir, entonces, que esos escritos, que Benjamin mismo ha considerado su "fisonomía más joven", iniciándola con *Dirección única* (Benjamin, 1978: 416), a continuación del cierre de su "ciclo productivo sobre literatura de habla alemana" y también después de esa cesura que calificó de "momento revolucionario de su pensamiento" [*Umwälzung seines Denkens*], son textos que hallándose bajo el signo de la Modernidad y conectados en mayor o menor medida con el proyecto de los Pasajes, se relacionan con problemas de la memoria de modo casi exclusivo.

Numerosos textos en torno de los Pasajes contienen reflexiones o imágenes de pensamiento simples sobre el complejo del recuerdo y la memoria que deben ser así considerados categorías con las que se verifican diferentes modelos y posibilidades de representación. En este proceso, Benjamin recurre a variados registros –a ideas tomadas, por ejemplo, de la arqueología, de la óptica y, sobre todo, de representaciones topográficas– para hacer manifiesta esa postura del sujeto frente a los rastros e imágenes de la historia, que en la génesis de sus reflexiones teóricas se perfila de modo cada vez más nítido en el sentido de un patrón de lectura específica. Dicha lectura de rastros e imágenes de la historia se sitúa en el escenario de una memoria colectiva e individual (que se considera análoga a una estructura) y se comprende como una actividad orientada al conocimiento que se ubica en el umbral entre la postura receptiva y la acción, entre la revelación y la historiografía, entre los sueños y la reflexión filosófica.

En este movimiento se muestra un claro cambio de paradigmas desde el primer estadio de los Pasajes, que lleva la marca de un patrón de memoria espacialmente topográfico, hasta una concepción escripto-topográfica de la memoria con impronta psicoanalítica, que es lo que estructura las anotaciones sobre los Pasajes durante los años '30. Como sitio de la escritura donde se documenta de modo fehaciente este cambio pueden citarse las

8. De la topografía a la escritura
El concepto benjaminiano de la memoria

**EL ESCENARIO DE LA MEMORIA
ENTRE ARQUEOLOGÍA Y ESCRITURA**

Cuando Benjamin en su último texto completo ("Sobre el concepto de historia") describe mediante imágenes de pensamiento la historiografía y el recuerdo como actividades análogas a estructuras, y las imágenes de "lo que ha sido" como imágenes del recuerdo, entonces se puede notar que se trata de una ocupación de larga data con la memoria [*Gedächtnis*] y el recuerdo [*Erinnerung*], en cuyo decurso el concepto de imagen (o su cognoscibilidad y legibilidad) se funde con una teoría de la memoria. El texto "Sobre algunos temas en Baudelaire" de 1939 –especialmente los Apartados I a IV, que son el lugar en los escritos benjaminianos en que se discuten de modo explícito diferentes modelos de memoria, y en concreto en el Apartado III, donde Benjamin polemiza con el concepto freudiano de impacto [*Chock*]*– marca de modo claro el carácter de una discusión *teórica* acerca de la memoria, sin embargo los rastros de su labor en una concepción de la memoria se remontan muy atrás, concentrándose especialmente en la primera fase de trabajo

---

* Freud y también Benjamin se dejan llevar por su cultura francesa y escriben "*chock*", como sinónimo de lo que luego se habría de internacionalizar con el término tamizado por la grafía inglesa en la palabra "*shock*". [N. del T.]

Tercera parte

La memoria y la escritura

"Imágenes que nunca vimos
hasta que las recordamos."

"Lo pasado, el ya no ser,
trabaja apasionadamente en las cosas."

Los pasajes de París son, por ello, *el* lugar paradigmático, porque allí se entrecruzan la escritura de la ciudad (su arquitectura y topografía) con las experiencias del sujeto del modo más heterogéneo y rico en sentidos: se trata de "ritos de pasaje", espacios oníricos, umbrales y lugares de transición. En este momento de la obra benjaminiana, así como en numerosos textos de otros autores, lo que domina son los esquemas topográficos de la escritura en imágenes de la Modernidad. En los pasajes vuelven una y otra vez las pautas topográficas desde los mitos, que pueden ser entendidos casi como una escritura en imágenes pre-alegórica. En tanto las estructuras topográficas provocan en un texto el movimiento de inclusión y exclusión, abren también a "lo otro" del sujeto un "espacio del cuerpo y de la imagen" en la escritura, presentándose como especialmente adecuadas para transformar "el otro discurso" en un "discurso del otro". En este proceso, sin embargo, se disuelve la alegoría de la Modernidad como en una escritura, que abriera su espacio a las estructuras del inconsciente. La huella de recuerdos en la distancia entre imagen (o texto) y significado, que caracterizaba el "otro discurso" de la alegoría clásica, representa una huella escondida, que Benjamin tenía en su mira con el carácter escriturario de la alegoría en el momento en que escribía su libro sobre el drama barroco. Esa huella avanza hasta ocupar el primer plano de la escritura en la Modernidad como "discurso del o/Otro", como lenguaje del inconsciente, que es descifrado en la historia primitiva de la Modernidad llevada a cabo por Benjamin como la escritura onírica del grupo humano colectivo.

"consideración por las condiciones de representabilidad" [*Rücksicht auf Darstellbarkeit*]); es decir, todos ellos conllevan una representación distorsionada. La distorsión es, sin embargo, uno de los conceptos psicoanalíticos a los que Benjamin se adhiere en sus trabajos sobre la Modernidad de manera directamente explícita: en primer lugar en su ensayo sobre Kafka, donde califica sus gestos y personajes como distorsionados, poniéndolos en relación con "lo olvidado" (*G.S.*, II.2.431 y sigs.), y más adelante en "Central-park", donde habla de una "distorsión hacia lo alegórico" [*Entstellung ins Allegorische*]:

> La engañosa transfiguración del mundo de la mercancía se contrapone a su distorsión en lo alegórico. La mercancía busca mirarse al rostro a sí misma. Su devenir persona es celebrado en la prostituta. ("Central-park", <20>; *G.S.*, I.2.671)

Del mismo modo en que en los textos de Freud se instauran las alegorías de segundo grado, también en Benjamin la alegoría de la Modernidad es una alegoría de segundo grado: alegoría y, al mismo tiempo, dispersión de la idea y de la representación de lo alegórico (alegoría de la estructura imaginaria que tiende un puente sobre el abismo que separa la imagen del significado). En tanto la destrucción de las relaciones orgánicas (o la desvalorización del "mundo de las cosas" [*Dingwelt*]) a través de la mercancía recuerda, por ejemplo, a la intención alegórica, así también su Aura, su apariencia de naturalidad se disuelve bajo la mirada del autor de la alegoría. Las personificaciones alegóricas también tienen sus sucesoras en esa historia primitiva de la Modernidad erigida por Benjamin en la figura de la prostituta tomada de las obras de Baudelaire, aunque no ya como corporeizaciones de una idea, sino como "la mercancía que más eficazmente cumple con la percepción alegórica", en cuyo cumplimiento se emplaza la disolución del halo alegórico, según lo aclara el propio Benjamin en una carta a Horkheimer de 1938 (Benjamin, 1978: 752).

Esta lectura sólo es posible gracias a un texto que decodifica la experiencia de la metrópolis moderna como escritura alegórica.

desconcertante"("La enseñanza de lo semejante"; *G.S.*, II.1.208-209). Ahora bien, no sólo la citada imagen como jeroglífico (cf.: *ein ägyptisches Traumbuch*) remite a las representaciones del inconsciente en el psicoanálisis, sino que todas las reflexiones benjaminianas se apoyan sobre una afinidad existente entre la alegoría y la concepción del inconsciente freudiano.

Freud se sirve con frecuencia justamente de los procedimientos alegóricos para representar los procesos del aparato psíquico, y tanto más cuanto que refuta la idea de localizar los procesos psíquicos en el cuerpo, para considerar el cuerpo como un "escenario" (*Schauplatz*) en el que se manifiestan las perturbaciones psíquicas (Starobinski, 1983). Freud debate así las funciones y estructuras de los procesos primarios como descripciones alegóricas, pero reflexionando al mismo tiempo sobre los modos de representación que ellos implican. Ya sea que la manera de funcionar de la memoria se represente según el modelo de una "pizarra mágica" [*Wunderblock*], ya sea que el lenguaje de los sueños sea analizado como escritura en imágenes y que se compare con enigmas figurativos o jeroglíficos, o ya sea que se eche mano a un esquema topológico para diferenciar los sistemas del aparato psíquico, o que el inconsciente aparezca como el escenario de la escritura, en todos los casos las descripciones freudianas de las estructuras del inconsciente se sirven de representaciones alegóricas. Y puesto que Freud no sólo *representa* alegóricamente las estructuras del inconsciente, sino que en su análisis de las articulaciones del inconsciente lee las producciones de imágenes del sujeto igualmente como alegorías –como si se tratara del "otro discurso", es decir: como otra representación, cuyo pensamiento propio, el así llamado pensamiento onírico [*Traumgedanke*] queda sin caracterizar–, Freud, en definitiva, hace sus lecturas como traducciones sin un original y, por lo tanto, *sus* propios textos son como alegorías *de segundo grado*.

Según Freud, entonces, lo normativo de la traducción entre el texto onírico manifiesto y latente no puede reconstruirse como un código, sino sólo describirse en sus modos de elaboración ("condensación" [*Verdichtung*], "desplazamiento" [*Verschiebung*],

LA ALEGORÍA MODERNA Y LA ESTRUCTURA DEL INCONSCIENTE

Las alegorías de la Modernidad colaboran justamente, por un lado, para salvar el carácter escriturario del lenguaje, mientras que, por otro lado, dejan abandonado al sujeto en la mayor inseguridad, y de modo radical, en cuanto a la relación entre texto (o imagen) y significado. Las huellas de una prehistoria de esta alegoría de la Modernidad se encuentran siempre allí, donde una *lectura* alegórica –no una exégesis erudita y ordenada tipológicamente o regulada de modo lógico-sistemático– permite que las imágenes o los textos se vuelvan escritura, una escritura de la que el sujeto se haga responsable. Esto significa que la alegoría de la Modernidad se constituye mediante la práctica de la lectura y la contemplación de textos e imágenes *como escritura*. En este sentido Benjamin habla de "imágenes leídas" y de un "instante crítico y peligroso que se halla en la base de toda lectura" (Anotaciones y materiales para "La obra de los Pasajes", Block N3,1; *G.S.*, V.1.578). El método alegórico que Benjamin ha diseñado para su proyecto de los Pasajes y que tiene evidentes puntos de contacto con el patrón de la "imagen dialéctica" y con la concepción teórica del "ahora de la cognoscibilidad" –es decir, con el segundo estadio de la teoría alegórica benjaminiana que surgió en el contexto de sus trabajos sobre la Modernidad–, se fundamenta, además, en una relectura psicoanalítica del carácter escriturario de la alegoría.

Así puede decirse que la mirada del autor de la alegoría en Benjamin es la que hace transformar las cosas en escritura, en tanto lee "el libro de lo acaecido" [*Buch des Geschehenen*] (*G.S.*, V.1.580), como si leyera el "libro egipcio de los sueños de alguien que no duerme" [*ägyptisches Traumbuch des Wachenden*] (*G.S.*, III.198). En el momento del desciframiento de las "imágenes desconcertantes" en la Modernidad, por el contrario, se define la relación de esa imagen con el texto literal de modo análogo a lo que sucede en el proceso alegórico: el texto literal como "el fondo en el que sólo y únicamente puede formarse la imagen

su *index* histórico? (Anotaciones y materiales para "La obra de los Pasajes", Block J24,1 y J24, 2; *G.S.*, V.1.347-348)

Sin embargo, esta huella de los recuerdos va siendo constantemente ocultada y recubierta en el procedimiento alegórico por un establecimiento de *translatio*, al mismo tiempo que la alegoría en su tendencia a lo esquemático adopta siempre la forma de un saber fijado:

> En su mano <en la mano del autor de la alegoría> la cosa se vuelve algo diferente, por ese proceso él establece un diálogo con ese algo diferente, mientras lo diferente deviene así una clave para el ámbito de un saber oculto que su autor reverencia como su emblema. Esto determina el carácter escriturario de la alegoría. <La alegoría> es un esquema y como esquema es objeto del saber, pero será imperdible sólo hasta que ese esquema se fije: una imagen fijada y un signo que fija, todo en uno. (*G.S.*, I.1.359)

Y si el autor de la alegoría y su actividad de creador de alegorías juegan un papel tan importante en la investigación de Benjamin –y no, en cambio, el esquema y la clave de la *translatio*–, y con ello el sujeto pasa a ocupar el lugar dominante en lugar de la autoridad que interpreta, es decir, en lugar de una instancia establecida que da las normas en las relaciones alegóricas, en este giro se anuncia ese aspecto de la escritura alegórica de la Modernidad,[13] donde el sujeto se halla completamente situado en "el abismo entre el ser y el significar de la imagen" (*G.S.*, I.1.342).[14]

---

13. Cf. para este aspecto Menke (1991: 180).
14. Heinz Schlaffer remite a la visión moderna que Benjamin habría llevado a su libro sobre el drama barroco, pero estableciendo los límites de validez de ese ensayo (Schlaffer, 1989: 186-190). Se podría argumentar, a la inversa –apoyándose históricamente en los trabajos de Foucault–, que Benjamin con la ayuda de la luz arrojada por su concepto de "*Jetztzeit*" ha descubierto aspectos en el drama barroco que prenuncian la Modernidad.

pensamiento debía recorrerla "en un zigzag infinito, desde lo similar a lo semejante a eso mismo" (Foucault, 1966: 45). Es justamente esta distancia, en mi opinión, la que circunscribe el territorio del "otro", un territorio que, al mismo tiempo, sirve de base para la constitución del "otro discurso": tanto como discurso regulativo sobre "lo otro" como discurso del "otro", que está cuestionando esa regulación.

Cuando Benjamin en su libro sobre el drama barroco hace semejante hincapié en el *carácter escriturario de la alegoría*, se ve claramente cómo está utilizando su procedimiento de una "crítica salvadora". Según Benjamin, entonces, la mirada alegórica transforma "las cosas y las obras en una escritura estimulante"[12] (*G.S.*, I.1.352). En una constelación histórica, donde la "*écriture*" (en sentido foucaultiano) sea reprimida a causa del dominio generalizado de los signos representativos, ella vendrá a dar y se salvará en la alegoría literaria (por "el carácter de escritura de lo alegórico" [*Schriftcharakter der Allegorie*] (*G.S.*, I.1.359). Así la alegoría proveía una huella mnemónica para la similitud perdida, una huella para esa literatura que Foucault ha asociado con una especie de contra-discurso (o discurso de un recuerdo) y de resurgimiento de esa similitud a partir de la Modernidad. La alegoría sería, por ello, un campo en la escritura, en el que –bajo el signo de la representación– se podría ver una huella mnemónica del sistema lingüístico ternario y del espacio abierto entre imagen (o texto) y significado, es decir: para ese espacio reprimido que retorna en la literatura de la Modernidad y que, entonces, no pocas veces es percibido como abismal, según lo que el mismo Benjamin anota en sus hojas sueltas para los Pasajes:

> El sentido "abismal" debe ser definido como "significado". Siempre será alegórico./ El abismo baudelairano es [...] un abismo secularizado: el abismo del saber y de las significaciones. ¿Qué es lo que constituye

---

12. En alemán: "*die Dinge und Werke in erregende Schrift*". [N. del T.]

como "abismo entre el ser y el significar de la imagen"[10] (*G.S.*, I.1.342), entonces se da por sentado, por una parte, que este abismo implica la pérdida de un sistema unívoco y de validez universal. Por otro lado, se inmiscuye así en el aspecto de la historia sémiótica* ese proceso que Foucault ha descrito como la pérdida de la similitud en el momento del fin del Renacimiento que él ha denominado "Edad Clásica" [*âge classique*]: como pasaje de un sistema sígnico más complejo y ternario a uno binario, es decir, a un sistema de un signo representativo que es definido como "unión entre un significante y un significado" (Foucault, 1966: 57).[11]

El sistema sígnico ternario como sistema unitario y triple había implicado antes "tres elementos perfectamente distintos: lo que estaba marcado, eso que se estaba marcando, y lo que permitía ver en esto la marca de aquello" (Foucault, 1966: 78). Como experiencia del lenguaje, Foucault entiende la disolución de estos tres elementos contenidos en una figura en: (1) "el ser bruto y primitivo, bajo la forma simple, material de la escritura, un estigma sobre las cosas"; en (2) "por encima de ésta, el comentario, que retoma los signos dados con una nueva intención"; y en (3) "por debajo, el texto del cual el comentario supone la primacía oculta debajo de las marcas visibles a todos. De aquí, tres niveles del lenguaje, a partir del ser único de la escritura" (Foucault, 1966: 57). Y es justamente, según Foucault, este tipo de *escritura* la que pierde su papel dominante con el comienzo de la "Edad Clásica" (en el siglo xvii).

Bajo el dominio de la similitud y de la escritura se había mantenido abierta, por lo tanto, una distancia entre el significante y el significado, de modo que, como Foucault formulaba, el

---

10. En alemán: "*Abgrund zwischen bildlichem Sein und Bedeuten*". [N. del T.]

* La presencia de esta palabra tan moderna para traducir el término "*Zeichen*" encuentra su apoyo en el hecho de que el mismo Benjamin ya había utilizado (en 1925) la entonces inusual denominación de "*semiotisch*" (semiótico) en su libro sobre el drama barroco (cf. *G.S.*, I.1.342). [N. del T.]

11. Este punto aparece tratado en detalle en el capítulo 3 del presente estudio.

a través de la glosa de la percepción figurativa de cualquier tipo en la experiencia y la cotidianidad de los individuos. Por este motivo, la alegoría desempeña un papel importante en la tradición de la memoria cultural, pero no sólo en esa línea de la tradición que ha señalado Frances A. Yates, al analizar las asociaciones específicas entre la categoría de *ars memoriae* y las pinturas alegóricas del Renacimiento (Yates, 1966: 91 y sigs.). Más bien se produce el caso contrario, cuando las imágenes y los esquemas alegóricos representan un repertorio de *topoi* establecidos, estructurados por el recuerdo y la experiencia, entonces se transforman en pilares del archivo de la memoria cultural:

> <La alegoría> es un esquema y como esquema es objeto del saber, pero será imperdible sólo hasta que ese esquema se fije: una imagen fijada y un signo que fija, todo en uno.[8] (*G.S.*, I.1.359)

De este modo, también el hecho de que la imagen de la mujer y los cuerpos femeninos lleguen a ser material privilegiado de la personificación alegórica, hasta tal punto que hayan desaparecido las figuras míticas del repertorio de las personificaciones, ejerce una influencia sobre la construcción simbólica del "otro sexo". En la personificación alegórica convergen la fijación del "otro discurso" y la consolidación de la idea de "otro sexo".[9]

Sin embargo, a partir del hecho de que tales fijaciones no poseen validez eterna y de que la distancia entre texto y significado no puede ser asegurada de modo duradero por un sistema de conocimiento coherente, sino que ese saber puede llegar a ser cuestionable, renace constantemente la actividad de la alegorización. Así, por ejemplo, cuando Benjamin en su libro sobre el drama barroco define el lugar de la inmersión alegórica

---

8. En alemán: "*Ein Schema ist sie, als dieses Schema Gegenstand des Wissens, ihm unverlierbar erst als ein fixiertes: fixiertes Bild und fixierendes Zeichen in einem*". [N. del T.]

9. Cf. el excurso sobre la forma femenina de la alegoría en Weigel (1990, 167 y sigs).

mandamiento que ordenaba destruir lo orgánico para recoger en sus trozos así esparcidos la verdadera significación según lo escrito y establecido.[...] La alegorización de la *physis* sólo puede imponerse enérgicamente gracias a los cadáveres. Y los personajes del drama barroco mueren, porque sólo así, como cadáveres, tienen acceso a la pequeña patria de la alegoría. (*G.S.*, I.1.391-392)

Esta tendencia desvalorizante en la representación alegórica tiene también su contracara en la *alegoresis*, dado que la génesis de las lecturas alegóricas –ya sea en el conflicto por una interpretación alegórica de los mitos, encendido en torno a las epopeyas homéricas, o ya sea en la glosa alegórica de determinados pasajes de las Sagradas Escrituras– se halla, por cierto, en la creencia de "otro sentido" que se basaría en el movimiento de defensa del significado literal de determinados pasajes (por ejemplo, la historia de Lot y sus hijas, la historia de Susana o el Cantar de los Cantares).[7] El establecimiento de una interpretación alegórica de los textos implica en origen, por lo tanto, una devaluación del sentido literal y, con ello, un acto de represión [*Verdrängung*].

EL SABER Y EL ABISMO: SOBRE EL CARÁCTER ESCRITURARIO DE LA ALEGORÍA

Por otra parte, se instaura un campo de interpretaciones a partir de la diferencia entre texto (o imagen) y significado y a partir de la distancia entre la lectura literal y la alegórica, que se halla enclavado en la historia de los sistemas de poder y conocimiento –tanto en su establecimiento como en su disolución–. En este sentido, se libra en este territorio de la interpretación alegórica una lucha explícita o tácita por el control del saber que, con la asistencia de las estructuras del imaginario, se inscribe

---

7. Julia Kristeva trata en su lectura del Cantar de los Cantares, por el contrario, de rescatar la simultaneidad de la significación literal y carnal, por un lado, y la alegórico-religiosa, por otro; véase: Kristeva (1983: 106-127).

ideas abstractas y conceptuales, que pueden entenderse también como una "corporeización" [*Verkörperung*] de concepciones inmateriales. Mientras que la contracara de este proceso permanece fuera del campo de la mirada, donde se produce una "descorporeización" [*Entleibung*] que se cumple en el material y en las imágenes que son consumados y consumidos en la alegorización. Aquí también se manifiesta una cierta indiferencia frente al "otro" en el "otro discurso".

Tomando como ejemplo el drama barroco alemán, Benjamin llevó a cabo un minucioso trabajo que resalta la tendencia de la desvalorización de los materiales, la cual lleva a que en la representación alegórica se llegue a "algo otro".[6] Para él la alegoría se asociaba con las prácticas de "desnudamiento de las cosas sensibles" [*Entblössung der sinnlichen Dinge*] (*G.S.*, I.1.360), de "rigidez" [*Erstarrung*], de "desmembramiento" [*Zerstückelung*] y de "privación del alma" [*Entseelung*]:

> [...] la personificación alegórica ha ocultado siempre el hecho de que a ella no le interesaba personificar la esencia de las cosas [*Dinghaftes*], sino más bien configurar la cosa como concreción [*das Dingliche*] en tanto persona y así dotarla de mayor imponencia. (*G.S.*, I.1.362-363)

> De una espiritualización de lo corporal no se halla ni el menor resquicio. Toda la naturaleza se personifica, pero no para interiorizarla, sino, por el contrario, para quitarle el alma ([Cita de Cysarz, 1924: 672, en el texto de Benjamin]; *G.S.*, I.1.363)

Benjamin va a agudizar justamente esta tendencia allí donde la alegoría y el emblema se sirven del cuerpo humano como materia prima, basándose en la idea de "la pía mortificación del cuerpo" [*fromme Mortifikation des Leibes*]:

[...] el cuerpo humano no iba a significar una excepción a este

---

6. Benjamin trabaja destacando claramente, por cierto, la dialéctica de realce y desvalorización del mundo profano, pero también la relación dialéctica entre trascendencia e inmanencia. Sin embargo, no deja de poner el acento –contra la opinión establecida frente a la alegoría– en la devaluación. Para este aspecto, cf. también Steinhagen en Haug (1979: 672).

traducción (*translatio*) entre palabra (o también imagen) y significado proviene, entonces, de un *saber* determinado y, de tal modo, arroja la cuestión del acceso a este saber. En la dedicación académica a la alegoría, el interés se dirige en primera instancia al establecimiento de tal sistema. Ello implica que el punto de atención sea el esfuerzo por lograr diferencias constitutivas en cuanto al significado que sean suficientes en la representación figurativa,[5] pero alternativamente también por reconstruir claves y códigos históricos. En este proceso, sin embargo, queda en el camino la cuestión por el significado del "otro" en la dimensión alegórica. Además, la experiencia demuestra que muchas pinturas alegóricas, independientemente de lo que deberían representar o de la búsqueda por parte del espectador de su significado escondido (es decir, sin conocimiento o clave del significado pretendido), ejercen una fascinación que las trasciende. A esto se agrega el hecho de que en el caso de muchos cuadros surge la pregunta de si la significación alegórica no habría sido simplemente una coyuntura moral para la representación o si el deseo del artista y del espectador no se dirige en primera instancia a esa *otra representación*, pues el deseo es desde siempre el deseo hacia "lo otro". Independientemente de la pregunta por el acceso al sistema del saber, regulado por la relación alegórica entre texto y sentido, las alegorías posibilitan diferentes lecturas en las que en el centro se hallan ya sea el sistema de "traducción" o la representación concreta.

CORPOREIZACIÓN Y DESCORPOREIZACIÓN

Sin embargo, olvidar el hecho de que la alegoría trata de una "traducción" a *otro* lenguaje, se corresponde con un modo de observación que se interesa mayormente por *un* plano de la constitución de sentido alegórico: por la "clarificación" [*Veranschaulichung*] o "simbolización" [*Versinnbild-lichung*] de

---

5. Compárese, por ejemplo, el sistema de representaciones alegóricas del arte en la *Iconologia* (1593) de Ripa.

que rara vez se pone sobre el tapete; y, en el caso de mencionar esta derivación, se la entiende rápidamente como la más normal de las concretizaciones, es decir, se trataría de una expresión figurativa). Así, si implícitamente la imagen aparece definida frente al concepto como "imagen de alteridad", es justamente en la distancia entre imagen y concepto donde se esfuma el juego de las significaciones, que sólo se constituye cuando se hace hincapié en la heterogeneidad de *logos* y materia, de significado y significante y en sus múltiples diferencias.

Basados en estos puntos de partida diferentes, sin embargo, los signos concretos visibles se definen a veces –desde la perspectiva de la representación– como otro en relación con el significado, mientras que, a la inversa, desde la perspectiva de la lectura, la imagen concreta o el sentido de la palabra del texto remite a otro significado. En un caso lo que se tiene *in mente* [*das Gemeinte*] se representa en una imagen *otra*, de tal modo que lo visible es "esta otredad", mientras que, en el segundo, lo representado obtiene un significado "otro", que no es visible o aparece en clave. En el plano semiótico, podría tomarse como punto de partida el hecho de que, por una vez, los significados son vistos como "otros", y que el significante parece ser unívoco (o propio) y original mientras que los significantes son tomados como punto de partida, es decir, que remiten a otro significado, además de a su sentido propio. Cuando la representación alegórica o la exégesis alegórica (o *alegoresis*) sitúan al "otro", lo hacen, por lo tanto, exactamente en el lugar inverso: en el significante *o* en el significado. Aquí surge naturalmente la pregunta de si dirigen su atención cada vez a algo diferente.[4]

Se considera, entonces, que la dimensión alegórica regula la relación entre la "palabra" y el "significado", según un sistema determinado, por lo general, según un sistema de normas tradicionales y concepciones (Kuhn, 1979: 207). La relación de la

4. Para poder responder a esta pregunta habría que considerar atentamente las relaciones triangulares entre: 1. imagen o texto; 2. significado; y 3. Sujeto; a continuación habría que analizar estas posibilidades y variantes sistemáticamente y, llegado el caso, realizar una tipología.

ciones y a la tesis mencionada antes, habría que plantearse la pregunta de qué significados del *otro* han precedido e impregnado la comprensión de la alegoría como "otro discurso" de esa alegoría moderna. Puesto que el significado del o/Otro remite no sólo al inconsciente, sino también a lo femenino, habría que preguntarse también si la idea de la alegoría como "otro discurso" aparece implícitamente asociada de alguna manera con las relaciones entre los sexos y si "el otro" del discurso tiene puntos de contacto con la construcción del "otro sexo".[3] En este cuestionamiento se introduce el convencimiento de que sólo cuando en la investigación alegórica se sobrepasa el marco de una historia del lenguaje de las formas [*Formensprache*] y se incluyen los diferentes aspectos del o/Otro, de la diferencia de los géneros sexuales, de la corporeidad y materialidad de los signos, recién en ese momento dicho estudio obtiene una dimensión que puede llamarse histórico-cultural. Sin embargo, la investigación alegórica tampoco se ha interesado hasta ahora por el sentido del "otro" en el proceso alegórico ni por las cuestiones de "*gender*" en las figuras alegóricas.

Todas las explicaciones sobre la alegoría y los procesos alegóricos están de acuerdo, por cierto, en la conocida derivación etimológica de la palabra a partir del griego, en el sentido de que en la "alegoría" se trata del "otro discurso" –*allos*: "otro"; y *agoreúo*: "hablar públicamente"–. Algunos críticos definen la relación entre "otro" y "discurso" de manera más concreta y traducen "alegoría" a partir del prefijo, entendido como adverbio, *allé*: "de otra manera". Esta segunda interpretación significaría, entonces, "hablar de otra manera que públicamente", es decir: "de otro modo que el que es comprensible para todos". Ahora bien, en cuanto a este "otro" es importante destacar la profundidad de sentidos según de dónde se haga derivar la palabra (algo

---

3. Éste fue el cuestionamiento de un simposio que con el título de "Das Geschlecht der Allegorien" ["El género sexual de las alegorías"] tuvo lugar en diciembre de 1991 en el Instituto Científico-Cultural de Essen. Cf. Schade,Wagner y Weigel (1994).

tación traslaticia[1] llega a ser una representación distorsionada o una traducción sin el original. Estas reflexiones más bien teóricas sobre las transformaciones de las formas alegóricas y de los procedimientos en el pasaje hacia la Modernidad se han motivado gracias al material histórico sobre la historia del imaginario de la ciudad, una historia que contiene algo así como los pilares de una genealogía histórico-cultural para el proyecto benjaminiano de los Pasajes.[2] En la literatura de la Modernidad son dominantes los textos que absorben o citan la tradición de las representaciones alegóricas de la ciudad, transformando esto en modos escriturarios que se entrecruzan de manera múltiple con las estructuras del inconsciente. Ya sea que la topografía de la ciudad llegue a ser escritura que puede ser leída como escritura onírica o como alegoría del inconsciente y del recuerdo, ya sea que el *flâneur* se mueva en la ciudad "como en otro escenario" [*auf einem anderen Schauplatz*] en el que se deja arrastrar por su impulso a mirar, o ya sea que la imagen de la escritura de la ciudad sea entendida como si fuera la condensación de las imágenes oníricas de una época, en todos los casos siempre la ciudad aparece como escenario de una escritura que en la lectura alegórica remite al o/Otro y al inconsciente. En lo que concierne a las relaciones de los sexos, se puede describir este proceso de cambio tanto como cambio de paradigmas, desde la personificación alegórica de la ciudad *como* mujer hasta la representación de la ciudad como un cuerpo sexualizado con connotación femenina. Con la vuelta hacia la escritura de la Modernidad de las estructuras topográficas provenientes de antiguas representaciones urbanas míticas se asocia también un regreso de las participaciones reprimidas en las personificaciones.

Si se quisiera adscribir con alguna convicción a estas observa-

---

1. También la alegoría literaria, entendida como metáfora continua (por ejemplo, en Quintiliano: *Institutio oratoria*, VIII, 8.40), o como serie de metáforas, se refiere al discurso traslaticio de las representaciones metafóricas.
2. Cf. Weigel (1990; especialmente Parte II).

7. El "otro" en la alegoría
Una prehistoria de la alegoría de la Modernidad en el barroco

SOBRE LA DESAPARICIÓN DEL "OTRO" EN EL DISCURSO DEL "OTRO"

Para obtener una idea clara sobre el concepto de alegoría, es imprescindible cuestionarse al mismo tiempo la formulación del "otro discurso" [*die andere Rede*]. Sin embargo, en este cuestionamiento queda siempre una opacidad en la significación del "otro" [*das andere*]. Tan pronto como se menciona la definición de la alegoría como "otro discurso", surge, en verdad, cierta oscuridad frente al sentido, proveniencia y función de ese "otro". Esto resulta particularmente llamativo en el pasaje hacia la Modernidad, cuando *el o/Otro* conquista su lugar en las múltiples e iridiscentes significaciones, monopolizando el primer plano de la literatura y el arte. Mi tesis, por lo tanto, consiste en que "el Otro" (en el sentido del psicoanálisis) se torna dominante en la *escritura alegórica de la Modernidad* y que los procedimientos alegóricos pre-modernos —como discurso indirecto, representación pictórica, personificaciones, esquemas alegóricos y estructuras narrativas— se introducen en forma transformada, de tal modo que del "otro discurso" se obtiene un "discurso del Otro" [*Rede des Anderes*]. En este sentido, las representaciones pictóricas se transforman en un lenguaje figurativo del inconsciente o en imágenes leídas, y las encarnaciones [*Verkörperungen*] devienen cuerpos semióticos [*semiotische Körper*], espacios del cuerpo y de la imagen para las imaginaciones del sujeto. Además, la represen-

En ella y gracias a la reflexión sobre ella se transforman no sólo las imágenes en imágenes dialécticas, las alegorías en representaciones distorsionadas, destruidas desde dentro la estructura imaginaria de la representación figurativa, sino que se produce también ese viraje materialista en el pensar en imágenes benjaminiano que hace visible la corporeidad y lo orgánico del hombre y de las cosas, constituyendo el concepto de "espacio del cuerpo y de la imagen".

Este devenir persona de la mercancía se funda, según la lectura de Benjamin, en el archivo de imágenes de la Modernidad sobre todo porque en las prostitutas es como si salieran al encuentro las imágenes que se han tornado corpóreas:

> En Baudelaire la forma de la mercancía se manifiesta como el contenido social de la forma en que se percibe la alegoría. Forma y contenido han llegado a ser uno en la síntesis de la ramera. (Anotaciones y materiales para "La obra de los Pasajes", Block J 59,10; *G.S.*, V.1.422)

Las prostitutas no son, entonces, solamente vendedoras y mercancía al mismo tiempo, son también imagen y cuerpo en una unidad. Las figuras de un "mirarse a sí mismo al rostro" define tanto una corporeidad o personificación de la imagen como también una autorreflexión de la imagen o su encarnación en cuerpos reales. La formulación recuerda los intentos, que son motivos dominantes en Benjamin, de hacer productiva la relación de la cercanía y la lejanía para una reflexión de diferentes modos de representación –como la Huella y el Aura, por ejemplo (cf. V.1.560)–, además de la conocida cita de Karl Kraus por la que cuanto más cerca es mirada la palabra, ella miraría más lejos (I.2.647). También nos encontramos aquí con que el esbozo de la categoría del "espacio del cuerpo y de la imagen" juega un papel importante:

> En todo lugar, donde la acción misma gesta la imagen y es la imagen, absorbiéndola y devorándola, donde la cercanía se mira con sus propios ojos [*wo die Nähe sich selbst aus den Augen sieht*], allí se abre el solicitado territorio de la imagen, un mundo de absoluta e integral actualidad. ("El surrealismo"; *G.S.*, II.1.309)

El espacio del cuerpo es este espacio de la imagen, en tanto obtiene su representación en forma de inervaciones corpóreas, es decir: a través del cuerpo del grupo colectivo. Tal convergencia de representación y percepción, de imagen y cuerpo, predestina a la prostituta a ser la figura central del trabajo sobre los Pasajes.

umbral? ¿una vacilación, que se justifica justamente por el hecho de que el umbral no conduzca a ninguna parte? Pero innumerables son los sitios en las grandes ciudades, donde estar en el umbral es no estar en ninguna parte y las prostitutas son como los Lares de este culto de la Nada, manteniéndose erguidas en los pórticos de los edificios de inquilinato y sobre el asfalto de los andenes que lanzan su eco por lo bajo.

En este contexto la topografía del umbral aparece asociada en primera instancia al motivo del despertar sexual, pero, sin embargo, la descripción de la escena como culto remite a ese significado de "ritos de pasaje" en el imaginario colectivo, que incluye en la historia primigenia de la Modernidad justamente la arquitectura de los pasajes. Junto con la constelación del Despertar como "el abc del pensar dialéctico" y con la concepción de la "imagen dialéctica", la prostituta ingresa, como alegoría de la Modernidad, en el escenario del proyecto de los Pasajes. Aquí, ella se halla justamente en el umbral, pero ha optado también por salir de un mundo primitivo para internarse en esa esfera de pasaje entre el sueño y la vigilia, que se manifiesta como la condición de posibilidad para el Despertar. Como "habitantes de los umbrales" (*G.S.*, V.617) las prostitutas ocupan así una posición en los escritos tardíos de Benjamin a la que el autor vuelve a dedicar sus esfuerzos sin cesar para descifrar las fantasmagorías, los símbolos del deseo y las imágenes materializadas del grupo colectivo.

Pero el interés en las mujeres no se origina en primer lugar porque ellas estén ligadas a "lo que ha sido" o a lo olvidado, sino que éste se origina en su capacidad expresiva que hace que se asocien las representaciones de lo femenino con aquello de "lo que ha sido" en ese momento de una representación distorsionada, que Freud analizó como estructura del lenguaje del inconsciente. Así sostiene Benjamin:

> La engañosa transfiguración del mundo de la mercancía se contrapone a su distorsión en lo alegórico. La mercancía busca mirarse a sí misma el rostro. Su devenir persona es celebrado en la prostituta. ("Central-park", <20>; I.2.671)

que las figuras femeninas kafkianas no son solamente criaturas de un mundo primitivo, sino también que participan en la forma de la distorsión.

"LA DISTORSIÓN HACIA LO ALEGÓRICO":
LAS PROSTITUTAS COMO "ESPACIO DEL CUERPO Y DE LA IMAGEN" PARA UNA ALEGORÍA DE LA MODERNIDAD

Entre los personajes del archivo benjaminiano de los años treinta, la figura de la prostituta [*Hure*] va sobresaliendo cada vez más para jugar el mismo papel que jugaba la ramera [*Dirne*] en los escritos tempranos.[31] Mientras que en los trabajos previos a *Infancia en Berlín* esta figura tiene todavía una gran importancia, va desapareciendo paulatinamente en las reelaboraciones posteriores de ese texto, que se constituye finalmente bajo la égida de lo materno.[32] El motivo así desplazado va a encontrar, entonces, su expresión, de alguna manera, en el proyecto de los pasajes y en el libro sobre Baudelaire. En el trabajo titulado "Crónica de Berlín" (de 1932) todavía aparecen las prostitutas tanto como "custodias del pasado" [*Hüterinnen des Vergangenen*], como también en calidad de "habitantes de los umbrales" [*Schwellenbewohnerinnen*] (*G.S.*, VI.472):

Pero, ¿se trataba realmente de un pasaje?, ¿no es más bien un empecinamiento obstinado y lúbrico de permanecer sobre el

31. En los escritos tempranos que aluden a las experiencias estudiantiles predomina la figura de la ramera, mientras que en los posteriores lo será la prostituta; por ello debe considerarse el segundo vocablo en su dimensión de imagen. Sin embargo, el uso idiomático en Benjamin no es siempre coherente. Por cierto que hasta *Dirección única* (de 1938) encontramos en sus textos el término de *Dirne*, mientras que en los esbozos para los Pasajes que son de la misma época aparece el de *Hure* (cf. *G.S.*, V.1023 y V.1057), pero ya en el mismo año de 1938 en los esquemas para el libro sobre Baudelaire en carta a Horkheimer (1978: 752), así como en las primeras notas para ese texto se habla nuevamente de *Dirne* (cf. VII. 2.739).

32. Para este punto, compárese mi trabajo sobre "Traum-Stadt-Frau. Zur Weiblichkeit der Städte in der Schrift" ["El sueño, la ciudad, la mujer: sobre la femineidad de las ciudades en la escritura"], en Weigel (1990: 204-229).

nios" [*eines ehelosen Muttertums*] descrito por Bachofen en la imagen de una vegetación cenagosa (Bachofen, 1948: 36),[29] que Benjamin traslada a la obra de Kafka:

> Sus novelas se desarrollan en un mundo de ciénagas. La criatura aparece en sus obras en el estadio que Bachofen designa como el hetáirico. El hecho de que este estadio se haya olvidado no impide que vuelva a mostrarse en la actualidad. Más bien: este estadio se halla presente justamente a causa de ese olvido. (*G.S.*, II.2.428)

En este mismo sentido las figuras femeninas en la obra de Kafka son designadas por Benjamin como criaturas de las ciénagas, que pertenecen, por ello, a una esfera de "exuberancia caótica" [*regellose Üppigkeit*]. Cuando se trata justamente del exotismo de las mujeres de apariencia prostituida (*G.S.*, II.2.413), estas figuras son diferentes de las prostitutas de los Pasajes, dado que no aparecen asociadas con el motivo de la negativa a la procreación. Por el contrario: en el mundo primitivo [*Vorwelt*] del hetairismo de Bachofen las ubicaciones de la prostituta y de la mujer aparecen sin distinguir. El procedimiento de la distorsión, sin embargo, vincula el ensayo sobre Kafka (con sus prostitutas) a esas figuras de los Pasajes, donde ellas serán la alegoría de la Modernidad.

Cuando Benjamin se sirve del término freudiano de "distorsión" [*Entstellung*] en su trabajo sobre Kafka, lo utiliza especialmente como categoría mnemónica: distorsión, entonces, como "forma que toman las cosas cuando yacen en el olvido"[30] (*G.S.*, II.2.431). Así también cuando Benjamin, un poco antes del pasaje mencionado, parte de la idea de que en los textos kafkianos de lo que se trata, en realidad, es del olvido y de que cada cosa olvidada se mezcle "con lo olvidado del mundo primitivo" [*mit dem Vergessenen der Vorwelt*] (*G.S.*, II.2.430). Por ello puede decirse

---

29. Para la recepción sobre Bachofen realizada por Benjamin, véase Plumpe (1979).
30. En alemán: "*Form, die die Dinge in der Vergessenheit annehmen*". [N. del T.]

Estos aspectos ponen en evidencia una semiótica de los diferentes lugares de lo femenino en la escritura. Ello sucede, por ejemplo, en la función mágica de aquellas esferas asociadas a lo femenino dentro de la casa (el costurero, el armario): los dominios subterráneos y pre-simbólicos a través del giro "las madres" [*die Mütter*], la figura mítica de Ariadna, que se confunde con la amiga deseada, y las alegorías petrificadas, como corporeidades de un recuerdo del mito y de la jungla urbana, a las que Benjamin denomina "sabias en umbrales" [*Schwellen-kundige*], identificándola de ese modo en su función figurativa como detentadora de lo pre-simbólico en el orden urbano (*Infancia en Berlín*; G.S., VII.1. 394-395).

La función figurativa de lo femenino aparece así desde la posición de guardianas del pasado asociada con *la escritura*. La expresión de "lo femenino-que ha sido" adquiere aquí no sólo su sentido, dado que las mujeres reales pertenecen a lo olvidado de la cultura, sino también porque las imágenes de lo femenino y las figuras de las mujeres representan en su mayor parte en la memoria cultural "lo que ha sido, lo olvidado y lo reprimido" [*das Gewesene, Vergessene und Verdrängte*]. Si, en un sentido, la marca de su proveniencia se origina en lo olvidado, las mujeres, sin embargo, dejan de habitar esa esfera en la figura del retorno de lo reprimido, tornándose la corporeidad de aquello que justamente se halla en el archivo figurativo de la Modernidad para ese territorio de lo olvidado.

Benjamin interpreta las figuras de mujeres kafkianas en su ensayo de 1934, por el contrario, como "configuraciones de un mundo primitivo" [*Vorwelt-Gestalten*]. Este ensayo sobre Kafka, por otra parte, acredita claras huellas de la lectura de Bachofen que Benjamin estaba realizando casi por la misma época, pero en este estudio no se interesa tanto por la "edad de oro" del matriarcado, como se encuentra en este autor, sino por su pintura de un mundo primitivo prehistórico de "hetairismo",* como un grado de desarrollo primario "de una maternidad sin matrimo-

---

* La palabra está formada sobre el término griego *hetaira* en el sentido de "compañera, cortesana". [N. del T.]

del Todavía alguna vez, del Volver a poseer, de lo Vivido. Por ello no ha de desear lo nuevo en ningún trecho más que en el trayecto de retorno, cuando lleve consigo a una nueva persona. Así como yo, apenas te vi por primera vez, volví de regreso contigo hacia el lugar de donde acababa de llegar. (*Escritos autobiográficos*; G.S., VI.523)

La mujer ya no aparece aquí situada en el pasado, tampoco *posee* ella el pasado, sino que abre el paso hacia el pasado, más bien como el retorno de "lo que ha sido". En este sentido, nos encontramos en muchos textos desde fines de los años veinte con mujeres que son las guardianas del pasado. En estos casos, sin embargo, su posición aparece trasladada claramente hacia el escenario de la escritura, siendo descifrable sobre la transparencia de una marca de lo femenino en lo imaginario. Ello aparece elaborado en relación con el motivo de la *flânerie*, que describe la escritura de la ciudad como escena del recuerdo, según lo exhiben también las imágenes de pensamiento de *Infancia en Berlín*. Entonces, aparecen siempre ya ligados entre sí la estructura del recuerdo y la significación de los lugares connotados femeninamente en el imaginario. El recuerdo se instaura como Musa de la *flânerie*, una rememoración del libre deambular [*ein Memorieren im Schlendern*]:

> Ella [la Musa] avanza por las calles y cada una la lleva hacia abajo. Va bajando y si no a la casa de las madres, por lo menos hacia un pasado que puede ser tanto más encantado en la medida en que no es el propio del autor, su pasado privado. ("El *flâneur*", G.S., III. 194)[28]

Siguiendo las imágenes y huellas del recuerdo, Benjamin trabaja en la reconstrucción de la genealogía de la función figurativa y sígnica de lo femenino. Esto sucede en *Infancia en Berlín*, en una de sus series de escenas primigenias, y en el proyecto de los Pasajes en una lectura de las imágenes oníricas de lo colectivo y de las ruinas de una cultura de la Modernidad.

28. También sucede esto en la reseña de Hessel; y, con pequeños desvíos, también en los esbozos tempranos para los Pasajes, surgidos desde 1927 (*G.S.*, V.1052).

pasado y en todo caso ninguna tiene presente"[23] (II.1.93); "su pasado nunca está cerrado"[24] (Parte VII; *G.S.*, II.1.95). En lugar de ello, cada una vive en una estructura, que conforma como su *future antérieur* –ese tornarse el haber sido– que ha sido definido por Lacan como una estructura temporal del deseo y tiempo histórico del sujeto,[25] como si fuera un recurso temporal: "El eterno presente que ha sido va a devenir de nuevo"[26] (Parte *G.S.*, IV; II.1.93). En relación con el pasado, sin embargo, la significación de la diferencia de género sexual en este texto llega a ser tan dominante que aparece sintetizada conceptualmente en la expresión de un "femenino-que ha sido" [*ein Weiblich-Gewesenes*], (Parte VIII; *G.S.*, II.1.95).

El entramado entre el retorno y "lo que ha sido", que aquí todavía se presenta como con una estructura mítica de lo femenino –"lo que ha sido eterno presente ha de devenir de nuevo"–, ha de aparecer más adelante, pero entonces con la configuración de un conflicto, para describir la estructura de un "deseo de dicha" [*Glückbegehren*] como nostalgia por una repetición de lo que "nunca ha estado aquí todavía" [*Noch-nie-da-gewesenen*]. Así sucede en el hermético texto titulado "Agesilaus Santander" (que repite la leyenda talmúdica de la innumerable cantidad de ángeles que son creados a cada momento, y que anuda el motivo del ángel nuevo con el *Angelus Novus* fijado a la pared), escrito por Benjamin en 1933 en Ibiza como regalo de cumpleaños a una de las mujeres que había amado:[27]

> Quiere la dicha: el conflicto, en el que el éxtasis de lo único, de lo Nuevo, de lo No vivido todavía se halla junto a esa bienaventuranza

---

23. En alemán: "*Denn jede Frau hat die Vergangenheit und jedenfalls keine Gegenwart*". [N. del T.]
24. En alemán: "*ihr Vergangnes ist nie beschlossen*". [N. del T.]
25. Cf. Samuel Weber, 1978: 10.
26. En alemán: "*Die ewig gewesene Gegenwart wird wieder werden*". [N. del T.]
27. Se trataba de la pintora holandesa Toet Blaupot ten Cate; cf. Wil van Gerwen: "Walter Benjamin 1932/33 auf Ibiza". Ponencia para el Congreso dedicado a Benjamin reunido en Osnabrück en junio de 1992.

puede verse como disolución de una estructura de imagen mental mal comprendida. Ello sería, pues, comparable con la elaboración benjaminiana de esa otra historia de dos décadas de fascinación que lo unió al *Angelus Novus* de Paul Klee: es decir, con la reflexión sobre la rigidez mítica de la imagen pictórica que se transforma en 1940 en la imagen dialéctica del "Ángel de la Historia".[21] Como un punto intermedio entre el mito de una creación no engendrada, según se lee en "La conversación", entre el Genio y la Ramera (de 1913) y la "imagen de pensamiento" sobre el Maestro de la primera mitad de la década del treinta se podrían considerar esas trece proposiciones sobre los libros y las rameras en el número 13 de *Dirección única*, en las que se comenta comparativamente su estatuto metafórico: "Libros y rameras: cada uno de ellos tiene su especie de hombre que vive de ellos y que los veja. Para los libros, los críticos."[22] (*G.S.*, IV.1.109).

"PUES CADA MUJER TIENE SU PASADO Y EN TODO CASO NINGUNA TIENE PRESENTE": LAS MUJERES COMO CUSTODIAS DE LOS UMBRALES

Otro rastro más nos conduce desde las mujeres de "La conversación" a los grandes proyectos más tardíos. Pues al mismo tiempo que con el cambio del pronombre personal en la Parte IV de "La conversación", se introduce en el texto el tema de presente y pasado. Mientras que el hablante se halla poseído por el presente, las mujeres se manifiestan como custodias del pasado en una posición superior al mismo Genio, de quien se dice que maldice sus recuerdos al configurarlos en su creación, pues es pobre en ellos y se encuentra indeciso (*G.S.*,II.1.93). Justamente a la inversa se da con las mujeres: "Pues cada mujer tiene su

---

21. Véase al respecto el capítulo 4 de este estudio.
22. En alemán: "*Bücher und Dirnen - sie haben jedes ihre Sorte Männer, die von ihnen leben und sie drangsalieren. Bücher die Kritiker*". [N. del T.]

dos décadas antes, donde se daba el tema de la falta de procreación en el diálogo entre el Genio y la Ramera (Parte V del texto). A la prostituta se acercan justamente aquellos que nadie ha engendrado y que no quieren engendrar, con lo que resulta vinculado el perfil que caracteriza al Genio. Éste dice de sí justamente: "Todas devinieron mis madres. Todas las mujeres me han dado el ser, no fue un hombre el que me engendró" (Parte V; G.S., II.1.94). Esta imagen que con la idea de una madre virginal coloca al Genio en rivalidad con el hijo de Dios, citando así un mito tradicional del Genio,[19] es sobrepasada porque también la madre es colocada fuera de toda competición como si hubiera sido descorporeizada, en tanto ella aparece como mujer de cuyas gestaciones sólo se han originado productos espirituales fracasados, poemas muertos: "Sólo pienso en mi madre. ¿Me permites que te hable de ella? Ella ha dado a luz como tú: cien poemas muertos".[20] Aquí se trata tanto de la rivalidad del Genio con Dios como también con la gestación femenina, es decir, se trata de una apropiación doble de la creación; y de tal modo esta idea del Genio aparece en la imagen de pensamiento posterior como si estuviera iluminada desde adentro. En la formulación que dice "el primogénito masculino de la obra que él mismo había antes concebido", el procedimiento es invertido: no es el Genio el que crea la obra, sino que el Maestro surge desde el mismo origen que la obra que se afirma independiente de la naturaleza.

Con este proceso que se desarrolla sobre un período de veinte años mostrando la transformación de una imagen (a la que el autor se sintió ligado con una especie de fascinación) en una imagen dialéctica, se hace evidente un desplazamiento que

---

19. Por ejemplo, durante el movimiento alemán del Sturm und Drang.
20. En relación con este imaginario puede verse, por ejemplo, la ironía romántica de Heinrich Heine en la poesía "Flor de loto" [*Lotusblume*], escrita en 1855 desde el lecho de enfermo –cuando estaba colocado perentoriamente (por así decirlo) en la posición de genio– y dedicada a su amada ("La Mouche") y a sí mismo: "Pero en lugar de la vida que fructifica/ella concibe [recibe] sólo un poema" [*Doch statt des befruchtenden Leben/ empfängt sie nur ein Gedicht*], en Heine (1993, 847).

Por el contrario, más bien se encuentran paráfrasis de su negación, por ejemplo, en la acentuación de la irrenunciabilidad a esa otra productividad, como en la representación de "Sócrates", donde Benjamin le critica al filósofo que degrade a la figura del *Eros* al papel de instrumento:

> En una sociedad compuesta por hombres no existiría el individuo genial; pues éste vive a través de la existencia de lo femenino. Es cierto: la existencia de lo femenino institucionaliza la asexualidad de lo intelectual en el mundo. (*G.S.*, II.1.130)

El énfasis de Benjamin en esa otra productividad de la mujer podría leerse quizás como una "crítica salvadora", como salvación de la diferencia de los géneros sexuales en el momento histórico de su desaparición. Sólo que a las mujeres les sigue quedando como territorio propio ese lugar mudo de una productividad "otra".

También estas concepciones aquí mencionadas van a pasar más adelante a imágenes dialécticas para ganar así un contenido fantasmagórico que va a leerse en su constructividad cultural y en sus condicionamientos, sobre todo gracias a un desmontaje o deconstrucción de las ideas de "genio" y de "obra maestra". Para este pasaje es necesario leer el texto titulado *Nach der Vollendung* ["Después de la terminación definitiva"] que forma parte de la serie de *Cuadros de un pensamiento*, donde Benjamin describe la constitución de la obra maestra como un desgaste de lo femenino y como deseo ferviente de superación de la naturaleza o de la propia proveniencia desde las "oscuras profundidades del seno materno". El Maestro aparece allí como "el primogénito masculino de la obra que él mismo había antes concebido"[17] (*G.S.*, IV.1.438).[18]

Esta imagen de pensamiento vuelve su mirada directamente a un fantasma que se había incorporado al arsenal benjaminiano

---

17. En alemán: "*Er ist der männliche Erstgeborene des Werkes, das er einstmals empfangen hatte*". [N. del T.]
18. Para esta idea, véase el capítulo 5 del presente estudio.

de símbolo– una deshumanización [*Entseelung*] de miles de mujeres poniéndolas como en una exhibición de obras de arte:

> Por un tiempo vamos a dejar de hablar sobre la "espiritualización" de lo sexual, sobre ese preciado inventario masculino. Vamos a hablar de la sexualización de lo espiritual: ésta es la moralidad de la que es portadora la prostituta. Ella representa a la cultura en el *Eros*, ese *Eros* que es el individualista más poderoso y más enemigo de la cultura; también él puede ser pervertido, también él puede servir a la cultura. (Benjamin, 1978: 67-68)

Contra las estrategias de la instrumentalización del *Eros* en el dominio de lo intelectual, así como contra una superación o absorción de la posición femenina en una *quasi* transubstancialización de lo sexual (según aparece en los proyectos representados por varones en teorías culturales contemporáneas),[15] Benjamin acentúa –apoyándose completamente en los recursos de las concepciones tradicionales de las relaciones de los sexos– la aparentemente invisible otra productividad de las mujeres que está ligada a su lenguaje inaudible y que, sin embargo, se presenta como el condicionamiento de la producción cultural. De manera similar, Kristeva habla de la productividad de las mujeres como de "un efecto que no dispone ni de poder ni de un sistema lingüístico, sino que es su muda apoyatura" (Kristeva, 1976: 167); pues en tanto es apoyo mudo del sistema, él mismo no puede aparecer como fenómeno visible.

Es por ello que el texto titulado "La conversación" condensaría la idea de que el silencio marca la posición femenina productiva. En esto se percibe la postura benjaminiana de *otra* productividad de la mujer, que en sus textos de este período juega un papel muy importante.[16] Sin embargo, costará encontrar en ellos una descripción positiva, o algo más concreto que en "La conversación".

---

15. Esto sucede del modo más flagrante en el esquema de "máquinas de solteros"; cf. Clair y Szeemann, 1975.

16. Por ejemplo en "La vida de los estudiantes" o en "Sócrates" (*G.S.*, II.1.84 y 130).

representa el motivo de un amor sin procreación en la autorrealización de un artista metido dentro de la relación histórico-cultural de la Modernidad. Sus lecturas de Baudelaire podrían verse, con todo, también como comentarios de sus propios escritos tempranos. En ellos el motivo de la prostituta así como el de la no procreación adquieren una importancia central para la figura del Genio y para la concepción de una creación intelectual que no vaya acompañada de la idea de un engendrar biológico.

Muchos de los escritos tempranos giran alrededor de la relación entre sexualidad y actividad intelectual, entre procreación y creación, y en torno del significado de la diferencia de los sexos para la "comunidad de los creadores" [*Gemeinschaft Schaffender*], (*Frühe Arbeiten zur Bildungs- und Kulturkritik: Das Leben der Studenten*; *G.S.*, II.1.84 ["Trabajos tempranos sobre crítica de la formación y la cultura: La vida de los estudiantes"]), donde las imágenes a menudo oscilan entre el plano de la creación corporal e intelectual. Así, mientras que los textos benjaminianos atestiguan una rara fascinación por los pasajes entre lo corpóreo-erótico y lo espiritual,[14] al mismo tiempo, Benjamin se afana en su argumentación con el fin justamente de contrabalancear la idea de una mezcla o de una sumisión de una esfera a la otra –especialmente en el trabajo intensivo con los mitos contemporáneos y tradicionales acerca de la creación intelectual y de las concepciones que pretenden una superación de la diferencia de los sexos o de lo femenino como representación del "otro" sexo, como, por ejemplo, en el *topos* de "la espiritualización de lo sexual"–. Así, Benjamin escribía en 1913 en una carta a su amigo Herbert Belmore, donde le echa en cara haber producido –a causa de la elevación de la prostituta al rango

---

14. Así, por ejemplo, en las imágenes de un silencio que se da a luz a sí mismo [*das Schweigen gebiert sich selber*], de una mirada que desflora [*sein Blick entjungfert*] (*G.S.*, II.1.92), de un paisaje que concibe [*die Landschaft empfängt*] (*G.S.*, II.1.99), de la matriz del tiempo [*Schoss der Zeit*] (*G.S.*, II.1.102) o del marchar preñado de sabiduría [*mit dem Wissen schwangergehen*] (*G.S.*, II.1.131).

"EL PRIMOGÉNITO MASCULINO DE SU OBRA": CREACIÓN Y GESTACIÓN

Pero justamente es el aspecto de lo maternal en los cuerpos de las mujeres sáficas benjaminianas lo que aparece escatimado: ese círculo femenino se halla más bien en una situación de amor, liberado de objetivos últimos. "El amor de sus cuerpos no conoce la gestación, pero ese amor es bello de ver"[13] (*G.S.*, II.1.96). En este motivo de un amor sin la gestación, no unido a objetivos, y de un erotismo no subsumido a la procreación, resuena ya un *topos* que en las figuras de la lesbiana y de la ramera –las heroínas de la poesía baudelairiana– ha de avanzar al primer plano en el proyecto de los Pasajes.

Como alegorías de la Modernidad esas figuras femeninas, sin embargo, aparecen reflejadas como imágenes dialécticas, al punto que Benjamin también discute las precondiciones que hacen de ellas el objeto de fascinación del autor que describe la vida moderna, quien se siente en un plano de igualdad con el héroe de la Antigüedad, en el sentido de que en él hay un rechazo de la naturaleza y de lo natural como reacción contra el desarrollo de la técnica y de la nivelación de las diferencias sexuales:

> Al tránsito sacrificial de la sexualidad masculina se debe al hecho de que Baudelaire deba considerar el embarazo hasta cierto punto como competencia impura. ("Central-park" <19>; *G.S.*, I.2.670)
> La impotencia masculina –figura clave de la soledad–: bajo su signo se cumple la suspensión de las fuerzas productivas, un abismo separa a los hombres de sus iguales. (<31>; *G.S.*, I.2.679)
> Baudelaire nunca ha escrito una poesía de prostituta desde la perspectiva de ella (compárese el *Libro de lectura para habitantes urbanos*, 5). (<21>; *G.S.*, I.2.672)
> Los lectores de Baudelaire son hombres. Son ellos los que han llevado a la fama al poeta y a quienes él se los compró. (Anotaciones y materiales para "La obra de los Pasajes", Block J57,9; *G.S.*, V.1.418)

Partiendo del ejemplo de la poesía baudelairiana, Benjamin

[13]. En alemán: "*Die Liebe ihrer Leiber ist ohne Zeugung, aber ihre Liebe ist schön anzusehen*". [N. del T.]

palabras [*zwischen den Leibern der Worte*]– y el lenguaje de los cuerpos [*Körpersprache*].

"La lengua de las mujeres ha quedado sin hacer. Cuando las mujeres hablan, su lenguaje está poseído por la demencia"[12] (*G.S.*, II.1.95), ésta es una afirmación de Benjamin a la que Luce Irigaray podría suscribir por completo con su descripción psicoanalítica, la cual sostiene que las mujeres no encuentran ningún lugar en el discurso establecido y que, por lo tanto, se sirven de la lengua sólo en forma de una mímesis desfigurada, puesto que:

> [...] como carencia, como falta, como pantomima o como repetición errada del sujeto –debe dar cuenta de que frente a esta lógica– <de una economía del *logos*, agregaría yo> es posible un exceso demencial por parte de las mujeres. (Irigaray, 1977)

También el importante aspecto del exceso tratado por Irigaray se halla en "La conversación" benjaminiana adjudicado a las mujeres:

> Pero las mujeres están en silencio. Hacia donde tiendan sus oídos, allí las palabras quedarán inexpresadas. Acercan sus cuerpos y se acarician unas a otras. Su conversación se liberó del objeto y de la lengua. [...] El silencio y el goce –siempre separados en la conversación– se tornan uno. (Parte VIII; *G.S.*, II.1.95-96)

La misma disimultaneidad entre el discurso y el goce del cuerpo femenino que aparece configurado en esa descripción benjaminiana –"voz sin cuerpo, cuerpo sin voz" (Kristeva, 1974a)– se dará en el capítulo final de la obra de Kristeva, *Des chinoises*, describiendo en una perspectiva histórico-cultural el distanciamiento y superación del cuerpo materno a través del *logos* masculino y colocado en el contexto de una historia del monoteísmo, esto es, del principio "de una comunidad simbólica, paterna y superyoica" (Kristeva, 1974a: 23).

---

12. En alemán: "*Die Sprache der Frauen blieb ungeschaffen. Sprechende Frauen sind von einer wahnwitzigen Sprache besessen*". [N. del T.]

cuya identidad se revela muy pronto como femenina. En lo personal del texto acontece, en su Parte IV, un significativo cambio de sexo. Así del género masculino (o neutro) montado en la escenificación anterior (el que habla y el que escucha, en la Parte II; el improductivo, el charlatán y el genio, en la Parte III) se pasa a una pareja sexuada que consiste en *el* Hablante y *la* Oyente [*der Sprechende-die Hörende*], que se transforma luego en una conversación entre el Genio y la Ramera [*das Genie-die Dirne*], en la Parte V, y en una observación general sobre la diferencia de los sexos en el lenguaje en la Parte VI.

Si la posición femenina aparece aquí conectada con el silencio, de ello resultan dos consideraciones. En tanto oyente la mujer es vista, desde la idea de "un lenguaje verdadero", como productiva –la mujer es la custodia "del sentido antes de la comprensión, desplegando su defensa contra el mal uso de las palabras y oponiéndose al engaño" (Parte IV; *G.S.*, II.1.93)–. En este contexto, la Mujer aparece como ocupando una posición de *pendant* frente al Genio. Como "agentes" [*Tätige*] aparecen en este texto benjaminiano tanto pensadores como mujeres (Parte III; *G.S.*, II.1.92). Por otro lado, aquí el silencio es la contracara del lenguaje, unido a la relación sexual de los sexos, como en el siguiente pasaje: "La otra conversación del silencio es goce"[11] (Parte IV, *G.S.*, II.1.93).

Pero, sin embargo, el hecho de que Benjamin asocie la posición femenina en el lenguaje con el silencio, no tiene como consecuencia que se comporte de modo indiferente frente al lenguaje de las mujeres. Justamente en las Partes VII y VIII de "La conversación" considera esta cuestión. Ambas partes empiezan con la misma pregunta: "¿Cómo hablaban Safo y sus amigas?" ["Wie sprachen Sappho und ihre Freundinnen?"], y cuestionando la utilidad de la lengua para su conversación –"Pues el lenguaje les quita el alma" [*Denn Sprache entseelt sie*]–, terminan marcando finalmente un tipo de locuacidad que se halla localizado entre el cuerpo del lenguaje [*Sprachkörper*] –entre lo corpóreo de las

---

11. En alemán: "*Des Schweigens anderes Gespräch ist Wollust*". [N. del T.]

1916) tanto como "símbolo de lo no comunicable" (*G.S.*, II.1.156) o como lo semiótico del lenguaje en tanto portador de lo mimético (en 1933) y, con ello, como condición de posibilidad para el vertiginoso destello de la "similitud no sensorial" ("Sobre la capacidad mimética"; *G.S.*, II.1.213). Estamos ante una especie de solución en los esfuerzos para superar la oposición entre el patrón de arbitrariedad en "la consideración burguesa del lenguaje", por un lado, y la creencia de que la palabra es la esencia de la cosa, en la "teoría mística del lenguaje", por otro (*G.S.*, II.1.150).

En el texto de 1916 –que se refiere a la lengua adámica en el Génesis– (bajo el título de "Sobre el lenguaje en general y sobre el lenguaje de los humanos")–, las mujeres, sin embargo, están completamente ausentes. Pero, por lo menos, en el pasaje sobre la otra mudez y tristeza de la naturaleza ahora ya denominada, pero sin capacidad para hablar después de la expulsión del paraíso del lenguaje, podría pensarse en Eva o en las mujeres que se hallan en la misma posición que la mencionada aquí:

> En el dolor intenso la profunda inclinación a la mudez es algo que va infinitamente mucho más allá de una incapacidad o falta de voluntad para comunicarse. Lo triste se siente transido y reconocido por lo irreconocible. Ser nombrado –aun cuando el que nombra sea alguien de la estatura de los dioses o un bienaventurado– resulta quizá siempre una sospecha de dolor. (*G.S.*, II.1.155)

Mientras que en la lectura que Benjamin realiza en su teoría del lenguaje de la primera historia del acto de la creación[9] el hombre aparece en uso de la palabra y, al mismo tiempo, se halla en el origen del lenguaje,[10] en "La conversación", en cambio, la productividad y el sentido del lenguaje salen de quien escucha,

---

9. Benjamin llama la atención sobre el hecho de que en la segunda historia de la creación se hable del material del que está hecho el hombre, pero pasa inmediatamente a considerar "la relación del acto de la creación con el lenguaje" (*G.S.*, II.1.148) en la primera historia de la creación.
10. Para una crítica de la tesis de M. Stoessel acerca de lo humano olvidado y de la estructura edípica en el artículo benjaminiano sobre el lenguaje, véase el capítulo 3 del presente estudio.

"¿CÓMO HABLABAN SAFO Y SUS AMIGAS?": LA MAGIA DEL LENGUAJE Y LA DIFERENCIA DE GÉNERO SEXUAL

"La conversación" significa la verificación de un género discursivo en el pasaje entre un pensar en imágenes y una reflexión teórica que habría de ser tan característico de la escritura de *Dirección única* y de *Infancia en Berlín* como del texto "Sobre el concepto de historia": una serie de escenas en prosa o de imágenes de pensamiento cortas y sucesivas pero cerradas cada una dentro de sí. Las ocho partes de "La conversación" giran en torno de la idea de otra lengua que aquí se denomina todavía "verdadera" [*wahre Sprache*; G.S., I.1.92)]; una lengua que más allá de lo dicho, tiende a ser pura cháchara [*Geschwätz*] –el hablante aparece en el texto como calumniando esa misma lengua (*G.S.*, II.1.91)–, que, con todo, no es independiente de la conversación, sino que aparece como si fuera posible en ella y gracias a ella, es decir, gracias al oyente o gracias a ese asentimiento tácito que la conversación va produciendo, donde el silencio resulta "el límite interno de la conversación" (*G.S.*, II.1.92).

Estas observaciones van a volver a aparecer tres años más tarde en la reelaboración de su teoría lingüística,[8] que ha encontrado su expresión en la carta a Buber como la conocida formulación programática de dirigirse "hacia lo denegado para la palabra" [*auf das dem Wort versagte*], o de "lo inefable en el lenguaje" hacia lo que está "dentro del lenguaje y, por lo tanto, ha de obrar por su intermedio" (Benjamin, 1978: 127). En "La conversación" esa otra lengua no aparece localizada como el polo opuesto a la conversación, sino *dentro de* ella. De este modo, esa concepción dialéctica de la teoría lingüística benjaminiana se manifiesta comprendiendo el carácter sígnico del lenguaje (en

---

8. Se podría denominarla magia del lenguaje o teología del lenguaje. Ambos aspectos, el de la magia y el de la teología, aparecen contenidos en "La conversación", como lo documenta el siguiente pasaje: "La conversación del genio es plegaria [...] El genio cuando habla es más silencioso que el que escucha, así como el que ora es más silencioso que Dios" (*G.S.*, II.1.93, Parte IV).

una escenificación del diario íntimo, que a nivel metafórico se halla enzarzada en un completo "ensamblaje de fuerzas contrarias" como en la imagen paradójica de la "ascensión al trono de quien abdica" (*G.S.*, II.1.101). Sin embargo, la figura de la amada que sale al encuentro del yo desde el paisaje del conocimiento, o mejor, la amada que es enviada desde el paisaje demuestra que esta escena está organizada desde la especificidad del género.

Mientras que no podría ser mayor la distancia de este paisaje de diario íntimo del Yo con el paisaje de los despojos de la multitud en la historia primigenia de la Modernidad (es decir: el pasaje de los textos juveniles sobre el Yo hasta la lectura de las imágenes de la memoria de la Modernidad), estos textos marcan, con todo, su constelación específica, en tanto ponen en escena una perspectiva contraria al tiempo histórico, así como la dramaturgia del texto temprano arroja una oculta relación con el proyecto de los Pasajes. La figura de la amada, como parte de lo mítico, en tanto paisaje del acontecimiento percibido, se destaca a veces de modo más claro, a veces sólo como una sombra, para indicarnos el camino en el laberinto de un texto en el que esa simbología no aprehendida se transforma en el poderoso archivo de un pensamiento dialéctico en imágenes. Como Ariadna o como Guardiana del Umbral, ella nos sale al encuentro aquí y en la mayoría de los textos de Benjamin.

Si hasta ahora estuvo siempre presente en la recepción de Benjamin la imagen de la "prostituta como alegoría de la Modernidad" –se nos aparece en el libro sobre Baudelaire y en el proyecto de los Pasajes– (siempre y cuando se hubiera prestado atención a la importancia de la diferencia genérica en sus textos), es mi intención ahora seguir las huellas de aquella Ariadna, de modo de descifrar la metamorfosis de las imágenes en imágenes dialécticas en ese laberinto textual.

dinamismo de lo profano y la intensidad mesiánica, la idea de dos fuerzas que proviniendo de direcciones contrapuestas tuvieran la capacidad, sin embargo, de impulsarse mutuamente (véase *supra*), como "*gegenstrebige Fügung*" [ensamblaje de fuerzas contrarias] (*G.S.*, II.1.204). En el ensayo sobre Kafka que data de 1934 esta misma figura aparece como una vuelta, como "dirección del estudio que transforma la existencia en escritura" (*G.S.*, II.2.437) o en la imagen del estudio como un galope que se lanza contra esa tormenta "que sopla desde el olvido"[2] (*G.S.*, II.2.436), mientras que esta misma constelación más adelante va a tomar la forma de una imagen dialéctica, como una figura de pensamiento sobre la disimultaneidad entre un enfoque de la cadena de acontecimientos y la mirada del ángel dirigida hacia la catástrofe (las ruinas del pasado), aplicada ahora a la teoría de la historia.[3]

El mismo ordenamiento dinámico estructuraba, sin embargo, ya el texto literario sobre el diario íntimo —posiblemente como una "simbología incomprendida"—. El Yo inmerso en un acontecimiento que "lo rodea *como* un paisaje"[4] (*G.S.*, II.1.99, el destacado es mío), se dirige hacia atrás; y la tormenta que se enfurece en el Yo en movimiento, a quien las cosas le hacen frente, hace surgir un "movimiento contrario de esas cosas en el tiempo del Yo"[5] (*G.S.*, II.1.102). Las expresiones referidas al tiempo, que sentimos "resonar violentamente contra nosotros de nuevo"[6] (*G.S.*, II.1.100) o a la mirada de las cosas, que nos impulsa hacia el futuro (*G.S.*, II.1.99), o la que sostiene que en "ese tiempo del Yo, en el que las cosas se nos oponen [...] Para él todo lo futuro ya ha pasado"[7] (*G.S.*, II.1.102) esbozan topográficamente

---

2. En alemán: "*Denn es ist ja ein Sturm, der aus dem Vergessen herweht. Und das Studium ein Ritt, der dagegen angeht*". [N. del T.]
3. Véase para este aspecto, el capítulo 4 del presente estudio.
4. En alemán: "*Als Landschaft umgibt uns alles Geschehen*". [N. del T.]
5. En alemán: "*Gegenbewegung der Dinge in der Zeit des Ich*". [N. del T.]
6. En alemán: "*gewaltig gegen uns wieder fluten*". [N. del T.]
7. En alemán: "*jene Zeit, in der die Dinge uns widerfahren [...] Ihr ist alle Zukunft vergangen*". [N. del T.]

marca en la estructura de los ensayos tempranos, de los artículos y de las anotaciones y que volveremos a encontrar en los escritos de la década del treinta. Si bien es cierto que con una pequeña pero efectiva diferencia en el modo de escritura, en el desplazamiento del uso de las imágenes, que permite ahora que la imaginería y las representaciones dialécticas lleguen a ser imágenes leídas. Se trata en sí –siguiendo al Foucault de *El orden del discurso* (1971a: 61)– de un "desplazamiento diminuto" [*mince décalage*] que obraría como "una pequeña (y quizás odiosa) maquinaria que permite introducir en la raíz misma del pensamiento el *azar,* lo *discontinuo* y la *materialidad*".[1]

La relación en la que en el texto citado de Benjamin se introduce "el Yo contra los padres" [*das Ich gegen die Väter*] y que indica en la perspectiva de la voz narrativa de un "nosotros" evidentemente la de un jovencito, caracteriza "La conversación" sin ninguna duda como perteneciente a la época temprana. Con todo, otras constelaciones –ésas en las que no hay una posición tomada desde el yo que escribe, sino que deben leerse como constelaciones *textuales*– anuncian claramente en su escenificación y en su ordenación topográfica imágenes de pensamiento que serán paradigmáticas en los escritos tardíos. Así el texto titulado "Das Tagebuch" ["El diario íntimo"], que debería conformar un ciclo junto con "La conversación" y "Der Ball" ["El baile"] –dado que aparecen agrupados bajo el título de *Metafísica de la juventud*–, prenuncia un ordenamiento en cuya configuración tanto filosófica como lingüística Benjamin ha estado trabajando desde siempre. Así también en el "Fragmento teológico-político" (escrito alrededor de 1920) Benjamin buscó resumir, en una imagen conceptual que fuera corriente y estuviera entre el

---

con el viejo sentido de "moza rústica y algo grosera", como todavía se ve en el diminutivo de "*Dirndlkleid*" (vestido típico de muchacha). La palabra "*Hure*", en cambio, tiene una connotación negativa más unívoca desde antiguo, como en inglés "*whore*". [N. del T.]

1. Foucault, 1971a: 61: "...*une petite (et odieuse peut être) machinerie qui permet d'introduire à la racine même de la pensée, le* hasard, *le* discontinu *et la* matérialité." [N. del T.]

sexuales, que en el presente se desarrollan más allá de los mitos de autenticidad, tienen que ver sólo con el plano de la *performance*, las imágenes dialécticas y el espacio del cuerpo y de la imagen benjaminianos incluyen la génesis y la representación de imaginarios corpóreos así como figuraciones lingüísticas.

"UNA SIMBOLOGÍA NO APREHENDIDA": ORÍGENES DE UN PENSAR EN IMÁGENES

> Una simbología no aprehendida nos esclaviza sin ceremonias. A veces, al despertar, nos acordamos de un sueño. Pero raramente la clarividencia ilumina los despojos de nuestra fuerza en la que el tiempo marcó su paso al vuelo. ("*Metaphysich-geschichtsphilosophische Studien*", G.S., II.1.91).

Estas observaciones sobre el momento del despertar, que echa luz sobre una simbología aprehendida, no provienen de las anotaciones del proyecto de los Pasajes, como podría creerse, sino que se hallan en el comienzo de un texto que Benjamin escribió cuando contaba con 21 años y que tituló entonces "La conversación". De esta y de otras anotaciones que han surgido en relación con sus actividades estudiantiles y en la época de los movimientos de las Asociaciones Juveniles, no es sólo la imagen particular ni la formulación concreta o su figuración lo que vincula sus escritos tempranos con el último gran proyecto de trabajo del modo más peculiar. El concepto de la experiencia, las ideas sobre la estructura del tiempo que incluyen el concepto del tiempo mesiánico, cercanía y distancia, el movimiento y la mirada de las cosas, el concepto de la revelación [*Offenbarung*], un lenguaje no-instrumental, la relación entre lo erótico y el conocimiento [*Erkenntnis*], muchas figuras femeninas –especialmente la de la "prostituta" [*Hure*], que en esta etapa todavía es llamada "ramera" [*Dirne*]*–, todos estos son motivos que ya dejan su

---

* La palabra "*Dirne*" en alemán actual tiene un sabor arcaico que la conecta

6. Desde las imágenes a las imágenes dialécticas
El significado de las diferencias de género en los escritos benjaminianos

Si en el capítulo anterior el acento se hallaba puesto en las figuras específicas de pensamiento y los movimientos de la teoría dialéctica de Benjamin como condición para una reflexión teórica sobre constelaciones de la diferencia de género, en este punto se ha de analizar su propio trabajo en imágenes que se relacionan con ese tema. Aquí se muestra justamente que las imágenes sobre femineidad, sobre los mitos de la creación y las metáforas sexuales representan uno de los archivos más importantes en los que se puede reconstruir de modo más fehaciente la génesis de las imágenes dialécticas en los escritos de Benjamin, y que su trabajo en la transformación de las imágenes en imágenes dialécticas adquiere justamente allí un perfil visible. Así podría decirse que en el marco del trabajo teórico benjaminiano las imágenes relacionadas con el género sexual representarían la alegoría de un procedimiento alegórico. No se trata solamente de que ciertos tipos que encarnan lo femenino aparezcan explícitamente delineados en el proyecto de los Pasajes y en el libro sobre Baudelaire, sino de que también su método de la alegoría moderna (del desvío que lleva hacia ella) o de la alegoría de la Modernidad obtiene un claro perfil gracias a las imágenes de lo femenino.

También la postura de la "crítica salvadora" [*rettende Kritik*] frente a los deseos [*gegenüber dem Begehren*], que aparece vinculada a las imágenes de lo genérico sexual, podría tornarse fructífera para las actuales teorías de "*gender*". Mientras que cada estrategia como el juego de máscaras o la parodia de los roles

ción y observación de la historia del sujeto femenino, más allá de las ilusiones creadas por un discurso emancipatorio o por una negativa hacia la historia. Las condiciones que ofrece Benjamin son un complemento importante a las posibilidades de la teoría de Kristeva, precisamente allí, donde deben trasladarse los cuestionamientos desde el campo psicoanalítico a uno histórico.

(hacia los espacios interiores y cocinas amueblados técnicamente durante el "milagro económico"), sería interesante tomar nota también de otro enfoque posible: la participación de la mujer en el trabajo de reconstrucción y en el despeje de las ruinas causadas por la catástrofe del nacionalsocialismo. También a las mujeres les concierne esa pregunta que formula Primo Levi en su texto de recuerdos, cuando describe su camino de regreso a través de la Alemania destruida en calidad de sobreviviente de un campo de concentración de Auschwitz: "Mientras deambulaba por las calles llenas de escombros de Múnich, en la cercanía de la estación, donde nuestro tren se hallaba de nuevo encallado, me sentí como si me moviera entre una multitud de deudores morosos, como si cada uno particularmente me debiera algo y se negara a pagármelo. Estaba entre ellos, en el campo de Agramante, entre el pueblo de los dominadores; pero había pocos varones, muchos de ellos eran lisiados, y muchos andaban en andrajos como nosotros. Me parecía que cada uno hubiera debido formularnos preguntas, leernos en el rostro quiénes éramos y escuchar humildemente nuestro informe. Pero nadie nos miraba a los ojos, nadie aceptaba la contienda: todos eran sordos, ciegos y mudos, encerrados en sus ruinas como en una fortaleza de voluntaria ignorancia, sintiéndose todavía fuertes, capaces siempre de odiar y despreciar, prisioneros de las antiguas ataduras de soberbia y culpa" ("Il resveglio"; Levi, 1963: 249).

los "hombres" o con el "sistema masculino", sino que tiene que incluir a las mujeres en esta perspectiva.[23] En todo caso, las mujeres (en base a su sexo biológico) comparten bastante de la perspectiva del ángel por la división específica genérica (en base al "sexo impuesto socialmente") del trabajo en la historia de la cultura occidental. Son justamente *ellas*, las que se hallan ocupadas mayormente con los cuerpos, tanto en la gestación como en su tarea de cuidado de los enfermos y en su duelo por los muertos. Sin embargo, no debe comparárselas con el "Ángel de la Historia", dado que como sobrevivientes, como participantes de esta historia y de esta cultura, sus rostros se ven necesitados de apartar la mirada del ángel.[24]

Sin embargo, hay una diferencia en tanto sean hombres o mujeres los que se enfrentan a esta imagen, una *diferencia* que es justamente esa tan difícilmente expresable a nivel conceptual que se pone en juego entre la dialéctica del Iluminismo y su variante femenina, siempre y cuando, con todo, la imagen benjaminiana del "Ángel de la Historia" se lea como dialéctica. Y si con ella no puede decirse que la filosofía de la historia de Benjamin erija una piedra miliar para una teoría de lo femenino, bien puede entenderse que ella propone las condiciones previas para una representa-

---

23. He tratado de expresar el específico lugar de la mujer dentro de una cultura en la que ella, al mismo tiempo en que es partícipe aparece también como excluida, con los conceptos de una "mirada bizca" [*schielender Blick*] y de una constelación en la imagen de la "voz de la Medusa" [*Stimme der Medusa*]; véanse Weigel, 1983 y 1987. Entre las autoras actuales en lengua alemana, puede mencionarse especialmente Anne Duden, quien parte de la posición de la mujer como víctima *y* agente; véanse sus publicaciones: *Übergang* [*Pasaje*], de 1982, y *Das Judasschaf* ["Piel de Judas"], de 1985. Cf. al respecto la conversación Duden y Weigel, 1989.

24. Si se estableciera la relación entre la escena del "Ángel de la Historia" con, por ejemplo, la situación histórica de las así llamadas *Trümmerfrauen* ["mujeres de los escombros"] después de 1945, ayudando a la reconstrucción en Alemania, el trabajo del recuerdo dentro de la investigación feminista (que se ha ocupado de estas mujeres) obtendría seguramente una acentuación diferente. Mientras que hasta ahora lo que interesó fue el aspecto de un trabajo no rentado, sobre todo en consideración con la subsiguiente expulsión de las mujeres del mercado laboral que las llevó exclusivamente al trabajo doméstico

este trabajo, en el significado de los tres diferentes ángeles y la dialéctica desarrollada entre sus respectivos lugares en el texto–,[22] se agregará ahora una nueva lectura hecha desde la perspectiva de las mujeres dentro de la historia de la emancipación. El punto de partida será, en consecuencia, la lectura del "Ángel de la Historia" como imagen dialéctica y como constelación de una disimultaneidad.

Cuando las mujeres leen hoy esta imagen, se hace evidente qué difícil es encontrar un lugar en esa dialéctica. Así, el primer ángel –la voz lírica en la poesía de Scholem– ofrece la aceptación de una perspectiva atemporal, en la que un Yo, colocado moralmente en una posición superior –que con una variante de lectura podría entenderse como: el mundo "masculino" o "patriarcal"–, le da la espalda al mundo de hoy. Esta lectura sería, claro, la versión de una salida de la historia, en la que el ángel completaría su representación, por ejemplo, girando su cabeza hacia un tiempo anterior supuestamente más feliz (matriarcal). El segundo ángel (representado en la rigidez de la figura aterrorizada de Paul Klee) se ofrece, por el contrario, a una mirada fascinante, a una identificación con una rigidez mítica, a un observador fascinado por el mito y captado en una identificación fascinada con la posición de víctima [*Opferposition*]. El tercero, el "Ángel de la Historia", por fin, aparece expresamente como diferente "de nosotros". Con la discordancia entre su posición y la "nuestra", se quiebra la estructura figurativa que se basa en el momento de la identificación en que se cae en el desconocimiento de lo heterogéneo. El "nosotros" puede referirse al "nosotros" que piensa en conceptualizaciones de Progreso o, simplemente, pero de modo necesario, puede referirse al "nosotros" de los sobrevivientes. Leído esto políticamente o desde el feminismo puede remitir también a la participación de las mujeres en el concepto de Progreso en tanto "emancipación". Sin embargo, en la medida en que las mujeres tomen parte en las instituciones dominantes, este "nosotros" no puede identificarse sin más con

---

22. Véase el capítulo 4 del presente estudio.

de una construcción, cuyo lugar no lo conforma un tiempo homogéneo y vacío, sino colmado por el *Jetztzeit*" (Reflexión XIV de "Sobre el concepto de historia"; *G.S.*, I. 2. 701).

Para una historia de las mujeres, así como para toda historiografía que no haga suya la mirada de los dominadores ("de los herederos de aquellos que han conquistado antes", como afirma Benjamin en la Reflexión VII), las observaciones benjaminianas representan un estímulo productivo, especialmente porque a las mujeres se las recuerda para citar sólo unos pocos aspectos o imágenes de su pasado, dado que ellas fueron en gran parte "olvidadas" en las tradiciones y minimizadas como sujetos. Así, mientras que la historiografía orientada a una concepción de desarrollo no dice absolutamente nada sobre los sujetos femeninos, sobre autoras, artistas, etcétera, se abre en la lectura de los mitos, de pinturas y de otras fuentes de la imagen una abundancia de correspondencias con vivencias y situaciones de las mujeres de hoy, como lo documentan también citas de figuras femeninas históricas y míticas en determinados textos de la literatura actual, en los que no se trata de representar "cómo ha sido realmente" la historia (según parodia Benjamin en su Reflexión VI), sino que lo que importa son las imágenes de pensamiento literarias, así como las constelaciones de una dialéctica femenina del Iluminismo, las imágenes del recuerdo de un pasado, donde se puede apresar a las mujeres en el momento del despertar (para las que ese instante es también un momento de peligro).[21]

UNA LECTURA DEL "ÁNGEL DE LA HISTORIA" DESDE LA PERSPECTIVA DE LAS MUJERES

Para concretar la práctica de la imagen dialéctica de Benjamin, refiriéndola a una problemática de una dialéctica femenina del Iluminismo, a la relectura de su conocida imagen del "Ángel de la Historia" –que ha sido desarrollada en páginas anteriores de

---

21. Para este aspecto, compárese Weigel, 1987, especialmente en el capítulo titulado "Literaturgeschichte in Bewegung" ["Historia de la literatura en movimiento"].

se separa tanto de una filología que permaneciera fijada a una "inspección" [*Beaugenscheinigung*] de un texto, hipnotizada por él, como también de una mitología,[20] estableciendo su procedimiento de una "lectura auténtica":

> La filología es ese tipo de inspección de un texto que se esmera en los detalles, atando al lector mágicamente a él... La apariencia de una facticidad cerrada, que queda aprisionada en la investigación filológica y que produce una hipnosis en el investigador, se volatiliza en la medida en que se construye el objeto en perspectiva histórica. Las líneas de fuga de esta construcción convergen en nuestra propia experiencia histórica. De este modo se constituye el objeto como mónada. Todo lo que cargado en el texto se encontraba en una parálisis mítica, se torna viviente en la mónada... Por ello, usted ha de encontrar que la crítica a la postura del filólogo es en mí una vieja preocupación —y que ella está íntimamente identificada con la preocupación por el mito. (Carta de Benjamin a Adorno del 9 de diciembre de 1938; Benjamin, 1978: 794-795)

Con la mirada puesta en la historia, este proceso aparece ligado a una negativa a imaginarse la continuidad y el progreso. Como alternativa a una lógica de desarrollo de una historiografía lineal, una lectura en el sentido benjaminiano se abre a las *correspondencias* entre el *Jetztzeit* y "lo que ha sido" (que son tanto de naturaleza dialéctica como figurativa, según lo había formulado Benjamin en su anotación sobre la "imagen dialéctica"). Las correspondencias del presente se refieren a "lo que ha sido" al "citar" los aspectos del pasado, haciéndolas saltar del *continuum* de la historia y "cargándolas" así con su *Jetztzeit*, por lo que el modo de la iluminación o carga se conforma a partir de la situación en la que se encuentran, de sus afectos y deseos, de sus expectativas (hacia una redención), pues: "La historia es objeto

---

20. En este contexto se inserta también su apartamiento de los *Paysans de Paris* de Louis Aragon, que Benjamin considera el modelo y lo opuesto de sus propios escritos sobre la ciudad: "Mientras que en Aragon permanece un elemento impresionista —'la mitología'— y a este impresionismo se lo hace responsable por los muchos filosofemas sin forma del libro; en mi caso se trata de una disolución de la 'mitología' en el espacio de la historia" (Anotaciones y materiales para "La obra de los Pasajes", Block N1,9; *G.S.*, V.1.571).

de un psicoanálisis estructural que dirige su punto de mira sobre fenómenos sociales y de historia cultural.

Justamente con el interés de Benjamin por los mitos de la Modernidad, pero también –lo que es más importante– con la perspectiva histórica de sus estudios, la teoría benjaminiana establece una complementariedad productiva con las tesis de Kristeva para la investigación de una dialéctica femenina del Iluminismo. Las imágenes dialécticas benjaminianas constituyen una *topografía histórica* independientemente del modelo gráfico como el del esquema triádico. Ellas deben leerse como superposiciones de imágenes iluminadas de modo diferente, *double exposures* del *Jetztzeit* así como de "lo que ha sido", en las que pueden ser leídas en todas sus contradicciones las constelaciones históricas, que incluyen la historia del sujeto femenino.[19]

En lo que respecta a la relación entre mito e Iluminismo, el enfoque de Benjamin se dirige hacia los aspectos de pasaje. Para esto una de las constelaciones centrales es la idea del *despertar*, que considera el caso paradigmático del pensamiento dialéctico, el umbral entre la noche y el día como transición entre el sueño y la conciencia. Es, por lo tanto, una constelación que se organiza topográficamente como un paso complejo (a nivel psicoanalítico como "umbral", a nivel temporal como "el ahora de la cognoscibilidad" e históricamente como superposición entre "lo que ha sido" y lo presente). Esta organización parece apropiada, así, para la presentación de un movimiento dialéctico en un acto suspendido, para la observación y el conocimiento como imagen dialéctica.

Al no escatimar los aspectos de lo mítico y del inconsciente ni negar su magia, estos aspectos abren el camino en la obra de Benjamin hacia una reflexión fructífera. En este proceso, Benjamin

---

19. Sus imágenes dialécticas se refieren, entre otras cosas, a la descripción topográfica del "aparato psíquico" según las "Notas sobre 'la pizarra mágica' " freudianas. En ese texto de Freud, aparece pensada la *disimultaneidad* entre percepción-conciencia y recuerdo tanto a nivel temporal como espacial (Freud, 1952; XIV). Cf. el capítulo 8 del presente estudio.

significativo la magia, el mito y una instrumentalización progresiva. Mientras que en Horkheimer y Adorno magia, mitos e Iluminismo son definidos esencialmente como estadios consecutivos de una evolución histórica, Benjamin, por su parte, pone el acento más bien sobre las disimultaneidades. Su teoría lingüística aparece, en consecuencia, impregnada por el duelo causado por la pérdida del carácter mágico del lenguaje, por la pérdida de su inmediatez, por ese "lenguaje paradisíaco" del hombre que era, al mismo tiempo, cognoscitivo y denominativo. Esa teoría lleva también la impronta del saber acerca de la lógica histórica de esta pérdida. Ella, además, se funda sobre una *praxis* de la *lectura* que acredita su "explosividad" [*Brisanz*] sobre todo en los mitos de la Modernidad, cuando Benjamin descubre, por ejemplo, "correspondencias entre el mundo de la técnica moderna y el mundo simbólico arcaico de la mitología" (Anotaciones y materiales para "La obra de los Pasajes", Block N2a,1; *G.S.*, V.1.576), o descifra en la topografía y arquitectura urbanas una estructura onírica, y, en este proceso, reflexiona sobre los aspectos de lo mítico y del inconsciente en la historia del progreso, de la tecnificación y del mundo de la mercancía y de las cosas.

A nivel metodológico se trata aquí de la significación de posiciones psicoanalíticas para una representación materialista de la historia, en la que Benjamin, en base a ese materialismo, insiste en incluir la *materia* que se halla condicionando las relaciones de producción, como, por ejemplo, el cuerpo humano. Al comprender la materialidad humana de modo físico y la corporeidad en lo colectivo con la categoría del espacio del cuerpo y de la imagen[18] en tanto base para una visión materialista, Benjamin distingue la organización técnica de la *physis* de su realidad política y objetiva, lo que suscita un traslado de su gestación al territorio de la imagen. En otras palabras: se produce así una reflexión acerca de la significación de lo *imaginario* para la realidad de lo físico. En este movimiento, las ideas benjaminianas se tocan con las perspectivas

---

18. Al respecto véase el capítulo 2 del presente estudio.

lo femenino en lo simbólico, dándole, a la vez, representación topográfica: la mujer se encuentra situada en la posición inferior con el cuerpo frente al *infans*, mientras que aquí encuentra su expresión tanto la relación de los sexos como también el nexo entre *Cuerpo* y *Nombre-Ley*. De este modo surge una teoría en la que, partiendo de la tríada y de sus personajes, se desarrolla un pensar en imágenes, donde las situaciones más variadas y las "soluciones" son aprehendidas y presentadas figurativamente como imágenes superpuestas de escenas primarias psicoanalíticas y sus repeticiones en lo simbólico o sus transformaciones hacia lo simbólico.[15] Ello se produce, sobre todo, en la ampliación de sus estudios sobre temas de historia cultural, allí donde Kristeva abandona el plano de la ontogénesis (como en el epílogo de *Des chinoises* o en sus *Historias de amor*), donde hace referencia de modo reiterado a figuras femeninas míticas.[16] En ese contexto, sus nombres vienen a nombrar constelaciones paradigmáticas y "soluciones" en el profusamente conflictivo devenir sujeto de la mujer.[17]

BENJAMIN: MITO Y MODERNIDAD

Benjamin ha desarrollado, en efecto, tal pensamiento en imágenes más allá del *tropos* de la metáfora. Ello se halla anclado en su teoría del lenguaje, en la que aparecen ordenados de modo

---

15. Por ejemplo, en tales giros como "la virginidad de la palabra", "la hija de su padre" o "la hija de su madre"; cf. "De nuestro lado", en Kristeva (1974b).
16. Sus *Historias de amor* tratan de mitos centrales de la cultura cristiana como la Virgen María, Romeo y Julieta o Don Juan. Por otro lado, el hecho de que la recepción de Kristeva sea más positiva en los países de habla alemana que en los anglófonos puede estar conectado con el fenómeno de que en Alemania su libro *La révolution du langage poétique* se consideró como el principio y la base para su lugar de enunciación teórica. De este modo sus textos que de modo explícito se refieren a la "femineidad" jamás han alcanzado la significación de su libro sobre poesía.
17. Cf. para ello el capítulo sobre la referencia a los mitos y al recuerdo de la historia en mi libro sobre la literatura actual de mujeres (Weigel, 1987).

las consecuencias de esa constelación para la comprensión de la mujer, tanto para la mujer en devenir, la niña [*das Mädchen*],[14][*] como también para el destino y significado de ese cuerpo femenino que sufre represiones y prohibiciones. En este proceso, Kristeva logra diferenciar varias funciones y posiciones femeninas, como, por ejemplo, "la función de la madre", que se halla asociada a un predominio del cuerpo materno en la fase preedípica, y también la función de la mujer en lo simbólico que denomina "el efecto mujer": "un efecto que no dispone ni de poder ni de un sistema lingüístico, sino que es su muda apoyatura" (Kristeva, 1976: 167); es decir: es el apoyo mudo del sistema pero él mismo no tiene visibilidad. Y ello es una imagen que hay que tomar completamente de modo literal y concreto.

El hecho de que a Kristeva le haya sido posible describir la conflictuada historia de la constitución del sujeto femenino con la carga de contradicciones necesariamente allí implícitas, se explica en su proyección de los conflictos analizados en el modelo de sujeto del psicoanálisis: *la tríada*. Los conflictos que acontecen en la dimensión de la historia del sujeto y de la cultura se representan ahora en una figuración triádica. Desde la perspectiva del *infans* femenino la constitución del sujeto de la mujer se va moviendo de ese modo en forma conflictiva entre los polos de la identificación con el padre, o mejor: con la *Ley* en Nombre del Padre, y de la identificación con la madre, o mejor: con el *Cuerpo* de la madre. La posición ocupada por el padre que se halla en la punta superior de la tríada se relaciona con la Ley y con el Nombre. La posición ocupada por la madre en este modelo hace imaginable la compleja problemática de un lugar de

---

14. La posición del *infans*, que en Freud y Lacan aparece casi únicamente descrita desde lo masculino, es analizada por Kristeva también desde el ángulo de lo femenino.

* En el caso de Freud, la coartada de la asexualidad del *niño* está dada por la adjudicación al género neutro de la palabra que lo designa [*das Kind*]. El idioma francés por su parte, en el caso de Lacan, no deja de mostrar su sexismo al denominar al niño con un masculino supuestamente indeterminado [*l'enfant*] [N. del T.]

historia descifrada como una imagen en tanto dialéctica en un acto suspendido.

...Y DIFERENCIAS: KRISTEVA Y LA TRÍADA PSICOANALÍTICA

En la conformación de la teoría feminista los escritos de Kristeva han logrado una incomparablemente mayor difusión que los de Benjamin. Al mismo tiempo, puede decirse que la recepción de Kristeva viene a ocupar el lugar de una recepción incompleta de Benjamin, que con ella ha ganado para el feminismo una dirección psicoanalítica de modo evidente. En las investigaciones acerca del complicado lugar de la mujer en su entrada en la historia –la historia del sujeto y la historia de la cultura–, a la toma de partido por la teoría kristeviana le corresponde un lugar tan central y productivo, justamente, porque su modo de continuar escribiendo el psicoanálisis en clave estructuralista hace representable las diferentes posiciones de los sexos en forma de tríada.

A la cuestión de una constelación problemática de una dialéctica del Iluminismo en Benjamin le corresponde en las reflexiones de Kristeva –ancladas en primera instancia en el terreno de la ontogénesis–, la de la complicada entrada de la mujer en lo simbólico. Como ya sucedía en la teoría del sujeto lacaniana, se trata ahora del desplazamiento del grado de desarrollo del "complejo de Edipo" freudiano (que todavía en Freud era parte de un modelo teleológico) hacia una constelación que se representa de modo topográfico y que se concibe como el pasaje del dualismo madre-hijo hacia una relación *triádica*, en la que la prohibición del incesto (para ambos sexos) se ve como la prohibición de la madre o como separación del cuerpo de la madre. Ello conlleva consecuencias también para la referencia mítica. La alusión al mito de Edipo ya no sigue teniendo lugar a modo de una identificación actualizante con la figura trágica griega, ni tampoco lo que interesa aquí es contar otra vez la historia antigua. En lugar de ello, esto es leído como la escena primaria de una constelación que ha devenido una estructura.

En oposición a Lacan, Kristeva se interesa especialmente por

de las similitudes no sensoriales" ("La enseñanza de lo semejante"; *G.S.*, II.1.209). Después de la desaparición de la magia del lenguaje originaria y la llegada del dominio del lenguaje sígnico, se manifiesta el costado mágico en determinadas *constelaciones* o *fases* en el aspecto comunicativo del lenguaje, de tal modo que lo similar se evidencia con la rapidez de un destello. Así se concreta el concepto benjaminiano de "similitudes no sensoriales" con la relación entre el carácter de una magia perdida del lenguaje y el lenguaje de signos predominante, donde aparece lo mimético ya sólo de modo pasajero o como un destello, es decir, en un parpadeo instantáneo [*im Augen-Blick*], de tal modo que en ese proceso se tornan visibles las imágenes desconcertantes [*Vexierbilder*] del inconsciente y de lo no todavía consciente. El costado mágico necesita, por lo tanto, al aspecto comunicativo del lenguaje para hacerse visible. Ese aspecto, en tanto fase venidera del lenguaje, previamente reprimida pero que ha retornado en diferente forma al nivel visible, no puede aislarse empíricamente. Como lo semiótico en Kristeva, la mímesis benjaminiana se halla vinculada a una concepción dialéctica.

En su función teórica el concepto benjaminiano de "similitud no sensorial" puede compararse con la concepción de Kristeva acerca de lo semiótico como "segundo retorno de la funcionalidad pulsional en lo simbólico". Sin embargo, a pesar de las analogías entre sus respectivas concepciones teóricas del lenguaje y del acto dador de sentido, a pesar de que ambos muestran interés por la ruptura con el mito de la creación, y por las consecuencias de esta ruptura, y por los aspectos perdidos de la escritura –los cuales se manifiestan de manera diferente después de haberse transformado–, es necesario destacar que existen diferencias significativas entre ambos. Así mientras que Kristeva se interesa, a nivel de lo semiótico, por un "sujeto en movimiento" y por una *praxis* textual específica que otorga su significación a lo discontinuo, al ritmo, a la gesticulación y al cuerpo lingüístico; Benjamin, por su parte, dirige su atención a la magia del lenguaje y a las "similitudes no sensoriales" con las imágenes y constelaciones, y también a la transgresión (Kristeva, 1974b: 68). Así, entonces, lo semiótico logra su expresión como ataque, como transgresión, como infracción, como explosión en lo simbólico. Ambas modalidades del proceso dador de sentido, sin embargo, no pueden aislarse empíricamente una de otra, puesto que la dialéctica con la que se hallan en relación posibilita este mismo proceso.

Lo "thético",* tanto como corte y como límite, ocupa en la teoría kristeviana estructuralmente el mismo lugar que tiene en la teoría lingüística benjaminiana "la expulsión del paraíso sufrida por el lenguaje". Benjamin separa, en efecto, "el 'lenguaje paradisíaco' del hombre" de la *media*-tez del lenguaje como signo. En referencia a la segunda versión del mito de la creación en la Biblia y como derivación del lenguaje creativo de Dios, Benjamin considera al lenguaje humano antes de la expulsión tanto cognitivo como denominativo. Su carácter mágico consiste en su capacidad para reconocer el lenguaje mudo de la naturaleza y de las cosas en el acto de nombrarlas. Se trata aquí de la descripción llevada a cabo en el mito bíblico de una situación lingüística previa a la inmediatez en la que todavía se hallaban sin separar la comunicación y lo comunicado: la magia del lenguaje y la mímesis. La pérdida de esta magia inmanente aparece vinculada con el origen de la abstracción como capacidad del espíritu del lenguaje en la expulsión del paraíso, pero también con el conocimiento del Bien y del Mal y con el surgimiento de un lenguaje, que, al participar *algo* (fuera de sí mismo), se torna puro signo. Con ello se traspasa la inmediatez hacia la abstracción, creando una nueva magia que ya no descansa en sí misma, una magia del Juicio, que tendrá sus raíces en la Palabra que descarga su Condena ("Sobre el lenguaje en general y sobre el lenguaje de los humanos"; *G.S.*, II.1.152).

El perdido don mimético del hombre, según Benjamin, "ha ido a dar, en su recorrido de siglos de desarrollo, muy paulatinamente al habla y a la escritura, creando en ellos el más perfecto archivo

---

* La palabra griega *thetikós* es traducida como "aquello que es materia de discusión; discutible" (A. Bailly, ob. cit.). [N. del T.]

(Kristeva) y la del lenguaje sígnico que funciona como un mediador (Benjamin). De aquí en adelante, la aparición de la modalidad anterior está ligada a la modalidad dominante de la etapa posterior en el texto o en la escritura, pero se presentará *sólo* como transgresión y corte, o como un destello y vertiginosa iluminación.

Según Kristeva, las articulaciones de lo semiótico pertenecen a la fase pre-edípica caracterizada por una relación arcaica con la madre. En este sentido, son consideradas como funciones pre-simbólicas y pre-lingüísticas predecesoras del discurso que las va a utilizar para apoyarse en ellas, pero tomando a su vez distancia. Dado que en esta concepción la constitución del sujeto, en el modelo psicoanalítico que sirve de base, se halla vinculada con la entrada en el lenguaje, es decir, en lo simbólico, Kristeva puede decir:

> Como lugar de engendramiento del sujeto, la *chora* semiótica es para él [el sujeto] el lugar de su negación donde su unidad retrocede ante el proceso de cargas y de *stasis** que la producen. (Kristeva, 1974b: 27)

Lo semiótico debe ser aislado de la teoría, sin embargo, sólo como elemento "previo" [*préalable*], particularizando su funcionamiento. Nos alcanza recién después de la "tesis" simbólica, es decir: después del "corte" [*coupure*] en el que confluyen las brechas semióticas y *stasis* de las pulsiones en la posición del significante, mientras que a causa de este corte se produce el engendramiento recursivo de lo semiótico, como un "segundo" retorno de la funcionalidad pulsional hacia lo simbólico, como una negatividad introducida en el orden simbólico, como su

---

y sobre el lenguaje de los humanos"(1916), "La enseñanza de lo semejante" (1933) y "Sobre la capacidad mimética" (1933).

* La palabra griega *stasis* es definida en como estabilidad, fijeza/ levantamiento, revuelta" (A. Bailly, ob. cit.), mientras que María Moliner la documenta para el español en el área de la medicina como "estasis"="detención" (M. Moliner, *Diccionario de uso del español*, Madrid, Gredos, 1990). [N. del T.]

tenido lugar después de 1968 (dedicada a buscar los rastros materialistas en ella) no dejó de hacer lo suyo para impedir una visión más clara.[12] La recepción incompleta, e incluso obstruida, de sus textos tiene en parte culpa de que hoy la Teoría Crítica y el posestructuralismo se encuentren en terrenos enfrentados entre sí, mientras que realmente pueden observarse puntos de contacto entre los escritos de Benjamin y los de Michel Foucault y Julia Kristeva, por ejemplo.

ANALOGÍAS ENTRE LAS CONCEPCIONES TEÓRICAS DE BENJAMIN Y KRISTEVA...

Benjamin y Kristeva podrían ser comparados dentro de sus reflexiones teóricas sobre todo en la concepción dialéctica del proceso dador de sentido en Kristeva (1974b) y en el caso del lenguaje en Benjamin. Es posible establecer un paralelo entre la dimensión del sujeto de la historia descrita por Kristeva como lo "Semiótico" y lo "Simbólico", y la relación establecida por Benjamin, en su representación de la historia cultural, entre el aspecto mágico del lenguaje (lo mimético) y su aspecto comunicativo, diferenciándolos uno de otro pero vinculándolos entre sí por su funcionamiento. La respectiva modalidad privilegiada en cada uno –los modos de articulación de la *chora* * semiótica en Kristeva y la magia del "lenguaje paradisíaco" del hombre en Benjamin–[13] se integra hasta desaparecer en el momento en que surge la siguiente modalidad: la de lo simbólico

---

"Occidentalización de nuestras orientaciones culturales de valor" es uno de los rasgos dominantes en la formación teórica de Alemania (Occidental) desde 1945 (Habermas, 1989).

12. Incluso Seyla Benhabib vuelve a olvidar a Benjamin en su historia de la Teoría Crítica; es decir, lo menciona de modo breve, pero desde la perspectiva de la crítica habermasiana (Benhabib, 1986).

* *Chora*: Kristeva toma este término de Platón en el sentido amplio de "espacio de tierra limitado / lugar ocupado por una persona" (cf. Bailly, ob.cit.). Para el concepto de "chora semiótica", véase pág. 132 del presente trabajo [N. del T.]

13. Especialmente en sus artículos titulados: "Sobre el lenguaje en general

a debérsela ahora a un reino más puro. De este modo, su patria no se halla donde ha nacido, sino que ha llegado al mundo donde se halla su patria. Él es el primogénito masculino de la obra que él mismo había antes concebido. (*G.S.*, IV.1.48)[9]

En este pasaje Benjamin describe una construcción, ligada a la idea de obra, que implica una creación masculina y que se erige autónomamente separada de la categoría *mater-materia*, y esto sucede de tal modo que el varón se adueña de la imagen (del nacimiento), haciéndola devenir reconocible como dialéctica. Es una cuestión todavía pendiente analizar qué consecuencias podría producir este modelo de creación para una artista mujer, y tampoco Benjamin nos dio, por cierto, más claves en este sentido.[10]

El hecho de que hasta ahora hayan merecido poca atención los trabajos y el modo de razonar de Benjamin en la formación de la teoría feminista, ya sea en línea sucesoria con la Teoría Crítica o en un acto de ruptura con ella (con excepción de la revista alemana *Frauen und Film* ["Las Mujeres y el Cine"]), en general tiene su origen seguramente en la demorada recepción de Walter Benjamin. Pero también, en la manera más bien violenta de apropiación de la herencia benjaminiana llevada a cabo por la Escuela de Frankfurt, dado que en esa recepción quedaron en el camino especialmente aquellos aspectos que no se podían integrar con la "orientación hacia la cultura occidental" [*Westorientierung*]* ni con la toma de partido por concepciones que hacían una particular utilización de la Razón y la Comunicación.[11] La recepción selectiva de la obra benjaminiana que ha

---

9. Para el trabajo benjaminiano con las imágenes en relación con el mito de la creación, véase el capítulo 6 del presente estudio. Para un análisis de las perspectivas que este mito ofrece a la historia cultural, véase Weigel, 1990.

10. Para el problema de las diferenciaciones en las condiciones de creación artística para el varón y la mujer, véase el caso ejemplar de Bellmer y Zürn en Weigel, 1990: 67-114.

* Resulta evidente que, visto desde Alemania, con el término de "Westen" (Oeste/Occidente) se quiere aludir especialmente a Francia y a los Estados Unidos que son los únicos modelos válidos para el eurocentrismo alemán. [N. del T.]

11. Jürgen Habermas considera que la "orientación hacia el Oeste" o la

titulado *Walter Benjamin und die Utopie des Weiblichen* ["Walter Benjamin y la utopía de lo femenino"], que para este fin interpreta muchas de las imágenes dialécticas o de crítica al Progreso benjaminianas como utópicas.[7] Más importantes que sus imágenes sobre la femineidad son hoy, en cambio, sus prácticas textuales en el tratamiento con las imágenes de lo femenino transformadas en imágenes dialécticas o en imágenes de pensamiento.

No es un hecho atribuible al azar, al fin y al cabo, que Benjamin en una de sus imágenes de pensamiento (mucho antes de las teorías de la "estética femenina" o "estética de lo femenino") haya encontrado una presentación convincente para el aprovechamiento y a la vez aniquilación de lo femenino en el mito masculino de la creación y, con ello, haya servido de antecedente en su imagen dialéctica para una de las tesis centrales de la crítica literaria feminista. *Cuadros de un pensamiento* culmina en un pequeño texto titulado *Nach der Vollendung* ["Después de la terminación definitiva"], donde Benjamin se ocupa de la metáfora del nacimiento en la conceptualización del "surgimiento de las grandes obras" [*die Entstehung der grossen Werke*], describiendo cómo la concepción de una creación mental ocupa el lugar de la natural, mientras que el aspecto necesariamente femenino para el acto de crear se consume a sí mismo, terminando por agotarse. De este modo el creador renace ya en el mismo momento de la terminación de la obra, pues "Él es el primogénito masculino de la obra que él mismo había antes concebido"[8] (*G.S.*, IV.1. 438). Con la sustitución de la Madre por la Obra, el creador ya no debe su existencia al lugar de donde proviene, sino a la terminación definitiva de su propia obra, y, con ello, no sólo logra independencia de la naturaleza sino que se presenta como superior a ella:

> Como el Bienaventurado, sobrepasa a la Naturaleza: pues esa existencia, que recibió desde el seno de la tierra por primera vez, va

---

7. Esto sucede especialmente con los tipos y motivos del/de la andrógino/a.
8. En alemán: "*Er ist der männliche Erstgeborene des Werkes, das er einstmals empfangen hatte*". [N. del T.]

No debe creerse que el pasado ilumine el presente y que el presente eche luz sobre el pasado, sino que la imagen es aquella en la que lo que ha sido entra en contacto con el ahora para formar una constelación de modo rápido como un destello. En otras palabras: la imagen es dialéctica en un acto suspendido. Pues mientras que la relación del presente con el pasado es puramente temporal, la de lo que ha sido con el ahora es dialéctica: no temporal, sino de naturaleza figurativa [*bildlicher Natur*]. Sólo las imágenes dialécticas son auténticamente históricas, es decir no arcaicas. <y el lugar en el que uno las encuentra es el lenguaje. Despertar.>[6] La imagen leída significa la imagen en el "ahora de la cognoscibilidad", cuando es portadora en sumo grado del sello del instante crítico y peligroso que se halla presente en toda lectura. (Anotaciones y materiales para "La obra de los Pasajes", Block N3,1; *G.S.*, V.1.576)

Para la comprensión de esta anotación en el proyecto de los Pasajes es importante tener en cuenta que en Benjamin la lectura se refiere a algo más que lo escrito y que "lenguaje" significa aquí no sólo las palabras escritas o dichas. Y esto no quiere decir que para Benjamin los fenómenos sociales aparezcan "reducidos" a un texto, sino que la capacidad de leer o la técnica de descifrar operan en un campo más amplio que el referido solamente a lo escrito. La imagen dialéctica benjaminiana, entonces, no contiene una dialéctica *congelada*, sino que representa más bien la toma instantánea de un movimiento en el que el conocimiento se ilumina [*in der... Erkenntnis aufleuchtet*] como en un destello al hacerse visible una constelación específica. Benjamin ha probado su procedimiento, por cierto, en multitud de temas y situaciones de la historia cultural (de modo detallado en el drama barroco, en el París del siglo xix y en el Berlín de su infancia). Al mismo tiempo, siempre ha dado muestras de una mirada escrutadora y muy atenta a los lugares y funciones de lo femenino en el mundo de las imágenes y de los signos que iba analizando. Con todo, no ha producido, por cierto, una teoría de la "femineidad", como podría hacer creer el estudio de Christine Buci-Glucksmann

---

6. En la variante marcada como Block N2a,3 se halla la frase agregada en este punto que colocamos entre ángulos (*G.S.*, V.1.577).

tación conceptual. Esto tiene como resultado que tanto esta búsqueda de un tercer lugar más allá del mito y del Iluminismo –que opera entre algunos del feminismo– como también las esforzadas tentativas de otro esbozo de sujeto (femenino) sean comprensibles, pero tengan poco sentido y no conduzcan, por ello, demasiado lejos. Ambas posibilidades –por lo menos en lo que concierne a las mujeres en los círculos culturales de Europa y los Estados Unidos– parecen salidas apropiadas para evitar caer en la problemática mencionada, pero no para solucionarla. En lugar de eso, partiendo de la consideración de la impropiedad del discurso académico para la compleja constelación de una dialéctica femenina del Iluminismo, lo que se impone es la necesidad de instituir modos específicos de pensar y representar, o sea: introducir una dimensión en el pensamiento dialéctico que *posea una perspectiva múltiple y sea topográfica*. La posición de la mujer dentro de y en relación con el pensamiento de la Ilustración no puede esclarecerse, en un análisis como totalidad y de modo total, con un enfoque que tenga una validez única y general, en consecuencia queda sólo una serie de observaciones –probablemente infinita–, en las que aparecen exactamente iluminadas las más diferentes situaciones y momentos del pasaje.

"IMAGEN DIALÉCTICA" Y DISCURSO DE LOS SEXOS

Para este proyecto nada hay más promisorio que una vuelta a los procedimientos benjaminianos en el tratamiento con los mitos y las imágenes, especialmente en su concepción de la "imagen dialéctica", una imagen que ha interpretado la dialéctica en un acto suspendido [*Dialektik im Stillstand*], o sea: como una instantánea extraída del *continuum* temporal, que oculta su historia previa y posterior dentro de sí como el "ahora de la cognoscibilidad". Sin ninguna duda, la imagen dialéctica benjaminiana es una imagen al servicio del conocimiento, que se conecta, sin embargo, con imágenes vistas, imaginarias o del inconsciente:

empresa de recuperar para la mujer la obtención de la individuación que se le ha negado o el trayecto ganado por el sujeto masculino en la carrera iluminista, tendría para ella consecuencias mucho más agudas que los daños y descompensaciones atestiguados del progreso que produce el varón para sí mismo. Mientras que para el varón se han cumplido las prácticas de apropiación y sumisión de la naturaleza en la materia y en la imagen del Otro, preferentemente *en el otro sexo*, para la mujer este trabajo civilizatorio se refiere a ella misma, según la etimología de *mater-materia*, dado que el dominio y la racionalización en primera instancia se dirigen a la autoconservación; el cuerpo de la mujer como el *escándalo* para una historia fundada sobre la racionalidad. La estructura sacrificial [*Opferstruktur*] de la historia del Iluminismo,[5] no sólo se repite aquí en el sujeto femenino de modo, por así decirlo, más corpóreo y cercano sino que la mujer siempre toma parte en las dos caras de la moneda a la vez. En ello la variante femenina de una dialéctica del Iluminismo –además del componente de la Razón y de lo Otro, que a esta altura puede tener un rostro femenino– parece como si introdujera una tercera posición en esa dialéctica: una posición muy inestable, por cierto, que mantiene relaciones hacia los dos lados, hacia la Razón y hacia lo Otro. Un motivo más para que en las teorías de lo femenino jueguen un papel tan importante los modelos triádicos y especialmente psicoanalíticos.

El lugar de *sujeto femenino* no sólo es mucho más complicado que el masculino, introduce también en la dialéctica una perspectiva *doblemente pervertida*: la mirada y el discurso del otro sexo que desea intercambiar su lugar con el primero, sin poder renegar simplemente de su proveniencia de otro lado, y que ni siquiera se siente tan seguro de en qué medida es deseable el lugar que se le ha impedido ocupar. La complejidad de esta constelación parece, por cierto, retraerse de modo constante a una represen-

---

5. Con vista a los efectos que esta estructura sacrificial tiene para "lo femenino", la historia del Iluminismo ha sido escrita de modo más convincente en el trabajo de Heinrich (1985) y en el estudio sobre Edipo de Kurnitzky (1978).

discurso contemporáneo en torno de un "futuro del Iluminismo" y de la "posmodernidad", que se desarrolla como una polémica con dos posturas contrapuestas,[3] muestra desde el comienzo qué difícil es, evidentemente, seguir escribiendo con continuidad histórica para el momento de hoy una *Dialéctica del Iluminismo*, esa obra de historia de la cultura que Horkheimer y Adorno publicaron en 1947. Las dificultades se agudizan, sin embargo, aun más cuando se halla en discusión la voluntad de la mujer de abordar el saber o a sí misma, o cuando se trata de su participación en la vida pública y política.

La situación de lo femenino en el texto de Horkheimer y Adorno aparece, sin embargo, como la contracara del Iluminismo y de la autoconservación. Más bien su ubicación se da en el dominio de la naturaleza. Es una naturaleza que aparecería superada por y para el individuo y transformada en parte como propia, y que ha sido puesta de relieve en numerosos estudios dentro de las investigaciones feministas y, entretanto, también confirmada con ejemplos concretos y matizados,[4] como en la referencia de la descripción y análisis de la historia en la que la mujer ha sido domesticada y lo femenino llevado a la cualidad de mito.

Cuando se trate, sin embargo, en ese texto de una historia obviada, cuando se trate del deseo de la mujer para devenir sujeto, como si fuera un discurso proferido desde el lugar de la contracara, se hará fácilmente evidente cómo esa dialéctica se pone en movimiento de tal modo, que ya no será posible pisar suelo firme. No se puede, en este caso, reconstruir el proceso por el que la mujer llega a ser individuo, ni tampoco transformar una cara de la situación en la otra o, en definitiva, pronunciarse. La

3. Muchos trabajos alemanes alrededor de este tema dan la impresión de que se tratara de tomar partido en pro o en contra del Iluminismo y de identificarse como partidario u opositor de la posmodernidad, en lugar de analizar históricamente el cambio en el desarrollo cultural. De otro modo se comporta, por ejemplo, Fredric Jameson (1984).

4. El texto de Max Horkheimer y Theodor Adorno no se halla, por cierto, libre de la creación de mitos sobre la mujer; véase especialmente el pasaje sobre la Megara en el apartado titulado "Mensch und Tier" ["El hombre y el animal"] (1969: 266).

son también respuestas a la estructuración mítica y artística del patrón y de la historia de la "femineidad" (como objeto del trabajo analítico del feminismo), y una reacción a la postura que sostiene que no se puede introducir simplemente en los mitos de la femineidad un discurso que sea "claro y esclaredor" (*aufgeklärter bzw. aufklärerischer*).*

El dilema aparece, como sucede tan habitualmente, en los polos contrapuestos. De un lado encontramos posiciones iconoclastas, para las que el patrón de la femineidad (y la imagen de la mujer) se condensa en una bella apariencia, una magia sospechosa y una perfidia maligna; se trata de posturas, en fin, que en tanto recurren a una verdad insondable o mismidad de la mujer, pueden valer como variaciones para los mitos del Iluminismo. De otro lado, se hallan las "nuevas puestas en mito" [*Remythisierungen*] o recursos al mito de un mundo femenino que habría sido mejor: por ejemplo, mitos de matriarcado o "mitos secundarios"[2] de los estudios de la mujer dentro de la sociología con su tendencia hacia descripciones positivistas de características (femeninas), que en su pretensión de superioridad moral y totalidad no pocas veces se manifiestan como la imagen especular invertida de los desarrollos masculinos. Tales polarizaciones son explicables a partir de la dificultad, e incluso imposibilidad, de obtener una propia y unívoca perspectiva, en lo posible, del modo de mirar y escuchar a la mujer. Estas dificultades se hacen todavía más acuciantes en el caso de que se trate del área de la razón y de lo que ella traspasa y reprime, pero también donde esté en juego la posición de las mujeres dentro de y en relación con el Iluminismo. La formación de bandos en el

---

* La autora realiza en todo este capítulo un juego de palabras tratando de "reescribir" en versión femenina el libro de Horkheimer y Adorno: *Dialéctica del Iluminismo*, apoyándose en el sentido de la raíz alemana "*aufklären*", como "iluminar, aclarar, esclarecer e ilustrar". [N. del T.]

2. Gudrun Axeli-Knapp utiliza este término en su crítica de estudios sociales recientes en la investigación feminista, en la que características particularmente femeninas aparecen evaluadas positivamente y, luego, elevadas a rango general. Véase Axeli-Knapp (1988).

texto, ya que se quedan atrás sin lograr alcanzarlo en toda su dimensión.[1]

Y lo que es más importante aún, la novela no se conforma con presentar la problemática entre Malina y la narradora en primera persona; además de esto, el texto da forma a otra constelación de la relación de los sexos en el nexo entre el Yo y el amante (Iván). No sólo Bachmann tematiza aquí la diferencia y relación de los sexos al nivel de la "razón", sino, al mismo tiempo, al nivel del "amor"; tejiéndose, sin embargo, ambos "niveles" en la trama literaria de la novela como en su textura.

El ejemplo de *Malina* ha de ser tomado aquí de modo paradigmático para discutir, contra ese telón de fondo, sobre las tendencias del discurso feminista hacia los modos expresivos literarios y de imágenes, así como sobre la referencia frecuente a episodios míticos y figuras artísticas, sobre el modo de tratamiento de los mitos y las posibilidades y perspectivas de un pensamiento en imágenes. Efectivamente, los aspectos "literarios" de las investigaciones feministas no siempre aparecen fundados en un aprovechamiento creativo de las posibilidades de la lengua poética en su capacidad para una multiplicidad de enfoques, de plurivocalidad y pluralidad de sentidos ni en la diferencia, "imaginería" [*Bildlichkeit*] y simultaneidad de lo distinto. Más a menudo hay razones en juego que abarcan desde una crítica necesaria a la rigidez [*Verfasstheit*] de la ciencia hasta una global hostilidad contra la ciencia y la teoría. Estas posiciones consideran que literaturidad e imaginería son características de una (así llamada) forma de expresión *femenina* y que el lenguaje de por sí debe unirse con la promesa de mayor subjetividad, concreción y vitalidad, mientras que se gesta una nueva formación de mitos —como se ha de reconocer fácilmente—, en los que "lo femenino" queda establecido como la oposición de la pretendida racionalidad de la ciencia. Al mismo tiempo, los préstamos en el arte y en los mitos

---

1. Los comentarios sobre *Malina* llenan ya estantes enteros; y, aunque en los últimos años se ha venido gestando un enfoque nuevo y completo de la novela, la crítica no logra debatir en las respectivas interpretaciones más que algunas de las capas de sentido del texto. Cf. Weigel, 1994a: 232-263.

En el diálogo con Malina se completa este enfoque en un episodio posterior a través de la seguridad de la voz que asume su Yo: "Llegaste *después de mí*, no puedes estar aquí antes que yo, eres pensable sólo recién después de mí" (III.247). Muy pocas veces se da tal acertada representación de la dialéctica del Iluminismo desde una perspectiva femenina como en la novela de Bachmann. En la constelación Malina/Yo se encuentra tanto la asimetría y jerarquía de una relación dicotómica de los sexos como también su vinculación con la relación entre lo racional y el "Otro" que se presenta como el productor de esa misma razón pero que aparece como subsidiario de esa categoría y escindido por ella. No por azar se trata aquí de un texto *literario* que logra dar articulación al complicado territorio de las mujeres y a la compleja función de lo femenino en la dialéctica del Iluminismo. Esto sucede a través del aprovechamiento de numerosas posibilidades expresivas propias del lenguaje poético. Allí donde textos crítico-académicos del feminismo tratan de nombrar y formular teóricamente como ejemplo el destino de lo femenino en el progreso de la ciencia europea, presentándola como "la simultánea apropiación y rechazo de lo femenino" (Fox Keller, 1986: 50), el texto de Bachmann coloca bajo la lupa, a partir de dos historias vinculadas dialécticamente entre sí pero separadas una de otra, una relación cuestionada cuya constelación recibe luz en una multiplicidad de cambiantes escenarios e iluminaciones. De este modo la relación entre el Yo y Malina no sólo se presenta como la de dos personajes, voces, historias y posturas, sino que aparece también representada como históricamente temporal y jerárquicamente espacial, como relación de posibilidad y de acotación posterior [*Nachträglickeit*], de afirmación y desaparición, de superioridad y decadencia. Las figuraciones en las que se mueven ambas instancias poseen muchos niveles y sentidos, de modo que son difíciles de aprehender en la univocidad, linealidad y estructura lógica del lenguaje conceptual así como en la argumentación científica. Y éste sería uno de los motivos por los que las interpretaciones y comentarios sobre *Malina* como texto novelístico todavía no están a la altura del

aquí de hacer fructífero el pensamiento de Benjamin para la teoría y la historia de "lo femenino" o de introducirlo en el debate teórico feminista.

SOBRE EL PROBLEMA DE LA IMAGINABILIDAD Y REPRESENTABILIDAD [*VOR- UND DARSTELLBARKEIT*]: LA POSICIÓN DEL SUJETO FEMENINO

> Desde el comienzo yo estaba colocada *debajo* de él, y tengo que haber sentido bien pronto que *él habría de tornarse mi perdición*: que el lugar de Malina ya estuviera ocupado por Malina, antes de que él se instalara en mi vida. (Bachmann: *Malina*, 1978: III. 17).(El subrayado es mío.)*

Con estas reflexiones la narradora (que debe ser percibida como voz femenina de un Yo sin nombre y neutro) de la novela *Malina* de Ingeborg Bachmann (1971) trata de expresar, en este pasaje en el que se presenta la relación entre la voz narrativa y Malina –donde Malina, el protagonista varón, representa la postura superior de la razón–, esa misma relación en palabras. En un pasaje posterior en el que la voz narrativa sigue reflexionando sobre la *diferencia* entre sí misma(-o) y Malina se dice:

> Me parece que su tranquilidad proviene del hecho de que yo sea un Yo demasiado poco importante y bien conocido, como si él me hubiera secretado a mí, un despojo, una superflua persona en devenir, como si yo hubiera sido hecho(a) de su costilla y fuera desde siempre prescindible, pero también como *una impostergable oscura historia, que acompaña a la suya, que quiere completarla, pero que hace que él se sienta separado de su clara historia y a la vez disociado de ella.* Por ello soy yo únicamente quien puede aclarar algo con él, y sobre todo debo y puedo aclararme ante él a mí misma(-o). Pero él, él no tiene nada que aclarar, él no. (III.22) (El destacado es mío.)

* Para la mejor comprensión de este pasaje conviene aclarar que en la novela de Bachmann Malina es el apellido de un funcionario estatal austríaco de origen esloveno que ha escrito un texto "apócrifo" donde aparece la propia voz narrativa que aquí se analiza. [N. del T.]

mujeres y hombres en la historia cultural se inscribieron y se siguen inscribiendo de modo extremo en los modelos de pensamiento y en las formas de expresión tradicionales, así como en las estructuras simbólicas e imaginarias, dominan en el estudio acerca de los géneros contribuciones necesariamente teóricas que reflexionan sobre los condicionamientos lingüísticos de la investigación. Por ello, ya sea de modo consciente o no, de modo expreso o tácito, los trabajos sobre cuestiones de género, son siempre trabajos sobre y dentro de las significaciones específicamente genéricas que se transportan al habla y a la escritura, a la conceptualidad y a los juicios de valor, a la percepción y al enfoque, a la determinación del objeto y a los elementos que han sido excluidos. "Quién habla" y "desde qué lugar se habla" tienen en esto el carácter de cuestionamientos insoslayables. Las teorías de "lo femenino", que deben entenderse como intento de dedicarse de modo explícito a estas relaciones, se refieren, por ello, de modo reiterado a la relación entre lenguaje y sexo o al lugar de las mujeres y al papel de lo femenino en las prácticas tradicionales de la constitución de sentido, pero sin poder situarse a sí mismas más allá de dicha problemática, en la que se están esforzando en desarrollar una reflexión. Y, sin embargo, parecería que la búsqueda de un lugar desde el que pudiera hablarse sigue desplazándose cada vez más y más.

Las siguientes observaciones no están pensadas, por lo tanto, como contribución a la historia cultural de las relaciones de los sexos, sino como una reflexión sobre el *modo* en que esas relaciones han sido (o pueden ser) expresadas en diferentes concepciones teóricas –especialmente en los trabajos de Julia Kristeva y de Walter Benjamin–.

Este intento se halla vinculado, además –en relación con el debate teórico actual–, a un interés doble. En primera instancia, refutar la (supuesta) oposición entre "Teoría Crítica" y la "teoría francesa" según parece presentarse en la irreconciliable formación de campos en el funcionamiento cultural y académico alemán. Como ejemplo de esta situación se traen a la discusión las posiciones de Kristeva y Benjamin de modo comparativo para marcar semejanzas y diferencias. En segundo lugar, por fin, se trata

5. Hacia una dialéctica femenina del Iluminismo
Julia Kristeva y Walter Benjamin

La contemporaneidad del trabajo teórico benjaminiano y de su pensar en imágenes podría manifestarse también y justamente en el discurso sobre las diferencias de género. Las relaciones de los géneros sexuales pueden considerarse como el emblema de la cultura occidental, y lo femenino en particular ha sido utilizado como material figurativo privilegiado para la representación de muchas "construcciones de la imaginación" [*Vorstellungen*] en ese sentido significativas, así como conceptos, ideas y valores. Por ello, el modo benjaminiano de pensar y de encarar la filosofía, su tratamiento dialéctico de las imágenes y la pasión ligada a ellos podría muy bien indicar un camino posible que sacara al discurso de los géneros (incluido también el discurso feminista) de las numerosas aporías en las que se halla enzarzado de modo reiterado: atrapado entre el trabajo de Iluminismo iconoclasta en la larga tradición de las imágenes femeninas, por una parte, y la permanente reproducción de las mismas imágenes, por otra; entre la crítica cultural y los esfuerzos de emancipación; entre el rechazo del "orden masculino" y la orientación hacia las significaciones allí institucionalizadas; entre la crítica del sujeto y el apasionamiento por el sujeto, etcétera.

Cada vez que se aborda el discurso sobre los sexos, las diferencias de los géneros sexuales definidas en y por el lenguaje están desde siempre vigentes, por esta razón los estudios sobre "femineidad" y sobre las mujeres o sobre la historia de los sexos tropiezan siempre en sus representaciones con limitaciones conceptuales. Dado que las diferentes posiciones e *imagines* de

Segunda parte

Otras lecturas de géneros

"Pero las mujeres están en silencio. Hacia donde tiendan sus oídos, allí las palabras quedarán inexpresadas. Acercan sus cuerpos y se acarician unas a otras."

lo que ha sido destruido en la historia, lo que ha sido usado y gastado en la producción artística y también "lo que se desvanece en el devenir" [*das im Werden Vergehende*]. Así como Hölderlin lo ha intentado en su lectura y traducción de las tragedias griegas, cuando tenía presente la "aparición incontrolada" [*wilde Entstehung*] de una forma razonada, pero, al mismo tiempo, se esforzaba en hacer resaltar "lo oriental" que el arte griego había reprimido;[13] sin llegar, sin embargo, a embarcarse (ni a querer embarcarse) en otra tradición que dejara de lado la griega. Aquí se trata, como lo ha formulado Hölderlin, de una "vuelta de todos los modos de imaginación y formas" [*Umkehr aller Vorstellungsarten und Formen*], no de un regreso total, pues: "Una vuelta total hacia esto, así como todo viraje absoluto, sin ningún apoyo, le está vedada al hombre, en tanto ser cognoscente" (Hölderlin, 1992: II.375).

En tal sentido, en la imagen de pensamiento benjaminiana sobre teoría de la historia es justamente el ángel –alguien que no es humano– quien se empecina en la posición de un viraje y con ello mantiene abierta la mirada también para nosotros durante algunos momentos.

---

13. Así lo declara el poeta en carta a Wilmans en 1803 (Hölderlin, 1992: II.925).

cionales y figuras de lenguaje usadas por él mismo, en las imágenes de pensamiento; una transformación, en suma, que no evalúa o denuncia esas imágenes mentales simplemente como falsa conciencia. El mismo Benjamin describe su trabajo como una reflexión en el instante del despertar; se trata, pues, de una reflexión que no se absorbe en la pasión por la condensación de imágenes ya utilizadas por los otros ni tampoco se esfuma aplicando la razón, sino que se integra en la imagen de pensamiento para llegar a ser una unidad que subsume un procedimiento alegórico y una crítica salvadora.

La figuración, en la que desemboca el texto de Benjamin y en la que se expresa la disimultaneidad de nuestra precepción así como la mirada del "Ángel de la Historia", se corresponde de la misma manera con la figura teórica de la disimultaneidad en el modelo freudiano, como ha sido expuesto en la alegoría de la "pizarra mágica" [*Wunderblock*].[11] La disimultaneidad entre la conciencia y la escritura que se transparenta desde las huellas duraderas del inconsciente constituye con ello la base para esa representación benjaminiana. Justamente la expresión "cadena de acontecimientos" [*Kette von Begebenheiten*] puede ser rastreada en la obra de Freud. En su ensayo titulado "Sobre los recuerdos encubridores" de 1899, se dice: "Que la vida de la memoria se reproduzca como una cadena de acontecimientos interconectados entre sí, es algo que no tiene lugar hasta la edad de seis o siete años, en muchos no antes de los diez"[12] (Freud, 1952: I.531-532). Dicha disimultaneidad se hace visible a través de la figura de la Vuelta como nuevamente podemos encontrarla en Hölderlin. La Vuelta, entonces, organiza una percepción, que –deteniéndose en el tiempo, pero tomando también una posición enfrentada– posibilita la mirada sobre lo que ha desaparecido en el movimiento,

---

11. Véase el capítulo 8 del presente trabajo, donde se trata detalladamente esta alegoría freudiana.
12. En alemán: "*Dass das Leben vom Gedächtnis als zusammenhängende Kette von Begebenheiten reproduziert wird, kommt nicht vor dem sechsten oder siebenten, bei vielen erst nach dem zehnten Lebensjahr zustande*". [N. del T.]

Dicha reflexión sobre imágenes mentales propias [*eigene Vorstellungsbilder*] significa una implicación de la reelaboración (*Bearbeitung*, un término freudiano) de los deseos ligados a estas imágenes y con ello del trabajo en la fascinación y "pasión por las imágenes" [*Bildbegehren*].

Con este texto sobre el "Ángel de la Historia" Benjamin ha elaborado, en rigor, probablemente también su propia historia de casi veinte años de fascinación que lo unía al cuadro de Paul Klee, reflexionando sobre ello en una imagen dialéctica, que, al mismo tiempo, representa un despertar de una fijación mágica en la pintura en forma de una continuada "inspección" [*Beaugenscheinigung*].[10] No por azar el período en el que Benjamin se encontró en posesión del cuadro se superpone con la historia −mantenida oculta y luego mencionada por él− del origen de la redacción de este texto en el año 1940 poco antes de su involuntario suicidio. En una carta dirigida a Gretel Adorno, Benjamin, haciendo referencia a este texto, le escribe que lo que le interesaba era "dar forma a algunos pensamientos, de los que puedo decir que ya llevo escondidos conmigo desde hace veinte años, y que por cierto he mantenido escondidos de mí mismo" (*G.S.*, I.3.1223). Así, la idea de Klee −documentada como anotación en 1925 en el *Libro de bosquejos pedagógicos*, donde comentó su *Angelus Novus* con la frase: "Medio alado y medio prisionero es el ser humano" (Klee, 1990: 100), una anotación que se mueve en el modelo de una concepción dicotómica de la imaginación y de la identidad−, ha logrado en la imagen de pensamiento benjaminiana del "Ángel de la Historia" liberarse de su rigidez como metáfora existencial, para llegar a convertirse en un elemento dinámico que se halla en tensión irreconciliable con la representación de la disimultaneidad.

La radicalidad del pensamiento benjaminiano se encuentra justamente en el trabajo en semejantes constelaciones, en la transformación de las imágenes convencionales, de las metáforas tradi-

---

10. Benjamin utiliza esta palabra para caracterizar la fijación mágica de cierto tipo de filología sobre el texto (1978: 794). Este punto aparece tratado especialmente en el capítulo 5 del presente estudio.

LA PASIÓN POR LA IMAGEN Y POR LA "VUELTA" [*UMKEHR*]

A través de esta constelación que sobre la base de esas relaciones múltiples se diferencia claramente de una simple descripción de un cuadro o de una representación figurativa, se pasa –gracias a un movimiento textual dialéctico– a una oposición entre las dos figuras previas, los ángeles mencionados de Scholem y Klee: con una imagen angélica que articula líricamente su deseo por el viraje, para el primero, y con otra que se inmoviliza en la mirada mítica y en la magia de una fijación rígida de medusa, para el segundo. Este procedimiento textual se basa, por cierto, en un esquema triádico, pero que no desemboca en una síntesis, sino en una constelación de la disimultaneidad. En ella se manifiesta la reflexión acerca de la incompatibilidad del deseo de mejoramiento ("recomponer lo destruido") y de la rigidez en el terror. En ella se representa la disimultaneidad y con ella la hostilidad hacia una comprensión histórica positivista, donde la historia aparece como serie de sucesos en un *continuum*, pero también como una percepción de la ruina, de la catástrofe en una imagen de pensamiento. El vendaval que sopla desde el paraíso y es llamado Progreso, aspecto original de un movimiento *histórico* por el que la historia es expulsada inexorablemente del paraíso (es decir, de un lugar mítico), marca una situación en la que el mesianismo y la filosofía de la historia ya no pueden marchar juntos.

Resulta claro que en este texto, de modo diferente a lo que sucedía en el "Fragmento teológico-político" de veinte años antes, la imagen no está ya al servicio de la ilustración de una lección de filosofía de la historia, es decir, de la relación del orden de lo profano con lo mesiánico (cf. *G.S.*, II.1.203-204). Más bien, ahora se trata del diseño de una imagen de pensamiento que toma como punto de partida, por un lado, una imagen poética, y por otro, un cuadro; es decir, ambas son imágenes que pueden valer como imágenes del deseo [*Wunschbilder*], pero cuya figuración no puede ya ser traducida ni de modo conceptual ni metadiscursivo.

encuentra con el tercer ángel, con el "Ángel de la Historia". Así puede decirse que el Angelus Novus representado por Klee no es idéntico al "Ángel de la Historia", y, por ello, no debe ser interpretado como su presentación figurativa. Más bien se trata aquí de una "imagen mental" [*Vorstellungsbild*)]:

> El Ángel de la Historia tiene que tener ese aspecto. Su rostro ha girado hacia el pasado. Hacia allí donde aparece ante *nosotros* una cadena de acontecimientos [*Kette von Begebenheiten*], allí ve *él* una catástrofe concreta que amontona sin cesar despojo sobre despojo y que forma un torbellino a sus pies. A él le gustaría permanecer allí un tiempo, despertar a los muertos y recomponer lo destruido. Pero sopla un vendaval desde el paraíso que se arremolina en sus alas y que es tan fuerte que el ángel ya no puede plegarlas. Ese vendaval lo impulsa inexorablemente [*unaufhaltsam*] hacia el futuro al que da la espalda mientras la montaña de ruinas llega al cielo. Lo que llamamos Progreso es *este* vendaval.

El movimiento del texto se origina sobre todo en un cambio múltiple de la perspectiva: entre la mirada del observador hacia el ángel y la perspectiva y los deseos del propio ángel ("le gustaría permanecer allí un tiempo"), pero también entre el "nosotros" y el "le" puestos en relación con los despojos ante sus pies y con el futuro a sus espaldas hacia donde es impulsado por el vendaval. En este movimiento se hace presente una disimultaneidad entre el "nosotros" y el ángel en una multiperspectiva de capas superpuestas: como constelación topográfica y espacial ("donde aparece ante nosotros", "allí ve él"), corporal (se habla de "rostro", "pies" y "espaldas"), temporal ("mientras", "inexorablemente" en el sentido de "sin cesar"), material ("muertos", "despojos/ruinas"), mítica ("el vendaval que sopla desde el paraíso") y, finalmente, como constelación conceptual o de filosofía de la historia ("lo que llamamos Progreso").

El Yo lírico de la poesía citada coincide, entonces, con la voz de ese ángel. En un regreso al origen histórico y dador de salvación, el tono de la frustrada búsqueda de felicidad (en el orden de lo profano) así como el *pathos*, valorando y marcando positivamente el viraje, determinan el ritmo lírico.[9] A diferencia de este ángel de Scholem –extremamente dotado para la palabra– el que aparece en el cuadro de Paul Klee, segundo ángel citado, es mudo. De él dice Benjamin que se llama "Angelus Novus" (o que ha sido denominado así por el pintor):

> Existe un cuadro de Klee, que se llama Angelus Novus. Allí esta representado un ángel que parecería como si estuviera a punto de alejarse de algo sobre lo que concentra su mirada. Sus ojos aparecen completamente abiertos, su boca se halla abierta y sus alas desplegadas.

En la descripción benjaminiana este ángel está dotado de atributos de una medusa: la boca abierta, así como sus ojos, y la mirada escrutadora. A la descripción de la imagen de Klee, así como a la representación del ángel del cuadro y la denominación dada por el pintor se añaden asociaciones: "parecería"/ "como si estuviera a punto de"... Con esta formulación el texto apunta a la lógica perceptiva del "como si" [*als ob*] en la representatividad aceptada de las imágenes materiales. Hay allí un movimiento que aparece solamente imaginado en la frontalidad de la imagen (que dirige al observador el rostro del Angelus Novus), pero a través del acto de mirar hay un *plus* que se agrega a la representación. El movimiento penetra realmente en el texto cuando se

---

9. Compárese la propia interpretación del "Ángel de la Historia" por Scholem. Importante para la comprensión de Benjamin es aquí el énfasis en su pensamiento de la huella de la tradición judía, que lleva la impronta de la esencial amistad con Scholem. En su artículo, sin embargo, Scholem quiere hacer abstracción de las diferencias entre su pensamiento y el de Benjamin, cuando le adjudica a éste una concepción histórica cíclica, donde origen y meta se encuentran en un punto. (Scholem, 1983; véanse especialmente págs. 63 y 71).

dialéctica. Este hecho es, por cierto, sintomático de la incomprensión con que se rodea el pensar en imágenes benjaminiano. Este fenómeno también está cargado de consecuencias, dado que en ese pasaje confluyen las diferentes líneas de sus trabajos y toman forma sus muy específicas reflexiones de la historia, del Progreso, de la expectativa de salvación como imagen en *una* constelación. Esta imagen de pensamiento puede ser comprendida, por lo tanto, de modo cabal como alegoría del trabajo teórico específico de Benjamin.

Leída como imagen *metafórica* –en la que, por ejemplo, el *Angelus Novus* de Paul Klee se interpretara como representación visual [*bildliche Repräsentation*] del "Ángel de la Historia"–, esa imagen de pensamiento benjaminiano no sería comprendida como dialéctica en un acto suspendido, sino que en esa interpretación su costado dialéctico se hallaría inmovilizado, paralizado.

Este tipo de acercamiento va acompañado desde el principio por una postura muy extendida que consiste en pasar por alto o no considerar el epígrafe del texto, una cita tomada de un poema de Gershom Scholem. Estos versos, sin embargo, son una parte constitutiva del movimiento en que se inscribe el texto, dado que marcan un punto de referencia de esa constelación hacia la que va a desembocar ese movimiento. En realidad, esta Reflexión IX de "Sobre el concepto de historia" (*G.S.*, I.2.697-698) exhibe no un ángel, sino tres completamente diferentes. El primero es justamente el presentado por los versos de Scholem así:

Mein Flügel ist zum Schwung bereit
ich kehrte gern zurück
denn blieb' ich auch lebendige Zeit
ich hätte wenig Glück.

[Mis alas se hallan listas para el vuelo
retornaría con gusto de nuevo
si permaneciera también el tiempo de los vivientes
tendría poca dicha.]

Gerhard Scholem, "Gruss vom Angelus"

enseñanzas esenciales de la filosofía de la historia. Esta relación está en la base de una concepción de la historia mítica, cuya problemática puede representarse con una imagen [*deren Problem sich in einem Bilde darlegen lässt*]. Cuando una flecha fija su meta en la dirección en la que actúa la *dýnamis* de lo profano (y otra marca la dirección de la intensidad mesiánica), entonces, por cierto, la búsqueda hacia la felicidad de una humanidad sin ataduras se lanzará contra la dirección mesiánica; pero así como una fuerza en su camino puede impulsar a otra que se dirige en dirección contraria, así también el profano orden de lo profano impulsa la llegada del reino mesiánico. (*G.S.*, II.1.203-204)

Lo que aquí se denomina "enseñanza de la filosofía de la historia", *representándoselo* como una imagen, es decir, como *ilustración* de una idea [*Einsicht*] formulada conceptualmente en una descripción figurativa, puede ser considerado como el intento de seguir los rastros de la elaboración de las imágenes de pensamiento en la obra de Benjamin. Así, el intento de hacer patente un problema filosófico gracias a la capacidad de imaginarse flechas en dirección a un blanco o de fuerzas contrarias que se impulsan recíprocamente hacia un camino determinado, tiene, por así decir, el carácter de la representatividad de una figura formulada conceptualmente sobre una imagen geométrica o topológica. Aquí se reconoce el esfuerzo de apresar la dialéctica en una imagen; una preocupación que ha de tener éxito realmente en la obra benjaminiana sólo con las imágenes leídas o escritas.

En este sentido la imagen de pensamiento del "Ángel de la Historia" podría leerse en un *continuum* con el "Fragmento teológico-político" comentado. Se trata, en efecto, del pasaje más citado de Benjamin de sus tesis sobre teoría de la historia, en las que esboza su crítica contra el historicismo convencional y contra la idea de Progreso del materialismo histórico; pasaje que ha sido repetidamente leído como metafórico[8] y no como imagen

---

8. El último estudio que presenta así este aspecto es el de Lindner (1992: 254).

ENSAMBLAJE DE FUERZAS CONTRARIAS [*GEGENSTREBIGE FÜGUNG*]: EL "ÁNGEL DE LA HISTORIA"

En el mismo sentido en que se conforma la figura del "ensamblaje de fuerzas contrarias"[6] en la que culmina la imagen de pensamiento del "Ángel de la Historia", expresada por un desfasaje de la sincronicidad entre *su* posición (y percepción) y *la nuestra* y, al mismo tiempo, por la disimultaneidad [*Ungleichzeitigkeit*] e incompatibilidad [*Unvereinbarkeit*] de la filosofía de la historia y del mesianismo, así también el "ensamblaje de fuerzas contrarias" tiene antecesores en una serie de constelaciones similares, de figuras de lenguaje e imágenes con las que Benjamin ha trabajado evidentemente durante la época de elaboración de su *"gegenstrebige Fügung"*.

En "Das Tagebuch" ["El diario íntimo"], de 1913, que se presenta como un texto *poético* lleno de metáforas, el Yo, por ejemplo, aparece situado en un movimiento contrario de cosas y tiempo, mientras ello se produce en medio de un acaecer que lo rodea como un paisaje, es decir, en medio de un entorno que se percibe como *mítico*.[7] La misma constelación que aquí se presentaba en medio de un texto subjetivo y literario provisto de un lenguaje metafórico reaparece en los más variados momentos de la obra y las figuras benjaminianas de lenguaje, por ejemplo como imagen conceptual en el contexto de un discurso filosófico sobre la relación de lo mesiánico y la filosofía de la historia en el "Fragmento teológico-político" (escrito entre 1920 y 1921). Después de acentuar la diferencia entre lo mesiánico y el dinamismo de la historia, Benjamin afirma allí:

> El orden de lo profano debe erigirse sobre la base de la idea de la felicidad. La relación de este orden con lo mesiánico es una de las

---

6. La idea proviene de Heráclito, pero *Gegenstrebige Fügung* es también el título del libro de Jacob Taubes sobre su fascinación por Carl Schmitt (Taubes, 1987).

7. Para una exposición más detallada del origen de esta constelación en el pensar en imágenes benjaminiano, véase el capítulo 6 del presente trabajo.

ción de un progreso" (*G.S.*, I.2.701) y "*el concepto* de un presente" (*G.S.*, I.2.702) (El destacado es mío.)

El texto aquí analizado se inicia con la muy controvertida imagen del autómata, cuya presentación se introduce con un esquema *dicendi* tradicional: "Como se sabe debe..." [*Bekanntlich soll es...*], para pasar a la detallada descripción del engranaje y, luego, continuar con la idea de una "contrapartida en la filosofía" [*ein Gegenstück in der Philosophie*]. Préstese atención a esto: una *contrapartida* (o "*pendant*") y no una comparación. "Frente a esta maquinaria [*Apparatur*] uno puede imaginarse un *pendant* en la filosofía" (*G.S.*, I.2.693). Las numerosas tentativas de lectura de este pasaje, que dan vuelta estas frases de Benjamin (cf. Habermas, 1973) para extraer de ellas un sentido unívoco, muestran a las claras que esta idea de un *pendant* en la filosofía frente a la imagen del autómata no se halla a un nivel de igualdad en una transferencia –(*metáphora*)– unívoca que pasara desde el objeto escrito hacia el concepto filosófico. Más bien, Benjamin describe aquí, en la correspondencia entre una cosa concreta y su *pendant* en la filosofía, justamente un territorio en el que la imagen se construye como similitud entre las figuras del mundo exterior y las del conocimiento. Es, por otro lado, éste el campo de su escritura donde desarrolla las imágenes de pensamiento que encuentran su lugar más allá de la oposición entre la lengua poética y el discurso filosófico, es decir, en el lenguaje de las imágenes de pensamiento que operan con las figuras tradicionales de ese pensar. Con todo, estas imágenes de pensamiento no se hallan en el principio de su actividad de escritor, sino que son el resultado de numerosos desvíos –porque "método es desvío" (*El origen del drama barroco alemán*; *G.S.*, I.1.208)– que surgen "del centro del mundo de sus imágenes".[5]

---

5. Así acuña Benjamin esta frase en su trabajo referido a Kafka (*G.S.*, II.2.678), con un giro que podría leerse, sin embargo, como una autorreflexión.

Sin embargo, las imágenes de pensamiento son también imágenes leídas, lecturas de imágenes por escrito, en las que el carácter escriturario de las imágenes –ya se trate de cuadros, de imágenes de recuerdos, de imágenes oníricas o de imágenes del deseo materializadas en la arquitectura o en las cosas– se transforma literalmente en escritura.

En las imágenes de pensamiento resulta evidente que escritura y modos de pensar en Benjamin no pueden separarse, pero también que su manera de pensar en imágenes constituye no sólo la vía específica de su configuración teórica, sino también de su filosofía y de su escritura, y, por último, que sus textos no pueden dividirse en forma y contenido. Mucho más puede extraerse todavía de las numerosas constelaciones de *Leitmotive* que forman sus textos, así como también puede descubrirse un modo particular de escribir logrado a partir de las tensiones entre la lengua poética y el metadiscurso conceptual, como si existiera un tercer elemento más allá de la oposición dualista entre literatura y filosofía. La aparición y construcción de este tercer lugar puede observarse tanto en la génesis de figuras particulares que se extienden a veces durante un gran lapso, como también en la construcción y modos de procedimiento de textos concretos.

Como ejemplo puede tomarse el procedimiento empleado en "Sobre el concepto de historia". La serie de dieciocho o veinte trozos breves –que no son, en realidad, tesis– no desarrollan un programa de filosofía de la historia, sino que más bien presentan reflexiones sobre *concepciones* históricas, imágenes de pensamiento sobre representaciones en las que se ha concebido la historia, y también sobre el concepto de *la* Historia. Es sobre esto donde Benjamin pone el mayor énfasis de que es capaz a través de afirmaciones como las siguientes: "la marioneta a la que *se denomina* 'materialismo histórico'" [*die Puppe, die man 'historischen Materialismus' nennt*] (*G.S.*, I.2.693); o "*la concep-*

[*Einmal ist keinmal*], que persiguen la huella de la constitución de sentido en mitos amorosos tradicionales; cf. "Cuadros de un pensamiento", *G.S.*, IV.1.368-369.

antigua, la desintegración necesaria y portadora de su carácter particular entre el ser y el no ser. En el estado entre el ser y el no ser, sin embargo, lo posible deviene, en todas partes, real y lo real deviene ideal; y esto es un terrible pero divino sueño de la libre imitación artística. (Hölderlin, 1992: II.73)

Cuando Hölderlin en el curso de su reflexión acentúa especialmente el recuerdo de lo desintegrado en lo nuevo, como también el abismo y el contraste entre lo nuevo y lo viejo, entonces –desde la perspectiva de lo posible que ha entrado en la realidad para formar parte de ella– sólo la visión retrospectiva hacia lo que se ha desvanecido durante el proceso es lo que posibilita "el recuerdo de lo desintegrado" [*die Erinnerung des Aufgelösten*]. Y justamente este tipo de recuerdo es central para las imágenes de pensamiento de Benjamin. La constitución de sentido que persigue Benjamin se diferencia de la "*Grammatologie*" que se orienta hacia un concepto moderno del signo. Tampoco se relaciona con la *différance* que opera, por su parte, con el más variado material lingüístico (Derrida, 1967b), sino con el origen de las ideas y su cristalización en figuraciones lingüísticas: imágenes lingüísticas, que preceden y se hallan en la base del archivo de las metáforas, de la retórica en general y de la iconografía. Por ello, Benjamin caracteriza también el lenguaje como el lugar de esas imágenes que define como "dialéctica en un acto suspendido", a la par que quiere hacer valer esas imágenes dialécticas en tanto imágenes *auténticas* (Anotaciones y materiales para "La obra de los Pasajes", Block N2a,3; *G.S.*, V.1.577). Ello concierne a esa escritura en imágenes en la que las imágenes del mundo se tornan la imagen del mundo. Y Benjamin mismo ha creado y escrito tales imágenes con sus "imágenes de pensamiento", de manera de deconstruir por ese medio "modos de pensar" [*Denkweisen*] y "concepciones" [*Vorstellungen*] tradicionales.[4]

---

[4]. Puede estudiarse muy especialmente el modo de escritura de estas imágenes de pensamiento en los textos breves en prosa reunidos bajo el título de "Sombras breves", por ejemplo: "Amor platónico" o "Una vez es ninguna vez"

desarrolla y se hace visible la dialéctica de imagen y pensamiento. En primer lugar se trata de representaciones lingüísticas de esas similitudes en las que "el mundo se amalgama con las figuras del conocimiento", como ha sostenido Mitchell, es decir, textos que toman forma partiendo de esas imágenes y figuraciones en las que se realiza el pensamiento y en las que se estructura y se expresa la historia, la realidad y la experiencia. Se trata, en fin, de representaciones de ideas [*Darstellungen von Vorstellungen*] en el sentido de que el movimiento dentro de ellas inmovilizado en el proceso de la imitación lingüística de la idea se torna nuevamente fluido. Con la ayuda de la capacidad mimética, la imagen, como dialéctica en un acto suspendido, se transforma en escritura, es decir, se pone de tal modo en movimiento que en ese proceso se hace visible el origen y las partes integrantes de esa determinada idea. Eso que ha precedido a la idea y se ha introducido en ella, desaparece y, al mismo tiempo, se transforma en invisible y sin valor, con la expresión de la idea en la imagen como su contracara. La mímesis de la escritura ha instaurado de esta manera su constitución de sentido como imagen.

La dialéctica que así obra no sigue ningún tipo de esquema triádico. Ella se ha constituido más en base a Hölderlin que a Hegel, pues en el primero puede constatarse el intento de una descripción lingüística exacta del proceso dialéctico y su iluminación en todos los aspectos, que justamente en ese proceso cambian su jerarquía y posición. Como ejemplo podría valer el texto de Hölderlin titulado *Vom Werden im Vergehen* ["Del devenir en lo que se desvanece"], cuya representación lingüística de una constelación "de lo que surge" [*des Entspringens*] y de lo que se origina, se realiza miméticamente, describiendo, al mismo tiempo, este movimiento como una transformación mutua entre el estatuto de lo posible y el de lo real (o de lo ideal):

> Pero lo posible que se ha entrometido en la realidad logrando su desintegración, ejerce una influencia en esto y produce no sólo la sensación de la disolución sino también el recuerdo de lo desintegrado [...] La nueva vida es ahora real, ésa que se ha de desintegrar y la que ya se ha desvanecido; posible, idealmente

Este concepto de imagen puede explicar por qué en la historia primigenia de la Modernidad emprendida por Benjamin, donde el modo de observación aparece, por cierto, ampliamente dominado por las imágenes y fundado en una teoría de las imágenes, la pintura ocupa un lugar tan secundario. E incluso en los momentos en que Benjamin se dedica a obras particulares de la historia del arte, como en el caso de la *Melancolía* de Durero o el *Angelus Novus* de Paul Klee, esas imágenes llegan a ser en sus manos puntos de partida para la meditación, como lo formula él mismo después de una exposición de cuadros de Klee (1978: 283), o imágenes de pensamiento que lo acompañan y lo ocupan por un largo tiempo.[3] Pero, se tornan imágenes de pensamiento en un doble sentido: imágenes en las que se desarrolla el pensamiento de Benjamin, es decir, sus reflexiones teóricas; e imágenes cuya representación se traduce en figuras de pensamiento (donde aquí la idea de "traducción" aparece de nuevo usada en un primer sentido, como el que Benjamin le ha dado en el contexto de un lenguaje adámico: como traducción del lenguaje de las cosas al lenguaje de las palabras).

IMÁGENES DE PENSAMIENTO [*DENKBILDER*]

La imagen de pensamiento [*Denkbild*] es un término que Benjamin ha utilizado como una especie de caracterización genérica para pequeños textos propios y puede ser considerado como el núcleo de su particular trabajo con ese pensar por medio de imágenes [*das Bilddenken*]. Sus imágenes de pensamiento son como imágenes dialécticas pero escritas; más precisamente: constelaciones que literalmente han devenido escritura, en las que se

---

3. Así, Benjamin se ocupa de la *Melancolía* de Durero ya en 1913, en ocasión de una visita al museo de Basilea, hasta que la lectura alegórica del cuadro se torna un importante pilar de su libro sobre el drama barroco (elaborado entre 1916 y 1925). En cuanto a la historia de la fascinación por el cuadro de Klee de dos décadas de duración, ella ha hecho, como es sabido, su propia historia teórica, que será tratada en el curso de este capítulo.

Y esta imagen sería la portadora de esa "frágil y preciosa realidad" de Proust; y no solamente ella. La imagen —como esa cualidad de lo tercero, como fenómeno no material de una similitud que es comparable a la estructura de la imagen del sueño— es para Benjamin esa conformación, en la que son reconocibles experiencias, la historia y la realidad, al manifestarse como una imagen del recuerdo.

En el momento en que Benjamin aprehende la imagen como constelación, cuando aquello "donde 'lo que ha sido' entra con la velocidad de un destello en contacto con el ahora para formar una constelación"[1] (Anotaciones y materiales para "La obra de los Pasajes", Block N2a,3; *G.S.*, V.1.576), entonces en ese instante la imagen describe una relación de similitud heterogénea y heteromorfa.[2]

> La imagen es el concepto general en el que se subsumen diferentes similitudes y correspondencias particulares (*convenientia, aemulatio, analogia, sympathia*), amalgamando el mundo con "figuras de conocimiento". (Mitchell, 1984: 503)

Según Mitchell, no antes del Renacimiento, con la creación de una perspectiva artificiosa que suscitó la ilusión de una representación fiel a la realidad, se produce la dominación de la imagen material y de la función representativa sobre el concepto de la imagen, que, a su vez, origina la jerarquización ahora hacia otro tipo de imágenes definidas como "mentales" [*geistige*] y consideradas como "secundarias o figuradas" [*sekundäre bzw. übertragene*]. El concepto benjaminiano de imagen, por el contrario, actualiza una tradición bíblica o judía que estaba desterrada a lo largo de este desarrollo histórico, por lo que la imagen aparece utilizada como sinónimo de similitud, pero para una similitud inmaterial y "no sensorial". Justamente dentro del seno de esta tradición las imágenes se tornan legibles, son aprehendidas como escritura.

1. En alemán: "*worin das Gewesene mit dem Jetzt blitzhaft zu einer Konstellation zusammentritt*". [N. del T.]
2. Para la relación entre imagen y similitud distorsionada, véanse los capítulos 8 y 9 del presente estudio.

enrollado en el interior con la mano) lo que me atraía hacia la profundidad. Cuando con el puño apretado me había apoderado con todas mis fuerzas de la suave masa de lana, comenzaba la segunda parte del juego que terminaba en la revelación. Entonces me dedicaba a desenrollar desde el bolsillo de lana "lo que me habían traído". Iba atrayendo el objeto cada vez más cerca de mí, hasta que ocurría lo desconcertante. "Lo que me habían traído" salía a la luz, pero "el bolsillo" en el que eso se había mantenido, ya no existía. No me cansaba así de repetir la prueba de este proceso. Eso me enseñó que forma y contenido, el envoltorio y lo envuelto son lo mismo. Esa lección me condujo así a retirar con igual cuidado la verdad [*Wahrheit*] desde dentro de la poesía [*Dichtung*] como la mano infantil retiraba la media sacándola del "bolsillo". (*G.S.*, VII.1.416-417)

A la misma historia ya se había referido Benjamin en su ensayo sobre Proust (en 1929), pero sólo para llegar allí a la conclusión de que la imagen sería un tercer elemento. El pasaje, que se ocupa con el apasionado juego proustiano del "culto de la semejanza", comienza con el concepto de similitud y desemboca –después de algunos rodeos– en la idea de la imagen. Así, partiendo del concepto de similitud, Benjamin hace también referencia al mundo de los sueños, "donde lo que sucede no surge de modo idéntico, sino similar: impenetrablemente similar a sí mismo" (*G.S.*, II.1.314), para hacer visible la "estructura del mundo de los sueños" en la historia de la media, introduciendo, al mismo tiempo, el concepto de "tercero" que le sirve para deslizarse hacia la analogía con la avidez por las imágenes que desarrolló Proust. Pues como los niños

[...] que nunca se sienten satisfechos, así ansían ambas cosas: con *un solo* movimiento del puño [*in einem Griff*] transformar el bolsillo y lo que se halla adentro en un tercer elemento [*etwas Drittes*]: en la media. Así era Proust de insaciable; esa caja de sorpresas [*Attrappe*], el Yo, había que vaciarlos de un solo golpe, para volver a llenarlos con ese tercer elemento: la imagen, que apaciguaba su curiosidad, no, no su curiosidad, sino su nostalgia. (*G.S.*, II.1.314)

4. Imágenes de pensamiento
Una relectura del "Ángel de la Historia"

EL CONCEPTO DE IMAGEN EN BENJAMIN

Con su teoría de la legibilidad y su definición de las imágenes dialécticas como signos leídos, Benjamin procede con las imágenes desde el aspecto de la escritura y no de la representación. El concepto benjaminiano de imagen, entonces, no presenta ninguna relación con la historia de las imágenes en su materialidad, pero tampoco con la idea de una "imagen mental", término que obtiene su delimitación frente a la imagen material en virtud de su caracterización como "imagen derivada" o "imagen impropia". El concepto benjaminiano, en cambio, recurre más bien a una función representacional que remite a una tradición previa "que ve el sentido *literal* de la palabra *imagen* como una noción absolutamente no pictórica o incluso anti-pictórica" (Mitchell, 1984: 521).

Benjamin mismo caracteriza la imagen como una "constelación de similitud" que obtiene su forma en un tercer elemento –más allá de una relación forma-contenido–. Con el objeto de mantener esta distinción vuelve a contar varias veces durante la década del treinta su historia sobre la media, que aparece desarrollada en *Infancia en Berlín hacia 1900* de este modo:

> Cada par tenía el aspecto de un pequeño bolsillo. Nada me interesaba más que el placer de meter la mano en su interior tan profundamente como podía. Pero no lo hacía por el calor que allí encontraba. Era siempre "lo que me habían traído" (que apresaba

la *distancia* de la imagen con respecto a la imaginación (1992: 90). Y fue esta distancia –considerada como distorsión– la que de modo creciente llegó a determinar la dirección de la lectura benjaminiana de las imágenes, por lo menos desde fines de la década del veinte. Así mientras que Foucault analiza aquí el acto de imaginar desde el lado de la producción como una actividad que precede a la imagen y que se detiene en ella, Benjamin, por su parte, se había esforzado –en un enfoque opuesto– por recuperar, a partir del instante de la "inmovilización" [*Stillstellung*] de las imágenes, su propia dialéctica, leyéndolas de tal modo que se tornara de nuevo visible lo que las ha precedido, lo que ha penetrado en ellas y lo que ha desaparecido. Pues para Benjamin la imagen es "dialéctica en un acto suspendido" (*Dialektik im Stillstand*; V.1.577). Y el hecho de hacer visible "lo que ha sido" inmovilizado dentro de la imagen, sólo puede ocurrir de un modo vertiginoso: "La imagen dialéctica tiene la velocidad del relámpago [*ist ein aufblitzendes <Bild>*]. Así, en la imagen relampagueante en el "ahora de la cognoscibilidad", es como debe ser apresado "lo que ha sido" (Anotaciones y materiales para "La obra de los Pasajes", Block N9,7; *G.S.*, V.1.591-592).

En cierto sentido, Benjamin ya había trascendido lo que Foucault señala –de nuevo de modo retrospectivo, aunque teóricamente como condición– como el punto oscuro de la fenomenología, en tanto el primero había desarrollado una teoría de la expresión, que según Foucault sólo era posible por una superación de la fenomenología (Foucault, 1992: 28): "A la fenomenología le ha sido posible hacer hablar a las imágenes; pero ella no ha dado a nadie la posibilidad de comprender su lenguaje" (1992: 29).

---

construidas de la conciencia colectiva. Así en un *exposé* sobre los pasajes: "Ellas son restos de un mundo onírico. La evaluación de los elementos del sueño al despertar es un caso ejemplar del pensamiento dialéctico" (*G.S.*, V.1.59).

descrito el sueño como origen y condición de posibilidad de la imaginación –utilizando una terminología ontológica, fenomenológica y psicoanalítica que desde un punto de vista teórico significaba una superposición infrecuente–, lo que le había servido de base para reflexionar acerca de la relación entre imaginación e imagen. En una explícita toma de distancia frente a *La interpretación de los sueños* freudiana,[19] Foucault construye una dialéctica en la que la imagen marca la cristalización del momento de colapso de la imaginación –como si fuera una repentina rigidez (por la que el "Fantasma" constituye aquí la forma más extrema, en la que la imaginación queda atrapada en la imagen)–, mientras que la imaginación se define como un movimiento "iconoclasta", como si fuera una actividad óntica que quebrara, destruyera e ingiriera las imágenes relacionadas con los deseos y el decurso de la existencia del sujeto (Foucault, 1992: 78 y sigs.). A Foucault le interesa aquí, por lo tanto, justamente ese momento de transición de los estímulos que no pueden ser aferrados –que denomina "imaginación" (donde Freud hablaba de "inervaciones" [*Innervationen*] o "apertura de brechas" [*Bahnungen*])–, que pasa hasta las imágenes cristalizadas, o sea hacia un lugar que obtiene una significación paradigmática, como el momento del despertar, el umbral entre el sueño y la vigilia, al representar un espacio relevante entre los Pasajes benjaminianos. Si se considera que en este prólogo Foucault afirma que "la imagen representa una visión hacia la imaginación en el acto de soñar" (1992: 89) y que la conciencia de la vigilia toma posesión por esa vía de los instantes del sueño, entonces podría caracterizarse la imagen del sueño recordada, siguiendo a Benjamin (y a Freud) como "representante sustituto" [*Stellvertreter*] del acto de soñar en la conciencia de la vigilia,[20] pero teniendo presente, además, que Foucault acentúa

19. En esta alusión explícita Foucault parte de una comprensión convencional de Freud, mientras que su propia dialéctica de la relectura de la obra freudiana a través de Laplanche y Pontalis (1985) lo coloca más cerca que lo que él mismo explicita, ya sea en cuanto al sueño o a las "fantasías originarias" [*Urphantasien/ phantasmes originaires*]. (Foucault, 1992: 52 y sigs.)

20. Ésta es una relación que Benjamin traslada a las imágenes materialmente

Pero si interpretar significa apropiarse por la fuerza o la astucia de un sistema de reglas, que en sí no posee ninguna importancia esencial, e imponerle una dirección para hacerlo servir a una nueva voluntad y así colocarlo en el nuevo juego de modo de dominar otras reglas, entonces el devenir de la humanidad es sólo una serie de interpretaciones. (1971b: 78)

En estas analogías, con la interpretación en el caso de Foucault y con la lectura y la cita en el caso de Benjamin, se evidencia una clara distinción que es característica para la diferencia entre los textos de los dos autores. Mientras Foucault hace hincapié en *reglas*, Benjamin se refiere casi exclusivamente a *imágenes*.

Y en lo que concierne al significado de las imágenes, puede observarse en la base de las reflexiones de ambos autores nuevamente otra inversión que sigue lo antes descrito en la relación del lenguaje como discurso y del lenguaje como literatura. Estas dos vías de pensamiento no dejan de tener, con todo, puntos de contacto, por ejemplo en el interés por el sueño como modo específico cognoscitivo y de experiencia, pero también en el interés en la "imagen", más allá de su función de copia, y de la historia de la imagen material. Pero el punto de cruce más significativo de estos dos movimientos teóricos contrarios se halla en el concepto de similitud. Sin embargo, en el marco de un modelo escénico de la historia, en el caso de Benjamin –en el contexto de una reformulación del escenario histórico (por ejemplo, en el libro sobre el drama barroco, donde la historia viene a terminar en el teatro) como teatro de la memoria (por ejemplo, en el proyecto de los Pasajes)–, las imágenes y su legibilidad llegan a ser el medio más importante para la historia. Por el contrario, las imágenes pasan a ocupar cada vez un lugar menos importante en los trabajos de historia del discurso de Foucault, aunque ellas habían jugado un papel central en el origen de sus reflexiones teóricas, cuando el psicoanálisis tenía todavía mayor relevancia.

En su introducción al libro de Ludwig Binswanger titulado *Traum und Existenz* [*Sueño y existencia*] de 1954, Foucault había

tragedia, es tragedia–, Benjamin describe una puesta en escena en la que la historia "viene a terminar en el teatro" [*in den Schauplatz hineinwandert*] (*G.S.*, I.1.271), es decir, en la que la historia obtiene su representación no en una dimensión temporal sino escenográfica. En este sentido, Benjamin identifica escenario histórico con escena de la escritura, por lo que las imágenes escénicas de la historia se tornan imágenes legibles, semejantes a las de la escritura. Desde este momento, por lo tanto, toma cuerpo su interés por lo teatral y su topografía, y también por la significación de las constelaciones como espacios en imágenes de la historia que es necesario descifrar, y que más adelante habrá de desarrollar en el proyecto de los Pasajes y en sus tesis de teoría de la historia.[17]

Las imágenes de la historia, sin embargo, devienen semejantes imágenes leídas (o dialécticas) únicamente a través de la actitud de la lectura, que sólo se establece como práctica esencial de la historiografía en virtud de la discontinuidad. Junto a "una mirada que desmenuza" es necesario también una inversión de "la relación entre lo cercano y lo lejano" frente a la historia tradicional (Foucault, 1971b: 81), o como afirma Benjamin: "una óptica dialéctica que reconozca lo cotidiano como impenetrable y lo impenetrable como cotidiano" ("El surrealismo"; *G.S.*, II.1.307).

En este cambio de enfoque habrá de cumplirse ahora el postulado nietzscheano acerca de la utilidad de la historia para la vida, en tanto se anule la diferencia entre la historia de los historiadores y la historia de los protagonistas, cuando coincidan lectura y acción, obrar e interpretar. Así como cuando Benjamin, considerando la relación de la Revolución Francesa con la antigua Roma,[18] afirmaba que la cita se tornaba el salto del tigre (de la Revolución), así también para Foucault una práctica específica de la interpretación se transforma en la condición de posibilidad para un cambio de la dirección histórica:

---

17. Para la genealogía del modelo topográfico de la memoria en Benjamin, véase el capítulo 8 del presente estudio.

18. Véase el capítulo 1 del presente trabajo.

la puesta en escena, del ritual, del ámbito de las regulaciones y de la lucha, pero también indica mecanismos complejos, en los que acaece la historia y en los que el enmascaramiento [*Maskierung*][16] representa una práctica específica en el tratamiento de las reglas que se imponen en ese teatro del no-lugar. Pues:

> Los diferentes surgimientos [*éminences*] no hacen a las conformaciones sucesivas de idéntico significado; más bien, ellos resultan de sustituciones y desplazamientos, conquistas y cambios. (1971b: 78)

Con todas estas figuras que podrían ser subsumidas bajo el título (psicoanalítico) de "distorsión" [*Entstellung*], en las que lo que emerge entra históricamente en el juego de las apariciones pero también con la caracterización de los efectos de este "gran juego de la historia" como huellas de marcas y recuerdos que se inscriben en las cosas y en los cuerpos (1971b: 77), Foucault funda su concepto de la historia como una contra-memoria dentro de un modelo de memoria, en el que ésta aparece en la conformación de huellas duraderas así como también en tanto escenario de la escritura.

Tal idea le debe mucho a la escuela fundada dentro del área del pensamiento psicoanalítico, y más precisamente a la descripción topológica de la relación entre percepción-conciencia, por un lado, e inconsciente, por otro, según fue elaborado por Freud, pero también a la concepción de la memoria como "escena de la escritura", según se halla en Derrida. En el caso del drama barroco –leído como expresión de la idea de la historia *en tanto* tragedia, o sea: la idea de una postura histórica en la que la historia deviene

---

16. Para la diferenciación en la interpretación del enmascaramiento entre Marx y Benjamin, véase el capítulo 1 del presente estudio. Para la idea de la historia como parodia y farsa en Foucault, véase el siguiente pasaje: "El buen historiador, el 'genealogista' sabe qué ha de entender de esta mascarada. No porque la deseche, considerándola poco seria; más bien porque querría llevarla hasta sus últimas consecuencias: organizaría, si por él fuera, el gran carnaval de todos los tiempos, en el que las máscaras retornaran sin cesar. [...] La genealogía es la historia como carnaval en gran estilo" (1971b: 85-86).

como un torbellino que arrastrara hacia su interior, en el ritmo que le es peculiar los mismos "elementos de la emergencia" [*Entstehungsmaterial*]. (*G.S.*, I.1.226)

El modo en que Foucault entiende, por lo tanto, la variante nietzscheana del concepto de origen (en sentido de *Entstehung*) aparece como homologable al uso benjaminiano de origen en el sentido de lo que surge [*von Entspringendem*], que aparece así en oposición a la idea de *Entstehung* en el sentido de comienzo. En tanto en el libro sobre el drama barroco el concepto de origen se conecta con ideas y contenido, cuando Benjamin pasa a su proyecto sobre la Modernidad se trata ahora de fenómenos de origen dentro de la historia, como, por ejemplo, el de las galerías o pasajes parisienses, en cuya topografía se superponen significados materiales, concretos y simbólicos.

ESCENAS E IMÁGENES DE LA HISTORIA

En rigor, la idea de origen habría que imaginársela, tanto en Benjamin como en Foucault, como algo percibido de modo *teatral*, como una entrada en el escenario de la historia, es decir como una entrada y aparición al mismo tiempo, o una "escena primaria" [*Urszene*]. Así, por ejemplo, en Foucault: "La emergencia es también la entrada de fuerzas en escena, su salto desde las bambalinas al centro del escenario" (1971b: 76). Foucault habla también del "lugar de la confrontación", pero de modo tal que para no caer con la palabra "escenario" en las aguas turbias de una *metáfora* que haga de la historia una obra teatral, caracteriza al mismo tiempo ese lugar como un no-lugar, diciendo: "En cierto sentido, la obra interpretada en ese teatro del no-lugar es siempre la misma" (1971b: 77). (La traducción alemana de Foucault es en este punto más específicamente teatral, dado que se dice: *auf diesem ortlosen Theater gespielten Stück*, "una obra interpretada en este teatro del no-lugar".) La idea de "interpretar" [en francés "*jouer*" y en alemán "*spielen*"] apunta más bien a figuraciones de territorio de la "expectativa" [*Erwartung*] y del "recuerdo" [*Erinnerung*] a través de esa "cita secreta entre los antepasados y nosotros", a través de esa "fuerza mesiánica *débil* [...] a la que el pasado tiene derecho" ("Sobre el concepto de la historia", Reflexión II; *G.S.*, I.2.694).

Todavía más estrecho es el contacto entre las reflexiones de Benjamin y Foucault en el campo de los conceptos de "origen" y "emergencia" [*Entstehung-émergence*]. Mientras que la "proveniencia" [*Herkunft-provenance*], según Foucault, se refiere, por lo tanto, a la idea de procedencia y se corresponde con una red de rastros [*marques*] que se cruzan en el individuo como las inscripciones de los acontecimientos en el propio cuerpo, en su obra la idea de "emergencia" aparece como aquello "que emerge": "*Entstehung* significa más bien surgimiento [*Auftauchen-surgissement*], como el principio y la ley particular de una súbita aparición [*Aufblitzen-apparition*]" (1971b: 75). La traducción alemana de este texto utiliza significativamente el término *Aufblitzen* (fenómeno súbito como la luz del relámpago), que en la obra de Benjamin tiene carácter de *Leitmotiv*, para reproducir el vocablo francés de *apparition*; este hecho remite, entonces, a una asociación que permitiría prestar atención a su trabajo sobre la idea de origen. En efecto, en el prólogo de carácter epistemológico que Benjamin redactó para su libro sobre el drama barroco, escrito cuando su autor se encontraba en una particular época de umbral –valiéndose de expresiones conceptuales metafísicas, pero realizando, al mismo tiempo, un giro mental que rompía con la metafísica–, se discute el concepto de "origen" [*Ursprung*] no sólo delimitándolo con respecto al de "comienzo" [*Anfang*], sino fundamentándolo como "emergencia" [*Entstehung*]:

> El origen [*Ursprung*] –a pesar de ser una categoría completamente histórica– no tiene, sin embargo, nada que ver con la emergencia [*Entstehung*]. En el origen no se halla el devenir de aquello que ha surgido [*des Entsprungenen*], sino más bien que con esta palabra se piensa en el devenir y el desaparecer de lo que está surgiendo [*Entspringendes*]. El origen se encuentra en el río del devenir

Yo que quisiera exhibir el movimiento de prestidigitación de una unidad substancial). El cuerpo es una masa que se desintegra sin cesar. La genealogía se halla, como análisis de la proveniencia, por lo tanto, allí donde el cuerpo se entrelaza con la historia. La historia debe mostrar, entonces, cómo el cuerpo es interpenetrado por la historia y cómo ella, por su parte, se empecina royendo al cuerpo. (Foucault, 1971b: 75)

En los textos de Benjamin no existe, por cierto, semejante estrecha asociación entre proveniencia y cuerpo. Así, si en su obra siempre se da un entrelazamiento de cuerpo e historia, ello sucede en el área de un espacio de la imagen, de tal modo que el cuerpo, en tanto matriz de la historia, aparece siempre estructurado como imagen. La *physis* ha de producirse sólo en el espacio de la imagen según su "realidad totalmente política y objetiva" ("El surrealismo"; *G.S.*, II.1.310) y, por ello, no podrán separarse el espacio de la imagen y el espacio corpóreo.[14] A pesar de ello, el concepto foucaultiano de la heterogeneidad de la proveniencia –con sus rasgos de disolución del Yo y de dispersión, etc. (Foucault, 1971b: 73)– aparecería indirectamente representado en los textos de Benjamin por ese *negarse* a aceptar la idea de una construcción de una proveniencia [*Herkunft*] que fuera portadora de unidad o identidad o que sirviera a fines político-ideológicos, por ejemplo, en el pasaje donde este autor pone el acento en el carácter artificial del recuerdo que le fue acordado al proletariado.[15] La dimensión que Foucault denomina "proveniencia" [*provenance*] en su lectura de Nietzsche –"la pertenencia a un estamento que se pierde en el tiempo" (1971b: 73)– aparece asignada en Benjamin en primera instancia al

---

14. Véase el capítulo 2 del presente estudio.
15. En los esbozos de "Sobre el concepto de historia" se encuentra la siguiente anotación: "Problema de la tradición II/ En el proletariado no existió una correspondencia histórica que concerniera a la conciencia de una misión nueva. No tuvo lugar ningún recuerdo. Se ha tratado de asignárselo artificialmente, en obras como la historia de las guerras campesinas de Zimmermann, entre otras..." (*G.S.*, I.3.1236). Cf. también I.3.1242.

negación del cuerpo" dentro del dominio de la filosofía (Foucault, 1971b: 81). Pues para ambos autores el cuerpo no se encuentra fuera de la historia, ni tampoco se lo entiende como perteneciente a la Naturaleza en oposición a la Cultura. También el cuerpo tiene una historia. El cuerpo es, al mismo tiempo, la matriz y el lugar de ajustes de cuentas de la historia.

En rigor, Foucault ha perseguido esta empresa en una serie de proyectos, desde el estudio de la locura, las prácticas para vigilar y castigar, el dispositivo de la sexualidad hasta, finalmente, los modos de la subjetivización en la Antigüedad y el cristianismo temprano. Pero ya antes, Benjamin había destacado de modo particularmente significativo la importancia de la historia para la materialidad y corporeidad (lo que es ahora un bastión tan relevante en la teoría actual), aun cuando esto no haya despertado la debida atención (con excepción de la alegoría del cadáver en el libro sobre el drama barroco).

En su artículo sobre Nietzsche, Foucault reflexiona sobre todo acerca del uso nietzscheano del concepto de "origen" [*Ursprung*], con el objeto de contrastarlo con la idea de principio histórico o de identidad primordial, al mismo tiempo que con el fin de diferenciar los aspectos afines a la idea de "origen" [*Ursprung-origine*] entendido ya sea como "proveniencia" [*Herkunft-provenance*] o "emergencia" [*Entstehung-émergence*]. En este sentido, el concepto de genealogía, capital para su investigación, se explica en el contexto de las ideas de proveniencia y emergencia, donde lo corpóreo aparece tratado en primera instancia bajo el aspecto del origen como proveniencia, así como se presenta en este pasaje:

> El cuerpo –y todo lo que lo roza– es el lugar de la proveniencia: en el cuerpo se encuentra el estigma de los acontecimientos pasados; de él provienen también los deseos, las impotencias y los errores. En el cuerpo los acontecimientos encuentran su unidad y su expresión, pero él también es el campo de disensión que puede llevar a los conflictos más insuperables.
> Los acontecimientos dejan su impronta en el cuerpo (fijados por el lenguaje y diluidos por las ideas). En el cuerpo se disuelve el Yo (ese

lo posible, del proceso de la transmisión de la tradición, tanto como su afirmación acerca de "la tarea de cepillar la historia a contrapelo"[12] ("Sobre el concepto de historia", Reflexión VII; *G.S.*, I.2.696-697), se tocan con el programa foucaultiano de hacer jugar a la historia contra su propio origen, de liberarla de los modelos metafísicos y antropológicos de la memoria y "de hacer una contra-memoria, desarrollando en ella una forma totalmente diferente del tiempo" (Foucault, 1971b: 85). El texto de Nietzsche al que aquí alude Foucault lleva por título *Vom Nutzen und Nachteil der Historie für das Leben* ["De la utilidad y la desventaja de la historia para la vida"], y es el mismo, en otro de sus pasajes, de donde Benjamin ha tomado el epígrafe de "Sobre el concepto de historia" (Reflexión XII), de modo que bien puede decirse que dicha obra establece un puente entre los dos autores aquí tratados,[13] aun cuando los textos de Nietzsche no ocupen en la obra de Benjamin la misma posición central como garantía de la Modernidad que tienen en Foucault. De todos modos, ambos proyectos de Foucault y de Benjamin podrían ponerse en relación con el famoso *dictum* nietzscheano:

> Hasta ahora todo lo que ha dado color a la existencia no tiene una historia: ¿o acaso habría una historia del amor, de la codicia, de la envidia, de la conciencia, de la piedad, de la crueldad? Incluso falta por completo una historia comparativa del derecho, o aun del castigo. (Nietzsche, *Die Fröhlische Wissenschaft* [*La gaya ciencia*]. 1988, III.1.7.378-379)

En virtud de esta intertextualidad, las obras de Benjamin y de Foucault se hallan en franca oposición a una "sistemática

---

12. En alemán: "*die Aufgabe, die Geschichte gegen den Strich zu bürsten*". [N. del T.]

13. Compárese sobre todo la confrontación crítica con la obra de Nietzsche *El nacimiento de la tragedia* en el libro de Benjamin sobre el drama barroco, que presenta como objetivo criticar a su autor por su negativa a considerar el valor de conocimiento del mito de la tragedia para una filosofía de la historia. Pfotenhauer, por su parte, ha señalado de modo sistemático los rastros de una lectura benjaminiana de Nietzsche (Pfotenhauer, 1985).

vas reflexiones críticas en torno al historicismo en cuanto a la *discontinuidad* y al *concepto del origen*. Estas coincidencias se manifiestan de modo más acabado en la comparación entre los textos benjaminianos del concepto de la historia y el Block N del proyecto de los Pasajes, por una parte, y el artículo titulado "Nietzsche, la genealogía, la historia", por otra, que Foucault escribió en 1971 para un homenaje a Jean Hyppolite, y donde dice:

> Todo lo que sirve de apoyatura para tratar la historia y abarcarla en su totalidad, todo lo que la hace aparecer como un movimiento paciente y continuo debe ser sistemáticamente demolido [...] La historia ha de ser "verdadera" en la medida en que introduzca en nuestro propio ser las discontinuidades. Dividiendo en pequeños trozos nuestros sentimientos, pondrá en escena nuestros instintos; tornará múltiple nuestro cuerpo haciendo que él se oponga a sí mismo. (Foucault, 1971b: 79-80)

Si aquí en los tópicos del cuerpo se podría constatar una cercanía con "el espacio del cuerpo y de la imagen" del ensayo benjaminiano sobre el surrealismo, donde al ser humano "no le quedará ningún miembro intacto" (II.1.309), con igual razón podrían hallarse pasajes en Benjamin sobre la idea de un dinamitar la cantera del *continuum*, por ejemplo, cuando éste afirmaba: "...que el hecho de que el objeto de la historia sea obtenido de la explosión del *continuum* del decurso histórico es algo que resulta de su propia estructura monadológica" (Anotaciones y materiales para "La obra de los Pasajes", Block N10,3; *G.S.*, V.1.594).

Foucault, por otro lado, habría de postular para este proceder una "mirada que desmenuza", lo que recuerda la idea benjaminiana de "cambio de la mirada histórica sobre lo que ha sido por una mirada política"[11] ("El surrealismo"; *G.S.*, II.1.300). Así también la recomendación benjaminiana de tomar distancia, en la medida de

---

11. En alemán: "*Auswechslung des historischen Blicks aufs Gewesene gegen den politischen*". [N. del T.]

lenguaje como literatura, para ir ganando espacio el lenguaje como discurso (según ocurre en sus proyectos arqueológicos e histórico-discursivos), este tipo de pasajes no pasa de tener un carácter episódico. El mismo título bajo el que este pasaje aparece ("La escritura de las cosas") podría muy bien figurar como título para un pensamiento que se desarrollara en el área entre los dos términos mencionados por el propio Foucault, que habrían representado muy diferentes recuerdos de una similitud perdida: la cábala y la literatura (moderna). Eso habría significado moverse en un territorio en el que Benjamin realmente había trabajado y donde las huellas de sus textos en alguna medida se han perdido. Justamente en ese espacio –no muy diferente quizá de un abismo– es donde ha operado Benjamin con su proyecto de la legibilidad. Es un espacio que se abre a causa de correspondencias entre dos diferentes recuerdos: la huella de una tradición escrituraria perdida, por una parte, y el surgimiento de otra similitud en la literatura de la Modernidad, de una "similitud distorsionada o no sensorial".[10] De tal modo, Foucault ha venido acotando y describiendo poco a poco justamente esos márgenes entre los que encontró su origen "el pensamiento completamente nuevo" de Benjamin.

ACERCA DEL ORIGEN Y DEL CUERPO EN LA HISTORIA

Dado que en el apartado precedente se trató de manera reiterada el tema del origen, se verá a continuación cuál es su importancia y su fundamentación teórica en el concepto de "historia auténtica" en el ámbito de Benjamin y Foucault. Las concordancias más explícitas en los proyectos teóricos de los dos autores se refieren, entonces, a la historiografía, y a sus respecti-

---

10. Para el significado del concepto de "similitud no sensorial", de "distorsión" y de una "segunda cesura" en la historia del lenguaje después de que fuera expulsado del paraíso el espíritu del lenguaje, véase el capítulo 9 del presente estudio.

nuestro saber, ni en nuestra reflexión para hacernos sentir el recuerdo de la 'coyuntura'. Nada más, salvo quizás la literatura –y ello de una manera más alusiva y diagonal que directa [...] [Ella] manifiesta la reaparición, allí donde no se la esperaba, del ser vivo del lenguaje" (Foucault, 1966: 58).

Sin embargo, en la manera en que Benjamin se refirió justamente a esa posibilidad de la reaparición de una similitud perdida y a una ambigüedad del lenguaje, se manifiesta en su obra también otro rastro del recuerdo, una huella de la memoria de las Sagradas Escrituras y de la tradición judía en la letra escrita que está proveyendo un modelo de similitud no basada en la copia. Y también Foucault sigue esta huella, especialmente en la sección titulada "La escritura de las cosas", en la que se refiere explícitamente al hebreo y a la cábala, y donde se acerca todavía más a la lectura benjaminiana del Génesis y a sus presuposiciones culturales. Si ambos autores se refieren al origen divino del lenguaje, llamando la atención sobre el polifacetismo y la confusión babélica como cesura, Foucault va a emplear la expresión de "*raison d'être*" del lenguaje, allí donde Benjamin sostiene que "el espíritu del lenguaje" ha sufrido la "expulsión del paraíso" [*Sündenfall des Sprachgeistes*]:

> Bajo su primera forma, cuando les fue dado a los hombres por Dios, el lenguaje era un signo de las cosas absolutamente cierto y transparente porque se parecía a ellas. [...] Todas las lenguas que conocemos no las hablamos más que sobre el fondo de esta similitud perdida, y en el espacio que ella ha dejado vacío. No existe más que una lengua que conserva esa memoria, porque deriva de manera directa de ese primer vocabulario ahora olvidado; porque Dios no ha querido que el castigo de Babel escapara al recuerdo del hombre; porque esta lengua ha debido servir para contar la antigua alianza de Dios con su pueblo; porque, en fin, es ésta la lengua en la que Dios se ha dirigido a aquellos que lo escuchaban. El hebreo conlleva, entonces, como los restos, las marcas de la primera denominación. (Foucault, 1966: 51)

En los propios escritos de Foucault en los que, en el curso de su investigación, ha ido quedando desplazado el tema del

la escritura. "Desaparece entonces esa capa uniforme donde se entrecruzaban indefinidamente lo *visto* y lo *leído*, lo visible y lo enunciable" (Foucault, 1966: 58), lo que produce el efecto de una separación entre las palabras y las cosas, donde el orden gana la partida por sobre la interpretación:

> [...] sobre uno de los márgenes se encuentran los signos que se han tornado instrumentos del análisis, marcas de la identidad y de la diferencia, los principios de la puesta en orden, claves para una taxonomía; sobre el otro borde, la semejanza empírica y murmurante de las cosas, esa similitud sorda que se halla por debajo del pensamiento y suministra la materia infinita para las divisiones y distribuciones. (Foucault, 1966: 72)

Sin embargo, la similitud perdida no tenía ninguna relación con la idea de copia, así como tampoco la tenía la perdida inmediatez del "lenguaje paradisíaco" benjaminiano. Por el contrario, era "la forma invisible de lo que hacía visible a las cosas desde la profundidad del mundo", de modo tal que lo visible era signo de las analogías invisibles, la cifra de un lenguaje mudo que había que descifrar. Desde la perspectiva de la historia del lenguaje, Foucault describe esta pérdida de la similitud como el pasaje de un sistema de signos *ternario* a uno *binario*, como pasaje de un signo, donde "se reconocía el significante, el significado y la 'coyuntura'[9] (*týnkhanon*)", a otro que se definía "por la unión entre un significante y un significado" (Foucault, 1966: 57). Aquí nos encontramos, en definitiva, ante un sistema de signos que domina la representación así como toda la época que Foucault designa como "*l'âge classique*".

Y en el umbral de la época moderna ya "no hay nada más en

---

9. La comparación de la relación entre Dios, la Naturaleza y el Hombre, que es dominante en el área del lenguaje del paraíso dentro de la teoría de la magia del lenguaje benjaminiana, parece acercarse, en virtud de este signo ternario y triádico, a la comparación con la tríada edípica, según la ha presentado M. Stoessel. (Cf. el capítulo 2, pág. 61). Para el tema de la "coyuntura" como condición de posibilidad para la teoría benjaminiana de la alegoría, cf. el capítulo 7 del presente estudio.

se inscriben en el lenguaje del hombre, terminan perdiéndose cuando el lenguaje es expulsado del paraíso; al mismo tiempo, en su caída el lenguaje se impregna de un carácter instrumental y comunicativo. Por otro lado, como consecuencia de la expulsión, el costado mágico del lenguaje se manifiesta sólo de modo efímero en el aspecto sígnico de la lengua, mientras la capacidad mimética del hombre se trans-substancia de tal manera en la escritura y la lengua como para hallar su expresión sólo en forma de la "similitud no sensorial" benjaminiana.

Con respecto a esta última idea se da ahora –de modo sorprendente incluso en la manera de sus formulaciones– la mayor cercanía de Foucault a Benjamin en su presentación de la similitud *perdida* en el segundo capítulo de *Las palabras y las cosas*, que se puede leer como una historización benjaminiana en tanto teoría del lenguaje derivada del mito. La ruptura con el lenguaje de la magia que en Benjamin había aparecido como una "escena primigenia *mítica*" [*mytische Urszene*], la expulsión del paraíso, se da en Foucault sólo concretizada como un movimiento *histórico* y situada en el pasaje del Renacimiento hacia la Edad Clásica, la época de la representación, como la primera de las dos constelaciones históricas de cambio analizadas en su libro *Las palabras y las cosas*. Pues las *episteme* del siglo XVI, que sufren un retroceso en dichos procesos, son descritas por Foucault dentro del paradigma de las similitudes:

> El mundo está cubierto de signos que es necesario descifrar y esos signos, que revelan sus semejanzas y afinidades, no son ellos mismos más que formas de la similitud. Conocer es, por lo tanto, interpretar: ir desde la marca visible a aquello que se dice por su intermedio, y que sin esa marca permanecería *palabra muda, dormida en las cosas* [*parole muette, ensomeillée dans les choses*]. (Foucault, 1966: 47) (El destacado es mío.)

Y donde una vez existió "un espacio de inmediata similitud" –un gran libro abierto, rodeado de signos escritos y mágicos–, allí mismo en el siglo XVII aparece disuelta la correspondencia entre lenguaje y mundo a la vez que suspendida la primacía de

formulaciones de la visión alegórica y de la estructura monadológica de los fenómenos.[8]

En esta forma de pensamiento la cita adquiere una materialidad y una independencia lingüísticas que la hacen legible en diferentes capas pero también resistente, en el sentido de una construcción de la historia. La cita da cuerpo al lenguaje como si fuera literatura, desgajándola de un discurso para hacerla devenir, como fragmento, parte de otra escritura. Pues la cita

> [...] llama a la palabra por su nombre, la recorta con violencia del contexto, pero precisamente aquí es donde la cita proclama su origen [...] En la cita ambos reinos –origen y destrucción– muestran su identidad ante el lenguaje. Y a la inversa: sólo allí –en la cita– es donde los dos dominios se interpenetran, allí es donde el lenguaje aparece consumado. En la cita se refleja el lenguaje de los ángeles, en el que todas las palabras, perturbadas en la relación idílica del sentido, devienen lemas en el libro de la creación. (*G.S.*, II.1.147)

Haciendo referencia a su propio origen en las figuras del contexto y la ruptura, la cita, con todo, también se resiste a tomar parte en la construcción de una nueva totalidad.

UNA SIMILITUD PERDIDA

En esta significación de la cita resuena la teoría benjaminiana de la *magia del lenguaje*, que Benjamin había absorbido en su lectura del Génesis bíblico, pero leído no como el sentido impuesto por la tradición o como "verdad revelada" ("Sobre el lenguaje en general y sobre el lenguaje de los humanos"; *G.S.*, II.1.147), sino como "una escena primigenia mítica" [*mythische Urszene*] para el nacimiento del lenguaje y del sentido. La inmediatez o la magia del lenguaje adámico, definidos como traducción del lenguaje mudo de la naturaleza o de las cosas que

---

8. Compárese sobre todo el Block N del proyecto de los Pasajes.

dispersión del lenguaje cada intento tendiente, efectivamente, a dominar la ruptura con el orden clásico no hace más que completar ese orden, puesto que en los esfuerzos, ya sea sistemáticos o analíticos, por definir el lenguaje en su totalidad, no se hace otra cosa que repetir ese quiebre. En este sentido, rivalizando con el cumplimiento de un saber sistemático, aparece postulada así la pregunta acerca de una forma absolutamente nueva de pensamiento:

> Volver a encontrar en un único espacio el gran juego del lenguaje podría significar igualmente dar un salto decisivo hacia una forma completamente nueva del pensamiento, como también significaría clausurar en sí mismo un modo de saber constituido en el siglo precedente. (Foucault, 1966: 318)

Mientras que Foucault, por su parte, por medio de la heterogeneidad del discurso y del lenguaje traza las líneas de una problemática que se halla estructurando la configuración teórica actual, en tanto se fundamenta sobre la teoría del lenguaje o sobre la semiología; y, además, con sus proyectos ha provocado las variaciones más diferenciadas tendientes a reducir el abismo y el enfrentamiento entre el discurso académico y la literaturidad;[7] la escritura de Benjamin ya se halla situada directamente en relación con esa heterogeneidad. Para la relación con el proyecto de los Pasajes, para la tentativa de la representación de una historia primigenia de la Modernidad lograda a partir de una colección de citas e imágenes de pensamiento podría tomarse en cuenta más bien la primera de las variantes metodológicas de Foucault. Benjamin trabajaba, en efecto, en una forma completamente nueva del pensamiento, por ejemplo, con la representación de la totalidad en el fragmento, concretado metódicamente en las

---

7. Así por ejemplo en el retrato estructural que traza Barthes en sus *Fragmentos de un discurso amoroso* o en los más recientes textos de Derrida con su fuerte tendencia a la metaforización, también en los juegos de palabras lacanianos, en los que, por ejemplo, resulta unívoca la referencia a lo simbólico o corporal.

lo que se coloca cada vez más en el centro del debate filosófico la tarea de una reflexión radical sobre el lenguaje (Foucault, 1966: 303 y siguientes). Foucault pone así los límites de "un lenguaje que no dice nada ni calla tampoco nunca y que se llama 'literatura'" (1966: 317) frente al discurso; *discurso* en el sentido de una unidad de la gramática general y como modelo de una representación simple que valía para la "Edad Clásica". Foucault entiende ese lenguaje como una especie de contradiscurso: la literatura es, entonces, un resurgimiento del "lenguaje según modos de ser múltiples, cuya unidad sin lugar a dudas no pudo ser restaurada", un surgir del lenguaje "según una multiplicidad enigmática" (1966: 315-316).

Foucault se dedicó en sus últimos estudios a una constelación histórica en la que encontraba *discursos* en su forma más distintiva, es decir como textos prescriptivos;[6] Benjamin, por el contrario, desplegó su teoría de la decodificación y legibilidad no sólo en base a textos *literarios* polivalentes de la Modernidad, sino también echando mano a textos culturales, a la topografía de la ciudad, a la arquitectura, a interiores, a los objetos, a la moda, etc. Benjamin comprendió, entonces, estos textos como la escritura onírica de la multitud, a la par que le importaba descifrar en esos textos el sueño de una época pasada en su propio origen; es decir, decodificar los símbolos del deseo del último siglo "antes de que los monumentos que ellos representaban se hubieran desintegrado" ("La obra de los Pasajes"-"Exposés"; V.1.59). Con este proyecto de lectura, Benjamin da el paso clave justamente sobre una frontera del saber que Foucault vincula al fin del discurso y al resurgimiento simultáneo de un lenguaje múltiple. Como consecuencia de la creciente fragmentación y

---

6. Hay que considerar que el hecho de que Foucault se limite en su historia de la sexualidad en el mundo antiguo a textos prescriptivos arroja algunos problemas. De ese modo cae muy bien bajo su enfoque el movimiento del *logos* (cf. Foucault, 1984b), pero recibe menor luz la representación de los conflictos y la contracara de una historia que más bien obtuviera su expresión en otro lenguaje, por ejemplo, en el mito o en las tragedias. Cf. Weigel, 1990: 187 y sigs.

destrucción (*G.S.*, V.1.587). En todo caso, en el decurso de los estudios de Foucault sus libros fueron perdiendo extensión –compárese, por ejemplo, *Las palabras y las cosas* o las investigaciones sobre las cárceles, la locura o la clínica con los tomos segundo y tercero sobre la *Historia de la sexualidad*–, de modo tal que la montaña de citas proveniente de los documentos analizados para el archivo han ido retrocediendo frente a la propia construcción, a su propia escritura. Benjamin, en cambio, sintió evidentemente la amenaza de la posibilidad de que paulatinamente se le perdiera la representación de su construcción en los casilleros de su proyecto de los Pasajes, aunque reiteradamente volvía a desarrollar, modificándolos, sus esquemas con tal de preservarlos. De todos modos, al parecer se dedicaba cada vez con mayor asiduidad a la labor de extractar citas particulares o fragmentos de las diferentes tradiciones, hasta el punto de quedar enredado finalmente en la trama de sus múltiples referencias e indicaciones.

EL FIN DEL DISCURSO Y LA VUELTA DE LA LITERATURA

Esta situación está conectada también, por cierto, con el intento de Benjamin de escribir una historia primigenia de la Modernidad, que históricamente se ubicaría en ese lugar de transición[5] que Foucault en *Las palabras y las cosas* describe como lugar de aparición de la literatura y como el instante en el que el lenguaje se presenta desligado de la representación, por

---

5. Esto concierne a la segunda de las dos situaciones de ruptura analizadas por Foucault: "Sin embargo, esta investigación arqueológica ha dejado a la vista dos grandes discontinuidades en la *episteme* de la cultura occidental; primeramente, la que inaugura la Edad Clásica (hacia la mitad del siglo XVII), y, luego, la que a comienzos del siglo XIX marca el umbral de nuestra Modernidad" (Foucault, 1966: 13). Ambas cesuras históricas fijan en Benjamin la diferencia entre la alegoría del libro sobre el drama alemán y sus estudios sobre la alegoría de la Modernidad. Cf. el capítulo 7 del presente trabajo. También Menninghaus (1980: 72 y sigs.).

1969: 169-170). Si Foucault ve concretizado ese archivo en su tratamiento del discurso histórico como esos sistemas "que introducen las afirmaciones como *acontecimientos* (que tienen sus condicionamientos y áreas de aparición) y *cosas* (que abarcan sus posibilidades y sus campos de aplicación)" (1969: 169), entonces podría decirse que Benjamin parte literalmente de las cosas y sucesos mismos, como si se tratara de una perspectiva inversa a cuya afirmación le siguiera la pista. Así, en todo caso, sucede en su historia primigenia de la Modernidad [*Urgeschichte der Moderne*], en la que él, a diferencia de un re-constructor de los discursos históricos, se coloca más bien en la postura del coleccionista de citas y de lecturas. Por el contrario, su libro sobre el drama barroco podría leerse realmente como la descripción de un archivo del teatro en sentido foucaultiano,[4] puesto que a Benjamin le interesaba allí la *idea* del drama barroco. Esta idea era entendida como la estructura más íntima y como configuración, como imagen de todos los dramas virtuales, como "círculo de todos los extremos posibles dentro de sí" (*G.S.*, I.1.227). Para Foucault, por su parte, el archivo es "en primera instancia la ley de lo que puede ser dicho; el sistema, que domina la aparición de las afirmaciones como sucesos únicos" (1972: 170).

El trabajo en ese archivo llevó a los dos autores comentados de modo constante al archivo como institución, como lugar de depósito de la tradición, en un sentido concreto topográfico sobre todo en la Bibliothèque Nationale, donde ambos periódicamente desaparecían detrás de verdaderas montañas de libros. Por este hecho es probable que nunca habrían podido encontrarse, aun cuando sus permanencias en esa biblioteca no hubieran estado separadas por varias décadas. Sólo que a Foucault parece haberle tocado una suerte extremadamente mejor en la sistematización u ordenamiento de su archivo y también en el logro del *dictum* benjaminiano que sostiene que la historia es objeto de una "construcción", que fue precedida por una

---

4. Menninghaus habla en este sentido con toda razón de "el estructuralismo práctico del libro sobre el drama alemán" (Menninghaus, 1980: 127 y sigs.).

[*Standort und Haltung*] del historiógrafo, una postura que justamente trascendiera la opinión privada o la convicción.[3] Foucault, por su parte, reflexiona sobre esto bajo el lema del "sentido histórico" como reconocimiento necesario de un "saber en perspectiva": para el historiador este hecho incluye el lugar desde el que mira, el momento en que se encuentra, el partido que toma, y la inevitabilidad de sus pasiones. Partiendo de la idea del lugar de la percepción, Benjamin habla en sentido parecido de un "ahora de la cognoscibilidad" [*Jetzt der Erkennbarkeit*] y supedita de modo extremo la imagen de "lo que ha sido" a las preocupaciones (psíquicas) y a la mirada del observador o lector del presente –"el sujeto del conocimiento histórico"–, pero también a la determinada luz bajo la que alguien revela las imágenes, decidiendo así su legibilidad. "La imagen leída significa la imagen en el 'ahora de la cognoscibilidad', cuando es portadora en sumo grado del sello del instante crítico y peligroso que se halla presente en toda lectura." (Anotaciones y materiales para "La obra de los Pasajes", Block N3,1; *G.S.*, V.1.578). Y también el historiador de Benjamin debe enfrentar las pasiones, que se le presentan de modo insoslayable en el pasado de las cosas mismas.

> El pasado, el ya no ser trabaja apasionadamente en las cosas. A ello confía el historiador su tarea. Se aferra a esa fuerza y reconoce las cosas como son en el momento del ya no ser. (Primeras anotaciones para "La obra de los Pasajes"/"Los pasajes parisienses"; *G.S.*, V.2.1001)

Para ambos autores, Benjamin y Foucault, el más importante lugar de trabajo y, al mismo tiempo, el objeto más esencial era el *archivo* [*Archiv*], pero no por cierto en el sentido de la tradición como "suma de todos los textos, que una cultura tiene en su posesión y ha guardado como documentos de su propio pasado o como testimonio de la conservación de su identidad" (Foucault,

---

3. Así escribía Benjamin en su ensayo sobre Karl Kraus: "Pues la opinión es la falsa subjetividad que se escapa de la persona a quien puede absorber la circulación de la mercancía" (*G.S.*, II.1.343).

un catedrático de la historia de los sistemas de pensamiento, como es el caso de Foucault, quien da sus clases en el prestigioso Collège de France, donde a causa de la magnitud de la asistencia a menudo se transmitía su voz por altoparlante para que su mensaje llegara a la gente que colmaba los pasillos, por una parte, con el así llamado autor independiente, cuya defensa del segundo doctorado [*Habilitation*] había fracasado en la Universidad de Francfort, y quien fue un judío en el exilio no sólo después de 1933; alguien, en definitiva, que debía preocuparse de manera creciente y con inmenso gasto de relaciones públicas para obtener posibilidades de publicación sobre las que se construía una existencia laboral tan precaria, como lo demuestra el hecho de que cuando en el exilio parisiense descubrió la pérdida de su lapicera fuente, semejante suceso lo arrojó al borde de la desesperación.

Esta breve semblanza digresiva sobre ambos pensadores debería parecer lícita, especialmente si se tiene en cuenta que dichos autores adscribían una particular importancia para la construcción y la lectura de las imágenes de la historia a la *ubicación y postura*

RETRATO DE DOS AUTORES DESDE SUS RESPECTIVOS ARCHIVOS

Y con estas dos diferentes constelaciones nuestros dos autores, Foucault y Benjamin, parecen haber arribado de modo absoluto cada uno a su propio continente, llevando consigo las marcas respectivas de sus propias experiencias y posturas. La primera impresión nos diría que no podría imaginarse un contraste más profundo que el que se da entre *las imágenes* y *los modos discursivos* de los dos teóricos: entre una mirada intrépida y sostenida, acompañada de una postura corporal decidida, en el uno, y la mirada contemplativa, algo soñadora, guiada por gestos de estilizada melancolía, en el otro; entre el análisis discursivo lúcido y sistemático, por un lado, y las imágenes de pensamiento sutiles y literarias, por el otro. A Benjamin, sin embargo, ambos retratos seguramente le hubieran gustado, en tanto podrían entenderse como el desarrollo del perfil del que cavila sin pausa y bajo cuya mirada el *continuum* acaba por desmoronarse. Tampoco parece posible un mayor contraste como se dio entre

reflexionando sobre ellas; Benjamin, por su parte, se referirá a un autor cuyos textos no posean ningún carácter proyectivo para la vida. Dando forma a la crisis de la percepción y de la experiencia en la Modernidad, el autor alemán habrá de operar más bien dentro del archivo de imágenes de una memoria colectiva.

Y, sin embargo, a pesar de la concordancia y continuidad de la perspectiva masculina, en el desplazamiento mencionado parece hallarse también un motivo para los movimientos entrecruzados de los intereses históricos en Benjamin y en Foucault –o mejor: de sus miradas y de los "sentidos históricos" (Nietzsche)– y de las genealogías de sus respectivos proyectos. Si los estudios foucaultianos tienen su punto de partida en un pensamiento moderno, donde la relación entre signo y sujeto se ha tornado problemática, y en una arqueología de las ciencias humanas (según se trata en *Las palabras y las cosas* de 1966), su itinerario en dirección hacia la así llamada Historia Antigua en su último gran proyecto tiene como meta un territorio en el que el hombre se constituye como sujeto tanto en las prácticas sexuales como también en las discursivas. Benjamin, en cambio, realizó la lectura de los clásicos al principio de su recorrido (sobre todo, la literatura del romanticismo y del barroco, como también la de Goethe y Hölderlin), para luego concentrarse en los textos de los siglos XIX y XX (como el de los surrealistas, entre otros, y especialmente en los de Proust, Baudelaire y Kafka). Sus lecturas acerca de Baudelaire fueron tornándose, en el marco del creciente proyecto de los Pasajes, los fragmentos de una "historia primigenia de la Modernidad" en los que la literatura y lo escrito –bajo la formulación de la legibilidad– aparecen rodeados por otras escenificaciones y personajes. El autor como héroe, que Benjamin entiende como "el verdadero sujeto de la *modernité*", se presenta así enfrentado a otros héroes, de tipos y caracteres de lo más diferentes en el seno de la metrópolis de la Modernidad, con posiciones que se distribuyen entre los dos sexos.

en que el autor detiene los golpes aparece en su obra descrita como "combate" [*Gefecht*] (*G.S.*, I.2.616).

Más allá de esto, existen correspondencias en las respectivas presentaciones de una escenificación de los sexos. Mientras que Foucault analiza los discursos en los que el sujeto masculino considera el uso de los placeres especialmente como puesta en escena de las relaciones con el compañero sexual masculino, donde la relación con la mujer resulta marginal, dado que ella aparece tan sólo bajo el rubro de la economía y así la interrelación de los sexos, por lo tanto, se tematiza sólo bajo el aspecto del engendramiento; Benjamin, por su parte, diseña algo así como la imagen inversa que da un espejo: el autor de la Modernidad visto "en el camino sacrificial de la sexualidad masculina"("Central-park"; *G.S.*, I.2.670), pues allí Baudelaire –en su negativa frente a lo natural, frente a un modelo de femineidad burguesa que se reduce a la familia y a la función maternal– estiliza a la lesbiana como heroína de la Modernidad en su sexualidad liberada de la función reproductora ("Charles Baudelaire. Un poeta en la época del capitalismo avanzado"; *G.S.*, I.2. 594, y "Central-park"; *G.S.*, I.2.667). En la figura del "retorno de lo igual" [*Wiederkehr des Gleichen*] –según Benjamin– *lo nuevo* en la relación entre Modernidad y Antigüedad sería portador de lo que Baudelaire habría de rescatar como "lo igual en eterno retorno" [*Immerwiedergleichen*; *G.S.*, I.2.673], y con ello las marcas [*Signaturen*] de la diferencia sexual. Pues en este punto se instaura entre las constelaciones analizadas por Foucault y Benjamin un claro desplazamiento de la homosexualidad femenina a la masculina, sin que ello traiga consigo, por cierto, un cambio de perspectiva del sujeto masculino al femenino, dado que, según Benjamin, Baudelaire habría dejado lugar en el marco de la Modernidad al amor lésbico; pero, en realidad, no lo trató en un plano de igualdad (*G.S.*, I.2.596). Esta observación de Benjamin llama la atención sobre otra diferencia, una *diferencia* en la escritura. Mientras que Foucault analiza textos prescriptivos, o sea, discursos, en los que el sujeto masculino se constituye como autor, diseñando en el texto sus propias artes de la vida o

análisis de esa "genealogía del hombre de deseo" proveniente de la Antigüedad (1984b: 20)– cerca, entre otros, de los estudios en torno a una "historia primigenia de la Modernidad", a los que Benjamin se había entregado durante más de diez años en los últimos de su vida, casi ya medio siglo antes de Foucault. Esta situación describe, en rigor, una doble inversión en y de la genealogía. En una relación de *addenda* historiográfica y teórica con respecto a Benjamin, Foucault estudia la Antigüedad en perspectiva histórica, como si fuera la pre-historia de aquellas artes de la existencia que para Benjamin se cristalizan en las posturas de Baudelaire como héroe de la Modernidad.

En realidad, se pueden observar numerosas correspondencias entre los dos proyectos no sólo porque Benjamin equipara al autor de la Modernidad, Baudelaire (que se halla expuesto a los bombardeos de sensaciones en la metrópolis, al mismo tiempo, que las reutiliza configurándolas dentro de su obra), con el héroe de la Antigüedad, mientras que Foucault haciendo una analogía entre la constitución de sí del sujeto y la estructura política, entre la ética de los placeres y el orden de la *polis*, se refiere a la formulación de Platón* acerca de que el filósofo debe "estructurarse como una ciudad" (984b: 97).[2] La correspondencia tampoco se agota porque Foucault subraye en la problematización de la Antigüedad acerca de las artes de la vida la clara utilización metafórica de la "lucha" (lucha con los propios deseos, donde el vencedor y el vencido entran en prácticas de una escenificación del placer), mientras que Benjamin caracteriza al autor de la Modernidad como "gladiador" [*Fechter*] (*G.S.*, I.2.570), y a todo el proceso de la creación misma como duelo, en tanto la manera

---

* En la traducción inglesa del presente trabajo la cita de Foucault sobre Platón aparece sustituida por otras dos que dicen así: "el 'paradigma' de la ciudad se encuentra en el cielo para el que quiera contemplarlo" y "el filósofo, al mirarlo, 'podrá reglamentar su propia ley'" (Foucault, 1984a: 97). [N. del T.]

2. Para la relación entre Foucault y Benjamin bajo el aspecto de la confluencia entre la ciudad y la topografía de los sexos, puede verse Weigel, 1990: 180-203.

Esta nota al pie es sintomática desde el punto de vista de la historia de la filosofía, en tanto configura esa típica tríada[1] en la que se coloca la *actual* formación teórica en Francia y en los Estados Unidos en relación con los trabajos teóricos *históricos* provenientes de Alemania. Por otro lado, sin embargo, da un indicio que tiene cierto peso; Foucault valora, en efecto, el trabajo de Benjamin, pero colocándolo junto al libro de Burckhardt sobre el Renacimiento, como pilares para una historia de "las artes de la existencia" y para aquellas técnicas de sí

> [...] con las que los hombres no sólo fijan las reglas de conducta, sino que buscan transformarse ellos mismos, modificarse en su singular manera de ser, y hacer de su vida una obra que sea portadora de ciertos valores estéticos y responda a ciertos criterios de estilo. (Foucault, 1984a: 18)

Para la construcción de la historia del sujeto como una historia de las problematizaciones y técnicas de sí, especialmente de la conducta sexual, a través de la que "el individuo se constituye y se reconoce como sujeto" (1984a: 13), Foucault menciona a autores, cuyos trabajos pueda anexar a su propio estudio sobre "las problematizaciones de la conducta sexual en la Antigüedad" (1984a: 19). Las técnicas de sí son por ello descritas como el propio cuerpo y como la relación de prácticas "eto-poéticas" (1984a: 21) concernientes a los otros. Delimitando sus representaciones crítico-ideológicas Foucault caracteriza su proyecto como "arqueológico y genealógico": "arqueológico" en relación con las formas de la problematización misma y "genealógico" en cuanto a "su formación a partir de prácticas y de sus modificaciones" (1984b: 19).

Juntamente con el esbozo de una *genealogía* y una arqueología de las técnicas de sí y modos de subjetivización, Foucault sitúa su propio trabajo como si fuera una *genealogía* de la historia de las artes de la existencia. Así, coloca su último gran proyecto –el

---

1. Véase a este respecto la Introducción al presente estudio.

3. Vasos comunicantes
Michel Foucault y Walter Benjamin

LAS ARTES DE LA EXISTENCIA: LA ANTIGÜEDAD Y LA MODERNIDAD

En uno de sus últimos libros, el segundo tomo de su *Historia de la sexualidad* (publicado en 1984), Michel Foucault dedica al autor del estudio sobre Baudelaire una nota al pie (Foucault, 1984a: 19). Según mi opinión, ésta es su única referencia explícita a Walter Benjamin, aunque también sus escritos anteriores revelan una gran afinidad con el pensamiento de Benjamin, ya sea en cuanto al concepto de "similitud" en la arqueología foucaultiana de las ciencias humanas, o en su lectura de Nietzsche, o también en su concepto de la historia, donde son de significativa importancia elementos como la ruptura de un *continuum*, la referencia a la corporeidad y la crítica al historicismo. La siguiente nota al pie puede ser leída en el marco de un entendimiento en el discurso filosófico franco-alemán después de 1945, pero más especialmente en el ámbito de una recepción tardía de Benjamin en Francia:

> Sería inexacto creer que después de Burckhardt, el estudio de estas artes y de esta estética de la existencia haya sido descuidada. Piénsese, por ejemplo, en el estudio de Benjamin sobre Baudelaire. Un análisis interesante se puede encontrar también en el reciente libro de S.Greenblatt: *Renaissance Self-fashioning*, 1980.

a una imagen "verdadera" y completa de la historia, o como Benjamin formularía más tarde: "sólo a la humanidad *redimida* le corresponde *saciarse* con su pasado"(*G.S.*, I.2.694) (El destacado es mío.) "El mundo mesiánico es el mundo de una absoluta e integral actualidad. Solamente en él se da una historia universal" (*G.S.*, I.3.1235); o "El auténtico concepto de la historia universal es uno mesiánico" (*G.S.*, V.608). Sin embargo, la idea de que la historiografía debe tomar en cuenta, en el desciframiento de las tradiciones, especialmente la forma de sus distorsiones resultaría todavía hoy entre la mayoría de los historiadores –por lo menos en el ámbito de habla alemana– una propuesta descabellada.

una estructura del inconsciente) representa una de las variantes con las que Benjamin realiza su viraje materialista desde modos de observación psicoanalítica. En el ensayo sobre Kafka, que prenuncia ya, no solamente con los motivos del vendaval [*Sturm*] y de la vuelta [*Umkehr*], las tesis de teoría de la historia de seis años más tarde, la distorsión aparece al mismo tiempo como diferencia con respecto a la redención [*Erlösung*], pues: "lo olvidado concierne siempre a la mejor parte, dado que concierne a la posibilidad de la redención" (*G.S.*, II.2.434). Por este medio, Benjamin consigue adscribir su lectura del mesianismo judío en la vía que lleva al materialismo y al psicoanálisis: "Nadie dice, por supuesto, que las distorsiones que el Mesías habría de enderezar con su aparición son solamente las de nuestro espacio. También lo son, ciertamente, las de nuestro tiempo" (*G.S.*, II.2.433). Y aquellas del cuerpo –como, en rigor, habría que completar–, de un cuerpo que fuera comprendido como memoria, y que, al mismo tiempo, muestra una/su diferencia hacia el origen –según la versión temprana de Benjamin acerca de la magia del lenguaje–.[22]

> Este hombrecillo (el jorobadito) es el habitante de la vida distorsionada; ha de desaparecer cuando llegue el Mesías, del que un gran rabino ha dicho que Él no habría de desear cambiar el mundo por medio de la violencia, sino enderezarlo solamente un poquito. (*G.S.*, II.2.432)

Mientras que la vida distorsionada marca aquí la diferencia con respecto a la redención, en esta reformulación psicoanalítica de la idea mesiánica resulta superada, al mismo tiempo, la posibilidad de una clara oposición de "la vida verdadera y falsa". De este modo en la condición de lo *incredento* tampoco puede accederse

---

22. Para el significado de la distorsión como lo que sería una segunda cesura en la historia del lenguaje, "después que es expulsado del paraíso el espíritu del lenguaje" [*nach dem Sündenfall des Sprachgeistes*]. Véase el capítulo 9 del presente estudio.

espalda de los culpables, superponiendo incisiones y amontonando ornamentos, hasta que la espalda de los culpables se torna vidente y puede descifrar ella misma la escritura, en cuyas letras el culpable puede deducir el nombre de la culpa desconocida. Es entonces la espalda la que carga con la culpa. (*G.S.*, II.2.432)

La "iluminación profana" [*profane Erleuchtung*] que conduce al espacio del cuerpo y de la imagen en el surrealismo puede ser comprendida así como la contrapartida a tales prácticas violentas de "clarividencia" [*Erhellung*] y, por lo tanto, ser interpretada una vez más como un concepto basado en el sentido de una reacción contra el impacto.

Mientras que el tema del ensayo sobre Kafka aparece estructurado por la relación entre el cuerpo y el olvido, el interés por la significación del cuerpo en el contexto de un lenguaje del inconsciente lo amalgama con otros textos de los años treinta, especialmente con el proyecto de los Pasajes y el libro sobre Baudelaire, donde se encuentra el mismo tema en el debate de las huellas constantes, de la "*mémoire involontaire*" y en la referencia a las imágenes de la memoria depositadas en los miembros del cuerpo, de las que habla Proust (*G.S.*, I.2.613). En el ensayo sobre Kafka es el concepto de la "distorsión" [*Entstellung*], tomado de la teoría freudiana del inconsciente, el que describe el modo de la vinculación entre el cuerpo, las cosas, los animales y lo olvidado:

> Odradek es la forma que toman las cosas cuando terminan en el olvido. Aparecen distorsionadas. Distorsionada es la "preocupación del padre de familia", de la que nadie sabe cómo es realmente; distorsionada aparece también la alimaña, de la que sabemos muy bien que representa a Gregor Samsa; distorsionado resulta también el gran animal, mitad cordero mitad gatito, para quien quizás el cuchillo del carnicero sería una salvación. Estas figuras de Kafka, sin embargo, están vinculadas con una larga serie de formaciones cuya imagen más acabada es la del jorobado. (*G.S.*, II.2.431)

Esta referencia al cuerpo, a las cosas, a lo orgánico y lo inorgánico como material para la distorsión (como modalidad de

sobre el espacio del cuerpo y de la imagen también como el intento de exorcizar revolucionariamente al terror dentro de la Modernidad. Partiendo de la situación del cuerpo en la ausencia mental hemos llegado por ese camino al concepto de una actualidad como presencia mental corpórea.

OLVIDO Y REDENCIÓN: PARA UNA REFORMULACIÓN PSICOANALÍTICA DE LO MESIÁNICO

En el ensayo sobre Kafka (1934), por el contrario, se hacen más articulables los aspectos de la extrañeza y del olvido que tienen que ver con el cuerpo: "la extrañeza más relegada de nuestro cuerpo: el propio cuerpo"[21] (*G.S.*, II.2.431). Aquí analiza Benjamin el significado de la gesticulación en Kafka, leyendo su literatura como "código de gestos", cuya comprensión no puede llevarse a cabo simbólicamente. Esto aparece formulado del modo más acabado con la leyenda talmúdica, en la que la aldea cuya lengua no se comprende, aparece interpretada como el propio cuerpo, como extrañeza que "se ha tornado su amo" –es decir, del nuevo individuo–, (*G.S.*, II.2.424). En esto se trata de un lenguaje del cuerpo, en el que lo olvidado se torna visible; pero cuyo sentido, sin embargo, no puede ser descifrado sin más. Se trata también del cuerpo como material y matriz de un lenguaje del inconsciente.

En este contexto se halla esa imagen que puede leerse como la contracara de las ideas revolucionarias del espacio del cuerpo y de la imagen; una imagen, en la que la confluencia de la representación y la percepción se manifiesta con el mismo material en un cuerpo, pero ahora como terror.

En *La colonia penitenciaria*, sin embargo, los que mandan se sirven de una antiquísima maquinaria que graba letras alambicadas en la

---

21. En alemán: "*die vergessenste Fremde unser Körper - der eigene Körper*". [N. del T.]

humano en la situación de la ausencia mental no posea ya la determinación de sus límites. Lo percibido, sobre todo aquello percibido en el rostro, penetra en el cuerpo [...] Un individuo en situación de inmenso terror puede entonces verse compelido a imitar justamente aquello que lo aterroriza. (*G.S.*, VI.76)

La misma constelación, como una especie de mímesis apotropaica,* que el individuo adjudica al efecto de protección contra el terror, ha de aparecer más tarde, cuando Benjamin se haya alejado[20] del constructo metafísico de una relación cuerpo-espíritu y utilice en lugar de ello un vocabulario psicoanalítico más corriente. En el libro sobre Baudelaire ha de surgir como la simultaneidad del impacto y el contragolpe originado por ese mismo impacto, al respecto, por ejemplo, de las muecas excéntricas del poeta francés (*G.S.*, I.2.616). De modo comparable al impacto del cine y de la nueva experiencia que la cámara torna posible, al hacer reconocible "lo ópticamente inconsciente" y hacer visible las posturas del individuo en centésimos de segundos, aparece ya en el espacio del cuerpo y de la imagen "en lugar de un espacio animado por el hombre con conciencia un espacio animado inconscientemente" (*G.S.*, I.2.500), un tópico que Benjamin va a analizar en su ensayo sobre la obra de arte. Sólo que el proceso en este caso no ocurre en la pantalla, es decir, no se representa como espacio del cuerpo sobre la imagen fílmica, sino en la multitud y en el espacio del obrar político; a lo que habría que agregar que este espacio se halla todavía en una situación pre-fascista. En este sentido, podría leerse el pasaje

---

* El término aquí utilizado deriva de la palabra griega "*apotrópaios*" que se toma con el significado de algo que "desvía los males"; cf. M.A.Bailly, *Abrégé du dictionnaire grec-français*, París, Hachette, 1901. [N. del T.]

20. Parecería que a través de ello más bien se desvaneciera el intento de una oposición analítica y sistemática entre "lo corpóreo" [*Leib*] y "el cuerpo" [*Körper*] que, por ejemplo, en los "Schemata zum psychophysichen Problem" jugaba todavía un importante papel. Sin embargo, cae fuera del interés de este trabajo llevar a cabo la investigación del uso idiomático benjaminiano acerca de la distinción entre *Leib* y *Körper*.

ciación de la reacción vital; sólo él es al mismo tiempo aprehendible según su animación psíquica. Toda excitabilidad psíquica puede localizarse en él de manera diferenciada, como pretendía la vieja antroposofía cuando realizaba la analogía del cuerpo y el macrocosmos. Una de las más importantes determinaciones de la diferenciabilidad la ofrece el cuerpo en la percepción. (*G.S.*, VI.81-82)

Junto a las diferencias entre placer y dolor, y a una discusión sobre las relaciones espaciales del cuerpo, sobre la cercanía y la lejanía, sobre la realidad del sueño y de la percepción, se encuentran ya en este texto todos los motivos que después en la fase de producción de los trabajos benjaminianos de la Modernidad han de aparecer investigados en detalle y concretizados a nivel de historia de los medios. En una anotación del ensayo acerca de la obra de arte se dice de modo explícito:

> El reconocimiento de que la primera materia donde la capacidad mimética se pone a prueba es el cuerpo humano, es un hecho que debería hacerse fructífero para la historia primigenia del arte con mayor energía de lo que se ha hecho hasta ahora. (*G.S.*, VI.127)

Benjamin formula con esto una perspectiva de investigación que recién fue recuperada en los años ochenta a partir de los numerosos estudios dedicados al lenguaje y a la historia del cuerpo.

Pero volvamos al origen de la idea de espacio del cuerpo y de la imagen en su obra temprana sobre antropología. La temprana anotación titulada "Über das Grauen I" ["Sobre el horror I"] puede leerse como una anticipación de la idea –comparable con la noción de *shock* o impacto–, de un cuerpo que ha perdido la noción de sus límites distintivos, tal como se representa en el ensayo sobre el surrealismo. Allí Benjamin describe la situación de la ausencia mental o la inmersión en lo extraño como negación de la potencia del cuerpo o descorporeización [*Entleibung*]. En estos casos el cuerpo queda:

> [...] sin la distancia separadora y diferenciadora de la esfera corporal <y> mental, lo que se manifiesta en el hecho de que el cuerpo

el *logos* divino", que habría de tener su representación en el triángulo edípico. Aun cuando se entendiera la relación entre Dios, la naturaleza y el hombre en la descripción del lenguaje adámico (similar a la del padre, la madre y el hijo) como triádica, le faltaría justamente ese aspecto que es el que caracteriza a la estructura edípica: la prohibición de la inmediatez entre el cuerpo de la madre y del hijo. La teoría benjaminiana de la magia del lenguaje parece más bien merecedora de una descripción a nivel de una concepción pre-analítica, como esbozo de una inmediatez lingüístico-teológica y no corpóreo-psicoanalítica.[19]

En la génesis de las anotaciones benjaminianas parecen tornarse importante poco después, y precisamente en el contexto de los estudios sobre Freud, las reflexiones sobre lo corpóreo y el cuerpo. Y cuando Benjamin se refiere al cuerpo en el desarrollo de su pensamiento, esto sucede siempre en relación con el *cuerpo en el lenguaje*: en el motivo del cuerpo hecho símbolo y desmembrado, del signo corpóreo, de las posturas y gestos, de la perdida capacidad mimética, de los asistentes corporales del recuerdo (involuntario) o en el motivo de la distorsión. Así en una de las más amplias anotaciones sobre el área temática de lo corpóreo y del cuerpo, que quizás ha surgido hacia 1922/1923 y que lleva por título "Schemata zum psychophysichen Problem" ["Esquemas sobre el problema psicofísico"] (*G.S.*, VI.78), Benjamin discute al mismo tiempo la función de una *différance* provocada por una excitación psíquica, describiendo el cuerpo como instrumento de diferenciación:

> Pues toda reactivación vital se halla ligada a la diferenciación, cuyo más afinado instrumento es el cuerpo. Esta determinación suya debe reconocerse como esencial. El cuerpo como instrumento de diferen-

---

[19]. Para una reformulación psicoanalítica de la teoría benjaminiana del lenguaje en "La enseñanza de lo semejante", véanse los capítulos 8 y 9 de este estudio. La semejanza estructural entre la concepción benjaminiana de la expulsión del paraíso en su relación con el lenguaje y la concepción de Julia Kristeva sobre el psicoanálisis, aparece tratada en el capítulo 5 del presente estudio.

de Stoessel va perdiendo su fuerza argumentativa, en tanto este olvido se aplica una vez tras otra al origen del hombre desde el punto de vista de la materia, a la hechura del hombre, a su *physis*, a lo femenino y al trabajo.[17]

Más bien parecería que en la teoría temprana de Benjamin sobre el lenguaje, los motivos del Aura –por ejemplo, en la imagen del encuentro de miradas– y de la Magia, o de la Inmediatez, todavía aparecen sin deslindar, mientras que la inmediatez en la concepción del espacio del cuerpo y de la imagen ha perdido su carácter, porque en ella ha sido superada la diferenciación entre lo percibido y el perceptor, entre lo denominado y el denominador, entre la naturaleza y el hombre, en el sentido de que ambas esferas del cuerpo y de la imagen son ahora inseparables. A ello apunta ya el hecho de que el espacio de la imagen devenido material en el cuerpo de la multitud, para Benjamin sólo parezca representable en una imagen de la mecánica (como lo muestra la ya mencionada imagen del despertador) lo cual no tiene nada que ver con una "reinstalación de la unidad paradisíaca entre concepción y espontaneidad" (Stoessel, 1983: 175). Ese cuerpo deviene no similar a la *naturaleza*, sino a las *cosas*, en la medida en que "la primera materia donde la capacidad mimética se pone a prueba: el cuerpo humano"[18] (*G.S.*, VI. 127) –perdida como material mimético en el decurso del desarrollo humano– hace su aparición en la constelación de la acción revolucionaria, y aquí despliega su fuerza mimética. Es decir, la confluencia entre el espacio del cuerpo y de la imagen en la Modernidad aparece en un abrir y cerrar de ojos como una "similitud corpórea" con una imagen de la mecánica.

También resulta problemático describir (Stoessel, 1983: 139) la temprana teoría del lenguaje benjaminiana como una idea preedípica de una "comunidad mágica del hombre y la naturaleza en

---

17. En realidad, aquí se produce una reconciliación de la diferencia entre la interpretación adorniana del *Aura* (como trabajo) y la benjaminiana (lo humano en las cosas), que aparecía al comienzo del estudio de Stoessel (1983: 27).

18. En alemán: "*erste Materie, an der sich das mimetische Vermögen versucht, der menschliche Körper*". [N. del T.]

la anotación "Percepción y cuerpo"(*G.S.*, VI.67), en la que también se debate el fenómeno de la incapacidad del propio cuerpo para la percepción del sujeto. Las reflexiones sobre la vergüenza encuentran su desarrollo en las anotaciones tituladas "Über Erröten in Zorn und Scham" ("Sobre el enrojecimiento en la ira y la vergüenza")(de 1920/1921; *G.S.*, VI.120), que, por lo demás, de nuevo están en relación con las notas a "Über die Malerei order Zeichen und Mal" ("Sobre la pintura o el dibujo y la marca"), escritas en 1918 (*G.S.*, II.2.603-604), de tal modo que ello viene a resultar en un tejido de reflexiones comparadas sobre diferentes signos –por ejemplo, sobre la imagen o el cuerpo, o también sobre el rostro–; signos que, por otra parte, se distinguen en cuanto a su materialidad y matriz. En este sentido, contra la opinión de Stoessel, es ya en esta etapa temprana de su producción donde el autor ha corregido sus observaciones sobre teoría del lenguaje, y no tan sólo en el estudio de 1929 sobre el "espacio del cuerpo y de la imagen" o en ambos ensayos de 1933 donde Benjamin ha continuado la escritura de su artículo sobre el lenguaje surgido diecisiete años antes. Por ello, es erróneo afirmar, como lo hace Stoessel, que había una "olvidada relación del hombre con su origen como materia" en el texto temprano (Stoessel, 1983: 69).

No debe creerse, en fin, que son sólo las anotaciones ahora publicadas el motivo de una corrección del cuadro global que describe Stoessel. Es, por supuesto, correcto, que en los dos artículos de 1933, "La enseñanza de lo semejante" y "Sobre la capacidad mimética", el cuerpo aparece recobrado explícita y teóricamente y que el discurso benjaminiano brinda una modificación de su teoría sobre la magia del lenguaje. También el concepto de la "similitud no sensorial", que Benjamin esboza en este contexto, representa aquí –como lo demuestran las anotaciones– evidentemente una delimitación del concepto de "similitud corporal" que ha quedado por el camino (*G.S.*, VI.193). Pero, de ninguna manera, puede ponerse esto en relación con una "substancialización de lo que Benjamin denomina Aura" (Stoessel, 1983: 16); cuando, por otro lado, en general la crítica a Benjamin de "lo olvidado humano" en el mismo estudio

Obras completas (aparecido en 1985) se ha tornado evidente, por lo menos qué importante papel juegan las reflexiones sobre el cuerpo ya en los apuntes tempranos de psicología y antropología, que han sido escritos sólo poco tiempo más tarde que el artículo (tampoco destinado para su publicación) "Sobre el lenguaje en general y sobre el lenguaje de los humanos" (1916). La observación de Marlen Stoessel respecto de "lo humano olvidado" en que Benjamin habría incurrido en su lectura del mito de la creación como magia del lenguaje, en tanto el origen del lenguaje del hombre aparecería allí como un proceso incorpóreo, debería ahora ser, si no anulada, por lo menos modificada, dado que Benjamin mismo había sido evidentemente consciente de este olvido y se ha dedicado a subsanarlo en otros trabajos. En este sentido, Benjamin subsume cuerpo y lenguaje –como lo demuestra un esquema antropológico de 1918– a esferas distintas del individuo pero pensadas como simultáneas. Cuerpo y lenguaje representan en este esquema los puntos contrapuestos de los vértices de una semiesfera, a partir de los cuales se constituyen exclusivamente los distintos círculos existenciales del hombre. Sin embargo, en las anotaciones surgidas en la misma época, en ocasión de sus lecturas freudianas, se trata, en cambio, de las relaciones entre lenguaje, percepción, lo corpóreo y el cuerpo. En este momento se encuentran también conexiones *directas* con su teoría sobre la magia del lenguaje, como, por ejemplo:

> La relación de la figura humana con el lenguaje, es decir, cómo Dios dando forma obra dentro de él, es el objeto de la psicología. Aquí hay que considerar también lo corpóreo, en tanto lingüísticamente Dios obra de modo directo –y quizás incomprensible– dentro de él. (*G.S.*, VI.66)

En este contexto a Benjamin le interesa la relación de la corporeidad con el lenguaje tanto en relación con el cuerpo como signo –por ejemplo, en sus anotaciones "Über die Schan" ("Sobre la vergüenza") (de 1919/1920; *G.S.*, VI.70)– como también en cuanto a la percepción, cuya historia trae a colación en un "Veränderung des Leibes" ("Cambio del cuerpo"), por ejemplo en

de la imagen oculto "correlativamente opuesto". Esto coincide con la atención que Benjamin presta a la materialidad y espacialidad de las imágenes y de la escritura, así como a lo no representable, que aparece de esta manera con ello sugerido, como se dice en otras anotaciones,[14] pero no más tardíamente que en el libro sobre el drama barroco, por ejemplo en relación con Johann Wilhelm Ritter, quien se torna allí una figura de análisis. Mientras que en las anotaciones sobre la pintura (que provienen probablemente del año 1921), se describe el cuadro como correlación entre fantasía y copia, la función de copia ya no juega ningún papel en el posterior concepto benjaminiano de imagen. Si la imagen es ese concepto que en Benjamin ocupa el lugar de perspectivas y combinaciones más polifacéticas, también su mención de la imagen de la escritura, la del sueño, las de la historia, la del recuerdo, la del pensamiento y la dialéctica se fundamenta en un concepto de imagen –más allá de la controversia en torno a la relación entre "imagen material y espiritual"– que remite a la palabra "imagen" [*Bild*] en su sentido originario y literal como similitud.[15] Y la conexión específica entre *imagen* y *espacio* desempeña un papel más importante en el contexto de los escritos benjaminianos sobre el recuerdo, entre los que habría que considerar la configuración textual de *Infancia en Berlín hacia 1900* como una de las más claras en su capacidad de hacer presente los espacios en imágenes y una topografía de las imágenes del recuerdo.[16]

Algo más ocultos y complicados son, en cambio, los rastros del cuerpo y del espacio del cuerpo en los textos benjaminianos. Desde la publicación de los "Fragmente vermischten Inhalts" ("Fragmentos de contenido miscelánico"), del tomo VI de las

---

14. Por ejemplo, en "Sobre la pintura o el dibujo y la marca" (II.2.603-604), que se consideran anotaciones surgidas alrededor de 1918.
15. Para la historia del concepto de imagen, véase Mitchell, 1984: 521; y para el concepto en Benjamin, véase el capítulo 4 del presente estudio.
16. Al respecto compárese el aspecto de la conexión entre la topografía de la ciudad, el recuerdo y la diferencia sexual en Weigel, 1990.

la construcción y su cobertura ya no pueden distinguirse con exactitud, pero también quizás porque deseaba esbozar con ello, en un gesto revolucionario del texto, la idea del proceso artístico como construcción y, de ese modo, comprometer al proceso histórico en toda la situación. "La historia es objeto de una construcción", como ha de sostener en las tesis de teoría de la historia, que fueron escritas en 1940 en el exilio con la impronta de una reflexión sobre la consideración de la historia y de las constelaciones revolucionarias, cuando ya ha cundido el fascismo nacionalsocialista.* Benjamin considera aquí la historia, entonces, como objeto de una construcción *teórica*, mientras que el gesto del texto de 1929 todavía se halla enfáticamente bajo el signo de una *praxis* revolucionaria del arte, en tanto se refería a los surrealistas y acrecentaba programáticamente la práctica que les era particular.

PARA LA GÉNESIS DEL CONCEPTO DEL "ESPACIO DEL CUERPO Y DE LA IMAGEN" EN LOS ESCRITOS BENJAMINIANOS

Hasta donde llegan mis investigaciones, la expresión de "espacio del cuerpo y de la imagen" en esta combinación y formulación sólo se encuentra en el ensayo sobre el surrealismo, donde aparece en el origen de las ideas benjaminianas como un punto de confluencia en el que vienen a tocarse rastros primeramente aislados. Uno puede toparse, por ejemplo, con el concepto de "espacio de la imagen" en las anotaciones no destinadas a la publicación ("Zur Malerei" ["Sobre la pintura"]; VI.113-114), en las que Benjamin diferencia distintos tipos de pintura, pero no recurriendo solamente al modo de representación, sino también a la relación entre "el espacio visual de su visión" y un espacio

---

* Se conserva en el texto el uso alemán de la especificación que hace del Nacionalsocialismo una subespecie entre los "fascismos", entendidos como el fenómeno a nivel general. [N. del T.]

esfuerzo por pensar juntos el psicoanálisis y el materialismo en relación con la Modernidad.

En ambos casos Benjamin realiza un gesto de fundición *material* o de viraje materialista en sus modos de observación *psicoanalítica*: en el caso del espacio del cuerpo y de la imagen en el surrealismo se produce una materialización de la imagen en inervaciones corporales. Es decir, una corporeidad de la expresividad del cuerpo por la cual el cuerpo humano deviene una materia en imagen, pero una forma literal, no ya alegórica de la corporeidad. En el caso de las imágenes dialécticas del proyecto de los Pasajes surge una materialización del lenguaje del inconsciente y una espacialización de la estructura onírica, es decir, una materialización de lo imaginario en el exterior orgánico e inorgánico, el cuerpo social.

Benjamin mismo fundamenta la creciente concentración en la imagen dialéctica y la constelación del despertar en el proyecto de los Pasajes como un "viraje copernicano de la memoria" o como "un viraje copernicano en la observación histórica", que serían imperiosamente necesarios por el hecho de que se habrían perdido los asistentes corpóreo-naturales de la memoria (*G.S.*, V.1.490 y sigs.). Allí donde habría retrocedido la asistencia corporal del recuerdo (que hoy se denominaría "memoria corporal"), en ese lugar Benjamin coloca el trabajo del recuerdo y del desciframiento del mundo de las cosas, el material del inconsciente colectivo (que hoy se denominaría "imaginario social"). Pero aun allí Benjamin trata todavía de dotar de un estatuto a la relación entre el espacio del cuerpo y de la imagen:

> La construcción tiene durante el siglo XIX [...] el papel del proceso corporal, en el que las arquitecturas "artísticas" se levantan entonces como sueños en torno del armazón del proceso fisiológico. (Anotaciones y materiales para "La obra de los Pasajes", Block K1a,7; *G.S.*, V.1.494)

En el ensayo sobre el surrealismo Benjamin, sin embargo, ha tratado de superar la diferencia entre armazón y cerramiento, entre construcción y arte, quizás porque en la esfera del cuerpo

En la historia de gestación de los textos benjaminianos los orígenes de las categorías de "el espacio del cuerpo y de la imagen" y "la imagen dialéctica" parecen ligados entre sí como vasos comunicantes. El preludio preparado por algunas imágenes de pensamiento aparece dado en *Dirección única* (de 1928),[12] donde ambas categorías son puestas por escrito a fines de la década del veinte. Aunque la categoría de "el espacio del cuerpo y de la imagen" se gesta más bien a partir de la idea de "la iluminación profana" y "la imagen dialéctica",[13] aparece especialmente conectada a la constelación del despertar. En rigor, son construcciones teóricas que tienen su base en el

---

Feerie]. Su anuncio, además, de que algunos motivos profanos de *Dirección única* [*Einbahnstrasse*] habrían de marchar en fila india en un *crescendo* infernal [*in einer höllischen Steigerung vorbeidefilieren*] para el proyecto de los Pasajes, puede hacerse valer por lo menos con la misma fuerza para el ensayo sobre el surrealismo, dado que el mismo Benjamin ha llamado a este último el "biombo" [*paravent*] puesto delante del proyecto de los Pasajes. Cf. la carta del 30 de enero de 1928 (Benjamin, 1978: I.455).

12. El mismo Benjamin –en carta a Scholem del 30 de enero de 1928– partía de la idea de que su *Dirección única* abriría un nuevo ciclo de producción: ese ciclo "habría de cerrarse con el ya planeado proyecto de los Pasajes, así como el drama barroco había cerrado el ciclo sobre literatura alemana" (Benjamin, 1978: I.455). Dos años antes, durante el trabajo en *Dirección única*, le escribía a Scholem que en ese libro se fundían "una fisonomía más vieja con otra más joven" (Carta del 5 de abril de 1926; en Benjamin, 1978: I.416). Este pasaje de un ciclo de producción de germanista –especialmente con los trabajos sobre la crítica romántica, pasando por el drama barroco, por Hölderlin y por las *Afinidades electivas* de Goethe– a un ciclo sobre la Modernidad puede asociarse con una cesura biográfica que siguiera paso a paso las diferentes dedicatorias de sus libros (el libro sobre el drama barroco aparece dedicado a su mujer, mientras que la dedicatoria de *Dirección única* se dirige a Asja Lacis). Esta cesura tiene que ver sobre todo con la nueva situación de Benjamin como autor libre, quien voluntariamente rechaza la carrera académica universitaria. Ello coincide, además, con el cambio que se produce en su vida familiar y que lo lleva a partir de entonces a vivir de sus escritos; para este aspecto, véase Fürnkäs, 1988: 10 y sigs.

13. El concepto surge, al parecer, por primera vez en Primeras Anotaciones para "La obra de los Pasajes"/"Los pasajes parisienses", cuya datación Rolf Tiedemann fija entre mediados de 1927 y fines de 1929 o comienzos de 1930 (*G.S.*, V.2.1073).

Pero así como el que duerme –que se iguala en esto al loco– franquea con su cuerpo el viaje macrocósmico, y los ruidos y sensaciones del propio interior (que a la persona sana en la vigilia se le presentan como la estructura de la salud: la presión arterial, los movimientos de las entrañas, el pulso y las reacciones musculares en su increíblemente agudizado sentido interior) engendran la locura o la imagen onírica que ellos *traducen* y explican, así le sucede a la multitud soñante que se ensimisma en su interior dentro de los pasajes. Debemos perseguirla para interpretar el siglo XIX en la moda y la publicidad, en la arquitectura y en la política como la consecución de la historia de sus sueños. (Anotaciones y materiales para "La obra de los Pasajes", Block [*Konvolut**] K1,4; *G.S.*, V.1.491-492) (El destacado es mío.)

En la gestación de las imágenes de los sueños por medio de procedimientos fisiológicos o en la evaluación de las imágenes oníricas como *traducción* de procesos corporales, el proyecto de los Pasajes sigue de cerca en su segunda fase de elaboración el modelo freudiano del inconsciente, trasladando este proceso a la multitud y a su cuerpo –la ciudad– , mientras que en la variante de la primera fase aparece el sueño todavía como un dominio interno.[10]

En este punto de las anotaciones para la prehistoria de la Modernidad, "el espacio del cuerpo y de la imagen", en lo que concierne a la multitud, aparece transferido a las galerías, que el autor recorre con su vista como quien lee con el propósito de descifrar, mientras que la secuencia correspondiente en el texto sobre el surrealismo presenta a la multitud por medio del espacio del cuerpo y de la imagen como un engranaje detonante: un verdadero "encantamiento dialéctico" [*dialektische Feerie*].[11]

* La palabra alemana "*Konvolut*" utilizada por los compiladores de las obras de Benjamin es un latinismo que implica la idea de una carpeta (o *dossier*) donde se han colocado materiales afines. Aparte de este término culto, circula en el ámbito de los estudios benjaminianos la palabra "Block", que es la que aquí se prefiere en virtud de su fácil comprensión. [N. del T.]

10. Para la diferencia teórica de los conceptos de memoria entre la primera y la segunda fase en "La obra de los Pasajes", véase el capítulo 8.

11. Benjamin comunicó primeramente a Scholem en una carta que el título del trabajo planeado sobre las galerías o "pasajes" habría de ser: "Los pasajes parisienses. Un encantamiento dialéctico" [*Die Pariser Passagen. Eine dialektische*

que menciona un "gestar echando fuera de sí" [*herausstellen*] y un "penetrar y devorar" [*hineinreissen und fressen*] se le opone la del proyecto de los Pasajes, con: "el verdadero método de hacer presentes las cosas", "representárnoslas en nuestro propio espacio (no a nosotros en el de ellas)" (*G.S.*, V.2.1014).

El espacio del cuerpo y de la imagen aparece así como una imagen onírica que se ha tornado real o como una fantasía original [*Urphantasie*] materializada.[9] Dos tipos de imágenes que se caracterizan por estar estructuradas por un sujeto en el que él mismo tiene participación en la escena que imagina. Y algo más todavía: en el espacio del cuerpo y de la imagen se hallan unidas la matriz y el material de la expresión y de la representación. Por el contrario, la imagen dialéctica es una imagen *leída*, una imagen en el código lingüístico, aun cuando el material para su representación pueda ser aquí multifacético: desde la fisonomía pasando por las imágenes oníricas, desde el mundo de las cosas hasta la arquitectura, lo orgánico y lo inorgánico. Todo lo ve Benjamin en el

> [...] paisaje de una galería. El mundo orgánico e inorgánico, la necesidad rastrera y el lujo desfachatado se enlazan en un maridaje que es el colmo de lo contradictorio. La mercancía se exhibe y se desplaza mezclándose sin complejos como las imágenes residuales de confusos sueños. (Primeras anotaciones para "La obra de los Pasajes"/"Los pasajes parisienses", *G.S.*, V.2.993)

En virtud de estas correspondencias entre el mundo exterior y el de los sueños, la galería en la metrópolis de la Modernidad se torna para Benjamin el paradigma topográfico de su investigación: en ella lee el mundo de las cosas como un sueño, pero efectuando una operación por la cual la oposición entre lo interno y lo externo aparece superada en una constelación dialéctica, al observar la topografía *externa* como *lo interno* del cuerpo de la multitud. Así, por ejemplo, el soñante en su viaje por el cuerpo:

---

9. Cf. Laplanche y Pontalis, 1985.

"EL ESPACIO DEL CUERPO Y DE LA IMAGEN"–"LA IMAGEN DIALÉCTICA"

La presente lectura exhibe, es cierto, una promiscua relación entre el discurso benjaminiano sobre *el espacio del cuerpo y de la imagen*, por un lado, y el gesto revolucionario del ensayo sobre el surrealismo, por otro. Este último texto se halla en cercanía temporal con la primera fase del proyecto de los Pasajes (1927-1929), en cuyo contexto Benjamin empieza a esbozar también la concepción de la *imagen dialéctica*, que va a continuar reelaborando en la segunda fase de trabajo (entre 1934 y 1940). La cercanía entre las dos concepciones trasciende la dimensión temporal. Pues, así como el discurso sobre el espacio del cuerpo y de la imagen nace de una distinción entre comparación e imagen, así la imagen dialéctica se deriva de una delimitación frente a la imagen arcaica.[8] En ambos conceptos conviven "representación e idea" [*Darstellung und Vorstellung*] y a ambos les es común el hecho de expulsar la dimensión Tiempo de la tradicional casilla del orden lineal. En la combinación entre imagen, cuerpo y espacio falta a la cita de modo flagrante la categoría Tiempo como cuarta dimensión de la cultura. Está simplemente ausente. Mientras que en la imagen dialéctica, por su parte, esa categoría aparece "superada" [*aufgehoben*] como Tiempo lineal, en el momento en el que el "ahora de la cognoscibilidad" [*Jetzt der Erkennbarkeit*], "lo que ha sido y lo de hoy" [*Gewesenes und Heutiges*] confluyen directamente, es decir, sin distancia. Y en ambos casos de lo que se trata es de la "presentificación" [*Vergegenwärtigung*] –contrapuesta a la "empatía" [*Einfühlung*]–, pero también de una técnica de la *cercanía* y de un metabolismo entre materia e imagen. A la terminología del ensayo sobre el surrealismo

---

8. Cf. por ejemplo, *G.S.*, V.1.577. La diferenciación entre imagen arcaica y dialéctica va unida a una distinción entre mitología y espacio histórico. Constitutivo para ello es la constelación del despertar que para Benjamin es el abc del pensamiento dialéctico o, en otras palabras, el caso ejemplar del acto de recordar.

antropológico –que no ocurre sin dejar rastros– , queda como resultado, según el texto: "...un resto. También el grupo colectivo tiene existencia corpórea"[6] (*G.S.*, II.1.310). De este modo, la esfera de la imagen no puede diferenciarse de una multitud corpórea, en tanto su realidad toma cuerpo en la misma esfera de la imagen, la que, por su parte, se refiere a la materialidad corporal de la multitud en su condición de matriz. Para hacer imaginable y representable esta idea, el texto remite a la concepción neurológico-psicoanalítica de energía como carga corporal:

> Y la *physis* que se organiza en la técnica para el grupo colectivo puede gestarse según su realidad política y objetiva sólo en ese territorio de la imagen, en el que la iluminación profana nos brinda familiaridad. Sólo cuando bajo esta profana iluminación, el cuerpo y el espacio de la imagen se interpenetran profundamente, de modo que la tensión revolucionaria se torne la inervación corporal colectiva y todas las inervaciones corporales del grupo colectivo devengan una descarga revolucionaria, sólo en ese momento la realidad se sobrepasará a sí misma como el Manifiesto Comunista lo requería. (*G.S.*, II.1.310)

Después de esta presentación de una carga detonante hecha cuerpo en la multitud revolucionaria sigue la imagen final del despertador que, por lo tanto, indica un quiebre: el paso gigantesco del "cuerpo" [*Leib*] al "engranaje" [*Apparat*].[7] En la continuación del texto benjaminiano sobre el surrealismo se vuelca asimismo toda la fuerza en la pendiente de la estación energética, haciendo fluir la escritura en el pasaje por el espacio del cuerpo y de la imagen, donde resulta tan reforzada que la imagen fluye en el cuerpo hasta hacer confluir cuerpo e imagen en uno para lograr, efectivamente, el salto en el "sistema de los engranajes" [*Apparatur*].

6. En alemán: "*ein Rest. Auch das Kollektivum ist leibhaft*". [N. del T.]
7. Esta mecanización aparece todavía enfatizada por una retórica que en algunos momentos roza la cadencia marcial, como "la orden de hoy" y "hombre por hombre".

ese sujeto mismo entra en funciones. En ese dominio de la imagen que "ya no puede abarcarse de ninguna manera contemplativamente" se anulan la distancia y las fronteras entre sujeto e imagen, en tanto el sujeto mismo ha penetrado en el espacio de la imagen, al participar en él con su propio cuerpo:

> En todo lugar donde la acción misma gesta la imagen y es la imagen, absorviéndola y devorándola, donde la cercanía se mira con sus propios ojos [*wo die Nähe sich selbst aus den Augen sieht*], allí se abre el solicitado territorio de la imagen, un mundo de absoluta e integral actualidad, donde ya no tiene sentido la sala burguesa. (*G.S.*, II.1.309)

Aquí ya no le queda al individuo ningún miembro en su lugar, después de su partición dialéctica entre el materialismo político y la naturaleza física, donde el espacio de la imagen se presenta, al mismo tiempo, como el del cuerpo.

Lo que aparece aquí descrito es la convergencia de los territorios de la imagen y del cuerpo como procedimiento de gestación o de incorporación, un recurso que en virtud de la falta total de distancia y de la construcción de cercanía autorreferencial –"*wo die Nähe sich selbst aus den Augen sieht*"– hace saltar por los aires la constelación benjaminiana, por lo regular tan significativamente dialéctica, de cercanía-lejanía[5] y, de ese modo, anula la frontera entre sujeto y objeto. El que lee ya no puede distinguirse del que actúa, y tampoco el que descifra una imagen del que la representa o *es* una imagen *in actu*. A lo largo del pasaje esto se va aplicando de la misma manera a un proceso colectivo, dado que en el traspaso del materialismo metafísico al

---

5. Esta característica se manifiesta especialmente en las concepciones benjaminianas de la *Huella* [*Spur*], definida como "la manifestación de una cercanía, por más lejano que sea lo que ella deja tras sí", y del *Aura* [*Aura*], como "manifestación de una lejanía, por más cercano que sea lo que ella provoca" (Anotaciones y materiales para "La obra de los Pasajes", Block M16a,4; *G.S.*, V.1.560). O en la famosa cita de Karl Kraus: "Cuanto más cerca se observa una palabra, más lejos mira ella" (Nota al pie en "Sobre algunos temas en Baudelaire"; *G.S.*, I.2.647).

de lo humano del hombre– , así como la sala burguesa abre sus puertas en ese cambio para devenir "el mundo de absoluta e integral actualidad". No por azar la imagen del despertador aparece engarzada con un pasaje en el que Benjamin desarrolla y complejiza sus ideas sobre el espacio del cuerpo y de la imagen, concepto que se menciona expresamente en el mismo lugar. En el comienzo de la argumentación aparece la distinción entre la comparación y la imagen, aunque el camino hacia ese desarrollo pasó por varios estadios conceptuales: por la "iluminación profana" [*profane Erleuchtung*], entendida como una inspiración materialista y antropológica, resultado de una "superación de la iluminación religiosa"[1] (*G.S.*, II.1.297) y encarnada en los tipos del que lee, del que piensa, del que espera y del que deambula (o *flâneur*, *G.S.*, II.1.308), pero también el texto nos ha llevado a considerar "el cambio de la mirada histórica sobre lo que ha sido"[2] por una mirada política (*G.S.*, II.1.300); o "el contraste frente a los compromisos anodinos de 'comunidad del sentimiento'"[3] (*G.S.*, II.1.304) o una "óptica dialéctica que reconozca lo cotidiano como impenetrable y lo impenetrable como cotidiano"[4] (*G.S.*, II.1.307).

Si estos estadios aparecen profusamente presentados en una terminología que se manifiesta en percepciones (mirada, visión, etcétera), por oposición a opiniones y sentimientos, el texto de Benjamin se abre también a una distinción entre comparación e imagen que franquea la entrada a un pasaje sobre las esferas del cuerpo y de la imagen como *dimensión espacial*. Aquí se hace visible un área de la imagen en la que el sujeto –Benjamin habla del artista o del intelectual revolucionario– penetra en el descubrimiento "del ciento por ciento del espacio de la imagen", donde

---

1. En alemán: "*Überwindung religiöser Erleuchtung*". [N. del T.]
2. En alemán: "*Auswechslung des historischen Blicks aufs Gewesene*". [N. del T.]
3. En alemán: "*Kontrast gegen die hilflosen Kompromisse der 'Gesinnung'*". [N. del T.]
4. En alemán: "*eine dialektische Optik, die das Alltägliche als undurchdringlich, das Undurchdringliche als alltäglich erkennt*". [N. del T.]

del despertador transmuta sonido y movimiento en permanencia, allí el ritmo textual llega en el mismo momento abruptamente a su detención. Y mientras "el despertador que en cada minuto resuena durante los sesenta segundos", por una parte, significa justamente lo contrario de los disparos contra los relojes en lo alto de los campanarios durante la Revolución de Julio "*pour arrêter le jour*" –según nos cuenta Benjamin en la Reflexión XV de "Sobre el concepto de historia" (*G.S.*, I.2.702)–, ambas imágenes producen el mismo efecto: *la función del despertador aumentada a una situación imposible de medir y la violenta detención de los relojes de las torres para hacer posible la memoria*. "*Irrités contre l'heure*" es la anécdota que condensa los disparos contra los relojes, como disparos del *Jetztzeit* a lo mensurable que se encuentra en su devenir de un tiempo lineal, como disparos contra el tiempo "homogéneo y vacío", según lo define Benjamin en sus tesis "Sobre el concepto de historia", que, en rigor, son una reflexión teórica sobre la historia. Y, sin embargo, se exhibe aquí una diferencia que puede leerse como alegoría de la distinción de la estructuración conceptual que impregna los textos respectivos de 1929 y de 1940: el *espacio del cuerpo y de la imagen* en el ensayo sobre el surrealismo y la *imagen dialéctica* en las tesis "Sobre el concepto de historia".

Si en el último texto se trata de la idea y construcción de la historia, pero también de aspectos recordados o citados del pasado, de imágenes del pasado o de correspondencias entre el *Jetztzeit* y "lo que ha sido" [*das Gewesene*] –que se representan y son reconocibles en imágenes dialécticas–, en el texto anterior se hace visible una imagen corpórea, que resuena por el cese de la temporalidad. Así, por ello, se le impone al sujeto una imagen sobre el cuerpo. En el traspaso que va del óvalo del reloj a las muecas del rostro humano se dio el cambio entre el espacio de la imagen al espacio corpóreo. Y el resonar contra el tiempo es igualmente un disparo contra la idea de oposición entre lo orgánico y lo mecánico, entre el individuo y los engranajes, que ahora aparecen todos sin fronteras –de una manera que causa impacto, por cierto, dado que el rostro funciona como símbolo

2. "El espacio del cuerpo y de la imagen"

Las huellas en los escritos de Benjamin

LOS PASAJES A TRAVÉS DEL ESPACIO DEL CUERPO Y DE LA IMAGEN EN EL SURREALISMO

"No es el que está junto al manantial el que puede abrevarse con plenitud en las corrientes espirituales, sino quien erguido en el valle alimenta sus energías de la pendiente, es decir de la distancia a la fuente". Esta imagen de la estación energética que domina el comienzo del texto benjaminiano "El surrealismo. La última instantánea de la inteligencia europea" (1929) aparece sustituida al final del ensayo por otra, igualmente tomada de la mecánica: el "óvalo de un despertador donde cada minuto suena durante sesenta segundos" (*G.S.*, II.1.310), que los surrealistas cambian por las muecas de su propia cara. Mientras que en la primera imagen la energía llega al sujeto por un movimiento situado fuera de él, en la imagen final la mecánica interpenetra directamente al individuo, pues su rostro mismo se ha tornado mecánico, embarcado en un movimiento ininterrumpido o en un resonar sin pausa, de tal modo que el tiempo está colmado completamente de una mezcla de sonido y movimiento y, por ello, termina anulándose. Esta imagen se halla, entonces, al final de un artículo que en su modo de escritura cumple miméticamente la transformación conjurada en el texto de la rebelión surrealista como una revolución, remontándose en un movimiento ascendente con ritmo creciente para resonar al final en un constante campanilleo. Sin embargo, allí donde la imagen de la campanilla equipara *memoria* e *historia*, como cuando escribe: "Articular históricamente el pasado significa [...] hacerse dueño de un recuerdo tal como destella en un momento de peligro" ("Sobre el concepto de historia", Reflexión VI; *G.S.*, I.2.695). En este concepto de historia, fundido en las imágenes del pasado que deben ser leídas como recuerdo, y no en la crítica benjaminiana de una ideología del progreso históricamente específica y limitada por su tiempo, es donde hay que leer la verdadera "actualidad" de sus obras.

enfrentados al "espíritu nuevo"; así como el lenguaje es el instrumento de un "nuevo espíritu", libre y puro y sin recuerdos:

> Es como el principiante que ha aprendido un idioma nuevo: lo traduce siempre a su idioma nativo, pero sólo se asimila el espíritu del nuevo idioma y sólo es capaz de producir libremente en él cuando se mueve dentro de él sin reminiscencias y olvida en él su lengua natal. (1971: 12)

Si en Marx el espacio en imágenes de lo político se torna por necesidad poesía o un dominio de lo metafórico en la estricta separación entre historia y recuerdo (por lo cual subyace una comprensión convencional de la metáfora en el sentido de discurso impropio o figurativo), ello no deja de aparecer unido, no por azar, a un uso particular de las imágenes, que no se da como cita, sino que puede leerse como la realización o reproducción de las metáforas tradicionales. Esto sucede, por ejemplo, cuando Marx pone en relación el concepto de la idea de pureza de lo históricamente nuevo en la conocida comparación de la nación y la mujer violada: "A la nación, como a la mujer, no se les perdona la hora de descuido en que cualquier aventurero ha podido abusar de ellas por la fuerza" (1971: 19).

Cuando Benjamin, por su parte, coloca la cita, como invocación de lo actual en la espesura de lo único, aparece con ello una vinculación con el concepto de la historia, por lo cual la construcción de la historia aparece entendida como trabajo en y con las imágenes del recuerdo,[13] que funde la cognoscibilidad del pasado en un modelo de la memoria y, de este modo, finalmente

---

13. En sus anotaciones Benjamin acentúa el carácter involuntario de las imágenes del recuerdo, cuando escribe: "La imagen del pasado que destella en el *Ahora* de su cognoscibilidad es, en una definición amplia, una imagen del recuerdo. Se asemeja a las imágenes del propio pasado, que les sobrevienen a los individuos en el momento de peligro. Estas imágenes surgen, como se sabe, de modo involuntario. La historia es, en sentido estricto, entonces, una imagen de la memoria involuntaria; una imagen, que en el momento de peligro se le hace súbitamente presente al sujeto de la historia" (*G.S.*, I.3.1243).

heredada. Así mientras que Benjamin cita la idea de Marx acerca de la revolución como un salto dialéctico, no puede pensarse una mayor diferencia con su propia interpretación de la esfera de la imagen de la Revolución Francesa. La diferencia proviene no tanto porque Marx se apoye sobre una familia de palabras referidas al teatro y a la vestimenta teatral (tragedia, farsa, disfraz, máscara, etcétera), con sus asociaciones de préstamo y traducción donde subyace la valoración de una expresión inauténtica, falsa o impropia; ni tampoco sólo porque Marx, hablando de pesadillas, de resurrecciones y de fantasmas o espíritus [*Geister*] de la revolución, haya situado las imágenes del pasado en la fase nocturna de la razón. La diferencia tiene más que ver con el modo explícito en que Marx esboza un concepto de la historia que apunta completamente hacia el futuro, donde todo recuerdo del pasado aparece valorado negativamente y cada referencia a una búsqueda hacia atrás[12] tiene que ser relegada al olvido, así como sucede con los muertos. Por ello para Marx el recuerdo aparece equiparado con un adormecimiento de los sentidos:

> La revolución social del siglo xix no puede extraer su poesía del pasado, sino solamente del porvenir. No puede comenzar su propia tarea antes de despojarse de toda veneración supersticiosa por el pasado. Las anteriores revoluciones necesitaban remontarse a los recuerdos de la historia universal para aturdirse acerca de su propio contenido. La revolución del siglo xix debe dejar que los muertos entierren a sus muertos, para cobrar conciencia de su propio contenido. Allí, la frase [*Phrase*] desbordaba el contenido [*Inhalt*]; aquí, el contenido desbordaba la frase. (1971: 15)

Esta valoración negativa del pasado y de los recuerdos va unida a un concepto del lenguaje logocéntrico que se basa en la oposición entre "espíritu" [*Geist*] y "espíritus" [*Geister*] en el sentido de "fantasmas". "Los espíritus del pasado" se hallan

---

12. Para el significado del concepto de "proveniencia" [*Herkunft*] en Benjamin y en Foucault [*provenance*] véase el capítulo 3 del presente estudio.

sa" (1971: 15), es decir, que se da una falsa conciencia. La misma constelación experimenta bajo la pluma de Benjamin, en el contexto de sus imágenes de la historia, una interpretación completamente diferente, sin buscar oponer su propio texto con el de Marx y sin adjudicarle, así, un análisis falso. Esto ya se percibe en la manera en que Benjamin instaura una cesura frente a un discurso forjado sobre la oposición de verdadero-falso, y en lugar de dicho juego de opuestos presenta otra lectura diferente de la constelación histórica en una imagen de pensamiento que mantiene una tácita intertextualidad con el *18 de Brumario* de Marx, como sucede en la Reflexión XIV de "Sobre el concepto de historia":

> La historia es objeto de una construcción, cuyo lugar no lo conforma un tiempo homogéneo y vacío, sino colmado por el *Jetztzeit*. Así para Robespierre la Roma antigua era un pasado marcado por un *Jetztzeit*, que él hacía saltar por los aires para extraerlo del continuo de la historia. La Revolución Francesa se veía como una Roma rediviva. Citaba a la vieja Roma exactamente como la moda cita una vestimenta del pasado. La moda posee el olfato para lo actual, moviéndose siempre en la espesura de lo pretérito. La moda es el "salto del tigre" [*Tigersprung*] hacia el pasado. Sólo que este salto se produce en un circo en el que la clase dominante domina. El mismo salto bajo el cielo libre de la historia es el dialéctico al que Marx entendió como el de la revolución. (*G.S.*, I.2.701)

El salto del tigre hacia el pasado, como movimiento por el que se salta el *continuum*, crea una inmediatez hacia el pasado, haciendo presente o citando una imagen del archivo de la memoria histórica (citándola en el sentido de darle cita entre nosotros o pidiéndole que se presente, pero no en el sentido de gestar así una referencia erudita que convoca el prestigio de la autoridad). Dicha figura muestra a las claras cuán estrechamente se hallan ligados en Benjamin el concepto de actualidad y la cita como prácticas de un obrar político en imágenes fuera del *continuum* histórico. Esta práctica es reconocible como un uso benjaminiano de la cita que se aparta de cualquier tradición

(*G.S.*, V.1.594). Se trata, pues, de aspectos insoslayables de la representación de la historia que han llegado a surgir gracias a la presencia de la actualidad (*G.S.*, V.1.587). Y si la actualidad representa esa carga detonante que produce la explosión de lo continuo o la tregua "de una constelación saturada de tensión"[10] (*G.S.*, V.1.595), ella gesta la estructura monadológica o la constitución de la historia como imagen. En relación con el concepto benjaminiano de la historia, debe decirse que su relectura de la historia como "escena de la memoria" [*Gedächtnisszene*][11] hace de la actualidad su condición de posibilidad para una representación dialéctica de los estados históricos de la cuestión (*G.S.*, V.1.587) y para la legibilidad de las imágenes de la historia (*G.S.*, V.1.577). Y justamente el pensar en imágenes es el núcleo de la *teoría* de la historia benjaminiana, que al aparecer transformada en *filosofía* de la historia y despojada de sus conceptos de actualidad e imagen, se ve desfigurada no hacia la cognoscibilidad, sino hacia lo cognoscible, es decir, reducida a lo conocido.

La distorsión benjaminiana del materialismo histórico que tiene lugar aquí se manifiesta en el modo paradigmático en que Benjamin ilumina las imágenes del imaginario colectivo frente a la interpretación marxista, hasta desplazar ese "conjurar a los muertos" [*Totenbeschwörungen*], que para Marx se encuadraba bajo la categoría de la falsa conciencia, en una práctica de la cita y en un obrar en la esfera de la imagen de lo político. Así, Marx en el famoso comienzo de su *18 de Brumario* describe las alusiones de los actores políticos a figuras e imágenes de acontecimientos históricos pasados –por ejemplo, la referencia de la Revolución Francesa a la Roma antigua–, atribuyéndolas a "las ilusiones que necesitaban para ocultarse a sí mismos el contenido burguesamente limitado de sus luchas" (Marx, 1971: 13), entendiendo que allí se producía una "veneración supersticio-

---

10. En alemán: "*einer von Spannung gesättigten Konstellation*". [N. del T.]
11. Este concepto es tratado en el capítulo 8 del presente estudio.

te llegan a su representación como distorsiones), las imágenes de la historia pueden llegar a ser reconocidas y leídas. Esto significa que en Benjamin se produce una metamorfosis que superpone el paradigma de Marx basado en la oposición "ser-conciencia" [*Sein-Bewusstsein*] con el de Freud "conciencia-inconsciente" [*Bewusstsein-Unbewusstes*],[9] y que culmina en la idea de la "presencia de espíritu" [*Geistesgegenwart*]. Pero recuérdese que decir "presencia de espíritu" implica decir "la postura del sujeto que permite la actualidad".

En este sentido, Benjamin pudo afirmar que la actualización y no el progreso debería ser el concepto central del materialismo histórico (*G.S.*, V.1.574). Y sobre este concepto básico se apoyan sus tesis e imágenes de pensamiento en "Sobre el concepto de historia", que nos hemos acostumbrado a denominar "Tesis de filosofía de la historia"; una denominación que tiende nuevamente a dejar de lado en los escritos de Benjamin el significativo trabajo con el pensar en imágenes.

IMÁGENES DE LA POLÍTICA – POLÍTICA DE LAS IMÁGENES: UNA LECTURA DE MARX

El modo en que Benjamin, tanto en su proyecto de los Pasajes como en "Sobre el concepto de historia", reformula el materialismo histórico, podría describirse literalmente como una "dis-torsión"; en este caso como una distorsión en el sentido freudiano, es decir en relación con los jeroglíficos del recuerdo, donde se halla la huella de los estímulos o una reelaboración psíquica. El abandono del elemento épico de la historia (*G.S.*, V.1.592) y el desmoronamiento de la historia en imágenes –no en "historias" (*G.S.*, V.1.596)– son las formas en las que se produce la explosión del objeto de la historia desde el *continuum* del decurso histórico

---

9. Lo mismo sucede con la relectura psicoanalítica de conceptos centrales de Marx (la fantasmagoría y el fetiche) que Benjamin hace girar diametralmente hacia los aspectos de significado y de expresión al entenderlos como imágenes.

lenguaje del inconsciente como un sistema de constitución de la significación con una sintaxis específica y, siguiendo las imágenes oníricas, clasifica diferentes modalidades de la elaboración de los sueños. En la marcha de su trabajo sobre los modos de funcionar del aparato psíquico se va eclipsando, sin embargo, una de esas alternativas: la de la "consideración por las condiciones de representabilidad" [*Rücksicht auf Darstellbarkeit*]. Esto concierne a la cuestión de la representación. Ahora bien, cuando Benjamin –apoyándose en Freud–,[8] concentra su atención en cuerpos, cosas, mercancías, monumentos, topografía, etc., para considerarlos como símbolos del deseo y materializaciones de la memoria colectiva, vuelve a colocar ese material en una posición central para el psicoanálisis y para los medios de expresión del lenguaje del inconsciente. Y, a la inversa, este procedimiento implica la introducción de un modo de observación –entrenado psicoanalíticamente– de determinantes históricos en la lectura del marxismo, que no es ajeno al modo en que Benjamin hace hincapié en la relación expresiva (entre economía y cultura) en contraposición con la relación causal que Marx intentaba reproducir. Al mismo tiempo, puede decirse que este modo funda su lectura específica –basada en el psicoanálisis– de las imágenes de la historia.

De este modo, Benjamin toma literalmente la afirmación de que "el mundo posee mucho tiempo antes el sueño de una cosa y solamente tiene que poseer esa conciencia para poseer la cosa realmente", para entretejer esa cita de Marx,* que anota en su proyecto de los Pasajes, con el concepto freudiano de los sueños (*G.S.*, V.1.583). Así, Benjamin sostiene que a través de la decodificación de los símbolos de deseo que se han tornado materiales (que, por cierto, como todos los signos del inconscien-

---

8. Para una lectura de Freud por parte de Benjamin véanse especialmente los capítulos 8, 9 y 10 del presente estudio.

* La cita de Marx proviene de sus *Escritos tempranos*, y más exactamente de una carta de Marx a Ruge Kreuzenach, fechada en septiembre de 1843; véase Marx: *Die Frühschriften*, Stuttgart, Kröner, 1953. [N. del T.]

"El mundo de una absoluta e integral actualidad" en Benjamin

casa"⁷ (*G.S.*, II.1.310), representa el momento de un *Jetztzeit* corpóreo que se ha tornado material. En tanto el *Jetztzeit* de la cognoscibilidad coincide con el *Jetztzeit* de una representación o acción corpóreas, esta escena puede tener para Benjamin el valor de "un mundo de absoluta e integral actualidad". La actualidad en sentido estricto sería "política como representación" [*Politik als Darstellung*]: presencia de espíritu hecha cuerpo.

Esta escena caracteriza, por decirlo así, en la fase revolucionaria de la confluencia del espacio de la imagen y del cuerpo, la idea de Benjamin sobre la actualidad. Pues, según lo desarrolla en su libro sobre el drama barroco, para él la representación de una idea:

> [...] no puede ser considerada de ningún modo como exitosa, en tanto no aparezca virtualmente cortado el círculo de sus posibles extremos [...] La idea es una mónada, o sea, simplemente: cada idea contiene la imagen del mundo. A su representación le concierne nada menos que transformar en signo la imagen del mundo en toda su concisión. (*G.S.*, I.1.227-8)

Los párrafos finales del artículo sobre el surrealismo, que diseñan un entramado entre los espacios de la imagen y del cuerpo hechos representación en las inervaciones corpóreas de la comunidad, deben leerse como una mónada de "un mundo de absoluta e integral actualidad". En ellos se entrecruzan dos operaciones teóricas de Benjamin, que deberían describirse como relectura materializada y como radicalización de conceptos teóricos previos, una vez en relación con el psicoanálisis y otra con el materialismo histórico, respectivamente.

Sigmund Freud, por su parte, había desarrollado primeramente su teoría del inconsciente en relación con la teoría de la histeria y en torno al síntoma corporal como símbolo del recuerdo. Freud pasa a describir, luego, en su *Interpretación de los sueños,* el

---

7. En alemán: "*in welchem die profane Erleuchtung uns heimisch macht*". [N. del T.]

PENSAR EN IMÁGENES: EL CUERPO Y LA ACTUALIDAD EN BENJAMIN

Hay que señalar que esta presentación en una imagen de pensamiento de una constelación difícilmente traducible en conceptos no debe confundirse con la poesía, y no es tampoco una cualidad extra del discurso filosófico, sino un modo de llevar adelante la reflexión filosófica que coloca fuera de juego al propio discurso filosófico considerado como metadiscurso. En la imaginería de Benjamin no se trata del arsenal metafórico, es decir, del así llamado discurso figurativo o discurso impropio, por el que una imagen ocuparía el lugar de un concepto o pensamiento pudiendo ser éstos también expresables de otra manera. Justamente aquí, en la diferenciación de la comparación –"la diferenciación entre comparación e imagen"[5] (*G.S.*, II.1.308)–, reside la condición de ese modelo de *Aktualität* que se desarrolla en el artículo sobre el surrealismo. Lo que se halla en juego no es, entonces, una "puesta en clave" [*Verschlüsselung*] de significaciones en las imágenes, según Habermas (1972: 189), sino la concepción que consiste en que memoria y acción se articulan en imágenes, que las ideas están estructuradas con imágenes y que, por lo tanto, de lo que se trata es de la práctica en el manejo de las imágenes: en definitiva, de una "política de las imágenes" [*Politik der Bilder*] y no de una "política modélica" [*bildliche Politik*].

En la esfera de la imagen benjaminiana confluyen las ideas y las acciones, las imaginaciones y las representaciones de sus actores. Y allí donde los sujetos dan cuerpo a sus ideas *in actu*, se enlaza para Benjamin el espacio de la imagen con el del cuerpo. Esta escena de la historia, el engendramiento "de la realidad política y objetiva"[6] de la *physis* en esa esfera de la imagen, "en la que la iluminación profana nos hace sentirnos en

---

5. En alemán: "*die Unterscheidung von Vergleich und Bild*". [N. del T.]
6. En alemán: "*der politischen und sachlichen Wirklichkeit*". [N. del T.]

pensar en imágenes puede rastrearse también en esta controvertida conferencia en aquellos pasajes en los que –en la presentación de las formulaciones [*Theoreme*] de Benjamin– palabras como "imágenes" [*Bilder*] o "miradas" [*Blicke*] aparecen sustituidas por el "pensar" [*Denken*] o los "pensamientos" [*Gedanken*] o, incluso, son directamente suprimidas. Así, por ejemplo, Habermas se refiere al "instantáneo destello de actualidad de un pensamiento que mantiene su dominio durante históricos segundos" (1972: 176)[3]. Mientras que la versión original de Benjamin, como es sabido, se refiere a imágenes súbitamente luminosas en la frase: "*Sólo como imagen*, que en su perderse de vista para siempre destella justamente en el momento de su cognoscibilidad, es como se puede apresar el pasado"[4] ("Sobre el concepto de historia", Reflexión V;* *G.S.*, I.2.695) (El destacado es mío.). O también Habermas pasa por alto imágenes de pensamiento centrales para la teoría benjaminiana, como, por ejemplo, cuando habla de "la promesa mesiánica de felicidad" (1972: 198), y mezcla el mesianismo con la búsqueda de la felicidad, mientras que por el contrario, en Benjamin se trataba de subordinar la búsqueda de la felicidad al orden de lo profano. La relación de lo profano con lo mesiánico se describe (en los "Fragmentos teológico-políticos") en la imagen de una estructura contra la corriente y en una *Denkbild* [imagen de pensamiento] de dos fuerzas que, aunque en direcciones contrarias, pueden transmitirse energía una a otra hacia su respectiva dirección ("Metaphysichgeschichtsphilosophische Studien" ["Estudios metafísicos y de filosofía de la historia"]; II.1.204): *eine gegenstrebige Fügung*.

---

3. En alemán: "*Der aufblitzenden Aktualität eines für historische Sekunden die Herrschaft antretenden Gedankens*".
4. En alemán: "Nur als Bild, *das auf Nimmerwiedersehen im Augenblick seiner Erkennbarkeit eben aufblitzt, ist die Vergangenheit festzuhalten*".
* Llamamos a estos textos "Reflexión" (cuando van acompañados del número respectivo), en lugar del apelativo de "tesis" con que se los conoce corrientemente, apoyados en que el mismo Benjamin se refiere a una de ellas, en carta a Gretel Adorno, llamándola "*die 17. Reflexion*" (cf. *G.S.*, I.3.1223). [N. del T.]

principalmente en ámbitos o dominios completamente diferentes de aquellos con los que se supone tendría que entrar en contacto. Con su concentración en imágenes se refiere Benjamin, por el contrario, a esa modalidad, en la que se transmite todo lo material y todo lo inteligible, es decir, el mundo y el saber. Tan importante como la falta de concordancia de conceptos básicos es, en este sentido, el hecho de que Habermas se haya evadido de la lectura de Benjamin para pasar por alto el concepto de *Aktualität* justamente en el momento en que introducía su propio concepto de actualidad. El punto oscuro de esa lectura, el cerrarse a una *Aktualität* señalada por "un ciento por ciento del espacio de la imagen" caracteriza así, la proveniencia del interrogante por la "actualidad" de Benjamin, pero, por otro lado, su consecución en ese pasaje retoma el hilo de una argumentación apoyada en genealogías. Y si se acepta que la mención de Brecht en la supuesta liberación de Benjamin de tendencias anarquistas servía a los mismos fines, entonces puede decirse también que en el séptimo y último párrafo (donde se proponía que la teoría benjaminiana de la experiencia se pusiera al servicio del materialismo histórico), se apuntaba a la teoría de la comunicación lingüística, un proyecto en el que Habermas venía trabajando desde el comienzo de los años setenta y que sella con estas palabras: "...una teoría de la comunicación lingüística que *retrotrae* la penetración de Benjamin a la teoría materialista de la evolución social" (Habermas, 1972: 220) (El destacado es mío.)

Si el llevar agua para el molino de un proyecto teórico es una característica de Habermas, también es sintomático dónde se halla el problema –y sólo por ese motivo resulta aquí interesante tratarlo–, pues, al mismo tiempo, esta lectura obra como un biombo frente al pensar en imágenes benjaminiano (que no es fácilmente traducible a categorías de un discurso filosófico), y, además, funciona como barrera para poder franquear la esfera de la imagen, en tanto se anula la separación entre sujeto y objeto, así como la distancia entre quien filosofa y el objeto de su discurso.

Un eclipse de la imagen y del trabajo benjaminiano con el

o sea "un mundo de una absoluta e integral actualidad". El arco completo de la argumentación del texto benjaminiano sobre el surrealismo, su discusión sobre las posibilidades de ese momento de una politización del arte, desemboca en una idea de actualidad, que se diseña como espacio del cuerpo y de la imagen.[2]

Habermas, sin embargo, en un párrafo de su conferencia, que, por su parte, confluye en un concepto de actualidad, no sigue la línea de pensamiento de Benjamin, sino que interrumpe su lectura del artículo sobre el surrealismo para citar la idea de la "preparación metódica y disciplinaria de la revolución" y así derivar en la interpretación de que Benjamin,

> [...] impulsado por su contacto con Brecht, se habría liberado de sus inclinaciones anarquistas del pasado, y en ese momento habría mirado la relación entre arte y práctica política fundamentalmente desde el punto de vista de la *utilidad* [*Verwertbarkeit*] organizativa y propagandística del arte para la lucha de clases. (1972: 215) (El destacado es mío.)

Si, por una parte, es difícil hallar apoyo a tales interpretaciones en los textos benjaminianos posteriores a 1929; por otro lado, hay que agregar sobre todo que el criterio de "utilidad" es ajeno al pensamiento de Benjamin, a quien, ya sea cuando contempla el lenguaje, la historia, el arte o el mundo de las cosas en la Modernidad, siempre le interesarán los aspectos de la inmediatez. En el mismo sentido, puede decirse que la oposición entre anarquismo y organización proviene, más bien, del repositorio de opuestos que el propio texto de Habermas presenta como una estructura continua: poesía y política, arte y lucha de clases, teología y marxismo, Iluminismo y mística. La figura de la "unión" [*Vereinigung*], sin embargo, en el contexto de lo que Benjamin se hubiera esforzado en unir, así como la cuestión de la relación de, por ejemplo, teoría y *praxis* o política y arte, se fundamenta todo ello en una postura y en un pensamiento que se constituyen

---

2. Para la significación y génesis de este concepto véase el capítulo 2 del presente estudio.

representación o incluso como política poética –cuando Benjamin vio estas realizaciones– ya no pudo negar esas diferencias de principio entre obrar político y manifestación callejera. (1972: 214)

Y en este punto continúa con las palabras de Benjamin:

> [...] eso significaría dejar la preparación metódica y disciplinaria de la revolución por completo en manos de una práctica que vacila entre ejercitación y triunfalismo. (Habermas, 1972: 214-5; y *G.S.*, II.1.307)

Si se abriera el artículo de Benjamin sobre el surrealismo en el pasaje citado, podría verse que no se trata allí de diferencias de principio entre la acción política y la celebración de la manifestación en la calle, sino de una delimitación frente a conceptos surrealistas que son muy puntuales y que destacan *exclusivamente* el componente del entusiasmo en los actos revolucionarios, lo que Benjamin finalmente evalúa como un "prejuicio romántico". En esta línea Benjamin continúa con un comentario sobre la "política poética" que pasa del tono crítico al sarcástico, pero no está dirigido –como afirma Habermas– contra una "política como representación" (1972: 55). Benjamin se ocupa, más bien, de criticar una política que se sirva de medios "poéticos", es decir, de aquellos artificios que provengan de la poesía [*Dichtung*], especialmente del recurso de la comparación:

> Pues: ¿qué pasa con el programa de los partidos burgueses? Es una mala poesía primaveral. Llena hasta reventar de comparaciones [...] ¿Y qué sucede con el depósito de imágenes a disposición de los poetas de los ateneos del partido socialdemócrata? (*G.S.*, II.1.308)

Y ahora le sigue el famoso pasaje sobre el pesimismo, sobre la desconfianza ante cualquier entendimiento y el postulado de "quitar de la vida política la metáfora moral y en el ámbito del accionar político descubrir un ciento por ciento del espacio de la imagen" (*G.S.*, II.1.309). Y exactamente allí donde ese espacio de la imagen se abre Benjamin descubre su concepto de actualidad,

QUIEBRES Y PUNTOS OSCUROS DE LA LECTURA

Habermas trata brevemente en el párrafo introductorio el concepto de actualidad, y en relación con esto cita justamente ese pasaje del "Anuncio de la revista *Angelus Novus*", en el que Benjamin explica lo efímero de la verdadera actualidad con la leyenda talmúdica de los innumerables ángeles que son creados en cada momento para luego desaparecer en la nada después de haber cantado su himno ante Dios (*G.S.*, II.1. 246). En la parte restante de su exposición el concepto de actualidad ya no desempeña un papel central, pues se trata más bien de una discusión en torno al concepto benjaminiano de crítica en relación con un concepto del arte como crítica ideológica. Finalmente, el sexto párrafo lleva agua para su molino cuando Habermas quiere demostrar el modo en que su antecesor utilizaba las categorías marxistas (Habermas, 1972: 208), argumentando que el intento de una vinculación de la política con el arte habría sido un fracaso en Benjamin, y desemboca nuevamente en la cuestión de la actualidad de este autor:

> La actualidad de Benjamin no se halla justamente en una teología de la revolución. Su actualidad se muestra, más bien, si intentamos, por el contrario, "poner al servicio" del materialismo histórico la teoría benjaminiana de la experiencia. (1972: 215)

Vale la pena detenerse con cierto detalle en el procedimiento retórico que permite ese viraje capital en lo referente a la temática, que pasa desde el concepto de actualidad en Benjamin a la actualidad de Benjamin. Con el fin de fundamentar el rechazo de una teología de la revolución, Habermas se refiere, en el mismo discurso ya citado, al artículo de Benjamin sobre el surrealismo (de 1929), para extractar de allí las objeciones de Benjamin contra las ideas de una "política poética", apoyándose en la básica refutación benjaminiana de los intentos surrealistas, en los que:

> El arte es llevado a un accionar expresivo, y resulta así anulada la separación entre un obrar poético y uno político. [...] La política como

antes una conferencia de homenaje por el octogésimo aniversario del nacimiento de Benjamin bajo el título de "La actualidad de Walter Benjamin" y la había comenzado expresamente con una genealogía, en la que él mismo tomaba posición en directa descendencia, pasando por Peter Szondi –el que "hubiera estado hoy y aquí sin lugar a dudas en mi lugar" (Habermas, 1972: 175)–, y por Adorno, quien aunaba en una persona al "heredero, interlocutor crítico y la personalidad que ha abierto brechas". Ello sucedía, con todo, en un lugar que pensaba compartir con los coordinadores editoriales Tiedemann y Schweppenhäuser. Sin embargo, contra tal tipo de homenaje se había expresado el propio Benjamin en sus anotaciones manuscritas para un texto como "Sobre el concepto de historia", cuando sostenía que el modo en que algo pasado es homenajeado como "la herencia" es más dañino que lo que podría ser su falta de consideración como tal (*G.S.*, I.3.1242).

Si las palabras de Habermas de 1972 son puestas a consideración aquí de nuevo, ello no sucede con el ánimo de continuar la disputa suscitada con respecto a los aspectos teológicos o marxistas de los textos benjaminianos, y tampoco para reabrir la discusión sobre las reflexiones de Benjamin bajo los paradigmas habermasianos de crítica ideológica y teoría cultural materialista. De ninguna manera tampoco interesa aquí ejercer la crítica –o la refutación– de tesis tales como la de que Adorno "ha sido con seguridad el mejor marxista" (Habermas, 1972: 211); una tesis cuya retórica puede ser explicada a partir del clima de discusión vivido en la constelación histórica del post-Mayo del '68.[1] Más bien es la intención del presente trabajo reconstruir, mediante una lectura renovada de la referida conferencia, justamente aquel aspecto en el que se reconoce un desconocimiento del concepto benjaminiano de actualidad. Por lo tanto, el texto de Habermas ha de ser tratado aquí sólo en relación con este tema.

---

1. Compárese, por ejemplo, la controversia entre la revista *alternative* (núms. 56/57, 1967; y 59/60, 1968) y la postura de la Escuela de Frankfurt frente al "marxismo de Benjamin".

"El mundo de una absoluta e integral actualidad" en Benjamin

La cuestión de la actualidad de Walter Benjamin es algo que acosa constantemente a los críticos, como se ha visto recientemente en ocasión de cumplirse los cien años de su nacimiento; y siempre está relacionada con la utilidad de su pensamiento para la problemática contemporánea, en el sentido de una posible ductilidad de sus formulaciones para aplicar a análisis y discusiones de hoy. Así, por ejemplo, Irving Wohlfahrt debatía, en la conferencia de apertura al Congreso Internacional sobre Benjamin realizado en Osnabrück en 1992, la validez de las reflexiones benjaminianas sobre la filosofía de la historia después del "fin del socialismo" o después del desmoronamiento del socialismo real, y terminaba rescatando a Benjamin para el pensamiento actual, claro está que después de realizar aquí y allá algunas correcciones en el discurso benjaminiano. A nuestro entender, se trata de un rescate cuestionable, en tanto no da en el blanco al realizar el gesto de búsqueda de la adaptación de la teoría pasada a las situaciones y discursos del momento, perdiendo de vista el concepto benjaminiano de actualidad. Con este proceder se pierde la oportunidad de considerar el presente quizá de otro modo a la luz de la postura benjaminiana de actualidad. Lo que está en juego, entonces, no es una crítica que salva [*eine rettende Kritik*], lo que se evidencia es más bien un desconocimiento de la obra de Benjamin, pues una auténtica lectura del concepto de actualidad en los textos benjaminianos llevaría a resaltar lo vano de semejante empresa, "la actualidad de Walter Benjamin".

La difundida cuestión de la actualidad de Benjamin, entonces, participa de un pensamiento que afinca su tradición y su desarrollo en la teoría a partir de una serie de nombres de autoridades y de su relación mutua. Esto lleva a una genealogía como historia de la obra de grandes autores y como herencia y continuidad en el decurso de las posturas teóricas y del conocimiento analítico. En este sentido, no fue una casualidad que Wohlfahrt intentara vincular a Benjamin (revisado en el tono del postsocialismo) con Habermas, quien representaría el modelo tácito, al que terminaría por mencionar directamente al final de su exposición. El mismo Habermas había realizado veinte años

cuestión de la actualidad de Benjamin implica ya una exclusión de su concepto de actualidad.

Con esta táctica se le quita a la discusión sobre la teoría crítica de la sociedad tal vez exactamente esos aspectos que, aunque todavía sin resolver, podrían constituir lo que ella tiene de específicamente actual. Y no se trata aquí de la conveniencia histórica de determinadas afirmaciones analíticas o de formulaciones particulares, y tampoco de la cuestión de la coherencia de las diferentes referencias filosóficas, culturales y epistemológicas de los textos benjaminianos. Se trata, más fundamentalmente, del modo de hacer filosofía, de pensar y de analizar que poseía Benjamin, de su postura frente a las ideas recibidas y a sus "constelaciones", de modos de tratamiento y de procedimiento de los signos y del material histórico y cultural; se trata, en definitiva, de "la obra de la presencia de espíritu en cuerpo" [*Werk leibhaftiger Geistesgegenwart*], (en *Dirección única*; G.S., IV.1.142).

El concepto de actualidad en Benjamin se constituye, en rigor, sobre la base de un pensar y obrar en imágenes. Ello se refiere al modo extraordinario y al material igualmente extraordinario de ideas y pensamiento en imágenes, pero representa también un concepto de acción del que Benjamin dice en su ensayo sobre el surrealismo de 1929 que las ideas representadas *in actu* aparecen permeadas por el cuerpo y la imagen (*G.S.*, II.1.310), que pensar y actuar confluyen y que así "se abre un mundo de absoluta e integral actualidad" (*G.S.*, II.1.309). No nos encontramos aquí ante una "teoría materialista de la sociedad" en el sentido tradicional de la frase, sino frente a una teoría que establece una relación de inmediatez con lo material de lo social o lo simbólico. No se trata, en rigor, de una materialismo *avant la lettre*, sino de una relectura literal de lo material –es decir, de las cosas, de la escritura, de los gestos–, que ha atravesado la escuela tanto del materialismo político como antropológico, para introducir en el espacio de lo político su materia primera –el cuerpo– y, viceversa, para hacer hincapié en la constitución y estructuración en tanto imagen de esa materia.

1. "El mundo de una absoluta e integral actualidad" en Benjamin

CONMEMORAR E IGNORAR

Sobre la actualidad de Walter Benjamin fue el título de uno de los libros conmemorativos sobre la obra de Benjamin, que se basaba en una serie de conferencias (Unseld, 1972). Este título no sólo fue uno de los textos más difundidos sobre el autor, sino también uno de los lugares de referencia más obligados de ahí en adelante. Con esta fórmula se anuncia en general una apropiación de las formulaciones e ideas benjaminianos, que se presentan en una mezcla entre homenaje e historización. Si bajo ese título se discute la significación *actual* de la obra de Benjamin, esto representa una consideración en la que, implícitamente, se da por sentado que su pensamiento padece de una limitación histórica y que su validez está sujeta a su tiempo, para luego pasar a actualizar dicha validez –relativizada o modificada, según los casos–. Y si en las siguientes páginas no se hará hincapié sobre la actualidad de Benjamin, no será para oponerle una validez que sería universal y transhistórica, sino porque el modo de formular el interrogante –que seguiría el paradigma de la conveniencia de la teoría para la situación histórica– lleva inscrito dentro de sí un desconocimiento del concepto benjaminiano de "actualidad" [*Aktualität*]. Tal pregunta sólo puede formularse bajo el desconocimiento de una conceptualización específica de "actualidad". La tesis de este estudio, por lo tanto, consiste en que formularse la

PRIMERA PARTE
La política de las imágenes y del cuerpo

"...la primera materia donde la capacidad mimética
es sometida a una prueba: el cuerpo humano..."

cuerpo y de la imagen para los pasajes parisienses la "constelación" del despertar, ya que también en el lenguaje de imágenes de la Modernidad pueden ser vistas como las sacerdotisas de una dialéctica entre la conciencia y el inconsciente (véanse los capítulos 5 y 6 del presente estudio); de una dialéctica, en suma, en la que similitudes instantáneas se tornan perceptibles (capítulo 8).

La desfiguración hacia lo alegórico que se desarrolla en el proyecto benjaminiano de una historia primigenia de la Modernidad –en analogía con el lenguaje del inconsciente– representa también una distorsión de la alegoría, como se percibe en la forma en que la idea domina en el libro sobre el drama barroco (capítulo 7). Por ello debe considerarse que la "similitud distorsionada", que aparece en el dominio del proyecto de la Modernidad, significa el viraje de una similitud reprimida, cuya desaparición histórica puede situarse, sobre el telón de fondo de la idea foulcaultiana del "orden de las cosas", dentro de un sistema de signos en el pasaje de lo binario a lo ternario. Desde el comienzo Benjamin rescata de ese punto de transición de la historia del lenguaje la similitud reprimida en el momento de su desaparición histórica, en el sentido de que en su libro sobre el drama barroco permitió que las cosas se transformaran bajo la mirada alegórica en una escritura excitante. Pero, además, Benjamin consigue dotar, finalmente, de un significado central dentro de la Modernidad a ese viraje en forma distorsionada (capítulos 3, 7 y 9) que él llamó la "similitud distorsionada" [*entstellte Ähnlichkeit*].

camente las cesuras y desplazamientos entre la así llamada obra temprana y la tardía, entre los estudios histórico-literarios y la "historia primigenia de la Modernidad" [*Urgeschichte der Moderne*], entre el "lenguaje puro" [*reine Sprache*] y las "imágenes desconcertantes" [*Vexierbilder*], entre las imágenes y las imágenes dialécticas. Dichas figuras y conceptos benjaminianos se tratarán aquí de modo reiterado desde diferentes perspectivas, en tanto forman puntos nodales del pensar en imágenes que postula la obra de Benjamin. Y, en tanto ellos se tornan significativos bajo diferentes enfoques, conformarán también los puntos clave de la presentación en este estudio, repitiéndose, incluso, algunas citas en páginas diferentes.

Junto con la categoría del "espacio del cuerpo y de la imagen" la noción de "distorsión" constituye uno de los elementos más importantes en los diferentes textos de Benjamin aquí analizados. La última noción es solamente uno de los términos psicoanalíticos centrales que se introducen en el pensamiento benjaminiano; tampoco surgen a partir de este concepto relaciones únicamente con la redención mesiánica. En forma de "similitud distorsionada" [*entstellte Ähnlichkeit*] esta idea constituye la base de la reformulación, llevada a cabo durante la década del treinta, de su más antigua teoría del lenguaje y, con ello, también sirve de apoyatura a los orígenes de la categoría de "similitud no sensorial" (*unsinnliche Ähnlichkeit*; véanse los capítulos 3, 8 y 9 del presente estudio). Esta última categoría se halla en el contexto originario del concepto benjaminiano de la memoria, que en esa ocasión aparece sistemáticamente tratado por primera vez. Y con la "desfiguración hacia lo alegórico" [*Entstellung ins Allegorische*], así como con la figura de la prostituta en el proyecto de los Pasajes [*Passagen-Projekt*], en la cual se impregna de sentido la alegoría de la Modernidad, juega también un papel de peso la distorsión en los desplazamientos discursivos y del imaginario en torno al concepto de lo "femenino": de las habitantes de "lo que ha sido" [*das Gewesene*] y del silencio –que se encontraban en los escritos tempranos– devienen "las habitantes de los umbrales" [*Schwellenbewohnerinnen*]. Ellas ocupan ahora en el espacio del

se habían ido perdiendo en el desarrollo de la teoría psicoanalítica. Esto sucede, sin embargo, sin que esa ruptura con el modelo que implicaba una simple descifrabilidad del signo cuerpo y la idea de "la brecha engramática" [*engrammatische Bahnung*]* desdeñe la estructura representativa del inconsciente: éstas son las "distorsiones" [*Entstellungen*] y las "imágenes desconcertantes" [*Vexierbilder*].** En este sentido, se trata de una "vuelta de todos los modos de imaginación y formas" [*Umkehr aller Vorstellungsarten und Formen*], Hölderlin, 1992, II: 375), lo que lleva a una vuelta al modelo de las lecturas y traducciones de las tragedias griegas hechas por Hölderlin, donde mirando hacia atrás y, al mismo tiempo, con la vista puesta en la "aparición descontrolada" [*wilde Entstehung*] de una forma racional, debía resaltar "lo oriental", que el arte griego había negado (Hölderlin, II: 375, 925).

Esta relectura de la obra de Benjamin aparece estructurada a través de los *Leitmotive* que forman algunos de los conceptos y figuras hasta ahora más bien descuidados por la recepción, los que, por cierto, tampoco aparecían en el centro de la atención del autor mismo, pero que –según la tesis de este estudio– representan una especie de tácita columna vertebral para ese "giro absoluto" [*vollkommene Umwälzung*], que "debía realizar con la masa de mis ideas e imágenes provenientes de la lejana época de un pensamiento directamente metafísico e incluso teológico" (Benjamin, 1978: 659). Se trata, en efecto, de figuras y conceptos que, al mismo tiempo que adquieren forma, fundamentan teóri-

---

* El concepto de *Engramm* es desarrollado por la autora en el capítulo 10 del presente estudio, en relación con las investigaciones del Warburg Institute. [N. del T.]

** La palabra "*Vexierbild*" ha sido conectada con la idea de "anamorfosis" y de "jeroglífico". Habría que agregar a esta serie de asociaciones la idea afín de "*Vexierspiegel*", espejos cóncavos deformantes, que, por otra parte, eran comunes en los parques de diversiones alemanes hacia 1900. En este contexto, pues, la traducción opta por la idea de: imágenes que desconciertan por su deformación y que deben ser rearmadas por el sujeto. Cf. en inglés: "*picture-puzzles*".

En lugar de acentuar las tan traídas y llevadas contradicciones en la obra de Benjamin, esta relectura hará más bien reconocible una serie de distorsiones, como producto de una elaboración con formulaciones y figuras de pensamientos de diverso origen; así, por ejemplo, una desfiguración del materialismo histórico (véanse los capítulos 1 y 3) o de la magia del lenguaje (capítulos 8 y 9). El significado central del concepto de "distorsión" [*Entstellung*] se manifiesta también claramente cuando Benjamin procede a superponer su sentido de "modalidad de representación en la estructura del sueño" [*Darstellungsmodalität der Traumstruktur*] con el de redención [*Erlösung*], como concepto tomado del mesianismo judío: así en el ensayo sobre Kafka surge la distorsión tanto como forma del olvido –como una especie de síntoma–, y como diferencia hacia la redención (véanse los capítulos 2, 9 y 10). Es posible que precisamente esta reformulación psicoanalítica benjaminiana de lo mesiánico, que se esconde en las figuras del mesianismo y del psicoanálisis como el rastro más escandaloso –bajo la máscara de la explícita reformulación programática del materialismo histórico– haya sido ocultada en "Sobre el concepto de historia". En todo caso, Benjamin no ha pasado de su cuaderno de notas al texto preparado para publicar justamente la frase que sostenía que la imagen dialéctica se definiría como el recuerdo involuntario de la humanidad redimida (*G.S.*, I.3.695).

Sin embargo, no se trata de que el psicoanálisis represente un punto de referencia estático para las reformulaciones, superposiciones y distorsiones aquí mencionadas dentro de la conformación teórica de Benjamin. Más bien debe considerarse que en su obra los modos de observación del psicoanálisis aparecen en una conformación claramente re-materializada, referidos precisamente a la primera materia del ser humano: el cuerpo (capítulo 2), tanto en su acentuación del lenguaje de las cosas y del cuerpo, como también en su concepto de "espacio del cuerpo y de la imagen" [*Leib- und Bildraum*]. En este proceso Benjamin opera con figuras psicoanalíticas en una especie de viraje, dado que se hacen más visibles los orígenes corporales que

procedimiento de Benjamin en su trabajo con las imágenes y en su transformación en imágenes dialécticas, en tanto las imágenes aparecen iluminadas desde adentro y sus modos de funcionar, interrumpidos y detenidos, según una operación por la que las estructuras establecidas se habitan internamente y, al mismo tiempo, son anuladas desde el interior. También podría compararse la descripción derridiana de la deconstrucción como "la última escritura posible de una época" con el procedimiento benjaminiano de la "crítica salvadora" [*die rettende Kritik*]. Sin embargo, una lectura deconstructiva en sentido retórico de los textos de Benjamin parecería forzada, en tanto su operativo "deconstructivo" con las imágenes no se refiere a ellas como tropos retóricos, sino como "constelaciones". El recurso aprehende en su representación al mismo tiempo lo *no representable*, el reverso de las figuras de pensamiento, la dialéctica de las cosas y de la historia. De este modo ese deseo de la imagen y el pensar en imágenes permanecen en la obra de Benjamin siempre ligados a la "fuerza mesiánica débil" de una esperanza histórica.

Las siguientes páginas se colocan, sin embargo, en el mismo plano de la lectura deconstructiva de Benjamin en el sentido de resistirse a la tendencia de ubicar su pensamiento en ideologemas establecidos o -*ismos*. Así, por ejemplo, durante largo tiempo la conocida discusión en torno a los elementos "marxistas" y "teológicos" ocultó que este binomio no puede ser leído en sus textos como una oposición y que, más bien, cuestionamientos y *topoi* que Benjamin ha tomado de ambos dominios pasan a ser figuras reformuladas a partir de un tercer territorio: figuraciones que provienen de conceptos del psicoanálisis (ya sea sobre la estructura del inconsciente o la dialéctica entre la conciencia y el inconsciente). Estas figuras psicoanalíticas aparecen en sus textos superpuestas en una especie de desfasaje imitativo en parte con ideas de otros ámbitos completamente diferentes –por ejemplo, la relación de la filosofía de la historia con el mesianismo, según se desprenderá de una relectura del "Ángel de la Historia" como imagen dialéctica que será expuesta en el capítulo 4 de este estudio–.

"límites de representación" en el contexto de la historia de la *Shoah* se basa en una noción demasiado esquemática de la teoría del lenguaje benjaminiana. A pesar de todo, esta relectura de Benjamin así como la de Paul de Man –que acusa rasgos problemáticos similares (véase el capítulo 9)– han suscitado evidentemente un nuevo interés por su obra en el marco de la teoría del discurso angloamericana y también internacional, con el llamativo efecto de que en algunos casos la relación franco-germana en el dominio del discurso filosófico se ha triangulado con la presencia de un mediador angloamericano.[7] Pero si la recepción en Alemania de la teoría francesa contemporánea, especialmente del post-estructuralismo, corre en parte por el carril transatlántico (gracias a la polea de transmisión del *Deconstructionism*), al mismo tiempo ocurre que en el contexto de habla alemana se llega por el desvío de una doble traducción, dado que muchos títulos clave de Derrida, Kristeva, Foucault, entre otros, se basan en una lectura de los clásicos alemanes, como Heidegger, Husserl, Freud, y también Hölderlin o Kafka. Y si hasta hace poco faltaban en esta lista los autores de la Teoría Crítica temprana, últimamente la cosa se ha revertido, por lo menos para el caso de Benjamin, con quien, sin embargo, la mencionada doble traducción hace sentir su influencia.

Aun cuando la tríada esbozada de un debate franco-angloamericano-germano en la actual teoría del discurso constituye el horizonte de la relectura propuesta para los escritos de Benjamin, esta interpretación no terminará siendo una versión "deconstructiva" de sus textos. En todo caso, no lo sería si la noción de "deconstrucción" toma como modelo la lectura de Paul de Man, que trata de integrar el texto benjaminiano sobre la traducción en la historia de la retórica, claro que al precio de expulsarlo de su mesianismo (véase el capítulo 9 de este estudio). Así sería posible denominar "deconstructivo", en el sentido de la "Gramatología" derridiana, al

---

7. También, como es sabido, la lectura derridiana de "Para una crítica de la violencia" fue originada en un simposio en The Cardozo Law School de Nueva York.

filosófico-social de la Teoría Crítica durante la era Habermas, que se caracterizó por una fuerte tendencia a la reducción de la categoría estética[5] y por el rechazo de todos los aspectos asociados con ella. En el camino quedó por ello también el trabajo benjaminiano sobre el pensar en imágenes.

Una segunda circunstancia es la que se relaciona con la tardía recepción de la obra de Benjamin en Francia, donde solamente recibió un fuerte impulso después de la publicación en francés de "La obra de los Pasajes" en 1982[6] y donde todavía hoy acusa rasgos de una recepción parcial y en parte basada en una información imprecisa. Así, por ejemplo, sucede con la lectura errónea hecha por Derrida del texto benjaminiano sobre la violencia, donde el autor francés se refiere a una "correspondencia entre Carl Schmitt y Walter Benjamin" (Derrida, 1990: 979, 1015), aunque, como es sabido, solamente existe una carta en cuestión enviada por Benjamin a Schmitt junto con su libro sobre el drama barroco. Resulta sugerente la relectura realizada por Derrida del texto benjaminiano de filosofía del derecho desde el punto de vista del significado, acentuando las figuras de "establecimiento" [*Setzung*] de la ley y "abolición" [*Entsetzung*] de la ley. Hay que señalar con toda claridad que tal lectura, sin embargo, no se articula en una vasta e intensiva investigación de la configuración teórica benjaminiana. Y esto sucede, justamente, en aquellos pasajes en los que se halla operando la propia teoría del lenguaje de Benjamin. Sin embargo, la contribución de Derrida a la cuestión de los

---

Sozialforschung [Instituto para la Investigación Social de Francfort] no exista hoy ni un único especialista de la teoría benjaminiana.

5. En la reducción que va de la estética como teoría de percepción sensorial a una teoría del arte o de lo bello se la coloca entonces en el campo opuesto a lo político, lo ético y lo social.

6. En este sentido puede ser que una publicación demorada de Benjamin (en primera instancia del original alemán y desde luego también de las posteriores traducciones) diera origen a la laguna existente durante largo tiempo en la recepción francesa de la filosofía alemana, en la que este autor, sin embargo, desempeña un papel importante. Es interesante agregar que en 1983 tuvo lugar en París un congreso multitudinario sobre "La obra de los Pasajes". Véanse los dos títulos compilados por Bolz y Faber (1985 y 1986).

de las Galerías]* que va de 1927 a 1929, y la recuperación del mismo proyecto a partir de 1934, un tiempo en el que igualmente se reconocen claras huellas de una lectura de Freud y la utilización de términos psicoanalíticos en los textos de Benjamin (véase el capítulo 9 de este estudio).

Como ejemplo de las autores elegidos del mencionado campo de la teoría francesa se tomará la obra de Michel Foucault y Julia Kristeva para señalar las correspondencias con la teoría de Benjamin de modo explícito y detallado (capítulos 3 y 5). Estos análisis deben entenderse como modélicos en el sentido de que su objetivo es suplir una laguna en el actual discurso teórico, la de las tácitas relaciones entre la temprana Teoría Crítica y el postestructuralismo (cf. Weigel, 1995b). El hecho de que estas relaciones se hallen hoy en su mayoría en el desván del discurso teórico se debe a varios factores. Primeramente debe considerarse la quizá violenta apropiación de Benjamin llevada a cabo por la Escuela de Frankfurt y su marginalización (que equivaldría a un segundo exilio) en la historia de la Teoría Crítica después de la muerte de Adorno,[4] especialmente en la fase de la reformulación

---

que tienen en cuenta la gestación (Anotaciones y materiales; primeras anotaciones, *exposés*, esbozos tempranos, etc.) [N. del T.]

 * En el caso de darse dos traducciones de una misma palabra, la primera remite a un concepto ya en circulación en las traducciones en español de la obra de Benjamin. Para el caso de la palabra clave benjaminiana *Passage*, sería importante señalar que los traductores españoles se han dejado atraer por un galicismo, para permitir las asociaciones implícitas en el verbo "pasar" (de un dominio a otro, pero también en el sentido de "progresión"). Benjamin utiliza, por lo menos una vez, el término "galería" (en alemán *Galerie*), como sinónimo de *Passage*, en *Infancia en Berlín hacia 1900*, en la apostilla titulada "La calle doblada" [*Die krumme Strasse*]: "El cuento habla a veces de pasajes y galerías que de cada lado tienen acondicionados negocios llenos de atractivos y peligros." [*Das Märchen redet manchmal von Passagen und Galerien, die beideseits mit Buden voller Lockung und Gefahr bestellt sind*; VII.1.415]. En rigor, en el siglo XIX en París circulaban los dos términos, *passage* y *galerie*, como lo señalan las notas tomadas por el propio Benjamin, quien registra: "les Galeries de Bois", "la Galerie d'Orléans", junto a "Passage de l'Opéra", "Passage des Panoramas". [N. del T.]

 4. El resultado de esta marginación puede verse en el hecho de que entre los herederos institucionales de la Teoría Crítica en el Frankfurter Institut für

(por ejemplo, entre los elementos "marxistas" y "teológicos"). Pero sobre todo, esas formulaciones surgen en el campo de reflexiones de la crítica de la razón como "orden de las cosas" para las estructuras de lo imaginario y lo simbólico, para el paradigma de la escritura y la lectura, para la constitución del sujeto bajo el lema de una "vuelta a Freud" (es decir, una relectura del psicoanálisis), pero también para los actuales paradigmas antropológico-culturales (como la diferencia sexual y la memoria cultural). En suma, dichas formulaciones constituyen el horizonte teórico de cuestionamiento sobre el que este estudio despliega una relectura del pensamiento benjaminiano.

El papel más importante lo cumple, por supuesto, Freud (y el psicoanálisis). Esto concierne a una lectura actual de Freud como condición de posibilidad de la relectura de las figuras de pensamiento benjaminianas aquí propuestas, pero se refiere también a la afinidad del pensamiento de Benjamin con ciertos modos freudianos de observación y su significación para la génesis de sus típicas figuras de pensamiento (esto vale especialmente para la estructura del sueño, la estructura topográfica de la memoria y la dialéctica entre la conciencia y el inconsciente). Esta afinidad hacia figuras psicoanalíticas del pensamiento no representa un tema limitado, sino un constante *Leitmotiv* en el presente estudio. Por ello, se hace hincapié sobre dicha afinidad en distintos momentos del análisis, por ejemplo en las tesis sobre la reformulación psicoanalítica de la teoría de Benjamin de la magia del lenguaje a comienzos de la década del treinta y en el mesianismo tratado en la misma época (véanse los capítulos 2, 9 y 10 de este trabajo). Esta afinidad se muestra de modo ejemplar y concentrado en la elaboración del concepto de memoria alrededor de 1930, es decir, entre la primera fase de trabajo en la serie de "La obra de los Pasajes"* [o

---

* La así llamada "Obra de los Pasajes" (*Das Passagen-werk*) es un texto fragmentario que ha tenido una singular suerte. Georges Bataille lo salvó ocultándolo en la Bibliothèque Nationale de Paris. Esta obra consiste básicamente en el trabajo de investigación llevado a cabo por Benjamin en ese mismo lugar, y ha sido agrupado por los editores alemanes siguiendo criterios temáticos y otros

de pensar y de escribir, la investigación genealógica de sus figuras y de sus imágenes de pensamiento representa, al mismo tiempo, un análisis de la formación de su teoría. Así, cuando ciertas formulaciones –que en los textos benjaminianos a menudo aparecen implícitas u ocultas en forma de citas– se refieren aquí a determinados autores (por ejemplo, a Freud, que es mencionado más como referente de un modo psicoanalítico de pensamiento que como nombre de autor) o también cuando dichas formulaciones aparecen relacionadas con un concepto (teórico), ello sirve para analizar la teoría benjaminiana a la luz del discurso teórico actual y no persigue el objetivo de trazar líneas de influencia.

En este sentido, el concepto de Benjamin de "legibilidad" [*Lesbarkeit*] aparecerá utilizado en relación con sus propios textos. "El índice histórico" [*der historische Index*] que caracteriza a una determinada época, en la que las imágenes logran legibilidad, significa, pues, para muchas de sus imágenes de pensamiento, que ellas puedan llegar en el *Jetztzeit** del discurso teórico actual a una cognoscibilidad quizá no nueva, pero sí seguramente diferente como sucede, por ejemplo, con un tipo de discurso post-Mayo del '68.[3] Especialmente a la luz de la así llamada teoría francesa, los textos de Benjamin pueden alcanzar una nueva legibilidad, que rompería con una localización identificatoria hacia líneas de la tradición y con la reiterada queja sobre las incongruencias y contradicciones de allí emergentes

---

* Se trata aquí de un término de Benjamin, quien lo entendía como la partícula del tiempo en que nos encontramos y que aúna la idea espacial, pero de modo que el lapso pueda ser entendido en conceptos relativos. Así, la civilización humana tendría un *Jetztzeit* (literalmente: "un tiempo del ahora") que es un período infinitesimal en la historia del universo. Se podría traducir con la expresión latina *hit et nunc* para hacer hincapié en las dos coordenadas pensadas por Benjamin, pero se ha optado, finalmente, por la expresión alemana, dado que así circula en los textos traducidos. [N. del T.]

3. Compárese, por ejemplo, la ubicación de la teoría benjaminiana en categorías de una "estética materialista" como punto de referencia para el discurso de homenaje de Habermas en 1972, y la recepción errónea del concepto benjaminiano de "actualidad" en el capítulo 1 del presente estudio.

apropiado para indicar el camino de salida de las aporías a las que han conducido los discursos basados en una crítica de las ideologías.[2]

Es por ello que en la propia configuración teórica de Benjamin a nivel discursivo o argumentativo hay poco lugar para reflexiones, tesis y figuras de otros autores, ya sea de textos literarios o científicos, así como también es raro encontrar en ella debates metateóricos o de historia de la teoría (salvo los párrafos acerca de diferentes teorías de la memoria en el libro sobre Baudelaire). Más bien es posible encontrar que lo que estructura su pensamiento son prácticas de la cita así como el redescubrimiento y la imitación distorsionada de figuras de pensamiento específicas en forma de relaciones temáticas a menudo completamente modificadas. Por lo tanto, reconstruir "influencias" o genealogías filosóficas de su pensamiento significaría perder de vista siempre la especificidad de su obra.

El enfoque sobre el origen de estas figuras de pensamiento no se halla tampoco aquí bajo la consigna de "perfección", sino del interés por el trabajo benjaminiano con determinados conceptos. Así, cuando se hable de cesuras en la conceptualización de determinados fenómenos (como, por ejemplo, en relación con la estructura de la memoria) o de reformulaciones de determinadas teorías (como, por ejemplo, acerca de la teoría lingüística, de lo mesiánico, de lo mimético), en esos casos, entonces, no se hablará tanto de una derivación discursiva o explícita, sino más bien de una "re-formulación" en el sentido literal de la palabra, es decir, una formulación diferente, un desplazamiento en la configuración lingüística, una representación modificada de una imagen ya utilizada a menudo en sus propios escritos. En tanto en la obra de Walter Benjamin no se pueden separar los modos

---

2. Ello parece particularmente apropiado para superar la categoría de la "falsa conciencia", que de modo reiterado gira en el vacío o tiende a juicios de valor morales y a oposiciones entre sujeto y objeto del conocimiento, porque ignora o desconoce las imbricaciones del pensamiento (también del propio) en las estructuras del deseo o del inconsciente.

interpretarse como un síntoma de la manera en que se ha pasado por alto la importancia central de las imágenes en la teoría benjaminiana. Para Benjamin, en efecto, las imágenes no son objeto, sino medio y matriz de su concepción teórica.

Si bien aquí se trata a este autor como teórico, no se lo hace intentando reconstruir su *sistema* teórico. Más bien se realiza en este estudio una búsqueda de los orígenes de sus figuras e imágenes de pensamiento, de las huellas de su trabajo con determinadas formulaciones en su confluencia con constelaciones específicas, puesto que es especialmente llamativo el modo en que determinadas imágenes, figuras lingüísticas, paradigmas o también palabras aisladas atraviesan sus escritos, comparables a aquellas piezas de coleccionista u objetos preciosos, con los que Benjamin describe las imágenes únicas en una tarea de reminiscencia arqueológica ("Crónica de Berlín"; *G.S.*, VI.486). En el marco de este estudio también se llama la atención acerca de cómo las imágenes llegan a dominar sus textos en algunos pasajes, para desaparecer completamente por un trecho del discurso hasta reaparecer luego de modo abrupto, mediante pequeños desplazamientos o desfiguraciones –que, sin embargo, se revelan muy efectivos–, o también en forma de constelaciones completamente nuevas. La historia de sus esfuerzos teóricos debería escribirse también como la historia de una fascinación: como un vínculo igualmente mágico con imágenes y fenómenos determinados y su apropiación, así como un trabajo intelectual con las implicaciones semánticas y las condiciones de posibilidad culturales de esa fascinación. De esta manera, cuando Benjamin parte de la idea (en *Dirección única*; *G.S.*, IV.1.116-117) de que no existiría "imaginación sin inervación" [*Keine Vorstellung ohne Innervation*], entonces modifica de modo significativo la conocida afirmación aristotélica de que no existe pensamiento sin una imagen mental: en este pasaje establece la base del pensamiento en procesos de excitación, sin cuya consideración toda reflexión se vería despojada de su matriz. En este sentido, su "pensar en imágenes" [*Bilddenken*] aparece fundido en un "deseo de la imagen" [*Bildbegehren*], y, por ello mismo, resulta el recurso

manifiesta en el hecho de que Benjamin no trata discursivamente las *oposiciones* tradicionales de las *episteme* establecidas (como aquellas de la forma y el contenido, pero tampoco de la teoría y de la *praxis*, de la política y del arte, del contexto y el texto, del individuo y de la colectividad, etcétera), sino que en sus imágenes de pensamiento las oposiciones se ven anuladas –no superadas [*aufgehoben*], sino literalmente anuladas– , en tanto alcanzan su configuración en ese tercer elemento, la imagen. En este sentido, sus escritos se concentran en la conceptualización y representación de los fenómenos que le preocupan, siempre en una búsqueda constante y en el trabajo con la legibilidad y representatividad de la dialéctica que mora en las cosas y en la existencia. Las imágenes de nuestras percepciones e ideas y las metáforas que nos rodean aparecen en Benjamin consideradas como "espacio del cuerpo y de la imagen" [*Leib- und Bildraum*]* donde se gesta nuestra realidad ("El surrealismo. La última instantánea de la inteligencia europea"; *G.S.*, II.1.309-310; véase el capítulo 2 del presente estudio), áreas que el autor atraviesa en su trabajo reflexivo y escriturario hasta hacerlas devenir el espacio de la escritura de una iluminación profana.

Y es precisamente en este franqueo del umbral del territorio de la imagen de nuestro pensar y obrar, en esta entrada del pensar en imágenes y de las imágenes de pensamiento en la teoría benjaminiana, donde se hallaría fundamentada realmente la actualidad de Walter Benjamin, allí donde se abriría "el mundo de una absoluta e integral actualidad" (*G.S.*, II.1.309). Que en la publicación de homenaje "Sobre la actualidad de Walter Benjamin" se ignorara justamente este genuino concepto benjaminiano de "actualidad" de modo consecuente (véase el capítulo 1), podría

---

* La relación conceptual de estos términos (nunca suficientemente definidos) supondría que el espacio del cuerpo (o corporeización del espacio) ha surgido de la aniquilación dialéctica del espacio de la imagen, pero conservando dentro de sí obligatoriamente rasgos de esta aniquilación. Véase Martin Roman Deppner: "Körperräume und Leibbilder. Die 'profane Erleuchtung' der Kunst", en Weigel, 1992: 119. [N. del T.]

figuras del pensamiento se amalgaman con las de la historia, con las de la experiencia o con las de la realidad (véase el capítulo 4).

La recepción de la obra de Walter Benjamin, caracterizada por una amplia compartimentación disciplinaria, ha llevado a una división de sus textos que suelen analizarse separadamente como discurso filosófico o como textos de crítica literaria; pero, además, esta división conduce a ubicar sus formulaciones [*Theoreme*] en ciertas coordenadas de tradición, encuadres y paradigmas,[1] de tal modo que con este proceder se pasa por alto precisamente ese campo en el que Benjamin se ha movido en primerísimo lugar, como si fuera un territorio invisible (al que se alude indirectamente, en el mejor de los casos): pensar en imágenes [*Bilddenken*]. Pero aquí la cuestión no pasa, justamente, por considerar este dominio como un *suplemento* que pueda agregarse a sus textos, como una cualidad particular (aun si se la considerase como una cualidad estética), de la que pudiera hacerse abstracción en el terreno de la recepción filosófica y sociológica (aunque ésta es la postura más generalizada). Tampoco sería interesante para nuestro estudio interpretar su "pensar en imágenes" como perteneciente a un archivo del repositorio de metáforas o de la retórica, para luego distanciarse del estatuto de teoría del conocimiento y de la historia de sus imágenes de pensamiento [*Denkbilder*] y volver a leerlos siempre como imágenes metafóricas o ilustraciones, o aun como traducciones de problemas que podrían ser articulados en conceptos.

Lo específico de la configuración teórica benjaminiana se halla, más bien, justamente en este pensar en imágenes, en la referencia a esas figuras en las que se presenta la realidad y se forja una tradición de imágenes de la historia, y, sobre todo, en el trabajo teórico y lingüístico que ellas llevan consigo, en la observación de sus orígenes y en sus condiciones de posibilidad, en sus implicaciones, exclusiones y efectos negativos. Ello se

---

1. Así, su texto "Sobre el concepto de historia" aparece tratado, por ejemplo, como filosofía moral o filosofía de la historia, mientras que su libro sobre el drama barroco alemán se evalúa según criterios de la historia de la literatura, etcétera.

Introducción
Una similitud distorsionada. Walter Benjamin como teórico

En este estudio se considera a Walter Benjamin como teórico y no como filósofo (ya sea de la historia o del arte). Por ello aparecerán en el centro del enfoque los modos específicos de su pensamiento y las figuras a través de las cuales ese pensamiento ha cobrado forma y que atestiguan la originalidad de su reflexión. Sus modos de escribir y de pensar no pueden disociarse, pues ambos dominios desembocan –más allá de la oposición entre forma y contenido– en un tercero: la imagen, que el mismo Benjamin caracterizó como un "tercer" elemento [*ein Drittes*], ("Una imagen de Proust"; *G.S.*, II.1.314).* Estamos ante una imagen que en su obra no adquiere, sin embargo, el *status* de una copia, de una "imagen mental" [*geistiges Bild*], sino de una constelación poseedora de una similitud heterónoma y heterogénea en la que las

---

* Las referencias bibliográficas entre paréntesis remiten a las obras completas de Walter Benjamin en el original alemán bajo el título de: *Gesammelte Schriften (G.S.)*, a cargo de Rolf Tiedemann y Hermann Schweppenhäuser, Francfort, Editorial Suhrkamp, en siete tomos separados en catorce libros o partes, cuya publicación se desarrolló entre 1974 y 1989. El orden de edición no es estrictamente cronológico, sino que sigue otras pautas: I. Ensayos terminados; II. Artículos aparecidos en publicaciones periódicas; III. Reseñas; IV. Breves textos literarios propios y traducciones; V. La obra de los Pasajes; VI. Fragmentos o escritos inacabados; VII. Notas a la edición y catalogaciones. En el presente estudio aparece, por lo tanto, indicado el texto que se cite de la obra de Benjamin siguiendo el orden de: número romano para el tomo, arábigo para el libro o parte y finalmente el número de la paginación. [N. del T.]

Nota preliminar del traductor

La presente traducción fue llevada a cabo a partir de un texto manuscrito alemán pero, al mismo tiempo, siguió de cerca las correcciones hechas sobre la versión inglesa, editada por Routledge de Nueva York en 1996 bajo el título de *Body-and Image-Space. Re-reading Walter Benjamin*. Otros ajustes al texto fueron posibles, además, gracias a una comunicación con la autora durante la última etapa del trabajo. Finalmente se tuvo en consideración la versión édita alemana, publicada bajo el título de *Entstellte Ähnlichkeit. Walter Benjamins theoretische Schreibweise* (que podría traducirse como: *Una similitud distorsionada. Los modos teóricos de escritura de Walter Benjamin*), aparecida en la casa editorial Fischer de Francfort en mayo de 1997, la cual contiene una disposición diferente de los capítulos. Las citas textuales de obras de Walter Benjamin se tradujeron directamente del original alemán. El mismo procedimiento se llevó a cabo en otros autores como Hölderlin, o no alemanes, como Foucault, Kristeva, De Man, Primo Levi, Adorno y otros, cuyos textos fueron considerados en sus respectivos idiomas.

TERCERA PARTE
La memoria y la escritura

8. De la topografía a la escritura
El concepto benjaminiano de la memoria 185
9. La lectura que ocupa el lugar de la traducción
La formulación psicoanalítica de la teoría sobre la magia
del lenguaje 213
10. Legibilidad
El lugar de Benjamin en los enfoques contemporáneos
sobre la memoria corpórea y pictórica 239
11. El estupor no filosófico o la escritura en perpetuo asombro
La posición de Benjamin después del Holocausto 259

Bibliografía 285
Índice analítico 297

Índice

Nota preliminar del traductor 9
Introducción: Una similitud distorsionada.
Walter Benjamin como teórico 11

Primera parte
La política de las imágenes y del cuerpo

1. "El mundo de una absoluta e integral actualidad"
   en Benjamin 29
2. "El espacio del cuerpo y de la imagen"
   Las huellas en los escritos de Benjamin 47
3. Vasos comunicantes:
   Michel Foucault y Walter Benjamin 69
4. Imágenes de pensamiento.
   Una relectura del "Ángel de la Historia" 97

Segunda parte
Otras lecturas de géneros

5. Hacia una dialéctica femenina del Iluminismo:
   Julia Kristeva y Walter Benjamin 117
6. Desde las imágenes a las imágenes dialécticas:
   El significado de las diferencias de género en los
   escritos benjaminianos 143
7. El "otro" en la alegoría
   Una prehistoria de la alegoría de la Modernidad
   en el barroco 167

Traducido del manuscrito original alemán *Entstellte Ähnlichkeit. Walter Benjamins theoretische Schreibweise* (Francfort, Fischer Ed., 1997), con consideración de la versión en inglés revisada por la autora, *Body- and Image-Space. Re-reading Walter Benjamin* Londres, Routledge, 1996

© 1996 Routledge
Cubierta de María Laura Piaggio
Traducción: José Amícola

1a. edición, 1999

La reproducción total o parcial de este libro, en cualquier forma que sea, idéntica o modificada, escrita a máquina, por el sistema "multigraph", mimeógrafo, impreso por fotocopia, fotoduplicación, etc., no autorizada por los editores, viola derechos reservados. Cualquier utilización debe ser previamente solicitada.

© 1999 de todas las ediciones en castellano

Editorial Paidós SAICF
Defensa 599, Buenos Aires
e-mail: paidos@internet.siscotel.com
Ediciones Paidós Ibérica SA
Mariano Cubí 92, Barcelona
Editorial Paidós Mexicana SA
Rubén Darío 118, México D. F.

Queda hecho el depósito que previene la Ley 11.723
Impreso en la Argentina. Printed in Argentina

Impreso en Gráfica MPS, Santiago del Estero 338,
Lanús, en julio de 1999

ISBN 950-12-3804-0

Cuerpo, imagen y espacio en Walter Benjamin

Una relectura

Sigrid Weigel

PAIDÓS
Buenos Aires
Barcelona
México

Género y cultura

Directoras de colección:
Ana Amado y Nora Domínguez

1. Luce Irigaray, *Ser dos*
2. Daniel Balderston y Donna J. Guy (comps.), *Sexo y sexualidades en América latina*
3. Néstor Perlongher, *El negocio del deseo*
4. Sigrid Weigel, *Cuerpo, imagen y espacio en Walter Benjamin*

CUERPO, IMAGEN Y ESPACIO EN WALTER BENJAMIN
Una relectura